T0186082

Lecture Notes in Computer Science 12377

More information about this series at http://www.springer.com/series/7409

Klaus Miesenberger · Roberto Manduchi ·
Mario Covarrubias Rodriguez ·
Petr Peňáz (Eds.)

Computers Helping People with Special Needs

17th International Conference, ICCHP 2020
Lecco, Italy, September 9–11, 2020
Proceedings, Part II

 Springer

Editors
Klaus Miesenberger ⓘD
Institute Integriert Studieren
JKU Linz
Linz, Austria

Roberto Manduchi ⓘD
Jack Baskin School of Engineering
UC Santa Cruz
Santa Cruz, CA, USA

Mario Covarrubias Rodriguez ⓘD
Dipartimento di Meccanica
Politecnico di Milano
Milan, Italy

Petr Peňáz
Support Centre for Students
with Special Needs
Masaryk University Brno
Brno, Czech Republic

ISSN 0302-9743   ISSN 1611-3349 (electronic)
Lecture Notes in Computer Science
ISBN 978-3-030-58804-5   ISBN 978-3-030-58805-2 (eBook)
https://doi.org/10.1007/978-3-030-58805-2

LNCS Sublibrary: SL3 – Information Systems and Applications, incl. Internet/Web, and HCI

This Springer imprint is published by the registered company Springer Nature Switzerland AG
The registered company address is: Gewerbestrasse 11, 6330 Cham, Switzerland

Preface

Since its inception in 1989, ICCHP has evolved to become the largest European conference on accessibility and inclusion, and in particular on technical aspects such as eAccessibility and Assistive Technology. ICCHP addresses the many unnecessary barriers, physical or otherwise, that impede opportunities for work, education, and participation by people with disabilities.

It capitalizes on progress in all areas of technology that can contribute to remove these barriers. Artificial intelligence has certainly captured the lion's share of attention for technological trends in accessibility. Smartphone apps now read text, recognize objects, and automatically describe the content of pictures. Ever-improving speech understanding algorithms enable hand-free control of computers, appliances, or devices, with research ongoing on the recognition of dysarthric speech. Autonomous cars may in the near future provide individualized transportation to those who cannot drive, while exoskeleton systems will enable ambulation to people with paraplegia. Intelligent homes offer opportunities for independent living to those with reduced motion control. At the urban scale, mapping and localization systems are being deployed in public spaces to support orientation and wayfinding, or to identify safe paths to traverse for wheelchair users. It is encouraging that all major information technology companies have committed to including accessibility features in their products, and even started their own research labs in access technology.

Yet, sometimes innovation comes from the grassroots. Communities of makers have taken on the challenges of designing low-budget assistive technology, often involving people with disabilities in exciting co-design experiments. Crowdsourcing and micro-volunteering projects have evolved into accessibility platforms with thousands of contributors and users. The scope of ICCHP encompasses all of these technologies, with the common goal to build a more accessible, inclusive, and participative world.

In 2020, the proceedings of the 17th conference are delivered to you as a compendium of new and exciting scholarly and practical work going on in our field. ICCHP runs a highly competitive process for selecting the contributions for publication and presentation. The Program Committee, including 130 experts, guarantees that each paper is reviewed by at least 3 experts. 1 member of the panel of 15 conference chairs assesses the review results of each contribution to come to a final decision, which was made during online meetings held over 3 days. This two-phase selection procedure guarantees high scientific quality, making ICCHP unique to our field. 107 contributions were accepted and you will find them in the two-volume proceedings embedded in the structure of thematically grouped chapters. The concept of organizing Special Thematic Sessions again helped to structure the proceedings and the program in order to support a deep focus on highly desirable selected topics in the field as well as to bring new and interesting topics to the attention of the research community.

Due to the COVID-19 crisis, we decided to run the conference online only. Although we do hope that the situation becomes better, at the time of writing this preface, travel and contact opportunities were frequently changing. We needed predictable organization and plannable programs, which could only be made available online. Running the conference virtually was challenging but also an important experience in terms of interaction and communication, in particular for accessibility. We still managed to host a high-quality and fully accessible meeting for scientists, users, practitioners, educators, and policy makers. We strive to be able to provide new and innovative opportunities for exchange and cooperation. The Service and Practice Track, organized in addition to scientific presentations, supported a cross-domain exchange and cooperation. ICCHP aims to support young researchers, the next generation of experts in our field, and encourages them to contribute. ICCHP accepts the challenge to provide new and innovative online conference spaces, aiming at less formal discussions. This important factor, supporting the transfer of knowledge so needed in our endeavors, must not be lost when moving online.

Thank you for your attendance at ICCHP 2020 and we hope that you and your colleagues to be regular participants in its most important mission, also recognized through patronage of the United Nations Educational, Scientific and Cultural Organization (UNESCO). It is here that research, innovation, and practical endeavors in important topics of Assistive Technologies and eAccesibility can come together to be shared, explored, and discussed.

September 2020

Klaus Miesenberger
Roberto Manduchi
Mario Covarrubias Rodriguez
Petr Peňáz

Organization

ICCHP Committees

Our special thanks go to those who have contributed in putting this conference together:

General Chair

Roberto Manduchi   UC Santa Cruz, Jack Baskin School of Engineering, USA

Publishing Chairs

Miesenberger, K.   JKU Linz, Austria
Covarrubias Rodriguez, M.   Politecnico di Milano, Italy
Peňáz, P.   Masaryk University Brno, Czech Republic

Program Chairs

Archambault, D.   Université Paris 8, France
Buehler, C.   TU Dortmund, FTB, Germany
Coughlan, J.   Smith-Kettlewell Eye Research Institute, USA
Debevc, M.   University of Maribor, Slovenia
Fels, D.   Ryerson University, Canada
Kobayashi, M.   Tsukuba University of Technology, Japan
Kouroupetroglou, G.   National and Kapodistrian University of Athens, Greece
Murphy, H. J.   California State University, Northridge, USA
Pawluk, D.   Virginia Commonwealth University, USA
Suzuki, M.   Kyushu University, Japan
Weber, G.   Technische Universität Dresden, Germany
Zagler, W.   Vienna University of Technology, Austria

Young Researchers Consortium Chairs

Archambault, D.   Université Paris 8, France
Chen, W.   University of Bergen, Norway
Fels, D.   Ryerson University, Canada
Fitzpatrick, D.   Dublin City University, Ireland
Kobayashi, M.   Tsukuba University of Technology, Japan
Morandell, M.   Health University of Applied Sciences Tyrol, Austria

Pontelli, E.	New Mexico State University, USA
Prazak-Aram, B.	Austrian Institute of Technology, Austria
Scaccabarozzi, D.	Politecnico di Milano, Italy
Weber, G.	Technische Universität Dresden, Germany
Zimmermann, G.	Hochschule der Medien, Germany

Service and Practice Track Chairs

Petz, A.	University of Linz, Austria
Pühretmair, F.	KI-I, Austria

International Programe Committee

Abascal, J.	Euskal Herriko Unibertsitatea, Spain
Abbott, C.	King's College London, UK
Abou-Zahra, S.	W3C Web Accessibility Initiative (WAI), Austria
Abu Doush, I.	American University of Kuwait, Kuwait
Andreoni, G.	Politecnico di Milano, Italy
Andrich, R.	Fondazione Don Carlo Gnocchi Onlus, Italy
Atkinson, M. T.	The Paciello Group, USA
Augstein, M.	University of Applied Sciences Upper Austria, Austria
Azevedo, L.	Instituto Superior Tecnico, Portugal
Banes, D.	David Banes Access and Inclusion Services, UK
Barroso, J.	University of Trás-os-Montes and Alto Douro, Portugal
Batusic, M.	Fabasoft, Austria
Bernareggi, C.	Universita degli Studi di Milano, Italy
Bernier, A.	BrailleNet, France
Bosse, I.	Technische Universität Dortmund, Germany
Bu, J.	Zhejiang University, China
Caruso, G.	Politecnico di Milano, Italy
Christensen, L. B.	Sensus, Denmark
Conway, V.	WebKitIT, Australia
Crombie, D.	Utrecht School of the Arts, The Netherlands
Darvishy, A.	Zurich University of Applied Sciences, Switzerland
Darzentas, J.	University of the Aegean, Greece
Debeljak, M.	University of Ljubljana, Slovenia
DeRuyter, F.	Duke University Medical Centre, USA
Diaz del Campo, R.	Antarq Tecnosoluciones, Mexico
Draffan, E. A.	University of Southampton, UK
Dupire, J.	CNAM, France
Emiliani, P. L.	Institute of Applied Physics Nello Carrara, Italy
Engelen, J.	Katholieke Universiteit Leuven, Belgium
Galinski, Ch.	InfoTerm, Austria
Gardner, J.	Oregon State University, USA
Hakkinen, M. T.	Educational Testing Service (ETS), USA
Hanson, V.	University of Dundee, UK

Haslwanter, T.	University of Applied Sciences Upper Austria, Austria
Heimgärtner, R.	Intercultural User Interface Consulting (IUIC), Germany
Höckner, K.	Hilfsgemeinschaft der Blinden und Sehschwachen, Austria
Inoue, T.	National Rehabilitation Center for Persons with Disabilities, Japan
Iversen, C. M.	U.S. Department of State, USA
Jitngernmadan, P.	Burapha University, Thailand
Kiswarday, V.	University of Primorska, Slovenia
Koumpis, A.	Berner Fachhochschule, Switzerland
Kozuh, I.	University of Maribor, Slovenia
Küng, J.	JKU Linz, Austria
Kunz, A.	ETH Zurich, Switzerland
Lee, S.	W3C Web Accessibility Initiative (WAI), UK
Lewis, C.	University of Colorado Boulder, USA
Lhotska, L.	Czech Technical University in Prague, Czech Republic
Macas, M.	Czech Technical University in Prague, Czech Republic
Magnusson, M.	Moscow State University, Russia
Mavrou, K.	European University Cyprus, Cyprus
McSorley, J.	Pearson, USA
Mihailidis, A.	University of Toronto, Canada
Mirri, S.	University of Bologna, Italy
Mohamad, Y.	Fraunhofer Institute for Applied IT, Germany
Moreira Silva Dantas, P.	Federal University Rio Grande do Norte, Brazil
Mrochen, I.	University of Silesia in Katowice, Poland
Müller-Putz, G.	TU Graz, Austria
Muratet, M.	INS HEA, France
Normie, L.	GeronTech - The Israeli Center for AT and Ageing, Israel
Nussbaum, G.	KI-I, Austria
Oswal, S.	University of Washington, USA
Paciello, M.	The Paciello Group, USA
Panek, P.	Vienna University of Technology, Austria
Paredes, H.	University of Trás-os-Montes and Alto Douro, Portugal
Petrie, H.	University of York, UK
Pissaloux, E.	Université Rouen, France
Rassmus-Groehn, K.	Lund University, Sweden
Raynal, M	University of Toulouse, France
Sanchez, J.	University of Chile, Chile
Sik Lányi, C.	University of Pannonia, Hungary
Simsik, D.	University of Kosice, Slovakia
Slavik, P.	Czech Technical University in Prague, Czech Republic
Sloan, D.	The Paciello Group, UK
Snaprud, M.	University of Agder, Norway
Stepankowa, O.	Czech Technical University in Prague, Czech Republic

Stephanidis, C.	University of Crete, FORTH-ICS, Greece
Stiefelhagen, R.	Karlsruhe Institute of Technology, Germany
Stoeger, B.	University of Linz, Austria
Tarabini, M.	Politecnico di Milano, Italy
Tauber, M.	University of Paderborn, Germany
Teixeira, A.	Universidade de Aveiro, Portugal
Teshima, Y.	Chiba Institute of Technology, Japan
Tjoa, A. M.	Vienna University of Technology, Austria
Truck, I.	Université Paris 8, France
Velazquez, R.	Panamerican University, Mexico
Vigo, M.	University of Manchester, UK
Vigouroux, N.	IRIT Toulouse, France
Wada, C.	Kyushu Institute of Technology, Japan
Wagner, G.	University of Applied Sciences Upper Austria, Austria
Waszkielewicz, A.	Foundation for Persons with Disabilities, Poland
Watanabe, T.	University of Niigata, Japan
Weber, H.	ITA, University of Kaiserslautern, Germany
White, J.	Educational Testing Service (ETS), USA
Yamaguchi, K.	Nihon University, Japan
Yeliz Yesilada	Middle East Technical University, Cyprus

Organization Committee

Andreoni, G.	Politecnico di Milano, Italy
Bieber, R.	Austrian Computer Society, Austria
Brunetti, V.	Politecnico di Milano, Italy
Bukovsky, T.	Masaryk University Brno, Czech Republic
Covarrubias Rodriguez, M.	Politecnico di Milano, Italy
Feichtenschlager, P.	JKU Linz, Austria
Heumader, P.	JKU Linz, Austria
Höckner, K.	Hilfsgemeinschaft der Blinden und Sehschwachen, Austria
Hrabovska, L.	Masaryk University Brno, Czech Republic
Koutny, R.	JKU Linz, Austria
Lepschy, C.	JKU Linz, Austria
Miesenberger, K.	JKU Linz, Austria
Murillo Morales, T.	JKU Linz, Austria
Ondra, S.	Masaryk University Brno, Czech Republic
Pavlíček, R.	Masaryk University Brno, Czech Republic
Peňáz, P.	Masaryk University Brno, Czech Republic
Petz, A.	JKU Linz, Austria
Salinas-Lopez, V.	JKU Linz, Austria
Scaccabarozzi, D.	Politecnico di Milano, Italy
Schult, C.	JKU Linz, Austria
Seyruck, W.	Austrian Computer Society, Austria
Stöger, B.	JKU Linz, Austria

Tarabini, M.	Politecnico di Milano, Italy
Válková, H.	Masaryk University Brno, Czech Republic
Verma, A.	JKU Linz, Austria
Wernerová, P.	Masaryk University Brno, Czech Republic

ICCHP Roland Wagner Award Committee

Dominique Burger	BrailleNet, France
Christian Buehler	TU Dortmund, FTB Vollmarstein, Germany
E. A. Draffan	University of Southampton, UK
Deborah Fels	Ryerson University, Canada
Klaus Höckner	Hilfsgemeinschaft der Blinden und Sehschwachen, Austria
Klaus Miesenberger	JKU Linz, Austria
Wolfgang Zagler	Vienna University of Technology, Austria

Once again, we thank all those who helped put the ICCHP 2020 conference together, thereby supporting the AT field and a better quality of life for people with disabilities. Special thanks go to all our supporter and sponsors, displayed at: https://www.icchp.org/sponsors-20.

Contents – Part II

ICT to Support Inclusive Education - Universal Learning Design (ULD)

Hearing Systems and Accessories for People with Hearing Loss

How to Improve Interaction with a Text Input System

Human Movement Analysis for the Design and Evaluation of Interactive Systems and Assistive Devices

Service and Care Provision in Assistive Environments

Contents – Part I

XR Accessibility – Learning from the Past, Addressing Real User Needs and the Technical Architecture for Inclusive Immersive Environments

Serious and Fun Games

Large-Scale Web Accessibility Observatories

Accessible and Inclusive Digital Publishing

AT and Accessibility for Blind and Low Vision Users

Art Karshmer Lectures in Access to Mathematics, Science and Engineering

Accessibility of Non-verbal Communication: Making Spatial Information Accessible to People with Disabilities

Accessibility of Non-verbal Communication: Making Spatial Information Accessible to People with Disabilities

Introduction to the Special Thematic Session

Andreas Kunz[1]([⊠]) [iD], Klaus Miesenberger[2] [iD], and Max Mühlhäuser[3] [iD]

[1] Innovation Center Virtual Reality, ETH Zurich, Zurich, Switzerland
kunz@iwf.mavt.ethz.ch
[2] Institut Integriert Studieren, Johannes Kepler University, Linz, Austria
Klaus.Miesenberger@jku.at
[3] Technische Universität Darmstadt, Darmstadt, Germany
max@tk.tu-darmstadt.de
https://www.icvr.ethz.ch
https://www.jku.at/institut-integriert-studieren/
https://www.informatik.tu-darmstadt.de

Abstract. Non-verbal communication (NVC) is challenging to people with disabilities. Depending on their impairment, they are either unable to perceive relational gestures within performed by sighted people, or they are unable to perform gestures by themselves in such an information space (in case of motoric impairments such as cerebral palsy). Also other 3D gestures such as sign language and other aspects of non-verbal communication could provide an accessibility problem during training, interaction, and communication. This summary paper gives an overview on new approaches, how computers could mitigate these various impairments. Based on this we discuss how the papers accepted for this session relate and contribute to this new and challenging domain.

Keywords: Non-verbal communication · Cerebral palsy · Finger spelling

1 Motivation

Following the classical *3C model* [10], collaboration among humans comprises communication, coordination (scheduling, turn-taking etc.), and cooperation. The latter leads to artifacts that represent the intermediate and final results of collaboration, suggesting to distinguish a task space where these artifacts reside from the communication space – both of which may be real, virtual and/or imaginary depending on the setting. Consider a typical brainstorming meeting as a well defined and structured example of interaction and communication full of non-verbal elements, control tends to happen implicitly, following a

K. Miesenberger et al. (Eds.): ICCHP 2020, LNCS 12377, pp. 3–10, 2020.
https://doi.org/10.1007/978-3-030-58805-2_1

social protocol (e.g., turn-taking by means of the first person to raise their voice after a sufficiently long pause); for simplicity, we will subsume it to happen in the communication space (for the case of brainstorming) hereafter. Turning to mixed brainstorming meetings between participants and people with disabilities, demanding challenges arise in both the communication and the task space (see Fig. 1). As the term *space* indicates, it can be enlightening to consider these two spaces in the narrow sense of the word, i.e. as three-dimensional (3D) constructs. As we will discuss below, serious disadvantages and even discrimination may result from restricting the mapping between participants and people with disabilities to one-dimensional accessible information what can be easily captured and conveyed in this form. Therefore, the session introduces suggestions to mitigate these deficiencies with a 3D approach.

In a lively brainstorming, artifacts such as sticky notes are generated, placed on common workspaces such as whiteboards and digital screens, and then discussed within the team (Fig. 1). While the artifacts are placed in the task space, the communication of the participants takes place in the communication space. Thus, the information flow in a team meeting is not simply on the generated artifacts and on the spoken explanations by the originator, but it is in particular a manifold of NVC, that could carry up to 55% of the overall information [3]. Gestures, facial expressions, postures, gazes, etc. are a huge repertoire of expressions performed in a three-dimensional space, from which some of them also refer to the 3D information space they are performed in.

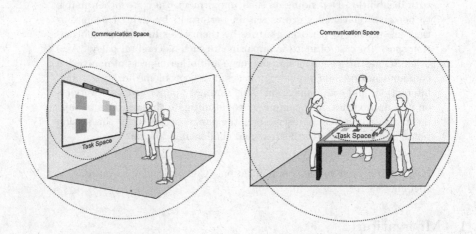

Fig. 1. Task and communication space within a team meeting [6].

While this interpersonal communication takes place in this communication space only, it typically also refers to artifacts in the task space. While this already shapes a three-dimensional information space, the artifacts in the task space make an additional dimension of complexity: The sizes of the artifacts, their distances to each other, as well as their position in the task space carry important information that also needs to be transferred to people with disabilities.

Within this session, three different accessibility problems will be addressed, and how they can be mitigated by means of assistive computer technology. While eventually future technology will allow these three different groups of handicapped people to communicate freely among each other, this session will introduce technologies to make 3D information accessible to (i) blind and visually impaired, (ii) motoric impaired (cerebral palsy), and (iii) deaf people.

2 Blind and Visually Impaired People

2.1 Related Work

There are multiple approaches to output the digital content of screens to BVIP, such as e.g. the outcome of the Tidia-Ae project [1], accessible classrooms [2, 12]. Many of the barriers described by [11] are still existent, or only partially addressed, for instance in an accessible tabletop [13,15], where natural pointing gesture of the sighted users on artifacts on a small interactive table could be detected and the relevant artifact's content output to a Braille display.

In order to detect a spatial relationship between artifacts, a Wii controller was used by [9], which outputs the proximity of artifacts to the blind user by vibration. Another approach by [16] uses cards with different tactile material, that again use near-field communication to communicate with smartphones. In order to allocate cards (of a mindmap application) on the table, [14] some active edge projection actuators to identify the card of interest on the table.

2.2 System Setup

During a brainstorming, sighted users refer to artifacts in the 3D task space by gazing or pointing gestures. These gestures are inaccessible for BVIP and thus need to be translated. Moreover, the task space is also continuously altered by adding artifacts or by clustering or removing them. The relationships of the artifacts to each other contains additional information, but this also has an influence on the NVCs. It is thus necessary to map all relevant NVCs to the artifacts on the common workspace and make their content accessible to BVIPs together with their spatial relationships. The proposed system consists of an interface for sighted users, as well as of an interface for BVIPs, which are both interconnected via the task space (Fig. 2).

The task space consists of two parts with two different views on the same content. For the sighted users it is the regular work space like an interactive whiteboard, while the part for the BVIP is a 2D horizontal output device that allows experiencing the spatial distances between the artifacts (Fig. 2).

2.3 Interface for the Sighted Users

The interface for the sighted users consists of the following components (Fig. 3):

- Input/editing device (smartphone or tablet) for editing the artifacts (cards),

– Screen for the facilitator to arrange cards in the task space (Fig. 1),
– Pointing gesture detection of the facilitator in front of the electronic whiteboard (Fig. 1).

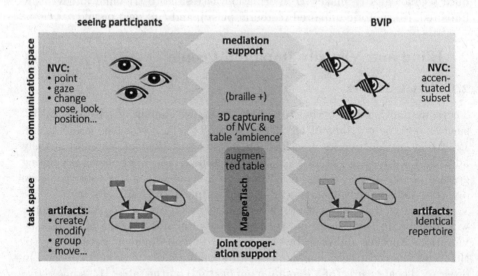

Fig. 2. Schematic system overview.

The card's are edited on a smartphone or tablet using the integrated keyboard of such devices. Only one or two words will be edited and then the card
will be submitted to the shared task space. There, it will be further processed by
the facilitator (Fig. 3). The facilitator will arrange the cards and initiate discussions. He is defining clusters and distances of the card's, as well as their positions
on the screen. While arranging the cards on the whiteboard, he will eventually
perform pointing gestures that need to be captured. While these pointing gestures are useless to the BVIP, they need to be related to areas on the screen
that contain the generated artifacts. However, since pointing gestures are typically not performed precisely, it is sufficient to only detect certain regions on the
screen. The system architecture is an open framework allowing to add new and
additional NVC features for better inclusion of people with disabilities.

2.4   BVIP Interface

The BVIP interface consists of an interactive table on which a copy of the whiteboard content, i.e. the clusters exist. The table has an integrated x−y actuation
system, which can magnetically pull a handle on the tabletop to any desired
position. As soon as a pointing gesture from a sighted user in a cluster of cards
is detected, the table is activated to move the handle to a region of interest. The
BVIP's hand is then guided to a correct position to provide spatial information

Fig. 3. Editing of a card on a mobile device and a meeting room with an integrated whiteboard.

to him. For more detailed information of a cluster's content, the BVIP could then read out the content of the individual cards on his Braille display, or by using text to speech.

3 People with Cerebral Palsy

Cerebral palsy is a permanent movement disorder. Symptoms include poor coordination, stiff muscles, weak muscles, tremor, spasms, athetosis, etc. While frequently not being able to control muscles in a coordinated way, as e.g. for pointing gestures (Fig. 1), the research is focusing towards an augmentative alternative communication (AAC).

3.1 Related Work

To regain the possibility of selecting artifacts from the environment, research is mainly focusing on interfaces such as head movement and speech recognition devices, brain-computer interfaces [5], or eye tracking [8]. However, such devices are either too expensive, or too cumbersome to be used in a daily routine.

3.2 System Setup

In order to overcome the drawbacks mentioned in the above, the proposed system makes use of a 3-axes gyroscope, an HC-05 Bluetooth module, and a microcontroller Arduino Nano to make a complete data collection system for detecting head orientation. Using these components the head movement could be used to select commands or words and confirm the selection by nodding. The corresponding selection is shown on a screen to guide the user and to allow for a correction of his head movements. First preliminary studies with people having cerebral palsy showed promising results of this comparatively low-cost system.

4 Hard of Hearing and Deaf People

Following the World Federation of Deaf [19], millions of deaf and hard of hearing people use sign or signing supported language for communication instead of and/or in combination with written/spoken language. As a first example we focus on finger spelling as an important component of sign language, in which words need to be spelled letter by letter, which is in particular important for properly spelling names or other uncommon words [4]. However, finger spelling needs practicing in order to fluently communicate important information to others.

4.1 Related Work

Finger spelling relies on the movement of hand and fingers, and is thus more than just a sequence of still images [7]. Thus, training tools that just show still images for practicing such as [18] are not sufficient to train a finger spelling motion. Here, using animated avatars seem to be a promising solution for training such movements. However, existing solutions either just show an artificial hand instead of a whole avatar, or the avatar's torso shows a "robot-like" behavior [17], or the whole training system was bound to one single operational system, which hindered a widespread distribution.

4.2 System Setup

To overcome these shortcomings, a web-based solution is introduced that can be accessed from various operation systems to achieve platform independence. It is planned as an extensible framework allowing to integrate more NVC access solutions. Based on JavaScript WebGL2, the app allows also controlling the camera's perspective so that the avatar speller can be seen from various viewpoints

5 Contributions to Non-verbal Communication

The above outline, still restricted to well defined scenarios, shows the broad domain of NVC. A broad range of R&D is needed to address the challenge of making more aspects of NVC accessible and integrating them into AT supported environments for better exchange and participation. Due to the broad aspects of NVC, the contributions by nature address considerably different issues and thereby underline the need for a more holistic and integrating theory and concept of non-verbal communication for improved accessibility and inclusion.

The first paper focuses on accessibility of brainstorming meetings. It shows how pointing gestures by sighted people are retrieved and transferred to BVIP on a novel spatial output device. As a well defined setting in terms of timing, location, infrastructure and meeting participants but also in terms of procedures, artefacts and roles, this kind of meetings is an ideal playground for starting studies on NVC. The paper demonstrates one of the first approaches managing to bring the complexity of a collaborative meeting into an experimental setting allowing to support non-verbal communication aspects for BVIP users.

The second paper presents how interacting with and using a brainstorming tool by blind and visually impaired people (BVIP) can be facilitated. By combining the brainstorming software with a pointing gesture recognition system

BVIP participants reach a new participation experience during the brainstorming meeting when gestures are conveyed using Braille display and speech synthesis for access. This still experimental approach provides a new and innovative field for experimenting with new ways of better access and participation.

The third paper makes an emphasis on relating Augmentative and Alternative Communication (AAC) where people with severe motor and speech disabilities need innovative approaches in using alternative, body or body-near non-traditional and non-verbal activities for interaction and communication and in particular Human-Computer Interaction (HCI) based communication. Pointing gestures, tracked by a miniaturized sensor help people with cerebral palsy to precisely point at visible targets to enable several information flows. Any progress in tracking and making sense out of non-verbal communication cues and activities of users can be seen as a potential for new supportive functionalities.

The fourth paper integrates the question of access to sign language and finger spelling for deaf and hard of hearing people as an aspect of NVC. Using a web based avatar better training and learning should be facilitated. This at first reads distinct to the rest of the session, but consideration of a resource hosting, explaining and providing training on non-verbal aspects of communication is seen as of interest for all groups of users with disabilities in terms of a) understanding b) producing and c) integrating non verbal communication aspects into interaction and communication. The extensive work in the domain of sign language is seen as a candidate for a more structured and standardized approach.

6 Summary and Future Research

It is interesting and motivating to see how broad and diverse the call for papers for a session on accessibility of non-verbal communication has been. Tracking, presenting, understanding, doing and managing non-verbal communication aspects seem to be of particular interest for almost all groups of people with disabilities and seem to be of particular importance for facilitating active participation and inclusion. It seems to come much closer to the essence of inclusion into the diverse domains of our social life all based on very rich communication going beyond pure access to content as text, images, videos or other artefacts. More R&D is needed to allow people with disabilities to access, master and actively contribute to the full and rich range of non-verbal communication aspects.

References

1. Freire, A., Linhalis, F., Bianchini, S., Forber, R., Pimentel, M.: Revealing the whiteboard to blind students: an inclusive approach to provide mediation in synchronous e-learning activities. Comput. Educ. **54**, 866–876 (2010)
2. Karlapp, M., Köhlmann, W.: Adaptation and evaluation of a virtual classroom for blind users. I-Com J. Interact. Media **16**(1), 45–55 (2017)
3. Mehrabian, A., Ferris, S.: Inference of attitudes from nonverbal communication in two channels. J. Consult. Clin. Psychol. **31**(3), 248–252 (1967)

4. Schembri, A., Johnston, T.: Sociolinguistic variation in the use of fingerspelling in Australian sign language: a pilot study. Sign Lang. Stud. **7**(3), 319–347 (2007)
5. Daly, I., Billinger, M., Scherer, R., Müller-Putz, G.: Brain-computer interfacing for users with cerebral palsy, challenges and opportunities. In: Stephanidis, C., Antona, M. (eds.) UAHCI 2013. LNCS, vol. 8009, pp. 623–632. Springer, Heidelberg (2013). https://doi.org/10.1007/978-3-642-39188-0_67
6. Alavi, A.: A Framework for Optimal In-Air Gesture Recognition in Collaborative Environments. Dissertation ETH Zurich, Zurich, Switzerland (2020)
7. Wilcox, S.: The Phonetics of Fingerspelling. John Benjamins Publishing, Amsterdam (1992)
8. Amantis, R., Corradi, F., Molteni, A.M., Mele, M.L.: Eye-tracking assistive technology: is this effective for the developmental age? evaluation of eye-tracking systems for children and adolescents with cerebral palsy. In: 11th European Conference for the Advancement of Assistive Technology, AAATE 2011, pp. 489–496. IOS Press (2011)
9. Cheiran, J., Nedel, L., Pimenta, M.: Inclusive games: a multimodal experience for blind players. In: Brazilian Symposium on Games and Digital Entertainment, Salvador, Brazil, pp. 164–172. IEEE (2011)
10. Fuks, H., Raposo, A., Gerosa, M. A., Pimentel, M., Filippo, D., Lucena, C.: Inter- and intra-relationships between communication coordination and cooperation in the scope of the 3C collaboration model. In: 12th International Conference on Computer Supported Cooperative Work in Design, Xi'an, China, pp. 148–153. IEEE (2008)
11. Köhlmann, W.: Identifying barriers to collaborative learning for the blind. In: Miesenberger, K., Karshmer, A., Penaz, P., Zagler, W. (eds.) ICCHP 2012. LNCS, vol. 7382, pp. 84–91. Springer, Heidelberg (2012). https://doi.org/10.1007/978-3-642-31522-0_13
12. Köhlmann, W., Lucke, U.: Alternative concepts for accessible virtual classrooms for blind users. In: 15th International Conference on Advanced Learning Technologies, Hualien, Taiwan, pp. 413–417. IEEE (2015)
13. Kunz, A., et al.: Accessibility of brainstorming sessions for blind people. In: Miesenberger, K., Fels, D., Archambault, D., Peňáz, P., Zagler, W. (eds.) ICCHP 2014. LNCS, vol. 8547, pp. 237–244. Springer, Cham (2014). https://doi.org/10.1007/978-3-319-08596-8_38
14. Pölzer, S., Miesenberger, K.: A tactile presentation method of mind maps in co-located meetings. In: Workshop Tactile/Haptic User Interfaces for Tabletops and Tablets, Dresden, Germany, p. 31. ACM (2014)
15. Pölzer, S., Kunz, A., Alavi, A., Miesenberger, K.: An accessible environment to integrate blind participants into brainstorming sessions. In: Miesenberger, K., Bühler, C., Penaz, P. (eds.) ICCHP 2016. LNCS, vol. 9759, pp. 587–593. Springer, Cham (2016). https://doi.org/10.1007/978-3-319-41267-2_84
16. Regal, G., Mattheiss, E., Sellitsch, D., Tscheligi, M.: TalkingCards: Using tactile NFC cards for accessible brainstorming. In: 7th Augmented Human International Conference, Geneva, Switzerland, pp. 1–7. ACM (2016)
17. Toro, J.A., McDonald, J.C., Wolfe, R.: Fostering better deaf/hearing communication through a novel mobile app for fingerspelling. In: Miesenberger, K., Fels, D., Archambault, D., Peňáz, P., Zagler, W. (eds.) ICCHP 2014. LNCS, vol. 8548, pp. 559–564. Springer, Cham (2014). https://doi.org/10.1007/978-3-319-08599-9_82
18. Vicars, B.: Fingerspelling Tool. https://asl.ms/. Accessed 21 Jun 2020
19. World Federation of the Deaf, Human Rights Toolkit. https://wfdeaf.org/wp-content/uploads/2017/01/7.-Human-Rights-Toolkit.pdf. Accessed 21 Jun 2020

Accessible Multimodal Tool Support
for Brainstorming Meetings

Reinhard Koutny[1]([✉])(iD), Sebastian Günther[2](iD), Naina Dhingra[3](iD),
Andreas Kunz[3](iD), Klaus Miesenberger[1](iD), and Max Mühlhäuser[2](iD)

[1] Institut Integriert Studieren, Johannes Kepler University, Linz, Austria
{Reinhard.Koutny,Klaus.Miesenberger}@jku.at
[2] Technische Universität Darmstadt, Darmstadt, Germany
{guenther,max}@tk.tu-darmstadt.de
[3] Innovation Center Virtual Reality, ETH Zurich, Zurich, Switzerland
{ndhingra,kunz}@iwf.mavt.ethz.ch
https://www.jku.at/institut-integriert-studieren/,
https://www.informatik.tu-darmstadt.de,
https://www.icvr.ethz.ch

Abstract. In recent years, assistive technology and digital accessibility for blind and visually impaired people (BVIP) has been significantly improved. Yet, group discussions, especially in a business context, are still challenging as non-verbal communication (NVC) is often depicted on digital whiteboards, including deictic gestures paired with visual artifacts. However, as NVC heavily relies on the visual perception, which represents a large amount of detail, an adaptive approach is required that identifies the most relevant information for BVIP. Additionally, visual artifacts usually rely on spatial properties such as position, orientation, and dimensions to convey essential information such as hierarchy, cohesion, and importance that is often not accessible to the BVIP. In this paper, we investigate the requirements of BVIP during brainstorming sessions and, based on our findings, provide an accessible multimodal tool that uses non-verbal and spatial cues as an additional layer of information. Further, we contribute by presenting a set of input and output modalities that encode and decode information with respect to the individual demands of BVIP and the requirements of different use cases.

Keywords: Blind and visually impaired people · Brainstorming · Business meeting · Non verbal communication · 2D haptic output device

1 Introduction

In recent years, the inclusion of persons with visual impairment or blindness has made significant strides towards an accessible society. Digital accessibility, in particular websites and applications found on stationary and mobile devices, has improved tremendously making the consumption of digital information, remote

K. Miesenberger et al. (Eds.): ICCHP 2020, LNCS 12377, pp. 11–20, 2020.
https://doi.org/10.1007/978-3-030-58805-2_2

communication and participation over the internet easier than ever before. In contrast, communication during in-situ meetings still heavily relies on non-verbal communication (NVC), which is hardly accessible to blind and visually impaired persons (BVIP) in most situations. In this context, sighted people do not only use their regular means of NVC, such as posture, gaze, facial expressions, or body language [22], but also make use of deictic gestures to refer to visual artifacts or other persons in the room during conversations [11]. While deictic gestures use arm and index finger for referencing points of interest [3,29] and are learned from childhood on [4,6], this form of NVC is not self-contained and requires knowledge about where a speaker is pointing at as well as the information which person or artifact a person refers to [1,7]. Hence, spatial aspects, in particular the location of people and artifacts, play an important role. These spatial aspects are also often inaccessible to BVIP.

Thus, unrestricted participation in group conversations, which additionally make use of visual artifacts like cards or sketches on whiteboards or digital presentations, is still found to be a huge challenge for BVIP. Therefore, a good part of group conversations in a business context is inaccessible for BVIP. Also, tool support for brainstorming meetings has not adequately met the needs of BVIP. In particular, offering means to include a broad variety of user interaction approaches and devices to cater for a wide spectrum of users and use cases as well as considering accessibility has been a shortcoming in this area to date.

In order to address this shortcoming, we propose and implement dynamic tool support for BVIP during business meetings as part of the MAPVI project [13][1]. Thereby, we allow BVIP to fully participate by providing necessary non-verbal and spatial information as well as providing an accessible user interface to actively contribute on whiteboards. As proof-of-concept, we implement tool support in the form of a Metaplan application used during a brainstorming meeting with an ongoing group conversation.

In this paper, we investigate the requirements of BVIP during brainstorming meetings and present an accessible multimodal tool that utilizes non-verbal and spatial cues as an additional layer of information. We further contribute by presenting a set of in- and output modalities that encode and decode this information with regards to the individual demands of BVIP and requirements of the different use-cases.

The paper is structured as follows: Sect. 2 discusses related work. Section 3 describes the methodology. Section 4 explains the conceptual solution. Section 5 outlines the architecture. Section 6 gives an overview of user-interaction methods possible with this type of approach. Finally, Sect. 7 concludes the paper and gives an outlook on future work.

---

[1] The MAPVI project including this publication was founded by the Austrian Science Fund (FWF): I 3741-N31.

2   State of the Art

Research investigated a large body of interactive systems which allow for body-based [22] or gesture interaction [8,35], as well as interfaces to allow intuitive world exploration techniques for BVIP [5,10,15,34]. However, during meeting situations, NVC has a tremendous amount of interaction possibilities that can enrich discussions for sighted persons during meeting situations, BVIP are often not able to fully access them and still rely on spoken information [13]. Further, business meetings nowadays usually make use of additional electronic tool support, such as digital presentations, and documents that can be collaboratively edited. Examples range from sticky notes [16] and mind map tools [21] to dedicated brainstorming and decision support software [12]. While all provide collaboration support, none of them provides specialized accessibility interfaces for BVIP.

To address these limitations, research has designed a variety of tools that allow for multimodal interfaces (e.g., [2,17,24,31]) and to support collaboration between BVIP and sighted people. For example, Thieme et al. [30] investigated how tools can assist during collaborative programming tasks. More recently, Shi et al. [28] presented a design tool for teachers to assist students with visual impairments to create interactive tactile maps. With regards to meetings, Regal et al. [27] presented an approach that uses NFC to map digital contents on tangible cards to support brainstorming meetings. Further, in a predecessor project [19], we investigated shortcomings of brainstorming meetings using mind maps and provided an accessible representation of them as an adaptive tree view for BVIP [25,26]. While this project already revealed great potential, it also exposed the need to support additional modalities to augment the perception of BVIP by providing further methods to handle NVC cues as well as spatial information within business meetings.

In summary, while there are a number of collaborative brainstorming tools that support BVIP through multimodal interfaces, there still remains a need in terms of business meetings, which helps BVIP to alleviate existing constraints that limit the access to non-verbal communication and spatial information, such as the location of participants, collaborative surfaces, or objects.

3   Methodology

User acceptance is one of the main success criteria of every project, tool or framework, therefore we involved users from the beginning of the project by interviews with (2 persons, both legally blind) and questionnaires (9 persons, 3 legally impaired and 6 visually impaired). According to these activities NVC is crucial in conversations, especially if more than two people are involved and that there might be disparity between NVC cues BVIP think are helpful during a first interview and after exposure to additional NVC cues. Observations show that the set of NVC cues perceived to be helpful is a very individual matter as well, pointing out the necessity of a highly customizable stream of information

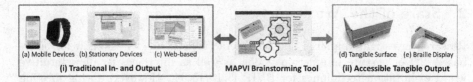

Fig. 1. Overview of the MAPVI brainstorming tool that supports (i) traditional in- and output modalities, such as (a) mobile devices, (b) stationary devices and (c) web-based interfaces, as well as (ii) accessible tangible output modalities, such as (d) a magnetic surface with tangible representations and (e) modern braille displays.

conveying NVC cues. The outcomes of these efforts suggest that there is indeed a strong need for technologies, which can improve and support the perception of spatial aspects of group conversations and non-verbal communication for BVIP and a highly customizable solution would be greatly appreciated, since which parts of non-verbal communication are of most interest to a person and which level of detail is necessary and workable is a very individual matter depending on the person and the situation. According to these interviews and questionnaires, an ontology has been developed to describe the information space that is of relevance in this setting. Based on this foundation, the MAPVI brainstorming tool and its architecture were designed to allow for an accessible, extensible and customizable platform supporting a vast amount of devices and methods for user interaction to cater to an as broad as possible user group.

4   Concept

The MAPVI Brainstorming tool is developed to manage and support brain-storming meetings together with BVIP. The process and requirements of this application are derived from meeting sessions inspired by the Metaplan method. Therefore, it relies on different roles of participants, in particular a moderator and other participants, referred to as regular participants. These regular partic-ipants can be sighted people as well as BVIP. They can create notes, actively participate in the discussion and make decisions, finding consensus as a group. The moderator, on the other hand, asks questions, elicits and organizes ideas and encourages and directs discussions towards specific topics and subtopics arising during this creative process. However, the moderator does not create content or make decisions.

These major two roles are also reflected in the brainstorming tool (see Fig. 1). The moderator has his or her own user interface, which allow him or her to organize, place and group notes, created by regular participants. Moderators can also delete notes if requested by participants and agreed upon as a group. This is all done in a web-based application, which shows a virtual whiteboard consisting of notes, groups of notes and relations between notes. Since, whiteboards can contain numerous notes, which can quickly confuse users if presented in one view, multi-view functionality was implemented. This allows multiple views on the same whiteboard, which run simultaneously and show different parts of the whole whiteboard at different zoom levels. The role of regular participants is deliberately restricted to create notes and edit their own notes. This is done via a mobile application, which pushes new notes and changes of existing ones to a server, which is also accessed by the web-based whiteboard application.

5   Architecture

5.1   Server-Backend

The brainstorming tool is a client-server application, which consists of two data interfaces: a RESTful API to create, read, update, and delete data (CRUD) and a Web-Socket service for real-time notifications.

RESTful-API: Since access to data is not solely be done by one application or framework but multiple different ones, namely, at this stage from a web application and an Android application, a standardized approach is highly beneficial. Therefore, we decided to implement a RESTful-API, which allows for platform-independent, easy access to all necessary data. Via this API, applications of any kind can perform CRUD operations. In particular, data can be accessed concerning meetings in general, users, notes of meetings, groups of notes and relations between notes.

Authentication: Typically, this access needs to be restricted to people who are allowed to consume and modify data. To ensure this, we use a token-based authentication mechanism for the RESTful API to ensure the security and privacy of the data entered into the system.

Web-Sockets: Because multiple moderator views are possible as well as multiple Android clients can enter and modify data, data gets created, updated and deleted from multiple clients simultaneously. To keep the displayed information updated and consistent, we use Web-Sockets to inform all applications of changes in the data. Applications can register to specific channels, corresponding to data sets. If data gets changed on the server, the server broadcasts this information to appropriate channels and the clients will be informed about these changes.

5.2   Web Interface

The web interface is implemented with Laravel[2] using Bootstrap and the dynamic part is generated using Konva[3] JavaScript Library. The web interface

---

[2] Laravel - PHP web framework: https://laravel.com.
[3] Konva - Javascript 2D Canvas Library: https://konvajs.org.

displaying the whiteboard view accesses data via the RESTful API and listens to changes via Web-Sockets, for instance, when notes get created by participants using the Android app or get deleted in another instance of the whiteboard view.

5.3 Android App

The Android app accesses data using the RESTful API as well. Changes are communicated via Web-Sockets. Since the role of regular participants is deliberately restricted by the Metaplan technique, the purpose of the Android application, which is only used by regular participants, is very specific and the feature set is comparatively low. Essentially, the Android app allows adding new notes and modify notes that the user-created and it also gives an overview of all notes that were created by an individual user.

6   Input and Output Modalities

6.1   General Accessibility of the User Interface

The brainstorming tool supports a broad variety of user interaction methods. Again, the two different roles, moderator and regular participant, play an important role in this context. The moderator user interface, which is, as mentioned before, a web interface, can be operated using a mouse and keyboard, but it can also be operated using a touchscreen. Therefore, big touch screen devices acting as whiteboards are directly realizable. Also, multiple views on the same whiteboard are possible to show different parts of the whole composition of notes and other items. The selected architecture also allows for a keyboard-only operation, if moderators cannot use mice or touchscreens for whatever reason. Screenreader accessibility for the moderator user interface is possible too, because of the way that data is cached and updated in the browser using Web-Sockets.

6.2   Recognition of NVC

One part of the MAPVI project and this software suite is the inclusion of gesture recognition. So far pointing gestures of participants can be recognized [9]. The brainstorming tool allows these pointing gestures to be fed into the system and shared with BVIP. The architecture of the system allows because of the use of an easily extendable RESTful API the implementation of other NVC cues as well. Facial expressions, eye gestures and other hand gestures are possible in the future. This information can be later offered to BVIP.

6.3   Gesture-Based User Interface for BVIP

Additionally, gesture based user interfaces tailored for BVIP are supported, in particular, user interfaces considering spatial aspects of meetings. A mobile application using smartphones in combination with a smartwatch, which is currently under development, can be used to retrieve information about artifacts or participants by pointing in the general direction of information sources using the smartphone or smartwatch as virtual index finger, once this is finished. This will enable BVIP to easier select pieces of information, without cognitively overloading them and shows great potential to improve their spatial perception of the environment including the location of people and artifacts.

6.4 Tangible Representation of the Information

Tangibles provide a haptic experience and are able to map the content of individual items of the digital whiteboard to a physical surface and are distinguishable for BVIP by different shapes and tactile characteristics [14,18]. Further, they can maintain the position and clustering of the digital cards analogously. Hereby, it is important that the tangibles consistently adapt to the spatial information correctly, which requires an additional mechanism that can move them on the physical surface of the table, e.g., through embedded motors (e.g., [23]) or external mechanical support (e.g., [20]). As tangibles with embedded functionality may increase complexity and are expensive, external mechanisms that can move custom 3D-printed objects are reasonable. For example, electromagnetic arrays (e.g., [32,33] or a magnetic gripper arm below the surface can precisely address tangibles with magnetic foundations individually and move each object according to the layout of the virtual whiteboard.

We implemented our prototype with a magnetic gripper arm to relocate tangibles to represent the digital content as cards. The spatial information of each card is maintained in real-time to make them physically accessible for BVIP and updates modifications of the spatial distribution of the cards dynamically. A top mounted camera detects the position of each tangible and recognizes changes by the user which triggers update commands to the tool. If a tangible is moved accidentally, the device can return it to its original location to keep the consistency. If a user touches a tangible with the index finger, the linked content of the virtual card of the brainstorming tool is readout.

7   Conclusion and Further Work

In this paper, we presented design considerations based on user involvement of members of the target group of BVIP and a proof-of-concept implementation of an accessible multimodal brainstorming tool for business meetings. A careful architectural design and selection of technology have ensured accessibility, extensibility, and customizability of this approach for brainstorming tool support. Multi-model user interface approaches including the tactile representation of information, gesture recognition or gesture-based user interfaces allow BVIP people to gain access to the vast information space of non-verbal communication and show great potential in helping them to participate in group conversations in a business context to the full extent. As the next step, existing user interface approaches will be refined and extended in close cooperation with people of the target group. In particular, gesture-based as well as tactile user interfaces will be investigated in more detail to explore how and to which degree they can help to deal with the immense amount of spatial and non-verbal information that gets generated during group conversations and prevent cognitive overloading blind and visually impaired people. Evaluations with the target group will be undertaken to study the benefits of this approach and reveal areas for improvements.

References

1. Alibali, M.W.: Gesture in spatial cognition: expressing, communicating, and thinking about spatial information. Spat. Cogn. Comput. **5**(4), 307–331 (2005). https://doi.org/10.1207/s15427633scc0504_2
2. Baldwin, M.S., Hayes, G.R., Haimson, O.L., Mankoff, J., Hudson, S.E.: The tangible desktop: a multimodal approach to nonvisual computing. ACM Trans. Access. Comput. **10**(3) (2017). https://doi.org/10.1145/3075222
3. Bangerter, A., Oppenheimer, D.M.: Accuracy in detecting referents of pointing gestures unaccompanied by language. Gesture **6**(1), 85–102 (2006). https://doi.org/10.1075/gest.6.1.05ban
4. Bates, E.: The Emergence of Symbols: Cognition and Communication in Infancy. Language, Thought, and Culture: Advances in the Study of Cognition. Academic Press, New York (1979). https://books.google.de/books?id=_45-AAAAMAAJ
5. Bolt, R.A.: Put-that-there: voice and gesture at the graphics interface. In: Proceedings of the 7th Annual Conference on Computer Graphics and Interactive Techniques, SIGGRAPH 1980, pp. 262–270. ACM, New York (1980). https://doi.org/10.1145/800250.807503
6. Brannigan, C.R., Humphries, D.A., Jones, B.: Ethological studies of child behaviour, pp. 37–64. Cambridge University Press, Cambridge (1972)
7. Butterworth, G., Jarrett, N.: What minds have in common is space: spatial mechanisms serving joint visual attention in infancy. Br. J. Dev. Psychol. **9**(1), 55–72 (1991). https://doi.org/10.1111/j.2044-835X.1991.tb00862.x
8. Dhingra, N., Kunz, A.: Res3ATN-deep 3D residual attention network for hand gesture recognition in videos. In: 2019 International Conference on 3D Vision (3DV), pp. 491–501. IEEE (2019)
9. Dhingra, N., Valli, E., Kunz, A.: Recognition and localisation of pointing gestures using a RGB-D camera. arXiv preprint arXiv:2001.03687 (2020)
10. Geronazzo, M., Bedin, A., Brayda, L., Campus, C., Avanzini, F.: Interactive spatial sonification for non-visual exploration of virtual maps. Int. J. Hum.-Comput. Stud. **85**, 4–15 (2016). https://doi.org/10.1016/j.ijhcs.2015.08.004. http://www.sciencedirect.com/science/article/pii/S1071581915001287. Data Sonification and Sound Design in Interactive Systems
11. Goffman, E.: Encounters: Two Studies in the Sociology of Interaction. Ravenio Books (1961)
12. Groupmap - collaborative brainstorming & group decision-making (1442020). https://www.groupmap.com/
13. Günther, S., et al.: MAPVI: meeting accessibility for persons with visual impairments. In: Proceedings of the 12th PErvasive Technologies Related to Assistive Environments Conference, PETRA 2019, pp. 343–353. ACM, New York (2019). https://doi.org/10.1145/3316782.3322747

14. Günther, S., Schmitz, M., Müller, F., Riemann, J., Mühlhäuser, M.: BYO*: utilizing 3D printed tangible tools for interaction on interactive surfaces. In: Proceedings of the 2017 ACM Workshop on Interacting with Smart Objects, SmartObject 2017, pp. 21–26. ACM, New York (2017). https://doi.org/10.1145/3038450.3038456

15. Guo, A., et al.: VizLens: a robust and interactive screen reader for interfaces in the real world. In: Proceedings of the 29th Annual Symposium on User Interface Software and Technology, UIST 2016, pp. 651–664. ACM, New York (2016). https://doi.org/10.1145/2984511.2984518

16. Ideaflip - realtime brainstorming and collaboration (1442020). https://ideaflip.com/

17. Iranzo Bartolome, J., Cavazos Quero, L., Kim, S., Um, M.Y., Cho, J.: Exploring art with a voice controlled multimodal guide for blind people. In: Proceedings of the Thirteenth International Conference on Tangible, Embedded, and Embodied Interaction, TEI 2019, pp. 383–390. Association for Computing Machinery, New York (2019). https://doi.org/10.1145/3294109.3300994

18. Ishii, H.: Tangible bits: beyond pixels. In: Proceedings of the 2nd International Conference on Tangible and Embedded Interaction, TEI 2008, pp. xv–xxv. Association for Computing Machinery, New York (2008). https://doi.org/10.1145/1347390.1347392

19. Kunz, A., et al.: Accessibility of brainstorming sessions for blind people. In: Miesenberger, K., Fels, D., Archambault, D., Peňáz, P., Zagler, W. (eds.) ICCHP 2014. LNCS, vol. 8547, pp. 237–244. Springer, Cham (2014). https://doi.org/10.1007/978-3-319-08596-8_38

20. Lee, J., Post, R., Ishii, H.: ZeroN: mid-air tangible interaction enabled by computer controlled magnetic levitation. In: Proceedings of the 24th Annual ACM Symposium on User Interface Software and Technology, UIST 2011, pp. 327–336. Association for Computing Machinery, New York (2011). https://doi.org/10.1145/2047196.2047239

21. Miro - mind map software built with teams in mind (1442020). https://miro.com/

22. Müller, C., Cienki, A., Fricke, E., Ladewig, S., Mcneill, D., Tessendorf, S.: Body - Language - Communication: An International Handbook on Multimodality in Human Interaction, vol. Bd. 38.1. De Gruyter Inc., Berlin/Boston (2013)

23. Pedersen, E.W., Hornbæk, K.: Tangible bots: interaction with active tangibles in tabletop interfaces. In: Proceedings of the SIGCHI Conference on Human Factors in Computing Systems, CHI 2011, pp. 2975–2984. Association for Computing Machinery, New York (2011). https://doi.org/10.1145/1978942.1979384

24. Pires, A.C., et al.: A tangible math game for visually impaired children. In: The 21st International ACM SIGACCESS Conference on Computers and Accessibility, ASSETS 2019, pp. 670–672. Association for Computing Machinery, New York (2019). https://doi.org/10.1145/3308561.3354596

25. Pölzer, S., Miesenberger, K.: Presenting non-verbal communication to blind users in brainstorming sessions. In: Miesenberger, K., Fels, D., Archambault, D., Peňáz, P., Zagler, W. (eds.) ICCHP 2014. LNCS, vol. 8547, pp. 220–225. Springer, Cham (2014). https://doi.org/10.1007/978-3-319-08596-8_35

26. Pölzer, S., Miesenberger, K.: A tactile presentation method of mind maps in colocated meetings. In: Proceedings of the International Workshop on Tactile/Haptic User Interfaces for Tabletops and Tablets, Held in Conjunction with ACM ITS 2014. ACM, New York (2014)

27. Regal, G., Mattheiss, E., Sellitsch, D., Tscheligi, M.: TalkingCards: using tactile NFC cards for accessible brainstorming. In: Proceedings of the 7th Aug-

mented Human International Conference 2016, AH 2016. Association for Computing Machinery, New York (2016). https://doi.org/10.1145/2875194.2875240

28. Shi, L., Zhao, Y., Gonzalez Penuela, R., Kupferstein, E., Azenkot, S.: Molder: an accessible design tool for tactile maps. In: Proceedings of the 2020 CHI Conference on Human Factors in Computing Systems, CHI 2020, pp. 1–14. Association for Computing Machinery, New York (2020). https://doi.org/10.1145/3313831.3376431

29. Taylor, J.L., McCloskey, D.I.: Pointing. Behav. Brain Res. **29**(1), 1–5 (1988). https://doi.org/10.1016/0166-4328(88)90046-0

30. Thieme, A., Morrison, C., Villar, N., Grayson, M., Lindley, S.: Enabling collaboration in learning computer programing inclusive of children with vision impairments. In: Proceedings of the 2017 Conference on Designing Interactive Systems, DIS 2017, pp. 739–752. Association for Computing Machinery, New York (2017). https://doi.org/10.1145/3064663.3064689

31. Yu, W., Kangas, K., Brewster, S.: Web-based haptic applications for blind people to create virtual graphs. In: 2003 Proceedings of the 11th Symposium on Haptic Interfaces for Virtual Environment and Teleoperator Systems, HAPTICS 2003, pp. 318–325 (2003)

32. Weiss, M., Remy, C., Borchers, J.: Rendering physical effects in tabletop controls. In: Proceedings of the SIGCHI Conference on Human Factors in Computing Systems, CHI 2011, pp. 3009–3012. Association for Computing Machinery, New York (2011). https://doi.org/10.1145/1978942.1979388

33. Weiss, M., Schwarz, F., Jakubowski, S., Borchers, J.: Madgets: actuating widgets on interactive tabletops. In: Proceedings of the 23nd Annual ACM Symposium on User Interface Software and Technology, UIST 2010, pp. 293–302. Association for Computing Machinery, New York (2010). https://doi.org/10.1145/1866029.1866075

34. Willis, S., Helal, S.: RFID information grid for blind navigation and wayfinding. In: Ninth IEEE International Symposium on Wearable Computers (ISWC 2005), pp. 34–37. IEEE, New York (2005). https://doi.org/10.1109/ISWC.2005.46

35. Zhai, S., Morimoto, C., Ihde, S.: Manual and gaze input cascaded (magic) pointing. In: Proceedings of the SIGCHI Conference on Human Factors in Computing Systems, CHI 1999, pp. 246–253. ACM, New York (1999). https://doi.org/10.1145/302979.303053

Pointing Gesture Based User Interaction of Tool Supported Brainstorming Meetings

Naina Dhingra[1]([✉])[iD], Reinhard Koutny[2][iD], Sebastian Günther[3][iD],
Klaus Miesenberger[2][iD], Max Mühlhäuser[3][iD], and Andreas Kunz[1][iD]

[1] Innovation Center Virtual Reality, ETH Zurich, Zurich, Switzerland
{ndhingra,kunz}@iwf.mavt.ethz.ch
[2] Institut Integriert Studieren, Johannes Kepler University, Linz, Austria
{Reinhard.Koutny,Klaus.Miesenberger}@jku.at
[3] Technische Universität Darmstadt, Darmstadt, Germany
{guenther,muehlhaeuser}@informatik.tu-darmstadt.de
https://www.icvr.ethz.ch,
https://www.informatik.tu-darmstadt.de

Abstract. This paper presents a brainstorming tool combined with pointing gestures to improve the brainstorming meeting experience for blind and visually impaired people (BVIP). In brainstorming meetings, BVIPs are not able to participate in the conversation as well as sighted users because of the unavailability of supporting tools for understanding the explicit and implicit meaning of the non-verbal communication (NVC). Therefore, the proposed system assists BVIP in interpreting pointing gestures which play an important role in non-verbal communication. Our system will help BVIP to access the contents of a Metaplan card, a team member in the brainstorming meeting is referring to by pointing. The prototype of our system shows that targets on the screen a user is pointing at can be detected with 80% accuracy.

Keywords: Brainstorming tool · Web application · Android application · Pointing gesture · Robot operating system · Kinect sensor · OpenPtrack · Localization · Recognition · Non-verbal communication

1 Introduction

Non-verbal communication plays an important role in team meetings, in which we use gestures along with speech to convey the full meaning of our ideas. Usually, those gestures are based on our inherited cultures, language we speak, etc. However, this non-verbal communication (NVC) is not accessible to blind and visually impaired people (BVIP) without additional aid. Thus, they are unable to participate in the meetings to a full extent. To better integrate BVIP in such meetings, we need to provide them with external aids that are able to capture

© The Author(s) 2020
K. Miesenberger et al. (Eds.): ICCHP 2020, LNCS 12377, pp. 21–29, 2020.
https://doi.org/10.1007/978-3-030-58805-2_3

and transfer the spatial information of artifacts as well as referring gestures and other non-verbal communication elements by sighted users.

Brainstorming meetings are used in many areas of business and academia, such· as medical diagnostics, scientific research, spin-offs, military operations; etc. Considering the wide use of brainstorming meetings, there is a need to build an autonomous system to help BVIP work independently in those meetings. Otherwise, it is very difficult for them to understand the full meaning of the conversation, mainly due to the non-verbal communication.

NVC in brainstorming meetings includes several kinds of gestures performed by the participants, such as nodding, shaking the head, head orientation, pointing gestures, sign language, eye contact, blinking of eyes, pointing with eyes, etc. Thus, the information flow in a team meeting is not simply based on generated artifacts and on spoken explanations, but it is in particular a manifold of NVCs that could carry up to 55% of the overall information [13]. These gestures refer to the 3D information space they are performed in.

Spatial aspects of brainstorming meetings also play a vital role in understanding and determining pointing gestures performed by the participants of a meeting. Most people tend to give an egocentric relative position of the objects in the meeting room when referring to them. Some of the spatial artifacts which are to be considered are whiteboards, items on the whiteboards, etc. For this paper, we developed a Metaplan brainstorming tool which is the basis of our spatial artifacts.

Thus, the goal is to transfer NVC elements to BVIP, and more particular pointing gestures that refer to artifacts in the 3D information space. For this, we use OpenPtrack along with robot operating system (ROS) [18] to detect the pointing direction of a user with regard to artifacts in a common work space. We have also developed a brainstorming tool which has a web interface (the "Moderator" interface) and android application for the digital interaction between the members of the brainstorming meeting. The content of the corresponding artifact could then be output on a blind user interface such as braille.

This paper is structured as follows: Related work is discussed in Sect. 2, while the methodology is described in Sect. 3. The experiments are elaborately illustrated in Sect. 3.1, results are discussed in Sect. 3.2, followed by suggestions for improvement in Sect. 3.3. Finally, Sect. 4 concludes our work.

2   State of the Art

Researchers have worked on technology to improve the experience of brainstorming meetings in particular for sighted people. Pictorial stimuli is used for supporting group conversation [22]. Graph-based web services are built for the solutions for various problems in meetings [6]. An automatic system to categorize and process the language used in meetings is described in [4]. Mobile phones are used for brainstorming sessions which act like a virtual mind map table [11]. There is also commercial as well as free tool support for brainstorming meetings. Approaches range from cards applications [5,10] and mind map applications [12,14] over dedicated brainstorming and decision support software [3,21] to virtual design spaces and visual management tools [15,20]. These various kinds of software allow for an improved workflow and help people to collaborate.

There is only little research to improve the integration of BVIP in brainstorming meetings. In [8], Mindmap-based brainstorming sessions are described to push the integration of BVIP in meetings. In [19], a Mindmap along with a LEAP sensor is described for tracking pointing gestures over an interactive horizontal surface. A prototypical system simulated gestures by sighted users and made them accessible to BVIP [16]. A system using a LEAP sensor and speech recognition was developed to improve the tabletop interaction for BVIP in [9] to better detect deictic gestures that are typically accompanied with specific words that hint to a geometric position. Another approach to detect pointing gestures in brainstorming meetings used a Kinect and a PixelSense table. It helped BVIP to understand the basic meaning of such gestures [7]. For this, an information infrastructure was developed by [17] to translate the natural behavior of sighted team members and thus reduce the information gap for the BVIP.

3   Methodology

Our approach includes the development of a brainstorming tool and an autonomous system for recognizing pointing gestures. Thereafter, the two systems are combined to know the output of pointing gestures made towards the digital screen showing the brainstorming tool. This combined system helps BVIP to access the content of the brainstorming tool app, i.e. the card on which a sighted user is pointing to.

3.1   Concept of the Brainstorming Tool

The brainstorming tool is software, which aims to support brainstorming meetings based on the Metaplan method. It mainly supports two different roles: a moderator and the other participants of the group. These participants can be sighted people as well as BVIP. The moderator organizes the input of the participants, leads the discussion, and asks participants to clarify and resolve input, but neither provides content nor makes decisions by himself. The participants on the other hand provide input by editing cards, and in a second step contribute to discussions and participate in the decision-making process. Consequently, the brainstorming tool has two different modes of operation, which will be used consecutively following the two different phases of Metaplan:

- Participants add cards via a smartphone Android application
- The moderator operates a web-based user interface, called whiteboard view, to organize cards of the participants

Android App for the Participants. The Android app for the participants has intentionally a relatively small feature set, since any detailed user interface would distract the user from his main task. The functionalities of the Android app are as follows:

– Participants can create cards and edit them.
– Providing an overview of all created cards by each individual user.
– Participants can submit cards to whiteboard. Once the card is submitted, it cannot be deleted anymore from the whiteboard by the participant.

Web-Based User Interface for Moderators. The web-based user interface for moderators includes the following functionalities for organizing and facilitating a meeting:

– Organization
  – Moderators are provided with an overview of meetings. They can create new meetings, invite participants to a meeting from the list of users, who registered to the system, and can modify and delete existing meetings.
  – Moderators can open meetings multiple times, which allows for multi-screen setups where screens show certain segments of the whole work space.
– Facilitation
  – In the whiteboard view, moderators can rearrange cards, which were created by the other participants using the Android app. New cards pop up in real time on a stack in a corner of the virtual whiteboard.
  – Moderators can create groups and relations between cards. However, they cannot decide to create these two types of entities themselves, but they are the output of group discussion.
  – Moderators can delete cards, groups and relations. This is the result of a group discussion among participants coordinated by the moderator.

Architecture and Technology. The brainstorming tool is based on a client-server architecture (see Fig. 1). The server is based on Laravel[1] which stores data in an SQL database. Laravel also provides the web-based user interface for the moderator. For the dynamic parts of the whiteboard view, which are supposed to change without page reloads, like real-time modifications of the size, orientation and position of user interface elements or repositioning and grouping of cards, the JavaScript Framework Konva[2] is used to display cards, groups of cards and their relation to each other. Konva allows the moderator to manipulate these items in a user-friendly manner using a mouse or touchscreen.

The server offers two kinds of APIs. Firstly, a RESTful API[3], which allows data, e.g. user data, cards, groups, relations and other data, to be created, read,

---

[1] Laravel - PHP web framework: https://laravel.com.
[2] Konva - Javascript 2D Canvas Library: https://konvajs.org.
[3] REST: https://en.wikipedia.org/wiki/Representational_state_transfer.

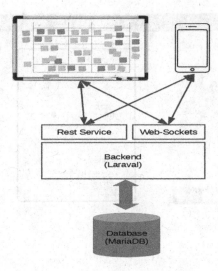

Fig. 1. Components of the brainstorming tool.

updated and deleted. Secondly, a Web-Socket[4] service, which allows broadcasting changes of such data following the publish-subscribe pattern[5]. Clients can subscribe to channels, which correspond to sets of data. If a set of data changes, the server publishes the fact that data was changed to these channels, and clients can react to these changes and for instance update their cached data.

3.2 Pointing Gesture Recognition System

The pointing gesture recognition system [2] uses a Kinect v2 sensor. The sensor data is given to ROS 1 (Robot Operation System) and analyzed by OpenPTrack [1] to get the joint coordinates of the pointing arm. These joint coordinates are then used for assessing the pointing gesture performed by the user. Each joint has a different ID and the x, y, z coordinates with different IDs are published. The sensor's reference frame is transformed to the world reference frame using the /TF ROS package. This package is used for rotation and translation, i.e. linear transformations, to have the world reference coordinate frame.

The pointing gesture consists of an arm movement towards the referral object, and the hand pointing towards the object. The hand gesture is usually accompanied with speech referring towards the same directional position. We calculated the pointing gesture from the elbow and hand position coordinates. These coordinates help to find the forearm vector which is used for calculating the pointing vector. We used the mathematical transformation as shown in Eq. 1. For this, we used a normal direction to the plane N_f, a predefined point on the ground plane P_f, the positions of hand H, and the position of elbow joint E, respectively.

---

[4] WebSocket: https://en.wikipedia.org/wiki/WebSocket.
[5] https://en.wikipedia.org/wiki/Publish-subscribe_pattern.

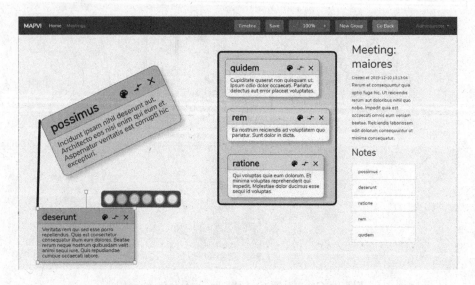

Fig. 2. Screenshot of the brainstorming tool.

$$P_p = H + \frac{(H - P_f) \cdot N_f}{EH \cdot N_f} \cdot EH, \tag{1}$$

The plane coordinate frame is the plane where the output screen (the common work space for the Metaplan) is placed. The coordinate position in the world reference frame is transformed to the plane coordinate frame of the output screen using a rotation matrix. The output values from OpenPtrack are converted to the whiteboard/matrix plane coordinate frame. The TF package in ROS is used for this coordinate transformation. These transformed output position values are analysed based on the position of the cards of the brainstorming tool being displayed on the screen. After getting the position of the card being pointed at, the card's content could be converted to speech and made available to the BVIP (Fig. 2).

3.3 Combination of Brainstorming Tool and Pointing Gesture Recognition System

After developing the brainstorming tool and the pointing gesture recognition system, these two systems are combined to better integrate BVIP in brainstorming meetings as shown in Fig. 3. The pointing gesture recognition system is used to assess the position of the card which is being pointed at by the moderator. This card carries the information which has to be conveyed to the BVIP. The system helps a BVIP to be better integrated and to access complete meaning of the conversation by knowing the contents the participants are talking about. So, it is a two-fold process: (1) The user points at the digital whiteboard where the contents of the web application of the brainstorming tool is displayed. The pointing

Fig. 3. Illustration of a user pointing at the digital screen with the brainstorming tool and RGB-D sensor is used for capturing pointing gesture.

gesture recognition system identifies the gesture and the target position of the pointing gesture. (2) The identified position is correlated to the content being displayed on the screen at that time to retrieve the contents of the corresponding artifact. Preliminary user studies on a screen with six equally distributed areas, this combined setup can offer 80 % accuracy in detecting the target position of pointing gesture.

4   Conclusion

We built a brainstorming tool and automatic pointing gesture recognition system, which can work together in an synchronous manner to help BVIP to access the integral meaning of NVC. The output of our system could be delivered to the BVIP via audio/speech or using a braille display.

The pointing gesture recognition system is based on the pre-developed software OpenPtrack and ROS. The output of the system gives the position of the pointing gesture towards the digital screen showing the web application of the brainstorming tool. Future work will also involve the output medium for the BVIP. We plan to use a magnetically driven 2D actuation system along with braille display and audio for the output of the system.

Acknowledgements. This work has been supported by the Swiss National Science Foundation (SNF) under the grant no. 200021E 177542/1. It is part of a joint project between TU Darmstadt, ETH Zurich, and JKU Linz with the respective funding organizations DFG (German Research Foundation), SNF (Swiss National Science Foundation) and FWF (Austrian Science Fund).

References

1. Carraro, M., Munaro, M., Burke, J., Menegatti, E.: Real-time marker-less multi-person 3D pose estimation in RGB-depth camera networks. In: Strand, M., Dillmann, R., Menegatti, E., Ghidoni, S. (eds.) IAS 2018. AISC, vol. 867, pp. 534–545. Springer, Cham (2019). https://doi.org/10.1007/978-3-030-01370-7_42
2. Dhingra, N., Valli, E., Kunz, A.: Recognition and localisation of pointing gestures using a RGB-D camera. arXiv preprint arXiv:2001.03687 (2020)
3. Groupmap - collaborative brainstorming & group decision-making (1442020). https://www.groupmap.com/
4. Huber, B., Shieber, S., Gajos, K.Z.: Automatically analyzing brainstorming language behavior with Meeter. Proc. ACM Hum.-Comput. Interact. 3(CSCW), 1–17 (2019)
5. Ideaflip - realtime brainstorming and collaboration (1442020). https://ideaflip.com/
6. Ivanov, A., Cyr, D.: The concept plot: a concept mapping visualization tool for asynchronous web-based brainstorming sessions. Inf. Vis. 5(3), 185–191 (2006)
7. Kunz, A., Alavi, A., Sinn, P.: Integrating pointing gesture detection for enhancing brainstorming meetings using kinect and pixelsense. In: Disruptive Innovation in Manufacturing Engineering Towards the 4th Industrial Revolution, 25–28 March 2014, Stuttgart, Germany, p. 28 (2014)
8. Kunz, A., et al.: Accessibility of brainstorming sessions for blind people. In: Miesenberger, K., Fels, D., Archambault, D., Peňáz, P., Zagler, W. (eds.) ICCHP 2014. LNCS, vol. 8547, pp. 237–244. Springer, Cham (2014). https://doi.org/10.1007/978-3-319-08596-8_38
9. Kunz, A., Schnelle-Walka, D., Alavi, A., Pölzer, S., Mühlhäuser, M., Miesenberger, K.: Making tabletop interaction accessible for blind users. In: Proceedings of the Ninth ACM International Conference on Interactive Tabletops and Surfaces, pp. 327–332 (2014)
10. Lino - sticky and photo sharing for you (1442020). http://en.linoit.com/
11. Lucero, A., Keränen, J., Korhonen, H.: Collaborative use of mobile phones for brainstorming. In: Proceedings of the 12th International Conference on Human Computer Interaction with Mobile Devices and Services, pp. 337–340 (2010)
12. Lucidchart - online mind map maker (1442020). https://www.lucidchart.com
13. Mehrabian, A., Ferris, S.: Inference of attitudes from nonverbal communication in two channels. J. Consult. Clin. Psychol. 3, 248–252 (1967)
14. Miro - mind map software built with teams in mind (1442020). https://miro.com/
15. Mural - online brainstorming, synthesis and collaboration (1442020). https://mural.co/
16. Pölzer, S., Miesenberger, K.: Presenting non-verbal communication to blind users in brainstorming sessions. In: Miesenberger, K., Fels, D., Archambault, D., Peňáz, P., Zagler, W. (eds.) ICCHP 2014. LNCS, vol. 8547, pp. 220–225. Springer, Cham (2014). https://doi.org/10.1007/978-3-319-08596-8_35
17. Pölzer, S., Schnelle-Walka, D., Pöll, D., Heumader, P., Miesenberger, K.: Making brainstorming meetings accessible for blind users. In: AAATE Conference (2013)
18. Quigley, M., et al.: Ros: an open-source robot operating system. In: ICRA Workshop on Open Source Software, Kobe, Japan, vol. 3, p. 5 (2009)

19. Schnelle-Walka, D., Alavi, A., Ostie, P., Mühlhäuser, M., Kunz, A.: A mind map for brainstorming sessions with blind and sighted persons. In: Miesenberger, K., Fels, D., Archambault, D., Peňáz, P., Zagler, W. (eds.) ICCHP 2014. LNCS, vol. 8547, pp. 214–219. Springer, Cham (2014). https://doi.org/10.1007/978-3-319-08596-8_34
20. Stormboard (1442020). https://www.stormboard.com/
21. Stormz - meeting software for demanding facilitators (1442020). https://stormz.me/de
22. Wang, H.C., Cosley, D., Fussell, S.R.: Idea expander: supporting group brainstorming with conversationally triggered visual thinking stimuli. In: Proceedings of the 2010 ACM Conference on Computer Supported Cooperative Work, pp. 103–106 (2010)

Communication Device for People with Cerebral Palsy Assisted with Head Movements

Sergio Arturo Rodriguez-Valencia[1], Iyari Alejandro Nava-Tellez[1],
Mario Covarrubias-Rodriguez[2], and Milton Carlos Elias-Espinosa[1(✉)]

[1] Tecnológico de Monterrey, Escuela de ingeniería y Ciencias,
México City, Mexico
mielias@tec.mx
[2] Politecnico di Milano, Dipartimento di Meccanica, Milan, Italy

Abstract. In this project we will address the design of a manipulated electronic Augmentative and Alternative Communication (AAC) device with simple head movements for Cerebral Palsy (CP) patients with level III or IV Viking Speech Scale (VSS) and a Gross Motor Function Classification System (GMFCS) level IV or V which means they are limited in their ability to control leg and arm movements and are therefore not candidates for the use of other conventional AACs. This was accomplished using a simple hierarchical word choice system as well as a inertia sensor mounted over the user's ear with the support of 3D printing technology as its primary manufacturing process.

Keywords: Cerebral palsy · AAC · Inertia sensor · Non- verbal · Communication

1 Introduction

Cerebral palsy can cause disturbances in sensory and cognitive development as well as in different motor disorders. This can directly affect those who suffer from it in their linguistic and communication development [1,2]. The lack of speech can in some cases be compensated by using an AAC (Augmentative and Alternative Communication), but for a patient to be a candidate for its use, it must have the cognitive and motor skills necessary to manipulate it. Currently 3 out of 1,000 children are considered to have cerebral palsy (CP) [3]. Children diagnosed with CP are generally affected in their cognitive and motor development making their motor skills fine, gross, and oral. In addition, it is considered that up to 30% of individuals with PC experience some impairment in listening, speaking, and language [4]. These are those patients who benefit from some type of AAC. AACs are all those devices that an individual use to send or receive messages [5]. Generally, they are focused on users being able to answer direct questions

Supported by APAC.

and the relatives of these patients try to make communication as simple as possible using yes or no questions. This negatively impacts patients because it renders them inactive at the time of communication and they will not be active in dialogue unless someone else starts it with them [6].

According to the study carried out by Tania Desai and Katherine Chow in Toronto District School Board, it was determined that the use of a simple electronic ACC adapted to a particular case within an iPad not only generated communication with a nonverbal child, but also over time brought the interest in the individual to communicate more and become more active with their teachers, peers, and family [8].

ACCs can be as simple as buttons with a single verbal output to deny or affirm, as well as image books in which the user searches from page to page until showing the iconography of what they need to express. Even something more complex that needs user navigation in a virtual environment such as the Go talk now application [7]. Regardless if it is something complex or simple, a prevailing problem and the reason why there are so many variants of ACC is the possibility that each individual has to manipulate it. There are cases in which the affect will be able to use an iTalk 2 [8] without any problem, but others in which having the buttons close together generates difficulties for the user to choose the correct option due to motor problems, which generates confusion with his interlocutor. In these cases, the user could choose to use a BigMack [9] device, but if this user is now unable to reach the button, history repeats itself and a new variant must be found. The way in which a person's movements ability is classified is through the Gross Motor Function Classification System (GMFCS) which provides a clear description of a patient current motor function. It goes from level I in which the person is able to walk in any place and also climb stairs without the use of a railing, all down to level V in which the person need the assistance of someone else to be transported and also has a clear limitation in his ability to control leg and arm movements [10].

Nowadays there is also electronic devices such as the Tobii [11] that can be used through eye seeking technology. However, most of the opinions about this system were about how expensive it was and how difficult it was to calibrate it because of constant sporadic tremors or even because the patient couldn't go through all the calibration process. So even though it was a great system most of the of the patients couldn't afford it or even using it so they wouldn't invest on it [12].

Communication in humans is essential for learning and for interaction with the people around us. Usually the use of a speech generating device in a common conversation can slow down the whole process while implementing dialogue patterns need learning time for both the sender and receiver of the message [13]. Therefore, this project aims to develop an AAC capable of being manipulated by unconventional movements. In this case we will address the use of basic head movements(turn the head up, down and sideways) in order to navigate through an electronic AAC with preloaded words in a hierarchical phrase system similar to the Go Talk Now app. This means that the user must choose between increasingly specific options until arriving to the phrase that is closest to what he wants to say. The use of head movements was decided because it is known that there these movements are known to be less common to be affected to the ones involving the upper and lower limbs [14]. In the same way we will be using an electronic model with inertia sensors because they have been successfully tested previously for the control of support devices for cerebral palsy during R. Raya research [15].

2   Arquitecture

During this project, direct support was received from the association for people with cerebral palsy or "APAC" in Mexico who managed to link us with a group of young people with cerebral palsy and most of them GMFCS level IV or V willing to help us in the validation of the entire project. Knowing the profile of each young person, we noticed that each one had different motor limitations, but instead of finding a solution that covered all cases, it was determined to carry out a generalized and parameterized system that could be adapted to any case, by generating a system capable of navigating a hierarchical digital CAA'without the need for fine movements, this would be easier to adapt in a future project. Once this has been defined, it was decided to develop this controlled system based on basic head movements (up, down and sideways). For this, it was first necessary to carry out the electronic design based on a gyroscope mounted on an over ear system to determine the direction in which the individual's head was moving. Only the gyroscope is mounted on the over ear system, the rest of the device is resting on the user's shoulders and neck like a necklace. It is important to also minimize the number of cables to prevent them from getting caught or hindered and limiting the patient's movement.

2.1   Electronic Design

The necklace features an Arduino nano that uses an Atmega328 microcontroller. This is programmed to obtain data from an MPU-6050 gyroscope, determine the direction of movement of the head and then send the information through an HC-05 bluetooth module also located on the collar to a Raspberry Pi card which has the purpose to process the information and display the graphical interface. This module uses the UART protocol to send information through the serial port. The MPU sensor, on the other hand, communicates using the I2C protocol. This system also has a vibrating motor to have a better interaction with the user. The entire data collection system is powered by 5 V battery as shown in Fig. 1.

   The MPU sensor detects changes from -2000 to 2000 per second. This information is sent in 16 bits, in 2 packets of 8 each. The microcontroller receives these 2 data packets and concatenates them to obtain an analog value that it can then interpret. The magnitude of the analog value represents the intensity of the movement made by the head; To perform the calibration of the device, repeated movements of each direction were recorded by the user, to determine

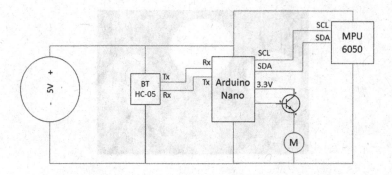

Fig. 1. Diagram of connections.

the minimum analog value required for the microcontroller to determine that a selection is being made in that direction. The microcontroller obtains data from the MPU every 0.2 s and makes a comparison with the value obtained in each axis of rotation with the minimum value to consider it a movement. If the minimum is exceeded, it is sent by the Bluetooth module to the terminal received by the screen. It was decided to use 3D printing technology with PLA in order to be able to easily redesign the entire over ear system in order adapt it as many times as necessary as shown on Fig. 2.

Fig. 2. Prototypes of over ear device.

2.2   GUI

This interface was designed in a hierarchical way so that at first four options are shown: yes, no, more and keyboard as shown in Fig. 3. The sides will say the affirmation or denial directly while the other two will redirect the user to a new screen.

In the case of the keyboard, it was placed so that if the user wanted to say a specific word, they could do so. Its operation is slow but effective, a vintage

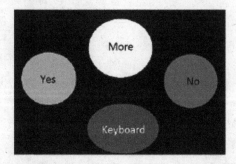

Fig. 3. Main screen.

cell phone keypad is displayed on the screen in which the cursor moves from number to number every two seconds. When this is in the number with the desired letter the user must send a downward movement to confirm his choice and now the cursor will move between the letters found in this number and the user will confirm the letter in the same way as previously did with the number. This process will be repeated until the user finishes forming his word and once this is done, he can confirm it to send it to a text to speech software and thus say a specific word that is not in the list of possible phrases. If the option of "More" is chosen, then a screen like the first one will be displayed in which there will be three options of branches to choose from and an option to return in case of eating an error. As the individual chooses options, these will lead him to more and more specific words until he meets a final phrase. Once this is done, the device will give the option in the form of a single audio output with the desired phrase. This not only allows the user to give specific ideas, but also allows them to be active in communication by not only focusing on giving a closed yes or no answer but also a complete sentence according to their idea. The phrase hierarchy flow is shown below in Fig. 4. This list was developed thanks to the team of therapists from APAC Mexico.

3   Results

The device shown in Fig. 5 was validated in the first instance by a user without any type of motor deficiency under a simple test on which he was asked to navigate freely through the screens and knowing the order of the hierarchy of dialogue he would reach specific phrases in a way that this test could function as a reference in test sessions with individuals affected with CP.

The testing phase was performed on individuals with a VSS level III and a GMFCS level IV and V who couldn't use of a conventional communication board due to their lack of control in their upper extremities. These individuals communicate through interpretation systems that only their relatives and nurses can comprehend, so the dialogue with them without the presence of someone who knows the system is null. During a span of 6 h of training distributed over a week,

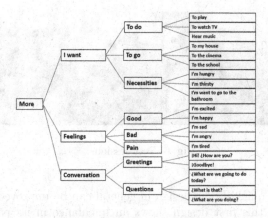

Fig. 4. Hierarchy flow of ideas.

Fig. 5. Prototype of the device.

the users shown in Fig. 6 were able to understand the operation of the system and navigate freely on the AAC, allowing them to have a more complex dialogue with the people around them without the need for an interpreter present. Despite being a dialogue limited by the number of sentences within the AAC, it showed acceptance by users and their therapists because they not only gave them a higher level of independence to express ideas, but also the complexity of the sentences and the use of recordings instead of a text-to-speech engine generated a feeling of belonging within their close groups so they urged us to continue recording and maintaining this modality within the AAC.

It is considered that this prototype has a minimum reach of 8 to 10 immediate users in APAC, this because to make a correct use of it, the user is required only to have mobility in the neck. This reach could be increased with the help of therapists and the continued use of the device by users. Since the familiarity to the device can be created with frequent use, the number of individuals capable of using it would rise. Also, it is known that with a good approach and training an individual who at first is not able to perform the correct use of an AAC with time will be able to do it [8].

Although the device was able to receive and transmit the movements of the head correctly, the calibration system must be done faster to make the person

Fig. 6. Test sessions.

adjustment more quickly. The design in general can be improved mainly in the necklace because this first design shows an imbalance in its parts that could eventually tire the user of its use. This also applies to the over-the-ear piece that could be printed on some other softer material to avoid user discomfort. Now, tests are still being carried out to verify its operation with more similar cases and thus have a more solid comparison against devices on the market in terms of variety of words and ease of use.

4   Conclusion

It was possible to design a first functional prototype of AAC focused on individuals with GMFCS level IV and V operated only with gross head movements. It is a simple interface that aims to encourage the operator to become communicatively active so that he can more easily get along with the people around him. This design was focused on neck movements, but its technology can be applied to any other type of movement and be as complex as the user's motor limitations allow. If, for example a patient can perform and control diagonal head movements the number of options per screen can be increased or otherwise decreased. This also applies to the cognitive skills of each patient. In this case the screen would display phrases, but it could also be arranged to show pictures or photos instead to be easier for less cognitive persons. We must remember that this condition affects each person who experiences it differently, so this device opens the doors to a generation of new AACs controlled uniquely by anyone with a communication or language impediments no matter his physical limitations.

The development of this work shows us that manipulation of support equipment is possible through unconventional means, in addition to one of its strongest advantages being its adaptability. It is even possible to modify the shape of the hardware to change the input movements and adjust them to those movements in which the individual has greater control. So a second step for this design is to address other types of movement such as those in the ankles or phalanges and check their operation to control supporting interfaces.

References

1. Kavlak, E., Tekin, F.: Examining various factors affecting communication skills in children with cerebral palsy. Neuro Rehabil. **44**(2), 161–173 (2019). https://doi.org/10.3233/NRE-182580
2. Choi, J.Y., Park, J., Choi, Y.S., Goh, Y.R., Park, E.S.: Functional communication profiles in children with cerebral palsy in relation to gross motor function and manual and intellectual ability. Yonsei Med. J. **59**(5), 677–685 (2018). https://doi.org/10.3349/ymj.2018.59.5.677
3. SCPE: Prevalence and characteristics of children with cerebral palsy in Europe. Dev. Med. Child Neurol. **44**(9), 633–640 (2002)
4. Pellegrino, L.: Cerebral palsy. In: Batshaw M.L. (ed.) Children with Disabilities, 5th edn. pp. 443–466. Paul H. Brookes Publishing Co., Baltimore (2002)
5. American Speech-Language Hearing Association: Roles and responsibilities of speech-language pathologists with respect to augmentative and alternative communication: technical report. ASHA Leader **24**(9), 8 (2004)
6. Pennington, L.: Cerebral palsy and communication. Pediatr. Child Health **18**(9), 405–409 (2008)
7. Muharib, R., Correa, V.I., Wood, C.L., Haughney, K.L.: Effects of functional communication training using GoTalk NowTM iPad® application on challenging behavior of children with autism spectrum disorder. J. Spec. Educ. Technol. **34**(2), 71–79 (2019). https://doi.org/10.1177/0162643418783479
8. Desai, T., Chow, K.: iPad-based alternative communication device for a student with cerebral palsy and autism in the classroom via an access technology delivery protocol. Comput. Educ. **79**, 148–158 (2014)
9. IRMA: Special and gifted education: concepts, methodologies, tools, and applications: concepts, methodologies, tools, and applications, IGI Global (2016)
10. Palisano, R., Rosenbaum, P., Bartlett, D., Livingston, M.: Gross motor function classification system expanded and revised. Can child centre for childhood disability research, MCMaster university. Dev. Med. Child. Neurol. **39** 214–223 (2007)
11. Valleau, M.J., Konishi, H., Golinkoff, R.M., Hirsh-Pasek, K., Arunachalam, S.: An eye-tracking study of receptive verb knowledge in toddlers. J. Speech Lang. Hear. Res. **61**(12), 2917–2933 (2018). https://doi.org/10.1044/2018_JSLHR-L-17-0363
12. Niehorster, D.C., Cornelissen, T.H.W., Holmqvist, K., Hooge, I.T.C., Hessels, R.S.: What to expect from your remote eye-tracker when participants are unrestrained. Behav. Res. Methods **50**(1), 213–227 (2017). https://doi.org/10.3758/s13428-017-0863-0
13. Cerebral palsy Alliance on Speech generating devices for children with cerebral palsy. https://cerebralpalsy.org.au/our-research/about-cerebral-palsy/interventions-and-therapies/speech-generating-devices-for-children-with-cerebral-palsy/
14. Wichers, M., Hilberink, S., Roebroeck, M.E., van Nieuwenhuizen, O., Stam, H.J.: Motor impairments and activity limitations in children with spastic cerebral palsy: a Dutch population-based study. J. Rehabil. Med. **41**(5), 367–374 (2009). https://doi.org/10.2340/16501977-0339
15. Raya, R., Rocon, E., Ceres, R., Harlaar, J., Geytenbeek, J.: Characterizing head motor disorders to create novel interfaces for people with cerebral palsy: creating an alternative communication channel by head motion. In: IEEE International Conference on Rehabilitation Robotics 2011, pp. 1–6, Zurich (2011). https://doi.org/10.1109/ICORR.2011.5975409

Enabling Real-Time 3D Display
of Lifelike Fingerspelling in a Web App

Jami Montgomery[1] ⓘ, John McDonald[2](✉) ⓘ, Eric Gong[1], Souad Baowidan[3],
and Rosalee Wolfe[2]

[1] Georgetown University, Washington, DC, USA
j.montgomery@georgetown.edu
[2] DePaul University, Chicago, IL, USA
jmcdonald@cs.depaul.edu, rwolfe@depaul.edu
[3] King Abdulaziz University, Jeddah, Saudi Arabia
Sbaawidan@kau.edu.sa
http://asl.cs.depaul.edu

Abstract. Fingerspelling receptive skills remain among the most difficult aspects of sign language for hearing people to learn due to the lack of access to practice tools that reproduce the natural motion of human signing. This problem has been exacerbated in recent years by the move from desktop to mobile technologies which has rendered prior software platforms less accessible to general users. This paper explores a web-enabled 3D rendering architecture that enables real-time fingerspelling on a human avatar that can address these issues. In addition it is capable of producing more realistic motion than prior efforts that were video-based and provides greater interactivity and customization that will support further enhancements to self-practice tools for fingerspelling reception.

Keywords: Sign language · Avatars · Fingerspelling · Educational tools

1 Introduction

Sign language is the preferred form of communication for millions of people around the world [2], and for many signers, written language is a second language. These factors contribute to the many challenges that Deaf and hard-of-hearing people face in day to day interactions with the hearing. For the millions of hearing people who interact with native signers, educational software can be an important part of the learning process and can provide valuable practice opportunities for many critical parts of sign language.

A component of many sign languages is fingerspelling, in which the hands convey the letters of an alphabet from a spoken language. The collection of hand configurations used in fingerspelling for a given spoken language is called a manual alphabet. By sequentially forming handshapes, words in the spoken language

© The Author(s) 2020
K. Miesenberger et al. (Eds.): ICCHP 2020, LNCS 12377, pp. 38–44, 2020.
https://doi.org/10.1007/978-3-030-58805-2_5

may be spelled letter by letter. Many sign languages incorporate fingerspelling as a key link to the spoken language, and while fingerspelling usage varies considerably among sign languages [11], most use fingerspelling for conveying

– Proper names of people and places,
– Loan worlds, such as technical terminology,
– Terms for which there is no commonly agreed-upon sign [1].

Fingerspelling is particularly important when signers are communicating with hearing people. For example, signers most often have sign names, but hearing people they interact with will tend not to have a sign name, and so fingerspelling will often be used for both participants.

In addition, fingerspelling can be an integral part of bi-lingual education for Deaf children, who continue to face challenges in early education, particularly with written forms of spoken languages. In the United States, the average reading level of deaf high school graduates has remained near the fourth-grade level for decades, and studies of early deaf education have shown that increased experience with fingerspelling positively influences a deaf child's reading ability [9].

Because of these factors, fingerspelling is an important component of both Deaf-hearing communication and early deaf education. Unfortunately, it can also be a difficult skill to learn, particularly for hearing people. This is somewhat ironic since it is the one part of signing that is actually borrowed from their spoken language. The problem lies not in the production of fingerspelling, but rather in its recognition or reception, i.e. reading a word being fingerspelled. Fingerspelling receptive skills are a notorious challenge for students in interpreter training programs and are often cited as the first skill learned but the last skill mastered. This is particularly true in ASL when the fingerspelling is rapid [8].

2   Limitations of Current Practice Tools

One important factor that exacerbates the challenge of learning fingerspelling reception is the lack of practice opportunities that are available to students in fingerspelling classes. The two most common practice methods are peer practice, which is practicing with other students, and watching videos of fingerspelling. Peer work between students can be ineffective for learning to read fluent fingerspelling as it involves watching non-native fingerspelling that is much slower and also inexpertly produced.

Video practice tools such as DVDs and https://www.handspeak.com/spell/ practice/ are problematic because of their immutability. They are limited to the words that have been recorded, and the fact that the cost of recording and distributing new fingerspelling recordings can be quite high, particularly for media such as DVD's, though online distribution does mitigate this somewhat. In any case, for video fingerspelling study, a student can end up learning or memorizing the specific productions of the particular words provided in the video. These limited recordings obviously cannot match the variability of productions they will witness in fluent discourse.

Several attempts have been made at computer and web-based fingerspelling recognition practice tools that attempt to display any fingerspelled word. Unfortunately, most of these are image-based tools such as [14], which provide sequentially shown still drawings or photos. As noted by [15], fingerspelling is conveyed, not by the still shape of the hand, but by its motion as it moves through the shapes in the word. Thus, it is the motion of the fingers that we perceive in a signer, not the individual handshapes when recognizing a word, and therefore, practice software that displays sequences of still pictures will not help students to recognize human fingerspelling motion at fluent speeds.

Increasingly, computer generated avatars have offered a compelling solution to this need as they are capable of producing the infinite variability of fingerspelling productions on demand and at variable speeds. However, prior practice tools leveraging 3D avatars have had several issues that hindered wider adoption including

- The display of an isolated 3D hand. When learning to recognize fingerspelling, it is important to have the whole visual field of the person or avatar [5]. In fact most still-frame tools have the same issue as they only show pictures or drawings of isolated hands
- Motion that did not prevent self-intersection of the fingers, such as seen in [3,12]. Human fingers will naturally move to avoid each other in transitions between letters, and any tool that does not prevent collisions in the fingers will not provide the realistic fingerspelling motion needed by students.
- Motion that was limited only to the arm and fingers of the avatar. The previously presented mobile drill and practice tool presented in [13] made great strides in providing natural motion of the fingers along with motion of the signer's arm for double letters using a single pre-rendered video of an avatar to display any word. Unfortunately, because of the nature of the video-clip splicing playback technique that was used in the app, the torso of the avatar was not able to move, which does not match the natural motion of a human signer. This resulted in a robotic appearance for the full avatar even as the motion of the hand was fluid and natural.
- Limited platform support. Even in the case of the full body avatar in [13], it was implemented as a native app that had the limitations of running only on Windows devices. Also, due to its technology relying on a large pre-recorded video of individual transitions between letters, it required a substantial amount of device storage. This is potentially problematic on some smaller devices like smartphones.

This paper introduces a novel web-based fingerspelling practice app that builds on the prior Fingerspelling Tutor technology in [13] by addressing these deficiencies. It does this by encapsulating the Fingerspelling Tutor experience in a web-app and implementing a 3D avatar display that provides fully interactive animations of one-handed fingerspelling in real-time to enhance the self-practice experience. Further, the app has been designed to support a variety of sign languages, and to allow the fingerspelling of any word in the chosen sign language.

In addition, it features interactive client control of the avatar with full camera movement so that fingerspelling may be viewed at a variety of speeds and viewing angles to simulate different conversation settings.

The previous Fingerspelling Tutor software was built, as described in [6] with the participation of interpreter training students, and its continued development has been driven by feedback from this target user group [16]. The current effort has also been driven by requests from users of the prior software, who indicated that wider platform support, more realism in the avatar's motion and increased interactivity with the avatar display.

3   Building a Better Practice Tool

To achieve a ubiquitously supported client, the new practice tool utilizes WebGL2 [4] to provide a responsive user interface that renders and animates the fingerspeller on the client's device. This mitigates the need to download or stream video and thereby significantly and reduces mobile bandwidth usage. The design requirements were:

1. Minimal data storage requirements on client device
2. Minimal initial data transmission between server and client
3. Minimal data transfer from client device to server when requesting an fingerspelling
4. Minimal data transfer from server to client when playing an animation

To accomplish all of these requirements, the new web app has been designed so that the server leverages the existing services from the prior Fingerspelling tutor software detailed in [13], which supported fingerspelling in a variety of sign languages in a native Windows app. This prior system utilized smooth motion controllers for the avatar's joints, and an exhaustive collection of inter-letter poses to avoid collisions between fingers during transitions to provide natural fingerspelling motions. The web app encapsulates this functionality on a native compiled Windows server but leaves the actual realization of these motions of the avatar to the client.

The client provides for interactive rendering and animation of the avatar which is supplied in an FBX format. To support ubiquitous access, the client is written in JavaScript and employs a WebGL2 JavaScript library called three.js for rendering [10], which is provided under the MIT software license. Communication between the client and server uses the standard HTTP2 protocol, and the data transmitted is encoded using the standard JSON format. A diagram of the architecture of this web app is provided in Figure 1.

In this diagram, the client-side application is implemented in JavaScript and relies on a mere eight megabytes to store the avatar data, including all geometry and surface textures. The server is implemented in C# on Windows.

As in our previous fingerspelling tutor, the new app will support a variety of options for input and interaction with the user including allowing the user to ask the avatar to fingerspell a word that the user types in, and also support a quiz

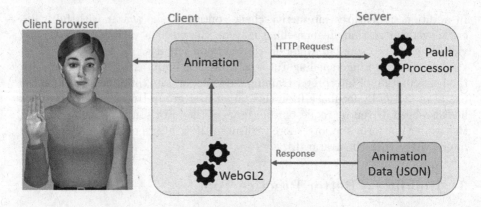

Fig. 1. Diagram of client-server architecture

facility with words coming randomly from a variety of word lists. In either case, the communication protocol for the system will require the client to request a word for fingerspelling and for the server to receive the word.

In order to minimize complexity in the JavaScript client, the server applies a variety of techniques to compose the animation data for the avatar

1. Sequencing the individual hand shapes in time, including the finger movements necessary for certain letters (e.g.. J and Z in ASL).
2. Computing interpolations that avoid collisions between the fingers and thumb via a library of artist-animated motion paths.
3. Adding motion of the arm for double letters either, e.g.. bounce or slide to the side depending on the sign language
4. Adding continuous ambient motion to the avatar to avoid a frozen robotic appearance

Scheduling these effects on the avatar is complex because many of these processes can affect the same joints and are computed with very different motion controls. For example, sequencing handshapes is done with traditional key-frame animation where settings for all of the hand's joints are applied at a given time. Then layering onto this ambient motion, which is an application of Perlin noise [7], requires a more complicated avatar structure than we desired on the client side.

In keeping with goals 1–4 above, the server pre-computes the animation on each of the avatar's joints by using a more complex internal representation and then sends frame-by-frame data to the avatar for playback. Since the client has full data for every bone at each frame, it does not have to perform interpolation and thus very simple animation controllers can be used, improving performance on slower hardware. Of course, by sending frame-by-frame data, we are increasing the amount of data being sent vs only sending keyframes, but since the Avatar has 25 bones in the torso and arm, the data for the body for a 10 s video is still less than 200 kilobytes as a clear-text JSON file, which can be reduced to less than 50k by using a binary encoding. Compare this to approximately 40 MB for a 10 s VGA resolution video at 30 fps. Thus, the web app requires less than 0.5% of the bandwidth required to transmit a video of the same animation, which results in a quick response time, even when internet connectivity is poor.

4 Conclusion and Next Steps

The new web app presented here builds upon prior Fingerspelling Tutor technology by providing greater platform access, greater naturalness in fingerspelling motion for receptive skill practice and allowing greater freedom for exploring fingerspelling contexts such as different points of view. The results reported in this paper concern an important technological advancement for a Fingerspelling reception practice tool which was designed and developed with input from the interpreter training community.

Once the new 3D display is completely integrated into the functionality of Fingerspelling Tutor, the software will be further tested with sign language students to determine the extent to which the added interactivity impacts student experience and learning.

References

1. Battison, R.: Lexical borrowing in American sign language (1978)
2. World Federation of the Deaf: WFD: who are we. http://wfdeaf.org/our-work/. Accessed 11 June 2020
3. Dickson, S.: Advanced animation in mathematica. Mathematica J. **15**(2), 15-2 (2013)
4. Ghayour, F., Cantor, D.: Real-time 3D Graphics with WebGL 2: Build Interactive 3D Applications with JavaScript and WebGL 2 (OpenGL ES 3.0). Packt Publishing Ltd. (2018)
5. Jamrozik, D., A.C.A.E.I.p.C.C.C.I.: Personal communication with Wolfe, R
6. Jamrozik, D.G., Davidson, M.J., McDonald, J.C., Wolfe, R.: Teaching students to decipher fingerspelling through context: a new pedagogical approach. In: Proceedings of the 17th National Convention Conference of Interpreter Trainers, San Antonio, TX, pp. 35–47 (2010)
7. Olano, M.: Modified noise for evaluation on graphics hardware. In: Proceedings of the ACM SIGGRAPH/EUROGRAPHICS Conference on Graphics Hardware, pp. 105–110 (2005)
8. Quinto-Pozos, D.: Rates of fingerspelling in American sign language. In: Poster presented at 10th Theoretical Issues in Sign Language Research conference, West Lafayette, Indiana, vol. 30 (2010)
9. Ramsey, C., Padden, C.: Natives and newcomers: gaining access to literacy in a classroom for deaf children. Anthropol. Educ. Q. **29**(1), 5–24 (1998)
10. Ricardo, C.: Threejs. http://threejs.org/. Accessed: 14 Apr 2020
11. Schembri, A., Johnston, T.: Sociolinguistic variation in the use of fingerspelling in Australian sign language: a pilot study. Sign Lang. Stud. **7**(3), 319–347 (2007)
12. Su, S.A., Furuta, R.K.: VRML-based representations of ASL fingerspelling on the world wide web. In: Proceedings of the Third International ACM Conference on Assistive Technologies, pp. 43–45 (1998)

13. Toro, J.A., McDonald, J.C., Wolfe, R.: Fostering better deaf/hearing communication through a novel mobile app for fingerspelling. In: Miesenberger, K., Fels, D., Archambault, D., Peňáz, P., Zagler, W. (eds.) ICCHP 2014. LNCS, vol. 8548, pp. 559–564. Springer, Cham (2014). https://doi.org/10.1007/978-3-319-08599-9_82

14. Vicars, W.: Fingerspelling tool. https://asl.ms/. Accessed 14 Apr 2020

15. Wilcox, S.: The Phonetics of Fingerspelling, vol. 4. John Benjamins Publishing, Amsterdam (1992)

16. Wolfe, R., McDonald, J., Toro, J., Baowidan, S., Moncrief, R., Schnepp, J.: Promoting better deaf/hearing communication through an improved interaction design for fingerspelling practice. In: Antona, M., Stephanidis, C. (eds.) UAHCI 2015. LNCS, vol. 9175, pp. 495–505. Springer, Cham (2015). https://doi.org/10.1007/978-3-319-20678-3_48

Cognitive Disabilities and Accessibility -
Pushing the Boundaries of Inclusion
Using Digital Technologies
and Accessible eLearning Environments

Cognitive Disabilities and Accessibility - Pushing the Boundaries of Inclusion Using Digital Technologies and Accessible eLearning Environments

Introduction to the Special Thematic Session

Susanne Dirks[1]([✉]) [iD], Christian Bühler[1], Cordula Edler[1],
Klaus Miesenberger[2] [iD], and Peter Heumader[2] [iD]

[1] TU Dortmund University, 44227 Dortmund, Germany
{susanne.dirks, christian.buehler}@tu-dortmund.de,
cordula.edler@icloud.com
[2] Institut Integriert Studieren, Johannes Kepler University,
Altenbergerstraße 69, Linz, Austria
{klaus.miesenberger, peter.heumader}@jku.at

Abstract. The aim of this session is to bring together researchers and developers who are engaged in the development and evaluation of digital technologies and e-learning environments to improve the conditions for social participation of people with cognitive disabilities and learning difficulties of all ages in all areas of life. In this session ideas, visions and projects for research, development and evaluation on the following topics will be presented and discussed: Digital technologies for people with cognitive disabilities, cognitive accessibility of everyday technologies and eLearning environments, eLearning environments for learners with learning difficulties (accessible MOOCs, LMS, VLEs), digital support systems for people with dementia and use of Augmented Reality, Virtual Reality or gaming elements in digital technologies for people with learning disabilities. The introduction integrates the different topics into the broader context of digital inclusion of people with cognitive disabilities. Even though much has improved in recent decades, there are still technological, structural and attitudinal characteristics that make it difficult for this target group to fully participate in society. Digital technologies and modern learning environments, if cognitively accessible, offer the possibility of overcoming barriers and enable people with cognitive disabilities to participate more actively in all areas of life.

Keywords: Digital inclusion · Cognitive disabilities · Digital accessibility · Assistive technology · eLearning environments

© Springer Nature Switzerland AG 2020
K. Miesenberger et al. (Eds.): ICCHP 2020, LNCS 12377, pp. 47–52, 2020.
https://doi.org/10.1007/978-3-030-58805-2_6

1 Introduction

The Internet and other digital resources have become a global standard for communication, learning, entertainment and exchange of information. Access to information and communication for people with disabilities through modern technologies is seen as an important prerequisite for social inclusion. People with disabilities should be able to use information and communication technologies just like everyone else.

In recent years, there has been a considerable advance in the public awareness of accessibility at all levels. A large number of countries have ratified the Convention on the Rights of Persons with Disabilities (CRPD), and WCAG 2.0 and WCAG 2.1 [1] have become the world standard for creating accessible digital content. The United Nations 2030 Agenda for Sustainable Development has called on all member states to take action to end poverty and disadvantage and improve living conditions for everyone. Of the 17 defined goals, goal 10 ('Reduce inequality within and among countries') focuses directly on improving the social, economic and political inclusion of people with disabilities [2].

Nevertheless, and especially in times like this Covid-19 crisis, when many aspects of public life are shifting into the digital space, it becomes obvious that far too many digital resources and learning environments are still not or only partially accessible to people with disabilities.

2 Digital Accessibility and Inclusion of People with Cognitive Disabilities

Digital accessibility has many different dimensions and, for its successful implementation, poses demands on technological, societal-social and psychological processes.

For people with motor and sensory impairments, the availability of assistive technologies and supporting hardware and software solutions plays an important role in the accessibility of digital information and services. For someone who is blind or severely visually impaired, a screen reader, for example, is a helpful device to gain access to previously inaccessible visual information. For a person with limited arm mobility, alternative input devices such as a joystick, an adapted keyboard or voice control are technical solutions that reduce access barriers [3].

On the social and attitudinal level, people with disabilities are affected by prejudices and social reservations. These barriers are very fundamental and lead to further barriers [4]. Although basic attitudes towards people with disabilities have improved significantly in recent decades because of changing concepts of health and disability [5], there are still a lot of stereotypes and systemic discrimination. People with cognitive disabilities are particularly affected by these barriers.

Experiences of social marginalization and disadvantage cause many people with cognitive disabilities to assess their skills and social significance negatively and to stigmatize themselves [6]. Therefore, these people have little confidence in their abilities to use digital resources. In order to overcome these barriers, structural conditions need to be improved and adapted learning opportunities need to be created.

People with cognitive disabilities not only need to learn how to use the new technologies, but also to change their attitudes towards their own abilities and their social significance to achieve full empowerment.

Society's challenge is to create the necessary conditions for inclusion in all areas of life and to support people with cognitive disabilities in the best possible way.

3   Potential of Digital Technologies and Accessible eLearning Environments for Inclusion

As already mentioned, the use of classical assistive technologies to support cognitive impairments is limited. People with cognitive disabilities can be restricted in many different cognitive functions to very different degrees. While some functions, such as memory, attention and planning processes can be successfully supported by both analog and digital aids, there are currently virtually no assistive technologies available for functions such as self-perception, emotional control and reasoning [7, 8].

Digital accessibility and in particular cognitive accessibility of digital resources is a complex issue. People with cognitive disabilities often have difficulties in understanding complex texts and are limited in their ability to deal with complicated user interfaces. Frequently used verification procedures, like logins or captchas, are also obstacles, which are difficult to overcome.

In recent years, various research and development projects have produced numerous digital solutions that support people with cognitive impairments in various areas of life. Using assistive functionalities intended for other target groups as e.g. Text to Speech (TTS), Augmented and Alternative Communication (AAC), captions, layout/design adaptation has supported new approaches to R&D and services [8]. Meta-browsers, such as the Mediata App [9], offer simple and cognitively accessible access to the Internet and to various communication functions (news, telephone, and calendar) on mobile devices. Electronic job coaches, such as the EJO App [10], support people with disabilities in work processes. They offer multimedia-based systematic instructions for different work processes and can be adapted to the individual needs of the user. The Easy Reading framework [8, 11] is a support tool that adapts web content in real time to the individual needs of the user. With Easy Reading, any user can modify an original web page so that they can understand all the content. The Easy Reading framework is available as a browser add-on or app and includes many different tools that can be used individually or combined. The framework is designed as an open source solution and can easily be extended with new functions.

For the social inclusion of people with disabilities, school education and vocational training are of particular importance. With increasing school and vocational qualifications, the proportion of people with disabilities is continuously decreasing. People with cognitive impairments are particularly affected by the lack of accessibility of education and vocational training opportunities. After graduating from a special needs school, they usually work in sheltered workshops or in state-supported employment.

Advances in computer-based education are seen as an effective way of remedying this situation by providing assistance and compensation for learners with specific needs. In principle, eLearning environments offer access to learning content to everyone. They enable learners to be more active across their lifespan by allowing them to choose how, when and where to study.

Cognitive impairments affect learning ability either in general or in specific areas and have negative effects on academic achievement and occupational training. The increasing spread of eLearning environments offers new possibilities for individual support in learning and training processes. To be used effectively, these environments must be cognitively accessible. In eLearning environments, cognitive accessibility can be achieved through different approaches [12]. Often adaptive user interfaces are developed that can be automatically fitted to the individual support needs of the learners. Serious Games or the integration of gaming elements is another way to improve the cognitive accessibility of eLearning environments. The use of virtual agents to assist learners with questions and support needs can also be helpful. Finally yet importantly, individually adapted interfaces are another way of enabling people with more severe cognitive impairments to access eLearning environments.

Various research and development projects have demonstrated that technologies that enhance the cognitive accessibility of digital content and accessible eLearning environments have great potential for improving the participation of people with cognitive disabilities. Nevertheless, many digital contents and learning environments are still not accessible. This Special Topic Session intends to provide the space for scientific discourse and the joint generation ideas for further research and development projects in this area.

4   Contributions

This Special Thematic Session presents a range of papers addressing the enhancement of digital inclusion for people with cognitive disabilities through accessible technologies and learning environments.

The first paper describes the development of adaptive user interfaces. These systems change their structure, functionalities, and content for the individual user in real time. Adaptive user interfaces show great potential towards enhancing the usability and accessibility of computer systems. The described user interface adaptations are realized within the Easy Reading framework. Easy Reading is a software tool that supports cognitive accessibility of web content and enables people with cognitive disabilities to better read, understand and use web pages.

The second paper addresses the issue of automatic assistance to users with cognitive disabilities. The author presents an approach to use reinforcement algorithms to automatically assist the user while surfing the web. Bio physiological data, like eye movements, blink rate and heart rate are collected to assess psychological stress of the user. The implemented reasoner learns to detect individual stress patterns and automatically evokes support functions, which are offered to the user. The system is also realized within the Easy Reading Framework.

Paper three presents a writing tool for dyslexic children. A word search function and a word prediction function for the Thai language are used to assist children to improve vocabulary and story writing. Based on the concept of 'Imagination Writing' pictures are introduced to facilitate writing processes in dyslexic children.

Paper four describes the preliminary evaluation for the design, implementation and use of a real-time interactive heart rate visualization application aiming at motivating to do physical activities for people with Autism Spectrum Disorder. The research demonstrates that visualization considerably impacts the level of engagement. The results of the evaluation suggest that improving fitness levels of individuals with ASD over time may potentially be enhanced through real-time interactive feedback of one's energy expenditure that aims to promote self-motivated physical activity.

The fifth paper presents a study (ethnographic analysis in two vocational programs) on the effect and value of compensatory technology in vocational rehabilitation and the effects on labor market participation by people with cognitive disabilities. The findings underline existing knowledge on the potential of technology and in particular the motivating factor. This needs considerable consideration in organization and management to exploit motivation and avoid distraction by compensatory technology.

The project described in paper six investigates the usability and engagement in a money management application for users' intellectual disabilities. The evaluation of the application revealed the common difficulties of people with cognitive disabilities when using digital technologies and emphasizes once more the special importance of the participatory development of digital technologies for usability and accessibility.

Paper seven focusses on modeling interpersonal proximity for children with ASD using a head-mounted camera to better cope in social communication and in particular to support therapy and training. From the experimental results, a high feasibility to use the system for therapeutic activities for children with ASD could be derived. It seems possible calculate a valid estimation of the interpersonal proximity from the evaluated computer vision approach (Tobii glass technology).

The last paper in this STS introduces a mobile app for supporting young adults with cognitive disabilities using public transport. It could be shown that the children understood the basic functions of the app very well and were able to use public transport more freely and independently using the app. In order to facilitate learning processes, new functions were developed that allow a systematic reduction of support.

5 Discussion

A very positive trend towards more interest and effort in taking up the challenges of cognitive accessibility and more efficient and professional support functionalities is identified. The flexibility and adaptability of systems also based on user tracking and AI for better understanding and managing the needs allows addressing complex context of this target group including users, their care and support environment and the intended inclusive settings. The better orientation towards user requirements of all stakeholders leads to a considerably increasing interest and work on including digital systems in service infrastructures. However, the papers also underline that much more interdisciplinary R&D, training, organizational and management changes and socio-psychological efforts are needed to exploit the digital potential to the fullest extent.

R&D and implementation include more and more all stakeholder groups and, even more, the initiative, leading role and decision-making come from the users and the sector itself. This clearly shows the positive trend towards closing the gap in cognitive accessibility in relation to general accessibility.

Acknowledgement. This session and this introduction has been facilitated in the frame of the Easy Reading project, which received funding from the European Union's Horizon 2020 research and innovation program under grant agreement No. 780529.

References

1. Web Content Accessibility Guidelines (WCAG) 2.1, June 2020. https://www.w3.org/TR/WCAG21/
2. United Nations Sustainable Development Goals, Goal 10 – Reduce inequality within and among countries, June 2020. https://sustainabledevelopment.un.org/sdg10
3. Cook, A.M., Polgar, J.M., Hussey, S.M.: Cook and Hussey's Assistive Technologies: Principle and Practice, 3rd edn. St. Louis (2008)
4. Centers for Disease Control and Prevention: Common Barriers to Participation Experienced by People with Disabilities, June 2020. https://www.cdc.gov/ncbddd/disabilityandhealth/disability-barriers.html
5. WHO International Classification of Functioning, Disability and Health (ICF), June 2020. https://www.who.int/classifications/icf/en/
6. Ali, A., King, M., Strydom, A., Hassiotis, A.: Self-reported stigma and its association with socio-demographic factors and physical disability in people with intellectual disabilities: results from a cross-sectional study in England. Soc. Psychiatry Psychiatr. Epidemiol. **51**(3), 465–474 (2015). https://doi.org/10.1007/s00127-015-1133-z
7. Gillespie, A., Best, C., O'Neill, B.: Cognitive function and assistive technology for cognition: a systematic review. J. Int. Neuropsychol. Soc. **18**, 1–19 (2012)
8. Miesenberger, K., Edler, C., Heumader, P., Petz, A.: Tools and applications for cognitive accessibility. In: Yesilada, Y., Harper, S. (eds.) Web Accessibility. HIS, pp. 523–546. Springer, London (2019). https://doi.org/10.1007/978-1-4471-7440-0_28
9. Dirks, S., Bühler, C.: Participation and autonomy for users with ABI through easy social media access. In: Cudd, P., de Witte, L.P. (eds.) Harnessing the Power of Technology to Improve Lives. Proceedings of the 14th European Conference on the Advancements of Assistive Technology. Studies in Health Technology and Informatics, vol. 242. IOS Press (2017)
10. Brausch, C., Bühler, C., Feldmann, A., Padberg, M.: Supported employment – electronic job-coach (EJO). In: Miesenberger, K., Bühler, C., Penaz, P. (eds.) ICCHP 2016. LNCS, vol. 9758, pp. 142–149. Springer, Cham (2016). https://doi.org/10.1007/978-3-319-41264-1_20
11. Easy Reading – Keeping the user at the digital original, June 2020. https://www.easyreading.eu
12. Cinquin, P., Guitton, P., Sauzéon, H.: Online e-learning and cognitive disabilities: a systematic review. Comput. Educ. **130**, 152–167 (2019)

Adaptive User Interfaces for People with Cognitive Disabilities within the Easy Reading Framework

Peter Heumader[✉], Klaus Miesenberger,
and Tomas Murillo-Morales

Institut Integriert Studieren, Johannes Kepler Universität Linz,
Altenbergerstraße 69, 4040 Linz, Austria
{peter.heumader,klaus.miesenberger,
tomas.murillo_morales}@jku.at

Abstract. Adaptive user interfaces are user interfaces that dynamically adapt to the users' preferences and abilities. These user interfaces have great potential to improve accessibility of user interfaces for people with cognitive disabilities. However automatic changes to user interfaces driven by adaptivity are also in contradiction to accessibility guidelines, as consistence of user interfaces is of utmost importance for people with cognitive disabilities. This paper describes how such user interfaces are implemented within the Easy Reading framework, a framework to improve the accessibility of web-pages for people with cognitive disabilities.

Keywords: Cognitive accessibility · Adaptive user interfaces · Web-accessibility

1 Introduction

The concept of user interfaces that have the ability to change according to the user's requirements, skills, environment, situation, or other criteria has been around for a long time. In general, these concepts can be categorized in adaptive user interfaces and adaptable user interfaces.

- Adaptive User Interfaces [1]: These systems change their structure, functionalities, and content for the individual user in real time. This is achieved by monitoring the user status, the system state, and the current situation that the user is facing. By using an adaption strategy (mostly rule based), the user interface is changed at run time.
- Adaptable User Interfaces [2]: This user interfaces are highly adjustable in terms of presentation of information, display of user interface and its components or user interaction/input concepts. The settings are usually stored in a user profile and the user is able to adjust those settings in advance, usually in a settings dialog. During runtime, in contrary to the adaptive user interfaces, these settings do not change.

© The Author(s) 2020
K. Miesenberger et al. (Eds.): ICCHP 2020, LNCS 12377, pp. 53–60, 2020.
https://doi.org/10.1007/978-3-030-58805-2_7

According to Laive [3], methods for user interface adaptations can further be assigned to the following categories:

- Adaptable/Manual: the user manages the process and performs all actions
- Adaptable with system support/user selection: the user dominates the adaptation process and the system supports it
- Adaptive with user control/user approval: the system dominates the adaptation process under the supervision of the user. The system initiates the action and notifies the user about the alternative that he/she has to choose
- Adaptive/Fully adaptive: the whole process is managed by the system, which decides and implements the action based on the preferential model and the main uses

Adaptive user interfaces show great potential towards enhancing the usability and accessibility of computer systems. User tracking with state-of-the-art sensors could give estimations about the current user's status, and could trigger adequate system reactions based on that [4, 5].

However, the added adaptability for user interfaces to improve accessibility might have some unwanted side effects. For example, increasing the font size to address the vision impairment of a person might result in longer text passages and the need to scroll, which in turn results in increased attention and memory demands for the user. Therefore, providing extensive adaptability is a highly complex task, as side effects and conflicts are difficult to locate [10]. Another unwanted site effect of fully adaptive user interfaces is the inconsistency caused by the dynamic changes to the user profile, which is then reflected in the user interface. This is another drawback, as consistency across webpages is very important for people with cognitive disabilities and also addressed in Guideline 2.1: Predictable of the W3C Web Content Accessibility Guidelines (WCAG2.1) [8, 11].

This paper describes how user interface adaptations are realized within the Easy Reading framework. Easy Reading is a software tool that supports cognitive accessibility of web content and enables people with cognitive disabilities to better read, understand and use web pages. This is achieved through functionalities as:

- Adjustment of the layout and structure of webpages,
- Explanation/Annotation of web content with symbols, videos or pictures,
- Automatic/supported Modification of web content e.g. by translating it into plain language or easy2read.

Easy Reading has been designed as a cloud based solution, allowing people to interact with clients implemented as browser extension or mobile applications. Within the framework, user interfaces, user interaction and the provided help are adaptable and, to a certain extent, also adaptive for the individual user.

2   State of the Art

In recent years several research projects have been dealing with the creation of adaptive user interfaces for people with disabilities. Among those projects, prominent examples are GPII [6] or MyUI [7].

GPII allows the personalization of user interfaces, by the use of cross-platform user profiles for user interface settings, and rule-based and statistical approaches for matchmaking [14]. The architecture of the GPII was developed by the Cloud4all project uses an ontology of user needs and preferences that are directly linked to user settings [9]. The linking is done with a rule based matchmaker (RBMM) that matches user preferences and needs, with solutions available to the system and settings supported by the solution. The matchmaker results therefore in a fully configured solution on the specific system based on the individual preferences and needs of a user [6].

MyUI on the other hand was an EU funded project that enabled the generation of individualized user interfaces that would adapt to the individual users needs in real-time, based on a user profile and the actual device [10, 12, 13].

These approaches all work with a user profile that is usually stored online. Once the user logs in, the profile is downloaded and a mechanism uses this profile to create a dynamic configuration of software, assistive technology, user interface or the whole operating system for the individual user. Adaptations can only be made on features and software that are currently available on the actual device or software, and therefore the user experience might change on different devices. While this approach is sufficient for most users, it is problematic for people with cognitive disabilities, as consistency of user interfaces is very important for them [8]. Another drawback of this solution is that features must be installed on the device first, before they can be used and adapted, which might be another obstacle for people with cognitive disabilities.

3   Approach

The Easy Reading framework allows users to obtain assistance for difficult to cope with content on any webpage. This is done by cloud based software-clients that inject a dynamically generated user interface directly in the current page. By this users are able to trigger different forms of help provided by the framework. The result of the support is then rendered again directly in the webpage – allowing the user to stay at the original content and learning to cope with it in the future.

Figure 1 shows a screenshot of Easy Reading on a Wikipedia page. The user interface is dynamically injected on the right – the result of triggering an assistance tool provided by the framework is directly rendered within the web-page. In this case the help was an automatically crated AAC[1]-version of the second paragraph accomplished by a text analysis cloud service in combination with an AAC library.

Adaptations within the Easy Reading framework can be applied to the user interface, the help that is provided, the user interaction (how help is triggered) and finally

---

[1] https://en.wikipedia.org/wiki/Augmentative_and_alternative_communication.

Fig. 1. Easy Reading on a webpage

how the help is rendered and presented within the web-page. Similarly to existing approaches, these adaptations are based on a user profile that stores user preferences and abilities. Currently the user profile hosts the following support categories for the help provided by the framework:

- Text Support: Indicates whether and how the user needs help with text and content in general.
- Layout Support: How the layout of Websites should be displayed for the user.
- Reading Support: If and how the user needs support in reading text
- Symbol Support: Indicates if and how the user needs support with symbol language

In addition, the profile holds categories for triggering and displaying the provided help:

- Input Support: Stores the preferred way to triggering help and to select where on the web-page help is needed
- Output Support: Specifies the preferred way of rendering the help provided

Based on these categories, once the user logs in with his or her user profile, a dynamically optimized configuration is created for the individual user (see Fig. 2). Unlike other approaches, this configuration is not created locally, but in the cloud, and it also includes personalized user interfaces, personalized help and a personalized way of displaying the help. In this manner, clients within the Easy Reading framework do not host the code for any feature provided by the framework, as this is dynamically created for each user.

This is a big advantage over other architectures, as no matter from which device the user logs in, the user experience is always the same. Another advantage is that no additional software needs to be installed, as every feature is prepared in the cloud and downloaded during user login. Finally this enables learning and improving personalization of service provision cross different web pages and over time.

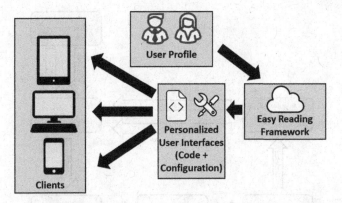

Fig. 2. User interfaces dynamically created and configured for the individual user

A drawback of the solution is however that it only works within a browser, while other solutions like GPII would also work across different applications or even operating systems. Here however each application has to be GPII-compliant and must implement its interfaces. Expanding the Easy Reading approach towards this broader application scenarios are considered as future challenges.

4 Update Strategies

As user skills, know-how and preferences change over time, the Easy Reading framework hosts a mechanism that automatically updates the preferences of the user profile based on user tracking and usage statistics (Fig. 3).

While the user is surfing the web, user interaction and tool usage is evaluated, and an updated profile is calculated. In addition, the system also hosts an additional optional user tracking component that creates an estimation on the users' current focus and detects and understands the situation the user faces (e.g. attention, stress, and confusion) at the moment. By this the additional feedback is created whether

- the user needs help for a part of the content,
- the help applied by the framework is accepted by the user
- the user has problems with the user interface or the user interaction required to trigger help of the framework

User tracking combines different sensors that feed into a software reasoner to calculate this estimation. Currently an eye-tracker that tracks the focus of the user on the web-page is used to detect cognitive load. Additionally, a smartwatch that detects heartbeats and heart rate variability is utilized to detect stress.

Based on this sensor data and the user interaction on the web-page, every hour the matchmaking component is triggered with the updated profile, resulting in a new dynamic configuration. Based on this a recommendation to add or remove functionality is triggered and presented via a dialog to the user.

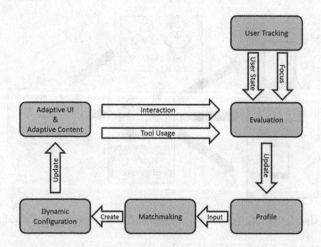

Fig. 3. Adaptive workflow within the Easy Reading framework

Figure 4 shows such a recommendation dialog. If the user accepts the dialog, the updated profile is saved and the tool is added into the current user interface. On the other hand, if the user rejects the recommendation, the changes to the profile are reverted. User approval of any changes is of utmost importance, as consistency of user interfaces and user interaction must be preserved.

Fig. 4. Tool recommendation within the Easy Reading framework

5 Current Results and Further Work

Currently the system is able to make recommendations for different tools to simplify web content as well as for different user interfaces that the framework provides. In the future recommendations on changing user interaction to trigger tools and displaying help provided by the framework will be implemented.

Due to the COVID-19 outbreak large scale user tests were not possible. Preliminary tests with 8 end users showed that a purely adaptive user interface without any user approval is not appropriate for end users. On the other hand, most users were able to understand the current implementation with user approval. Once the COVID-19 situation allows it, more exhaustive user tests are planned.

Acknowledgments. This project has received funding from the European Research Council (ERC) under the European Union's Horizon 2020 research and innovation programme (grant agreement No. 780529).

References

1. Benyon, D.I.: System Adaptivity and the Modelling of Stereotypes. National Physical Laboratory, Division of Information Technology and Computing (1987)
2. Hook, K.: Evaluating the utility and usability of an adaptive hypermedia system. Knowl. Based Syst. **10**(5), 311–319 (1998)
3. Lavie, T., Meyer, J.: Benefits and costs of adaptive user interfaces. Int. J. Hum. Comput. Stud. **68**, 508–524 (2010). https://doi.org/10.1016/j.ijhcs.2010.01.004
4. Brusilovsky, P., Maybury, M.T.: From adaptive hypermedia to the adaptive web. Commun. ACM **45**(5), 31–33 (2002)
5. Peissner, M., Schuller, A., Spath, D.: A design patterns approach to adaptive user interfaces for users with special needs. In: Jacko, J.A. (ed.) HCI 2011. LNCS, vol. 6761, pp. 268–277. Springer, Heidelberg (2011). https://doi.org/10.1007/978-3-642-21602-2_30
6. Loitsch, C., Weber, G., Kaklanis, N., et al.: A knowledge-based approach to user interface adaptation from preferences and for special needs. User Model. User-Adap. Inter. **27**, 445–491 (2017). https://doi.org/10.1007/s11257-017-9196-z
7. Peissner, M., Häbe, D., Janssen, D., Sellner, T.: MyUI: generating accessible user interfaces from multimodal design patterns. In: Proceedings of the 2012 ACM SIGCHI Symposium on Engineering Interactive Computing Systems, EICS 2012 (2012). https://doi.org/10.1145/2305484.2305500
8. WCAG2.1 – Web Content Accessibility Guidelines. https://www.w3.org/WAI/standards-guidelines/wcag/. Accessed 16 Apr 2020
9. Madrid, J., Peinado, I., Koutkias, V.: Cloud4all Priority applications and User Profile Ontology (D101.1). Public Deliverable of the Cloud4all Project (2012). http://cloud4all.info/render/binarios.aspx?id=90. Accessed 16 Apr 2020
10. Peissner, M., Edlin-White, R.: User control in adaptive user interfaces for accessibility. In: Kotzé, P., Marsden, G., Lindgaard, G., Wesson, J., Winckler, M. (eds.) INTERACT 2013. LNCS, vol. 8117, pp. 623–640. Springer, Heidelberg (2013). https://doi.org/10.1007/978-3-642-40483-2_44
11. Solovieva, T., Bock, J.: Monitoring for accessibility and university websites: meeting the needs of people with disabilities. J. Postsecond. Educ. Disabil. **27**(2), 113–127 (2014)
12. García, A., Sánchez, J., Sánchez, V., Hernández, J.A.: Integration of a regular application into a user interface adaptation engine in the MyUI project. In: Miesenberger, K., Karshmer, A., Penaz, P., Zagler, W. (eds.) ICCHP 2012. LNCS, vol. 7382, pp. 311–314. Springer, Heidelberg (2012). https://doi.org/10.1007/978-3-642-31522-0_46

13. Peissner, M., Schuller, A., Ziegler, D., Knecht, C., Zimmermann, G.: Requirements for the successful market adoption of adaptive user interfaces for accessibility. In: Stephanidis, C., Antona, M. (eds.) UAHCI 2014. LNCS, vol. 8516, pp. 431–442. Springer, Cham (2014). https://doi.org/10.1007/978-3-319-07509-9_41
14. Zimmermann, G., Strobbe, C., Stiegler, A., Loitsch, C.: Global Public Inclusive Infrastructure (GPII) – Personalisierte Benutzerschnittstellen. i-com. **13**, 29–35 (2014). https://doi.org/10.1515/icom.2014.0027

Automatic Assistance to Cognitive Disabled Web Users via Reinforcement Learning on the Browser

Tomas Murillo-Morales[✉], Peter Heumader,
and Klaus Miesenberger

Institute Integriert Studieren, Johannes Kepler University, Altenbergerstraße 69,
4040 Linz, Austria
{Tomas.Murillo_Morales,Peter.Heumader,Klaus.
Miesenberger}@jku.at

Abstract. This paper introduces a proof of concept software reasoner that aims to detect whether an individual user is in need of cognitive assistance during a typical Web browsing session. The implemented reasoner is part of the Easy Reading browser extension for Firefox. It aims to infer the user's current cognitive state by collecting and analyzing user's physiological data in real time, such as eye tracking, heart beat rate and variability, and blink rate. In addition, when the reasoner determines that the user is in need of help it automatically triggers a support tool appropriate for the individual user and Web content being consumed. By framing the problem as a Markov Decision Process, typical policy control methods found in the Reinforcement Learning literature, such as Q-learning, can be employed to tackle the learning problem.

Keywords: Cognitive accessibility · Affect detection · Assistive technology

1 Introduction

1.1 Cognitive Accessibility on the Web

Accessibility to the digital world, including the Web, is increasingly important to enable people with disabilities to carry out normal lives in the information society, something that has been acknowledged by the United Nations and many individual governments to be a right for people with disabilities. This is as true for people with cognitive, language, and learning differences and limitations as it is for anyone else [6]. Nowadays, many Web users suffering from a cognitive or learning disability struggle to understand and navigate Web content in its original form because of the design choices of content providers [6]. Therefore, Web content often ought to be adapted to the individual needs of the reader.

Currently available software tools for cognitive accessibility of Web content include Immersive Reader [4], the Read&Write browser extension [13], and Easy Reading [3]. These tools embed alternative easy-to-read or clarified content directly into the original Web document being visited when the user requests it, thereby enabling persons with a cognitive disability to independently browse the Web. Access

K. Miesenberger et al. (Eds.): ICCHP 2020, LNCS 12377, pp. 61–72, 2020.
https://doi.org/10.1007/978-3-030-58805-2_8

methods may be tailored to the specific users based on personal data, generally created by supporting staff or educators [8]. Besides these semi-automatic tools, current approaches to making websites accessible to people with cognitive and learning impairments still mostly rely on manual adaptations performed by human experts [8].

1.2 The "Easy Reading" Framework

The Easy Reading framework[1] improves cognitive accessibility of original websites by providing real time personalization through annotation (using e.g. symbol, pictures, videos), adaptation (e.g. by altering the layout or structure of a website) and translation (using e.g. Easy-to-Read, plain language, or symbol writing systems) [3].

The main advantage of the Easy Reading framework over existing cognitive support methods is that the personalized support tools are provided at the original websites in an automatic fashion instead of depending on separate user experiences which are commonly provided to users in a static, content-dependent manner and that must be manually authored by experts.

Easy Reading software clients have been designed as Web browser extensions[2] (for Mozilla Firefox and Google Chrome) and mobile OS apps (Android and iOS). The main interaction mechanism between the user and the client consist on a graphical user interface (GUI) that the user may choose to overlay on top of any Website being currently visited. A number of tools, personalized to the specific user, are available to the user in Easy Reading's GUI (see Fig. 1). The user may choose at any time to use some of the available framework functions by triggering their corresponding tool by clicking on the available buttons of the GUI.

1.3 Problem Statement

Given the special needs of Easy Reading's user base, having a traditional GUI as the only interaction mechanism between the user and the browser extension may not suit the specific needs of all users. Some users, especially those suffering from a profound cognitive disability, may not possess the necessary expertise and/or understanding to interact with Easy Reading's GUI. This is particularly the case if there are many tools being overlaid on the GUI, as this may overwhelm the user given the considerable amount of personalization mechanisms to choose from. The use of Easy Reading is also restricted for those suffering from additional physical disabilities making interaction slow or impossible when no easy to use AT solutions are at hand.

We therefore aim to assist the user in choosing and using the right cognitive support tool when he or she is in need of help while navigating Web content which appears to be confusing or unclear. We have expanded the Easy Reading framework so that it supports the automatic triggering of any support tool with the addition of two components; namely, (1) a user data collection module and (2) a client-based reasoner that

---

[1] https://www.easyreading.eu/.

[2] We recommend downloading the Easy Reading extension for Firefox at the following URL: https://addons.mozilla.org/en-US/firefox/addon/easy-reading-for-firefox/.

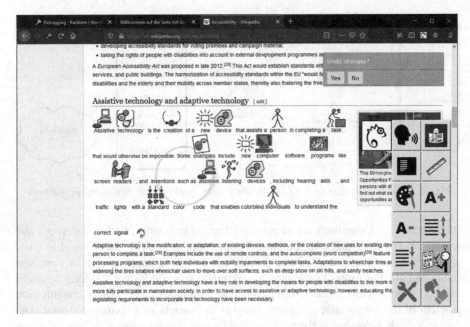

Fig. 1. The Easy Reading graphical user interface (GUI) overlaid on a website. The symbol support tool has been automatically triggered on a text paragraph by the Easy Reading reasoner, adapting its content automatically with symbol annotations over the original text. The user may reject automatically given help by means of an onscreen dialogue (top right). Any of the available tools on the Easy Reading GUI may be also manually triggered by the user at any given time by clicking on its corresponding button.

learns about the mental state of the user based on the gathered data and previous experiences, and reacts accordingly by triggering support tools when necessary. Figure 2 displays the interaction between these two components within the Easy Reading framework.

The next section gives a short overview on current methods for automatically detecting the cognitive load/affect of a person from collected user data. Based on some of these results, the design of the Easy Reading User Tracking and Reasoning framework is outlined in the remaining of this document.

2   Affect Detection: State of the Art

Affect recognition is the signal and pattern recognition problem that aims to detect the affective state of a person based on observables, with the goal of, for example, providing reasoning for decision making or supporting mental well-being [14]. Terms such as affect and mood elude a precise definition in the literature, but some working definitions may be characterized. Namely, **affect** is a neurophysiological state that is consciously accessible as the simplest raw, nonreflective, primitive feeling evident in mood and emotions e.g. the feeling of being scared while watching a scary movie [7].

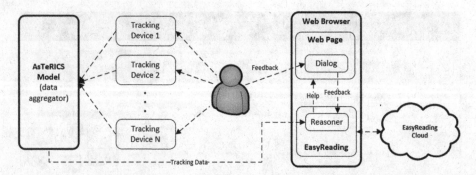

Fig. 2. Main components of the Easy Reading User Tracking and Reasoning Framework

On the other hand, **emotions** are intense and directed indicators of affect e.g. shock and scream are emotions that indicate the affect of being scared [7]. As opposed to emotions, **moods** are less intense, more diffuse, and last for a longer period of time than emotions [14]. For example, the emotion of anger, which does not last long by itself, can lead to an irritable mood [14]. On this paper we focus on the binary classification problem of the user's affect, namely, whether the user is in a confused mental state during a Web browsing activity. This problem is closely related to that of stress detection, in which data is analyzed to predict the stress level of a person, generally as a binary variable (stressed/unstressed). Stress detection is a well-researched problem that can be reliably undertaken by analyzing user physiological signals provided by e.g. a wrist-worn device such as a smartwatch [16].

Affect is a subjective experience of a person which is generally detected through self-reporting. Nevertheless, numerous approaches that aim to infer a person's affective state in an automatic fashion can be found in the literature. These approaches can be divided into four categories depending on the kind of data they process:

- Contextual approaches learn from the interaction between the user and a software system by e.g. analyzing mouse gestures or page visit times.
- Physiological approaches collect and analyze physiological data from the user, such as heart beat rate or skin temperature.
- Text-based approaches process and interpret the textual contents of speech spoken or written by the user using natural language processing (NLP) techniques for sentiment analysis generally based on supervised machine learning methods.
- Audio-visual approaches study recorded audio (generally speech) or video (of e.g. the user's face or full body) while the user interacts with the system.

Preferably, affect recognition systems should employ multimodal data i.e. fusion analysis of more than one input modality, since multimodal affect recognition system are consistently more accurate than unimodal methods [1]. A collection of state-of-the-art methods for affect recognition can be found in [1, 12, 14]. The vast majority of these methods rely on supervised machine learning models such as Deep Neural Networks (DNN) for image analysis e.g. for analyzing the user's facial expressions; or Random Forests (RF) and Support Vector Machines (SVM) for analysis of physiological signals e.g. heart rate variability. What these methods have in common is that they require of big amounts of training data that the learning model must be trained on. Available datasets such as the well-known DEAP dataset [5] aim to simplify this process by providing a large amount of pre-labelled training data for affect recognition tasks. For a list of available datasets the reader is directed to [12] and [14]. However, these approaches, especially those relying on physiological signals, suffer from a number of drawbacks that hinder their application in practice:

- Even if supervised models perform well when tested on known users, they exhibit high generalization errors when tested on unknown users, and thus models must be fine-tuned to the specific user [9].
- Available datasets have been collected using a specific combination of devices and sensors e.g. a specific wristband. Therefore, end users are forced to acquire a very similar combination of devices to make use of models trained on such datasets. Preferably, the reasoner model should adapt to the available hardware, not the other way around.
- Many tracking devices employed to collect data for these datasets are too expensive or obtrusive to be used in an informal home/office setting by end users, such as EEG headsets.

3 Easy Reading User Tracking and Reasoning

This section introduces our approach to automatic affect detection tailored to the specific user and available devices that aims to overcome some of the issues described in the previous section.

3.1 User Tracking Data Collection

In order to detect whether the user is confused or mentally overwhelmed by the content he or she is visiting during an ordinary Web browsing activity, user data needs to be collected in a transparent, unobtrusive manner to the user. In addition, specific tracking devices whose presence in a common household or office environment would normally be unwarranted (due to e.g. high cost) ought to be avoided. Therefore, after a study of the relevant literature and filtering out those tracking devices which did not satisfy these requirements, the following signals were considered:

- **Eye movement and position**. The current position of the user's gaze on the screen and the voluntary or involuntary movement of the eyes can be collected with the use of inexpensive eye trackers, commonly used in gaming, that can be mounted near a computer's screen in close distance to the user. Eye movement data is of great utility to ascertain cognitive load. Some authors even argue that eye movement data suffices to infer the cognitive demand of tasks being carried out by a person [15].
- **Blink rate**. The time period between two or more consecutive eye blinks can be a good indicator of task difficulty as well. For example, a poor understanding of the subject matter in a lecture on mathematics resulted, for some persons, on an

increased number of rapid serial blinks [10]. Blink frequency can be easily measured by, for example, analysing a video of the user's face recorded with a typical laptop webcam.

- **Heart Rate**. The current heart rate (HR) of the user, measured in beats per minute (BPM), and especially heart rate variability (HRV), which describes the variation of the time between heartbeats, is a rather simple but effective measure of the current affective state and stress level of the user [14]. These dimensions can be easily determined with the use of commercial smartwatches and fitness trackers, which are the most popular wearable devices being sold nowadays.

- **Implicit behavioural information**. Several measures of user behaviour on websites that aim to predict disorientation, task difficulty and user preferences can be found in the information retrieval literature. For example, time spent on site and click-through rates have been used to measure the cognitive load of users visiting a web search engine [2]. It is however important to note that other studies have concluded that user disorientation on websites is only weakly related to user behaviour [2]. Therefore, physiological signals are employed as the main data source employed by Easy Reading's reasoner module.

User data are processed and gathered by the Easy Reading framework as follows. Eye fixation duration (in milliseconds) and current x and y coordinates of the user gaze on the screen is measured by a Tobii 4C Eye Tracker[3]. To measure HR and HRV, the Vivoactive 3 smartwatch[4] by Garmin was selected as a good compromise between accuracy and affordability. Blink rate can be measured from video data recorded from any standard webcam, whether integrated in a laptop or an external one. Input signals are gathered and processed in an easy, flexible, and tailorable manner by means of an AsTeRICS model.

AsTeRICS [11] is an accessible technology (AT) construction set that provides plug-ins for many common input devices and signal processing operations. By combining already existing and newly developed plug-ins into an AsTeRICS model, raw input physiological signals are pre-processed before being sent to the reasoning module. Pre-processing includes methods for synchronization of data streams, handling of missing values (e.g. if the user does not possess some of the input devices), noise removal, and segmentation of the collected data into batches. Several pre-processing parameters can be adjusted directly in the AsTeRICS model by end-users or carers without the need of possessing technical skills. For example, batch (temporal window) size is by default set to 120 s (e.g. 12 samples aggregated after 10 s each) following state-of-the-art recommendations [16], but can be easily adjusted by modifying the relevant parameters of the Easy Reading AsTeRICS Data Collector plug-in. Collected batches are next converted to JSON objects and sent to the Easy Reading browser extension via a secure WebSocket connection maintained by the AsTeRICS Runtime Environment (ARE) Web server.

---

[3] https://gaming.tobii.com/tobii-eye-tracker-4c/.

[4] https://buy.garmin.com/en-US/US/p/571520/.

3.2 Easy Reading Reasoner

The Easy Reading Reasoner is the client-based module in charge of solving the problem of inferring the affective state of the user from the current readings of physiological signals collected by a running AsTeRICS model. The reasoner is hosted on the client in order to minimize the amount of messaging needed between the distributed components of the user tracking and reasoning framework, which in turn results in more responsive reasoner actions. This however comes at the cost of a more limited computational capacity, as the whole learning model has to run on the user's browser.

We have adopted a Markov decision process (MDP) as the framework for the problem, which allows it to be theoretically solved using a number of well-established control learning methods in the reinforcement learning (RL) literature. As previously stated, research shows that affection/stress recognition methods must be tailored to the individual differences of each person. Given that RL is specially well suited to problems in which the only way to learn about an environment is to interact with it, we model the environment shown in Fig. 2 as a MDP to be solved for a specific user. For a detailed characterization of MDPs and RL, the reader is directed to [17], Chapters 1 and 3. Like every MDP, our problem consists of an agent, (intractable) environment, state set (S), action set (A), and policy (π), characterized as follows.

The agent in a MDP is the learner and decision maker. It corresponds to the reasoner module being executed in the background script of the browser extension, as shown in Fig. 2. At any given time step, t, the reasoner observes the current state of the user, s_t, as specified by each sample being delivered by the AsTeRICS model, and decides on an action, a_t, to be taken with probability p i.e. $\pi(a_t|s_t) = p$. The current status, s_t, is the JSON object produced by the data collector model, which consists on a number of features e.g. HRV, and the current value of the user readings for that feature. Note that t does not correspond to an exact moment in time, but rather to the latest time window that has been aggregated by the data collector. Depending on the feature, the data collector sets its value to the latest received input or an aggregation thereof, such as the average or most common value (mode) during the time window.

The reasoner may next take one of three actions (a_t), namely:

1. No action (**NOP**). The reasoner has inferred that the user is not in need of help at the moment, and thus no further action is necessary.
2. Help user (**Help**). The reasoner has inferred that the user is in need of help with some content of the website being currently visited, and a suitable framework tool needs to be triggered. Figure 1 displays an example of this action being triggered on a website.
3. Ask user explicitly for the next action to take (**Ask**). The reasoner is unsure about the next action to take, as it expects both NOP and help actions to yield a low reward. In this case, it asks the user, via an onscreen dialogue, about which of these two actions to take next.

The user gives feedback, which may be implicit or explicit, on the action just taken by the reasoner and a numeric reward, r_{t+1}, is computed as a function of a_t and the user feedback, as shown in Table 1. This reward function heavily penalizes the case in which the agents fails to help a user in need. However, to prevent the agent from

Table 1. Reward function of the Easy Reading reasoner

a_t	Implicit user feedback		Explicit user feedback			
	User does not react/browses as usual for a given time	User manually triggers a tool	User accepts automatic help	User rejects automatic help	User requests help in dialog	User rejects help in dialog
No action	0	−200	N/A	N/A	N/A	N/A
Help user	+10	N/A	+10	−20	N/A	N/A
Ask user	−10	−10 (+10 to a_t = help user)	N/A	N/A	−10 (+10 to a_t = help user)	−10

persistently asking the user for explicit feedback on the best action to take, asking the user is always given a (low) negative reward as well. Moreover, since the correct (s_t, a_t) pair is known after the user has answered a feedback dialogue, this combination is accordingly rewarded in order to speed learning up. The agent is only positively rewarded in the case that it manages to predict that the user is currently in need of help and automatically triggers the correct tool for his or her needs.

Currently, the support tool triggered by the reasoner is the most frequently used tool by the user for the content type (text or image) that has been stared at the longest during the last time window t. Use frequency for each tool is computed and stored in each user's profile on Easy Reading's cloud backend.

In the subsequent time step, $t + 1$, the agent receives, along with the reward signal r_{t+1}, a new user state, s_{t+1}. This state is an aggregation of user data representing the user's reaction to a_t. Therefore, the Easy Reading extension does not start collecting a new state until the user's feedback has been gathered. Consequently, any user data incoming during the processing of s_t, and after a_t has been yielded but before the user feedback has been inferred, is discarded. This whole process is summarized in the workflow diagram shown in Fig. 3.

The goal of the agent (reasoner) is to learn which sequence of actions leads to a maximum reward in the long run. This behavior is encoded in a so-called policy, which the reasoner has to learn. The policy, $\pi(a|s)$, specifies which action to take on a given state, or, in the nondeterministic case, the probability of each action of the action space for a given state.

The Easy Reading reasoner keeps an estimation of the value, in terms of future expected returns, of each action a performed on each state s it has seen so far, $q_\pi(s, a)$, known as the action-value function of π. This function can be stored as a table in memory if the set state is small. In this case, input observables are further pre-processed in the browser extension via data binning to obtain a manageable state set. Otherwise, the state-value function can be approximated via function approximation methods e.g.

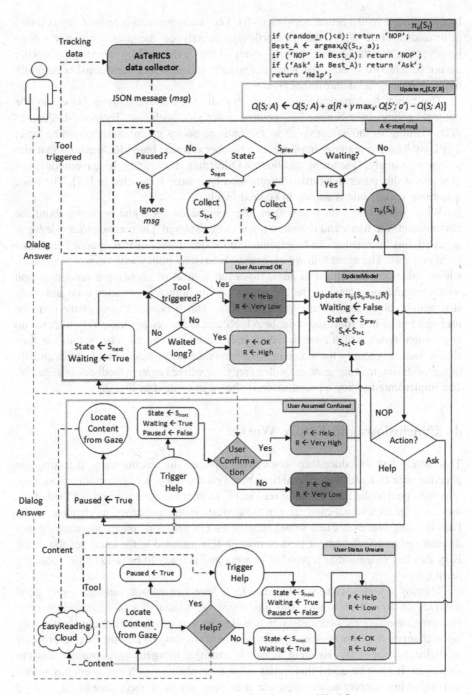

Fig. 3. Simplified Easy Reading Reasoner Workflow

by modelling it with a neural network (NN). The latter approach is possible by defining actor and/or critic NNs with Tensorflow.js directly on the user's browser[5]. Note however that due to the strict security policy of the Firefox add-on store this possibility cannot be included in officially listed extensions, and therefore our extension currently only implements a tabular q-function.

The policy that maximizes $q_{\pi^*}(s, a)$, for all states and actions is known as the optimal policy, π^*. Some RL control methods, such as Temporal-Difference (TD) learning methods, converge to the optimal policy given enough training time. The Easy Reading reasoner implements a number of value-based RL methods that aim to find π^*; namely, Q-learning and double-Q-learning. Describing these methods is out of scope of this paper, for further information the reader is directed to [17]. The basic q-learning update rule is shown in context in Fig. 3.

When interacting with a new user, the agent does not know anything about the environment (the user), and therefore it has to be explored. Once enough knowledge is acquired, this knowledge can be exploited to maximize the rewards obtained from this point onwards. The agent follows a ε-greedy behavioral policy with respect to $q_\pi(s, a)$, whose values are initialized to zero. However, instead of choosing a random action with ε probability, it chooses the "no action" action both at exploration time and when state-action values are tied at exploitation time. This way, since most of the time the user will not be in a confused state, help tools and dialogues are less likely to come up at unsought times, which aims to reduce user frustration overall. The system can then slowly learn to identify the states in which the user needs help as tools are manually triggered during training sessions with a caregiver where negative feedback is acquired. The implemented policy's pseudocode is shown in context in Fig. 3.

4   Conclusions and Future Work

This article has introduced an innovative approach to automatically detecting the affective state of a web user in real time based on the analysis of physiological signals. The main goal of the Easy Reading reasoner is to infer the current cognitive load of the user in order to automatically trigger the corresponding assistance mechanism of the Easy Reading framework that would help the user in getting a better understanding of a difficult piece of Web content (text or image). It is included in the latest version of the Easy Reading extension as a proof of concept and is ready to be tested with voluntary participants.

Training sessions with synthetic data have been carried out, yielding a very good accuracy of around 90% after 150 time steps i.e. around 5 h of real training time. However, detecting user confusion on actual users may prove much more challenging, since changes in physiological signals may be too subtle or complex to be properly modelled by the Easy Reading reasoner and the inexpensive consumer devices employed. It must be noted that initial informal evaluation with end users has shown that triggering support tools when the user does not need them should be avoided

---

[5] https://www.tensorflow.org/js.

altogether, since it frustrates and confuses them to the point where they refuse to keep using the Easy Reading extension with reasoner support enabled. After this observation, we modified the agent's policy from a traditional ε-greedy policy to the modified policy shown in Fig. 3. The next step is to test our approach with end users in a laboratory setting.

Acknowledgments. This project has received funding from the European Research Council (ERC) under the European Union's Horizon 2020 research and innovation programme (grant agreement No. 780529).

References

1. D'mello, S.K., Kory, J.: A review and meta-analysis of multimodal affect detection systems. ACM Comput. Surv. (CSUR) **47**(3), 1–36 (2015)
2. Gwizdka, J., Spence, I.: Implicit measures of lostness and success in web navigation. Interact. Comput. **19**(3), 357–369 (2007)
3. Heumader, P., Miesenberger, K., Reinhard, K.: The EasyReading framework - keep the user at the digital original. J. Technol. Pers. Disabil. **6**, 33–42 (2018)
4. Immersive Reader. Microsoft Azure. https://azure.microsoft.com/en-us/services/cognitive-services/immersive-reader/. Accessed 7 July 2020
5. Koelstra, S., et al.: DEAP: a database for emotion analysis using physiological signals. IEEE Trans. Affect. Comput. **3**(1), 18–31 (2012)
6. Lewis, C., Seeman, L.: Policy and standards on web accessibility for cognitive and learning disabilities. In: Yesilada, Y., Harper, S. (eds.) Web Accessibility. HIS, pp. 281–299. Springer, London (2019). https://doi.org/10.1007/978-1-4471-7440-0_16
7. Liu, B.: Many facets of sentiment analysis. In: Cambria, E., Das, D., Bandyopadhyay, S., Feraco, A. (eds.) A Practical Guide to Sentiment Analysis. Socio-Affective Computing, vol. 5, pp. 11–39. Springer, Cham (2017). https://doi.org/10.1007/978-3-319-55394-8_2
8. Miesenberger, K., Edler, C., Heumader, P., Petz, A.: Tools and applications for cognitive accessibility. In: Yesilada, Y., Harper, S. (eds.) Web Accessibility. HIS, pp. 523–546. Springer, London (2019). https://doi.org/10.1007/978-1-4471-7440-0_28
9. Nkurikiyeyezu, K., Yokokubo, A., Lopez, G.: Importance of individual differences in physiological-based stress recognition models. In: 15th International Conference on Intelligent Environments, IE 2019 (2019)
10. Nomura, R., Maruno, S.: Rapid serial blinks: an index of temporally increased cognitive load. PLoS One **14**(12), e0225897 (2019)
11. Ossmann, R., et al.: AsTeRICS, a flexible assistive technology construction set. Procedia Comput. Sci. **14**, 1–9 (2012)
12. Poria, S., Cambria, E., Bajpai, R., Hussain, A.: A review of affective computing: from unimodal analysis to multimodal fusion. Inf. Fusion **37**, 98–125 (2017)
13. Read&Write Literacy Support Software. Texthelp. https://www.texthelp.com/en-gb/products/read-write/. Accessed 7 July 2020
14. Schmidt, P., Reiss, A., Duerichen, R., van Laerhoven, K.: Wearable affect and stress recognition: a review, 21 November 2018
15. Shojaeizadeh, M., Djamasbi, S., Paffenroth, R.C., Trapp, A.C.: Detecting task demand via an eye tracking machine learning system. Decis. Support Syst. **116**, 91–101 (2019)

16. Siirtola, P.: Continuous stress detection using the sensors of commercial smartwatch. In: Proceedings of the 2019 ACM International Joint Conference on Pervasive and Ubiquitous Computing and Proceedings of the 2019 ACM International Symposium on Wearable Computers, London, UK, 9–13 September 2019, pp. 1198–1201. The Association for Computing Machinery, New York (2019). https://doi.org/10.1145/3341162.3344831

17. Sutton, R.S., Barto, A.G.: Reinforcement Learning: An Introduction, 2nd edn. A Bradford Book. MIT Press, Cambridge (2018)

Developing of Kid Can Write as Assistive Technology for Students with Learning Disabilities

Onintra Poobrasert[(⊠)] and Natcha Satsutthi

A-MED, NSTDA, Khlong Luang, Pathumthani, Thailand
{onintra.poo,natcha.sat}@nstda.or.th

Abstract. A learning disability child (LD) is a child who needs special treatments in one or more areas of learning such as reading, writing and/or calculating. Each child has different difficulties. Some children have reading and writing difficulties, but he or she can learn mathematics without a problem. Otherwise, some children have only a difficulty to learn mathematics or calculation. In addition, for some children, they have all three problems: reading, writing and calculating which are the important skills for learning. If a child has a learning problem, it will influence his pursuit of knowledge and his education. There are different characteristics of a learning disorder. Because there is no adequate supportive equipment to help this group of children in Thailand and there are increasingly LD children, Assistive Technology and Medical Devices Research Center (A-MED) improves the Kid Can Write system in order to help the children to improve their story-writing and vocabulary-writing capacities. The Kid Can Write system was already used with the LD children and there are many good perspectives from guardians, teachers and the LD children. The result of the experiments showed that the Kid Can Write system helps LD children improve on writing a story. The children can achieve a high score with a statistic significance at .05. Moreover, most of the guardians and teachers told that the Kid Can Write system is practical, and it satisfies the children.

Keywords: Assistive technology · Dysgraphia · Imagery · Learning disabilities · Writing tool

1 Introduction

Dyslexia child often has reading difficulties such as reading incapability, reading with difficulty, slow reading, must-spelling reading or unskilled reading [1]. Some LD child can read but have a difficulty to understand. On the other hand, the dysgraphia child always has problems relating to writing such as misspelled writing, incorrect-direction writing, incorrect writing, non-beautiful handwriting, line writing incapacity, instability of font characters [2]. Additionally, the dyscalculia child often has a problem concerning calculating such as numbers confusion, difficulties relating to quality, mathematic symbol misunderstanding, whole-idea misunderstanding and incapability of

K. Miesenberger et al. (Eds.): ICCHP 2020, LNCS 12377, pp. 73–80, 2020.
https://doi.org/10.1007/978-3-030-58805-2_9

addition, subtraction, multiplication, and division [3]. Furthermore, there are other learning problems in some LD children. From the study, it found most of the LD children have writing and reading disorders. The calculating disorder is the second problem found in the research. Therefore, the assistance for these children will focus on teaching them how to read and how to write because they are important skills of learning. If the child cannot read, it will be an obstacle for education. Nowadays, self-education is very practical for everyone because of the modern and advanced technologies such as a computer, smartphone or other equipment. If the LD child has a writing or reading disorder, he cannot access to the information as a normal child does.

Hence, writing is important because it is one of the ways of communication and emotion, idea and experience transmission to the receiver [4]. In Thailand, the educational curriculum sets eight group of subjects as the fundamental education. The Thai language is the 1st group of subjects which kids must learn in order to be capable of listening, speaking, reading and writing. The writing standard was fixed in the 2nd point of the subject named "standard T 201": a kid should be effectively capable of writing a story, essay, communication, brief story, information report and research [5].

2 Methodology

The development of Kid Can Write system was inspired by the *Imagination Writing*, work of an American educator, Nanci Bell. In the research of Nanci Bell, it stated about the linguistic processing that it is necessary to do a sound and character processing in the reading and spelling of human beings [6]. It was called *phoneme awareness* and *symbol imagery* [7]. Another research accelerates an awareness by applying phonological awareness method and symbol imagery [8]. So, Nanci Bell and her team designed a program™ V/V: THE VISUALIZING AND VERBALIZING PROGRAME by having an idea that imagination is the smallest part of linguistic processing [9]. The Program V/V™ uses *Picture to Picture* as a target to improve capacity relating to vocabulary by watching and explaining the pictures in respecting the 12 steps of the procedure [10]. The research teams from A-MED use similar technique to apply with the Thai LD children. The children start watching pictures and think about the pictures by using the 12 steps. They write to explain the pictures following these orders that are tangible substances: what (is the picture about?), size, color, number, shape, where, movement, mood, sound, when perspective, and background. Then, they explain intangible things: the procedure, when, picture perspective and background [11]. The result of the research concludes that the LD children practicing this method are more capable of writing than the others who do not apply this method.

Thus, A-MED develops the Kid Can Write system to help to improve a vocabulary writing and a story writing of the LD children. The system consists of the inscription process, accessing detail, works, and scores of each student. The function applied to help the student in searching a vocabulary is the Thai Word Search Function and Thai Word Prediction Function [12]. Whereas Thai Word Prediction is a function that aims to assist students with learning disabilities in their writing [13]. The 12 steps that mentioned earlier are included along with the use of mind mapping [14]. The development has an objective to help the LD children to learn by using technologies.

3 Experiment

To study the efficiency of the Kid Can Write system, which will be used with the LD students between 4th grade and 6th grade before and after using the Kid Can Write system, including:

1. To study the story-writing and vocabulary-writing capacities of the LD students
2. To compare the story-writing capacity and the vocabulary-writing capacity of the LD students.
3. To study satisfactions of the LD students.

3.1 Population and Sample

The population is the students, who have learning disabilities in writing, studying in 4th grade and 6th grade in the schools, which affiliated in Bangkok Education Department.

The sample group is 16 LD students between 4th grade and 6th grade from two schools (school A and school B). We selected the sample group using the Purposive Sampling Method [15]. Therefore, we assume that

1. After using the Kid Can Write system, the vocabulary-writing capacity of the LD students (in this study) is at a good level.
2. After using the Kid Can Write system, the story-writing capacity of the LD students (in this study) is at an average level.
3. After using the Kid Can Write system, the vocabulary-writing capacity of the LD students (in this study) is better (higher).
4. After using the Kid Can Write system, the story-writing capacity of the LD students (in this study) is better (higher).
5. After using the Kid Can Write system, the satisfaction of the LD students (in this study) is at highest level.

4 Analysis and Results

1. The vocabulary-writing capacity of the LD students between 4th Grade and 6th Grade before and after using the Kid Can Write system.

Table 1. Scores, average and deviation standard of the vocabulary-writing capacity of the LD students between 4th Grade and 6th Grade before and after using the Kid Can Write system (N = 16).

School	Class level	Student number	Pretest	Capacity	Post test	Capacity
A	4th Grade	1	1	Weak	4	Weak
		2	0	Weak	5	Weak
		3	3	Weak	11	Fair
		4	0	Weak	3	Weak
	5th Grade	5	1	Weak	17	Excellent
		6	0	Weak	4	Weak
		7	0	Weak	5	Weak
		8	2		10	Weak
B	4th Grade	9	10	Weak	20	Excellent
		10	0	Weak	17	Excellent
		11	11	Fair	18	Excellent
	5th Grade	12	1	Weak	18	Excellent
	6th Grade	13	1	Weak	18	Excellent
		14	0	Weak	17	Excellent
		15	0	Weak	15	Very good
		16	8		19	Excellent
x̄		N	2.38	Weak	12.56	Good
SD		16	3.76		6.39	

According to Table 1, it found that the capacity of the students before using the Kid Can Write system had scores between 0 to 11 points with the average of 2.38 and the deviation standard of 3.76. Therefore, their capacity was weak. Otherwise, after using the Kid Can Write system, they had scores between 3 to 20 points with the average of 12.56 and the deviation standard of 6.39. Their capacity is at a *fair* level. That is in accordance with the 1st hypothesis which assumed that the capacity of the students after using the Kid Can Write system would be at a *good* level.

2. The story-writing capacity of the LD students between 4th grade and 6th grade before and after using the Kid Can Write system.

Table 2. Scores, average and deviation standard of the story-writing capacity of the LD students between 4th grade and 6th grade before and after using the Kid Can Write sys tem (N = 16).

School	Class level	Student number	Pretest	Capacity	Post test	Capacity
A	4th grade	1	0	Weak	5	Weak
		2	0	Weak	4	Weak
		3	0	Weak	10	Weak
		4	0	Weak	4	Weak
	5th grade	5	0	Weak	12	Fair
		6	0	Weak	5	Weak
		7	0	Weak	5	Weak
		8	0	Weak	12	Fair
B	4th grade	9	2	Weak	15	Excellent
		10	0	Weak	12	Fair
		11	10	Weak	18	Excellent
	5th grade	12	0	Weak	13	Good
	6th grade	13	2	Weak	12	Fair
		14	1	Weak	14	Good
		15	1	Weak	14	Good
		16	5	Weak	16	Excellent
$\bar{x}$		N	1.31	Weak	10.69	Fair
SD		16	68.2		4.63	

According to Table 2, it found that the capacity of the students before using the Kid Can Write system had scores between 0 to 10 points with the average of 1.31 and the deviation standard of 2.68. Therefore, their capacity was weak. After using the Kid Can Write system, they had scores between 4 to 18 points with the average of 10.69 and the deviation standard of 4.63. Their capacity is at a *fair* level. That is not in accordance with the 2nd hypothesis which assumed that the capacity of the students after using the Kid Can Write system would be at a *good* level.

3. The comparison of a vocabulary-writing capacity among the LD students between 4th grade and 6th grade before and after using the Kid Can Write system.

Table 3. The comparative result of vocabulary-writing scores of the LD students between 4th grade and 6th grade before and after using the Kid Can Write system.

Test	N	$\bar{x}$	SD	t	df	sig
Pre test	16	2.38	3.76	7.37*	15	0.00
Post test	16	12.56	6.39			

*There is a statistic significance at .05.

According to Table 3 "the comparative result of vocabulary-writing scores of the LD students between 4th grade and 6th grade before and after using the Kid Can Write system", it found that the capacity of the student after using the Kid Can Write system has ameliorated with a statistic significance at .05 which is in accordance with the 3rd hypothesis.

4. The comparison of a story-writing capacity among the LD students between 4th grade and 6th grade before and after using the Kid Can Write system.

Table 4. The comparative result of story-writing scores of the LD students between 4th grade and 6th grade before and after using the Kid Can Write system.

Test	N	x̄	SD	t	df	sig
Pre test	16	1.31	2.68	10.43*	15	0.00
Post test	16	10.69	4.63			

*There is a statistic significance at .05.

According to Table 4 "the comparative result of story-writing scores of the LD students between 4th grade and 6th grade before and after using the Kid Can Write system", it found that the capacity of the student after using the Kid Can Write system has ameliorated with a statistic significance at .05 which is in accordance with the 4th hypothesis.

5. The satisfaction of the LD students between 4th grade and 6th grade before and after using the Kid Can Write system.

According to the Evaluation of Satisfaction of the LD students between 4th grade and 6th grade after using the Kid Can Write system, it found that the satisfaction is at a highest level. Its average is 4.34 which is relevant to the 5th hypothesis. The satisfaction of the LD students between 4th grade and 6th grade after using the Kid Can Write system is at a highest level.

Thai Word Search Function Evaluation has a highest level of satisfaction in 4 aspects: 1) The easy-to-use screen designs, 2) The suitability of choosing the character type on the monitor, 3) The suitability of choosing the font size on the monitor, and 4) The suitability of choosing the text colors.

Thai Word Prediction function Characteristic Evaluation has a highest level of satisfaction in all 5 aspects: 1) The easy-to-use screen designs, 2) The suitability of choosing the character type on the monitor, 3) The suitability of choosing the font size on the monitor, 4) The suitability of choosing the text colors, and 5) The suitability of using a sound communication.

12 Teaching Steps Evaluation has a highest level of satisfaction in all 4 aspects: 1) The clarity of the steps, 2) The use of the comprehensible language, 3) The suitability of the steps and 4) The relevance between questions and figures.

Overall Satisfaction Evaluation has a highest level of satisfaction.

5 Concluding Remarks

According to the study on the effectiveness of Kid Can Write system, the results have been found as follows:

1. After using the Kid Can Write system, the vocabulary-writing capacity of the LD students (in this study) is at a good level, and the story-writing capacity of the LD students (in this study) is at an average level.
2. After using the Kid Can Write system, the vocabulary-writing capacity of the LD students (in this study) is better (higher), and story-writing capacity of the LD students (in this study) is better (higher).
3. After using the Kid Can Write system, the satisfaction of the LD students (in this study) is at highest level.

Acknowledgements. The authors would like to convey our thanks and acknowledge the assistance of the Artificial Intelligence Research Unit (AINRU), National Electronics and Computer Technology Center. Additionally, the authors would like to give our special thanks to Ms. Wantanee Phantachat, Dr. Putthachart Pothibal, Dr. Daranee Saksiriphol, Dr. Bunthita Likkasit, and the Directors, the teachers, and the students at the school in Bangkok who participate in this research.

References

1. Pařilová, T.: DysHelper – the dyslexia assistive approach user study. In: Miesenberger, K., Kouroupetroglou, G. (eds.) ICCHP 2018. LNCS, vol. 10896, pp. 478–485. Springer, Cham (2018). https://doi.org/10.1007/978-3-319-94277-3_74
2. Graham, S., Harris, K., MacArthur, C.A., Schwartz, S.S.: Writing and writing instruction with students with learning disabilities: a review of a program of research. Learn. Disabil. Q. **14**, 89–114 (1991)
3. Freda, C., Pagliara, S.M., Ferraro, F., Zanfardino, F., Pepino, A.: Dyslexia: study of compensatory software which aids the mathematical learning process of dyslexic students at secondary school and university. In: Miesenberger, K., Klaus, J., Zagler, W., Karshmer, A. (eds.) ICCHP 2008. LNCS, vol. 5105, pp. 742–746. Springer, Heidelberg (2008). https://doi.org/10.1007/978-3-540-70540-6_108
4. Logsdon, A.: Learning Disabilities in Written Expression: Difficulty Using Writing in School and Everyday Situations (2019). https://www.verywellfamily.com/what-are-learning-disabilities-in-writing-2162443
5. Ministry of Education.: Basic Education Core Curriculum: Standard T201 (2017). http://academic.obec.go.th/newsdetail.php?id=75
6. Bell, N.: Visualizing and Verbalizing® Program for Cognitive Development, Comprehension, & Thinking (2019). https://lindamoodbell.com/program/visualizing-and-verbalizing-program
7. Bell, N.: Seeing Stars. Symbol Imagery for Phonemic Awareness, Sight Words and Spelling. Gander Educational Publishing, San Luis Obispo (1997)
8. Simmons, F.R., Singleton, C.: Do weak phonological representations impact on arithmetic development? A review of research into arithmetic and dyslexia. Dyslexia (2007)

9. Lindamood – Bell.: Visualizing and Verbalizing (2019). http://wakefieldlearningcenter.com/VisualizingandVerbalizing.html
10. Visualizing and Verbalizing: For Language Comprehension and Thinking Gander Publishing 2nd edn, p. 440 (2007)
11. Bell, N.: Visualizing and Verbalizing for Language Comprehension and Thinking. Gander Educational Publishing, San Luis Obispo (1986)
12. Poobrasert, O., Wongteeratana, A.: Assistive technology: writing tool to support students with learning disabilities. In: Miesenberger, K., Karshmer, A., Penaz, P., Zagler, W. (eds.) ICCHP 2012. LNCS, vol. 7383, pp. 346–352. Springer, Heidelberg (2012). https://doi.org/10.1007/978-3-642-31534-3_52
13. Poobrasert, O., et al.: Technology-enhanced learning for students with learning disabilities. In: 11th IEEE International Conference on Advanced Learning Technologies, ICALT, Athens, Georgia, USA (2011)
14. Buzan, T.: Mind Mapping For Kids: An Introduction, p. 128. HarperCollins Publishers, London (2005)
15. Robinson, R.S.: Purposive sampling. In: Michalos, A.C. (ed.) Encyclopedia of Quality of Life and Well-Being Research. Springer, Dordrecht (2014). https://doi.org/10.1007/978-94-007-0753-5_2337

Improving Fitness Levels of Individuals with Autism Spectrum Disorder: A Preliminary Evaluation of Real-Time Interactive Heart Rate Visualization to Motivate Engagement in Physical Activity

Bo Fu[1]([⊠]), Jimmy Chao[1], Melissa Bittner[2], Wenlu Zhang[1],
and Mehrdad Aliasgari[1]

[1] Computer Engineering and Computer Science, California State University
Long Beach, Long Beach, USA
{Bo.Fu, Wenlu.Zhang, Mehrdad.Aliasgari}@csulb.edu,
Jimmy.Chao@student.csulb.edu
[2] Kinesiology, California State University Long Beach, Long Beach, USA
Melissa.Bittner@csulb.edu

Abstract. Individuals with autism spectrum disorder (ASD) face significant challenges such as motor impairment in their daily lives that considerably restrict their abilities to persistently remain physically active or engage in recreational activities. As a result, many of these individuals may become overweight or obese that pose a multitude of health risks such as cardiovascular disease and Type II diabetes. A potential solution to reduce such risks is by promoting physical activity to individuals with ASD given its abundant health and cognitive benefits. As such, this research proposes a mobile application: *Heart Runner* developed for individuals with ASD to visualize their heart rates generated during physical activity in real time and to encourage them to achieve higher energy expenditure in a competitive social environment with their peers. We demonstrate preliminary evaluations of the *Heart Runner* application in real-world user studies, and present encouraging results indicating increased physical activity levels in those who completed exercise sessions using the Heart Runner compared to those who did not. These findings suggest that improving fitness levels of individuals with ASD over time may potentially be enhanced through real-time interactive feedback of one's energy expenditure that aims to promote self-motivated physical activity.

Keywords: Self-motivated engagement in physical activity · Individuals with autism spectrum disorder · Real-time heart rate visualization

1 Introduction

According to the Centers for Disease Control and Prevention, ASD is one of the most commonly diagnosed disabilities for individuals in the United States and the fastest growing developmental disability that may result in significant social, communication,

K. Miesenberger et al. (Eds.): ICCHP 2020, LNCS 12377, pp. 81–89, 2020.
https://doi.org/10.1007/978-3-030-58805-2_10

and behavioral challenges. ASD prevalence estimates increased from an average of 4 per 10,000 individuals in the mid-60s [1] to 1 per 59 in 2018[1]. In addition, motor impairment is common in those with ASD [2, 3], who are also almost 1.5 times more likely to be overweight or obese compared to their typically developing peers [4]. These deficits may be exacerbated by their tendencies to adopt sedentary lifestyles and activities that lack social play [5]. A growing number of individuals with ASD may not possess the skills needed to be physically active and participate in sport and recreational activities [6]. While there is evidence indicating that physical activity has positive effects on the overall health (e.g., weight, motor skills) of individuals with ASD [7] as well as physical and cognitive benefits [8, 9], there is limited research in providing innovative environments to engage individuals with ASD in physical activity. This is further complicated by the difficulties experienced by individuals with ASD when estimating their relative efforts invested in physical activity. To this end, this research proposes an interactive mobile application: *Heart Runner* designed specifically for individuals with ASD to comprehend real-time information of their energy expenditures during physical activities by means of interactive heart rate visualization. Furthermore, the *Heart Runner* aims to provide an engaging environment where individuals with ASD can compete with one another in sustaining accelerated heart rates with the overall goal of stimulating extended durations of a physical activity. In the context of this paper, physical activity is defined as bodily movement that results in energy expenditure. We present preliminary evaluations of the *Heart Runner* with promising results suggesting increased heart rates for those who completed a given physical activity using the application compared to those who did not. This finding indicates the potential benefits of utilizing mobile applications in providing engaging environments and enhancing self-motivation for individuals with ASD in physical activity.

2 Related Work

A brief overview of related work is presented in this section, for detailed systematic reviews of the literature, see [8, 10]. Technology has been shown to have a positive effect on engagement of individuals with ASD when used simultaneously with exercise [11], suggesting predictable environments and visual stimulation created by technology may increase the potential for independent participation. As an established evidence-based practice (EBP), technology has also been shown to be highly motivating and reinforcing [12]. Prior experiments have demonstrated that through the use of technology-aided instruction, individuals with ASD are able to engage in more on-task behaviors and may learn physical activity skills at a faster rate than those without technology-aided instruction [13]. Notable applications[2] have demonstrated successful

---

[1] https://www.cdc.gov/ncbddd/autism/data.html.

[2] Examples include, but are not limited to: ExerciseBuddy (http://www.exercisebuddy.com), Lazy Monster (https://apps.apple.com/us/app/workouts-exercises-at-home/id882240858), NFL Play 60 (https://aha-nflplay60.discoveryeducation.com), and Adventures of Super Stretch (http://adventuresofsuperstretch.com).

integrations of technology in enhanced physical activities though not always designed specifically for individuals with ASD. One observation is the notion of exergaming used in these applications, whereby gaming and technology are coupled to engage individuals in aerobic exercise, as body movements, reactions, and energy expenditure are tracked through participation in the game [14]. Exergaming is further investigated in [15], where findings have shown significant improvements in attention and working memory and decreases in stereotypical behaviors in individuals with ASD immediately after participating in a 20-min exergaming intervention. Motivated by these prior research findings, the *Heart Runner* implements the exergaming concept as discussed below.

3 *Heart Runner*: Design and Development

The *Heart Runner*[3] is a cross-platform mobile application. The trial implementation shown in this paper runs on the Android operating system. It utilizes the NativeScript[4] library to create interfaces and to access utility functions such as Bluetooth and phone cameras. The *Heart Runner* is compatible with heart rate monitors that support optical sensing technology when reading heart beats such as the Heart Zone[5] heart rate monitor used in the trials presented in this paper. The *Heart Runner* bases its architecture on the Model-View-ViewModel design pattern[6] that aims to support code reuse and extensibility. The application collects a user's heart rate data in real-time during physical activity and visualizes changes to this person's heart rate intensity as an avatar climbing up and down a mountain, as shown in Fig. 1a. The features shown in the *Heart Runner* follow several EBPs reported by the National Professional Development Center on ASD[7] that are specific to individuals with ASD, as discussed below.

The mountain is segmented into four colored zones, where each zone indicates a particular range of heart rate intensity. More specifically, the red zone indicates light exercise (at least 50% but below 60% of recommended maximum heart rates), the yellow zone indicates moderate exercises (at least 60% but below 70% of recommended maximum heart rates), the green zone indicates vigorous exercise (at least 70% but below 90% of recommended maximum heart rates), and the white zone indicates a danger zone (90% or above recommended maximum heart rates). The recommended maximum heart rate is determined by the age of an individual, where for those 16 and over: *Maximum Heart Rate* = 220 − *Current Age* and for those under 16: *Maximum Heart Rate* = 208 − 0.7 × *Current Age* [16]. The *Heart Runner* then calculates an increase in one's heart rates as a percentile value: *Heart Rate Activity (%)* = *Current Heart Rate* ÷ *Maximum Heart Rate*. The application allows a maximum of four players at a time with their respective avatars. As a player's heart rates are elevated, this person's avatar will synchronously climb up the mountain in the *Hear Runner*

---

[3] Open-source codebase hosted at https://github.com/Lazer7/Heart-Runner.

[4] https://www.nativescript.org/.

[5] https://heartzones.com.

[6] https://docs.microsoft.com/en-us/windows/uwp/data-binding/data-binding-and-mvvm.

[7] https://autismpdc.fpg.unc.edu/evidence-based-practices.

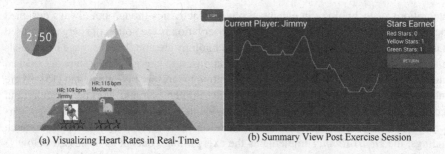

(a) Visualizing Heart Rates in Real-Time   (b) Summary View Post Exercise Session

Fig. 1. *Heart Runner* interface

application in real-time. In addition, players can view their current heart rates in BPM (beats per minute) and collect stars as they spend a target amount of time in a particular zone on the mountain. For instance, a red star indicates a player has spent 30 s completing light exercise, a yellow start indicates a player has spent 15 s completing moderate exercise, and a green star indicates a player has spent 10 s completing vigorous exercise. Finally, *Heart Runner* provides a circular timer (top left corner of the screen) as a visual cue to assist players understanding the target duration of their exercise, and allows terminations of an exercise session at any given time (via the Stop option located at the top right corner of the screen). Once an exercise session has ended, a summary page presents an overview of a player's heart rates recorded during the entire duration of the exercise. An example of such a summary page is shown in Fig. 1b. Summary pages are intended for caretakers to gain insights of the completed exercise, and to recommend or adjust desirable parameters accordingly such as a subsequent activity type and future target exercise durations.

4   Preliminary Evaluation

We conducted two trials of real-world user studies to evaluate whether the *Heart Runner* was effective in increasing heart rate intensity levels for individuals with ASD during physical activity. Trial one is a pilot study with the overall goal of testing technical feasibilities of the proposed application as well as refinement on experimental procedures. Trail two aims to overcome technical and procedure issues discovered in trail one and to provide additional results in the evaluation of the *Heart Runner*. Participants were drawn from different cohorts.

4.1   Trial One

A total of 20 individuals with ASD from a Southern California Transition school between the age of 18 and 21 took part in trial one. They were randomly assigned to join either the control group or the application group. Both groups were asked to exercise on stationary bicycles for a targeted duration at 20 min, with the only different being that those in the application group were asked to complete the exercise using the *Heart Runner* application. In the application group, the participants could select from several preset images as their avatars. Based on their age group discussed earlier, their recommended heart rate ranges would be 100–170 BPM with an optimal heart rate for vigorous activity reaching 144 BPM.

We experienced connection drops and range interferences for some participants during this trial, where their heart rate data had to be discarded as a result. The remaining dataset contains heart rates recorded for 15 participants, as shown in Fig. 2. We found that those in the application group (Fig. 2b) generated a higher average heart rate that is within the recommended ranges at 101.66 BPM, compared to those of the baseline group at approximately 90.63 BPM below the recommend ranges (Fig. 2a). The peak average heart rate in the baseline groups was at approximately 54.70%, which is outperformed by the application group at approximately 62.14%. Although none of the participants' heart rates in trial 1 reached the optimal 144 BPM, we found the heart rates of the application group to be less dispersed compared to those of the baseline group, with standard deviations of 14.80 and 23.09 respectively. In addition, Fig. 2c presents a timeline view of the average heart rates generated for each group throughout the exercise in trial 1. The heart rate differences between the two groups are amplified

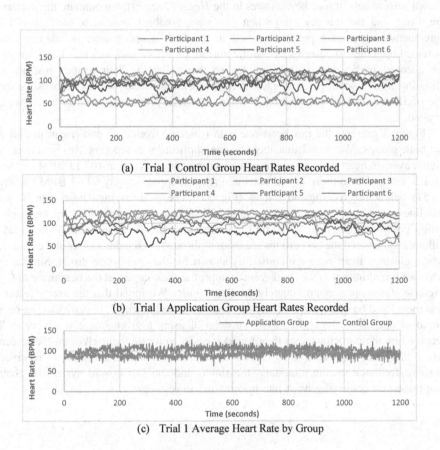

(a) Trial 1 Control Group Heart Rates Recorded

(b) Trial 1 Application Group Heart Rates Recorded

(c) Trial 1 Average Heart Rate by Group

Fig. 2. Trial 1 results

throughout, where elevated heart rates are constantly shown for the application group, and particularly at the beginning such as the first 10 min of the exercise session.

To elicit further feedback from the participants regarding the usability of the *Heart Runner* application, participants were asked to complete the System Usability Scale (SUS) questionnaire [17]. Instead of Likert Scales, we used a 3-point Smiley Face Likert Scale [18] as recommended for children with medical conditions. The usability feedback from the participants was generally very positive where most cited the application was "easy to use", "fun", and therefore "would like to keep playing". Although it may be necessary to recognize that not all participants were able to comprehend the purpose of the SUS questionnaire, since some commented on dislikes of sweating and the exercise itself. Nonetheless, the findings from trial 1 were encouraging and the experiment provided us an opportunity to identify areas of improvement.

4.2   Trial Two

We made changes to the usability questionnaire in trial 2, where participants were shown screenshots of four key features in the *Heart Runner* (the mountain, the avatars, the timer, and the star rewards) when providing feedback instead of statements for agreement/disagreement previously used in the SUS questionnaire. In addition, we provided upgrades to ensure successful connections before each session. Furthermore, we allowed participants to take photos of themselves as their avatars instead of choosing from a set of given images. A total of 12 individuals with ASD between the age of 18 and 21 took part in trial 2, where the same procedures used in trial 1 were applied.

Figure 3 presents the raw heart rate data collected from each participant in trail 2 for both groups. We found that those in the application group (Fig. 3b) generated a higher average heart rate that is within the recommended ranges at 107.11 BPM (StDev 16.12), compared to those of the baseline group at approximately 94.67 BPM (StDev 16.57) below the recommend ranges (Fig. 3a). The peak average heart rate in the baseline groups was at approximately 60.50%, which is outperformed by the application group at approximately 62.60%. Furthermore, Fig. 3c shows that the heart rate differences between the two groups are evident throughout the duration of the exercise, where elevated heart rates are constantly shown for the application group. Similar to what we found in trial 1, these differences appear at their largest at the beginning of the exercise session (e.g. approximately the first 8 min). We found that the avatar feature was most liked based on the usability feedback collected in trial 2. In particular, using a photo of oneself as the chosen avatar instead of using a given image was very well received by the participants, as they found it easier to locate themselves on the screen where there may be several other players in the same session. In addition, we received positive feedback on the mountain, the timer, and the star reward system on their helpfulness in conveying heart rate information in real-time.

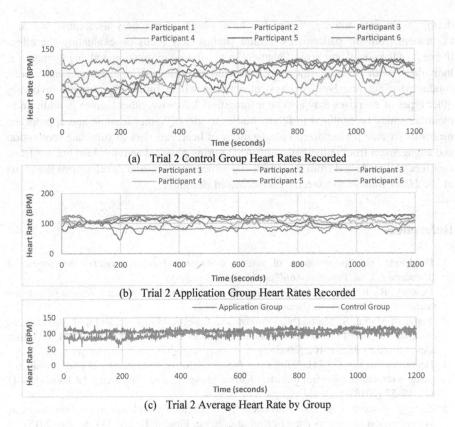

(a)   Trial 2 Control Group Heart Rates Recorded

(b)   Trial 2 Application Group Heart Rates Recorded

(c)   Trial 2 Average Heart Rate by Group

Fig. 3. Trial 2 results

5   Conclusions and Future Work

The evaluation results collected in both trials have provided preliminary evidence suggesting the potential benefits of visualizing heart rate data in real-time in an effort to potentially promote engagement and self-motivation among individuals with ASD during physical activity. In particular, we have consistently found higher average heart rates in those who used the *Heart Runner* application during physical activity compared to those who did not. Although these differences were not shown to be statistically significant ($p>0.05$) given the small sample sizes of both trials, further experiments may be necessary to verify this observation with larger number of participants. In addition, notable differences in heart rates of the two groups were especially found at the beginning of an exercise session, suggesting statistically significant differences may vary depending on a specific phase of physical activity. Future experiments may focus on measuring whether the *Heart Runner* application is effective at engaging individuals with ASD in extended exercise durations and at promoting user acceptance over a period of time. Moreover, the *Heart Runner* has provided a social environment and a reward system where players could compete with one another during a physical activity, where we have observed not only awareness but also excitement from the participants. Future studies may focus on evaluating the effectiveness of the social and reward element in generating motivation and engagement for individuals with ASD. Furthermore, the studies presented in this paper have been conducted using one type of physical activity, where future experiments involving other types of exercises may also be informative. Likewise, other themes in addition to mountains may be explored in future studies to identify other feasible and appropriate means to provide personalized visualizations of heart rate data to stimulate motivation and engagement from individuals with ASD during physical activity. Last but not least, user feedback collected from these trial experiments will inform development iterations of the *Heart Runner* to exercise user-centered design.

References

1. Fombonne, E.: Epidemiology of autistic disorder and other pervasive developmental disorders. J. Clin. Psychiatry **66**(Suppl. 10), 3–8 (2005)
2. Downey, R., Rapport, M.J.: Motor activity in children with autism: a review of cur-rent literature. Pediatric Phys. Therapy **24**, 2–20 (2012)
3. Vernazza-Martin, S., Martin, N., Vernazza, A., Lepellec-Muller, A., Rufo, M., Massion, J., Assaiante, C.: Goal directed locomotion and balance control in autistic children. J. Autism Dev. Disorders **35**, 91–102 (2005)
4. Healy, S., Aigner, C.J., Haegele, J.A.: Prevalence of overweight and obesity among US youth with autism spectrum disorder. Journal of Autism and Developmental Disor-ders **47**(1), 49–57 (2018)
5. Pace, M., Bricout, V.A.: Low heart rate response of children with autism spectrum disorders in comparison to controls during physical exercise. Physiol. Behav. **141**, 63–68 (2015)
6. Healy, S.: Does physical activity have special benefits for people with autism? (2018). https://www.autismspeaks.org/expert-opinion/does-physical-activity-have-special-benefits-people-autism. Accessed 25 07 2020
7. Datka, A.: What are the benefits of physical education in school? (2015). http://www.livestrong.com/article/529108-what-are-the-benefits-of-physical-education-in-school/
8. Bittner, M., McNamara, S., Adams, D., Goudy, L., Dillon, S.R.: Exercise identified as an evidence-based practice for children with autism spectrum disorder. Palaestra **32**(2), 15–20 (2018)
9. Zeng, N., Ayyub, M., Sun, H., Wen, X., Xiang, P., Gao, Z.: Effects of physical activity on motor skills and cognitive development in early childhood: a systematic review. Biomed. Res. Int. (2017)
10. Dillon, S.R., Adams, D., Goudy, L., Bittner, M., McNamara, S.: Evaluating exercise as evidence-based practice for individuals with autism spectrum disorder. Front. Public Health **4**, 290 (2017)
11. Wong, C., et al.: Evidence-based practices for children, youth, and young adults with autism spectrum disorder: a comprehensive review. J. Autism Dev. Disorders **45**(7), 1951–1966 (2015). https://doi.org/10.1007/s10803-014-2351-z
12. Takeo, T., Toshitaka, N., Daisuke, K.: Development application softwares on PDA for autistic disorder children **12**, 31–38 (2007)
13. Case, L., Yun, J.: Visual practices for children with autism spectrum disorders in physical activity. Palaestra **29**(3), 21–26 (2015)

14. Trout, J., Christie, B.: Interactive video games in physical education. J. Phys. Educ. Recreat. Dance **78**(5), 29–45 (2007)
15. Anderson-Hanley, C., Tureck, K., Schneiderman, R.L.: Autism and exergaming: effects on repetitive behaviors and cognition. Psychol. Res. Behav. Manag. **4**, 129–137 (2011)
16. Williams, L.: How Do I Find My Maximum Heart Rate and Use It For Training? (2019). https://www.runnersworld.com/health-injuries/a20791648/max-heart-rate/
17. Brooke, J.: SUS: A Quick and Dirty Usability Scale. Usability Evaluation in Industry. Taylor & Francis, London (1996)
18. Hall, L., Hume, C., Tazzyman, S.: Five degrees of happiness. In: Proceedings of the 15th International Conference on Interaction Design and Children, pp. 311–321 (2016)

Introduction of Compensatory Technology in Vocational Rehabilitation: A Practice Study About the Value of Technology and the Values that Shape These Practices

Gunnar Michelsen[✉]

The Norwegian Labour and Welfare Service,
Nordland Center for Assistive Technology, Bodø, Norway
gunnar.michelsen@gmail.com

Abstract. Job seekers with cognitive impairments, for example Asperger's syndrome and/or ADHD, have greater challenges in entering the labour market com-pared with other groups with impaired functional capacity. Introducing Cognitive Support Technologies (CST) can improve the competitiveness of job seekers with cognitive challenges. Compensatory technology has proven to be an underutilized tool in vocational rehabilitation for people with cognitive challenges. The data are taken from a two-year ethnographic fieldwork study at two vocational rehabilitation companies. Both companies placed special focus on introducing technology in the vocational rehabilitation process. The study shows that the introduction of compensatory technology has been valuable both in the individual empowerment process and for the participants upon completion of the vocational rehabilitation programme. The inhibiting factors described may be related to the diagnosis of the typical challenges faced by adults suffering from ADHD and/or Asperger's, such as organizational challenges, procrastination or general difficulty in doing things in a new way. The article describes the motivational value associated with CST in a vocational rehabilitation perspective, provides new knowledge about values in public management and reveals how efforts to achieve quantitative performance requirements inhibit the introduction of CST.

Keywords: Cognitive Support Technologies (CST) · Empowering · Affinity spaces

1 Introduction

The lower labour force participation rate among people with cognitive impairments compared to the population as a whole is a societal challenge [1–4]. Impaired cognitive functioning can entail challenges related to mastering basic skills in working life, such as using time wisely, organizing work tasks, interpreting and under-standing social interaction, and feeling comfortable in the social environment of the workplace [5]. The use of compensatory technology, including consumer technology, for individual adaptation in the workplace has been shown to have a moderately positive effect on

© Springer Nature Switzerland AG 2020
K. Miesenberger et al. (Eds.): ICCHP 2020, LNCS 12377, pp. 90–95, 2020.
https://doi.org/10.1007/978-3-030-58805-2_11

how people with cognitive challenges cope with the demands of working life, and thus contribute to inclusion in the workplace [6–9]. Compensatory technology has proven to be an underutilized tool in vocational rehabilitation for people with cognitive challenges [10, 11]. The explanations given for not fully exploiting the potential for inclusion that can be realized through the introduction of compensatory technology are partly a lack of knowledge of the opportunities afford-ed by the technology [12], a lack of user training [13], and the generally limited use of technology in the workplace [14].

2 Purpose

The low labour force participation rate in the user group, the underutilization of available technology and the lack of knowledge about the prerequisites for success have motivated the study's researchers to explore the factors that inhibit and pro-mote the introduction of compensatory technology in vocational rehabilitation. In-creasing the number of people with an impaired functional capacity in employment is a welfare policy goal. A recurring theme at national and international conferences on assistive technology, working life and people with an impaired functional capacity is that the technology is available, but that knowledge is lacking on the prerequisites for the optimal introduction of the technology to users and their networks.

The purpose of the study is to describe how values shape selected practices where technology is introduced, and the value of introducing compensatory technology to users and the field of social work.

The research question in this study relates to exploring the values in and the value of social work practice in the introduction of compensatory technology in vocational rehabilitation. The purpose is to develop knowledge about what promotes or inhibits the introduction and use of technologies as a tool in the inclusion of job seekers with cognitive challenges. The following research questions were formulated: 1) How is compensatory technology introduced in vocational rehabilitation for people with cognitive disabilities? 2) What values prevail in the negotiations concerning the introduction of technology in vocational rehabilitation? 3) What value does the introduction of compensatory technology have for social work and for persons with disabilities themselves?

Compensatory technology is introduced through contextual sociotechnical practices that are negotiated in relationships between a variety of actors – both techno-logical and human. In order to describe these sociotechnical practices, an exploratory ethno-graphic research design was used. The researchers take an inside look at how social order and relationship are developed in order to examine the networks of connections and negotiations between the actors. The study is also designed as a case-based practice study, which provides scope for more comprehensive descriptions of practices.

3 Methods

This study uses a practice-based approach to explore the values in and the value of social work practice in the introduction of compensatory technology. This practice study places itself within the field of vocational rehabilitation and assistive technology. The ethnographic study was conducted as fieldwork in two vocational rehabilitation programmes over a period of 24 months. The study uses theories, perspectives and approaches from practice research. The analysis uses concepts and resources from sociotechnology and the interdisciplinary field of science, technology and society (STS) studies.

Both of the rehabilitation enterprises offer the vocational rehabilitation programme « Subsidized employment in sheltered firms » (Arbeidspraksis i skjermet virksomhet- APS). The enterprises were selected as strategic cases because they emphasize the use of compensatory technologies to improve the working-life opportunities of participants with cognitive challenges. They also develop technology themselves and are involved in social innovation in the form of individually adapted vocational rehabilitation programmes. Both enterprises have employees with a combination of social work and IT skills, and the employees also have knowledge of technology-based adaptation.

All participants in the vocational rehabilitation programmes in the study had a reduced work capacity, were deemed to have especially tenuous aptitudes for coping with working life and were in need of comprehensive and close follow-up. Most of the participants in both enterprises had cognitive impairments associated with Asperger's syndrome, ADHD or a mental disorder. In line with this, we have started not from diagnoses, but from the challenges people experience in their daily lives. Diagnosis is not a criteria for inclusion in the rehabilitation programs we have followed and neither has it been a criteria for inclusion in this study. We have not asked for or registered any diagnoses, everything that is said about diagnoses has been part of what employees, management and some participants have shared and reflected upon, in general terms, in interviews and conversations.

The participants were mainly men, approx. 8/10. The age spread was considerable, the youngest in their early 20's. Most participants were between the ages of 25 and 40 who either struggled to get into work, or to complete an education, and some who have had a career in IT- industry, but for various reasons have fallen completely out of work. Both case enterprises rehabilitation programs were established as a comprehensive service for adults with cognitive problems. This means that the enterprises' value basis, recruitment of staff, organization and hours of work and the design of the physical and digital working environments were tailored to this target group. The objective of this customized rehabilitation was to prepare and qualify the participants for a job in the IT industry. The case-companies are here superficial described due to anonymity reasons.

The study describes how technology is introduced as a work tool to improve job seekers' self-organization skills, to help them cope with social interaction and to give them greater security in the working day. The enterprises introduced the technology in their information about the programme and in the initial interaction with the participants. The introduction of the technology is shaped by the enterprises' understanding of the technology's inherent compensatory potential, and is based on social policy guidelines on how new technology can help increase the number of people with impaired functional capacity in the labour force.

Training in the use of technology is a compulsory part of the vocational rehabilitation programme, and participants, supervisors and management all use the same technology. Virtually all activity and production at both enterprises takes place digitally: production, development, communication and reporting take place on digital platforms.

The enterprises provide training for participants in the use of digital tools and compensatory technology. The technology was introduced through exercises and adaptation of the technology to each participant. The compulsory training in the use of the technology took place either individually, in small groups or in plenary sessions. The purpose was for the functionality of the technology to serve as a support in the development of participants' working life skills and coping strategies. The introduction of the technology was based on the expectations and demands that the participants would encounter in ordinary working life. The efforts to introduce compensatory technology were therefore an integral part of the social education work aimed at developing the participants' ability to cope with disabilities and challenging life situations.

4   Results

The study found that the participants' cognitive challenges, such as executive difficulties, procrastination, general difficulties in changing patterns of action and establishing new routines, were a barrier to the introduction of technology. These are known challenges associated with diagnoses such as Asperger's syndrome and/or ADHD. Some participants were reluctant to use compensatory technology that was new to them, such as new phones or new software. During the participant observation fieldwork period, some participants never used compensatory technology that was new to them.

Successful implementation of technology first and foremost requires sufficient time to be spent on introducing it to the users, and for the professionals to have the necessary IT skills and social work expertise in relevant areas, such as the challenges faced by adults with cognitive difficulties. The value of mutual recognition is also a factor that promotes the introduction of compensatory technology.

If the participant has confidence in the professionals' IT competence and the professional can demonstrate that he or she genuinely believes that the participant's IT abilities are sufficient to work in the IT industry, this relational aspect could facilitate the process of introducing technology. The enterprise's supervisors show that they have faith in the participants and recognize their IT knowledge by giving them real development and learning tasks based on their abilities. The participants, in turn, recognize the professionals as supervisors, including in terms of having a common vocabulary and frame of reference in relation to IT.

Ensuring that compensatory technology is introduced within a framework that is perceived as inclusive also helps to facilitate its implementation. The fieldwork from these specialized rehabilitation practices explores how aspects of the design of the working environment can promote the inclusion of job seekers with cognitive difficulties. The work tasks, the community of interest and diagnosis, and the inclusive working environment seemed to have a motivating effect and made it possible to include participants who were at different stages in the rehabilitation process.

The study has generated new knowledge on how the process of introducing compensatory technology in itself has value for some of the participants, and how it has contributed to individual empowerment processes. The access to compensatory technology when and where they have a need for it is valuable for participants when they go out into the workplace. Being able to solve challenges using technology seems to facilitate the empowerment of the participants, regardless of the frequency of use. The study shows that just having the app as a backup has increased the participants' experience of greater control and autonomy. The study shows that in order for the technology to function as an actor in the empowerment process, the supervisors must have expertise in the technology and knowledge of the participants' individual challenges.

The study complements existing knowledge on how the introduction of compensatory technology can have professional value in social work practices with adults with cognitive challenges. The study has shown that the introduction of the technology can have a value as a motivating factor. The participant's relationship to technology, how it is implemented in the vocational rehabilitation programmes and the participants' experience of mastering the technology are factors that have helped motivate participants to develop new coping strategies. A surprising finding of the study was participants' indication that compensatory technology and the process of introducing it had a motivational value to them, and was not primarily viewed as an aid for performing isolated cognitive challenges.

The participating enterprises felt forced to reduce the efforts to introduce compensatory technology due to performance requirements and incentive schemes. Time and resources had to be allocated to activities that could help meet the management's target figures. The study has generated new knowledge on how the management's values inhibit the introduction and use of compensatory technology in vocational rehabilitation.

References

1. McDonough, J.T., Revell, G.: Accessing employment supports in the adult system for transitioning youth with autism spectrum disorders. J. Vocat. Rehabil. 32, 89–100 (2010). https://doi.org/10.3233/JVR-2010-0498
2. Steindal, K.: Arbeidstakere med Asperger syndrom. Metodeutvikling og kompetanseheving i NAV. Et samarbeidsprosjekt mellom NAV og Nasjonal kompetanseenhet for autisme. Sluttrapport. (Employees with Asperger's. Methodological development and competence building in the Norwegian Labour and Welfare Administration [NAV]. A collaborative project between NAV and the Norwegian Resource Centre for Autism, ADHD, Tourette Syndrome and Narcolepsy. Final Report). Hentet fra (2010). https://docplayer.me/24805083-Arbeidssokere-med-asperger-syndrom-metodeutvikling-og-kompetanseheving-i-nav-et-sam arbeidsprosjekt-mellom-nav-og-nasjonal-kompetanseenhet-for-autisme.html

3. Taylor, J.L., Seltzer, M.M.: Employment and post-secondary educational activities for young adults with autism spectrum disorders during the transition to adulthood. J. Autism Dev. Disord. **41**(5), 566–574 (2011). https://doi.org/10.1007/s10803-010-1070-3
4. Bø, T.P.: Arbeidskraftundersøkelsen – tilleggsundersøkelser om funksjonshemmede. Fire av ti funksjonshemmede i arbeid. Samfunnsspeilet, Statistisk sentralbyrå, 1. (2016)
5. Attwood, T.: The complete Guide to Asperger's Syndrome. Jessica Kingsley, London (2007)
6. De Jonge, D., Scherer, M.J., Rodger, S.: Assistive Technology in the Workplace. Mosby Elsevier, St. Louis (2007)
7. Hallberg, P.: The mobile phone as aids for adults with ADHD. Linköping University (2009)
8. Gentry, T., Kriner, R., Sima, A., McDonough, J., Wehman, P.: Reducing the need for personal supports among workers with autism using an ipod touch as an assistive technology: delayed randomized control trial. J. Autism Dev. Disord. **45**(3), 669–684 (2014). https://doi.org/10.1007/s10803-014-2221-8
9. Smith, D.L., Atmatzidis, K., Capogreco, M., Lloyd-Randolfi, D., Seman, V.: Evidence-based interventions for increasing work participation for persons with various disabilities. OTJR: Occup. Participation Health **37**(2_suppl), 3S–13S (2017). https://doi.org/10.1177/1539449216681276
10. Hansen, I.L.S.: IKT – et underutnyttet potensial i strategien for et inkluderende arbeidsliv? I J.Tøssebro (red.), KT – et underutnyttet potensial i strategien for et inkluderende arbeidsliv? i "Funksjonshemming – politikk, hverdagsliv og arbeidsliv Funksjonshemming – politikk, hverdagsliv og arbeidsliv.": Universitetsforlaget (2009)
11. Chen, J.L., Sung, C., Pi, Sukyeong: Vocational rehabilitation service patterns and outcomes for individuals with autism of different ages. J. Autism Dev. Disord. **45**(9), 3015–3029 (2015). https://doi.org/10.1007/s10803-015-2465-y
12. Søderstrøm, S.: Socio-material practices in classrooms that lead to the social participation or social isolation of disabled pupils.Scandinavian J. Disabil. Res. (2014). http://dx.doi.org/10.1080/15017419.2014.972449. ISSN: 1501-7419
13. Bureau of Labor Statistics. Persons with disability: Labor force characteristics – 2011. USDL-12-1125. United States Department of Labor (2011)
14. Jaeger, P.T.: Disability and the Internet : Confronting a Digital Divide. Lynne Rienner Publishers, Boulde (2012)

Investigating Usability and Engagement in a Money Management Application for Users with Intellectual Disability

Marian McDonnell$^{(\boxtimes)}$ (iD), Ryan Dowler, and Irene Connolly (iD)

Institute of Art, Design and Technology, Dun Laoghaire, Dublin, Ireland
marian.mcdonnell@iadt.ie

Abstract. Despite the many ways in which assistive technology could benefit users with cognitive impairments, many existing digital applications remain cognitively inaccessible in their design. Research has consistently found that Persons with Intellectual Disability (PwID) are less self-determined than their non-disabled peers, owing not to any reduced capacity for self-determination but to fewer opportunities for decision-making. Managing one's own money is important for self-determination and is an area where PwID may need support. My Money Counts is a visual money management application designed for use for individuals with an Intellectual Disability. An evaluation of the usability of My Money Counts application was conducted with the intended user group of PwID over two iterations of development. Feedback from phase one resulted in changes to accommodate the user group more appropriately. A mixed methods approach in Phase 2 used controlled observations, self-report questionnaires and a focus group. This paper reports on the application's evaluation with eight individuals with mild to moderate intellectual disability, who took part in the Phase 2 evaluation. The testing compared observational with self-reported evaluations for both usability and engagement, as well as exploring participants' views on spending and saving money. The final iteration of my Money Counts resulted in providing an appropriate method for PwID to budget their income independently.

Keywords: Intellectual disability · Money management · Usability

1 Introduction

1.1 Intellectual Disability

Intellectual disability (ID) refers to a disability that is limiting to intellectual function, and may be defined as having an IQ of 70 or below, impacting on reasoning, learning and problem solving [1]. ID may affect adaptive skills required in everyday life, e.g. social skills, communication, basic literacy and numeracy skills, including money management [2]. It has been well documented how assistive technologies (AT) could provide support in education or employment for people with ID [3, 4]. Additionally, use of technology in practice, can increase independence for activities of daily living such as shopping or using public transport [5, 6]. There are few ATs aimed at money

© Springer Nature Switzerland AG 2020
K. Miesenberger et al. (Eds.): ICCHP 2020, LNCS 12377, pp. 96–103, 2020.
https://doi.org/10.1007/978-3-030-58805-2_12

management. The POSEIDON Project, which develops customisable smart solutions for persons with Down Syndrome [3] developed a money handling training (MHT) application in response to a survey identifying money management as one of the primary areas needing support [7]. Results were positive: users liked the gamification approach while carers felt that it would help to improve financial understanding and promote safe handling of money. Garcia [8] identified that money management is a concern for Irish people living with ID, possibly also for their families, as people with ID may be reliant on support at home. Obviously, this has an impact on independence. Money management applications which assist in coin identification and balancing of cheque books have been found to be successful with users with ID in the past [5].

1.2 Usability and Engagement of My Money Counts

The original idea for this type of application began in February 2010, when St John of God Community Services for PwID and MABS, the Irish Money Advice and Budgeting Service, launched www.MoneyCounts.ie, an on-line money management training programme for people with intellectual disabilities. This older resource was web-based and was available free of charge to those wishing to use it. In 2017, seven years later after the launch, some issues with the original MoneyCounts in its current form were highlighted to the Institute of Art, Design and Technology, Dun Laoghaire, Dublin by the stakeholders. An important consideration was that the original tool in 2017 was not responsive as it was flash based. As it had become obsolete, it does not work well on mobile or tablet screens. Initial work involved establishing requirements for the proposed new mobile application, now called **My Money Counts**. Some of these new requirements included:

- An individual budgeting feature that will educate on how to manage income, expenditure and savings
- Suggested visualisations for disposable income when money is spent
- Use of rewards (e.g. badges) when money is saved
- Storage of previous budgets linked to login details.

See Fig. 1 and Fig. 2 for sample screenshots of the most recent iteration of this new application. Efficient usability is an essential component of any design if a product is to be used effectively. This is especially significant for PwID, who may already struggle to navigate the internet and other applications [9]. For the general population, usability may be measured by the System Usability Scale (SUS). This tool measures effectiveness, efficiency and satisfaction in the form of a questionnaire [10]. However, as ID often incorporates difficulties with reading and writing, the standard SUS is not an appropriate measure of usability in this case. While there is no clearly defined method for usability testing for PwID, Caliz, Martinez and Caliz [11] recommend observational research for detailed recording of the testing. Data can then be analysed and changes to the application made accordingly. Use of adapted SUS questionnaires to overcome problems posed by cognitive deficits is suggested. Therefore, the present study implemented use of a "smileyometer", based on a 5-point Likert scale to measure usability, using an adapted version of the SUS. O'Brien and Toms [12] describe engagement as encompassing an individuals' experience of technology. Therefore, it is subjective in nature and may depend on traits like aesthetics and appeal, ability to engage and hold attention, feedback and interaction.

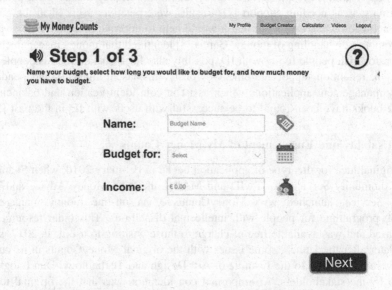

Fig. 1. Final iteration of budget creator in My Money Counts

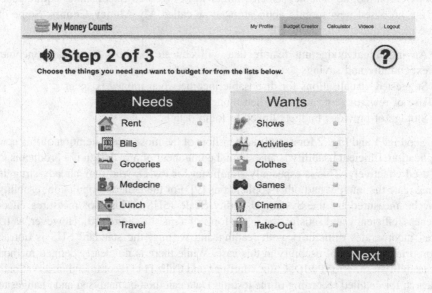

Fig. 2. Final iteration of select from needs and wants screen

The main purpose of the present study is to evaluate the usability and engagement of the My Money Counts application. Caliz, Martinez and Caliz [11] emphasise that it is the natural affinity of people with ID, particularly those with Down syndrome, to be open and friendly. This may impact on the reliability of self-reported usability as they may be inclined to report only in a positive manner. For this reason, the present study observes similarities between observations and self-reports. The research questions this study addresses are:

1. What are the usability and engagement issues relating to My Money Counts?
2. Is there a similarity between observed and self-reported usability?
3. Is there a similarity between observed and self-reported engagement?

2   Method

2.1   Research Design

A mixed methods research design was implemented for this study. Structured task observations, a focus group and completion of an adapted questionnaire were the methods employed for data collection. Lepisto and Ovaska [13] report that when conducting usability testing involving PwID, observational methods work well for researchers to understand the needs of the users. Small focus groups, of less than 10, allow for greater attention to be given to the participants [14]. Qualitative analysis was conducted on the data collected from observations and the focus group. The adapted System Usability Scale (SUS) was informed by Caliz, Martinez and Caliz [11] and used to measure the participants' opinions of the application. This adapted scale followed a Likert format and employed a "smileyometer" [15] to measure response. Although the smileyometer is generally used as a measure with children, Macedo and Trevisan [16] acknowledge that it could be implemented as an appropriate measure where intellectual disability is a factor. The range spanned from "very easy" to "very hard" to measure usability, and "liked a lot" to "disliked a lot" to measure engagement. See Fig. 3.

Fig. 3. Smileyometer to measure usability

2.2   Participants

The participants were recruited from St John of God (SJOG) Carmona Services, Glenageary, Co. Dublin. Prior to commencement of the research study, ethical approval was granted by Carmona Services under the terms of the SJOG Ethics submission and the Department of Technology and Psychology Ethics Committee (DTPEC) at IADT. Selective sampling was employed as the study required particular attributes from the participants, i.e. to possess an intellectual disability (ID), yet with the ability to communicate with the researcher. The sample consisted of 8 adults (4 females, 4 males), aged between 20 and 31 years (M = 23.25, SD = 3.23) with mild to moderate ID.

2.3 Accessible Materials

All materials used during the course of the testing were deemed accessible for the participants, having being informed by Moloney [17] in a study of accessible information for individuals with intellectual disabilities. Coded observation sheets were developed to measure usability and engagement during the user testing. Positive and negative descriptions were stated on the sheets relating to participant's ability to complete tasks, whether help was required or not and tasks completion. Positive and negative descriptions related to engagement included statements of participant interest, focus or boredom, vocalisations and behaviours during task completion. The observation sheets were informed by Macedo and Trevisan [16] who developed an evaluation method to measure usability and interaction of children with Down syndrome. This coding scheme was successfully adapted in that study. Based on Hookham's [18] comparison of usability and engagement, three of the actions (Dislike, Passive, Bored) were considered better suited as measures of engagement along with the addition of codes to measure Positive/Negative Vocalisations and Positive/Negative Behaviour. The researcher and assistant researchers awarded a point for each action observed and recorded relevant notes or comments made by the participants. Hookham [18] method demonstrated reliability with a Cohen's kappa of 64% as well as inter rater agreement. A similar method was employed by Hoe, Hisham and Muda [19] with children with Down syndrome and found to be successful. Desktop computers, pre – prepared with access to the My Money Counts application and headphones were provided for participants. Camtasia software was installed on the computers to observe and record participants' key strokes as they performed the tasks using the application. No identifying characteristics of participants were recorded.

3 Results and Discussion

3.1 Usability of and Engagement with My Money Counts

Overall, participants engaged moderately well with the application despite usability issues encountered. Furthermore, participants were observed to be interested and focused during testing. A popular task was to play the video, as some of the participants recognised somebody they knew. Another popular task was "paying for a drink", with positive behaviour and vocalisation observed. The two tasks, of the five tasks, completed by participants that proved to be the most problematic were using the budget creation tool and changing the password/managing account aspect. Other issues were with navigation generally. Changing passwords and logging in remains a concern. Kumin, Lazar, Feng, Wentz and Ekedebe [20] have highlighted the difficulties this action causes for some users with ID. They describe how users will log in from a home device, where passwords are often remembered by the device. However, in a real-world setting, to develop a mobile application for safe and secure use, on the go, the problem of account protection via passwords remains. The Norwegian e-Me project aim was to provide new knowledge that can significantly improve the usability and accessibility of identity management and authentication mechanisms in electronic services [21]. There was a discrepancy between observed and self-reported factors. The observational analysis reflecting the usability issues experienced by participants, did not correlate with the completed SUS forms. For example, four participants declared that they found creating the budget process very easy, yet observational analysis demonstrates that no participant found that task particularly easy. Caliz, Martinez and Caliz [11] suggest that this particular user group do not like to criticise, owing to their naturally friendly and open dispositions. In this regard, the observers hand written notes together with Camtasia screen recordings, helped with confirming any discrepancy between the two methods.

3.2   Strengths and Limitations of the Present Study

While not flawless, the present study has a number of strengths, not least that the research aims to include the target group for which the application is intended to serve [8, 22]. Adapting the "nothing about us, without us" motto, aims to understand the lived experience of users with ID in trying to access technology as cited in Noel [23]. The ongoing and deep analysis of the usability experience of the My Money Counts application is pioneering in nature. The project aims to address some of the usability barriers that those with ID encounter in trying to maximise the potential benefits of assistive technology in activities of daily life [4]. This study found Camtasia screen recordings a practical tool for confirming the observers hand written notes. The lack of inter–rater reliability is a potential limitation of the study. Additionally, it was found that ideally, there would be two observers per participant during observation, to maximize data collection. Unfortunately, this was not possible due to lack of resources.

4   Conclusion

The final iteration of my Money Counts resulted in providing an appropriate method for PwID to budget their income independently. The present study has contributed to the area of usability and disability through gaining knowledge of the users' experience. The voices of eight participants were heard, and their opinions and experiences will work towards creating greater e – inclusion. My Money Counts is a community research initiative undertaken to educate and support people with intellectual disabilities in financial matters. This includes a budgeting web tool which has been designed for accessibility. Further research and development is presently investigating whether the budgeting tool could be extended to people with lower subjective numeracy. Another issue that deserves further research is the issue surrounding managing secure accounts and passwords for PwID. As we, as societies, go ever more online, the importance of a safe environment for vulnerable users becomes ever more essential. Furthermore, although the literature highlights the importance of including people with ID in research, Kaehne and O'Connell [22] raise an interesting conundrum; the severity of the intellectual disability impacts on the success of any research involving this community. Perhaps this reality does not accurately represent wider groups of people with ID, as the voices heard are likely to be those with the ability to participate.

References

1. American Association on Intellectual and Development Disorders. (n.d.). http://aaidd.org/intellectual-disability/definition
2. Brue, A.W., Wilmshurst, L.: Essentials of Intellectual Disability Assessment and Identification (2016). https://ebookcentral.proquest.com
3. Augusto, J.C., et al.: Personalized smart environments to increase inclusion of people with down's syndrome. In: Augusto, J.C., Wichert, R., Collier, R., Keyson, D., Salah, A.A., Tan, A.-H. (eds.) AmI 2013. LNCS, vol. 8309, pp. 223–228. Springer, Cham (2013). https://doi.org/10.1007/978-3-319-03647-2_16
4. Owuor, J., Larkan, F.: Assistive technology for an inclusive society for people with intellectual disability. Stud. Health Technol. Inform. **242**, 805–812 (2017)
5. Rus, S., Caliz, D., Braun, A., Engler, A., Schulze, E.: Assistive apps for activities of daily living supporting persons with down's syndrome. J. Ambient Intell. Smart Environ. **9**(5), 611–623 (2017)
6. Dekelver, J., Daems, J., Solberg, S., Bosch, N., Van de Perre, L., De Vliegher, A.: Viamigo: a digital travel assistant for people with intellectual disabilities: modeling and design using contemporary intelligent technologies as a support for independent travelling of people with intellectual disabilities. In: Proceedings from IISA2015: 6th International Conference on Information, Intelligence, Systems and Applications, Corfu, Greece (2015). https://ieeexplore.ieee.org
7. Rus, S., Braun, A.: Money handling training-applications for persons with down syndrome. In: Paper presented at Intelligent Environments (IE) 12th International Conference, London, United Kingdom, September 2016. http://ieeexplore.ieee.org
8. Garcia Iriarte, E., O'Brien, P., McConkey, R., Wolfe, M., O'Doherty, S.: Identifying the key concerns of Irish persons with intellectual disability. J. Appl. Res. Irel. **27**, 564–575 (2014)
9. Chadwick, D., Wesson, C., Fullwood, C.: Internet access by people with intellectual disabilities: inequalities and opportunities. Future Internet **5**(3), 376–397 (2013)
10. Brooke, J.: SUS: A retrospective. J. Usability Stud. **8**(2), 29–40 (2013)
11. Caliz, D., Martinez, L., Caliz, R.: "USATESTDOWN" a proposal of a usability testing guide for mobile applications focused on persons with down's syndrome. In: Proceedings from ITCS2017: 6th International Conference on Information Technology and Services, Sydney, Australia (2017). http://aircconline.com/csit/csit765.pdf
12. O'Brien, H.L., Toms, E.G.: What is user engagement? a conceptual framework for defining user engagement with technology. J. Am. Soc. Inf. Sci. Technol. **59**(6), 938–955 (2008). https://doi.org/10.1002/asi.20801
13. Lepisto, A., Ovaska, S.: Usability evaluation involving participants with cognitive disabilities. In: Proceedings of the Third Nordic Conference on Human – Computer Interaction, vol. 82, pp. 305–308 (2004). https://doi.org/10.1145/1028014.1028061
14. Nind, M.: Conducting qualitative research with people with learning, communication and other disabilities: methodological challenges. ESRC National Centre for Research Methods (2008). http://eprints.ncrm.ac.uk/491
15. Read, J., MacFarlane, S., Casey, C.: Endurability, engagement and expectations: measuring children's fun. Interact. Des. Child. **2**, 1–23 (2009)

16. Macedo, I., Trevisan, Daniela G.: A method to evaluate disabled user interaction: a case study with down syndrome children. In: Stephanidis, C., Antona, M. (eds.) UAHCI 2013. LNCS, vol. 8009, pp. 50–58. Springer, Heidelberg (2013). https://doi.org/10.1007/978-3-642-39188-0_6

17. Moloney, M.: Accessible information: advocating the use of technology for individuals with intellectual disability on their path to individualised services (Masters dissertation). Dublin Institute of Technology, Dublin (2012). https://arrow.dit.ie/scschcomdis/45/

18. Hookham, G., Nesbitt, K., Kay-Lambkin, F.: Comparing usability and engagement between a serious game and a traditional online programme. In: Proceedings from ACSW 2016: Australasian Computer Science Week Multiconference. Canberra, AUS (2016). http://dx.doi.org/10.1145/2843043.2843365

19. Hoe, L.K., Hisham, S., Muda, N.: Assessing usability and fun of speech articulation training for children with down syndrome. J. Netw. Innovative Comput. **3**, 29–37 (2015)

20. Kumin, L., Lazar, J., Feng, J.H., Wentz, B., Ekedebe, N.: A usability evaluation of workplace-related tasks on a multi-touch tablet computer by adults with down syndrome. J. Usability Stud. **7**(4), 118–142 (2012)

21. Fuglerud, K.S., Røssvoll, T.H.: Previous and related research on usability and accessibility issues of personal identification management systems. NR-notat DART/10/10 from (2010). https://www.nr.no/en/nrpublication?query=/file/5371/Fuglerud_-_Previous_and_Related_Research_on_Usability_and_Acc.pdf

22. Kaehne, A., O'Connell, C.: Focus groups with people with learning difficulties. J. Intellect. Disabil. **14**(2), 133–145 (2010)

23. Noel, L-A.: Promoting an emancipatory research paradigm in design education and practice. In: Proceedings from DRS2016: Design Research Society 50th Anniversary Conference, Brighton, UK (2016). http://www.drs2016.org/355

Towards Modeling of Interpersonal Proximity Using Head-Mounted Camera for Children with ASD

Airi Tsuji[1(✉)], Satoru Sekine[2], Soichiro Matsuda[3], Junichi Yamamoto[4], and Kenji Suzuki[3]

[1] Tokyo University of Agriculture and Technology,
2-24-16 Nakacho, Koganei, Tokyo 184-8588, Japan
atsuji@go.tuat.ac.jp
[2] The University of Tokyo, 4-6-1 Komaba, Meguro-ku, Tokyo 153-8505, Japan
ssekine@keio.jp
[3] University of Tsukuba, Tennodai, Tsukuba, Ibaraki 305-8573, Japan
matsuda@ai.iit.tsukuba.ac.jp, kenji@ieee.org
[4] Keio University, 2-15-45 Mita, Minato-ku, Tokyo 108-8345, Japan
yamamotj@flet.keio.ac.jp

Abstract. This study suggests a novel method to clarify interpersonal proximity from the area occupied by a target person in the visual field. We use the size of the area as an index of interpersonal proximity to support therapeutic activities for the developmental support for children with ASD. We investigate the relationship between physical and interpersonal distance and its proximity as a sense of distance. Head-mounted camera and Mask-RCNN used as the measurement. The pilot experiment shows the possibility of measurement and experimentation in actual therapy showed a difference between interpersonal distance and interpersonal proximity.

Keywords: Chidren with ASD · Human recognition · Interpersonal proximity · Head-mounted camera · Machine learning

1 Introduction

Interpersonal proximity (a sense of distance) is an element of nonverbal communication and indicates aan dequate physical and social distance from communication targets. The concept of interpersonal distance as the physical distance was proposed by Hall [1] which is measured via the stop-distance and observation methods. It is widely used as one of evaluation of communications in psychology and sociology. To maintain a reasonable degree of distance from others requires spatial awareness that is regarded as the link between understanding proximity to others (interpersonal proximity) and social contexts. The concept is related to a sense of direction and spatial cognition [2]. However, it is known that the physical distance between two parsons is related to interpersonal proximity, but

© Springer Nature Switzerland AG 2020
K. Miesenberger et al. (Eds.): ICCHP 2020, LNCS 12377, pp. 104–111, 2020.
https://doi.org/10.1007/978-3-030-58805-2_13

these two factors are not the same. The interpersonal proximity is considered even in verbal communication and does not necessarily depend only on physical distance.

Children with autism spectrum disorder (ASD) experience difficulties in establishing social communication and interpersonal interaction with restricted interests and repetitive behaviors, which is defined in the Diagnostic and Statistical Manual of Mental Disorders, Fifth Edition published by the American Psychiatric Association [3]. Moreover, it has become clear that social communication skills can be improved by providing appropriate comprehensive developmental support for children with ASD [4].

In order to support the development of communication skills, it is important to assess the communication in terms of behavior and interaction in a quantitative manner. Previous work has been studied about physical and interpersonal distance that is measured as the target and used as an evaluation index. There are several therapeutic activities to help children to control the interpersonal distance to the appropriate degree in order to support the development of children with ASD. As an attempt to quantify the interpersonal proximity has been reported in the research on the interpersonal distance on VR space, which is originated from Bailenson [5]. It clarified that the interpersonal proximity is highly dependent upon visual perception. We consider that it is helpful for therapists or caregivers to observe to change the interpersonal proximity during sessions. We then try to explore a computational model to estimate the interpersonal proximity based on the measured interpersonal distance between two persons.

The main contribution in this study is to find a certain correlation between the image size of the target person in the image sequence obtained from first-person view and the physical interpersonal distance obtained by the motion capture system. The current study aimed to quantify interpersonal proximity to support the development of children with ASD. To this end, we aimed to identify a method via which to clarify interpersonal proximity from the area occupied by a target in the visual field of a first-person viewing camera.

2   Method

2.1   Interpersonal Proximity

Interpersonal distance refers to the physical distance between two persons and should be established to build interpersonal relationships. Hall divided personal space into close, individual, social, and public distance [1]. As the intimacy between the two persons increases, this distance decreases. Reducing distance, rather than intimacy, could cause others to experience strong discomfort. Children with ASD are often closer to or further away from each other relative to typically developing children. However, it is difficult to adjust their interpersonal distance or create appropriate distance from them [6,7].

The concept of interpersonal distance also exists in VR space involving the manipulation of interpersonal distance and behavior change [5]. The manipulation of interpersonal distance, using augmented reality in the real world, reduces

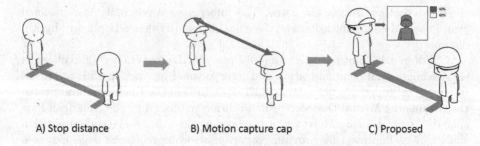

A) Stop distance   B) Motion capture cap   C) Proposed

Fig. 1. Previous and proposed measurement methods

discomfort or pressure [8]. It is noted that interpersonal distance is perceived and recognized mainly via vision, because visual interpersonal distance manipulation, using a head-mounted display, affects recognition and behavior in the actual interpersonal distance.

However, it is not simply considered to be another representation of interpersonal distance but is evaluated subjectively based on more types of information rather than physical distance. The term of interpersonal proximity is also used in the remote exchange of text information. It may be possible to obtain different interpersonal proximity to two persons maintaining the same interpersonal distance. Interpersonal proximity can be acquired even in communication in a virtual space, using only visual information; therefore, it is possible to clarify interpersonal proximity using visual information. We assume that an index of interpersonal proximity can be described in relation to the peer within the field of view from the participant.

2.2   Proposed System

We proposed the use of the area around the person in a first-person view as a method for estimating interpersonal proximity between two people. The images from the first-person viewpoint is acquired from the head-mounted camera. Figure 1 shows an overview of previous methods and the proposed method compared to conventional methods.

The conventional method to measure the interpersonal distance in a quantitative manner is the stop-distance method shown in Fig. 1A [9]. This method requires two persons to approach one another until they feel discomfort or unpleasantness; the distance between their toe positions at the final point is then measured. Although this method enabled quantitative measurement of interpersonal distance, it was difficult to measure changes in interpersonal distance dynamically during activity.

Then, a method using the motion capture system [10], allows us to measure the interpersonal distance in several activities, as illustrated in Fig. 1B. It measures the distance between the heads of two persons. However, this was limited to physical distance measurement and did not allow consideration of the influence of the field of view.

On the other hand, in the proposed method as illustrated in Fig. 1C, the head-mounted camera is used to acquire the first-person view field and the area occupied by the target person. We consider that we can estimate the interpersonal proximity that reflects actual feelings most closely.

2.3   Measuring Human Area

Mask-RCNN [11] is an object-recognition method using deep learning. The proposed system used this method to calculate the area occupied by the target person in the image sequence from a first-person view. The outline of the process is shown in Fig. 2. In Fig. 2, X means the position of each person, D means the distance between two persons and S means the area occupied by the target person in each frame. The area around each object each the image is calculated by processing the first-person view images taken with the head-mounted camera, using Mask-RCNN. Learning models use Common Objects in Context Dataset [12]. The only area occupied by the target person (the largest human tagged by the mask) is used as the index of interpersonal proximity. In addition, interpersonal distance measurement in motion capture was performed, to compare it with the existing method.

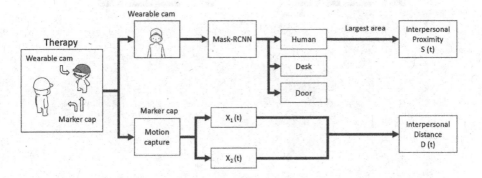

Fig. 2. Overview of system

3   Experiments

An experiment was conducted to verify the proposed method. In the experiment, the eye gaze and first-person images are acquired by using Tobii glass (Tobii Technology K.K.) [13] that is a glasses-type, head-mounted, first-person viewpoint camera with a small burden on the experiment participants. The motion capture marker cap used in a previous study was attached and interpersonal distance measurement was conducted at the same time. We will show the relationship between interpersonal distance and interpersonal proximity was examined using the proposed method. The experiment was conducted with two participants wearing the Tobii glass and marker caps. Participants were asked to perform the stop-distance method as a classical measurement of interpersonal distance. One participant was standing or sitting, and the other moved to approach him until discomfort was felt by one participant. The approaching participant stopped upon feeling discomfort or when the standing/sitting person raised a hand to indicate discomfort.

3.1 Result

Figure 3 shows the plots that represent interpersonal distance measured via motion capture and the area obtained by the proposed method. Blue lines represent the closest position. Table 1 shows the measurement results obtained via the stop-distance method. The interpersonal distance measured via motion capture and the frame obtained by the proposed method were acquired every second. Figure 4 shows the correlation between interpersonal distance and interpersonal proximity for the standing/sitting participants. Both correlation coefficients were higher than .50.

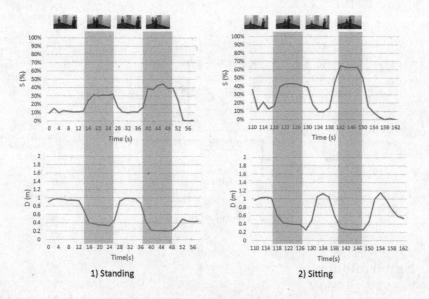

Fig. 3. Result of preliminary experiment

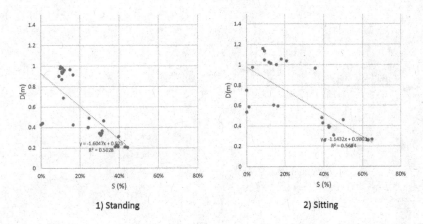

Fig. 4. Correlation between interpersonal distance and interpersonal proximity in preliminary experiments

Table 1. Result of each method

Standing/Sitting	Standing		Sitting	
Limit decision	Approaching	Non-approaching	Approaching	Non-approaching
Stop distance	43 cm	25 cm	40 cm	15 cm
Motion capture	35.72 cm	26.02 cm	37.05 cm	27.00 cm
Proposed	29.8%	40.59%	41.18%	57.99%

4 User Study with Children with ASD

We conducted an experiment for actual therapy for children with ASD. Participants in such therapy are children diagnosed with ASD. The chronological age was 5 years, 1 month, while the developmental age was 3 years, 4 months. The developmental age was calculated via the Kyoto Scale of Psychological Development [14], which is used in Japan as the standardized diagnosis scale. This experiment was approved by the Institutional Review Board of Anonymous Institute, and participants joined the experiment after providing informed consent.

4.1 Result

Figure 5 shows the results for interpersonal distance and interpersonal proximity. Figure 6 shows the correlation between interpersonal distance and interpersonal proximity. The correlation coefficient was .33.

4.2 Discussion

From the result of the pilot experiments, a certain correlation between the interpersonal distance obtained from motion capture and the proposed method was

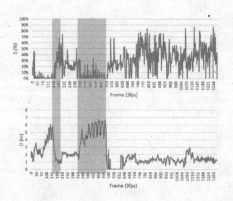

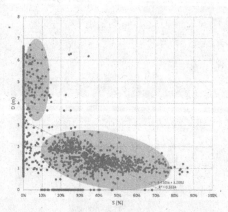

Fig. 5. Result of actual therapy

Fig. 6. Correration between interpersonal distance and interpersonal proximity of actual therapy

observed, as shown in Fig. 4. This result explains the target person looks larger as the distance is shorter when the target person appears within the field of view. We carefully checked if the head-mounted camera disturbed the therapeutic activities, but there was no critical problem during the experiment.

On the other hand, the results of the user study did not show a strong negative correlation compared to the pilot experiment, as shown in Fig. 6. We consider that there are several times when the participant was not looking at the therapist although they are actually at a close distance. However, except for that area which is illustrated the upper gray circle, a certain correlation also appears in the lower gray-circle area in Fig. 6. We assume that the participant may consider close proximity, although the target person does not appear in the field of view, the participant may consider close proximity if s/he knows well the target person stands behind or beside. However, its proximity may decrease compared with the target person standing in front of them. We may develop a time-varying algorithm that includes temporal characteristics of proximity. Although further analysis is needed, our findings provide insights between the interpersonal distance and interpersonal proximity.

5   Conclusion

In this study, we proposed a method via which to measure interpersonal proximity using an image sequence from a first-person view. From experimental results, we found high feasibility to use the system for therapeutic activities and also the possibility to estimate interpersonal proximity from the computer vision approach. In the future, we will conduct long-term therapy measurements to determine whether the proposed method can be used to measure changes in interpersonal proximity in therapy and verify the resultant effects.

References

1. Hall, E.T.: The hidden dimension (1966)
2. Kozlowski, L., Bryant, K.: Sense of direction, spatial orientation, and cognitive maps. J. Exp. Psychol.: Human Percept. Perform. **3**, 590–598 (1977)
3. American Psychiatric Association, et al.: Diagnostic and statistical manual of mental disorders (DSM-5®). American Psychiatric Pub (2013)
4. Rogers, S.J., et al.: Effects of a brief early start Denver model (ESDM)-based parent intervention on toddlers at risk for Autism spectrum disorders: a randomized controlled trial. J. Am. Acad. Child Adolescent Psychiatry **51**(10), 1052–1065 (2012)
5. Bailenson, J.N., Blascovich, J., Beall, A.C., Loomis, J.M.: Interpersonal distance in immersive virtual environments. Pers. Soc. Psychol. Bull. **29**(7), 819–833 (2003)
6. Rogers, A.L., Fine, H.J.: Personal distance in play therapy with an autistic and a symbiotic psychotic child. Psychotherapy: Theory Res. Pract. **14**(1), 41 (1977)
7. Kennedy, D.P., Adolphs, R.: Violations of personal space by individuals with Autism spectrum disorder. PLoS ONE **9**(8), e103369 (2014)
8. Maeda, M., Sakata, N.: Controlling the interpersonal distance using the virtual body size. IPSJ Interact. **2016**, 47–53 (2016). (in Japanese)
9. Gessaroli, E., Santelli, E., di Pellegrino, G., Frassinetti, F.: Personal space regulation in childhood autism spectrum disorders. PLoS ONE **8**(9), e74959 (2013)
10. Tsuji, A., Matsuda, S., Suzuki, K.: Interpersonal distance and face-to-face behavior during therapeutic activities for children with ASD. In: Miesenberger, K., Bühler, C., Penaz, P. (eds.) ICCHP 2016. LNCS, vol. 9759, pp. 367–374. Springer, Cham (2016). https://doi.org/10.1007/978-3-319-41267-2_52
11. He, K., Gkioxari, G., Dollár, P., Girshick, R.: Mask R-CNN. In: Proceedings of the IEEE International Conference on Computer Vision, pp. 2961–2969 (2017)
12. COCO - Common Objects in Context. http://cocodataset.org/
13. Tobii pro glass. https://www.tobiipro.com/ja/product-listing/tobii-pro-glasses-2/
14. Ikuzawa, M., Matsushita, Y., Nakase, A.: Kyoto scale of psychological development 2001. Kyoto International Social Welfare Exchange Centre, Kyoto (2002)

"ADAPEI-TRANSPORT": A GPS Based Mobile App for Learning Paths and Improving Autonomy for Young Adults Having Intellectual Disabilities to Take Public Transport

Jesus Zegarra Flores[1]([✉]), Gaelle Malnati[2], Jean Jaques Stevens[2], Eric Bournez[1], Leandra Boutros[1], Nadia Laayssel[2], Gilbert Geneviève[2], Jean-Baptiste de Vaucresson[2], Remi Coutant[2], Jean Paul Granger[2], and Jean-Pierre Radoux[1]

[1] Medic@, Département de recherche d'Altran, Parc d'Innovation, Boulevard Sébastien Brandt, Bât Gauss, CS 20143, 67404 Illkirch, France
{jesus.zegarraflores, eric.bournez, leandrajeane.boutros, jeanpierre.radoux}@altran.com
[2] ADAPEI du Territoire de Belfort, 11 rue de Phaffans, 90380 Roppe, France
{g.malnati, jj.stevens, n.laayssel, jb.devaucresson, r.coutant, jp.granger}@adapei90.fr,
gilbert.genevieve90@orange.fr

Abstract. Children and young adults with intellectual disabilities (from 10–20 years old) are trained by educators for their journeys taking public transport (buses). This training is done teaching them the different steps and actions to do in a sequential way using photos, pictograms, times, texts (e.g. walk to the bus stop Roppe and take the line 21 direction République, do not forget to press on the stop button to alert to take off, take off at the stop station République, etc.). Currently, specialists from ADAPEI association in Belfort (France) use booklets in which all the steps to follow are printed. With the increasing of the use of mobile apps in Assistive Technology, the aim of this partnership between Altran and ADAPEI from Belfort is to develop new supports to teach children (from the least to the most autonomous) the paths using GPS mobile and tablet apps before and while doing the journey. Moreover, for the most autonomous children familiarized with the use of apps, two ways of navigation using GPS have been developed. Either using maps showing the path or without using maps showing strategically the actions to do in an ordered way when the user is close to a point of interest. In this article, we will show the first results of the use of the app as a teaching system based on observations with disabled children in different situations, and the difficulties found to detect change of directions in noisy GPS data in cities.

Keywords: GPS · App · Intellectual Disability · Transport · Mobility

K. Miesenberger et al. (Eds.): ICCHP 2020, LNCS 12377, pp. 112–119, 2020.
https://doi.org/10.1007/978-3-030-58805-2_14

1   Introduction

The complexity of the public transport network and the management of unexpected situations cause that children having intellectual disabilities experience difficulties to become autonomous to take buses. Some examples to illustrate this can be that the bus does not arrive at the expected time or the bus has to change its normal path because of unexpected problems. Moreover, children can be stressed when they are lost without finding any help. Additionally, the process of learning different steps to take public transport in a sequential way may be long and depends on the capability of each child's memorization. Currently, specialists are creating paper supports by using different software tools. However, the creation of a path is normally time-consuming. Additionally, specialists practice the path with the child as much as possible until they consider that the child is autonomous to follow the path by himself/herself.

In order to develop new technological supports (apps) for learning the paths and for the adapted navigation to children with disabilities, researchers and engineers from Altran Technologies are working in collaboration with the specialists of the transport workshop from the ADAPEI association (http://adapei90.fr/) where they teach the different actions to do to arrive to a destination using the bus. ADAPEI is an association and educational institution that helps children and adults having intellectual disabilities to become autonomous in different activities (for example cooking workshops, etc.) in daily life.

In this article, we will explain the different parts of the developed mobile app and some tests done with end users in different situations. We will complete our analyze showing the difficulties found using real GPS data in cities and the filters used to reduce errors.

2   State of the Art

The state of the art presents some examples of how technology has been used to improve autonomy of people having disabilities.

Irma Alaribe, from the Montreal University, has worked on the creation of a serious game to support the learning of fixed routes for people with intellectual disabilities [1]. This article explains how the development of a serious game encourages the transition between theory and practice.

Price R et al. [2] have investigated the way on facilitating the use of public transport for young adults with intellectual disabilities. This study shows the interest of Google Maps as a help for improving navigation skills to take public transport. Four young adults were involved in this study, with different ID (Intellectual Disabilities) types. The results show an increase of the navigation skills, but also at different speeds of acquisition. The main factors are background with electronic devices or smartphones, natural skills with navigation, learning capabilities in addition with ID types. One of the young adults helped herself with visual indications in addition with Google Maps. The article highlights that a navigation app like Google Maps may be very useful for the autonomy of people with intellectual disabilities but depending on their social and technological background they may need some training. People also need eye contact with the environment which confirms the interest of Augmented Reality in navigation apps.

Don D. McMahon et al. [3] have studied the comparison on the levels of independence in navigation between two groups of adults with intellectual disabilities, helped with 3 tools: paper map (printed from Google Maps), Google Maps (on a mobile device), Augmented Reality app (Navigator Heads Up Display). 6 adults with ID (Intellectual Disability) were involved on different travels with each tool. The way of evaluating them was to score if the patients needed help or not to go from spot A to spot B. It was clearly seen that people have far better results using the Augmented Reality app.

There is an application called way2B [4] invented by two Trinity College graduate engineers in Ireland. This is a mobile app and watch that gives directions, which means that way2B gives users simple step-by-step instructions that are inputted by a carer who is then able to monitor their progress on the journey.

As it was described before, we have found research papers about intellectual disability people using mobile apps for navigation. However, they are based on people with intellectual disabilities who are already autonomous, and they can be familiarized easily with the use of apps on phones and connected watches.

Our objective using ADAPEI transport is to focus on the way to accompany children (early ages) to become autonomous using the app from a learning phase to an autonomous navigation phase in the transport workshop.

3   ADAPEI Transport App

In order to develop the app, specialists from the transport workshop in the association were involved, using the interfaces developed and giving us feedback. The information given about colors of the buttons, the type of pictograms and the prioritization of the information was important to develop a more intuitive app for them and disabled children.

Our app has been developed in the Android Operative system, with three main parts: (1) an interface for the creation of the path mainly used by the specialist where they can add information about the time, GPS coordinates, a pictogram, a photo about the point of interest and a recorded voice of the action to do. This path can be modified by changing the elements in case of errors. (2) A second part is the visualization of the path in which the children can watch all the steps and if they click on a step, the app shows more information about the step itself (for learning before doing the path). (3) The third part is the navigation part, in which the children can choose between a classical map with the path and markers indicating the steps, and another way to show the information displaying in a bigger spot the current step to do using pictograms and photos (Fig. 1).

The app in the tablet is used during theoretical workshop. It is connected to Internet in order to show the map and the marker with the information of the step. However, disabled children in the workshop do not use last generation smartphones and they do not have internet connection. This is the reason why another user navigation interface has been created without using maps and just showing the current actions to do with pictograms and photos when we are close to a landmark prerecorded in the app (* in Fig. 1).

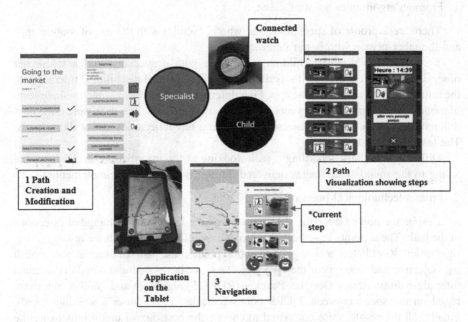

Fig. 1. Different parts of the app (1) path creation and modification, (2) path visualization and (3) navigation part.

4   GPS Data in Cities

We collect the GPS coordinates to save the whole path (every 5 s) done by the specialist while recording the information of every step (landmark) of the path. One of the main problems of the GPS data is that in the city there are plenty of reflections on buildings so that the signal recovered by the GPS antenna from the mobile phone induces errors in the position (Fig. 2) when the person is walking.

Fig. 2. GPS errors close to a bus station.

5 Methodology

The methodology has been divided into 2 parts.

1. From an ergonomics point of view:

There are 2 profile of specialists: one who is familiar with the use of mobile apps and the other person who is not familiar with it.

Tests with the disabled children were done with a specialist and a researcher observing the way children (with medium level of intellectual disabilities) interact with the information coming from the app. Five different children with an intermediate level of mobility between 14 and 20 years old were part of the tests. The tests were done on 4 different days with different trajectories including bus trajectories and walking parts. The tests took about 1 h.

Different situations: recording a path, looking at the information on the map, listening to the sounds and images delivered during navigation were implemented.

2. From a technological point of view:

Despite the noisy GPS data, we have worked on detecting the change of directions in the path. These points have been used to deliver information about the arrow turning right or left 30 m before a change of direction point in the path. In order to accomplish our objective and to segment the GPS trajectory, we have used and compared kalman filter algorithms, Ramer Douglas Peucker (RDP) [5] algorithm and another algorithm based on the speed between 2 GPS points (calculated speed/user's walking speed). Finally, all the results were compared to choose the best mix of algorithms using the quantity of true positive (tp) and false positives (tp/tp + fp).

6 Results

From an ergonomic point of view:

- The alarms for advising to press the stop button in the bus were understood by the children and automatically they pressed on the button.
- The information on the map, like the current position and the arrows for turning right or left, seem to be understood by the children once their meaning has been explained to them. For example, while they were doing the pedestrian path, we have asked them what actions to do when arrows appear and they answered correctly.
- It seems important to do and record the path with the child, in this case the specialist can record the voice saying the action to do or to report a danger. The specialist can ask the child if he understands the message or not to change it.
- Another test was to make a child record a path. In order to avoid stress while saving the path, the child was not asked to record the GPS coordinates for every landmark. They were asked to record the message, the pictogram, the photo and the message voice. Two children have done the test: one who knows how to read and the other who does not know. For the child who knows how to read, she was able to record the path just by indicating her at what moment she had to add the information. After

2 steps of explanation, she was able to record the steps by herself. On the other hand, for the person who did not how to read, it was more difficult for her to follow all the instructions. A more specific user interface including more pictograms will be developed in order to enable children who do not how to read to record the path. We think it can be a good exercise to record the path for memorizing the steps to do.

From a technological point of view

- The segmentation of the GPS data was done in two different walkable paths using a specific pipeline: RDP algorithm along with the filter of speeds followed by angle detection give better results. There are more true positives than false positives in the detection than using the other algorithms (more than 20% of better results in the change direction detection) (Fig. 3).

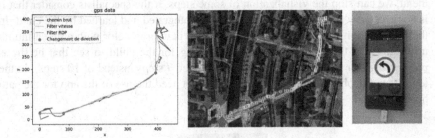

Fig. 3. On the left, the results (pink circles show changes of direction detected) after each part of the pipeline. In the middle, the map with the real path and the real changes of directions. On the right, the image of the arrow on the screen of the app. (Color figure online)

As we can see in the figures above, our algorithms were able to detect all the changes of directions except for one. We have observed that the most difficult detection was the change of directions in small spaces.

7 Conclusions and Future Work

- In this article, we have shown the efficiency of ADAPEI transport having encouraging results with the information given by the children. Tests were made on the creation and modification of the path, visualization and the navigation of the path with no technical errors.
- Children have understood different information like alarms and images which appear on the screen during navigation confirming their accuracies. Additionally, a child who knows how to read was able to understand the sequential way to record a path.
- Using just a type of filtering between kalman, speed filtering or RDP cannot give the ultimate result for a noisy data set, especially in the domain of navigation where GPS data are influenced by multiple factors such as: buildings perturbation and atmosphere. After multiple researches and applications of different methods of

filtering, we found that applying a filter based on speeds followed by an RDP segmentation can give better results. We are going to test this pipeline with more data in different situations in order to validate our approach.

- The most difficult case in change detection is found in small spaces. In this case, an idea is to ask specialists to record different steps in the creation of the paths, when the changes of directions are very close. Another idea is to use augmented reality, but in this case the smartphone should be more powerful than a low cost one.

- In order to avoid children to lose the phone while doing navigation, we have associated the smartphone to a smartwatch using a Bluetooth connection. If the smartphone is separated more than 15 m, the phone will send a SMS with its GPS coordinates to a prerecorded phone number to know its last position.

- In order to test the learning improvement and the autonomy of the children, a way to reduce the number of steps in the path has been developed. Using the modification menu, we can stop the visualization of some steps, if the specialists consider that it is not necessary anymore because it has been integrated and learned by the child. In the visualization part, we observe that the step is in gray color with a green thumb up (Fig. 4). In this way, it can be encouraging for the child to see that he/she is progressing (for instance, in the same path I need 7 steps instead of 10 steps). In the long term, the objective is that the child will not need the use of the app for the path he/she learned.

Fig. 4. Visualization path with 2 learned steps (steps with the thumbs up in green). The child has learned to cross the street and push the button to alert the driver to get off the bus. (Color figure online)

- We have also added the information of the GPS coordinates of the different bus stops, thanks to the collaboration with Optymo (the bus network company). The idea is to give information not only from the bus stop to get into or to get off from at a determined schedule, but also to deliver the name of the intermediate bus stop stations for learning. Moreover, warning information when the bus comes out from its regular itinerary will be delivered.

References

1. Alaribe, I.: Design a serious game to teach teenagers with intellectual disabilities how to use public transportation. Procedia-Soc. Behav. Sci. **176**, 840–845 (2015)
2. Price, R., Marsh, A.J., Fisher, M.H.: Teaching young adults with intellectual and developmental disabilities community-based navigation skills to take public transportation. Behav. Anal. Pract. **11**(1), 46–50 (2018). https://doi.org/10.1007/s40617-017-0202-z
3. McMahon, D.D., Smith, C.C., Cihak, D.F., Wright, R., Gibbons, M.M.: Effects of digital navigation aids on adults with intellectual disabilities: comparison of paper map, Google maps, and augmented reality. J. Spec. Educ. Technol. **30**(3), 157–165 (2015)
4. RTE News: TCD student engineer develop app to help people with an intellectual disability (2017). https://www.rte.ie/news/technology/2017/1218/928312-waytob-app/
5. Douglas, D.H., Peucker, T.K.: Algorithms for the reduction of the number of points required to represent a digitized line or its caricature. Cartographica: Int. J. Geogr. Inf. Geovisual. **10**(2), 112–122 (1973)

ICT to Support Inclusive Education - Universal Learning Design (ULD)

ICT to Support Inclusive Education

Introduction to the Special Thematic Session

Marion Hersh[1(✉)], Barbara Leporini[2], and Marina Buzzi[2]

[1] Biomedical Engineering, University of Glasgow, Glasgow G12 8LT, Scotland
Marion.Hersh@glasgow.ac.uk
[2] ISTI-CNR, via Moruzzi, 1, 56124 Pisa, Italy
Barbara.Leporini@isti.cnr.it, marina.buzzi@iit.cnr.it

Abstract. This short paper introduces five papers about different ways in which technology can be used to support the education of disabled children and young people. The topics covered include music education (two papers), for children with intellectual impairments in orphanages and autistic learners respectively, science education for hearing impaired students, classroom participation at a distance for autistic students and a recommender app for open learning resources. The approaches used include games, exercises, body motions, animations, a quiz and a robot based system with audio, video and vibro-tactile interfaces. Most of them were successful, but only tested with a small number of children and young people. The presentation of these papers is introduced by a brief discussion of the role of ICT in making education accessible to disabled people. It notes that there has been a tendency to develop learning technologies for specific groups of disabled people rather than for all learners and this is borne out in the papers.

Keywords: ICT · Inclusive education · Disabled people

1 Introduction

There are an estimated 93-150 million disabled children [15] and about a billion disabled adults. Education is a basic right, but many disabled people experience multiple barriers to accessing it, including learning environments which are not fully accessible [16], their right to education not being fully recognised legally [2], negative attitudes and low expectations [10, 12], and limited financial support [5]. Inclusive education has been recognised as a human right in the Convention of the Rights of Persons with Disabilities[1], but progress to it has been variable across different countries.

ICT can be used to support inclusion by providing many different ways of representing information, expressing knowledge and engaging in learning, including assessment, to increase the groups they are accessible to. This involves both general

---

[1] https://www.unicef.org/disabilities/files/Factsheet_A5__Web_REVISED(1).pdf.

© Springer Nature Switzerland AG 2020
K. Miesenberger et al. (Eds.): ICCHP 2020, LNCS 12377, pp. 123–128, 2020.
https://doi.org/10.1007/978-3-030-58805-2_15

learning technologies and assistive technologies designed specifically for disabled people. The use of ICT in education has the further advantages of teaching ICT skills, which are becoming increasingly important, and drawing on the increasing popularity and motivating effects of using ICT, particularly amongst young people.

However, ICT is a means not an end in itself or a universal solution and it needs to be supported by appropriate pedagogical strategies, which consider student diversity, as well as appropriate teacher education and career-long learning. Learning technologies need to be fully accessible to disabled and other students and take account of gender and the social and cultural issues, values and sensitivities of the diverse populations that might use them [4, 14]. For instance, a mathematics computer game with a young female central figure has been found to be popular with girls and also enjoyed by boys [1]. The inclusion of disabled people from different cultures as central characters in games and other learning activities could support the inclusion of disabled learners.

Rather than developing learning technologies which can be used by all learners, both disabled and non-disabled, there has been a tendency to develop specific technologies for particular groups of disabled learners. A number of learning technologies developed for disabled learners also have a therapeutic or rehabilitation focus. However, many technologies developed specifically for disabled learners could also be used by non-disabled learners and learning technologies for the general population should be designed to be accessible, useable and otherwise suitable for as wide a range of disabled learners as possible. For instance, educational games are increasingly popular, but their design does not necessarily consider the needs of disabled people, though accessibility and usability conditions have been developed [7].

Many disabled people require assistive technologies to overcome social, infrastructural and other barriers to participating in learning and to carry out learning activities 'safely and easily' [6]. Assistive technology availability varies greatly both between and within countries. The main factors that affect it are income, language and urban/rural area, with most of the assistive technologies available in English or the more dominant European languages and in urban rather than rural areas [8].

Education in science, technology, engineering and mathematics (STEM) is important, including for many careers, understanding the increasingly important public debates and policy formulation on issues such as cybersecurity/privacy management and genetically modified organisms, and daily living activities such as budgeting. However, disabled students are underrepresented in STEM [11]. Blind and partially sighted students often experience particular difficulties in accessing STEM [9]. This includes challenges experienced by screenreader users in accessing formulas, graphs and figures and carrying out exercises.

It has been suggested that new accessibility solutions for emerging technologies will tend to focus on the needs of people with cognitive impairments and learning disabilities, as well as technologies on mobile devices [17].

2   Session Papers

The session consists of five papers. Two present technologies for learning music and the other three for learning science, classroom participation at a distance and obtaining and presenting recommendations for learning resources. Two of the papers present technologies for autistic learners, one for disabled learners in general and the other two for hearing impaired learners and intellectually disabled learners in an orphanage. The music papers consider the value of developing music skills and creativity. However, there is a greater focus on the therapeutic aspects of music and the use of music to improve mood than there would be in the case of non-disabled people.

Information technology in the musical and speech development of mentally retarded (sic) children in an orphanage by Natalia Taligtseva, Svetlana Konovalova and Valerii Lutkov from a pedagogical university in Russia discusses the use of information technology such as SmartBoard and the LiteBim light and sound system to develop several games and exercises. They include reproducing the sounds of animals or objects, mnemonic diagrams to support learning songs and producing different rhythmic accompaniments to music. The exercises and games were tested by seven 8–11 year old children with intellectual disabilities living in an orphanage and led to a significant improvement in their musical skills. They learnt to correlate previously unfamiliar sounds with objects, sing more confidently and produce correct rhythmic accompaniments, which only a few of them were able to do previously.

Promoting creative computer-based music education and composition for individuals with autism spectrum disorders by Georgios Kyriakos from an English university presents a version of the Terpsichore software built with SuperCollider and able to convert code into sound clips, sequences, visual structures and buttons able to carry out various actions. The interface was transformed into a standalone app for Mac computers. There are two modes. The TOM mode supports composing original tonal music phrases. The SIP mode is intended to make learners concentrate on overall sound content rather than its tonal components. The software was tested by 28 autistic students aged 12 to 29 in Greece in a four months pilot study with the support of three tutors. The majority of the autistic students liked Tepsichore's graphical layout and generally reacted positively to it. Participants performed better on modifying musical phrases than composition, but that was probably to be expected, as original composition requires specific talent. Use of the software was generally found to improve participants' emotional state.

WebMoti by F.S. Asmy, A. Roberge-Milanese, M.C. Rombaut, G. Smith and D.I. Feis from two Canadian universities describes a software and hardware robot-based system that supports the classroom participation of autistic students when they are unable to attend in person. In addition to other factors that may prevent in person attendance, many autistic people experience high levels of stress and anxiety [3] and are distressed by noise which seems not to disturb non-autistic people [13]. The student uses an XBox game controller to control a small classroom based robot from a remote location such as their home. They can start and end the live video conference, and control the sensory input by turning video, audio and vibrotactile elements (provided through two pillows) on and off, control the camera and use an animated hand to indicate they want to participate. This allows personalisation of the educational session. The system was tested weekly for about five weeks with a first year autistic university student and two 8–10 year old autistic primary school students. Pre, midway and post study questionnaires indicated that WebMoti helped the students follow the lesson plan with their class without sensory overload. However, further tests with more students are required. It would also be useful to investigate modifications for different age groups.

Development of a learning support system for science using collaboration and body movement for hearing-impaired children: learning support for plant germination and growth conditions by Ryohei Egusa and colleagues from five different Japanese universities uses a game based approach involving body movements, animations and a quiz. It is aimed at correcting misconceptions and teaching correct information about plant germination and growth, but could be generalised to other science areas. It was tested with 17 6–9 year old hearing impaired children. The system was found to support collaborative game playing and collaborative approaches to learning science for hearing impaired children. However, the proportion of correct answers is not stated and the authors indicate that the participants were strongly influenced by other students' moods when playing the quiz and that there is a need for further development to encourage children to use scientific ideas in decision making.

Promoting inclusive open education: a holistic approach towards a novel accessible OER recommender system by Hejer Brahim, Mohamed Khribi and Mohamed Jemni from a Tunisian university proposes a recommender system for teaching, learning and research materials that are available under an open licence with no or minimal restrictions. The aim is to propose resources which are best suited to the particular learner's needs and characteristics. The recommender involves data acquisition and processing, data modelling, the learner's profile and the recommendation. It also covers accessibility tasks. However, further work is required to develop and test the recommender.

3 Conclusions

The five papers presented here cover diverse areas of education, including music, science and distance participation in classes. Several of them use multimodal or alternative interfaces and/or games of different types. Accessibility to all groups including disabled people, particularly those with sensory impairments, can generally be improved by offering multiple and multi-modal options for accessing the system. At the same time there need to be easy options for turning off modalities to avoid sensory overstimulation to autistic people in particular. A personalised approach to learning and customization features offered by educational tools can be particularly beneficial to disabled learners better and fit their learning rhythms and needs.

The results of tests of the technologies presented here have been positive, but have generally only involved small numbers of participants. The distance participation system was tested by two 8–10 year olds and a first year university student. This raises questions as to whether there are both learning technologies which are suitable for all ages and those which should be adapted to make them age appropriate. New education strategies could exploit the fast dissemination of technology, including virtual reality, the internet of things and tangible environments to make the learning experience more immersive, multimodal and engaging. However, care will be required to ensure that the resulting learning approaches take account of the accessibility and other needs of disabled learners.

There is thus a need to consider the compatibility of assistive and other technologies to enable disabled learners and teachers to use the full range of available tools and technologies and get the most out of them. This may require new approaches to design that take this need for compatibility into account. Finally, further research will be required to investigate how best to use ICT to support universal inclusive education and meet the needs of the full diversity of disabled and non-disabled learners and teachers.

References

1. De Jean, J., Upitis, R., Koch, C., Young, J.: The story of Phoenix Quest: how girls respond to a prototype language and mathematics computer game. Gend. Educ. 11(2), 207–223 (1999)
2. Forlin, C., Lian, M.G.J.: Reform, Inclusion and Teacher Education: Toward a New Era of Special Education in the Asia Pacific Region. Routledge, London (2008)
3. Gillott, A., Standen, P.J.: Levels of anxiety and sources of stress in adults with autism. J. Intell. Disabil. 11(4), 359–370 (2007)
4. Heemskerk, I., Brink, A., Volman, M., Ten Dam, G.: Inclusiveness and ICT in education: a focus on gender, ethnicity and social class. J. Comput. Assist. Learn. 21(1), 1–16 (2005)
5. Hernandez, G.: Assessing El Salvador's capacity for creating inclusive educational opportunities for students with disabilities using a capacity assessment framework. University of Maryland, College Park (2006)
6. Hersh, M.A., Johnson, M.A.: On modelling assistive technology systems - part I: modelling framework. Technol. Disabil. 20(3), 193–215 (2008)
7. Hersh, M.A., Leporini, B.: An overview of accessibility and usability of educational games. In: Student Usability in Educational Software and Games: Improving Experiences, pp. 1–40. IGI Global (2013)
8. Hersh, M., Mouroutsou, S.: Learning technology and disability—overcoming barriers to inclusion: evidence from a multicountry study. Br. J. Educ. Technol. 50(6), 3329–3344 (2019)
9. Leporini, B., Buzzi, M.: Education and STEM on the Web. In: Yesilada, Y., Harper, S. (eds.) Web Accessibility. HIS, pp. 651–674. Springer, London (2019). https://doi.org/10.1007/978-1-4471-7440-0_33
10. McGrew, K.S., Evans, J.: Expectations for students with cognitive disabilities: is the cup half empty or half full? Can the cup flow over? (Synthesis Report 55). University of Minnesota, National Center on Educational Outcomes, National Center on Educational Outcomes (2004)
11. Martin, J.K., et al.: Recruitment of students with disabilities: exploration of science, technology, engineering, and mathematics. J. Postsecondary Educ. Disabil. 24(4), 285–299 (2011)
12. OPM Removing barriers, raising disabled people's living standards (2014). https://www.opm.co.uk/wp-content/uploads/2014/05/Removing-barriers-raising-living-standards.pdf. Accessed 17 June 2020

13. Remington, A., Fairnie, J.: A sound advantage: increased auditory capacity in autism. Cognition **166**, 459–465 (2017)
14. Tondeur, J., Forkosh-Baruch, A., Prestridge, S., Albion, P., Edirisinghe, S.: Responding to challenges in teacher professional development for ICT integration in education. Educ. Technol. Soc. **19**(3), 110–120 (2016)
15. UNICEF Children and young people with disabilities (2013). https://www.unicef.org/disabilities/files/Factsheet_A5__Web_REVISED(1).pdf. Accessed 27 August 2020
16. World Health Organization (WHO): World Report on Disability (2011). http://www.who.int/disabilities/world_report/2011/en/. Accessed 17 June 2020
17. Yesilada, Y., Harper, S.: Futurama. In: Yesilada, Y., Harper, S. (eds.) Web accessibility. HIS, pp. 791–803. Springer, London (2019). https://doi.org/10.1007/978-1-4471-7440-0_40

Information Technology in the Musical and Speech Development of Children with Learning Disabilities in an Orphanage

Nataliya G. Tagiltseva[1]([⊠]), Svetlana A. Konovalova[1],
Lada V. Matveeva[1], Oksana A. Ovsyannikova[2],
Lidiya Z. Tsvetanova-Churukova[3], and Valerii V. Lutkov[4]

[1] Ural State Pedagogical University, Yekaterinburg, Russia
musis52nt@mail.ru, konovsvetlana@mail.ru,
lada-matveeva@yandex.ru
[2] Tyumen State University, Tyumen, Russia
sergeiovsiannikov@yandex.ru
[3] South-West University "Neofit Rilski", Blagoevgrad, Bulgaria
lidycveta@swu.bg
[4] Children's Art School No. 7, Ural State Pedagogical University,
Yekaterinburg, Russia
valeriylutkov@yandex.ru

Abstract. For children from mild to moderate mental retardation, living in an orphanage, require specific educational conditions. The absence of families of these children imposes their own conditions for the organization of their development. One of the effective forms of such development is information technology that allows a child with varying degrees of mental retardation to "go" outside the orphanage and find out what they could not find out at their place of residence. The socialization and development of such children can occur in the process of various types of activities, one of which is musical activity, which allows the child to hear the sounds of the world, get acquainted with various objects that have their own voice, learn to pronounce words correctly when singing children's songs, listen to music. The article reveals the possibilities of musical and speech development of a child from a mild to moderate degree of mental retardation when using such information technologies as SmartBoard and LiteBim. Exercises are presented for searching for sound analogs, singing according to mnemonic diagrams of the game – vocal ones: for playing various sounds in a voice, rhythmic ones: for accompaniment of a musical composition "stick to the beat", "play music". Diagnostic results of the musical, musical, rhythmic and speech development of such children showed positive dynamics, which allows us to recommend the exercises and games used in the sequence determined by the authors of the article to teachers working with mentally retarded children in these institutions.

Keywords: Information technology · Children with mental retardation · Pupils of orphanages · Musical and speech development · Musical games and exercises

© Springer Nature Switzerland AG 2020
K. Miesenberger et al. (Eds.): ICCHP 2020, LNCS 12377, pp. 129–135, 2020.
https://doi.org/10.1007/978-3-030-58805-2_16

1 Introduction

Nowadays in Russia, despite the annual decrease, there still remain a certain number of orphanages in which children with disabilities are brought up. These are children whose parents abandoned immediately after birth, due to the fact that they had defects in physical and mental development. These are children whose parents fell into a difficult everyday situation and, not having the strength to raise such a child, give him to an orphanage. As a rule, such children subsequently fall into foster families, where new parents are already engaged in their upbringing. But, before entering new families, such children live and study in the orphanage, where they socialize, acquire communication skills, knowledge about life, and certain skills. Among the many ways of such socialization, researchers [1–4] particularly emphasize musical activity that promotes both the musical and speech development of the child. Unfortunately, to date, musician teachers in orphanages, despite the SmartBoard existing in orphanages, interactive systems such as the LiteBim sound and sound system, computer programs, etc., use them not often enough and expediently. However, the introduction of just such technologies into the process of musical activity helps a child with a varying degree of mental retardation to learn about life phenomena, learn to listen to sounds, pronounce clearly the words denoting a particular subject, i.e. to find out and understand what they brought up in the orphanage did not even know about. The purpose of this article is to present a series of exercises and games for children with moderate and severe mental retardation when using SmartBoard, LiteBim sound and sound system for their musical and speech development. All these games and exercises were tested and proved effective in the Yekaterinburg orphanage for mentally retarded children by the teachers of the children's music school No. 8 and the children's art school No. 7 of the city of Yekaterinburg, teachers and graduate students of the Ural State Pedagogical University, Department of Music Education (Yekaterinburg, Russia).

2 Theoretical and Methodological Grounds for the Introduction of Information Technology for Children with Moderate and Severe Mental Retardation

Modern scientific research reveals various areas of work with children with health problems. Music and musical activity in such studies are considered by the authors as an effective means of developing such children, namely, their communicative and verbal skills, musical abilities [5–8]. The authors of [9] develop musical games for children with disabilities, aiming them at the perception of the sounds of certain objects, for example, a clock, a moving car, the sounds of a steam locomotive, forming their skills of precise movement with colored ribbons to music, developing skills of accompaniment of music to noise tools. Some works emphasize the importance of selecting a classical musical repertoire to improve the emotional state of children with a slight degree of mental retardation [2].

Recognizing the importance of music education in children with disabilities for their development, authors increasingly began to pay attention to the need to use information and communication technologies. Although, according to Thompson, G. A., McFerran, K.S. [4] the possibilities of music therapy and the inclusion in its content of information and communication technologies in working with children who have certain developmental problems are still poorly understood. So, Thompson, G.A., McFerran, K.S. For children with profound intellectual disabilities, video recordings were used in music therapy, which led to a closer interaction between the children and the formation of their communication skills. Other authors, Maria-DoloresCano and RamonSanchez-Iborra, developed a special music course using multimedia (PLAIME) for adolescents and achieved the following goals when introducing this course: they formed musical knowledge in such children, taught them how to work with information technologies, significantly improved communication skills with peers [7]. A study by Hillier, A., Greher, G., Queenan, A., Marshall, S., Kopec, J. proved the effectiveness of adolescent music education using information technology, namely the touch screen [5]. In working with children with disabilities authors Anopkina E.N. and Sakharova E.K. use a computer to demonstrate mnemonic schemes when graphic or pictorial content of the verbal material of a song is shown on a smart board [10]. For a better perception and understanding of the meaning of life sounds and music sounds, the authors include color and light combinations [11–13], including when using the touch screen [5]. In some works, the authors of pay attention to the musical education of children with varying degrees of mental retardation, who are brought up in special boarding houses [1]. At the same time, the authors indicate not only the methodological directions of work, but also justify certain musical material for listening to it by mentally retarded children in order to manifest positive emotional states in them. Analysis and generalization of these works allowed us to develop a strategy for introducing information technology into the musical development process of children with mental retardation brought up in an orphanage.

3 An Experiment on the Introduction of Information Technology in the Musical Development of Mentally Retarded Children in an Orphanage

To conduct an experiment in which 7 children of primary school age (8–11 years old) with mild and moderate degrees of mental retardation were brought up at the Yekaterinburg orphanage for mentally retarded children, teachers of children's music school No. 8, children's art school No. 7 from city of Yekaterinburg, teachers and postgraduates of the Ural State Pedagogical University have developed the following strategy for the actions of a teacher in music education:

- identify the criteria by which the diagnosis was made as a musical, musical and rhythmic development, and the development of speech abilities;
- identify games and exercises that include information technology that contributed to the improvement of these types of development;

- determine the sequence of the introduction of games and exercises in music classes in the orphanage;
- to analyze the initial and final diagnosis.

The criteria by which the participants in the experiment were diagnosed included the following skills:

- correctly name the object whose sounds the child hears in the process of their demonstration presented by a computer;
- sing a fragment of a familiar children's song (note that the children participating in the experiment had music lessons from the age of seven, so they proposed the songs they performed in these classes);
- remember the words of the song, based on the presented mnemonic schemes, and, then, correctly pronounce them when singing;
- rhythmically accompany music (getting into a strong share of a piece of music).

Based on the results of the diagnosis in children according to all four criteria, as well as relying on the analysis of studies by a number of authors on working with children [2–4, 9, 14] from mild to moderate degree of mental retardation, games and exercises using information technology, as well as the sequence of introducing these games into music classes with pupils of the orphanage is determined.

Due to the fact that children who are brought up in an orphanage have never seen objects that can be used as "sounding" in the lesson, as well as animals that make certain sounds, the first step was to familiarize them with various smartboards such objects and animals. Images were produced on the screen, depicting a train, cars, bells, clocks, as well as animals - cows, cuckoos, frogs, roosters. Together with the demonstration of the picture, the children perceived the sounds that were characteristic of the object or animal displayed on the screen. The children not only tried to repeat these sounds with their voices, but after listening to the names of objects imprinted in the picture, they repeated them. This activated the speech capabilities of each child. At the same stage, empty squares were shown on the SmartBoard, below were pictures with various images. Each child, after listening to a sound, found the object to which this sound corresponded. To activate the sound perception, the LiteBim light and sound system was actively used, when at the intersection of the light beam an image of one of the animals is displayed on the screen and the sound that this animal makes is reproduced. Then the children themselves found the right pictures corresponding to this or that sound.

The next step in working with children was the use of voice games. On the SmartBoard screen, images of an animal or an object already known to the child were shown, and he reproduced in his voice those sounds that were characteristic of these animals or objects. In the case of a true imitation of the voice of the sound of an object, quiet music began to play, performed by a celesta or a bell. In the case of incorrect onomatopoeic sound was absent. The child, expecting the sound, listened to the possible sounds of music, which, undoubtedly, formed his ability to listen.

Another stage of working with children was the use of mnemonic schemes - drawings of song heroes, some items about which the song was composed, which were shown to the child, after which he performed the song. Before including children in singing, children were offered singing exercises, when certain carriages were shown on SmartBoard, a song sounded, and the child picked up this song. Before these exercises, children were offered mnemonic diagrams, on which were images of certain objects that the child called. In the case of an incorrect answer, the teacher helped recall the name of the subject and pronounce its name. Such exercises developed children's speech abilities. Mnemonic schemes were displayed on SmartBoard, in parallel with the sound of only the melody of the song. According to the mnemonic scheme and the sounding melody of a song without a vocabulary, it was necessary to guess the song, remember its words, and then sing it together with the teacher.

More difficult in content was an exercise-game for the rhythmic accompaniment of a child to a musical work. At this stage, the LiteBim light and sound system was used, various music was included in the arsenal of this program. In the initial classes, in order to eliminate the children's toys from the installation, only light spots designed from four of its lights were shown to children. The teacher demonstrated the capabilities of reflective sticks and rackets. The next stage was a game with sticks and rackets, which were given alternately to children. This play with light by children was accompanied by musical accompaniment, for which calm lyrical music was chosen. Finally, after the children got acquainted with the lighting fixtures, games were introduced in the classroom with a "wand to the beat", "play music." The game "stick to the beat" was carried out using the intersection of the rays, when the child first reproduced dimensional tapping with a soft reflective stick on the floor. At the beginning of the work, light rhythmic patterns were used, for example, measured tapping with a stick, which is a reflection of a strong share in the metro-rhythmic pattern of a particular music. At the same time, the teacher can do this together with the child. Then the child independently chose the specific sound of one or another percussion instrument to perform the easiest scheme. Such a scheme may initially be a reflection of the metro rhythm, when at a certain musical piece, the pace the child notes only a strong share. As he mastered this simple pattern, the child was offered another rhythmic combination, including a combination: a quarter to two-eighths, and then, having mastered this rhythmic pattern, the child proceeded to master a more complex pattern: two-eighths and a quarter. The latter combination is more difficult to reproduce the rhythm not only for children with mental retardation, but also for a normally developing child of preschool and primary school age. At the same time, the children, for playing various combinations, choose the rhythm of the percussion instrument they like most for rhythmic accompaniment. The LiteBim program presents various tones of musical instruments. The game "play music" was introduced when the children mastered the ways of rhythmic performance of a particular piece of music. For this game, both instrumental and vocal works-songs were used, which were sung by the teacher, while the child performed the rhythmic accompaniment with his chopsticks along with the music. The implementation of the designated games and exercises took place in two classes per week for four months.

4 Key Findings

The results of the initial and final diagnostics, which were carried out respectively in November and February 2020, are shown in Table 1.

Table 1. Comparative characteristics of performing tasks at the beginning and at the end of training after using information technologies in the musical and speech development of children.

Criteria	Initial stage		Final stage	
	Task completed	Task not completed	Task completed	Task not completed
Correctly name the object whose sounds the child hears	2	5	4	3
Sing a fragment of a familiar children's song	1	6	3	4
Remember the words of the song	0	7	2	5
Rhythmically accompany music	3	4	7	0

If at the first stage the object was correctly named only by two children, but at the last stage there were already 4 children. The most successfully completed task is the rhythmic accompaniment of music in a light rhythm. At the beginning of the training, only 3 children tried to do such an accompaniment, at the end of the training all the children did it. This task aroused the greatest interest among children. The dynamics of improving the accuracy of the task was also according to the second criterion - to sing a fragment of a song and according to the third task - to memorize the words of the song. Of course, the children did not pronounce all the words of the song absolutely correctly, but when they looked at the mnemonic diagram on a smart board, they correctly pronounced the main words of the song.

The results obtained during the work on the musical and speech development of children with mental retardation, brought up in an orphanage, allowed us to determine the prospects for further work on this problem, namely, to determine games and exercises for developing the ability to reflect more complex rhythmic complexes, on rhythmic accompaniment of only slow, but fast-paced musical material, the ability to read the words of a song first as a poem, and then to sing them, the ability to listen to small musical pieces eniya using visual range. At the same time, the development of the outlined prospects will undoubtedly be associated with the active use of information technology, namely, the inclusion of certain music programs.

Acknowledgments. The authors of the article are grateful to Tatiana Borisovna Strizhak, a music teacher at the Yekaterinburg orphanage for mentally retarded children, who introduced the participants to the experiment with the information technology capabilities available in this institution, as well as providing advice to the authors of the article on the psychological characteristics of children brought up in this boarding house. Our gratitude to the director of this boarding house - Natalya Gennadyevna Pechenek for understanding the importance of the implementation of the work described in the article.

References

1. Evtushenko, I.V.: The system of work on musical education in special (correctional) boarding schools of the VIII type. Bull. Univ. Russ. Acad. Educ. **3**(37), 58–60 (2007). (in Russian)
2. Evtushenko, I.V.: The use of regulatory music in raising children with mild mental retardation. Mod. Prob. Sci. Educ. **6**, 258–274 (2013). (in Russian)
3. Tagiltseva, N.G., Konovalova, S.A., Kashina, N.I., Matveeva, L.V., Suetina, A.I., Akhyamova, I.A.: Application of smart technologies in music education for children with disabilities. In: Miesenberger, K., Kouroupetroglou, G. (eds.) ICCHP 2018. LNCS, vol. 10896, pp. 353–356. Springer, Cham (2018). https://doi.org/10.1007/978-3-319-94277-3_55
4. Thompson, G.A., McFerran, K.S.: Music therapy with young people who have profound intellectual and developmental disability: four case studies exploring communication and engagement within musical interactions. J. Intellec. Dev. Disabil. **40**(1), 1–11 (2015)
5. Hillier, A., Greher, G., Queenan, A., Marshall, S., Kopec, J.: Music, technology and adolescents with autism spectrum disorders: the effectiveness of the touch screen interface. Music Educ. Res. **18**(3), 269–282 (2016). http://apps.webofknowledge.com/full_record.do?product=WOS&search_mode=GeneralSearch&qid=2&SID=D6BZCfuyBtRl6pMefFJ&page=1&doc=6&cacheurlFromRightClick=no
6. Korobeinikova, I.Y., Tarasenko, N.I.: Kinesiological and musical rhythmic exercises as a means of developing verbal sensorimotor children with disabilities. Innov. Sci. **2**(4), 90–93 (2017). (in Russian)
7. Cano, M.-D., Sanchez-Iborra, R.: On the use of a multimedia platform for music education with handicapped children: a case study. Comput. Educ. **87**, 254–276 (2015)
8. Ovchinnikova, T.S.: Musical education of preschool children with disabilities in an inclusive education. Bull. Leningrad State Univ. A.S. Pushkin. **3**(2), 96–104 (2015)
9. Bean, D., Woldfel, A.: The magic pipe: 78 educational music games. Terevinth, 114 (2015) https://www.books-up.ru/en/book/volshebnaya-dudochka-3756524/. (in Russian)
10. Anopkina, E.N., Sakharova, E.K.: The musical development of children with disabilities of senior preschool age through the use of interactive musical and didactic games and mnemoshems. Bull. Sci. Conf. **4–2**(32), 10–12 (2018). (in Russian)
11. Aires, E.J.: Child and sensory integration. Understanding the hidden development challenges. Terevinth, p. 272 (2009). (in Russian)
12. Kirsanenko, Y.N., Dolgova, A.A.: Correctional work with children with disabilities in secondary school. Sci. Almanac. **1**(12), 245–248 (2015). (in Russian)
13. Tolkova, N.M.: Art-therapeutic methods and techniques in working with young children with disabilities in a preschool organization. Prob. Mod. Pedagogical Educ. **62-2**, 233–235 (2019). (in Russian)
14. Buzmakova, A.F.: The use of copyright and authorized presentations in the work of a speech therapist teacher with children with disabilities. Dev. Mod. Educ.: Theor. Methodol. Pract. **3** (1), 129–131 (2015). (in Russian)

Promoting Creative Computer-Based Music Education and Composition for Individuals with Autism Spectrum Disorders: The Terpsichore Software Music Interface

Georgios Kyriakakis[✉]

Center for Music and Audio Technology, University of Kent, Chatham, UK
gk232@kent.ac.uk

Abstract. In an effort to improve the quality of life for individuals with Autism Spectrum Disorders (ASD) by harnessing the therapeutic power of music, the *Terpsichore* software interface constitutes a proposal to center music-oriented activities around the development of compositional skills instead of the passive appreciation of music through the reproduction of existing content. This interface aims to assist learners with ASD in composing original tonal music and soundscapes, with a view of additionally contributing to the accomplishment of non-musical goals. To assess the software's effectiveness, a pilot study was conducted in which twenty-eight adolescents and adults diagnosed with ASD, participated in a series of software instruction sessions administered at four institutions in the Attica region of Greece. The study attested that participants generally responded to *Terpsichore* in a positive manner, with regards to their comfort in completing required tasks and their shifts in behavior, communication and emotional state.

Keywords: Autism Spectrum Disorders (ASD) · Information and Communications Technology (ICT) · Computer-aided learning · Music therapy · Music education for special needs · Creative composition · Interactive education · Computer-based accessible music applications

1 Introduction

Autism Spectrum Disorders (ASD) are developmental disabilities of a pervasive nature, encountered in a number of sub-conditions and variations [1, 2] and affecting diverse aspects of cognitive, social and emotional integrity [3]. Notable symptoms include, but are not limited to, communication skill deficiency [3], irregular behaviors or interaction patterns [4] and adherence to stereotypical activities [3]. The origin of ASD incidence in humans cannot be precisely determined, and may be attributed to hereditary factors coexisting with environmental ones [5].

Over the last few years, the familiarization of individuals with ASD with music education and performance practices, has acquired particular interest. Music has been identified as a helpful medium in stimulating emotions and nurturing imaginative behaviors for people with ASD [6]. The active engagement of ASD learners with music

© Springer Nature Switzerland AG 2020
K. Miesenberger et al. (Eds.): ICCHP 2020, LNCS 12377, pp. 136–148, 2020.
https://doi.org/10.1007/978-3-030-58805-2_17

may assist in highlighting their personality qualities and confronting unfavorable patterns induced by the disability [7]. In addition, music therapy, as a strategy for ASD treatment, possesses the potential to enhance awareness of musical concepts and regulate everyday behaviors [8], foster interpersonal communication [9] and stimulate eagerness to perform activities, especially in the cases of impromptu music performance and composition [10]. Moreover, the increasing dependence of music therapy interventions on Information and Communications Technology (ICT) [11, 12] constitutes an important impetus for debate and practical experimentation regarding the use of computer software to instruct creative concepts of music. Specifically, the hypothesis behind imagining an ideally practical approach to computer-based musical activities derives from the inherent appreciation of music as a factor positively affecting the learner's capacity to engage in creative music composition, for purposes of wellbeing improvement and rehabilitation [13], rather than resort to the reproduction of existing musical content.

Considering the above, the current paper is devoted to how the *Terpsichore* software music interface, named after the Muse for dance and musical theater in Ancient Greek mythology, attempts to serve the above objectives, while operating as a tool potentially helping learners compose original tonal music and soundscapes. This procedure ideally aims to nurture the development of various non-musical skills associated with behavior, communication, concentration and emotional state, while preserving an educational character and satisfying a reciprocal relationship between music education and therapy.

2   Related Work

In the last two decades, a number of research projects have attempted to incorporate aspects of music education in digital technology, to provide comprehensive assistance to individuals with ASD. To begin with, the SoundBeam [14] simulates the execution of orchestral instruments by utilizing the auditory effect caused by body gestures on an electrically conductive surface. It provides a series of tools enabling users to engage in entry-level composition tasks [15], and was most recently employed in a 'holistic' educational practice for preschool children with special needs [16]. Benemin [17] and Octonic [18] were designed to offer advanced reproduction and composition capabilities based on interpretative music phraseology, in the attempt to stimulate emotional consciousness and promote carefree music education. In addition, Google's Chrome Music Lab online platform [19] concentrates on the instruction of fundamental music notions including rhythm, basic composition and spectral analysis of instruments, while it encourages users to combine and manipulate different types of audio signals.

Research endeavors in the 2010s attempted to employ forward-thinking technological means related to interactive music performance and composition. One of these is the Skoog [20], a cubic tactile and pliable interface that allows the composition of phrases in the form of free improvisation, exploiting the translation of hand-based interactions into MIDI messages as means of sound emission from the computer. This interface has provided structural inspiration for the VESBALL [21], which emphasizes on simplicity in operation for the average instructor and learner and expressivity through piezoelectric sensor interaction, although its didactic features are not extensive. The Music Spectrum software [22] allows users to interact with various musical instruments on a fundamental level, and is particularly tailored to individuals with ASD with a view of alleviating their disability-specific symptoms and fostering their social inclusion. PLAIME [12] is designed to acquaint disabled learners with music theory principles, while placing increased emphasis on action monitoring and feedback. The SoundScape project [23] concentrates on the familiarization of adolescents and adults with various concepts of music and composition in a collaborative environment, and utilizes the iPad as means for mediation amongst users with ASD to enhance social integration through music. Meanwhile, the requirement of inserting explicitly didactic elements in the music cognition and composition processes has led to such endeavors as ImmertableApp [24] and Suoniamo [25]. In the former, participants familiarize themselves with sound synthesis in a simplified but immersive manner, whereas the latter exploits the power of online interaction to facilitate music note recognition and execution processes.

3   Rationale

The projects presented above exemplify the persistent evolution of research in the popularization of creative music practices or associated theoretical elements for mentally disabled people. However, they do not address the simulation of a detailed music curriculum, designed to implement a stepwise and targeted approach towards the composition of original tonal melodies and environmental soundscapes. The proposed curriculum-based approach should ideally encourage learners with ASD to occupy themselves regularly with music in their quotidian life, with an eventual purpose of externalizing their emotions, regulating their behaviors, and improving their quality of life. This statement is justified by the role of music education in empowering the learner's motivation to perform diverse activities through 'sensory stimulation' [26].

The rationale behind the construction of *Terpsichore* is based on two arguments. Firstly, an ASD diagnosis should by no means inhibit the acquaintance with knowledge fields and techniques that a musically literate neurotypical person normally takes for granted. To render musical notions understandable for learners with ASD, emphasis should be placed on images, contrasting colors and symbols associated with such concepts as notation. This proposal is intended to mitigate possible emotional and cognitive challenges that impact learning potential and cause unnecessary distractions or confusion. Secondly, it is necessary to provide participants with an environment characterized by versatility in activities offered, while still possessing a coherent structure with a focus on user-friendliness and creativity. This includes the interpretation of music as either a succession of notes and consonances, adhering to Western or other tonal conventions, or as any form of sound combination, irrespective of whether its pitch content is clearly defined, similar to the principle of 'organized sound' [27].

In general terms, the following three factors were taken into consideration so that *Terpsichore* possesses an acceptable format worthy of preliminary use and testing:

- Inclusion of two distinct working modes, labeled as *Tonal* or *Definite Pitch*, and *Soundscape and Indefinite Pitch (SIP)*, in order to adapt learning methods as desired, without exclusively resorting to pitch-defined auditory sequences.
- Ability to automatically provide on-screen feedback to learners, on various actions performed within the interface.
- Emphasis on practical areas related to the learner's mental condition and sensitivity, such as frequency filtering and time limitation in interface use, to prevent computer addiction and other adverse consequences in wellbeing.

4 The Terpsichore Software

The version of *Terpsichore* employed for testing in actual participants with ASD was constructed in 2018, using SuperCollider (version 3.9.3), a choice justified by the ability of the language to convert appropriate code to sound clips, sequences, visual structures and button arrangements, all designed to perform various actions [28]. The interface was transformed, using Platypus [29], into a standalone application for computers running on Mac OS X Snow Leopard (10.6) and above. Figure 1 displays the main menu of the software, from which four different environments can be accessed, starting from the top right and moving clockwise: Tonal Mode, SIP Mode, Software Termination and Options. It is worth mentioning that the Options window allows practitioners to modify time- and frequency-dependent parameters in the software levels prior to making them available to learners, as also shown in Fig. 1.

Fig. 1. Left: Main menu of *Terpsichore*. Right: 'Options' window

The objective of the Tonal Mode is to progressively instruct compositional tasks compliant with Western music conventions, such as representation of notes as symbols and letters from A to G. Included activities allow creative freedom to a significant extent, due to some learners with ASD possessing an unconventional perception of musical structure and tonal relationships [30]. However, the potential of tonal music to enhance analytical skills, concentration and overall brain functionality [31] was taken into close account while designing levels. Participants are familiarized with the necessary procedures that allow them to create their own music, and exploit this activity for purposes that extend beyond strict compositional frameworks, such as the understanding of various social situations and prompts given by peers to encourage activity completion [32].

The structure of the Tonal mode follows a distinct direction from fundamental music knowledge towards the modification of existing patterns and the composition of original melodies without a reference song being required. Specifically, Levels 1 through 5 refer to the instruction of notes and durations in music, Levels 6 to 10 concentrate on the modification of existing melodies, and Levels 11 to 14 prepare the ground for unconstrained music composition, which is the clear objective of Levels 15 to 18. Figure 2 presents screenshots of four levels, one for each goal mentioned above. It should be noted that instructors may activate, in most levels, an embedded User Manual, which provides them with on-screen guidelines on how to operate each level; these can be disabled to prevent unnecessary distractions on the learner's part. The same applies to the Reward Mode, which assigns tasks that learners need to complete successfully to prevent the software from ceasing operation altogether.[1]

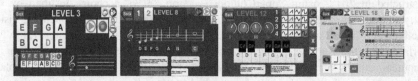

Fig. 2. Screenshots of four representative levels in the Tonal Mode. In the Level 8 screenshots, observe that the User Manual (person with book) and Reward Mode (cup) have been activated.

The functionality of the SIP mode is principally centered around audio stimuli that comply with soundscapes lacking a definitive temporal and frequency content, including sea waves, moving tree leaves and urban environment sounds. Its objective is to shift the concentration of learners to the overall sound rather than its tonal constituents, especially when lexical cue overload or the process of learning notation induces cognitive challenges. In the mode's fifteen levels, the areas predominantly addressed are the combination of environmental stimuli encountered in everyday life, the arrangement of sounds on a timeline, the real-time composition of audio through granular synthesis, and the manipulation of externally recorded sounds. This mode adopts previous therapeutic practices used to complement the familiarization of learners with sound. One such example is Level 3, whose reliance on the auditory representation of various emotions assists learners in identifying them through the facial expressions and actions of peers [33]. Likewise, Level 9 pertains to the ability to change the position of sounds in the stereo field, in an effort to assist learners in approximating the origin of sounds and mitigating auditory localization issues [34]. Screenshots of the above levels, alongside Level 7 (percussive phrase composition) and 11 (granular synthesis) are shown in Fig. 3.

---

[1] A number of screenshots for both *Terpsichore* modes is available via this link: t.ly/9SJm.

Fig. 3. Screenshots of four representative levels in the SIP Mode. Exactly as in the Tonal Mode, all text can be disabled to accommodate the needs of learners with ASD.

5 Methodology

During the *Terpsichore* research, key emphasis was given to the assessment of software efficiency in the creativity development and mental health treatment domains. To achieve this, a four-month pilot study was conducted, which involved a sample of N = 28 adolescent and adult participants (16 males and 12 females) from four different institutions in the Attica region of Greece, aged between 12 and 29. The severity of their ASD condition was specified, by each of the three tutors, 2 as 'mild' for 13 learners, 'moderate' for 12 and 'severe' for the remaining three. Moreover, the vast majority of HP have not been professionally occupied with music, although none has reported aversion to or irritation by music. Prior to the study's onset, a number of sessions were dedicated to the familiarization of tutors with the software, who were assisted by a detailed walkthrough video.

Throughout the study, instructors were mainly responsible for incorporating the software in conventional music and general education curricula, and identifying the responsiveness of learners to various aspects of the Tonal and SIP Modes, their ability to compose music and soundscapes, and the evolution of their behavior, communication and emotional state. Tutors 1 and 3 devoted eighteen sessions of roughly 45 min each to the software, while Tutor 2 employed *Terpsichore* in six hourly sessions administered for her four assigned participants. Assessment was completed thanks to a comprehensive semi-structured questionnaire, which includes multiple-choice questions in numerical (0 to 10) and Likert ('fully negative' to 'fully positive') scales, and optional open-ended questions where tutors provided extensive input and explanation to standardized responses. Sections in the questionnaire involve pre-*Terpsichore* evaluations of behavior, mental health attributes and relationship with music, performance and operation comfort in the Tonal and SIP Modes, and post-*Terpsichore* assessment of areas previously addressed.

6 Results

The majority of participants were impressed by the graphical layout of *Terpsichore*, including colors and shapes, and seemed enthusiastic about engaging in a novel creative activity, after tutors informed them of their prospective occupation with the software. The lexical content was generally more comprehensible for participants with milder ASD symptoms; for this reason, tutors occasionally disabled the on-screen User Manual and Reward Modes to prevent potential distractions. Moreover, through the respective open-ended responses recorded by tutors, it was determined that they intended to employ *Terpsichore* mainly in the treatment of emotional state, task concentration and music improvisation or composition.

The responsiveness of participants to the Tonal Mode's demands may be evaluated as generally favorable (M = 6.96, SD = 1.74), while ratings of 7 or above in this area account for three-quarters of the sample. According to questionnaire scores, provided by tutors and based on the quality of produced melodies, participants tended to display more efficient performances in levels where the modification of default phrases is possible (M = 7.68, SD = 2.04) than in levels associated with unconstrained composition from point zero (M = 7.00, SD = 2.05). In other words, learners performed better whenever required objectives were paired with compositional guidelines, rather than requiring full independence in formulating musical phrases. Half of the study's participants managed to complete all Tonal Mode tasks without particular difficulties or distractions. Main issues reported with regards to the remaining learners include complexity of certain levels towards the end of the mode. More precise estimates for learner performance in the Tonal Mode may be provided through the magnitude of Average Performance per Human Participant (APHP) across all levels, indicating overall good ratings (M = 7.43, SD = 2.02). Participants recorded values as high as 9.32 out of 10, while an APHP of 7 and 8 is respectively consistent with the sample's 21st and 45th percentile, demonstrating that the resourceful operation of the Tonal Mode is a manageable task for learners. Furthermore, in groups of levels and tasks associated with a specific knowledge area, performances generally increased when activities involved less initiative-taking and greater feedback or guidance from the software environment.

As far as the SIP Mode is concerned, responsiveness of learners to demands was rated, on average, slightly higher than in the Tonal Mode (M = 7.57, SD = 2.08), while an 82% of participants scored 7 or above across the board. The most preferred levels pertained to the organization of environmental stimuli into a moving timeline, and the alteration of amplitudes and panning positions of audio sources rotated around a virtual sound map. The only areas in which participants were particularly susceptible, were levels associated with granular synthesis as a means of constructing an electroacoustic soundscape. The assessment of SIP Mode performance via APHP scores yielded almost identical results to the Tonal Mode (M = 7.45, SD = 1.78). This denotes that the existence of symbols and letters to represent notes, does not negatively affect understanding and performance. In the SIP Mode, average ratings per participant are as high as 9.31 out of 10, while overall scores of 7 and 8 refer to the sample's 20th and 52nd percentile respectively. The above arguments designate that, although Tonal Mode levels tended to exhibit higher complexity than the ones of the SIP Mode, efficiency was almost equal amongst participants. In fact, no significant differences in learner performance were detected for detected for the two constituent modes of *Terpsichore*, as the associated non-parametric Friedman test yields $\chi^2(28) = .143, p = .705$.

Responses of tutors to questions pertinent to post-*Terpsichore* evaluation, indicate that emotional state, behavior towards peers, elementary communication and concentration on basic everyday tasks, have improved in twenty-four participants focused on the software. No noticeable positive changes have occurred for the four learners

Table 1. Influence of *Terpsichore* sessions on notable aspects of mental condition.

Post-*Terpsichore* aspect	Average	Median	St. deviation
Externalization of emotions	8.36	9	1.82
Interpretation of others' feelings	7.82	8	1.89
Overall emotional state	8.26	9	1.97
Behavior towards peers	8.25	9	1.94
Communication with peers	8.25	9	2.01
Perception of others in space	8.21	9	1.80
Overall response to *Terpsichore*	8.43	9	1.95

supervised by Tutor 2, mainly due to the serious nature of their ASD condition and the reduced time devoted to *Terpsichore*. Table 1 presents the overall influence of software-based sessions on key aspects related to the development of their mental state, while Table 2 refers to changes in musical literacy and compositional potential as a result of this four-month occupation.

Table 2. Influence of *Terpsichore* sessions on music cognition and composition skills.

Post-*Terpsichore* aspect	Average	Median	St. deviation
Acquisition of theoretical knowledge	7.52	8	2.35
Independent composition	7.18	8	2.54
Interest in composing tonal music	7.93	9	2.91
Interest in composing soundscapes	7.86	9	2.73

Changes in emotional state, behavior, communication and concentration are all strongly correlated with APHP in both working modes, as linear correlation analysis yields $[r(28) \geq .824, p < .001]$ for the Tonal Mode and $[r(28) \geq .85, p < .001]$ for the SIP Mode. This denotes that participants tended to translate more efficient performances into a more comprehensive short-term satisfaction of diverse non-musical goals, suggesting a discrete relationship between music education and therapy, even though larger sample sizes are needed to further verify this statement. Tutor reports on the performance of learners establish that the software contributed to the acquisition of entry-level music theory knowledge, while it considerably sparked the participants' eagerness to engage in the composition of tonal music and soundscapes more regularly.

Responses of learners to *Terpsichore*, as displayed in Tables 1 and 2 above, were regarded as highly promising, while instructors approve of the software's potential to nurture creativity and support mental state treatment in a constructive manner. Indicatively, Tutors 1 and 3 reported, following the study, that her learners were eager and impatient to use the software in class, thanks to the multiple interesting activities included, while Tutor 2 highlighted the breadth of capabilities offered in diverse disciplines of music, despite the limited time she had to instruct the interface. Overall, tutors strongly recommend *Terpsichore* to practitioners and music therapists, and concur that further development may lead to the software possessing a pronounced social impact.

7 Discussion

In this paper, we examined the principal characteristics of the *Terpsichore* software and the effect it had on various adolescents and adults with varying intensities of ASD and relevant symptoms. The results from the study demonstrate, in principle, that the interface is capable of fulfilling the desired education and therapy objectives, while maintaining a manageable level of complexity for the majority of participants. *Terpsichore* exhibits a compact nature, determined by its operation directly through a personal computer, without the requirement of adding and calibrating external objects. Thanks to the use of different colors and clearly defined learning components, learners are motivated to perform various compositional tasks without pre-existent knowledge of music being necessary, and are empowered to achieve pleasantly sounding musical results.

Following the instruction procedure on learners, the emotional state of most participants has improved noticeably, as has their behavior, interpreted as reduction of tantrums and impulsive actions, motivation to compose music, and excitement to use the software again. A prominent factor for these outcomes may be the classification of diverse knowledge fields into levels, in similarity to sequences of music therapy 'events' [35] designed to address principal areas of wellbeing. In the *Terpsichore* case, the gradual familiarization with core composition-oriented disciplines ensured that learners were continuously encouraged to control the musical content they produced, instead of perceiving music therapy as a commonplace extracurricular process. Moreover, occupation with the software increased the comfort of learners in communicating, at least to a fundamental extent, with individuals they encounter in everyday surroundings. The Tonal Mode was also deemed convenient in the instruction of music theory, as most participants exhibited reasonably good performances in this field, translating into an eagerness to compose melodies either independently or with occasional support from the peer tutor. In addition, the absence of a definite musical language framework in the SIP Mode, certainly affected the slightly increased ability of learners, on average, to independently operate environments associated with soundscapes and environmental audio, without actively seeking guidance from their instructors.

Although the occupation of most learners with *Terpsichore* can be positively evaluated, the four participants under the supervision of Tutor 2 exhibited less promising performances throughout both modes, while three of these discontinued use with the software at approximately the 70% mark, principally due to tiredness. This finding is responsible for statistical significances in various ratings, for the three distinct conditions of mild, moderate and severe ASD, even if the sample size is relatively small. Performances across both modes were significantly higher when the software was instructed for at least fourteen hours in total, in contrast to the six hours dedicated by Tutor 2 (one-way ANOVA yielded $p < .001$ in both cases). Obviously, less serious manifestations of ASD are congruent with an increased ability in meeting the software's demands. However, it is interesting to investigate, in future endeavors, whether general difficulties in maintaining attention can be alleviated through extensive training or are consistent with aversion to the software altogether.

8 Contributions to the Field

Terpsichore attempts to further the development of sound and music composition interventions in such a manner that didactic and therapeutic elements coexist, so that the above occupation is ideally complemented with the achievement of alternative goals depending on the learner's personality. The software intends to foster the establishment of an education-therapy loop, where development of compositional principles and techniques elicits appreciation and enthusiasm, inciting the user to employ *Terpsichore* on a more sustained basis. This can be confirmed by the reactions of most participants, whose positive attitude was coupled with remarks of impatience expressed towards tutors, on when the software would be employed in prospective classes. Most importantly, software sessions and associated performance ratings attest that a standard computer-based structure is sufficient and practical for the purposes served, especially considering that modes and levels are arranged according to discrete knowledge fields and entail task requirements capable of being completed without external connectivity options. Given that the software's operational principles are not constrained to music education reinforcement, but are also consistent with the alleviation of disadvantageous conditions caused by ASD, *Terpsichore* opens up new possibilities for caregivers and practitioners who do not have music as their primary area of specialization. In short, the interface advances such special education environments as [19–21] by increasing functional convenience for both users with ASD and supervising individuals with varying musical competence levels, while simultaneously placing multiple forms of regulated and freeform composition at the forefront of mental health treatment endeavors.

9 Conclusion and Future Development

Terpsichore constitutes a sustained effort in constructing a software interface that would not exclusively serve as a supplementary classroom or extracurricular aid for ASD special education routines, but would rather favor the composition of original musical phrases and soundscapes, with an eventual objective of rendering the music instruction process engaging and beneficial for the learner's quality of life. A subsequent step towards software optimization is the extension of research to broader and more sizeable target groups of participants, whose disability is not necessarily congruent with ASD. Moreover, calibration of remote interaction with MIDI, TouchOSC and touchless gestural mechanisms, is another initiative intended to increase the software's versatility, as is the translation of *Terpsichore*'s Graphical User Interface (GUI) to various spoken languages and such coding systems as Braille for learners with impaired sighting. Finally, it is important to establish prospective research on prolonged occupation with the software, in order to assess sustainability in music education development and mental health treatment, something that would represent a crucial stepping stone en route to distributing *Terpsichore* for commercial use.

Acknowledgments. Special thanks to the three tutors based in Attica, Greece (Ms. Persefoni-Alexia Sergi, Mrs. Panagiota Kyriakidou, Mrs. Chrysoula Papakirykou) who assisted with the pilot study and contributed to its successful completion. This work was partially funded through a bursary by the A.G. Leventis Foundation (Zurich), as part of the associated doctorate degree undertaken by the author at the University of Kent; the author would like to acknowledge the Foundation's invaluable support.

References

1. Trevarthen, C., Aitken, K., Papoudi, D., Robarts, J.: Children with Autism: Diagnosis and Interventions to Meet Their Needs, 2nd edn. Jessica Kingsley Publishers, London (1998)
2. Allen, R., Heaton, P.: Autism, music, and the therapeutic potential of music in alexithymia. Music Percept. **27**(4), 251–261 (2010). https://doi.org/10.1525/mp.2010.27.4.251
3. DSM-V: Diagnostic and Statistical Manual of Mental Disorders, 5th edn. American Psychiatric Publishing, Washington, DC (2013)
4. Marom, K.M., Gilboa, A., Bodner, E.: Musical features and interactional functions of echolalia in children with autism within the music therapy dyad. Nord. J. Music Ther. **27**(3), 175–196 (2018). https://doi.org/10.1080/08098131.2017.1403948
5. Hoekstra, R.A., Bartels, M., Verweij, C.J.H., Boomsma, D.I.: Heritability of autistic traits in the general population. Arch. Pediatr. Adolesc. Med. **161**(4), 372–377 (2007). https://doi.org/10.1001/archpedi.161.4.372
6. Sloboda, J.A., O'Neill, S.A.: Emotions in everyday listening to music. In: Juslin, P.N., Sloboda, J.A. (eds.) Series in Affective Science, Music and Emotion: Theory and Research, pp. 415–429. Oxford University Press, Oxford (2001)
7. Gold, C., Wigram, T., Mössler, K., Elefant, C.: Music therapy for people with Autism spectrum disorder (review). Cochrane Database Syst. Rev. **3**, 1–54 (2014). https://doi.org/10.1002/14651858.CD004381.pub3
8. Boso, M., Emanuele, E., Minazzi, V., Abbamonte, M., Politi, P.: Effect of long-term interactive music therapy on behavior profile and musical skills in young adults with severe Autism. J. Altern. Complement. Med. **13**(7), 709–712 (2007). https://doi.org/10.1089/acm.2006.6334
9. LaGasse, A.B.: Effects of a music therapy group intervention on enhancing social skills in children with Autism. J. Music Ther. **51**(3), 250–275 (2014). https://doi.org/10.1093/jmt/thu012
10. Kim, J., Wigram, T., Gold, C.: Emotional, motivational and interpersonal responsiveness of children with Autism in improvisational music therapy. Autism **13**(4), 389–409 (2009). https://doi.org/10.1177/1362361309105660
11. Drigas, A., Theodorou, P.: ICTs and music in special learning disabilities. Int. J. Rec. Contr. Eng. Sci. IT **4**(3), 12–16 (2016). https://doi.org/10.3991/ijes.v4i3.6066
12. Cano, M.D., Sanchez-Iborra, R.: On the use of a multimedia platform for music education with handicapped children: a case study. Comput. Educ. **87**, 254–276 (2015). https://doi.org/10.1016/j.compedu.2015.07.010

13. McDermott, J., Hauser, M.: The origins of music: innateness, uniqueness, and evolution. Music Percept. **23**(1), 29–59 (2005). https://doi.org/10.1525/mp.2005.23.1.29
14. Ellis, P., Van Leeuwen, L.: Living sound: human interaction and children with Autism. In: ISME Commission on Music in Special Education, Music Therapy and Music Medicine, Regina, Canada, July 2000
15. The Soundbeam Project (2003). http://www.soundbeam.co.uk. Accessed 15 Mar 2020
16. Lee, L., Ho, H.J.: Exploring young children's communication development through the Soundbeam trigger modes in the 'Holistic music educational approach for young children' programme. Malays. J. Music **7**, 1–19 (2018)
17. Challis, B.P., Challis, K.: Applications for proximity sensors in music and sound performance. In: Miesenberger, K., Klaus, J., Zagler, W., Karshmer, A. (eds.) ICCHP 2008. LNCS, vol. 5105, pp. 1220–1227. Springer, Heidelberg (2008). https://doi.org/10. 1007/978-3-540-70540-6_184
18. Challis, B.: Octonic: an accessible electronic musical instrument. Digit. Creat. **22**(1), 1–12 (2011). https://doi.org/10.1080/14626268.2011.538703
19. Google: Chrome Music Lab (2017). http://musiclab.chromeexperiments.com Accessed 15 Mar 2020
20. Skoogmusic Website (2020).. http://skoogmusic.com. Accessed 15 Mar 2020
21. Nath, A., Young, S.: VESBALL: a ball-shaped instrument for music therapy. In: Proceedings of the International Conference on New Interfaces for Musical Expression, Baton Rouge, 31 May–3 June 2015
22. Lima, D., Castro, T.: Music spectrum: a music immersion virtual environment for children with Autism. Procedia Comput. Sci. **11**(5), 1021–1031 (2011). https://doi.org/10.1016/j. procs.2012.10.013
23. Hillier, A., Greher, G., Queenan, A., Marshall, S., Kopec, J.: Music, technology and adolescents with Autism spectrum disorders: the effectiveness of the touch screen interface. Music Educ. Res. **18**(3), 269–282 (2016). https://doi.org/10.1080/14613808.2015.1077802
24. Baldassarri, S., Marco, J., Bonillo, C., Cerezo, E., Beltrán, J.R.: ImmertableApp: interactive and tangible learning music environment. In: Kurosu, M. (ed.) HCI 2016. LNCS, vol. 9733, pp. 365–376. Springer, Cham (2016). https://doi.org/10.1007/978-3-319-39513-5_34
25. Buzzi, M.C., et al.: Which virtual Piano keyboard for children with Autism? A pilot study. In: Stephanidis, C. (ed.) HCII 2019. LNCS, vol. 11786, pp. 280–291. Springer, Cham (2019). https://doi.org/10.1007/978-3-030-30033-3_22
26. Hoemberg, V.: A neurologist's view on neurologic music therapy. In: Thaut, M., Hoemberg, V. (eds.) Handbook of Neurologic Music Therapy, pp. 7–12. Oxford University Press, Oxford (2014)
27. Paynter, J.: The school council secondary music project (1973–82). In: Mills, J., Paynter, J. (eds.) Thinking and Making: Selections from the Writings of John Paynter on Music in Education, pp. 51–82. Oxford University Press, Oxford (2008)
28. Koutsomichalis, M.: Mapping and Visualization with SuperCollider. Packt Publishing, Birmingham (2013)
29. Thordarson, S.: Platypus Website (2018). http://sveinbjorn.org/platypus Accessed 25 Mar 2020
30. Matasaka, N.: Neurodiversity, giftedness, and aesthetic perceptual judgment of music in children with Autism. Front. Psychol. **8**, 1595 (2017). https://doi.org/10.3389/fpsyg.2017. 01595
31. Schlaug, G., Norton, A., Overy, K., Winner, E: Effects of music training on the child's brain and cognitive development. Ann. N.Y. Acad. Sci. **1060**, 219–230 (2005). https://doi.org/10. 1196/annals.1360.015

32. Pasiali, V.: The use of prescriptive therapeutic songs in a home-based environment to promote social skills acquisition by children with Autism. Music Ther. Perspect. **22**, 11–20. https://doi.org/10.1093/mtp/22.1.11

33. Tanaka, J.W., et al.: Using computerized games to teach face recognition skills to children with Autism spectrum disorder: the 'Let's Face It!' program. J. Child Psychol. Psychiatry **51** (8), 944–952 (2010). https://doi.org/10.1111/j.1469-7610.2010.02258.x

34. Skewes, J.C., Gebauer, L.: Brief report: suboptimal auditory localization in Autism spectrum disorder: support for the Bayesian account of sensory symptoms. J. Autism Dev. Disorders **46**, 2539–2547 (2016). https://doi.org/10.1007/s10803-016-2774-9

35. Møller, A.S., Odell-Miller, H., Wigram, T.: Indications in music therapy: evidence from assessment that can identify the expectations of music therapy as a treatment for autistic spectrum disorder (ASD): meeting the challenge of evidence based practice. Br. J. Music Ther. **16**(1), 11–28 (2002). https://doi.org/10.1177/135945750201600104

WebMoti

F. S. Asmy[1], A. Roberge-Milanese[2], M. C. Rombaut[2], G. Smith[2],
and D. I. Fels[2(✉)]

[1] Ontario Tech University, 2000 Simcoe St. N., Oshawa, Canada
[2] Ryerson University, 350 Victoria St., Toronto, Canada
dfels@ryerson.ca

Abstract. People with Autism Spectrum Disorder (ASD), particular young people often can be overwhelmed by too much environmental stimulation such as sound and complicated visuals. WebMoti, a hardware/software robot presence system, links students in real-time with their regular classes when they are unable to attend. Students with ASD have control over how much sensory stimuli is delivered to them by controlling the pan of the robot head, and the tilt and zoom of the robot's camera as well as on/off of the audio, video and vibrotactile stimuli from their remote location using an XBox game controller. Three students used WebMoti once per week for about five weeks each. Data were collected through pre and post study questionnaires as well as audio/video recordings during randomly selected classroom sessions to determine participant's experiences with and preferences of the various WebMoti functions. Results from the qualitative analysis of the video data indicate that students can follow the lesson plans along with their classmates without being overwhelmed by the audio/visual/tactile stimuli. They were also able to gain their teachers' and classmate's attention independently. Through WebMoti, participants could adjust and control the amount of sensory stimulation that they receive.

Keywords: Video conferencing · Robotics · Autism spectrum disorder · Inclusive design

1 Introduction

Individuals with Autism Spectrum Disorder (ASD) experience a vast array of characteristics that can vary widely. For example, some students can be hypersensitive and may display reactions into sensory stimuli, while other ASD students may not react at all, and/or have difficulty reading situations and understanding social cues or express unusual responses with social situations [1]. As a result of these behaviours, ASD students may have difficulties in school when interacting with their peers or adults. This can be due to their environment being loud during group work, breaks, or even when classmates are taking notes, the classroom lighting, and scents or movements of others [1]. These factors can reduce their attention span and make it difficult for them to cope with their environment resulting in disruptive behaviours.

Through the use of technology and various interventions, ASD students can receive support while attending school in order to mitigate some of the issues. Some involve peer-mediated interventions, which has shown to improve social skills in children [2].

K. Miesenberger et al. (Eds.): ICCHP 2020, LNCS 12377, pp. 149–156, 2020.
https://doi.org/10.1007/978-3-030-58805-2_18

Various software applications available to support different needs of students with ASD; there are at least 20 apps supporting children with ASD on the App store. One example, apps such as iCommunicate allow for ASD students to create picture schedules, flashboards and speech cards [3]. My Video Schedule or First Then Visual Schedule allows students to take their own pictures and organize them into a picture schedule of the day, showing routine. The apps also allow for voice recordings, messages as well as a checklist option for when the student completes a task [3]. The applications offered on the App store allow for a collaboration between the ASD students and another individual like a teacher, parent/guardian or speech pathologists. These applications are catered for a specific purpose and can be utilized whenever the student wants [3]. However, WebMoti challenges these aspects, this device is specifically designed for ASD students to use by themselves when attending class from a remote location. The device is synchronized with the activities that are going on in the classroom, which enables them to follow along in real time. The purpose of WebMoti is to provide ASD students with the option of learning remotely without losing their sense of presence within the classroom.

Remote education may have technical issues that may occur, but it can also provide many benefits such as reducing time and cost spent on travel, or social distancing that maybe required by students with ASD. It can create ongoing, flexible and regular support, and enhance the connection between the remote student and others [4]. Shafer et al. [5] showed that using a remote microphone setup with students with ASD improved listening ability as well as tolerance for noisier environments from the classroom. However, due to technical difficulties that may arise, such as intermittent audio or video connections, it tends to be used as an augmentation rather than a replacement for the classroom form of education for students [4].

The objective of the research reported in this paper is to study the interactions, activities, participation of participants and the usability of the system to support these activities. The WebMoti system description and the analysis of the video data captured during three user studies are reported in this paper.

2   System Description

WebMoti is a hardware/software system that links students with ASD to their regular classroom when they are unable to attend. The student controls a small robot (see Fig. 1) from a remote setting such as from home. Controllable functionality includes starting and ending the live video conference functions, controlling a motor so the "head" of the system pans left and right, a digital zoom, animated hand to indicate that student would like to take a turn, and a motorised tilt. In addition, the student can start/stop audio, video and vibrotactile elements of the system. The vibrotactile stimuli is provided through two pillows that can be placed around the student (e.g., on a chair seat and back).

The software portion of the WebMoti project is a browser-based, platform-independent cloud application written in Javascript. It leverages WebRTC for high fidelity, peer-to-peer audio and video. The backend of the application runs on Cloud Firestore, a real-time database. Authentication is federated using the student's Google account.

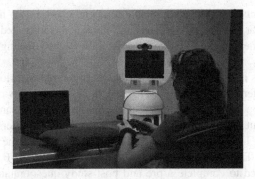

Fig. 1. Complete WebMoti system. The robot portion of the system would be placed in the classroom. The laptop, game controller and pillows would be used by a student located outside of the classroom. Student controlled functions include panning the robot head, camera tilt and digital zoom, off/on of audio, video and tactile stimuli, and activating animated hand for turn-taking.

The visual interface follows Google's Material Design guidelines [6] while attempting to reduce the cognitive load placed on the student. WebMoti maintains customisable interface elements, but also provides defaults in the absence of user preferences. For instance, the student is able to modify the frequency of notifications, presence of sound, video, and duration of the animated hand.

3 Methodology

WebMoti was installed with three students (two male) of different ages (two in the 8–10 age group and one in the 17–19 group) and academic progress. The first and second students, P1 and P2, were in grade 5 at different schools and used the system once per week for about five weeks. The third student, P3, was in the first year of university and used the system once per week. Students were asked to complete a pre-study questionnaire that consisted of 13 questions (4 demographic questions, 2 regarding computer use, 4 questions about communication and school activity preferences or challenges, and three questions about sitting and vibrotactile preferences). Students were also asked to complete a 7-question questionnaire midway through and once the study was complete about their use of WebMoti. Remote students were expected to use WebMoti to attend class, perform lesson tasks, and follow the classroom procedures, schedule and practices. For example, if they wanted to ask a question or make a comment, they usually were expected to "raise their hand", wait for the teacher to acknowledge them, and then to make their contribution; they were not to shout out comments.

P1 preferred using verbal and written forms of communication, P2 showing, and P3 drawing. All participants indicated it was easy to attend school, eat lunch, and sitting on a chair. At least one of the participants found it more difficult to talk to others, sit beside others, listening to others, going outside for a break, moving classrooms, sitting beside others and being still. All students found it more difficult to meet others. When asked what participants missed most when unable to attend classes, two missed friends, one missed the instructor and one missed learning. Participants indicated that they sought a quiet space, used headphones or did other activities when feeling uncomfortable in school.

The participants in this study were recorded on two-three occasions during their use of WebMoti to determine how they were able to control the device, as well as how useful it was in supporting their connection to school. A thematic analysis of the video data was carried out and resulted in six main themes and modifiers for four of those themes (see Table 1). Two independent raters coded 20% of the video material to ensure reliability. The inter-rater reliability rating was above 0.6 for all themes. Teachers were asked to complete a pre and post study questionnaire to provide their opinion of having WebMoti in their classroom. There were also able to provide comments, recommendations or challenges before or after the class during which WebMoti was being used.

Table 1. Themes for WebMoti student data

Themes	Definitions
Distraction	Prevents the WebMoti student (WMS) from paying attention to the teacher, what is being taught, or what is to be done independently *Example:* classmates talking to the WMS while the teacher is teaching
Attention getting (Modifiers: teacher, classmates, multiple attempts, inappropriate attention getting)	WMS attempts to gain the teacher's attention for assistance. This can be verbal or gestural. WMS is successful or unsuccessful after more than one attempt. They are able or unable to gain classmates' attention when the teacher has allowed student interactions to occur. WMS distracting the teacher from teaching, or seeking attention from classmates when students are learning *Successful:* Teacher responds to attention requests in a positive way *Example:* verbally calling the teacher or waving hand
Work with class on assigned academic activities (Modifiers: positive & negative)	WMS following or not following class activities *Example:* taking notes, filling in the worksheets
Allowed socializing with classmates (Modifiers: positive & negative)	WMS talking with classmate(s) during breaks or between classes. Or when WMS not allowed, or the conversation is not friendly/appropriate *Example:* WMS talking in the middle of a lesson
Technical issues	WebMoti is not working as intended *Example:* issues with volume, speaker, microphone, camera, motors, and internet connection
WebMoti controls (Modifiers: positive & negative)	Using controls correctly or incorrectly *Example:* wants to pan left but uses pan right control instead

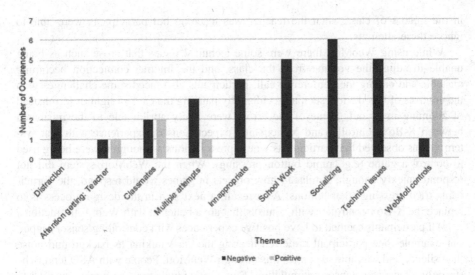

Fig. 2. Number of occurrences for each theme.

4 Results and Discussion

With WebMoti the participants were able to follow along with their classmates with the lesson plan and take notes without overwhelming their sensors. While the participants were using this device, they enjoyed getting their classmates' attention to talk to them. This occurred while the teacher taught the class and during breaks or in between subjects. As seen in Fig. 2, 6 instances of the 37 themes involved WebMoti participants engaging in socializing while the teacher was teaching. This was followed by five instances of technical issues and 5 instances of not doing schoolwork. The WebMoti participants were able to adapt to the controls and only had 1 instance of incorrectly using the WebMoti controls. This also indicates that participants did not become too distracted by their surroundings or the technology when talking to others through WebMoti. For example, when P1 was asked to zoom into the board by a guardian P1 tried to zoom in, and immediately zoomed out saying "I don't want to zoom in" preferring to have a full view of the classroom. Participants did, however, make multiple attempts to gain their teachers attention during teaching time compared with requesting attention for assistance. This could be related to not "understanding social cues or situations" as suggested by [1], or that they liked having attention from the teacher regardless of the situation.

Participants were also somewhat successful in gaining their classmate's attention whether it was permitted or not. P1 often gained their classmates attention by making many repetitive sounds or noises and by trying to talk to their classmates even when the teacher was teaching. Sometimes their classmates were able to ignore the participant while the teacher taught and responded to the participant when there were breaks. However, classmates would occasionally try to initiate a reaction from the participant in the middle of class when the teacher was teaching but participants were able to ignore these attempts.

While using WebMoti there were some technical issues that arose such as being unable to adjust the volume from the class, and the Internet connection becoming unstable and ending the conference call. Participants also faced some challenges with the controls of this device, such as accidentally panning the camera right or left instead of zooming in or out. Some of the errors were likely attributable to the mismatch between X-Box controller and participant's expectations or experience with that system. It was observed that participants would press buttons as though it were being used to control a game (e.g., rapid button pressing). When the WebMoti system did not respond quickly enough, similar to how objects in games would respond, the participants tried pressing other buttons. As a result, a next step in the design process is to replace the X-Box controller with controls that are a better fit with WebMoti functions.

All participants seemed to have positive experiences with controlling sensory input. For example, one participant preferred hearing the class talking as background noise than silence and was able to control this through WebMoti. People with ASD tend to be strongly affected by sensory stimulation. Some individuals may be hyper-sensitive to one or more senses and may require reduced levels of sensory stimulation, while others may be more hypo-sensitive and want enhanced sensory experiences [1, 3]. P1 prefered hearing their classroom activities and tended to use repetitive sounds to gain their classmate's attention for conversation. P2 displayed vestibular hypersensitivity indicated by constantly moving around in their chair, a common behaviour for individuals experiencing vestibular hypersensitivity [1, 3]. P3 displayed signs of visual hypersensitivity and as they preferred focusing the camera on the board, and hyposensitivity for audio and vestibular senses stating he/she was "more comfortable in environments with reduced levels of sensory stimulation." WebMoti was able to support the different needs for sensory input by the participants. Although the X-Box controller may be mismatched to the WebMoti control tasks, participants were still able to successfully and eventually adjust and control the amount of sensory stimulation that they received by adjusting the volume, using the pan and zoom features, and controlling the vibrotactile pillows.

WebMoti has allowed P2 who used to go to school part-time to be able to attend school more and keep up with the curriculum, in hopes of being able to attend school full time. WebMoti also benefited P1 who used to go to school part time before not going at all. WebMoti also has attracted the interest of both participants and parents/guardians who are not able to go to school full time or at all. As this system is easily deployable from home and school.

From the questionnaires, the teachers of the participants outlined various advantages of using WebMoti. For example, the teacher of P2 benefited from being able to interact with the student and answer questions right away. WebMoti made it possible for P1 to learn at the same pace as the rest of their class. It also increased P1's opportunity to learn when they could not attend class. The participant's teachers did face some challenges, for example, P2 often turned the camera towards the students in the classroom thus distracting them. P1 faced some technical difficulties, specifically audio, which also distracted the classroom students and teacher. According to the survey, P1's teacher had to modify the class timetable in order to accommodate the use of WebMoti which caused distraction and affected class management. P2's teacher also found that their ability to move around the classroom and away from the front when teaching was limited as the WebMoti student was unable to follow them easily.

4.1 Limitations

There are several important limitations in this project. The first is that the participant numbers are limited, and that the data reported in this paper are incomplete; there are additional videos to be coded, which will be completed for the final paper, if accepted. A second limitation is that this first WebMoti prototype could not be connected by teachers/students independently so that the frequency of use could only be once per week due to research team availability. Future versions of the system will be usable without research team support. Finally, network capacity, bandwidth and availability in elementary classrooms are limited, and require special permission to use. As a result, connections are often dropped or intermittently unavailable which then has an impact on WebMoti's performance and the student's ability to use it. Allowing additional setup time for a study may assist in determining the extent of these issues as well as how to compensate for them.

5 Future Work

Future work for WebMoti includes modifying the control system to fit the functionality; alternatives include dedicated keyboard controls or a modified joystick controller. Given that remote education is becoming a greater reality for many students, designing a simple and easily deployed system that could meaningfully represent and be controlled by a student who is unable to physically attend the classroom is one of our future aims. Finally, we would like to carry out additional studies with more users with ASD as well as other.

Acknowledgements. Funding was generously provided by the Advancing Education Program, administered by the Ontario Centres of Excellence. We also thank Ryerson University and le Conseil scolaire Viamonde for their support and partnership. Finally, we thank all of the participants in our study.

References

1. Ministry of Education. Effective Educational Practices for Students with Autism Spectrum Disorders. Toronto, Ontario (2019). https://collections.ola.org/mon/17000/274887.pdf
2. Chang, Y.C., Locke, J.: A systematic review of peer-mediated interventions for children with autism spectrum disorder. Res. Autism Spectr. Disord. **27**, 1–10 (2016). https://doi.org/10.1016/j.rasd.2016.03.010
3. Krause, J., Taliaferro, A.: Supporting students with autism spectrum disorders in physical education: there's an app for that. (Report) (Cover Story). Palaestra **29**(2), 45–51 (2015)

4. Ashburner, J., Vickerstaff, S., Beetge, J., Copley, J.: Remote versus face-to-face delivery of early intervention programs for children with autism spectrum disorders: perceptions of rural families and service providers. Res. Autism Spectr. Disord. **23**, 1–14 (2016). https://doi.org/10.1016/j.rasd.2015.11.011

5. Schafer, E.C., et al.: Assistive technology evaluations: remote-microphone technology for children with autism spectrum disorder. J. Commun. Disord. **64**, 1–17 (2016)

6. Google Inc. Material design (2020). https://material.io/design/. Accessed 13 Apr 2020

Development of a Learning-Support System for Science Using Collaboration and Body Movement for Hearing-Impaired Children: Learning Support for Plant Germination and Growth Conditions

Ryohei Egusa[1]([⊠]), Naoki Komiya[2], Fusako Kusunoki[3],
Hiroshi Mizoguchi[2], Miki Namatame[4], and Shigenori Inagaki[5]

[1] Meijigakuin University, Shirokanedai, Minato, Tokyo, Japan
egusa@psy.meijigakuin.ac.jp
[2] Tokyo University of Science, Yamazaki, Noda, Chiba, Japan
7517641@ed.tus.ac.jp, hm@rs.noda.tus.ac.jp
[3] Tama Art University, Yarimizu, Hachioji, Tokyo, Japan
kusunoki@tamabi.ac.jp
[4] Tsukuba University of Technology, Amakubo, Tsukuba, Ibaraki, Japan
miki@a.tsukub-tech.ac.jp
[5] Kobe University, Tsurukabuto, Nada, Kobe, Hyogo, Japan
inagakis@kobe-u.ac.jp

Abstract. In this study, we aimed to develop a full-body gaming-style collaboration and learning support system for a proxy topic of plant germination and growth conditions while focusing on improving the learning experiences of hearing-impaired children. The system is based upon a quiz game activity in which participants learn about plant germination and growth conditions via collaboration and question-answering with their friends. Through the use of a collaborative gaming environment, hearing-impaired learners can repeatedly simulate experiments and observations on germination and growth to accelerate and enhance learning. The system is built with standard information and communications technologies and is evaluate the system to assess its effectiveness. The evaluation experiment revealed the system supported collaborative game play with enjoyment, empathy for others, and interaction for hearing-impaired children. We conclude that the system is useful in supporting hearing-impaired children in learning science through collaboration. Furthermore, we believe that system, which uses body movement and collaboration, might be applicable to other learning areas.

Keywords: Science education · Hearing-impaired children · Collaboration

K. Miesenberger et al. (Eds.): ICCHP 2020, LNCS 12377, pp. 157–165, 2020.
https://doi.org/10.1007/978-3-030-58805-2_19

1 Introduction

In this study, we develop a full-body gaming-style collaboration and learning support system for a proxy scientific topic of plant germination and growth conditions while focusing on improving the learning experiences of hearing-impaired children. For this purpose, we leverage standard information and communication technologies (ICT) to provide a learning environment within which children play and learn with their fellow students using sensing and animation capabilities. We evaluate the system in terms of the total effect of the collaborative and full-body gaming experience on learning for hearing-impaired children.

Science education for children is vital to promoting a culture of scientific thinking, problem-solving competency, and innovation. It further encourages accession to scientific careers and other professions underpinned with knowledge and innovation [1]. Based on the rights of persons with disabilities [2], this issue becomes even more critical for hearing-impaired children, who face significant obstacles to learning via collaboration, owing to their difficulty in obtaining audio information [3, 4]. Thus we pursue a partial solution to overcoming this learning deficit by tackling the proxy topic of scientific naivety related to plant germination and growth conditions.

Education researchers have often addressed the challenge of eradicating naïve concepts held by young science students [5, 6]. Naïve concepts regarding plant germination and growth are common misconceptions [7]. In Japan, learners are quite likely to carry their naïve conceptions into their scholastic experiments. For example, many young people assume that sunlight and soil are the basic requirements needed by seeds to germinate. Thus, they often confuse the distinction between plant germination and growth conditions [8]. The challenge, therefore, is providing an enjoyable system that helps children learn about the three plant germination conditions and the five successful growth conditions during elementary school [9]. The three germination conditions are water, oxygen, and appropriate temperatures. The five growth conditions are water, sunlight, oxygen, appropriate temperatures, and fertilizer. Children can learn about these things through a variety of experiments and observations. However, doing so requires considerable time and effort. This poses an even greater problem for hearing-impaired children.

To address these problems, we aim to develop a support system based on gaming activity using body movement and animation. Through the use of a gaming environment, hearing-impaired learners can repeatedly simulate experiments and observations on germination and growth to accelerate and enhance learning. Moreover, in a collaborative learning environment, participants work on tasks together to promote interaction and knowledge building and build a shared conceptualization of problem solving [10]. We believe that, by using body movements, hearing-impaired children can be further enabled to communicate and interact with others. Body movement is a helpful method of expressing ideas and it helps participants understand one another using visual imagery. Past studies have reported that hearing-impaired children who participated in interactive experiences involving collaboration and body movement (e.g., a puppet show) demonstrated heightened feelings of enjoyment, presence, participation, absorption, and immersion [11, 12]. Research has also shown that collaboration and physical activity enhance immersion in these situations.

2   Game System

2.1   Framework

Figure 1 illustrates the framework of the system used to create the gaming experience. The setup comprises two screens, two projectors, a Kinect sensor, and one control computer. The system is based upon a quiz game activity in which participants learn about plant germination and growth conditions via collaboration and question-answering. One set of a screen and projector is applied to a wall, and the other is applied to the floor. The wall screen in Fig. 1 displays the seeds or seedlings of the plant referred to in the quiz and the area for participant responses. The floor screen shows the quiz answer options. Figure 2 shows the display contents image of the wall screen. Figure 3 illustrates the display contents of the floor screen (i.e., nine answer options displayed in a 3 × 3 configuration. When standing upon the answer options, participants' movements and locations are captured by a Kinect sensor. Players' answers are then displayed on the wall screen and synchronized.

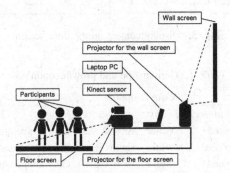

Fig. 1. System overview

2.2   Quiz Game Overview

Table 1 provides an overview of the germination and growth conditions quiz based on carrots, tomatoes, potatoes, and pepper seeds. The germination quiz offers nine answer options at a time. For the growth conditions portion of the quiz, participants are presented with "oxygen" and "appropriate temperature" as two given conditions, and they are asked to choose the remaining three from a set of nine valid or invalid options (i.e., "water," "sunlight," "wind," "caterpillars," "birds," "fertilizers," "earthworms," "electricity," and "music"). The correct answers include "water," "sunlight," and "fertilizer."

At the start of the game, participants are divided into groups of three. As one group plays the game, the two other observe and collaborate on how they will play when it

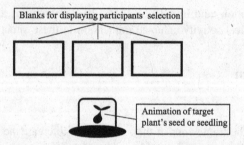

Fig. 2. Display content image on the wall screen

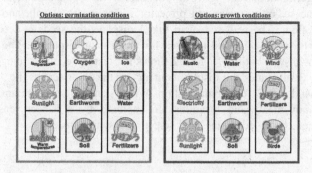

Fig. 3. Display content on the floor screen

Table 1. Germination and growth conditions.

Plants	Correct options		
Germination conditions			
Carrot seed	Water	Air (oxygen)	Cool temperatures
Tomato seed	Water	Air (oxygen)	Warm temperatures
Potato seed	Water	Air (oxygen)	Cool temperatures
Pepper seed	Water	Air (oxygen)	Warm temperatures
Growth conditions			
Carrot seedling	Water	Sunlight	Fertilizers
Tomato seedling	Water	Sunlight	Fertilizers
Potato seedling	Water	Sunlight	Fertilizers
Pepper seedling	Water	Sunlight	Fertilizers

becomes their turn. The group playing the game is shown nine options in the 3 × 3 grid projected on the floor. There is only one correct answer per column, and each player selects one answer from their three options by standing on it. The participants can change their positions during collaboration, selecting different floor-screen options and deciding upon their final answers to the quiz.

Finally, when a player decides upon an answer, he/she presses the appropriate selection point on the floor screen, signaling the system to judge whether their answer is correct. If all three players are correct, the system then projects an animation of the seed (or seedling) growing on the wall screen. If an answer is incorrect, the system displays "incorrect" and the players try again.

3 Evaluation Experiment

3.1 Methods

Participants: Participants included 17 hearing-impaired children in their 1st-to-3rd years of elementary school (6–9 years of age).

Tasks and Procedures: The participants were divided into six groups of three. A supporter joined the group lacking a participant. Each group played the game at least twice. Figure 4 shows one group playing the quiz game. They all had chosen invalid answers and been promoted to try once again by game characters. Following the activity, each student completed a paper questionnaire. 10 items were developed based on the Game Experience Questionnaire's [13, 14] social presence module, which is used to examine game players' psychological and behavioral participation in social gaming experiences from three perspectives: psychological involvement-empathy, psychological involvement-negative feelings, and behavioral involvement. In this evaluation, each of the three perspectives was further divided into specific options to make answering easier for the participants and to examine the effectiveness of collaborative playing. Discussions were held with teachers from the special support schools attended by the participants to help understand the question options.

Fig. 4. Game playing

Psychological involvement-empathy featured five options related to enjoyment with, understanding of, and gaining information from other participants: 1) "I empathized with the other;" 2) "I paid close attention to others during the quiz game;" 3) "I found it enjoyable during the quiz game to be with others;" 4) "When the others seemed to be having fun, I also enjoyed myself;" and 5) "I admired the others."

Psychological involvement-negative feelings featured one option: 6) "I was influenced by the mood of others during the quiz game."

Behavioral involvement included five options related to interaction and cooperation to solve the quiz: 7) "My actions depended on the actions of others while playing the quiz game;" 8) "The actions of others depended on my actions while playing the quiz gam;" 9) "I felt connected to others while playing the quiz game;" and 10) "the others paid close attention to me."

For each item, the participants replied using a seven-stage Likert scale with the following options: "strongly agree," "agree," "somewhat agree," "no strong opinion," "somewhat disagree," "disagree," and "strongly disagree."

Study date: The study was conducted on November 1, 2018.

3.2   Results

Participant replies were classified into positive responses of "strongly agree," "agree," and "somewhat agree." Neutral or negative responses of "no strong opinion," "somewhat disagree," "disagree," and "strongly disagree" were also classified. Reverse scoring was necessary so that lower scores indicated higher positive affectivity. The results show that the number of positive answers was higher than that of neutral or negative answers for all items. We analyzed the differences in count between positive, neutral, and negative replies for each item using a 1×2 Fisher's exact test.

Table 2 shows participant responses to the questions. In all items, the number of positive answers was higher than that of neutral or negative answers. From the perspective of psychological involvement-empathy, there was a significant difference in two population proportions in all five items. As expected, responses favored more positive answers than neutral or negative replies. This indicates that, in the collaborative quiz game play of the developed system, the participants experienced empathy toward others in the game experience of discussion and answering.

From the perspective of psychological involvement-negative feelings, there was a significant difference in the two population proportions for an item. Positive answers were favored over neutral or negative replies. This suggests that, in the game, the participants were strongly influenced by the moods of others.

From the point of view of behavioral involvement, there was a significant difference in two population proportions for all items with the exception of item 7. It revealed more positive answers than neutral or negative replies. This indicates that, in the collaborative quiz game play of the developed system, the participants experienced interaction with others via multiple players. However, participants felt that others did not depend on their action while playing the quiz game.

Table 2. Germination and growth conditions.

	Items	Strongly agree	Agree	No strong opinion	Disagree	Strongly disagree
	Psychological Involvement-Empathy					
1	I empathized with the other**	11	2	2	0	1
2	I paid close attention to others during the quiz game**	12	3	1	0	0
3	I found it enjoyable during the quiz game to be with others**	14	2	0	0	0
4	When the others seemed to be having fun, I also enjoyed myself**	13	2	1	0	0
5	I admired the others**	13	1	1	1	0
	Psychological Involvement – Negative Feelings					
6	I was influenced the mood of others during the quiz game**	11	2	2	1	0
	Behavioral Involvement					
7	My actions depended on the actions of others while playing the quiz game[n.s]	9	1	3	0	3
8	The actions of others depended on my actions while playing the quiz game*	10	1	2	0	3
9	I felt connected to others while playing the quiz game**	9	3	2	1	1
10	The other(s) paid close attention to me**	12	3	1	0	0

$N = 16$, $p** < 0.01$, $p* < 0.05$, n.s.: non-significance

4 Conclusions

In this study, we developed a learning science-support system specifically for hearing-impaired children. We designed the system to support collaboration and body movement using ICTs while focusing on plant germination and growth conditions.

The evaluation experiment revealed that the system supported collaborative game play with enjoyment, empathy for others, and interaction. However, while playing the quiz game, the participants were strongly influenced by others' moods. Results suggest that the atmosphere of the group supported the notion that scientific thinking could strongly influence the decisions of participants. Conversely, participants did not appear to be convinced that their actions affected those of others.

Based upon these study results, we can conclude that the system we developed can be used as a successful way to support hearing-impaired children's learning science with collaboration. Furthermore, we believe that our system, which uses body movement and collaboration, might be applicable to other learning areas.

Moving forward, we need to evaluate the effectiveness of the system's success in learning support in greater detail. In addition, we need to improve the system and/or quiz game format to encourage children to make decisions based upon scientific ideas.

Acknowledgements. This work was supported by JSPS KAKENHI Grant Number JP 17H02002 & JP18H03660.

References

1. European Commission: Science Education For Responsible Citizenship. European Union, Luxembourg (2015)
2. United Nations: Convention on the Rights of Persons with Disabilities (2006). https://www.un.org/development/desa/disabilities/convention-on-the-rights-of-persons-with-disabilities.html. Accessed 31 Mar 2020
3. Marchark, M., Hauser, P.C.: How Deaf Children Learn. Oxford University Press, Oxford (2012)
4. Kato, Y., Hiraga, R., Wakatsuki, D., Yasu, K.: A preliminary observation on the effect of visual information in learning environmental sounds for deaf and hard of hearing people. In: Miesenberger, K., Kouroupetroglou, G. (eds.) ICCHP 2018. LNCS, vol. 10896, pp. 183–186. Springer, Cham (2018). https://doi.org/10.1007/978-3-319-94277-3_30
5. McCloskey, M.: Naïve theories of motion. In: Gentner, D., Stevens, A. (eds.) Mental Models, pp. 299–324. Lawrence Erlbaum Associations, Hillsdale (1983)
6. Taylor, A.K., Kowalski, P.: Naïve psychological science: the prevalence, strength, and sources of misconceptions. Psychol. Rec. **54**(15), 15–25 (2004)
7. Wynn, A.N., Pan, I.L., Rueschhoff, E.E., Herman, M.A.B., Archer, E.K.: Student misconceptions about plants – a first step in building a teaching resource. J. Microbiol. Biol. Educ. **18**(1), 1–4 (2017)
8. Tanaka, S., Une, K.: Children's concept formation in the continuity of plant life - based on the learning analysis of germination of plant. Memoirs of Osaka Kyoiku Univ. ser. IV Educ. Psychol. Spec. Needs Educ. Phys. Educ. **62**(1), 43–52 (2013)
9. Ministry of education, culture, sports, science and technology Japan: National curriculum standards (2017–2018 Revision) section 4 science. https://www.mext.go.jp/component/a_menu/education/micro_detail/__icsFiles/afieldfile/2019/03/18/1387017_005_1.pdf. Accessed 31 Mar 2020
10. Stahl, G., Koschmann, T., Suthers, D.: Computer-supported collaborative learning. In: Sawyer, R.K. (ed.) The Cambridge Handbook of the Learning Sciences, 2nd edn. Cambridge university press, Cambridge (2014)
11. Egusa, R., et al.: Designing a collaborative interaction experience for a puppet show system for hearing-impaired children. In: Miesenberger, K., Bühler, C., Penaz, P. (eds.) ICCHP 2016. LNCS, vol. 9759, pp. 424–432. Springer, Cham (2016). https://doi.org/10.1007/978-3-319-41267-2_60

12. Egusa, R., et al.: A full-body interaction game for children with hearing disabilities to gain the immersive experience in a puppet show. In: Koch, F., Koster, A., Primo, T. (eds.) SOCIALEDU 2015. CCIS, vol. 606, pp. 29–38. Springer, Cham (2016). https://doi.org/10.1007/978-3-319-39672-9_3

13. De Kort, Y.A.W., IJsselsteijn, W.A., Poels, K.: Digital games as social presence technology: development of the social presence in gaming questionnaire. In: Proceedings of PRESENCE 2007, pp. 195–203 (2007)

14. IJsselsteijn, W.A., De Kort, Y.A.W., Poels, K.: The game experience questionnaire. Technische Universiteit Eindhoven, Eindhoven, Nederland (2013)

Promoting Inclusive Open Education: A Holistic Approach Towards a Novel Accessible OER Recommender System

Hejer Ben Brahim[1]([⊠]), Mohamed Koutheair Khribi[1],
Mohamed Jemni[2], and Ahmed Tlili[3]

[1] Technologies of Information and Communication Lab,
Higher School of Sciences and Technologies of Tunis,
University of Tunis, Tunis, Tunisia
Benbrahim.hejer@gmail.com, koutheair@gmail.com
[2] ICT Department, ALECSO, Ave Mohamed Ali Akid, Centre Urbain Nord,
Cité El Khadhra, PO Box: 1003, Tunis, Tunisia
mohamed.jemni@alecso.org.tn
[3] Smart Learning Institute of Beijing Normal University, Beijing, China
ahmed.tlili23@yahoo.com

Abstract. OER can pave the way to reach equitable and inclusive access to education for all. However, unleashing its full potential is disrupted due to the disregard of the special needs and learning characteristics of certain user groups such as people with disabilities by the mechanisms delivering OER. A potential solution lies within helping each final user to find the "best" OER that embraces his/her individual needs and specific characteristics. Recommendation accomplishes that as it could offer a significant support assisting learners with disabilities in recognizing and retrieving the most relevant accessible OER within the system delivering the educational content. This paper lays the foundation to an approach for building an accessible OER recommender system that delivers, to online learners, the most relevant accessible OER responsive to their needs, abilities, and disabilities, based on their contextual and usage data.

Keywords: Open Educational Resources · OER · Accessibility ·
Recommendation systems · People with disabilities · PWD · OER repositories ·
Inclusive education · Open education

1 Introduction

According to the United Nations 2030 agenda for sustainable Development, "The spread of information and communication technologies and global interconnectedness has great potential to accelerate human progress, to bridge the digital divide and to develop knowledge societies". This vision spurred the inception of Open Educational Resources (OER) movement which aims to remove all barriers to education [18]. OER refer to teaching, learning, and research materials that are either in the public domain or available, under an open license, for free access, use, adaptation, and redistribution by others with no or limited restrictions [33]. OER hold the promise of inclusive and

K. Miesenberger et al. (Eds.): ICCHP 2020, LNCS 12377, pp. 166–176, 2020.
https://doi.org/10.1007/978-3-030-58805-2_20

equitable access to education through enabling, via its transformative potential, educational content to be adapted to fit the specific needs of people with disabilities [38]. People with disabilities are vulnerable to the deficiencies in educational opportunities recognizing their particular needs. This reinforces their exclusion especially from formal education, resulting in unemployment, poverty, inequality, and instability [14, 33]. To that extent, the OER paradigm fosters inclusive education through holding a transformative potential supporting the adjustments to be performed on the educational content and adding more flexibility to the educational environment [7, 14]. Despite that several research focused on OER, little attention was paid to OER accessibility. Learners with disabilities are still facing the "non" accessible educational content. This is induced by the fact that OER producers seem oblivious to the importance of adopting accessibility requirements when creating OER, and the non-support of the adjustments that need to be done within learning environments and OER delivery systems, that are intended to facilitate the search, use and exploitation of OER for people with disabilities [2]. Confirming that, an analysis performed in [2] exposed two main barriers impeding open inclusive access to OER for all users. The first barrier concerns the non-consideration of personalization mechanisms as an OER delivery system should enable each learner – in particular those with disabilities – to locate and retrieve educational content matching his/her learning needs, abilities/disabilities, and individual characteristics. While the second barrier is related to a non-effective or a total discard of accessibility standards, showing that most of existing OER delivery systems do not involve people with disabilities. In short, existing OER delivery systems provide generally the same content, mostly not in compliance with accessibility principles, to all learners, not considering that they learn with not only different needs but also different abilities, disabilities, and learning characteristics. Which deepens the digital divide and exclusion from educational opportunities [2].

A potential way to balance this out is enacting personalization paradigms such as recommendation systems. These systems hold the promise to help and assist users, especially those living with a disability, to easily find and retrieve the most relevant educational content responding to their needs and interests [4, 24]. In this context, this study presents a new approach instrumentalizing the general recommendation paradigm towards recommending personalized accessible OER within OER delivery systems for people with disabilities. Additionally, the proposed approach aims to explore and exploit the growing number of existing non-accessible OER through enabling their conversion before providing learners with the most suitable and accessible personalized OER recommendations.

To this end, this paper unfolds 4 sections. After the introduction, Sect. 2 gives an overview of the scope of this work covering OER and accessibility and their related concepts. Section 3 presents the recommendation paradigm in education and accessibility. Section 4 finalizes the paper through a conclusion.

2 Open Inclusive Education

2.1 Accessibility

Through its world report on disability, WHO[1] (World Health Organization) revealed that over a billion people live with a form of disability. However, despite their significant number people with disabilities are one of the most marginalized groups in the world [36]. They endure difficulties in daily life aspects emphasized by the "non" adaptation of services, products or environments to their particular needs and specific characteristics. The accessibility paradigm counters these difficulties through providing concrete recommendations and practices to enable people with disabilities to achieve, on equal basis with others, access to education, employment, transportation, housing, etc.) [14]. Accessibility grants the "ability to access" to devices, services, products or environments for people living with a disability through the use of assistive technologies [15]. In line with that, Microsoft scaffolded that "There are no limits to what people can achieve when technology reflects the diversity of everyone who uses it" [20] proving that enabling equal access to technology especially for people with disabilities provides them with limitless opportunities to actively participate in society and empower them to overcome the difficulties they face in everyday life.

Falling in the scope of disability rights movement [14], the 9th article of United Nations Convention on the Rights of Persons with Disabilities consolidated this idea through advocating the crucial importance of universal access to technology especially the web. In this scope, accessibility in general, and web accessibility in particular, rhymes with democratizing access to Information and Communication Technologies (ICT) for People With Disabilities PWD through promoting the design, development, production and distribution of accessible web technologies. Web accessibility fosters the ability of people with disabilities to use and contribute to the web [14]. To this end, the Web Accessibility Initiative (WAI), which is a wing of the World Wide Web Consortium (W3C), is established and aims to lead the Web to its full potential to be accessible, enabling people with disabilities to participate equally on the Web. The Web Accessibility Initiative (WAI) "develops strategies, guidelines, and resources to help making the Web accessible to people with disabilities" [14]. The Web Accessibility Initiative (WAI) encompasses guidelines and recommended practices regarding the accessibility of: content through the Web Content Accessibility Guidelines (WCAG), authoring tools through Authoring Tools Accessibility Guidelines (ATAG) and user agents through User Agent Accessibility Guidelines (UAAG) [14].

Through its 26th article, the UN Convention on the Rights of Persons with Disabilities recognizes education as a fundamental human right highlighting its importance in everyone's sustainable personal development. People with disabilities are vulnerable to the deficiencies in educational opportunities recognizing their particular needs. This reinforces their exclusion from education which generates skill gaps and causes unemployment, poverty, inequality, and instability [37]. In education, accessibility promotes flexible and personalized learning for PWD through fostering the design and

---

[1] http://www.who.int/en/.

development of educational content, activities and services meeting their requirements and characteristics. In the same scope, given a re-definition of the term disability by the IMS Global Learning Consortium describing it as a mismatch between the needs of the learner and the education offered, accessibility refers to the ability of the learning environment to adjust to the needs of all learners. It is determined by the flexibility of the educational environment and the availability of adequate alternative-but-equivalent content and activities [14].

In this context, the OER paradigm fosters inclusive education through holding a transformative potential supporting the adjustments to be performed on the educational content and adding more flexibility to the educational environment [8].

2.2   Open Educational Resources (OER)

The urging need to open up, share freely and give wider access to information and technology, has motivated a range of open philosophies such as: Open source, Open access, Open Content, Open Data, Open Education, etc. The OER concept falls in the scope of the Open Education movement covering cost and constraint free resources, tools and practices that foster open sharing to broaden access to education [19]. The emergence of this concept encouraged and spurred the educational institutions to work on making education available for all. The Massachusetts Institute of Technology (MIT) was one of the first institutions to join the 'Open' wave through making nearly all its courseware freely available for all in 2001. Later, the number of institutions offering free or open courseware kept increasing. That is when UNESCO organized the 1st Global OER Forum in 2002 where the term Open Educational Resources (OER) was first coined and presented as: *"The open provision of educational resources, enabled by information and communication technologies, for consultation, use and adaptation by a community of users for non-commercial purposes"*. Then and with the constant growth of the OER movement, other efforts were made to define and describe the term and the concept of OER. In the Cape Town Open Education Declaration, during the conference on open education in 2007, OER were defined as follows *"open educational resources should be freely shared through open licenses which facilitate use, revision, translation, improvement and sharing by anyone."*

However, it was not formally adopted until 2012 through the Paris OER Declaration [31] which defined OER as: *"teaching, learning and research materials in any medium, digital or otherwise, that reside in the public domain or have been released under an open license that permits no-cost access, use, adaptation and redistribution by others with no or limited restrictions. Open licensing is built within the existing framework of intellectual property rights as defined by relevant international conventions and respects the authorship of the work"*.

Keeping in mind the aforementioned definitions, OER are cost-and-constraint (or limited constraints) free, flexible educational materials for all. OER are intended to foster and promote educational transformation. Besides, the most powerful asset of open educational resources is its ability, when digitalized, to be easily accessed, used, re-used and shared online.

Both OER and Accessibility are important pillars holding great potential to effectively build inclusive knowledge societies through removing the barriers that may hold back the expansion of education for all especially people with disabilities.

2.3   Accessible OER

Stemming from recognizing accessibility as a main design requirement when creating educational content, several research initiatives investigated the potentials of providing accessible educational content tailored to learners with disabilities' needs and characteristics. These initiatives gave life to a number of systems aiming to foreclose digital exclusion such as: The EU4ALL project [9], MoodleAcc+ platform [17], etc.

Following the same line and along with the tidal wave of designing for inclusion, researches took further the efforts towards maximizing flexibility and customization capabilities of the educational content to meet the individual needs of each and every learner. Which led to developing educational content as Open Educational Resources [10] fulfilling the promise of not only flexibility and transformability but also ruled out several financial, technical and access barriers.

As OER represent an important milestone to achieve equitable inclusive education, UNESCO[2] was proactive releasing OER-based inclusive guidelines and recommendations to promote and empower equitable inclusive access to education. The most important are:

- The "Guidelines for OER in higher Education"[3] in collaboration with CoL (Commonwealth of Learning) which highlighted, on one hand, that OER should be open and accessible to students with a diversity of learning needs. On the other hand, the guidelines pinpointed that the latter is achieved through the resource delivery system which will handle any "transformation" the educational resource might require to match the individual learning needs of the students.
- The Ljubljana OER Action Plan 2017, released as an outcome of the 2nd OER world congress and which described concrete actions to develop and use accessible inclusive OER. The suggested actions shed the light on the need to acknowledge the principle of inclusiveness when creating, accessing and sharing OER [21].
- And last but not least, UNESCO has recently furthered its efforts through releasing a draft recommendation on OER [7] in which it presents a specific list of important measures to scaffold the creation, use and adaptation of inclusive and quality OER [7].

Thus, two main facts can be revealed: One recognizing that increasing accessibility is crucial to reach inclusive knowledge society and the other proving that the latter can only be achieved through a close implication of OER creators and OER delivery systems.

---

[2] https://en.unesco.org.

[3] https://unesdoc.unesco.org/ark:/48223/pf0000213605.

2.4   OER Delivery Systems

To find OER, the user needs to explore the different kinds of facilities and services collecting, storing and supplying user communities with OER. These facilities support web-based management of OER through easing the search, retrieval and access to learning resources [26, 27]. Underpinning that, Sampson et al. [26, 27] assert that the main aim of OER delivery systems is to manage the use, organization, classification and share of OER in the form of Learning Objects (LO) and their associated metadata [26].

There is no shortage of optimism about the potential of OER in reducing barriers to education and improving the learning quality of PWD. However, a serious engagement from the mechanisms delivering OER is crucial to bring out and explore this potential through the functionalities and access features they offer. That's why there's a dire need to pursue a close investigation of the OER delivery systems commitment degree to OER main goals for providing broader, more equal and barrier free access to knowledge and education for all users.

Within this scope, a close analysis of a representative sample of twenty existing OER delivery systems in [2] exposed two main drawbacks; the first covering the non-consideration of personalization since OER delivery systems should enable each learner– in particular those with disabilities – to locate and retrieve educational content matching his/her learning needs and individual characteristics. While the second revealed a non-effective or a total discard of accessibility standards showing that most of these OER delivery systems do not involve people with disabilities through delivering the same content to all learners not considering that students learn with not only different needs but also different abilities, disabilities, and learning characteristics. Which deepens the digital divide and exclusion from educational opportunities [2].

A potential avenue to counter the lack of personalization for PWD in OER delivery systems is considering content discovery mechanisms like recommender systems. These systems can provide a significant support guiding learners with disabilities through locating as well as retrieving the most relevant accessible open educational resources meeting their disabilities and learning objectives. A special focus should be oriented consequently towards investigating the challenges of deploying recommendation services to foster people with disabilities' learning within OER delivery systems.

3   Accessible OER Recommendation

3.1   OER Recommendation and Accessibility

One of the most recurrent dilemmas facing users searching for educational content is the tremendous number of learning resources available on the internet which makes finding the content they need more difficult. Unwin, in [34], confirms that the real issue is not the lack of content but the inability of end users to effectively locate relevant learning resources [34]. Recommender systems emerge like the answer most likely to address this issue. The main purpose of these systems is to help users through preselecting resources that respond to their needs, interests and objectives [16]. Confirming that, Burke, R. [4] states that a recommender system is any system that produces personalized recommendations as output or has the effect of guiding the user in a personalized way to interesting or useful objects in a large space of possible options. In education, personalized recommender systems assist and support learners in achieving an optimal personalized learning experience through their ability to antici-pate learners' needs and to provide them with matching information and content. According to Resnick and Varian [24], recommendation in learning environments relies on using the experience of a community of learners to help individual learners in that community to identify and retrieve more effectively learning content from a wide spectrum of choices.

Recommenders can be applied to a variety of web based learning environments such as OER systems [16]. In that context, embodying recommenders into OER-based learning environment federates the personalization and adaptation features offered by the recommendation paradigm along with the transformative potential of OER. This would pave the way to OER-based personalized learning experiences for learners with disabilities recognizing their evolving and special needs, and taking into account the wide range of their accessibility requirements and preferences. Which represents a step forward towards equitable inclusive education.

3.2 Approach Towards a Novel Accessible OER Recommendation System

The proposed approach was built upon the Generic Meta-Level GML Framework for Technology Enhanced Learning (TEL) Recommendation Systems described in [16]. This approach (see Fig. 1) follows several steps beginning with retrieving, federating then pre-processing learners' and content data to build learner and OER models, to be used later within the recommendation engine. Afterward the OER conversion process, whenever required, is launched to perform the conversion of appropriate recommended OER into accessible ones responding to the active learner profile and her contextual characteristics. The output of the recommendation engine is then delivered to the learner through a specific accessibility viewer/delivery tool acknowledging his output device considering the potential use of assistive technologies.

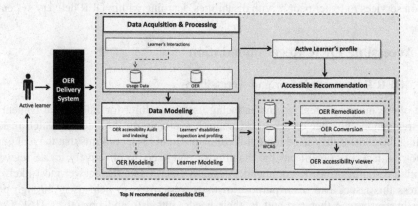

Fig. 1. Proposed accessible recommendation approach.

As described in Fig. 1, the proposed approach involves the following primary phases:

- **Data acquisition and processing:** This phase handles acquiring and mining the data describing the learners' characteristics and usage data (learners' usage activities, learners' disabilities and characteristics, contextual data such as space-time features (location, luminosity, sound level, time, etc.), used device, etc. [1, 35], assistive technologies' usage, etc.) and the educational content (OER and the metadata). It represents the system's learning phase handling the acquisition, retrieving, filtering and exploitation of data towards building learner and content profiles.
- **Modeling phase:** This phase is performed offline. It covers the modeling processes of learners and OER. (1) Learner modeling: The previously processed data is used to build learner models through the use of machine learning algorithms. Thereafter, learner models are grouped into several collections gathering similar learners with very much alike characteristics and preferences, to be used later on in the recommendation phase. (2) OER modeling: this process handles the automated exploration, crawling, analysis and indexing of OER features and content toward building an entire index representing all available resources in the repository taking into account accessibility issues. In order to consider the accessibility aspect of OER modeling, we include an offline auditing phase of OER to check and inspect their compliance with known accessible requirements and then generating a specific report explaining results and stating possible curation and remediation. This output is used either for modeling and conversion phases.
- **Accessibility tasks:** It represent tasks related to accessibility issues and covering mainly services of auditing, converting and viewing accessible OER. It encompasses the following tasks: (1) OER auditing: This process is performed offline and manages the accessibility evaluation, checking and testing of OER available in the repository, verifying thus their compliance with the WAI-WCAG requirements. Reporting templates are then used to report the evaluation results which will be processed with the OER features to build the OER model. (2) OER Conversion: covers the on-demand conversion of the "non" accessible OER. The conversion applies, whenever it is possible, the remediation options and strategies referring to the techniques addressing the learning resource's accessibility flaws. An automatic update of the content model as well as the OER repository is then performed. (3) OER viewing: it aims to display the recommended accessible OER with respect to the features of the assistive technologies used by the learner and its output device.
- **Recommendation phase:** This will ensure the prediction of the learning content, anticipating the learners needs and disability characteristics. In fact, it needs to be preceded by the identification of the active learner's profile through extracting the relevant information characterizing him/her. Once the active profile is recognized, the recommendation process is launched, and a prediction list of suitable OER is generated based on the learner's needs and disability characteristics. If not already accessible and appropriate to be used by the learner, the recommended OER is then converted-whenever it is possible, into accessible OER based on the remediation options and strategies provided as a result to the OER audit task. The top

N recommended accessible OER are then provided to the active learner through the accessibility viewer in a format compliant to the output device and assistive technologies he/she used.

- **Active learner profile identification:** The active learner refers to the current online learner using the OER delivery system. Identifying his/her profile is essential to guarantee the accuracy of the prediction process. It ensures recognizing the present request, needs and characteristics of the learner requiring recommendation. Through the active learner's interactions with the OER delivery system, his/her relative activities and contextual data, the assistive technologies' usage and the disability characteristics are identified (in an implicit and/or explicit manner) and extracted, processed and delivered to the recommendation engine toward providing the active learner with appropriate content matching his/her preferences and disabilities' requirements.

4   Conclusion

This paper gave an overview of a proposed approach towards recommending personalized accessible Open Educational Resources. We highlighted the core modules and functionalities leading the proposed approach. Our future works involve furthering our studies of each module and each step of the targeted recommendation system to explore and select most suitable techniques and algorithms to be used within each phase, which will pave the way to the development of a prototype of an accessible OER recommendation service to be deployed and experienced within existing OER delivery systems.

References

1. Adomavicius, G., Tuzhilin, A.: Context-aware recommender systems. In: Ricci, F., Rokach, L., Shapira, B., Kantor, Paul B. (eds.) Recommender Systems Handbook, pp. 217–253. Springer, Boston (2011). https://doi.org/10.1007/978-0-387-85820-3_7
2. Ben Brahim, H., Khribi, M.K., Jemni, M.: Towards accessible open educational resources: overview and challenges. In: The Sixth International Conference on Information and Communication Technology and Accessibility (ICTA 2017), Muscat, Sultanate of Oman, 19–21 December 2017 (2017)
3. Ben Daamech, R., Khribi, M.K.: Towards a framework for building automatic recommendations of answers in MOOCs' Discussion Forums. In: The Seventh International Conference on Information and Communication Technology and Accessibility (ICTA 2019), Hammamet, Tunisia, 13–15 December 2019 (2019)
4. Burke, R.: Hybrid recommender systems: survey and experiments. User Model. User-Adap. Inter. **12**(4), 331–370 (2002)
5. Downes, S.: Models for sustainable open educational resources. Interdiscip. J. E-Learn. Learn. Objects **3**(1), 29–44 (2007)
6. Drachsler, H., Hummel, H.G.K., Rob, K.: Identifying the goal, user model and conditions of recommender systems for formal and informal learning. JODI J. Digit. Inf. **10**(2), 1–17 (2009)

7. Draft Recommendation on Open Educational Resources. https://unesdoc.unesco.org/ark:/48223/pf0000370936. Accessed 29 Mar 2020

8. Education for All 2000–2015: achievements and challenges; EFA global monitoring report (2015). https://unesdoc.unesco.org/ark:/48223/pf0000232205. Accessed 06 Apr 2020

9. EU4ALL—Project. https://www.eu4all.info. Accessed 14 June 2020

10. Fletcher, G., Levin, D., Lipper, K., Leichty, R.: The accessibility of learning content for all students, including students with disabilities, must be addressed in the shift to digital instructional materials. SETDA Policy Brief. State Educational Technology Directors Association (2014)

11. Hu, J., Zhang, W.: Community collaborative filtering for e-learning. In: International Conference on Computer and Electrical Engineering, pp. 593–597. IEEE (2008)

12. Huang, R.H., Liu, D.J., Tlili, A., Yang, J.F., Wang, H.H., et al.: Handbook on facilitating flexible learning during educational disruption: the Chinese experience in maintaining undisrupted learning in COVID-19 outbreak. Smart Learning Institute of Beijing Normal University, Beijing (2020)

13. IMS AccessForAll Meta-data Overview|IMS Global Learning Consortium. https://www.imsglobal.org/accessibility/accmdv1p0/imsaccmd_oviewv1p0.html

14. Introduction to Web Accessibility|Web Accessibility Initiative (WAI)|W3C. http://www.w3.org/WAI/intro/accessibility.php. Accessed 19 Mar 2020

15. Kanwar, A., Cheng, R.: Making ODL inclusive: the role of technology (2017

16. Khribi, M.K., Jemni, M., Nasraoui, O.: Recommendation systems for personalized technology-enhanced learning. In: Kinshuk, H.R. (ed.) Ubiquitous Learning Environments and Technologies. Lecture Notes in Educational Technology. Springer, Heidelberg (2015). https://doi.org/10.1007/978-3-662-44659-1_9

17. Laabidi, M., Jemni, M., Ayed, L.J.B., Brahim, H.B., Jemaa, A.B.: Learning technologies for people with disabilities. J. King Saud Univ. Comput. Inf. Sci. 26(1), 29–45 (2014)

18. Lane, A.: Open education and the sustainable development goals: making change happen (2018)

19. Open Education and the Sustainable Development Goals: Making Change Happen. http://jl4d.org/index.php/ejl4d/article/view/266/256?platform=hootsuite. Accessed 19 Mar 2020

20. Microsoft Accessibility. https://www.microsoft.com/en-us/accessibility/default.aspx. Accessed 17 Mar 2020

21. Ministerial Statement, 2nd edn. Second World OER Congress, Ljubljana, pp. 1–2 (2017)

22. Ochoa, X., Duval, E.: Quantitative analysis of learning object repositories. IEEE Trans. Learn. Technol. 2(3), 226–238 (2009)

23. Open Education SPARC. https://sparcopen.org/open-education/. Accessed 02 Apr 2020

24. Resnick, P., Varian, H.R.: Recommender systems. Commun. ACM 40(3), 56–58 (1997)

25. Richter, T., McPherson, M.: Open educational resources: education for the world? Distance Educ. 33(2), 201–219 (2012). https://doi.org/10.1080/01587919.2012.692068

26. Sampson, D.G., Zervas, P.: Supporting accessible technology-enhanced training: the eAccess2Learn framework. IEEE Trans. Learn. Technol. 4, 353–364 (2011)

27. Sampson, D.G., Zervas, P.: Learning object repositories as knowledge management systems. Knowl. Manag. E-Learn. 5(2), 117–136 (2013)

28. Sekhavatian, A., Mahdavi, M.: Application of recommender systems on e-learning environments. In: EDULEARN11 Proceedings, pp. 2679–2687 (2011)

29. Sustainable development goals - United Nations. United Nations Sustainable Development. http://www.un.org/sustainabledevelopment/sustainable-development-goals/. Accessed 27 Mar 2020

30. Tebbutt, E., Brodmann, R., Borg, J., MacLachlan, M., Khasnabis, C., Horvath, R.: Assistive products and the Sustainable Development Goals (SDGs). Global. Health 12(1), 1–6 (2016). https://doi.org/10.1186/s12992-016-0220-6
31. The Paris OER Declaration 2012. https://en.unesco.org/oer/paris-declaration. Accessed 23 Mar 2020
32. Tlili, A., Jemni, M., Khribi, M.K., Huang, R., Chang, T.-W., Liu, D.: Current state of open educational resources in the Arab region: an investigation in 22 countries. Smart Learn. Environ. 7(1), 1–15 (2020). https://doi.org/10.1186/s40561-020-00120-z
33. UNESCO and Education Above All Foundation join forces to prioritize inclusive quality education. https://en.unesco.org/news/unesco-and-education-above-all-foundation-join-forces-prioritize-inclusive-quality-education. Accessed 25 Mar 2020
34. Unwin, T.: Towards a framework for the use of ICT in teacher training in Africa. Open Learn. 20, 113–130 (2005)
35. Verbert, K., et al.: Context-aware recommender systems for learning: a survey and future challenges. IEEE Trans. Learn. Technol. 5(4), 318–335 (2012)
36. WHO: 10 facts on disability. https://www.who.int/features/factfiles/disability/en/. Accessed 15 Mar 2020
37. Wiley, D.: Openness as catalyst for an educational reformation. Educause Rev. 45(4), 15–20 (2010)
38. Zhang, X., et al.: Accessibility within open educational resources and practices: a systematic literature review. Smart Learn. Environ. 7, 1–19 (2020). https://doi.org/10.1186/s40561-019-0113-2

Hearing Systems and Accessories
for People with Hearing Loss

Hearing Systems and Accessories for People with Hearing Loss

Introduction to the Special Thematic Session

Matjaž Debevc[1]([⊠]) and Christian Vogler[2]

[1] University of Maribor, Maribor, Slovenia
matjaz.debevc@um.si
[2] Gallaudet University, Washington, D.C., USA

Abstract. The Special Thematic Session on hearing systems and accessories is made up of a wide range of papers that illustrate different aspects of using such technologies in different environments. Studies shows the possibilities for improvements in higher education, captioning, sign language interpretation, communication for deaf-blind people and in museums.

Keywords: Hearing systems · Accessibility · Deaf and hard of hearing

1 Introduction

People with hearing loss (hard of hearing people, deaf and deaf/blind) are in the category of individuals who need specifically designed Information and Communication Technology (ICT), with emphasis on support in visual form, or sound amplification to enhance communication abilities, educational achievement and sociocultural characteristics [1]. Hearing loss is a condition where the ability to hear is reduced, and individuals require medical, educational, and psychological attention. Studies in Europe and the USA show that around 9–16% of the population in these countries have some type of hearing loss and the prevalence is increasing, especially since the population is getting older [23]. Another study shows that there are approximately millions of people in the world (14.6 million in the USA, for example) with a very high cost for an untreated disabling hearing loss, which are between 8,000 USD (Europe) to 9,000 USD (USA) per person each year [14]. In this way, it is important to lower this cost and support the use of hearing accessories, since they contribute to better health, higher income, and better family and social life [16].

Deafness is unique among disabilities, since it is the only disability in which most deaf sign language users share a common language, which is not equalled by the dominant hearing society. However, a minority of deaf and hard of hearing people speak sign language [15]. Additionally, most sign language users are users who learned sign language as their first language. Therefore, most deaf sign language users are bilingual, and, in this way, their primary need is to have bilingual support [11].

Deaf blindness is a separate disability from deafness and blindness. Usually, deaf-blind people experience some level of both hearing and vision disability and complete

K. Miesenberger et al. (Eds.): ICCHP 2020, LNCS 12377, pp. 179–185, 2020.
https://doi.org/10.1007/978-3-030-58805-2_21

deaf-blindness is very rare. However, age-related vision and hearing loss is going to become a serious problem with population aging. For them, hearing systems can be combined with haptic technology to enhance tactile perception [5].

As found in other studies, the development of accessible ICT holds great promise in supporting the communication needs, language, and social development in people with hearing loss [4, 12, 13].

According to the study, hearing systems and accessories include three broad classes of devices [8]:

- Hearing technology
- Alerting devices
- Communication Support Technology

Today's ICT supported *hearing technology*, which includes hearing devices, Assistive Listening Devices (ALD) and Personal Sound Amplification Products (PSAPs), are powerful miniaturized computing systems, on the one hand, and increasingly offer options for coupling and connectivity with modern communication devices to expand their capabilities on the other [8]. However, even the most sophisticated ICT technology may be of little use if it does not fit well to a person's individual hearing requirements and usage needs [19]. There are other various types of hearing technology that can benefit those with a hearing loss: Smart hearing instruments, adaptive and user-controlled hearing systems, machine learning-based hearing systems for individualization of the listening experience, algorithms for improving the acoustics of sound, and other types of cutting-edge technology which can assist people with hearing loss with listening, speaking and reading.

Alerting devices support visual modalities with the use of light and, in some cases, vibrations, or a combination of them, to alert users to specific events (clock alarm, fire alarm, doorbell, IoT devices, baby monitors). However, such devices need to be developed in strong connection with the end users according to the Universal Design principles, and adapted for the users who will be using them [9].

Communication Support Technology, also known as Augmentative and Alternative Communication (AAC), are devices and tools for improving communication skills, like telecommunication services, person-to-person interactions, collaborative and cooperative services. Using accessible AAC for communication and collaborative activities can encourage a group of persons to improve their use of language and their understanding of concepts as they plan and carry out their work. Despite many advances in this field, there remain challenges like the marginalization of people with severe hearing loss, and the need for research-driven technical development to optimize technology and precision of AAC devices [10].

Other emerging hearing systems and accessories include eXtended Reality (XR) glasses, real-time captioning systems with Automatic Speech Recognition and advanced computer vision algorithms. Furthermore, accessible and adaptive hearing systems, as, for example, in XR environments, can support visual modalities with avatars, pictures, signs or text on screen, allowing individuals to extend both their general knowledge and use of language without listening [20].

The following sections of the paper examine the challenges discussed by authors working in Communication Support Technology in higher education and in interpretation, as well as in human factors.

2 Support in Higher Education

Bogdanova (2020) [3] present the challenge of integrating people with disabilities into society, which requires not only the technical and informational implementation, but also to implement legislative initiatives as well. It is evident that, for example in Russia, all Russian universities are taking care in the development of the methodological tools which promote inclusion of students with disabilities. For example, for students with hearing loss it is needed to develop individual educational paths on collectivism and dialogical principles. These methods include a preview of learning material on the Learning Management System platform, together with quizzes and answering questions in essays. Another method defines the organization of the group activities together with hearing students, where students with hearing loss read the assignment and give results in a collaborative way in the shared document. Such combined group activities with the ICT support is claimed to reduce hearing workload and promote visual support. Additionally, in the study, they found that hearing students learn more successfully communication with students with hearing loss, which, at the same time, increases the tolerance in communication.

3 Sign Language to Text Interpretation

Live sign language to captioning interpretation is seen as a challenge, since the usual method involves sign language users, a sign language interpreter, who reads and vocalizes the sign language of the speaker and a high speed typist, who generates captions from the vocalization. Tanaka [17] noted that such method doubles labor costs and delays captioning provision. He proposes to use a crowdsourcing method with a non-expert typist, but who can perform sign language interpretation. In his study, where live video segmentation in short videos has been used, he found that non-expert users took approximately three times a segment's length to finish text captioning via a website. In this way, at least 11 users would be required to reduce the necessary workload for captioning. Crowdsourcing captioning illustrates that the idea of using multiple users for writing captions can be an effective way of performing captioning by a wide range of users with different skills and abilities.

4 Captioning

Captions allow translation of the auditory information into a visual representation on the screen. They give all viewers, including those who are deaf or hard of hearing people, a visual medium to follow video content that includes an auditory track. Usually, the live captioning quality is affected by the delay of a human stenographer's response in listening and transcribing live speech, and, consequentially, has a higher error rate due to transcribing under pressure. To help this challenge, Automatic Speech Recognition (ASR) has become used widely. While ASR is fast, its performance in transcribing and punctuating live speech has been less accurate than transcribing pre-recorded speech, as it has less time to make a decision on what has been said, and is unable to take the words that follow an utterance into account [6]. However, as ASR services have become more accurate and complex, these services have begun to incorporate reliable automatic punctuation into their transcriptions, through a combination of lexical and prosodic features, such as pause length in speech. Before the widespread adoption of ASR solutions, captions for television, education or courtroom reporting were generated by human-powered captioning services such as stenography or re-speaking, that usually generated punctuated captions [7]. Datta et al. [6] noted that the issue of evaluating punctuation versus unpunctuated captions was not considered until the advent of ASR. In their study, they found that viewers reported that punctuation improves the "readability" experience for deaf, hard of hearing and hearing viewers, regardless of whether it was generated via ASR or humans. In this way, the results of the study show the importance of using punctuation in the ASR systems as well.

In another study, done by Wakatsuki et al. [21], the authors investigated the tendency and characteristics of gaze behavior in deaf and hard of hearing people during captioned lectures. Additionally, they created hybrid captions, where part of the slides had been inserted into the captioning text, and made comparison between classical captioning and hybrid captioning. The study showed that there was no significance difference in the average gaze count between classical and hybrid captioning. Results from the experiment supported the findings from Behm et al. [2], where they argued that trailing captions that are positioned close to the instructor as the information source are easier to read and understand.

5   Distance Communication for Deaf Blind People

The field of Communication Support Technology for distance communication in various public or outside places for the deaf-blind is not well researched according to Onishi et al. [18] even though there are commonly used methods of communication for the deaf-blind, like tactile sign language and Braille. There are researchers working with solutions for supporting distance communication, like using hand tracking technology and a 3D-printed bio inspired robotic arm, or using wearable technology using telecommunication solutions. However, deaf-blind people have to be able to master Tactile Sign Language for the first case, or a stable and high-speed Internet supported single mobile telephone line for the second case.

Onishi et al. proposed a system for casual and remote communication between many users which incorporated hearing and non-hearing users. The interface of the system includes Braille display and WebSocket communication in a way that information can be shared between hearing users, who are not familiar with Tactile Sign language and are able to be connected using voice input or chat keyboard input. With the proposed interface, users can speak in chronological order and avoid conflicts of simultaneous talking. With this proposed system, there is no need to involve an additional person, who is in charge to work as a relay user for deaf-blind users.

6 Visiting Museums for Hard of Hearing People

Visiting museums is one of the important activities for lifelong learning, especially for people with disabilities. In Japan, Wakatsuki et al. [22] found that, in Japan, there are almost no museums which are working on accessibility. For speeding up the process, the authors prepared a 27 item questionnaire for deaf and hard of hearing people, with the aim to find accessible factors, which this target group need when visiting museums. As a result, visitors with hearing loss noted that, in a museum, they could not understand spoken explanations or announcements, and that there was a need for sign language interpretation. Additionally, they found that participants would generally prefer to navigate in the museum at their own pace with the help of accessible technology. In this way, the authors prepared videos with sign language for triggering by the QR code, which has been proposed as a proof-of-concept experiment.

7 Discussion and Conclusion

The thread that appears from all the papers presented in the session Hearing Systems and Accessories for People with Hearing Loss is in the support with Communication Suppor Technology. This applies captioning, sign language video presentation and interpretation and communication at the Higher Education Institution.

From the studies undertaken by the various authors, it is evident that there remains the need to make adaptations to standard forms of communication and presentation for deaf and hard of hearing persons. Ease of access and strategies that offer extra support in terms of captioning, sign language video, visual presentation of text based materials, for example, is one of the main important goals for universal design for the deaf and hard of hearing.

References

1. Brauer, B.A., Braden, J.P., Pollard, R.Q., Hardy-Braz, S.T.: Deaf and hard of hearing people. In: Sandoval, J.H., Frisby, C.L., Geisinger, K. F., Scheuneman, J.D., Grenier, J.R. (eds.) Test Interpretation and Diversity: Achieving Equity in Assessment, pp. 297–315. American Psychological Association (1998)
2. Behm, G.W., Kushalnagar, R.S., Stanislow, J.S., Kelstone, A.W.: Enhancing accessibility of engineering lectures for deaf & hard of hearing (DHH): real-time tracking text displays (RTTD) in classrooms. In: ASEE Annual Conference & Exposition, Seattle, Washington (2015). https://doi.org/10.18260/p.23995
3. Bogdanova, S.: Forms and methods of work with hard of hearing students at technical higher educational institutions in the "jurisprudence" discipline. In: Unpublished Paper for the 17th International Conference on Computers Helping People with Special Needs (2020)

4. Capitão, S., Almeida, A.M.P., Vieira, R.M.: Connecting families and schools of students with deafness: describing the ICT and internet use in education. Procedia Comput. Sci. **14**, 163–172 (2012)
5. Dammeyer, J., Nielsen, A., Strøm, E., Hendar, O., Eiríksdóttir, V.K.: A case study of tactile language and its possible structure: a tentative outline to study tactile language systems among children with congenital deafblindness. J. Commun. Disord. Deaf Stud. Hear. Aids **3** (2), 1–7 (2015)
6. Datta, P., Jakubowicz, P., Garcia, J., Hwang, C., Vogler, C., Kushalnagar, R.: Readability of punctuation in both automatic and human-generated subtitles. In: Unpublished Paper for the 17th International Conference on Computers Helping People with Special Needs (2020)
7. Downey, G.: Constructing "Computer-Compatible" stenographers: the transition to real-time transcription in courtroom reporting. Technol. Cult. **47**(1), 1–26 (2006)
8. EPRS: Assistive technologies for people with disabilities, Part II: Current and emerging technologies. European Parliament, Brussel (2018)
9. Gjøsæter, T., Radianti, J., Chen, W.: Universal design of ICT for emergency management. In: Antona, M., Stephanidis, C. (eds.) UAHCI 2018. LNCS, vol. 10907, pp. 63–74. Springer, Cham (2018). https://doi.org/10.1007/978-3-319-92049-8_5
10. Light, J., et al.: Challenges and opportunities in augmentative and alternative communication: research and technology development to enhance communication and participation for individuals with complex communication needs. Augmentative Altern. Commun. **35**(1), 1–12 (2019)
11. Marschark, M., Tang, G., Knoors, H.: Bilingualism and Bilingual Deaf Education. Oxford University Press, USA (2014)
12. Nordin, N.M., Zaharudin, R., Yasin, M.H.M., Din, R., Embi, M.A., Lubis, M.A.: ICT in education for deaf learners: teachers' perspective. Res. J. Appl. Sci. **8**(2), 103–111 (2013)
13. Pyfers, L.: Sign 2.0: ICT for sign language users: information sharing, interoperability, user-centered design and collaboration. In: Miesenberger, K., Karshmer, A., Penaz, P., Zagler, W. (eds.) ICCHP 2012. LNCS, vol. 7383, pp. 188–191. Springer, Heidelberg (2012). https://doi.org/10.1007/978-3-642-31534-3_29
14. Ruberg, K.: Untreated disabling hearing loss costs billions – in the US and the rest of the world. The Hearing Review (2019)
15. Samčović, A.: Accessibility of services in digital television for hearing impaired consumers. Assistive Technology (2020)
16. Shield, B.: Hearing loss – Numbers and costs. evaluation of the social and economic costs of hearing impairment. Brunel University, London (2019)
17. Tanaka, K.: A study examining a real-time sign language-to-text interpretation system using crowdsourcing. In: Unpublished Paper for the 17th International Conference on Computers Helping People with Special Needs (2020)
18. Onishi, J., Miura, T., Okamoto, T., Matsuo, M., Sakajiri, M.: Distance communication assistant system for deaf blind person. In: Unpublished Paper for the 17th International Conference on Computers Helping People with Special Needs (2020)
19. Vestergaard, K.L., Öberg, M., Nielsen, C., Naylor, G., Kramer, S.E.: Factors influencing help seeking, hearing aid uptake, hearing aid use and satisfaction with hearing aids: a review of the literature. Trends Amplification **14**(3), 127–154 (2010)
20. Waldow, K., Fuhrmann, A.: Addressing deaf or hard-of-hearing people in avatar-based mixed reality collaboration systems. In: IEEE Conference on Virtual Reality and 3D User Interfaces Abstracts and Workshops (VRW), pp. 595–596. IEEE (2020)
21. Wakatsuki, D., Arai, T., Shionome, T.: Analysis of the gaze behavior in deaf and hard-of-hearing students during a captioned lecture. In: Unpublished Paper for the 17th International Conference on Computers Helping People with Special Needs (2020)

22. Wakatsuki, D., Kobayashi, M., Miyagi, M., Kato, N., Namatame, M.: Survey for people with visual impairment or hearing loss on using museums in Japan. In: Unpublished Paper for the 17th International Conference on Computers Helping People with Special Needs (2020)
23. WHO and ITU: Safe Listening Devices and Systems: A WHO-ITU Standard. Geneva: World Health Organization and International Telecommunication Union (2019)

A Study Examining a Real-Time Sign Language-to-Text Interpretation System Using Crowdsourcing

Kohei Tanaka[(⊠)], Daisuke Wakatsuki, and Hiroki Minagawa

National University Corporation Tsukuba University of Technology,
4-3-15 Amakubo, Tukuba-shi, Ibaraki-Ken 305-0005, Japan
{a193101,waka,minagawa}@a.tsukuba-tech.ac.jp

Abstract. The current study examined how to use crowdsourcing to convert sign language-to-text. Generally in Japan, a sign language interpreter reads and vocalizes the sign language of the speaker, and caption typists generate captions from the vocalization. However, this method doubles labor costs and delays caption provision. Therefore, we developed a system that interprets sign language-to-caption text via crowdsourcing, with non-experts performing interpretations. While many individuals classified as deaf/hard-of-hearing (DHH) who can read sign language are suitable for this task, not all of them possess adequate typing skills. To address this, our system divides live sign language video into shorter segments, distributing them to workers. After the worker interprets and types the segments to text, the system generates captions through integration of these texts. Furthermore, we provide a user interface for playback speed control and one second rewinding in order to improve the ease with which tasks are completed. Our system can establish an environment that not only allows the interpretation of sign language-to-caption text, but also provides an opportunity for DHH individuals to assist those that are unable read sign language. We conducted a test using our prototype system for sign language-to-text interpretation. The mean time it took a worker to finish a task was 26 s for a 9 s segment. The combined total rate of missing text and collision between segments was 66%. Analysis of questionnaire responses found that workers assigned fewer tasks considered the tasks more enjoyable.

Keywords: Crowdsourcing · Deaf and hard-of-hearing · Real-time sign language-to-text interpretation

1 Introduction

The current study examined how to use crowdsourcing to convert sign language to text. Generally, in Japan, a sign language interpreter reads and vocalizes a speaker's sign language, and caption typists generate captions from the vocalization. However, this method doubles labor costs and delays the provision of captioning. Therefore, we

This study was partially supported by JSPS KAKENHI Grant Number JP15K01056 and JP19K02996.

developed a system that interprets sign language-to-caption text via crowdsourcing, with non-experts performing interpretations. Here, a non-expert is defined as a person who can read sign language with no experience as a captioner or otherwise.

While many individuals classified as deaf/hard-of-hearing (DHH) who can read sign language are suitable workers for this task, not all of them possess adequate typing skills. To address this, our system divides live sign language video into shorter segments, distributing them to workers. After the worker interprets and types the segments to text, the system generates captions through integration of these texts. Our system can establish an environment that not only allows the interpretation of sign language-to-caption text, but also provides an opportunity for DHH individuals to assist those that are unable read sign language. In this report, we describe a prototype system for sign language-to-text interpretation and provide results from the evaluation of the experiment.

2 Related Works

2.1 Speech-to-Text Captioning via Crowdsourcing

Communication access real-time translation (CART) [1], which uses stenography and a special keyboard, and C-Print [2], which uses a common PC, have been developed to provide real-time speech-to-text captioning. In Japan, IPtalk [3] is often used to make captions by having typists collaborate with each other. The web version of captiOnline [4] has also been used recently. Furthermore, SCRIBE [5] is a real-time captioning system that uses crowdsourcing. The system divides the audio stream into equal length segments. A worker, who is a non-expert, types the text from an assigned segment. Texts generated by workers are merged and provided to users as captions. By overlapping adjacent segments, words appearing in the text will be partially the same. A caption with the fewest number of errors is generated by merging them together. In addition, TimeWarp to improve performance of captioning task was also proposed [6]. The idea is to slow down the playback speed while working on a task and speed up the playback speed while waiting. This mechanism works well when there is a large difference between the worker's typing speed and speaker's talking speed. However, it is not obvious that this method is effective for sign language. One of the reasons is that, unlike transcription of speech, transcription of sign language requires translation. That is, depending on the words selected for translation, it may not be possible to merge them.

2.2 Sign Language-to-Text Captioning via Crowdsourcing

A study on direct sign language-to-text interpretation via crowdsourcing has been conducted [7]. Since sign language captioning requires translation that is distinct from speech transcription, it is difficult to use textual merging with overlap between segments. So, one worker takes charge of the task of creating segments in semantic unit. A segment is assigned to a group of workers. Each worker in the group interprets the segment and types text, that is, multiple texts are generated in the group. One text representing the segment is selected from the group by a vote of workers responsible for evaluating the quality of the texts. However, the workload of workers typing text and the quality of the caption depends on the skill of each worker creating segments. Because signs are read visually, workers sometimes overlook them while typing. Since the system is based on live speech in sign language at the scene, workers are not supported when they overlook signs.

Four studies on the expansion and improvement of this system have been reported.

The first method was to give workers as little stress as possible while swapping the number of workers in a group to equalize the number of workers in a worker group when they joined or left the group [8]. The second method was to swap workers in a worker group while balancing the skills of workers as they joined and left the group [9]. The third method was for a group of workers to execute the task of interpreting text and, if incomplete, complete the words that were not written by referring to other workers' translations [10]. The fourth method was to assign tasks to workers that were commensurate with their abilities while keeping the number of tasks assigned to workers as even as possible [11]. However, these studies have not improved the workload of the worker creating segments or prevented sign language oversight while typing.

3   Captioning System

3.1   System Structure

First, our system divided a live video of a sign language speaker into shorter and equal length segments, distributing them to workers via crowdsourcing. Second, a worker interpreted the sign language performed in a given segment, and created the appropriate text by typing it as a crowdsourced task. Finally, the system generated captions through integration of the texts created by workers. Workers were inserted into a queue to accept interpretation tasks. Workers who finished a given task were requeued. Therefore, faster workers received an more segments.

Shorter segments of sign language video made it easier for workers to create text, even if they were not adept at typing. Furthermore, we provided a user interface for playback speed control and one second rewinding in order to improve the ease in which tasks were completed.

Sign language video segments were automatically edited to equal lengths within our system, and the task of each segment was assigned to a different worker. Therefore, to eliminate missing text between segments, our system overlapped adjacent segments for a period of one second. Furthermore, the worker's task environment included live typing progress for workers who were assigned to the previous and next segments. This allowed for collaboration between workers, and we could expect natural connections between segments.

The system architecture was designed with YouTube Live [12] and a task control page, task execution page, and caption display page (see Fig. 1). The task control page divided segments of the speaker's live sign language video and assigned tasks to workers. The task execution page provided a user interface for interpreting and typing sign language while the worker watched a live sign language video of the speaker. The caption display page displayed the results of a worker's captions for an assigned task on the screen in the order of the task. The system's server was implemented in the platform Node.js [13]. The client was created via the website and used the YouTube Player API [14] to allow the website to view and control the video.

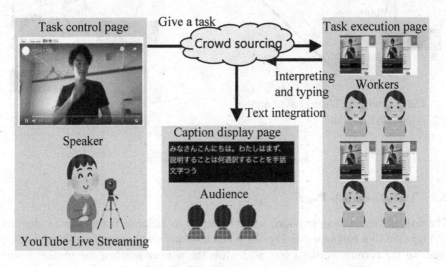

Fig. 1. A real-time sign language-to-text interpretation system architecture

3.2 Task Control Page

When the speaker clicked the "Start" button on the "Task Control" page, it started to divide the sign language video into segments of predetermined length and assign tasks to workers (see Fig. 2). At that time, the video playback time of the workers' interface was synchronized with the video playback time of the task control page. The segments were all set to an equal length. In this system, the real time was based on the playback time of the task control page. Workers in the worker queue were waiting to watch the video in real time. A task was assigned to a worker de-queued in the worker queue and that worker started the task.

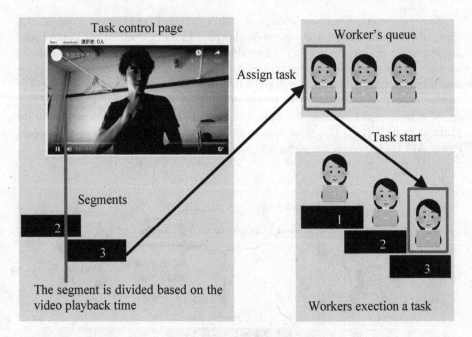

Fig. 2. Task control page structure

3.3   Task Execution Page

The task execution page provided a user interface to facilitate the worker to interpret and type the sign language (see Fig. 3). When a worker was assigned a task, the worker typed in the current worker's text field while the worker watched the speaker's sign language video. The previous and next segments displayed the live typing progress of a worker and allowed them to see missing or duplicate characters between segments. Workers alternated between reading sign language videos and typing text, sometimes overlooking the speaker's sign language. To address this, there were buttons and shortcut keys for the video controls, and the functions were 1-s rewind, pause, and playback speed control. Instructions on what the worker should do were displayed in the instruction frame. There are three types of instructions: "Start your sign language to text task," "Fast forward and wait until you make up for the delay," and "Wait for next task." "Start your sign language to text task" instructions were displayed in the instruction frame when the worker was assigned a task. Then the worker started interpreting and typing the speaker's sign language. "Fast forward and wait until you make up for the delay" instructions were displayed in the instruction frame when the worker completed the task. When workers used the video control functions, there was a delay from the live speech of the speaker. Workers made up for the delay with the fast forward playback based on the playback time of the video on the task control page in order to get the context. "Wait for next task" instructions were displayed when the worker caught up. Then the worker waited until the next task was assigned.

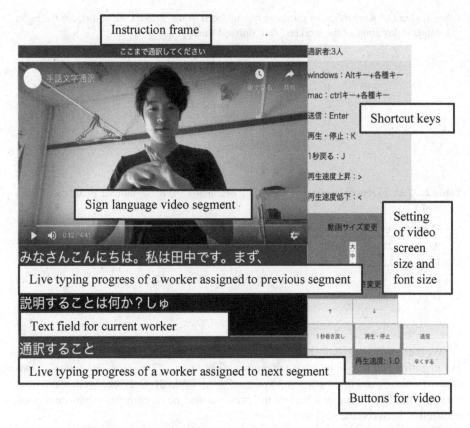

Fig. 3. Task execution page for sign language-to-text interpretation.

4   Experiments and Results

We conducted a test using our prototype system for sign language-to-text interpretation. Workers were four university students with DHH, who could read sign language. The workers had been using sign language for over 7 years. The video used for interpretation was 6 min, 54 s in length. Each segment of video was set to 9 s in length. The 9 s length was determined by the mean delimitation time of the task in a previous study [7]. When a worker was given the instruction "Fast forward and wait until you make up for the delay", the video playback speed was 1.5 speed. Before the test, the typing speed of the workers was measured. We analyzed workers' behavior logs in the task environment and their responses to questionnaires.

The mean Japanese character typing speed of workers was 1.9 CPS (characters per second; SD 0.3 CPS), with the highest and lowest being 2.4 CPS and 1.6 CPS, respectively (see Table 1). The mean time it took for workers finish tasks was 26.0 s (SD 13.1 s). Missing text and collision rates between segments were both 33%. The mean number of times a worker was assigned to a task was 12.3 (SD 5.4) with the highest and lowest being 21 and 7, respectively (see Table 2).

Table 1. Data of workers (m_c is the mean typing speed of the workers. m_s and σ_s are the mean and standard deviation of the workers' task finished times.)

Workers	m_c [CPS]	m_s [sec]	σ_s [sec]
A	2.4	16.7	2.2
B	1.9	25.7	9.9
C	1.7	45.2	8.3
D	1.6	33.6	14.7
All	1.9	26.0	13.1

Table 2. Task execution count and subjective evaluation (n_t is the number of times of tasks executed.)

Workers	n_t [time]	Ref. of next and prev. segment [Y/N]	Enjoyment of task [score]
A	21	No	2
B	12	No	3
C	7	No	3
D	9	Yes	4

Workers were asked in a questionnaire about the enjoyability of the task, with 1 = *negative* and 5 = *positive*. Results were one "2 = *weak negative*", two "3 s = *neither*", and one "4 = *weak positive*" (see Table 2). Only one worker reported checking the live typing progress of the previous and next segments to ensure a good connection between the segments.

"Ref. of next and prev. segment" was measured by the response to "Did you check the live typing progress in the previous and next segments?" "Enjoyment of task" was measured by the response to "Did you have a good time?"

5 Discussion

The mean time it took a worker finished a task was 26 s in a 9 s segment. In other words, workers took approximately three times as long as the segment's length to finish the translation to transcription task. Analysis of workers' behavior logs showed that slow typing was a major factor in the time it took. Workers with good typing skills finished tasks faster, whereas those with poor skills finished slower. In the future, we would like to try to experiment with methods to dynamically control the time of a task so that each worker's delay time is the same as the working memory retention time.

To reduce the text missing between the segments, we overlapped adjacent segments for one second, and allowed workers to check the live typing progress of previous and next segments. However, the combined total rate of missing text and collision between segments was 66%. After surveying the questionnaire, only one worker checked the progress of live typing in the previous and next segments. It is still considered that non-expert workers did not have time to check for missing or collisions between segments and sign language-to-text interpretation at the same time. In future studies, we would like to try to reduce these problems by adding a new worker task to revise text for missing segments and collisions and errors. In addition, we would like to evaluate the quality of the caption generation to demonstrate the feasibility of a sign language-to-text interpretation system.

Because only four workers participated in this experiment, all workers were immediately assigned to new tasks after being requeued. Given this, there was an approximate three-fold difference in finished tasks between the fastest and slowest workers. Analysis of questionnaire responses found that workers assigned fewer tasks considered the tasks more enjoyable. To determine the workforce required for optimum enjoyment, a simulation was conducted based on the slowest worker. We estimate the number of workers required by our system. The required number of workers Nw can be expressed as the sum of the time Tt that a worker spends on the task and the time Tc spent on the chasing replay afterwards, divided by the time of the segment Ts:

$$Nw = (Tt + Tc)/Ts \qquad (1)$$

where $Tc = (Tt - Ts)/(Rc - Rs)$, where Rc is the playback speed of the chase. Rs is the standard playback speed, i.e., 1x. Based on the slowest worker, $Nw = 14.85$, with a worst-case scenario of about 15 workers needed ($Tt = 45.2$ s, $Ts = 8$ s (because of the 1 s overlap), $Rc = 1.5$x). Results found that 15 workers would be required to reduce workload and increase enjoyment. In the future, we would like to evaluate workers' impressions by measuring system usability scale of worker interfaces.

6 Conclusion

We developed a system that interprets sign language-to-caption text via crowdsourcing, with non-experts performing interpretations. We conducted a test using our proto-type system for sign language-to-text interpretation.

The test results showed three findings: first, the slow typing of the workers was a major cause of slower workflow; and second, the non-expert workers did not have time to check for missing and collisions between segments of text and interpret from sign language-to-text at the same time; finally, 15 workers would be required to reduce the workload and increase workers' enjoyment.

In the future we would like to achieve four things. First, we would like to experiment with a method to dynamically control the time of the task so that each worker's delay time is equal to the working memory retention time; second, we would like to try to mitigate these problems by adding a new task for workers to revise the missing text and collisions between segments, and text errors in the task results; third, we would like to evaluate the quality of the caption generation and demonstrate the feasibility of a sign language-to-text interpretation system; finally, we would like to evaluate worker impressions by measuring the system usability scale of the worker interface.

Acknowledgements. We would like to thank Editage (www.editage.com) for English language editing.

References

1. Preminger, J.E., Levitt, J.E.: Computer-Assisted Remote Transcription (CART): a tool to aid people who are deaf or hard of hearing in the workplace. Volta Rev. **99**(4), 219–230 (1997)
2. Elliot, L.B., Stinson, M.S., McKee, B.G., Everhart, V.S., Francis, P.J.: College students' perceptions of the c-print speech-to-text transcription system. J. Deaf Stud. Deaf Educ. **6**(4), 285–298 (2001)
3. Kurita, S.: Development of CART software "IPtalk" and captioning services via personal computers: Communication support for the hearing-impaired. J. Inf. Process. Manag. **59**(6), 366–376 (2016). https://doi.org/10.1241/johokanri.59.366
4. Wakatsuki, D., Kato, N., Shionome, T., Kawano, S., Nishioka, T., Naito, I.: Development of web-based remote speech-to-text interpretation system captionline. JACIII **21**(2), 310–320 (2017). https://doi.org/10.20965/jaciii.2017.p0310
5. Lasecki, W.S., et al.: Real-time captioning by groups of non-experts. In: Proceedings of the ACM Symposium on User Interface Software and Technology (UIST 2012), pp. 23–34 (2012)
6. Lasecki, W.S., Miller, C.D., Bigham, J.P.: Warping time for more effective real-time crowdsourcing. In: Proceedings of the International ACM Conference on Human Factors in Computing Systems (CHI 2013), pp. 2033–2036 (2013)
7. Shiraishi, Y., Zhang, J., Wakatsuki, D., Kumai, K., Morishima, A.: Crowdsourced real-time captioning of sign language by deaf and hard-of-hearing people. Int. J. Pervasive Comput. Commun. **13**(1), 2–25 (2017)
8. Kumai, K., Zhang, J., Shiraishi, Y., Wakatsuki, D., Kitagawa, H., Morishima, A.: Group rotation management in real-time crowdsourcing. In: Proceedings of 19th International Conference on Information Integration and Web-based Applications & Services (iiWAS 2017), pp. 23–31 (2017)
9. Kumai, K., et al.: Skill-and-stress-aware assignment of crowd-worker groups to task streams. In: The sixth AAAI Conference on Human Computation and Crowdsourcing (HCOMP2018), pp. 88–97 (2018)
10. Shionome, T., et al.: Complement of incomplete task results for real-time crowdsourcing interpretation. In: Proceedings of 21th International Conference on Asian Language Processing (IALP 2017), pp. 359–362 (2017)
11. Hashimoto, H., Matsubara, M., Shiraishi, Y., Wakatsuki, D., Zhang J., Morishima, A.: A task assignment method considering inclusiveness and activity degree. In: Proceedings of The Second IEEE Workshop on Human-in-the-loop Methods and Human Machine Collaboration in BigData (IEEE HMData2018), pp. 3498–3503 (2018)
12. YouTube Live. https://www.youtube.com/live?gl=JP&hl=ja. Accessed 4 June 2020
13. Node.js. https://nodejs.org/. Accessed 4 June 2020
14. YouTube Player API. https://developers.google.com/youtube/iframe_api_reference?hl=ja. Accessed 4 June 2020

Readability of Punctuation in Automatic Subtitles

Promiti Datta[2], Pablo Jakubowicz[1], Christian Vogler[1],
and Raja Kushalnagar[1(✉)]

[1] Gallaudet University, Washington, DC 20002, USA
raja.kushalnagar@gallaudet.edu
[2] University of Toronto, Toronto, ON, Canada

Abstract. Automatic subtitles are widely used for subtitling television and online videos. Some include punctuation while others do not. Our study with 21 participants watching subtitled videos found that viewers reported that punctuation improves the "readability" experience for deaf, hard of hearing, and hearing viewers, regardless of whether it was generated via ASR or humans. Given that automatic subtitles have become widely integrated into online video and television programs, and that nearly 20% of television viewers in US or UK use subtitles, there is evidence that supports punctuation in subtitles has the potential to improve the viewing experience for a significant percentage of the all television viewers, including people who are deaf, hard of hearing, and hearing.

Keywords: Subtitles · Deaf · Hard of hearing

1 Introduction

Subtitles allow translation of auditory information into a visual representation on the screen. Subtitles give all viewers, including those who are deaf or hard of hearing a visual medium to follow video content that includes an auditory track. Improving the availability and accuracy of subtitles offers benefits for everyone, regardless of whether they are deaf, hard of hearing or hearing or not. In fact, nearly 20% of the population in the US or UK use subtitles; and 80% of them are hearing [3, 4]. Many hearing viewers who watch subtitles do so because they are learning English as a second language or watching TV in noisy settings such as pubs. Before the widespread adoption of Automatic Speech Recognition (ASR), subtitles for television, education, or courtroom reporting were generated by human-powered subtitling services such as stenography or re-speaking, that usually generated punctuated subtitles [2, 6, 7]. So, the issue of evaluating punctuation versus unpunctuated subtitles was not considered until the advent of ASR.

Live subtitling is challenging, as the text needs to be produced immediately, with almost no time for reaction and correction. The accuracy of ASR services with low latency has vastly increased the amount of television programming that can be subtitled. However, some ASR services include punctuation while others do not. While it seems intuitively true that subtitles will be harder to read without punctuation, this has

© Springer Nature Switzerland AG 2020
K. Miesenberger et al. (Eds.): ICCHP 2020, LNCS 12377, pp. 195–201, 2020.
https://doi.org/10.1007/978-3-030-58805-2_23

not been widely investigated, because human-generated subtitles are usually punctu-ated. Our study investigates how punctuation in subtitles is related to ease of reading and contributes to the overall "readability" experience. It compares viewer experiences for both human and ASR generated punctuated and unpunctuated subtitles.

2 Related Work

ASR is being integrated into television and video streaming services. For example, YouTube offers 'automatic subtitles' using its ASR services. Other streaming services use Google's 'Cloud Speech-to-Text'[1], Microsoft's 'Speech Services'[2], or Amazon's 'Amazon Transcribe'[3], and video players are integrating ASR in their options. While ASR is fast, its performance in transcribing and punctuating live speech has been less accurate than transcribing pre-recorded speech, as the machine has less time to make decisions on what has been said and is unable to take the words that follow an utterance into account. However, as automatic speech recognition services have become more accurate and complex, these services have begun to incorporate reliable automatic punctuation into their transcriptions, through a combination of lexical and prosodic features, such as pause length in speech. In live stenography for television, the stenographers utilize the same training as a court stenographer [2], with. For live television subtitling, speakers tend to speak with less structure and more variance than in court, so subtitling quality is usually inferior to court reporting. The subtitling quality is affected by the delay of a human stenographer's or re-speaker's response in listening and transcribing live speech, and usually has a higher error rate due to transcribing under pressure [1, 5].

3 Methods

3.1 Video

For the study, we gathered four videos with different subtitle generation and formatting: 1) punctuated subtitles generated by re-speakers, 2) unpunctuated subtitles generated by re-speakers, 3) punctuated subtitles generated by Google Live Transcribe[4], and 4) YouTube Automatic Subtitles[5]. All video clips were taken from live television broadcasts. Each video was trimmed into a two to four-minute clip that contained one segment of the television show. For the purpose of this experiment, the clips were categorized into news segments, and talk show segments (Table 1).

---

[1] https://cloud.google.com/speech-to-text/.

[2] https://azure.microsoft.com/en-us/services/cognitive-services/speech-services/.

[3] https://aws.amazon.com/transcribe/.

[4] https://www.android.com/accessibility/live-transcribe.

[5] https://support.google.com/youtube/answer/6373554?hl=en.

Table 1. Methodology

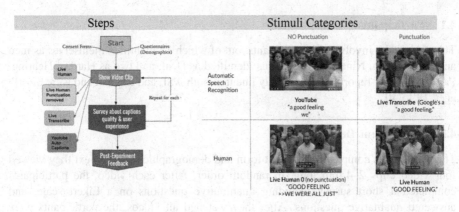

3.2 Types of Subtitling

Live Human Generated Subtitles with and without Punctuation. Television networks hire professional stenographers or re-speakers to generate live subtitles as a show is broadcasted. The subtitles are comprehensive and contain very few grammatical mistakes but may use paraphrasing and do not follow the exact words of the speaker. The subtitles were downloaded from recorded videos using CCExtractor. For these subtitles, the re-speakers have explicitly added punctuation. For this experiment, one version of the subtitles contained all the original punctuation, and one had all commas, periods, exclamation marks, and question marks removed.

Auto-generated Subtitles with and without Punctuation. The auto-generated subtitles were made using either Google's YouTube auto-subtitling service, or Google's Live Transcribe app. Both had similar word accuracies for each of the videos, however Live Transcribe provided automatic punctuation and YouTube subtitles did not (Table 2).

Table 2. Subtitle type

	Human	ASR
Punctuation	Live human subtitles	Live transcribe
No punctuation	Live human subtitles, punctuation removed	YouTube auto-generated subtitles

4   User Evaluation

4.1   Participants

The experiment involved 21 participants, out of which 12 identified themselves as men and 9 as women. Nineteen participants identified as Deaf, and two as Hard of Hearing. Participants self-reported being mostly fluent in both ASL and English and were mostly ages 18 to 40.

4.2   Experiment Design

The participants completed a consent form and demographic survey. Next they viewed four video clips 2–4 min long, in random order. After each video, the participants completed a short survey including quantitative questions on a Likert scale, and answered qualitative questions. After they watched all videos, the participants were invited to provide feedback doing an overall comparison of all the video subtitles (Table 3).

Table 3. Counterbalancing

G1	G2	G3	G4
LH	LT	LH_0	YT
LT	LH_0	YT	LH
LH_0	YT	LH	LT
YT	LH	LT	LH_0

Each of the subtitle types - live human (LH), live human with no punctuation (LH0), YouTube (YT), and Live Transcribe (LT), were counterbalanced using a Latin Square design with four groups. In each group, the type of video (news or talk show) alternated for each video.

5   Study Results

The videos were chosen to be easy to follow along, so that the viewers could focus on punctuation quality and readability, and not be distracted by too many incorrect words or difficult content. After completing the video section of the experiment, participants were asked to give short answers describing their experience reading punctuated subtitles vs. non-punctuated subtitles, as well as how much they were able to tolerate punctuation errors. There were common themes across most answers, as 16 out of 21 participants reported that they prefer some level of punctuation in subtitles over no punctuation.

5.1   Ability to Follow Along

Participants reported their ability to follow along with each type of subtitle as shown below. Most people were able to follow along with all four subtitle types, reporting scores of mostly fours and fives, with a bit more variability for the non-punctuated subtitles (YT and LH_0), as shown below, did not have a big impact.

5.2   Subtitle Readability by Format

Punctuated subtitles (LT and LH) were easier to read than non-punctuated subtitles (LH_0 and YT), which had more variability, but overall harder to read. Even with the same exact words, getting rid of punctuation had a noticeable negative impact on readability.

5.3   Comparison

Punctuated subtitles (Live Human and Live Transcribe) had a positive impact on readability compared to non-punctuated subtitles (LH - No Punctuation and YouTube). Many people did not feel the lack of punctuation had a great impact on readability.

5.4   Punctuation in Human Generated Subtitles

In a 2-sample t-test against overall readability scores for Live Human written subtitles versus the same subtitles with the punctuation removed, there was not a significant difference between scores.

5.5   Punctuation in Auto-Generated Subtitles

The 2-sample t-test between readability scores for the punctuated Live Transcribe versus non-punctuated YouTube subtitles, there was a significant preference towards the punctuated subtitles (Table 4).

Table 4. Average ratings by caption type

Question	LH	LH_0	YT	LT
Ability to Follow Along with Captions	4.6	3.6	4.2	4.4
Comprehension of Video	4.5	3.9	3.9	4.2
Word Accuracy	4.3	3.9	3.7	4.1
Readability and Grammar	4.1	3.3	2.7	4.0

5.6   Human Generated Subtitles vs. Auto-Generated Subtitles

There was a stronger preference toward human generated subtitles when human and auto generated subtitles either both had or punctuation or both did not have punctuation. A comparison showed significant preference for the punctuated auto-generated subtitles. Overall, subtitles with punctuation scored significantly higher than non-punctuated subtitles.

The figure above highlights the success of the punctuated Live Transcribe (LT) subtitles over the non-punctuated human subtitles (LH0). These conclusions are further reinforced by a follow up question asked of all participants: "Would you prefer punctuated subtitles with some punctuation errors over non-punctuated subtitles?", 83% said yes.

Common feedback with non-punctuated subtitles was that participants had trouble understanding grammar and sentence structure, run-on sentences, and identifying who was talking. Four people said non-punctuated subtitles were too hard to read.

Participants' comments generally indicated that they spent less effort on reading subtitles with punctuation. "When I read the non-punctuated subtitles, they look like run-on sentences and I have a hard time trying to figure out when they stop talking," "[Punctuated Subtitles] also help me separate concepts, sentences, paragraphs and so on. It makes everything much more transparent". "For non-punctuated subtitles, it made me lose motivation to understand everything because I lost track," "[Non-Punctuated Subtitles] wear my eyes out when I keep reading and notice there is no period. It affects my writing and reading skills".

6   Conclusion

Many DHH users prefer perfect subtitling with punctuation over no punctuation. In some cases, proper punctuation had a greater impact on readability than higher word accuracy. In the survey results and feedback, they mentioned that subtitles with punctuation errors are harder to read due to run-on sentences, not being able to tell who is speaking, and difficult reading complex sentence structures. Punctuation plays a very important role in conveying intended meaning to the language. Errors in punctuation or even wrong placement can change the meaning of the sentence completely and sometimes convert to confusion. Viewers reported they found it much easier to follow subtitles with punctuation.

Acknowledgements. We thank the National Science Foundation, grant #1757836 (REU AICT) and the National Institute on Disability, Independent Living, and Rehabilitation Research (NIDILRR #90DPCP0002). NIDILRR is a Center within the Administration for Community Living (ACL), Department of Health and Human Services (HHS). The contents of this paper do not necessarily represent the policy of NIDILRR, ACL, HHS, and you should not assume endorsement by the Federal Government.

References

1. Arumi-Ribas, M., Romero-Fresco, P.: A practical proposal for the training of respeakers. JoSTrans: J. Spec. Transl. **10**, 106–127 (2008)
2. Downey, G.: Constructing "computer-compatible" stenographers: the transition to real-time transcription in courtroom reporting. Technol. Cult. **47**(1), 1–26 (2006). https://doi.org/10.1353/tech.2006.0068
3. Jordan, A.B., Albright, A., Branner, A., Sullivan, J.: The state of closed captioning services in the United States. Washington, DC (2003). https://dcmp.org/learn/static-assets/nadh136.pdf
4. United Kingdom Ofcom. Television Access Services: Review of the Code and Guidance (2006)
5. Romero-Fresco, P., Martinez, J.: Accuracy Rate in Live Subtitling – the NER Model (2011). https://roehampton.openrepository.com/roehampton/bitstream/10142/141892/1/NER-English.pdf
6. Stinson, M.S., Elliot, L.B., Kelly, R.R.: Deaf and hard-of-hearing students' memory of lectures with speech-to-text and interpreting/note taking services. J. Spec. Educ. **43**(1), 52–64 (2008). https://doi.org/10.1177/0022466907313453
7. Wald, M.: Using automatic speech recognition to enhance education for all students: turning a vision into reality. In: 2005 Proceedings 35th Annual Conference on Frontiers in Education. FIE 2005, pp. 22–25 (2005). https://doi.org/10.1109/FIE.2005.1612286

Analysis of the Gaze Behavior of Deaf and Hard-of-Hearing Students During a Captioned Lecture

Daisuke Wakatsuki[1]([✉]), Tatsuya Arai[1], and Takeaki Shionome[2]

[1] Tsukuba University of Technology, Amakubo 4-3-15, Tsukuba City, Ibaraki, Japan
{waka,tatsuya}@a.tsukuba-tech.ac.jp
[2] Teikyo University, Toyosatodai 1-1, Utsunomiya City, Tochigi, Japan
shionome@ics.teikyo-u.ac.jp

Abstract. Captions are key tools for allowing deaf and hard-of-hearing audiences to obtain aural (audio) information. In a classroom setting, people with normal hearing can listen to the lecture while referencing the white/blackboard and documents to effectively combine the information, whereas those with hearing impairments cannot. During lectures, people with hearing impairments need to move their eyes (gaze direction) more than those with normal hearing. The purpose of this study is to investigate the tendency and characteristics of gaze behavior of deaf and hard-of-hearing persons during captioned lectures. In the experiment, we analyzed the gaze behavior, in terms of the gaze count and duration, in relation to the following gaze targets (points of gaze): a lecturer with slides (L), handouts (H), and captions (C). Furthermore, we created hybrid captions, wherein parts of the slide were cut out and inserted between chunks of text to reduce eye movement (EM). The study compared the gaze behavior of subjects viewing the hybrid captions to that of subjects viewing normal text-only captions. The gaze behavior for both captions was essentially similar. The analysis of the findings showed that the gaze behavior was not cyclic; instead, it was roundtrip-type behavior centered around L, the source of the lecture content. Additionally, the study suggested that hybrid captions were seamlessly accepted and used in a similar manner as normal captions, even though they did not reduce fatigue caused by EMs.

Keywords: Gaze behavior · Eye movement · Captioned lecture · Deaf and hard-of-hearing · Hearing loss

1 Introduction

Captions are key tools for deaf and hard-of-hearing audiences to obtain aural (audio) information. Many students with hearing loss at Japanese universities

This study was partially supported by JSPS KAKENHI Grant Numbers JP15K01056 and JP19K02996 and was carried out with the permission of the Research Ethics Committee of the Tsukuba University of Technology (approval number: H28–10).

absorb lectures using captions transcribed from the lecturer's voice. People with normal hearing can listen to the lecture while referencing the white/blackboard and documents to effectively combine the information, whereas those with hearing impairments cannot. During lectures, people with hearing impairments need to move their eyes (gaze direction) more than those with normal hearing. A study of eye-tracking of deaf and hard-of-hearing persons is useful to examine the efficacy of caption display and positioning, as well as the fatigue associated with eye movement (EM). The purpose of this study is to investigate the tendencies and characteristics of gaze behavior in deaf and hard-of-hearing persons during captioned lectures. In the experiment, we analyzed gaze behavior, in terms of the gaze count and duration, in relation to the following gaze targets (points of gaze): lectures, handouts, and captions. Furthermore, we created hybrid captions, where parts of the slide were cut out and inserted between chunks of text to reduce EM. The study compared the gaze behavior of subjects viewing the hybrid captions to that of subjects viewing normal text-only captions.

2   Related Works

Communication access real-time translation (CART) [1], which uses stenography and a special keyboard, and C-Print [2], which uses a common PC, have been developed to provide real-time speech-to-text captioning. They have been used and evaluated in educational settings since the 1990s [3]. In recent years, some researchers have proposed introducing new speech-to-text methods into the classroom, such as speech recognition and crowd-sourcing performed by non-experts [4,5]. In science classes, lecturers often refer to mathematical formulas and figures, frequently using indicator words like "this formula" and "that figure." In order to facilitate the integration of mathematical formulas into the captions, cutting the formulas out of the video images of the slides and inserting them between the sentences of the captions has been proposed [6].

However, there is still little research on how people with hearing loss make use of captions. A previous study on gaze behavior analyzed patients with hearing loss who were presented with captions. The study arranged a one-on-one video conference between a person with normal hearing and a person with a hearing impairment and analyzed the EMs of the subjects as they viewed a video with automatic captioning, generated by speech-recognition technology. The study described the relationship between EMs and captions displayed in varying fonts and colors [7]. Furthermore, researchers have developed a presentation device that allows the captions to follow after speaker with a small EM range, and it has been shown to be more advantageous than conventional captions displayed in a fixed position [8]. Many studies have presented techniques to improve text positioning and methods for displaying captions. However, few studies have analyzed how a person with hearing loss utilizes the captions. In this study, we analyzed the gaze behavior of people with hearing loss in a general lecture delivered with captions.

3　Experiment

The purpose of this study is to investigate the gaze behavior of students with
hearing impairments reading captions during simulated mathematics lectures
that present many mathematical formulas and diagrams. The lecture topics
were Apollonius's theorem ($l1$) and Ptolemy's theorem ($l2$) in geometry. The
lecture was approximately 15 min long, including explanations of the theorems
and examples. The lecturer explained the concepts by projecting the slides on
a whiteboard and writing on the board where necessary (Fig. 1). The scene was
filmed and made into a lecture video. The slides were printed onto handouts.
The normal captions ($c1$) were a transcription of the lecturer's speech (Fig. 2),
and the hybrid captions ($c2$) included mathematical formulas and diagrams from
the lecture inserted between chunks of the text from $c1$ (Fig. 3). Both captions
were created using captiOnline, a web-based remote speech-to-text captioning
system [9].

Fig. 1. Simulated mathematics lecture

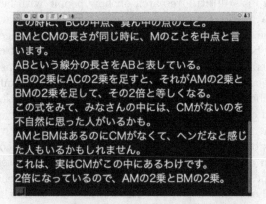

Fig. 2. Ordinary caption

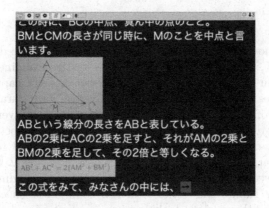

Fig. 3. Hybrid caption

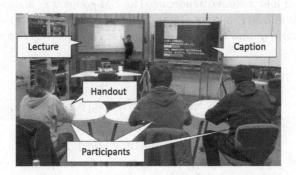

Fig. 4. Condition of experiment

Participants for the experiment were 11 deaf and hard-of-hearing students in their sophomore through senior years of college who absorb daily lectures using normal hearing-impaired captions. Before the study, we verified that the subjects were unfamiliar with the lecture topic used in the experiment. We divided the 11 participants into four groups and evenly allocated them to the four conditions ($l1c1$, $l2c1$, $l1c2$, $l2c2$) so that all the subjects encountered both types of captions. The lecture and video captions were displayed on two 60-in. screens placed side by side (Fig. 4). We filmed the subjects sitting through the lecture video and recorded the gaze targets [caption (C), lecture video (L), handouts (H), and other (O)] along with the lengths of time for which the targets were viewed. The recording was conducted by two people who were not participants in the experiment, and the combined data were used for analysis. For each gaze target, we analyzed the gaze count and duration and EM count, which refers to the number of gaze movements between two gaze targets (e.g., $C \rightarrow L$). The gaze count is defined as the number of times each gaze target is viewed. The gaze duration is the time spent gazing at one target before shifting the gaze to another target.

4   Results

Tables 1 and 2 show the average gaze count and average gaze duration for the gaze targets C, L, H, and O. We performed a t-test to examine whether there were differences in gaze count or gaze duration between the caption types. Significant differences were observed only in the average gaze duration for C at a significance level of 5%. Analysis of the variance between the average gaze count and average gaze duration showed significance in the main effects of all the targets. As a result of multiple comparisons, $c1$ and $c2$ tended to share similar figures for the average gaze count and average gaze duration. L had the highest gaze count, followed by C, H, and O. H had the longest gaze duration, followed by L, C, and O. Table 3 shows the total EM count between each target. We considered O to be the subjects looking away (gaze aversion) and excluded the instances from the data as they made up only 1% of the overall gaze count. As a result, $c1$ and $c2$ had a shared tendency. The EM count was highest in the C–L segment ($C{\rightarrow}L + L{\rightarrow}C$, approx. 55%), followed by the L–H segment ($L{\rightarrow}H + H{\rightarrow}L$, approx. 35%), and the H–C segment ($H{\rightarrow}C + C{\rightarrow}H$, approx. 10%).

Table 1. Average gaze count for each target (times).

Gaze target	$c1$ (%) [SD]	$c2$ (%) [SD]	p(t-test)
C	79.1 (31%) [17.7]	81.0 (34%) [27.8]	$n.s.$
L	114.7 (45%) [20.0]	107.0 (45%) [22.5]	$n.s.$
H	57.4 (23%) [24.6]	49.6 (21%) [26.0]	$n.s.$
O	3.5 (1%) [6.2]	2.6 (1%) [5.6]	$n.s.$
p(ANOVA)	$<.01$	$<.01$	–

Table 2. Average gaze duration for each gaze target (s).

Gaze target	$c1$ [SD]	$c2$ [SD]	p(t-test)
C	2.29 [0.70]	2.73 [1.25]	$<.05$
L	3.67 [1.14]	3.93 [1.67]	$n.s.$
H	5.56 [2.15]	5.76 [2.23]	$n.s.$
O	1.26 [1.31]	0.80 [1.28]	$n.s.$
p(ANOVA)	$<.01$	$<.01$	–

Table 3. Average EM count between gaze targets (times).

EM	c1 (%) [SD]	c2 (%) [SD]	p(t-test)
$C{\rightarrow}L$	66.5 (27%) [22.2]	68.3 (27%) [29.4]	n.s.
$L{\rightarrow}C$	68.2 (27%) [19.1]	68.8 (28%) [26.4]	n.s.
$L{\rightarrow}H$	45.0 (18%) [18.6]	37.1 (15%) [22.0]	n.s.
$H{\rightarrow}L$	46.6 (19%) [24.4]	37.5 (15%) [24.8]	n.s.
$H{\rightarrow}C$	10.3 (4%) [6.3]	11.7 (5%) [10.2]	n.s.
$C{\rightarrow}H$	12.0 (5%) [7.8]	12.4 (5%) [7.8]	n.s.
p(ANOVA)	<.01	<.01	–

5   Discussion and Conclusion

As Table 1 shows, there was no difference in the gaze count between normal captions $c1$ and hybrid captions $c2$. The study suggested that hybrid captions were seamlessly accepted and used in a similar manner as normal captions, even though they did not reduce fatigue caused by EMs. Moreover, as Table 2 illustrates, $c1$ and $c2$ showed differences in the average gaze duration for C. One must carefully read mathematical formulas and figures to understand geometry; therefore, we conclude that the gaze duration increased as the figures, tables, and mathematical formulas were simultaneously read with the text in the hybrid captions.

Positive and negative opinions about the hybrid captions were obtained from the post-experiment comments, such as:
"With the chart, I can understand what the teacher is talking about while watching the video."
"It was easy to see the formulas."
"Because of the limited scope of the text on the screen, I felt that it disappeared quickly from the screen."
"I don't need figures in the captions because it is in the lecture video."
From these comments, we can see individual preferences for different types of captions, as well as problems in viewing hybrid captions.

As can be seen from Table 1 and 2, the gaze count for C accounted for approximately 30% of the total gaze count, second only to L. The gaze duration for C was approximately 2–3 s, shorter than L or H. The subjects looked at C in short bursts. The gaze count for H was low, making up approximately 20% of the total count, but the gaze duration was the longest at 5–6 s, and the variation was significant. We believe this is because the gaze duration for H includes the time spent taking notes and checking documents.

L was viewed the greatest number of times, accounting for approximately 45% of the total gaze count, and the gaze duration was approximately 4 s. Table 3 shows that the mutual EM count, that is, the EM count in the C-L segment (between $C{\rightarrow}L$ and $L{\rightarrow}C$) was approximately evenly split. The same could be said for the segments between L-H and H-C. Furthermore, because the ratio of mutual EM between H-C was low at approximately 10%, the study suggests the gaze behavior was not cyclic behavior, such as viewing L, referencing C, taking notes with H, and viewing L again. Additionally, because the ratios of the mutual EM were high in the C-L and L-H segments, we believe the subjects engaged in roundtrip-type gaze behavior centered around L, the source of the lecture content. Behm et al. argued that trailing captions that are positioned close to the instructor (information source) are easier to read and understand. [8] The data from this study support this argument, that is to say, a high number of EMs in the C-L segment (approximately 55%) validates the appropriate positioning of visual information in lectures.

This study has described the gaze behavior of people with hearing loss during captioned lectures. The findings from this study can facilitate the consideration of what constitutes suitable caption positioning and content and contribute to an environment wherein deaf and hard-of-hearing students can absorb lectures.

Acknowledgements. We would like to thank Editage (www.editage.com) for English language editing.

References

1. Preminger, J.E., Levitt, J.E.: Computer-Assisted Remote Transcription (CART): a tool to aid people who are deaf or hard of hearing in the workplace. Volta Rev. **99**(4), 219–230 (1997)
2. Elliot, L.B., Stinson, M.S., McKee, B.G., Everhart, V.S., Francis, P.J.: College students' perceptions of the C-print speech-to-text transcription system. J. Deaf Stud. Deaf Educ. **6**(4), 285–298 (2001)
3. Marschark, M., et al.: Benefits of sign language interpreting and text alternatives to classroom learning by deaf students. J. Deaf Stud. Deaf Educ. **11**(4), 421–437 (2006)
4. Elliot, L.B., Stinson, M.S., Easton, D., Bourgeois, J.: College students learning with C-print's education software and automatic speech recognition. In: American Educational Research Association Annual Meeting (2008)
5. Lasecki, W.S., et al.: Real-time captioning by groups of non-experts. In: Proceedings of the 25th Annual ACM Symposium on User Interface Software and Technology, pp. 23–34 (2012)
6. Takeuchi, Y., Ohta, H., Ohnishi, N., Wakatsuki, D., Minagawa, H.: Extraction of displayed objects corresponding to demonstrative words for use in remote transcription. In: Miesenberger, K., Klaus, J., Zagler, W., Karshmer, A. (eds.) ICCHP 2010. LNCS, vol. 6180, pp. 152–159. Springer, Heidelberg (2010). https://doi.org/10.1007/978-3-642-14100-3_24
7. Rathbun, K., Berke, L., Caulfield, C., Stinson, M., Huenerfauth, M.: Eye movements of deaf and hard of hearing viewers of automatic captions. In: 32nd Annual International Technology and Persons with Disabilities Conference Scientific/Research Proceedings, San Diego, California, pp. 130–140 (2017)
8. Behm, G.W., Kushalnagar, R.S., Stanislow, J.S., Kelstone, A.W.: Enhancing accessibility of engineering lectures for Deaf & Hard of Hearing (DHH): Real-Time Tracking Text Displays (RTTD) in classrooms. Paper presented at 2015 ASEE Annual Conference & Exposition, Seattle, Washington, June 2015. https://doi.org/10.18260/p.23995
9. Wakatsuki, D., Kato, N., Shionome, T., Kawano, S., Nishioka, T., Naito, I.: Development of web-based remote speech-to-text interpretation system captiOnline. JACIII **21**(2), 310–320 (2017). https://doi.org/10.20965/jaciii.2017.p0310

Survey for People with Visual Impairment or Hearing Loss on Using Museums in Japan

Daisuke Wakatsuki[1](✉), Makoto Kobayashi[2], Manabi Miyagi[3],
Masami Kitamura[1], Nobuko Kato[1], and Miki Namatame[1]

[1] Faculty of Industrial Technology, Tsukuba University of Technology,
Amakubo 4-3-15, Tsukuba City, Ibaraki, Japan
{waka,m-kitamr,nobuko,miki}@a.tsukuba-tech.ac.jp
[2] Faculty of Health Sciences, Tsukuba University of Technology,
Kasuga 4-12-7, Tsukuba City, Ibaraki, Japan
koba@cs.k.tsukuba-tech.ac.jp
[3] Research and Support Center on Higher Education for People with Disabilities,
Tsukuba University of Technology, Kasuga 4-12-7, Tsukuba City, Ibaraki, Japan
mmiyagi@k.tsukuba-tech.ac.jp

Abstract. Museums are among the most important institutions for fostering lifelong learning. Recent years have seen legal reforms leading to an improvement in access to museums and relevant information. In fact, some museums are currently preparing barrier-free checklists, accessibility programs for visitors, and universal guidelines on how exhibits are to be held. Unfortunately, there are still few museums in Japan that have successfully implemented this kind of action. As an initial step to ameliorate this situation, we conducted a questionnaire for people with visual impairments or hearing loss with the aim of identifying how museums might assist visitors with visual impairments or hearing loss to enjoy a more educational and pleasant experience. The questionnaire results showed that museums are important venues for people with visual impairments or hearing loss. In the case of services, a low proportion of participants desired accompanied guidance, support at the time of entry, or tours designed to take disabilities into account. Additionally, responses to other questions also indicated that some participants do not wish to increase staff members' workloads. Rather, the most desired feature of the services desired in museums was that staff be understanding toward people with disabilities. Showing understanding toward visitors with a visual impairment or hearing loss and learning the appropriate means of communication and methods of support would help staff to achieve a more "universal" museum experience for visitors. Finally, we introduce details of activities that were carried out on the basis of the questionnaire results.

This study was supported by JSPS Kakenhi JP18H01046 and was carried out with the permission of the Research Ethics Committee of Tsukuba University of Technology (approval number: H29–16).

Keywords: Visual impairment · Hearing loss · Museum accessibility

1   Introduction

Museums are one of the most important institutions for fostering lifelong learning. Recent years have seen legal reforms that have improved access to museums and relevant information [1,2]. In fact, some museums are currently preparing barrier-free checklists, accessibility programs for visitors, and universal guidelines on how exhibits are to be held. For example, the Smithsonian National Museum is preparing a manual for designing accessible exhibits [3]. In Berlin, not only museums but the entire city is engaged in barrier-free activities to convey culture [4]. The Louvre offers a variety of services for people with disabilities [5]. The Deutsches Hygiene-Museum permits barrier-free access by people with disabilities [6]. The Omero Museum in Italy was established as a museum for the visually impaired [7]. Finally, some museums actively offer sign language talks and tours, as well as real-time captioning for the deaf and hard of hearing [8–10].

Most museums in Japan have also tried to prepare accessible contents and exhibition design. However, it seems that the number of visitors with visual impairment or hearing loss is still small. For example, information provided via tactile graphics or braille, equipment for assisted hearing (magnetic loops, directional speakers, etc.), and museum tours designed to take disabilities into account have been implemented. However, these may not be reaching people with disabilities and may be out of sync with current real needs. Without more visits from people with disabilities, a museum cannot obtain feedback or improve services. As an initial step toward ameliorating this situation, we administered a questionnaire to identify how museums (defined broadly) might assist visitors with visual impairments or hearing loss to enjoy a more educational and pleasant experience. We will also introduce details on activities that were carried out on the basis of what was learned from the questionnaire results.

2   Methodology

The museums that we targeted for our questionnaire included art galleries, science and history museums, culture centers, botanical gardens, zoos, and aquariums. We prepared 27 questions on a range of topics, including visitors' interest in museums, difficulties experienced during their visits to museums, and changes they hoped to see. The questionnaire participants included 25 individuals with visual impairments and 70 individuals with hearing loss, from middle school age and above. The details of the participants are shown in Table 1. We requested responses from associations related to visual impairments/hearing loss for working people, Tsukuba University of Technology for university students, and schools for the blind/the deaf for junior and senior high school students. Responses to the questionnaire were solicited from January 30 to February 21, 2018.

Table 1. Breakdown of participants.

	Visual impairment	Hearing loss	Total
Junior and senior high school students	18	49	67
University students	4	14	18
Working people	3	7	10
Total	25	70	95

By analyzing the resultant data, we sought to clarify two general topics: First, what kind of experience do individuals with visual impairments or hearing loss have when visiting a museum in Japan today? Second, what improvements would they like to see? After outlining the results of our analysis, we will introduce activities we undertook to meet visitors' requests.

3   Results

From the 27 questions included in the questionnaire, we will provide an overview of six particularly important questions: (a) "Types of museums that you have used"; (b) "Experiences of being assisted at museums"; (c) "Difficulties that you have faced when visiting a museum"; (d) "Conveniences needed at museums"; (e) "Services you would like museums to provide"; and (f) "Exhibitions or events that you would like museums to hold."

With respect to (a), all questionnaire respondents had visited a museum, with no discernible difference between the visual impairment or hearing loss groups by venues frequented. Table 2 shows the result for (b): "Experience of being assisted at museums." Visually impaired visitors who received assistance used dedicated guide terminals, tactile charts, and curators' accompanying services. For those with hearing loss, sign language interpretation services and dedicated captioning terminals were used. A summary of reasons for "no experience of receiving assistance" are shown in Table 3. Among the "Other" responses, there were the comments "Because it might be a hindrance" and "I didn't know that there was such support." Common responses to (c) are displayed in Table 4.

Table 2. Experience of being assisted at museums.

	Visual impairment	Hearing loss	Total
I have experience receiving assistance	4(18%)	8(13%)	12(15%)
I have no experience receiving assistance	18(82%)	52(87%)	70(85%)

Table 3. Reason for not receiving assistance.

	Visual impairment	Hearing loss	Total
I simply didn't need any assistance	11(48%)	29(42%)	40(43%)
I didn't need assistance because I had a companion	11(48%)	30(43%)	41(45%)
I needed assistance, but I couldn't request it	0(0%)	4(6%)	4(4%)
I needed assistance and requested it, but a support system was not available	0(0%)	2(3%)	2(2%)
Others	1(4%)	4(6%)	5(5%)

Table 4. Difficulties encountered when visiting a museum.

Visual impairment	Hearing loss
– Upsetting to be told: "as you can see" or "please have a look at this" – Floor maps are hard to read – Locations within the museum are hard to find. It takes a long time to reach a destination – The elevator does not have voice guidance	– Anxious because almost all explanations and commentaries are spoken – There is no sign language interpretation or subtitles so I cannot learn what I want to know – I cannot hear the museum announcements

Table 5. Conveniences needed at museums.

	Visual impairment	Hearing loss	Total
1. Signs or guidance in the museum	9(41%)	18(31%)	27(3%)
2. Pamphlets with enlarged characters or braille	6(27%)	3(5%)	9(11%)
3. Information provided via tactile graphics or braille	3(14%)	1(2%)	4(5%)
4. Equipment for rendering sound into text (museum announcements, videos, etc.)	3(14%)	34(57%)	37(46%)
5. Equipment for assisted hearing (magnetic loops, directional speakers, etc.)	1(5%)	2(3%)	3(4%)
6. Other	0(0%)	0(0%)	0(0%)

Table 5 shows the results for (d): "Conveniences needed at museums." Naturally, differences in impairment lead to differences in the kinds of convenience required. Table 6 shows the results for (e): "Services you would like museums to provide." Table 7 shows the results for (f): "Exhibitions or events you would like museums to hold."

Table 6. Services you would like museums to provide.

	Visual impairment	Hearing loss	Total
1. Staff should be understanding toward disabilities	13(59%)	25(43%)	38(48%)
2. It should be possible to access barrier-free information in advance	2(9%)	2(3%)	4(5%)
3. There should be museum tours designed specifically for people with disabilities	1(5%)	5(9%)	6(8%)
4. Staff should give accompanied guidance	2(9%)	0(0%)	2(3%)
5. Staff able to respond with sign language or communication via writing.	0(0%)	23(40%)	23(29%)
6. Prioritized entry or support at the time of entry	4(18%)	3(5%)	7(9%)
7. Other	0(0%)	0(0%)	0(0%)

Table 7. Exhibitions or events you would like museums to hold.

	Visual impairment	Hearing Loss	Total
1. Exhibits or events where you can enjoy touching objects	11(58%)	20(34%)	31(40%)
2. Exhibits or events where you can enjoy different aromas	0(0%)	2(3%)	2(3%)
3. Exhibits or events where you can enjoy sound	4(21%)	4(7%)	8(10%)
4. Exhibits or events with supplementary sound	2(11%)	2(3%)	4(5%)
5. Exhibits or events where you can enjoy text or sign language	2(11%)	29(50%)	31(40%)
6. Other	0(0%)	1(2%)	1(1%)

4   Observations

The questionnaire results show that museums are important venues for people with visual impairments or hearing loss. In response to a different question not included in this report, many participants indicated that they had been afforded the opportunity to learn at a museum thanks to family members or a schoolteacher.

A few respondents had been assisted at museums. For most of them, assistance was simply unnecessary and they had companions to help them. However, some had been unable to request assistance. Others were unaware that there was a support system in place, and still others were concerned about being a burden to staff members. This indicates a lack of public awareness of support for visitors with disabilities and a lack of penetration of a barrier-free mentality.

Visually impaired respondents encountered difficulties when visiting museums such as difficulty understanding explanations using demonstrative words, learning the location of destinations within the museum, or moving to those destinations. Visitors with hearing loss noted that they could not understand spoken explanations or announcements and that there was a need for sign language interpretation. These points also appeared in responses to questions on conveniences or services that museums need. With regard to conveniences, a particularly high proportion of participants desired signs or guidance in the museum, as well as the rendering of announcements or video audio into text. In the case of services, a low proportion of participants desired accompanied guidance, support at the time of entry, or tours designed to take disabilities into account. We surmise that participants would generally prefer to roam the museum and enjoy the exhibits at their own pace. Responses to other questions also indicated that some participants do not wish to increase staff members' workloads.

With respect to museum services, the most desired feature was that staff be understanding toward people with disabilities. Showing understanding toward visitors with a visual impairment or hearing loss and learning the appropriate means of communication and methods of support would help staff to achieve a more "universal" museum experience for visitors. With respect to the types of exhibitions or events that participants would like museums to hold, both those with visual impairment and those with hearing loss were interested in exhibits or events where objects can be touched. For the visually impaired, being able to touch exhibits may lead to greater understanding. We found that touching objects was also considered important by respondents with hearing loss.

On the basis of the questionnaire results, we implemented the following types of activities. First, we conducted a workshop for museum staff to help them learn how to respond to visitors with sensory impairment [11]. Second, we conducted a proof-of-concept experiment, where we attached QR codes to exhibit explanations that linked to videos with sign language interpretation [12]. We hope that our efforts may contribute to the realization of a more universal museum experience for all.

Acknowledgements. We would like to thank Editage (www.editage.com) for English language editing.

References

1. Hamraie, A.: Building Access: Universal Design and the Politics of Disability, 3rd edn. University of Minnesota Press, Minneapolis (2017)
2. Paciello, M.: Web Accessibility for People with Disabilities, 1st edn. CRC Press, Boca Raton (2000)
3. Smithsonian guidelines for accessible exhibition design. https://www.sifacilities.si.edu/ae_center/pdf/Accessible-Exhibition-Design.pdf. Accessed 30 May 2020
4. Berlin barrier-free: museums + art. https://www.visitberlin.de/en/berlin-barrier-free-museums-art. Accessed 30 May 2020
5. Accessibility — Louvre museum. https://www.louvre.fr/en/accessibility. Accessed 30 May 2020

6. DHMD: Accessibility. https://www.dhmd.de/ihr-besuch/barrierefreiheit/. Accessed 30 May 2020
7. Home Page - Museo Tattile Statale Omero. http://www.museoomero.it/main. Accessed 30 May 2020
8. Deaf and hard of hearing visitors—museums association. https://www.mu seumsassociation.org/museum-practice/deaf-and-hard-of-hearing-visitors. Accessed 30 May 2020
9. For visitors who are deaf—the metropolitan museum of art. https://www. metmuseum.org/events/programs/access/visitors-who-are-deaf. Accessed 30 May 2020
10. National palace museum-visiting > gallery tours. https://www.npm.gov.tw/en/ Article.aspx?sNo=02007003. Accessed 30 May 2020
11. Kobayashi, M. et al.: Workshop for staffs of museums and aquariums to learn how sensory impaired visitors feel via experiences. In: ICETC 2019: Proceedings of the 2019 11th International Conference on Education Technology and Computers, pp. 196–199. (2019). https://doi.org/10.1145/3369255.3369305
12. Namatame, M., Kitamula, M., Wakatsuki, D., Kobayashi, M., Miyagi, M., Kato, N.: Can exhibit-explanations in sign language contribute to the accessibility of aquariums? In: Stephanidis, C. (ed.) HCII 2019. CCIS, vol. 1032, pp. 289–294. Springer, Cham (2019). https://doi.org/10.1007/978-3-030-23522-2_37

Mobile Health and Mobile Rehabilitation for People with Disabilities: Current State, Challenges and Opportunities

Mobile Health and Mobile Rehabilitation for People with Disabilities: Current State, Challenges and Opportunities

Introduction to the Special Thematic Session

Frank DeRuyter[1] , Mike Jones[2(✉)] , and John Morris[2(✉)]

[1] Duke University Medical Center, Durham, NC 27514, USA
frank.deruyter@duke.edu
[2] Shepherd Center, Atlanta, GA 30309, USA
{mike.jones, john.morris}@shepherd.org

Abstract. Over the past decade, technologies have transformed society, education, entertainment, business and now healthcare. Today, digital health technologies are reaching a level of maturity that supports the robust and broad scope of healthcare. It has only been recently that mobile devices, wearables and connected virtual assistants are common in every aspect of healthcare. However, solutions for people with disabilities are just emerging. This Special Thematic Session will address mHealth/mRehab advances, challenges and opportunities for people with disability from several disease, disorder and technology perspectives.

Keywords: mHealth · mRehab · Mobile healthcare · Mobile rehabilitation · Apps · Disability

1 Overview of MHealth/MRehab

Innovative digital applications in the use of mobile devices, wearables and connected virtual assistants are increasingly common in every aspect of various industries such as transportation, finance, retail, manufacturing, and healthcare. The pace of innovation and the disruptions that have transformed each of these industries has been epic. In spite of their ubiquity, the variety of digital technologies are still considered by many as being in their early development [1]. Although digital technological developments are often viewed as still early stage, their use is anything but in its infancy. As of April 2020, over 59% (4.57 billion) of the worldwide population were considered active internet users. A remarkable 4.2 billion of these individuals were unique mobile internet users and part of the worldwide digital population [2]. As a result, a large portion of this global digital population have become informed consumers in the various industries.

Digital health has not been immune to innovation, disruption and informed consumers. In fact, despite healthcare being widely viewed as a laggard in digital intensity and adopting new technologies [3], digital health has in recent years been booming as

K. Miesenberger et al. (Eds.): ICCHP 2020, LNCS 12377, pp. 219–223, 2020.
https://doi.org/10.1007/978-3-030-58805-2_26

evidenced by the sheer number of wearable devices and health apps available to consumers and providers. This is further supported by the amount of global venture capital funding that has recently gone into digital health startups, mergers and acquisitions. Consumers, healthcare providers, health systems, and payers alike are all realizing the value of remote monitoring digital health solutions to improve patient outcomes.

For example, in the United States over the past 10 years, $58 B (USD) has been invested into digital health, with $8.9 B (USD) in 615 deals just in 2019. In the recently ended first quarter of 2020, over 80 funding deals were announced totaling $2.9 billion (USD) [4]. Without a doubt, the value of digital health solutions is in their ability to collect, analyze and act upon data obtained using various mobile devices, wearables and connected virtual assistants has become realized.

Tremendous growth has also occurred in the management of chronic health conditions with digital health applications. Despite these significant gains, there are still issues to be resolved surrounding connectivity, interoperability, integration, privacy, security, data mining, proper analytics, and adoption within the digital health space. In addition, not every digital solution provides clinical or evidence based support. While uptake is growing, the U.K.'s ORCHA recently reported, that only 43 apps out of over 327,000 health apps currently available account for over 83% of all health app downloads. Of those 43 apps, 65% had not been updated in over 18 months [5]. Furthermore in 2019, in a review of 104 peer-reviewed published papers on digital health products and services, only "28% of the studies targeted patients with high-burden, high-cost conditions or risk factors" and that only 15% of all the peer-reviewed studies actually examined the clinical effectiveness of their subjects [6].

This clearly further illustrates the need to study the prevalence of significant health disparities between the general population and people with disabilities, particularly with respect to chronic health conditions [7]. These underlying issues are the key themes for this Special Thematic Session.

While there have been many terms and definitions to describe digital health it was only in March of this year, that HIMSS (the global leader supporting the transformation of the health ecosystem through information and technology) put forth a new definition of digital health for the global health community [8]. That definition states:

Digital health connects and empowers people and populations to manage health and wellness, augmented by accessible and supportive provider teams working within flexible, integrated, interoperable and digitally enabled care environments that strategically leverage digital tools, technologies and services to transform care delivery [9].

Within the disability community, digital health delivery has traditionally been referred to with greater specificity as either mHealth (mobile healthcare), eHealth (electronic healthcare), and mRehab (mobile rehabilitation) [10]. All describe the practice of using information and communication technologies (ICT) such as mobile devices, wearables and connected virtual assistants to support diverse aspects of specific healthcare delivery. The terms are similar and overlapping, but refer to distinct aspects of remote delivery of healthcare services: mHealth is the delivery of general healthcare via mobile devices; eHealth is a broader term that describes healthcare practice supported by electronic processes that may not necessarily be mobile related;

and mRehab is the delivery of rehabilitation services via mobile communication devices.

At present, mHealth solutions for people with disabilities are just emerging. Evidence suggests that up until recently, people with disabilities have not been well represented in the growth of digital health [11]. This is particularly the case with the proliferation of mobile health apps for smartphones, wearables and connected virtual assistants.

While omission could lead to further health disparities, current technical, social, economic and policy trends are pointing to emerging opportunities to significantly broaden access to enhanced rehabilitation services for people with disabilities [12]. Furthermore, there is growing consensus that digital health can expand healthcare access to greater numbers of people. According to a recent statement on rehabilitation research priorities within the United States: *"The use of ICT eliminates distance barriers and can make rehabilitation and healthcare services available to people who have limited access to transportation and other access issues"* [13].

Clearly the value of digital health solutions is in the ability to collect, analyze and act upon data obtained through the use of various mobile devices, wearables and connected virtual assistants. If executed successfully, mobile health (mHealth) and rehabilitation (mRehab) strategies have the potential to address the key challenges of access and affordability. For example, digital health using ICT devices and strategies can provide information to enable home rehabilitation interventions between outpatient visits.

This could fill the gaps and changes that occur in patient care as well as afford the possibility of:

1. prescribing interventions/instructions to the patient and caregiver,
2. gathering just-in-time data on patient status instead of relying on imprecise recall during clinic visits,
3. presenting data to the patient and clinician in a timely manner, and
4. developing big data repositories with algorithms that will enable updating of prescribed in-home therapy and recommendations.

These types of mHealth and mRehab digital health innovations also have the potential to address challenges to effective and efficient delivery of outpatient rehabilitation by increasing patient motivation and adherence to recommended therapy regimens, improving patient engagement, and permitting more rapid progression between clinic visits.

2   Session Papers

This Special Thematic Session consists of 6 Scientific Papers and 2 Service and Practice Forum papers, which range from development of new consumer focused mobile technologies and applications, to disability consumer and provider survey research to updates of funded mHealth/mRehab research and development centers. The papers include assessment and care management for specific congenital and acquired disorders for children and adults, as well as general disability areas. The following summarize the Scientific Papers presented:

- Pulmonary rehabilitation has proven effective in COPD. The paper by Colombo and colleagues describes the design, development and results of MyDA, a mobile health app for improving management of COPD, which enabled 12 COPD patients to follow personalized pulmonary rehabilitation programs at home.
- A user study about designing a mobile app for motivating multiple sclerosis patients for conducting self-rehabilitation exercises at home is presented by Chassan and colleagues.
- The results of the development of a classification algorithm derived from accelerometer data collected to improve the classification of posture movements (laying, reclining, sitting, standing, walking) for hospitalized older adults is presented by Jarvis et al.
- Morris and colleagues present data and analysis of a survey of over 500 rehabilitation providers examining both the barriers and critical use cases for mRehab adoption.
- A survey of 412 people with various types of disabilities looking at use and unmet needs related to mobile apps for mHealth will be presented by Lippincott and colleagues. The paper focuses on user experience and maps behaviors, interests and needs to type of disability.
- The research and user-centered design and development of the SwapMyMood app to support executive function for military service members with traumatic brain injury and post-traumatic stress disorder will be presented by Wallace and Morris.

In addition to the above, the following 2 Service and Practice Forum papers are included in this Special Thematic Session and published within the digital edition of the ICCHP 2020 open access compendium "Future Perspectives of AT, eAccessibility and eInclusion":

- A paper by DeRuyter and colleagues provides highlights of research and development related to ICT access for persons with disability conducted in the just completed 5-year federally funded LiveWell Project.
- The newly funded Rehabilitation Engineering Research Center on Mobile Rehabilitation (mRehab RERC), which promotes accessible digital health and mobile rehabilitation applications for people with disabilities, will be described by Jones and colleagues.

These 8 papers illustrate the complexity and diversity of this topic area and demonstrate numerous possible mHealth/mRehab solutions. The key to understanding the possibilities of mHealth and mRehab is to understand better the technologies and how they can come together to create new opportunities for people.

As we create those opportunities, we must continuously ask ourselves what impact these digital health developments will have on people with disabilities beyond the delivery and monitoring of care and especially on improvements in their quality of life and full participation.

Acknowledgements. The organizing chairs of this Special Thematic Session wish to thank all who contributed papers to this session for presentation, publication and the exemplary work that they have conducted. The response to this session was overwhelming during this time of unprecedented social and economic disruption. It reinforces the importance of this emerging area of focus. Finally, a special thank you to the ICCHP Organizing Team for providing not only a platform to address this important topic but also for implementing a virtual online event.

References

1. Guidance for Wearable Health Solutions. CTA and HRS White Paper released at CES January 2020. https://shop.cta.tech/products/guidance-for-wearable-health-solutions. Accessed 30 May 2020
2. Global Digital Population as of April 2020. Statista: https://www.statista.com/statistics/617136/digital-population-worldwide/. Accessed 17 July 2020
3. Rowlands, D.: What is digital health and why does it matter? (2019). https://www.hisa.org.au/wp-content/uploads/2019/12/What_is_Digital_Health.pdf?x97063. Accessed 30 May 2020
4. Venture Capital Funding Digital Health Sector. BusinessWire 15 January 2020. https://www.businesswire.com/news/home/20200115005574/en/Venture-Capital-Funding-Digital-Health-Sector-Reaches. Accessed 30 May 2020
5. The Challenge: Getting the Right Apps to the Right People at the Right Time. ORCHA. https://www.orcha.co.uk/the-challenge/. Accessed 30 2020
6. The Oversell and Undersell Of Digital Health. Health Affairs Blog, 27 February 2019. https://doi.org/10.1377/hblog20190226.63748
7. DeRuyter, F., Jones, M.: Mobile healthcare and mHealth apps for people with disabilities. In: Miesenberger, K., Kouroupetroglou, G. (eds.) ICCHP 2018. LNCS, vol. 10897, pp. 449–456. Springer, Cham (2018). https://doi.org/10.1007/978-3-319-94274-2_65
8. HIMSS Who We Are. https://www.himss.org/who-we-are. Accessed 30 May 2020
9. HIMSS Defines Digital Health for the Global Healthcare Industry. https://www.himss.org/news/himss-defines-digital-health-global-healthcare-industry. Accessed 10 March 2020
10. Morris, J., Jones, M., DeRuyter, F., Putrino, D., Lang, C.E., Jake-Schoffman, D.: LiveWell RERC state of the science conference report on ICT access to support community living, health and function for people with disabilities. Int. J. Environ. Res. Public Health **17**(1), 274 (2019). https://doi.org/10.3390/ijerph17010274
11. Jones, M., DeRuyter, F., Morris, J.: The digital health revolution and people with disabilities: perspective from the United States. Int. J. Environ. Res. Public Health **17**(2), 381 (2019). https://doi.org/10.3390/ijerph17020381
12. DeRuyter, F., Jones, M.: Mobile healthcare and mHealth apps. In: Miesenberger, K., Kouroupetroglou, G. (eds.) ICCHP 2018. LNCS, vol. 10897, pp. 445–448. Springer, Cham (2018). https://doi.org/10.1007/978-3-319-94274-2_64
13. Frontera, W.R., et al.: Rehabilitation research at the national institutes of health moving the field forward (executive summary). Am. J. Phys. Med. Rehabil. **96**, 211–220 (2017)

A Mobile Diary App to Support Rehabilitation at Home for Elderly with COPD: A Preliminary Feasibility Study

Vera Colombo[1,2]([✉]), Marta Mondellini[1], Alessandra Gandolfo[3],
Alessia Fumagalli[3], and Marco Sacco[1]

[1] Institute of Intelligent Industrial Technologies and Systems for Advanced
Manufacturing, National Research Council, 23900 Lecco, Italy
vera.colombo@stiima.cnr.it
[2] Department of Electronics, Information and Bioengineering,
Politecnico di Milano, 20133 Milan, Italy
[3] Pulmonary Rehabilitation Unit, National Institute on Health
and Science on Ageing, 23880 Casatenovo LC, Italy

Abstract. The paper describes the design, development and preliminary evaluation of a *mobile* diary app for elderly with Chronic Obstructive Pulmonary Disease (COPD). The application, called My Daily Activity (MyDA), allows patients to follow personalized rehabilitation, based on physical training, cognitive stimulation and an educational program. MyDA is based on four different modules: configuration, exercise, assessment and education. The first version of the application has been developed for tablets based on Android OS. As a preliminary feasibility evaluation, 12 elderly with COPD have used the system at home for 3 months. Both objective and qualitative data have been analyzed. Preliminary results suggest that, despite some improvements should be applied, MyDA represents a feasible and valuable solution for motivating elderly with COPD to continue rehabilitation at home. Future works should focus on making the app more usable, more interactive and more attractive – especially for the technology rejecting users.

Keywords: mHealth · Home-based rehabilitation · Physical exercise · Cognitive training · COPD · Elderly

1 Introduction

Chronic Obstructive Pulmonary Disease (COPD) is a chronic and progressive disease, affecting over 300 million people worldwide, characterized by respiratory function decline and an umbrella of extra-pulmonary manifestations and comorbidities, which makes it a disabling condition. People with COPD often suffer from skeletal muscle disfunction, limited physical performance, cognitive decline, anxiety and depression. Pulmonary rehabilitation, with physical training as a cornerstone, is a comprehensive and effective intervention aimed at improving the patient's physical, psychological and social status. Pulmonary rehabilitation is usually carried out in hospital, where patients follow a personalized and integrated program for a limited period of time (2–3 weeks)

© Springer Nature Switzerland AG 2020
K. Miesenberger et al. (Eds.): ICCHP 2020, LNCS 12377, pp. 224–232, 2020.
https://doi.org/10.1007/978-3-030-58805-2_27

[1]. One of the main challenges for chronic respiratory diseases is the continuity of care: once returned home, patients should perform physical exercises on a daily basis, they should follow a controlled nutritional plan and should maintain themselves socially and physically active. However, the positive effects of the intervention tend to decline in the long-term period due to lack of adherence and lack of direct supervision at home.

2 Related Works

Researchers are investigating how to keep COPD patients motivated proposing safe and customized solutions such as telemedicine systems based on web-based applications, mobile apps, wearable sensor devices, as well as exergames (i.e. exercise + games). Mobile applications show a great potential to improve healthcare delivery especially when dealing with chronic conditions – as COPD is – even if lack of compliance with the use of technology is still a challenge [2]. Long term compliance could be achieved only whether information is provided correctly and appropriately, whether users feel empowered while using technology and – on the contrary – do not experience the perception of "being too difficult to use". To meet these requirements a patient-centered design approach – allowing personalization of interventions and considering natural variations in patient's behavior – is crucial, even if not always easy to be applied. Healthcare professionals, who also guarantee reliability and security of contents proposed, should be involved in the process; however, they are often included neither in the design nor in the validation of existing mobile health applications. Most of the currently available apps for COPD focus on education; other functionalities are: symptoms tracking, support for medication or treatment and a diary or calendar for reporting activities [3]. Although some studies prove that mobile and computer-based interventions are feasible and well accepted by patients, no firm conclusions can be drawn due to some methodological limitations. As recommended by a recent review, studies should cover a longer period of time, should consider subgroups (e.g. age, education level), should include outcomes as self-efficacy, cost-effectiveness and anxiety or depression and should provide also subjective data to explain participants' perspective towards the adoption of technology [4].

Within this context, we present MyDA (My Daily Activity), a mobile application for supporting COPD patients in performing rehabilitation at home. Unlike most of the existing applications, our solution allows the personalization of exercises based on the patient's needs and report of physiological parameters and symptoms. Another strong point is that MyDA has been designed by a multidisciplinary team formed of developers, clinicians and psychologists. Moreover, it has been evaluated, even if in a preliminary way, on a 3 month-period including also subjective experiences of participants.

3   Design of the Application

MyDA has been designed by our multidisciplinary team – including developers, clinicians and psychologists – considering end-users' perspective analyzing their specific needs and capabilities. The application has been designed to foster continuity of care: the same protocol followed during hospitalization is continued at home. The training program has been defined following the current practice, based on the ATS/ERS[1] guidelines on pulmonary rehabilitation. MyDA contains a weekly training timetable showing daily activities as configured by the physical therapist that can set specific parameters for each activity, monitor the patient's activities and update the prescription adjusting goals, if needed. The foreseen activities are: endurance exercise, consisting in cycling on an ergometer at constant intensity; strength exercises for upper and lower limbs, specifically arm raises, sit-to-stand, calf raises and supine arm-cross; and a serious game allowing users to train their cognitive functions in a virtual scenario representing a daily life activity (doing grocery). Patient's performance – represented by exercise-specific parameters – and self-reported data – breathlessness, perceived fatigue, heart rate and oxygen saturation – should be recorded in a report available to caregivers. A separate section of the app provides educational content, such as useful information on the disease, tips on how to manage its symptoms and guidelines for a healthier lifestyle. Users interact with the application through a Graphical User Interface (GUI), providing simple instructions and reducing the complexity of tasks thus minimizing risks of unintended actions. The application is accessible via tablet; this device has been preferred because it has a wider screen than smartphones and a higher portability than PC desktops/laptops, that makes the exercise setting more flexible. Motivation is addressed giving proper suggestions and instructions to the patients and showing them – through a simple color-based representation – accomplished tasks and future goals. Moreover, patients are aware that they are monitored and that a doctor or a physiotherapist evaluates their actions. Having an active role in reporting activities, feelings and symptoms helps improving mastery on the disease and, as a consequence, self-efficacy and independence.

4   MyDA

The application has been developed using Unity3D[2], based on C# language. The choice of using a game engine is mainly related to the development of the 2D serious game for cognitive training. Moreover, Unity3D is a cross-platform engine allowing to easily deploy the application on different platforms, such as Windows OS, Android OS, iOS etc. This makes MyDA accessible to a wider user audience with different preferences. In our study we provided patients with a tablet based on Android OS. MyDA is organized in five modules working as follows.

---

[1] American Thoracic Society/European Respiratory Society.

[2] https://unity.com/.

The **configuration** module consists in a dedicated section – secured with password – with access limited to clinicians. They can create the patient profile, specifying personal data and training data, setting the recommended frequency of training for the three activities and specific parameters for each of them (e.g. duration of the cycling exercise, number of sets and repetitions for the arm raises, duration of rest etc.).

The **activity** module contains all the classes and functionalities for managing the three training modalities with specific functions for each of them. When starting the application, in the "Home" panel, the patient selects the activity he/she wants to perform among the scheduled ones for that given day. Tapping on the activity icon, he/she begins the session. While performing the physical activities, patients are encouraged to listen to music, choosing among three different tracks provided by MyDA, according to their preferences. If endurance is the scheduled exercise, the patient, after setting the preferred track, receives instructions on the duration and intensity of the cycling activity and prepares the cycle-ergometer accordingly. When he/she declares to be ready (by tapping on a "START" button), a timer is displayed on the screen and the music starts playing. In a similar way, the patient receives support for strength exercises with proper instructions – both text and a video tutorial – on the correct starting position and execution and the task to be accomplished. The duration of each sets of movements is recorded as the time passing between a "tap" on "START" and a subsequent "tap" on "STOP" button. The cognitive training consists of completing a shopping task in a virtual supermarket. The patient, given a list of products to collect, has to select, first, the correct lane – i.e. the one containing the required products, as in a real supermarket – and then the product on a shelf by tapping on the corresponding image. As the levels of difficulty change, the number of products on the list, the number of lanes, the number of items on the shelf and the position of the product to find increase. Patients can pause the activity for a short time (e.g. if they need to rest) or interrupt the exercise session (Fig. 1).

Fig. 1. Some screenshots of the application: a) training timetable; b) educational program; c) symptoms assessment; d) warm-up of the endurance session; e) strength exercises session; f) virtual supermarket for cognitive training.

The **assessment** module manages the insertion and recording of the patients' health condition before and after each physical activity session. The self-assessment consists in a brief questionnaire focusing on four relevant issues: heart rate (HR), oxygen saturation (SpO2), breathlessness and muscle fatigue. The patient manually inserts HR and SpO2 values, measured by a finger pulse oximeter, through the GUI. In addition, the patient self-reports the levels of breathlessness and muscle fatigue by choosing on a 10-point Borg modified scale the symbol that corresponds to the perceived dyspnea or muscle fatigue at that given time.

The **education** module is organized as a "School of COPD" with 10 chapters. Each chapter is focused on a specific topic regarding different aspects of the disease and the strategies to handle with activities of daily living (e.g. travelling, preparing meals, social life, etc.). The educational contents combining images, text and videos have been realized by a group of lung specialists and physical therapists working at IRCCS INRCA (National Institute of Health and Science on Ageing).

The diary report includes the representation of the personalized schedule through a weekly timetable where each activity is identified by a representative icon; past activities are reported with an additional symbol – a red cross, a yellow bar or a green tick – indicating if the activity has been missed, interrupted or completed respectively. Report files contain the log data describing the patient's behavior during the training period. These data include the number and type of sessions interrupted/completed, the time spent exercising, the self-reported health assessment and specific information associated with each of the three activities. All the information gathered is available to professional caregivers and provides a comprehensive overview to track the patient's condition over time. This enables clinicians to discuss with the patient on his/her improvement or worsening and to adjust the prescribed program accordingly.

5   Preliminary Evaluation

5.1 Procedure

A preliminary feasibility study has been performed involving a group of patients with mild/moderate COPD, who used the app at home for 3 months. Participants were enrolled at IRCCS INRCA; after a period of rehabilitation in the hospital, they were given an Android based tablet with the application installed. At discharge, the physical therapist configured the app for each patient and showed him/her the main function-alities. All patients also received a user manual containing all the instructions, potential errors and troubleshooting written by the app developers. During the study, patients had the chance to phone call the physical therapist and developers to communicate technical problems and, eventually, ask for help. All participants were encouraged to follow the same training protocol, which was as follows: 20 min of endurance exercise (on a cycle-ergometer) for 5 days/week; 3 sets of 10 repetitions for each of the strength exercises for 3 days/week; cognitive serious game at least 3 times/week as they like; educational content as they like. After 3 months, patients returned the devices. The study protocol has been approved by the Ethical Committee of IRCCS INRCA.

The primary feasibility outcome was the frequency of use of the MyDA-based training program defined as: (number of attended sessions/number of planned sessions) %. Frequency of use for each type of activity (endurance, strength or cognitive) was also measured. Objective measures were obtained analyzing the log data of the application. Use of the application is classified as follows: very frequently (frequency of use > 95%); frequently (75–95%); occasionally (50–75%); rarely (25–50%); very rarely (5–25%); never (<5%). Qualitative responses were collected with semi-structured interviews carried out at the end of the three months and analyzed in combination with objective measurements to explain patients' behavior.

5.2   Results

Twelve elderly (6 male; age: 71 ± 7.3) with mild COPD participated in the study. Two participants encountered technical problems with the tablet; their data are incomplete so that they are not presented hereinafter. Results from the remaining 10 subjects (6 male; 4 female) are summarized in this section.

Considering the overall use of the application with no distinction on the activity performed, 2 patients never used the application for following the rehabilitation program and 1 patient very rarely used it. With respect to the first two users, the interviews revealed a total rejection of a technological tool. In particular, one subject declared: "I'm not inclined for technology, I don't even use a smartphone". The other subject instead reported that, in his opinion, the application was useless: the user carried out the motor exercises without the support of MyDA and he considered the cognitive task to be of little use. On the other hand, the patient who used the app very rarely, reported a problem with the usability ("difficulty using the device") and in particular that he was unable to navigate the interface, and this is why he only used MyDA when his grandchildren could help him. The remaining 7 participants used it for at least 65% of the planned activities. Among these, 3 patients trained with the support of the app exactly as planned (frequency of use > 100%).

The analysis of endurance sessions shows that 3 patients very rarely performed exercise with a minimum of 0 sessions to a maximum of 6 sessions performed; 1 patient occasionally followed the prescribed training. The remaining (n = 6) patients frequently (n = 3) or very frequently (n = 3) used the app. The first type of users reported they had the opportunity to perform physical exercise outdoor and therefore they did not always use the tablet for training. The subject who used MyDA occasionally, declared that he preferred cycling while watching television because time seemed to him to run faster. Among those who frequently used the app, users reported feeling more monitored and involved than in a standard situation, and found the device useful, especially at a general level and not specifically in the endurance session; the problem most frequently encountered by them was that the app was slow in loading a new session.

Regarding strength exercise sessions, 6 patients adhere to less than 50% of planned activities: 5 patients never used the application and 1 patient used it very rarely. During the interview, these subjects did not report any particular problem related to the tablet but they stated that they performed the exercises following the paper instructions given by the physiotherapist before discharge. The two subjects who were less inclined to the use of a technological device were part of this group. 1 patient occasionally and 1 frequently used MyDA to perform strength exercises. These users explained that they did not always perform the exercises with the app for different reasons: one due to muscle pain, while the other one carried out the exercises following the personalized indications of the physiotherapist. Only two patients adhere to the program as expected, with frequency of use higher than 95%. These users considered the app as very usable and they found easy to understand both the explanation of the exercises and how to interact with the tablet during the strengthening session.

Finally, the analysis of the cognitive sessions shows that 2 patients never used the application, 3 patients used it only rarely and 1 subject occasionally used it. The first two subjects, the same ones not using the tablet also for the previous activities, considered the cognitive exercise useless, despite the doctor's advice. Patients who accessed the serious game very rarely or occasionally said they found it boring ("I felt like I was falling asleep") and they found some usability problems; specifically, not being able to properly select the right objects on the shelves. This problem, in their opinion, led them to frustration and to a subsequent less use of the game. The remaining 4 patients very frequently accessed the serious game for cognitive training. These patients stated that the tablet was a support for training their memory and that it could improve their speed in shopping in reality.

5.3   Discussion

Overall, MyDA was well accepted by the majority of our sample. In general, patients showing aversion toward technology at the beginning of the study did not change their attitude. In some cases, especially considering the muscle strength sessions, the non-use of the device is likely to be related to an unclear communication between caregivers and patients. Not all patients completely understood the expected use and the functionalities (exercise video tutorials and timing recording) of that area of the application. It is likely that a smaller number of strength sessions than performed were recorded because some patients did not use the section correctly. In fact, the system recorded numerous interrupted sessions lasting more than 10 min and not registered as "completed sessions". It is possible that patients performed all the exercises without interrupting the training at the end of each session. Efficient communication on the importance of training and of being monitored, together with an effective training on the use of technology are essential to persuade both the technology rejecting users and the less physically active patients. Problems of usability emerged among those who infrequently used MyDA even if they were not averse to use it; in particular, a delay in loading the sessions, which did not allow an agile use, was reported. Finally, those using the app very frequently have played the serious game for cognitive training more than three times a week, finding it both useful from the point of view of enhancing their mnemonic skills and an enjoyable way to spend their time.

6 Conclusions and Planned Activities

The present work describes the design and development of a mobile health application enabling COPD patients to follow personalized pulmonary rehabilitation programs at home. Our solution includes a training diary with a personalized schedule and self-report of symptoms and vital signs, a support for physical exercises and an education session. We have considered the users' needs and capabilities applying a user-centered approach based on the cooperation among developers, psychologists and clinical experts. End users are elderly people with mild/moderate COPD, with no serious cognitive or motor impairment preventing to independently follow a rehabilitation program. Preliminary results on a group of 12 elderly reveal that – although some improvements could be applied – MyDA represents a valuable and feasible solution for home-based pulmonary rehabilitation. Main improvements should make the app more usable more interactive and more attractive – especially by the technology rejecting users. Moreover, thanks its modular approach, additional functionalities may be added to the application both in terms of proposed exercises and in terms of provided feedback. For example, audio feedback and voice instructions may be added to allow those patients with mild visual impairment to interact more easily with the application. One of the main limitations of our study is the sample size: although the recruited participants are a discrete number to evaluate the usability of the application, a larger population should be studied to demonstrate the acceptability of our solution. Furthermore, it is necessary to carry out further assessments to evaluate if our solution motivates users and involves them in the long-term rehabilitation process at home. For this reason, a long-term randomized trial will be performed and psychological variables as intrinsic motivation will be measured; we will compare the results reported by MyDA users with a control group, with the aim of better understanding the effectiveness of mobile-based training intervention in improving COPD continuity of care. Finally, despite mostly positive feedback from users, our study highlighted some usability issues that did not allow some patients to use MyDA; these problems will be resolved to allow for a more satisfying experience.

Acknowledgements. This work was supported by Lombardy Region and Fondazione Cariplo within the EMPATIA@Lecco project, Rif 2016-1428 Decreto Regione Lombardia 6363 del 30/05/2017.

References

1. Spruit, M.A., et al.: An official American thoracic society/european respiratory society statement: key concepts and advances in pulmonary rehabilitation. Am. J. Respir. Critical Care Med. **188**(8), e13–64 (2013). https://doi.org/10.1164/rccm.201309-1634st
2. Vaportzis, E., et al.: Older adults perceptions of technology and barriers to interacting with tablet computers: a focus group study. Front. Psychol. **8**, 1687 (2017). https://doi.org/10.3389/fpsyg.2017.01687

3. McCabe, C., et al.: Computer and mobile technology interventions for self-management in chronic obstructive pulmonary disease. Cochrane Database Syst. Rev. **5**(5), CD011425 (2017). https://doi.org/10.1002/14651858.cd011425.pub2
4. Sobnath, D.D., et al.: Features of a mobile support app for patients with chronic obstructive pulmonary disease: literature review and current applications. JMIR mHealth and uHealth **5** (2), e17 (2017)

A User Study About Designing a Mobile App for Motivating Multiple Sclerosis Patients for Self-rehabilitation

Clémence Chassan[1,2(✉)], Céline Jost[1], Marc Sévène[2], Olivier Cras[2], Thomas De Broucker[2], and Dominique Archambault[1]

[1] Université Paris 8-Vincennes-Saint-Denis (EA 4004 CHArt), Saint-Denis, France
clemence.chassan@gmail.com
[2] Centre Hospitalier de Saint-Denis, 93200 Saint-Denis, France

Abstract. Rehabilitation is essential to the treatment of Multiple Sclerosis (MS). Self-rehabilitation is rather a good way to keep it effective but its execution turns out to be often uncertain. A mobile application could help people suffering from MS practice those self-rehabilitation exercises at home. Indeed, therapists could manage and program exercises, and patients could follow therapists' programs through a mobile app. We are reporting the results of a study aimed at guiding the conception of a mobile application that would be attractive to people with MS. Therefore, a survey was carried out among users. We did one-on-one interviews with people with MS and focus groups to discuss with their therapists. The results are leading to an application that should be centered on people's occupation, and with playful components in order to provoke interest and investment.

Keywords: Multiple sclerosis · Motivation · Mobile app · Self-rehabilitation

1 Introduction

Multiple Sclerosis (MS) is a chronic degenerative neurological disease. 2.3 million people were affected in 2013 in the world [1]. This disease is the main non-traumatic cause of severe disability among young patients in many countries. MS begins between 25 and 35 years old and 2/3 of people affected are women [2]. There is no treatment to cure MS, but only actions to slow down its progression. Symptoms can be very different from a person to another. They can be visual, sensitive, motor or cognitive impairment, and the disease can progress to an irreversible disability [3]. The most common symptom reported by people with MS (pwMS) is fatigue [4]. Actually, it is one of the main reasons for inability to work for affected people [5]. Quality of life of pwMS decreases more and more while the disease progresses. Then self-rehabilitation and physical activities are widely recommended [6]. PwMS evolves into the loss of ability and thus of autonomy without appropriate regular physical exercises [7]. However, fatigue and depression are important symptoms linked to MS. As a

K. Miesenberger et al. (Eds.): ICCHP 2020, LNCS 12377, pp. 233–241, 2020.
https://doi.org/10.1007/978-3-030-58805-2_28

consequence, pwMS may prove less motivated and invested in rehabilitating and physical activities, which has a direct impact on their daily autonomy and overall life quality [8].

In this way, our project aims at developing and testing a prototype of a mobile app to make pwMS practice exercises, that have been selected by their therapists. The goal of the research presented in this article, is to choose conception's directions of the app we want to develop by questioning users (pwMS and therapists). This study consists of an investigation on how the mobile app can motivate pwMS to practice exercises and to manage their fatigue. Therefore, our central research question is about the motivation of pwMS. In view of the risk of fatigue and depression, how can we motivate pwMS to practice physical exercises or their self-rehabilitation while they are at home? We hypothesized that a mobile app could solicit pwMS' motivation to follow self-rehabilitation. We previously conducted a preliminary study with pwMS and therapists, to establish the needs of pwMS to practice exercises [9]. It allowed us to confirm that a mobile app where therapists program exercises could be a good way to motivate pwMS. Consequently, we add hypothesis about how the mobile app would have to be developed. First, we suppose that the use of gamification-the concept which uses design and elements that are usually specific to games in another context [10] could be a mean to motivate pwMS to practice exercises. Furthermore, one of occupational therapy's theory used to motivate patients, considers that each person has an intrinsic motivation linked with performance and self-efficacy in occupation [11]. So, choosing a concrete goal of patients' daily life could enhance their motivation to practice exercises. Then, we also hypothesize that if exercises programed in the app are linked with pwMS' daily life activities or personal goal, it could make more sense and make them doing their self-rehabilitation and being motivated.

2 Related Works

Guinti et al. [12] studied all mobile applications made for pwMS, available in the American and Spanish Android and iOS markets. They found a lack of mobile applications dedicated to help pwMS manage fatigue and to motivate them to practice physical activities. In France for pwMS, to our knowledge, only some mobile apps exist to improve compliance of medicinal treatments, but nothing about physical exercises or self-rehabilitation. Furthermore, Thirumalai et al. [13] tried an app with generalized exercises programs with pwMS and showed that it is necessary to offer adapted and specific exercises for each person to have a better acceptance of the application, and to motivate pwMS to use it. The study conducted in [14] brings to light the fact that an official "professional endorsement" seems to be a necessary condition for pwMS to accept and to use mHealth solutions. For the pwMS' acceptance of the app, Giunti et al. [15] developed a mobile app for the fatigue self-management based on gamification. A literature review studying elements of gamification used in mHealth for chronic diseases showed that adding gamification elements facilitates self-management of disease for people with chronic conditions [16]. Moreover, Geurts et al. [17] tested a mobile app to encourage pwMS to walk more and showed that if the objectives are adapted to the person and if the fatigue is taken in account, pwMS can be motivated and regular in the practice of exercises (walking, in this study). Lastly, the study described by Ehling et al. [18] aimed at trying to use a mobile app to decrease spasticity of pwMS by practicing exercises on their own at home, that were chosen by their physio therapist. This study showed good results. Indeed, the exercises were selected by physio therapists, therefore they are adapted to the individual capacity and the fatigue's level of each participant.

It appears that a mobile app might be a solution for making pwMS practice exercises, if their therapists are involved in the selection of exercises, if fatigue is taken into account for the choice of exercises, and if it uses gamification elements.

3   Method

One of the steps in the design methodology for developing the prototype has been to perform a qualitative study to investigate among future users the conditions that would make a mobile app to motivate patient. The user-centered methodology is presented on Fig. 1. There are two groups of users: the pwMS who use the mobile app and the therapists who establish the program of exercises in the app. First of all, we conducted a preliminary study to set out the needs of pwMS for the practice of their exercises [9]. Then we conducted focus groups with therapists to guide the conception of the mobile app and to build a second investigation with patients. This article presents the confrontation of these two surveys. Next, we will establish a prototype and present it to the users, and then we will develop and test it. All the qualitative studies of this project will be conducted with therapists and patients at the hospital of Saint-Denis. We have an agreement with the hospital so the local rehabilitation team takes part to this project.

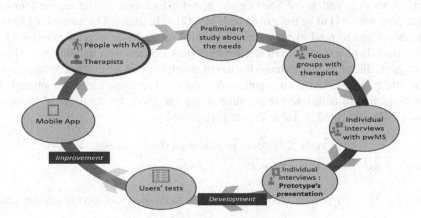

Fig. 1. Design methodology.

4 Participants

4.1 Therapists

Participants were volunteer therapists of the hospital of Saint-Denis. Inclusion criteria for each therapist were: (1) participant has been working with pwMS since more than 3 years; (2) participant is a mobile phone user. We built 3 groups of participants gathered by profession as they had different availabilities depending on their occupation. Our actual 3 groups are described in Table 1.

Table 1. Table of profiles of focus groups.

Therapists	Gender	Ages	Number of years of experience
6 physiotherapists	3 women 3 men	From 25 to 38 (average 29.8 standard deviation 4.5)	From 3 to 8 (average 4.8 standard deviation 1.9)
4 speech therapists 1 neuropsychologist	5 women	From 26 to 52 (average 37 standard deviation 8.6)	From 3 to 31 (average 11.6 standard deviation 9.9)
7 occupational therapists	7 women	From 25 to 49 (average 32.8 standard deviation 7.2)	From 3 to 23 (average 7.4 standard deviation 6.4)

All the participants have given their agreement to be recorded during the discussion.

4.2 PwMS

Participants were patients of Saint-Denis' hospital. Inclusion criteria required for each participant were: (1) to be diagnosed with MS; (2) to be affected by an evolved form of the disease and to need exercises in a rehabilitation center or physiotherapists; (3) to have a mobile phone and to self-declare having experience with mobile apps (4) have no physical disability that restrains the use of smartphone or means of adaptation to use their smartphone; (5) have no cognitive disability that restrains the use of smartphone. The evaluation of ability to use the smartphone was made by the patients' therapists. Four pwMS presented in Table 2 have participated.

Table 2. Table of profiles of pwMS interviewed.

PwMS	Age	Gender	Year of diagnose	Displacement
P1	38	Woman	2004	2 sticks for short way, electric wheeling chair for long way
P2	61	Woman	2016	Walking
P3	37	Woman	2018	Walking
P4	47	Man	1997	2 sticks

Each of them gave agreement to be recorded during the discussion.

5   Tools and Means

5.1   Investigation with Therapists

A methodology based on focus groups has been chosen for this investigation because it is a good way to open a large discussion about motivation, which seems relevant to have among professionals. The moderator had to begin with the explanation of the project to the therapists: *"Our project is to develop a prototype of a mobile app to make pwMS to practice their self-rehabilitation. The exercises in the app will be chosen by you: therapists"*, and then the moderator opened the discussion. The first subject of the discussion was mentioned with a question: *"How can we motivate pwMS to practice exercises with a mobile app?"*. This large question has been chosen to collect therapists' spontaneous ideas. The second subject of the discussion was gamification, the moderator had to define the concept and investigate about the integration of this concept in the mobile app's prototype. It will enable to confront therapists' and pwMS' opinion with literature, and then to give elements to confirm or not our hypothesis about the use of gamification. The third subject to evoke concerned exercises directly linked with disabilities in daily life activities. It will also enable to compare therapists' and pwMS' opinion with literature, and to have elements to confirm or not our second hypothesis about exercises linked with pwMS' daily life activities. Finally, to conclude, the moderator had to ask if therapists have others ideas to motivate pwMS to practice exercises with a mobile app. Each focus group has been recorded and has lasted one hour.

5.2   Investigation with PwMS

We chose individual interviews because it was not possible to group the patients for logistical reasons. Our interview grid was based on the results of therapists' investigations. The interviewer had to begin with the explanation of the project to the patients: *"Our project is to develop a prototype of a mobile app to help you to practice your self-rehabilitation's exercises. The exercises in the app will be chosen by your therapists"*. The first part of the interview began with an open question to know the spontaneous ideas of pwMS: *"How could you be motivated to practice exercises with a mobile app?"*. The second part was about gamification, to know pwMS' opinion about adding game elements in the mobile app. It will enable to confront pwMS and therapists' opinion with literature and then to give elements for our hypothesis about the use of gamification. For the third part the interviewer evokes exercises' program directly linked with their disabilities in their daily life activities and if they think it can motivate them. It will also enable to compare pwMS and therapists' opinion with literature and to give elements for our second hypothesis about exercises linked with daily life activities. Then, the fourth part was based on spontaneous ideas of therapists to motivate pwMS. So, the interviewer asked about relationship with the therapist through the mobile app, daily notifications, and videos guiding exercises. It will enable to confront pwMS' and therapists' opinions with literature. To conclude pwMS were asked if they had others ideas to motivate themselves to practice exercises with a mobile app.

6 Results and Analysis

6.1 Gamification

The spontaneous first answer of the therapists about how to motivate pwMS with a mobile app that was spontaneously was to add some game to the app. They talked about gamification without naming it. They mentioned some gamification elements like giving some challenge to the patients or building a system using levels. Nevertheless, one physiotherapist drew attention on the difficulty to talk about progress with pwMS because of the likely course of this disease. For one of the occupational therapists, it is delicate to broach the subject of game while dealing with such a severe disease. They finally agreed that using a system of levels can be motivating but it must be linked with the number of executed exercises or time spent to work and not with progress. Moreover, P1, P3, and P4 described themselves as sensible to games and thought that gamification could motivate them. However, P2 said that she does not like games and thinks it will not help her practicing exercises at home. P4 stated that he is competitive, but he does not have too much time and it might be a problem. P3 was very enthusiastic and said that she loves challenges and she is very competitive. Added to that, literature showed very good results of gamification in m-Health to improve self-management of chronic disease or progress to a healthy life behavior [16]. Therefore, gamification can be a solution to motivate pwMS to practice exercises with a mobile app, but some elements have to be taken into account. Gamification will not be adapted to all people. Moreover, we have to be attentive to the fact that MS is a degenerative disease and we cannot use progress of the person to gamify the app like it is done in sports mobile app.

6.2 Occupational-Centered

The second topic discussed was the process of working on daily life goals through the mobile app. The therapists thought it could give a sense to the exercises and motivate patients to achieve a goal which means something for them. All patients answered that having a concrete goal would interest them. P1 told us that it would help motivating her because it would be something she wants to do, something that makes sense for her. One therapist also added that it could make patients more active on their exercises because they can make the link to a concrete goal. This is a theory of occupational therapy to motivate patients for their rehabilitation [11]. According to this theory, patients could have a better engagement and investment in their rehabilitation exercises at home. The Canadian Model of Occupational Performance and Engagement is a mean to work for occupational therapists based on this theory [19]. Moreover, P4 talked about a problem of time because he has a baby to carry on and does not find time and energy to practice exercises. He liked the idea to direct exercises towards exercises linked with his activities, like changing a diaper. Finally, occupational therapists brought the light on the need of adaptation of each objective and exercise for each patient. However, they feared that it would be too time-consuming for them to configure a different program for each patient. Therefore, the app will have to be built by considering this fact.

6.3   Relationship with Therapists

The three groups of therapists all agreed that choosing exercises according to the abilities of their patients is essential. Then, one speech therapist explained that, knowing the therapist can check what exercises patients have done or not, might be motivating. One occupational therapist talked about a "supervisory comforting" towards the mobile app. For pwMS, the maintenance of the relationship thanks to the app is motivating. P1 told us that she needs to be encouraged by her therapist to make her exercises. The 4 pwMS told that they are reassuring their exercises would be chosen by their therapist who would select exercises depending on their capacities. P2 mentioned she always feels alone when she has to practice exercises at home without any guideline. The literature confirms that if exercises are adapted and specific to each patient, the acceptance to the app is better [13, 18].

6.4   Others Aspects Motivating

Lastly, others feature emerged from the investigations to motivate pwMS to practice exercises. All the therapists mentioned daily notifications to remind to make exercises, and all pwMS answered that notifications can help to not forget the exercises. A speech therapist added that some supportive and friendly sentences could be even motivating to remind the exercises. Videos and photos to explain guidelines of the exercises also created unanimity with all participants to help and motivate pwMS. In several studies daily notifications and videos are also used and are well accepted by pwMS [13, 18].

7   Conclusion and Perspectives

To conclude, the results of this study show that m-health can be a good solution to motivate pwMS to practice exercises but also that the following points are very important and should be taken into account: (1) exercises have to be chosen and programmed for each pwMS by the therapists who work with them, and know their individual specificity and their abilities; (2) some specific aspects of gamification can be used, but in respect with the disease evolution to avoid discouraging patients; (3) the programs of exercises focused on pwMS' occupations seem to be an interesting approach to motivate them. As perspectives, we will design 2 interfaces: one web site for therapists to manage exercises, and one mobile app for patients to follow therapists' programs. The therapists' interface will be designed to be the minimum time-consuming possible, and as specific as possible for each patient. The prototype is in the developing phase. Next, we will test it beyond the hospital of Saint-Denis and then we will conduct a larger study.

References

1. Browne, P., Chandraratna, D., Angood, C., et al.: Atlas of multiple sclerosis 2013: a growing global problem with widespread inequity. Neurology **83**(11), 1022–1024 (2014). https://doi.org/10.1212/WNL.0000000000000768
2. France's government of health [page on the Internet]. Paris, [updated 30 May 2018, consulted 16 July 2019] (2018). https://solidarites-sante.gouv.fr/soins-et-maladies/maladies/maladies-neurodegeneratives/article/la-sclerose-en-plaques
3. Richard, N., Waqar, R.: Multiple sclerosis: clinical evidence handbook. Am. Fam. Phys. **87**(10), 712–714 (2013)
4. Langeskov-Christensen, M., Bisson, E.J., Finlayson, M.L., Dalgas, U.: Potential pathophysiological pathways that can explain the positive effects of exercise on fatigue in multiple sclerosis: a scoping review. J. Neurol. Sci. **373**, 307–320 (2017). https://doi.org/10.1016/j.jns.2017.01.002
5. Schiavolin, S., Leonardi, M., Giovannetti, A.M., Antozzi, C., Brambilla, L., Confalonieri, P., et al.: Factors related to difficulties with employment in patients with multiple sclerosis: a review of 2002–2011 literature. Int. J. Rehabil. Res. **36**(2), 105–111 (2013). https://doi.org/10.1097/MRR.0b013e32835c79ea
6. Latimer-Cheung, A.E., Martin, G.K., Hicks, A.L., Motl, R.W., Pilutti, L.A., Duggan, M., et al.: Development of evidence-informed physical activity guidelines for adults with multiple sclerosis. Arch. Phys. Med. Rehabil. **94**(9), 1829–1836 (2013). https://doi.org/10.1016/j.apmr.2013.05.015
7. Edwards, T., Pilutti, L.A.: The effect of exercise training in adults with multiple sclerosis with severe mobility disability: a systematic review and future research directions. Multiple Sclerosis Relat. Disord. **16**, 31–39 (2017). https://doi.org/10.1016/j.msard.2017.06.003
8. Alsaadi, T., et al.: Depression and anxiety as determinants of health-related quality of life in patients with multiple sclerosis. Neurol. Int. **9**(4), 7343 (2017). https://doi.org/10.4081/ni.2017.7343
9. Chassan, C., Sévène, M., Cras, O., Archambault, D.: Application smartphone, sclérose en plaques et auto-rééducation. In: Actes du Colloque JCJC'2019, pp. 7–12. IFRATH, Université Paris8, Saint-Denis (2019)
10. Deterding, S., Dixon, D., Khaled, R.: Gamification: toward a definition. In: 2011 The ACM CHI Conference on Human Factors in Computing Systems, pp. 12–15 (2011)
11. Sharrott, G.W., Cooper-Fraps, C.: Occupation theory motivation: theories of motivation in occupational therapy: an overview. Am. J. Occup. Ther. **40**, 249–257 (1986)
12. Giunti, G., Guisado Fernández, E., Dorronzoro Zubiete, E., Rivera, R.O.: Supply and demand in mHealth apps for persons with multiple sclerosis: systematic search in app stores and scoping literature review. JMIR Mhealth Uhealth **6**(5), e1051 (2018). https://doi.org/10.2196/10512
13. Thirumalai, M., et al.: TEAMS (Tele-Exercise and Multiple Sclerosis), a tailored telerehabilitation mHealth app: participant-centered development and usability study. JMIR Mhealth Uhealth **6**(5), e10181 (2018). https://doi.org/10.2196/10181
14. Giunti, G., Kool, J., Rivera Romero, O., Dorronzoro, Z.E.: Exploring the specific needs of persons with multiple sclerosis for mHealth solutions for physical activity: mixed-methods study. JMIR Mhealth Uhealth **6**(2), e37 (2018). https://doi.org/10.2196/mhealth.8996
15. Giunti, G., Mylonopoulou, V., Rivera, R.O.: More stamina, a gamified mHealth solution for persons with multiple sclerosis: research through design. JMIR Mhealth Uhealth **6**(3), e51 (2018). https://doi.org/10.2196/mhealth.9437

16. Miller, A.S., Cafazzo, J.A., Seto, E.: A game plan: gamification design principles in mHealth applications for chronic disease management. Health Inform. J. **22**(2), 184–193 (2016). https://doi.org/10.1177/1460458214537511. Medline: 24986104

17. Geurts, E., Van Geel, F., Feys, P., Coninx, K.: WalkWithMe: personalized goal setting and coaching for walking in people with multiple sclerosis. In: 27th Conference on User Modeling, Adaptation and Personalization (UMAP 2019), Larnaca, Cyprus, 9–12 June 2019, p. 10. ACM, New York (2019). https://doi.org/10.1145/3320435.3320459

18. Ehling, R., et al.: Successful long-term management of spasticity in patients with multiple sclerosis using a software application (APP): a pilot study. Multiple Sclerosis Relat. Disord. **17**, 15–21 (2017). https://doi.org/10.1016/j.msard.2017.06.013

19. Polatajko, H.J., Townsend, E.A., Craik, J.: Canadian model of occupational performance and engagement (CMOP-E). In: Townsend, E.A., Polatajko, H.J. (eds.) Enabling Occupation II: Advancing an Occupational Therapy Vision of Health, Well-Being, & Justice Through Occupation, pp. 22–23. CAOT Publications ACE, Ottawa (2007)

Accelerometer-Based Machine Learning Categorization of Body Position in Adult Populations

Leighanne Jarvis[1][(⊠)] , Sarah Moninger[1] ,
Chandra Throckmorton[2] , Juliessa Pavon[1] , and Kevin Caves[1]

[1] Duke University, Durham, NC 27710, USA
leighanne.jarvis@duke.edu
[2] Signal Analysis Solutions, Bahama, NC 27503, USA

Abstract. This manuscript describes tests and results of a study to evaluate classification algorithms derived from accelerometer data collected on healthy adults and older adults to better classify posture movements. Specifically, tests were conducted to 1) compare performance of 1 sensor vs. 2 sensors; 2) examine custom trained algorithms to classify for a given task 3) determine overall classifier accuracy for healthy adults under 55 and older adults (55 or older). Despite the current variety of commercially available platforms, sensors, and analysis software, many do not provide the data granularity needed to characterize all stages of movement. Additionally, some clinicians have expressed concerns regarding validity of analysis on specialized populations, such as hospitalized older adults. Accurate classification of movement data is important in a clinical setting as more hospital systems are using sensors to help with clinical decision making. We developed custom software and classification algorithms to identify laying, reclining, sitting, standing, and walking. Our algorithm accuracy is 93.2% for healthy adults under 55 and 95% for healthy older adults over 55 for the tasks in our setting. The high accuracy of this approach will aid future investigation into classifying movement in hospitalized older adults. Results from these tests also indicate that researchers and clinicians need to be aware of sensor body position in relation to where the algorithm used was trained. Additionally, results suggest more research is needed to determine if algorithms trained on one population can accurately be used to classify data from another population.

Keywords: Activity · Accelerometers · Older adults · Machine learning · Classification

1 Background

Accelerometer-based activity monitors produce an automated, objective, valid and reliable measure of mobility [1], and are used frequently in both research and clinical environments. Several studies have used accelerometry in inpatient and assisted living settings to gather activity data [2–5]. Recent studies support that wearable device-

K. Miesenberger et al. (Eds.): ICCHP 2020, LNCS 12377, pp. 242–249, 2020.
https://doi.org/10.1007/978-3-030-58805-2_29

measured activity in hospitalized patients predicts readmission risk, length of stay, and disability [5–10].

While accelerometers are popular amongst researchers and clinicians to capture activity and mobility in patient populations, other sensors and platforms have also been used with various levels of success [11–13]. A commercial accelerometer was used for this study due to its low cost, high frequency data collection, flexibility in sensor placement, small size, and ability to maintain patient privacy (in comparison to camera activity monitoring platforms). While many commercial accelerometer sensors and platforms have been validated with younger, healthy people and some patient populations, many of these devices are not validated in specialized populations, such as hospitalized older adults.

Hospital providers make clinical decisions that depend in part on activity (e.g. whether a patient is physically improving or declining, or if discharge should be to home versus skilled nursing facility). Often there is little verifiable objective data upon which to guide these decisions because hospital health care providers must depend on patient report and/or other chart documentation, which has been shown to be suboptimal [14, 15]. Accelerometry has the potential to provide clinicians with objective information to gauge a patient's activity more accurately. Higher accuracy allows providers to detect early immobility and take timely clinical action to mitigate the risk of functional decline. Commercially available devices such as smart watches and activity trackers are robust and reliable devices that collect activity data, but these devices do not offer movement classification accuracy and flexibility within specialized populations (e.g. the acutely ill or other populations with varied health issues).

Clinicians and researchers at Duke University Medical Center are working to better understand the movement in an acutely ill population. This is especially important for hospitalized older adults because better outcomes, such as reduced need for post-acute care and decreased risk of death are directly linked to increased mobility while hospitalized [16, 17].

The aim of our work is ultimately to collect and use accelerometer data to train a machine learning algorithm to classify posture and movement changes in acutely ill, hospitalized patients. In this study we develop technology and software to reliably collect activity data and establish procedures to create machine learning models. Specifically, our algorithm uses accelerometer data to classify a patient's movement as laying, reclining, sitting, standing, or walking to better reflect specific activity movements during hospitalization.

2 Research Design and Methods

2.1 Participants

We recruited two cohorts from convenience samples at two locations in Durham, NC, under the review of the Duke University Medical Center Institutional Review Board. The first cohort (N = 15), consisting of older adults, 55 years or older (7 males 70.7 ± 6.3; 8 females 63.3 ± 8.7 years old) were recruited from the GeroFit program, an older adult exercises program run in conjunction with the Durham VA but held at a private health club, for older veterans. The second cohort (N = 15), were adults between 22 and 54 years (4 males 35.5 + 10.3; 11 females 30.9 + 9.3 years old) and were recruited from administrative offices at Duke University Medical Center. Due to the high sampling rate of the sensors, the small sample size (N = 30) was determined to be appropriate by our machine learning expert to be sufficient for model training and testing for this proof of concept development. Subjects with physical, cognitive, or behavioral impairment that would prevent the safe completion of the testing or be unable to follow study directions were excluded from participation. All subjects were required to be able to 1) lay supine, 2) reclined, 3) sit, 4) stand, and 5) walk in 1-min intervals, twice, and transition between positions independently, with or without the use of an assistive device (e.g. cane or walker).

2.2 Study Design

To train our machine learning algorithm to detect the five test positions (laying, reclining, sitting, standing, and walking), ten minutes of labeled sensor data was collected on each subject. Two small wireless 3-axis commodity accelerometers (Meta-MotionR; MbientLab, San Francisco, CA) were used. The data was streamed at 25 Hz to a custom iOS mobile application connected via Bluetooth Low Energy (BLE) 4. While the sensor allows for gyroscope, accelerometer, and temperature measurements, for this study data was only collected from the accelerometer. Since most typical human movements are less than 10 Hz [18], we selected a sample rate of 25 Hz based on a 12.5 Hz Nyquist frequency needed to abstract meaningful data. The Nyquist Theorem states that a sample rate at least two times higher than the highest frequency input signal is required for accurate measurements [19]. Data logging speed and long battery life of the Mbient sensors allowed us to record at a frequency higher than minimally required by the Nyquist Theorem for our study.

One sensor was worn on the upper front of the chest under the right clavicle attached with cloth tape. A second sensor was worn on the anterior of the right thigh attached with self-adhering bandage (e.g. sport wrap). Once instrumented, subjects were directed through the test positions in 1-min intervals, twice. The order of positions was laying, reclining, sitting, standing, walking - walking, standing, sitting, reclining, and laying. Each position was indicated to the subject with verbal instructions by the investigators and can be identified by: laying prone on a flat surface, reclining at an approximately 125–135° angle (assisted by a raised PT table or PT wedges), sitting with legs hanging off of bed/table height surface with back approximately at 90°, standing straight without movement, and walking at a normal pace.

2.3 Data Processing

Prior to beginning data collection, a non-identifying subject ID was entered into the mobile app. Each reading streamed from the accelerometer included x, y, and z axes and a timestamp. As the app collected the readings and persisted them into on-device storage, it displayed a stop-watch-style timer for each position duration. An investigator used the app to manually label the subject's position as it changed. This data was aggregated into a single CSV file on the mobile app and exported via email for post-processing. Data was processed offline after the collection from all participants.

The triaxial accelerometer data was buffered into 4-s time windows with magnitude-and-variance-based features extracted (e.g. trimmed-mean position and standard deviation of position). A Random Forest classifier was trained to automatically discriminate between the positions using leave-one-subject-out cross-validation to ensure robust performance estimates. This validation means that each participant's data was held aside for testing against the remaining participants' data that was used to train the classifier. This process was repeated for each participant and the results pooled across participants to estimate classifier performance.

3   Results

This paper describes the results of three tests: Comparison of performance of 1 vs. 2 sensors, importance of custom trained algorithms to classify for the given tasks, and overall classifier accuracy between older adults (55 or older) and adults under 55.

3.1   Comparison of Performance of 1 vs. 2 Sensors

To confirm reports, literature, and past studies, the data was analyzed to determine if one sensor would provide the accuracy needed to capture all posture movements. By using data recorded form a single sensor, we concluded that a single sensor worn on the chest or thigh would not provide reasonable accuracy for all posture movements. Specifically, when wearing only a chest sensor, sitting and standing were indistinguishable from each other. Using only a thigh sensor, laying, reclining, and sitting were indistinguishable from each other (Fig. 1).

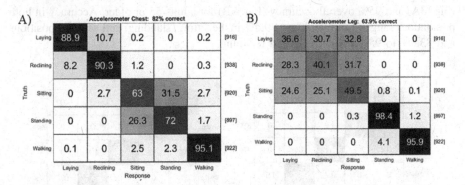

Fig. 1. Confusion matrices showing posture task with only one sensor used to identify body position. A) Only chest sensor used. B) Only leg sensor used.

3.2   Importance of Training for Task

To verify that sensor position and task performed are important to algorithm performance, we trained the classification algorithm based on one sensor location and tested the accuracy using data obtained from a different sensor location. Using a sensor on the leg when the classifier had been trained with a chest position sensor shows poor results (Fig. 2A) with only an 82.7% accuracy for standing/walking. However, using a sensor on the chest when the classifier had been trained on the leg did not have a negative impact (Fig. 2B) when comparing prone (laying/reclining) vs. upright (sitting, standing, and walking).

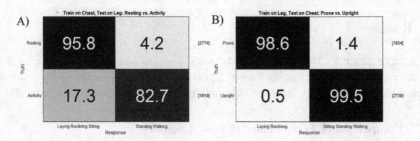

Fig. 2. Confusion matrices showing results of switching sensor locations after a classifier has been trained for the sensor placed on another location.

3.3   Classifier Accuracy – Older Adults and Adults

After confirming one sensor would not provide accuracy for each posture position, labeled data pooled from both sensors were used to train the classification algorithm for the test positions in a controlled setting. Accuracy for adults under 55 is overall 93.2% (Fig. 3A) and 95% overall accuracy (Fig. 3B) for adults 55 or older. Accuracy in both populations ranged from 96.5% to 99.4% in the sitting, standing, and walking positions and 83.5% to 95.1% for laying and reclining.

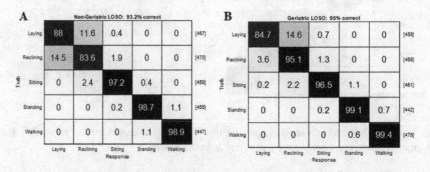

Fig. 3. Confusion matrices depicting classification accuracy in percent for older adults and adults wearing two sensors, one on the thigh and one on the chest. A) Adult (non-geriatric) results showing overall 93.2% accuracy. B) Older adults (geriatric) showing overall 95% accuracy.

To observe classifier accuracy based on training within a different population than the testing population, the algorithm was trained using labeled data from older adults and tested on data from adults under 55. The classifier accuracy for this condition is 93.7% accuracy (Fig. 4A). The accuracy for an algorithm trained on labeled data from adults under 55 and tested using data from older adults, yielded a 94% accuracy (Fig. 4B).

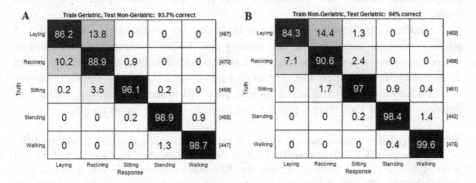

Fig. 4. Confusion matrices depicting classification when training algorithm on one population and testing on another population. A) Train on older adult (geriatric), test on adult (non-geriatric). B) Train on adult (non-geriatric), test on older adult (geriatric).

4 Discussion and Implications

When training and testing the algorithm within a specific population while wearing two sensors, we showed a 93.2% accuracy for adults and a 95% accuracy for older adults across the five positions. Performance using a single sensor worn on either the chest or thigh to classify multiple posture positions was less accurate. This indicates that more than one sensor may be needed to classify granular movement, and that multiple sensors may be needed to identify laying, reclining, sitting, standing, and walking posture movements with accelerometry.

By observing new classification tasks and using one sensor to distinguish all posture movements, we showed that sensor position is important to the specific task (e.g. walking). Specifically, changing a sensor position without retraining the algorithm proves to get inaccurate results, depending on the specific task. This is an important implication when using commercially available sensors because the algorithm must have the ability to be trained on data collected at that specific body position. Commercially available sensor and software packages only allow users to place the sensors in specific locations on the body which might not be sufficient for some research projects. For example, the Actigraph wGT3X-BT and ActiLife software limits sensor position to the wrist, waist, ankle, and thigh [20]. These results and discussion underscore the need for a customizable software solution that allows the user to generate their own algorithm based on training data specific to a population and sensor location.

Our results comparing algorithm performance using an algorithm trained on one population and tested on another population proved to be almost as accurate as training and testing within the same population. This is likely due to the similarities in these populations, both abled bodied and mobile, and the fact that subjects were performing specific constrained tasks. More research is needed to make an accurate statement regarding training within one population and testing in another. We speculate that testing on a population significantly different from the training group (e.g. mobility compromised, acutely ill, hospitalized subjects) would show poor classification accuracy.

To address this, structured testing is underway on hospitalized older adults and adults. Although more analysis and testing are needed, preliminary data analysis demonstrates the importance of training classifiers with data from the target population as speculated in this paper. The next step of this project is to finish testing on hospitalized adults and older adults. Additionally, we will further validate our findings by testing movement for different population groups in at-home environments.

Acknowledgement. This work was supported by the National Institute on Disability, Independent Living and Rehabilitation Research in the U.S. Department of Health and Human Services [grant number *90RE5028*]; and the National Institutes of Health [grant number *P20AG028716*]. The authors would like to thank the Claude D. Pepper Older Americans Independence Center (OAIC) at Duke University for their continued support on this project.

References

1. Pruit, L.A., et al.: Use of accelerometry to measure physical activity in older adults at risk for mobility disability. J. Aging Phys. Act. **16**(4), 416–434 (2008). https://doi.org/10.1123/japa.16.4.416
2. Brown, C.J., Roth, D.L., Allman, R.M.: Validation of the use of wireless monitors to measure levels of mobility during hospitalization. J. Rehabil. Res. Dev. **45**(4), 551–558 (2008). https://doi.org/10.1682/jrrd.2007.06.0086
3. Brown, C.J., Redden, D.T., Flood, K.L., Allman, R.M.: The underrecognized epidemic of low mobility during hospitalization of older adults. J. Am. Geriatr. Soc. **57**(9), 1660–1665 (2009). https://doi.org/10.1111/j.1532-5415.2009.02393.x
4. Hall, K.S., Cohen, H.J., Pieper, C.F., Fillenbaum, G.G., Kraus, W.E., Huffman, K.M., et al.: Physical performance across the adult life span: correlates with age and physical activity. J. Gerontol. Ser. A **72**(4), 572–578 (2017). https://doi.org/10.1093/Gerona/glw120
5. Pavon, J.M., Sloane, R.J., Pieper, C.F., Colón-Emeric, C.S., Cohen, H.J., Gallagher, D., et al.: Accelerometer-measured hospital physical activity and hospital-acquired disability in older adults. J. Am. Geriatr. Soc. **68**(2), 261–265 (2020). https://doi.org/10.1111/jgs.16231
6. Agmon, M., Zisberg, A., Gil, E., Rand, D., Gur-Yaish, N., Azriel, M.: Association between 900 steps a day and functional decline in older hospitalized patients. JAMA Intern. Med. **177**(2), 272–274 (2017). https://doi.org/10.1001/jamainternmed.2016.7266
7. Cohen, Y., Zisberg, A., Chayat, Y., Gur-Yaish, N., Gil, E., Levin, C., et al.: Walking for better outcomes and recovery: the effect of WALK-FOR in preventing hospital-associated functional decline among older adults. J. Gerontol. Ser. A: Biomed. Sci. Med. Sci. **74**(10), 1664–1670 (2019). https://doi.org/10.1093/gerona/glz025

8. Daskivich, T.J., Houman, J., Lopez, M., Luu, M., Fleshner, P., Zaghiyan, K., et al.: Association of wearable activity monitors with assessment of daily ambulation and length of stay among patients undergoing major surgery. JAMA Netw. Open 2(2), e187673 (2019). https://doi.org/10.1001/jamanetworkopen.2018.7673

9. Fisher, S.R., Graham, J.E., Ottenbacher, K.J., Deer, R., Ostir, G.V.: Inpatient walking activity to predict readmission in older adults. Arch. Phys. Med. Rehabil. 97(9 Suppl), S226–S231 (2016). https://doi.org/10.1016/j.apmr.2015.09.029

10. Sallis, R., Roddy-Strum, Y., Chijioke, E., Litman, K., Kanter, M.H., Huang, B.Z., et al.: Stepping toward discharge: level of ambulation in hospitalized patients. J. Hosp. Med. 10(6), 384–389 (2015). https://doi.org/10.1002/jhm.2343

11. Banerjee, T., Peterson, M., Oliver, Q., Froehle, A., Lawhorne, L.: Validating a commercial device for continuous activity measurement in the older adult population for dementia management. Smart Health 5–6, 51–62 (2018)

12. Zhan, K., Ramos, F., Faux, S.: Activity recognition from a wearable camera. In: 12th International Conference on Control, Automation, Robotics, & Vision, pp. 365–370. IEEE, Guandzhou (2012)

13. Guraliuc, A.R., Barsocchi, P., Potorti, F., Nepa, P.: Limb movements classification using wearable wireless transceivers. IEEE Trans. Inf. Technol. Biomed. 15(3), 474–480 (2011)

14. Resnick, B., Galik, E., Gruber-Baldini, A.L., Zimmerman, S.: Perceptions and performance of function and physical activity in assisted living communities. J. Am. Med. Directors Assoc. 11(6), 406–414 (2010). https://doi.org/10.1016/j.jamda.2010.02.003

15. Hodgson, C.L., Denehy, L.: Measuring physical function after ICU: one step at a time. Intensive Care Med. 43(12), 1901–1903 (2017). https://doi.org/10.1007/s00134-017-4939-1

16. Hastings, S.N., Sloane, R., Morey, M.C., Pavon, J.M., Hoenig, H.: Assisted early mobility for hospitalized older veterans: preliminary data from the STRIDE program. J. Am. Geriatr. Soc. 62(11), 2180–2184 (2014). https://doi.org/10.1111/jgs.13095

17. Ostir, G.V., Berges, I.M., Kuo, Y.F., Goodwin, J.S., Fisher, S.R., Guralnik, J.M.: Mobility activity and its value as a prognostic indicator of survival in hospitalized older adults. J. Am. Geriatr. Soc. 61(4), 551–557 (2013). https://doi.org/10.1111/jgs.12170

18. Welk, G.J.: Use of accelerometry-based activity monitors to assess physical activity. In: Physical Activity Assessments for Health-Related Research. Human Kinetics, Champaign, IL, pp. 125–141 (2002)

19. Weik, M.H.: Nyquist theorem. In: Weik, M.H. (ed.) Computer Science and Communications Dictionary, p. 1127. Springer, Boston (2000). https://doi.org/10.1007/1-4020-0613-6_12654

20. ActiGraph wGT3X-BT page. https://www.actigraphcorp.com/actigraph-wgt3x-bt/. Accessed 8 Aug 2019

Survey of Rehabilitation Clinicians in the United States: Barriers and Critical Use-Cases for mRehab Adoption

John Morris[1]([⊠]), Nicole Thompson[1], Tracey Wallace[1] [iD],
Mike Jones[1] [iD], and Frank DeRuyter[2] [iD]

[1] Crawford Research Institute, Shepherd Center, Atlanta, GA 30309, USA
john.morris@shepherd.org
[2] Duke University Medical Center, Durham, NC 27705, USA

Abstract. This paper presents data and analysis from survey research conducted by the Rehabilitation Engineering Research Center on Information and Communications Technology Access for Information and Communications Technology (ICT) Access for Community Living, Health and Function (LiveWell RERC) on the perceptions and attitudes of clinical professionals in rehabilitation medicine regarding mobile health (mHealth) and mobile rehabilitation (mRehab) practices, techniques and technology in the United States. The analytical focus of this paper is on two key survey questions related to specific barriers and opportunities (most critical use-cases) for adopting mHealth/mRehab interventions. We present response data to these two questions segmented by clinical specialty – physical, occupational, speech and recreation therapy – to identify possible variation between and among these rehabilitation professions. This analysis provides a detailed map of the terrain of clinician expectations and experiences for the adoption and implementation of mHealth/mRehab interventions in the United States, and possibly other countries. Results show substantial support for mRehab interventions and technologies across all four clinical specialties. The most frequently identified barriers to effective use of mobile and internet technologies to support patients remotely focused on patients (ability to learn and use the technology, and internet access), not clinicians. The was more variability among clinical specializations regarding best use-cases. Tracking patient adherence to prescribed activities and supporting patients in the home and community were the most frequently cited best use cases across the whole sample.

Keywords: eHealth · mHealth · Clinician attitudes · Technology

1 Introduction

This paper presents data and analysis from survey research conducted by the Rehabilitation Engineering Research Center on Information and Communications Technology Access for Information and Communications Technology (ICT) Access for Community Living, Health and Function (LiveWell RERC) on the perceptions and attitudes of clinical professionals in rehabilitation medicine regarding mobile health

K. Miesenberger et al. (Eds.): ICCHP 2020, LNCS 12377, pp. 250–257, 2020.
https://doi.org/10.1007/978-3-030-58805-2_30

(mHealth) and mobile rehabilitation (mRehab) interventions and technology in the United States. We focus on two key survey questions related to specific barriers and best use-cases for mRehab interventions identified by clinicians:

- What barriers might limit or detract from mobile and internet technology's effectiveness in supporting post-acute and between-visits therapy interventions?
- What do you believe are the most critical use cases for mobile or internet technology support in post-acute or between-visits therapy interventions?

We provide summary results from all respondents and analysis of responses by four core clinical specializations: physical, occupational, speech and recreation therapy to identify possible variation between clinical professions. This analysis provides a detailed map of the terrain across multiple dimensions for the adoption and implementation of mRehab interventions in the United States, and possibly other countries.

2 Background

Mobile health and mobile rehabilitation (mHealth and mRehab) services and technologies have attracted considerable interest from healthcare providers, technology vendors, rehabilitation engineers, investors and policy makers in recent years [1–3]. Successful adoption and use of mHealth/mRehab interventions requires clinician support and engagement, including the ability to identify appropriate use cases and possible barriers to use for rehabilitation clinicians and their patients, and acquire adequate knowledge and confidence using mHealth/mRehab interventions. We present results from a survey of rehabilitation clinicians in the United States on their attitudes, experience, expectations, and concerns regarding mHealth/mRehab interventions and technologies. Over 500 clinicians in physical, occupational, speech, recreation therapy professions, among others, participated in the survey.

Mobile healthcare and mobile rehabilitation offer the potential to dramatically expand services to patients in need. Indeed, the World Health Organization (WHO) views "digital health" solutions as a key tool to support the goal of Universal Health Coverage (UHC). According to the WHO: "Digital technologies provide concrete opportunities to tackle health system challenges, and thereby offer the potential to enhance the coverage and quality of health practices and services" [4].

This view is reflected in the World Federation of Occupational Therapists (WFTO), whose Statement of Position states: "Telehealth is an appropriate delivery model for occupational therapy services when in-person services are not possible, practical, or optimal for delivering care and/or when service delivery via telehealth is mutually acceptable to the client and provider" [5]. In the United States the main professional organization for each of the 3 core therapy specializations (physical, occupational and speech therapy) have published statements that support use of telehealth/mHealth [6–8]. Like the WHO and WFTO, these organizations emphasize the ability to extend therapy services to more patients in a more flexible way to the home and community by using technology-supported interventions.

3 Methodology

With input from our clinical advisors and informed by a review of the available literature on barriers to adoption of digital health interventions, we developed the "Clinician perspectives on mRehab interventions and technologies" survey questionnaire consisting of 22 questions to address four broad topics:

1. Perceived need for mRehab interventions based on patients' therapy needs post-discharge from inpatient rehabilitation or between outpatient clinic visits
2. Perceived barriers to use of mRehab, including personal interest or reservations about mRehab interventions
3. Perceptions regarding the potential utility of mRehab interventions including the most important use cases for the technology
4. Current interest in, knowledge about, or actual experience using mRehab strategies

Data were collected from January 22 to March 10, 2019. Participants were recruited through the researchers' personal networks at Shepherd Center, Duke University Medical Center, the American Congress of Rehabilitation Medicine, American Physical Therapy Association, American Occupational Therapy Association, American Speech-Hearing Association, and others. Data were collected using convenience sampling methods and online data collection on the Survey Monkey web-based platform. Although no protected health information (PHI) was collected in this survey, the Survey Monkey platform does meet the privacy and security requirements of the United States Health Insurance Portability and Accountability Act of 1996 (HIPAA), which establishes essential policies and practices for protecting patient health information from unnecessary and unauthorized access.

Efforts were made to ensure that relative balance in the number of respondents among the 4 core clinical therapy professions (physical, occupational, speech therapy and recreation therapy) by creating unique "collectors" in Survey Monkey and setting limits on the number of respondents to each. A small incentive—a $5.00 Starbucks gift card sent electronically—was offered to respondents to encourage higher levels of completeness in survey responses. The Research Review Committee at Shepherd Center reviewed and approved this research to ensure protection of participants.

4 Results

Response data were analyzed using SPSS version 22. A total of 505 rehabilitation clinicians across multiple rehabilitation specialties completed the questionnaire. About half of respondents reported between 5 and 19 years of experience in their profession, and slightly more than half (55%) personally owned a wearable fitness tracker, smart watch, or other wearable device with sensors. Table 1 provides a summary of survey respondents by profession. The "Other" category includes physical therapy assistant, certified occupational therapy assistant (COTA), medical assistant, rehabilitation instructor, experimental psychologist, and others.

Many respondents reported treating multiple patient populations including those with acquired brain injury (ABI), neurodegenerative diseases (NDD), musculoskeletal

Table 1. Respondents by profession (number and percentage of sample).

Disability type	Number	Percent
Physician	13	2.6
Non-Physician Medical (Phys. Asst, Nurse Practitioner, Nurse)	13	2.6
Physical Therapist	72	14.3
Occupational Therapist	104	20.6
Speech-language Pathologist	166	32.9
Recreational Therapist	57	11.3
Mental Health (Psychologist or Counselor)	54	10.7
Other professions	26	5.1

injury or disorder, cardiovascular disease (CVD), cancer, spinal cord injury (SCI) and other conditions (Table 2).

Table 2. Respondents by rehabilitation population served (number and percentage of sample).

Disability type	Number	Percent
Acquired Brain Injury (ABI)	375	74.3
Neurodegenerative Disease (NDD)	300	59.4
Musculoskeletal injury/disorder	198	39.2
Cardiovascular Disease (CVD)	181	35.8
Cancer	178	35.2
Spinal Cord Injury (SCI)	172	34.1
Other populations	119	23.6

Similarly, many respondents reported working in multiple clinical environments, including inpatient and outpatient environments, as well as skilled nursing facilities, home health and other environments (Table 3).

Table 3. Clinical environments of respondents (number and percentage of sample).

Disability type	Number	Percent
Inpatient acute	146	28.9
Inpatient rehab	203	40.2
Outpatient clinic	243	48.0
Skilled nursing facility	72	14.3
Home health	48	9.5
Other environments	73	14.5

To map the challenges and opportunities for implementing new mHealth and mRehab interventions for people with disabilities and chronic conditions, respondents were asked to: 1) select the 3 most likely barriers or concerns that might limit or detract from the effectiveness of mobile and internet technology to support post-acute and between-visits therapy interventions; and 2) to identify the 3 most critical use cases for technology-based remote interventions.

For each question, respondents were provided a list of barriers and use cases, respectively, with the option to specify additional barriers and use cases in an open-ended comment field. Tables 4 and 5 show the response rates for barriers and use cases for the core therapy specializations (physical, occupational, speech), plus the small but growing field of recreation therapy.

Table 4. What barriers might limit or detract from mobile and internet technology's effectiveness in supporting post-acute and between-visits therapy interventions? (Select 3).

Barriers to use	Physical therapy	Occupational therapy	Speech therapy	Recreation therapy	All 4 specializations
Patients unable to learn and/or correctly use technology	72.2%	77.9%	78.3%	73.7%	76.4%
Patients with limited or no access to internet services	50.0%	64.4%	74.1%	63.2%	65.7%
Cost vs. reimbursement	26.4%	36.5%	35.5%	22.8%	32.8%
Hassle and time commitment for clinicians to adopt	36.1%	26.9%	18.7%	19.3%	24.1%
Patient concern over security and privacy	22.2%	19.2%	23.5%	33.3%	23.6%
Concerns over accuracy and reliability	31.9%	18.3%	21.1%	15.8%	21.6%
Improvement in outcomes or efficiency not sufficient	12.5%	11.5%	11.4%	10.5%	11.5%

Respondents in all four professions identified concerns over the ability of patients to learn and use the mRehab technology correctly (76.4% of all respondents in these professions) and access to internet services (65.7%) as the top 2 potential barriers to the effectiveness of mobile and internet technology to support their patients. Physical therapists were notably less concerned with internet access compared to the other four professions.

Table 5. What do you believe are the most critical use cases for mobile or internet technology support in post-acute or between-visits therapy interventions? (Select 3).

Use cases	Physical therapy	Occupational therapy	Speech therapy	Recreation therapy	All 4 specializations
Support patient adherence to prescribed exercises/activities	73.6%	61.5%	72.9%	57.9%	67.9%
Support patient functioning at home and in the community	51.4%	70.2%	78.9%	59.6%	68.9%
Real-time, direct observation, communication with patients	56.9%	51.9%	46.4%	50.9%	50.4%
Remote biometric monitoring of patient activity with apps or wearable tech	48.6%	33.7%	24.7%	24.6%	31.3%
Patients' self-reporting of outcomes	33.3%	26.0%	30.7%	28.1%	29.6%
Remote environmental monitoring using sensors in homes	23.6%	27.9%	13.9%	12.3%	19.0%

There was some variation in the secondary barriers identified among the four professions. Physical therapists were more concerned with the hassle and time commitment required of clinicians for set-up (36.1%), and the accuracy and reliability of the technology (31.9%). Occupational and speech therapists were more concerned with the cost of the solutions and reimbursement by insurance providers (36.5% and 35.5%, respectively). Recreation therapists identified security and privacy of the technology as their leading secondary concern (33.3%).

There was greater variation in the most critical use cases identified by respondents in each of the four therapy professions. Almost three-fourths (73.9%) of physical therapists identified supporting patient adherence to prescribed exercises and activities. Notably, a similar percentage of speech therapists (72.9%) also identified this as a critical use case. But, speech therapists' most frequently cited use case was supporting patient functioning at home and in the community (78.9%). This was also the most frequently cited use cases for occupational and recreation therapists (70.2% and 59.6%, respectively).

Approximately half of the respondents in each profession cited real-time, direct observation and communication with patients as a critical use-case, making this the third most cited use-case. Also noteworthy, almost half of the physical therapists (48.6%) cited remote biometric monitoring as a critical use case. Patient self-reporting of outcomes and remote environmental monitoring using sensors in the home were least frequently cited overall.

5   Conclusion

Clinical professionals often serve as "gatekeepers" for new healthcare technologies [9]. They are the ones who must prescribe a technology-based intervention to a specific patient, or not. Within a large clinical facility (hospital or large clinic), clinicians are often engaged in technology reviews and planning for implementation of new patient-care technologies. Consequently, it is critical to identify their perceptions of the barriers and best uses for new technologies such as those used for mRehab.

The survey data presented here on the perceptions of rehabilitation clinicians indicates broad acceptance of mHealth technologies and interventions for specific use-cases. There was consensus among respondents in the four rehabilitation therapy professions analyzed here in favor of using of mHealth technologies to support patient adherence to prescribed exercises and activities and to support patient functioning in the home and community. There was much less support for use-cases involving wearable or environmental sensors and patient self-reporting.

There was strong consensus that the main barriers to adoption related to *the patients*, not the clinicians. Patients' ability to learn and use the technology correctly and patient access to the internet were the top perceived barriers. Other potential barriers such as reimbursement from insurance providers, hassle and time commitment on the part of clinicians, security and privacy, accuracy and reliability of data collected, and improvement in health outcomes were much less frequently identified as barriers.

The low levels of concern for these other potential barriers is noteworthy, as these have been identified as concerns in earlier studies of physician perspectives on digital health. In a 2016 survey of physicians in the U.S., most respondents reported being concerned about potential liability, reimbursement, technical problems, and patient privacy [10]. Similarly, a survey of physicians in Europe cited patient privacy and data security as major concerns [11]. A scoping review of the literature on physician attitudes toward eHealth conducted by Canadian researchers identified technology design, training, liability, and patient privacy as key issues [12].

It is possible that rehabilitation therapists are more likely to utilize a wider range of technologies, especially mobile and internet technologies, than physicians. Also, rehabilitation therapy usually involves more frequent and longer-duration interactions with patients. That degree of engagement with patients may motivate rehabilitation clinicians to be more concerned about patient access than they might be regarding reimbursement, time commitment on the part of the clinician, privacy, etc.

The survey of clinician perspectives on mRehab interventions and technologies serves as the cornerstone for our long-term commitment to engage clinicians regularly regarding their experiences using new methods and modalities of interacting with their patients and using newly emerging technologies. We plan to update and refine this cornerstone survey with the goal of tracking clinician perceptions and experiences over time. Additionally, we plan to conduct more targeted research on topics such as experiences implementing a cloud-based digital therapeutics system for prescribing home exercise programs (HEPs) and tracking progress; and using specific consumer platforms to track patient activity such as smartwatches, fitness trackers, camera-based systems, smart speakers and other smart home devices.

Acknowledgements. The authors thank the hundreds of rehabilitation clinicians from multiple specialties who participated in this research project. This research is supported by the Rehabilitation Engineering Research Center on Information and Communications Technology Access for Community Living, Health and Function (LiveWell RERC), which is funded by a 5-year grant from the National Institute on Disability, Independent Living and Rehabilitation Research (NIDILRR) in the U.S. Department of Health and Human Services (grant number 90RE5028). The opinions contained herein are those of the mRehab RERC and do not necessarily reflect those of the U.S. Department of Health and Human Services or NIDILRR.

References

1. Frontera, W.R., et al.: Rehabilitation research at the National Institutes of Health: moving the field forward (executive summary). Am. J. Phys. Med. Rehabil. **96**, 211–220 (2017)
2. Dobkin, B.H., Dorsch, A.: The promise of mHealth: daily activity monitoring and outcome assessments by wearable sensors. Neurorehabil. Neural Repair **25**, 788–798 (2011)
3. Jones, M., Morris, J., DeRuyter, F.: Mobile healthcare and people with disabilities: current state and future needs. Int. J. Environ. Res. Public Health **15**, 515 (2018)
4. World Health Organization: WHO guideline: recommendations on digital interventions for health system strengthening. World Health Organization, Geneva (2019). Licence: CC BY-NC-SA 3.0 IGO
5. World Federation of Occupational Therapists: World Federation of Occupational Therapists' Position statement on telehealth. Int. J. Telerehabil. 6 (2014)
6. American Occupational Therapy Association: The American Occupational Therapy Association Advisory Opinion for the Ethics Commission Telehealth. https://www.aota.org/~/media/Corporate/Files/Practice/Ethics/Advisory/telehealth-advisory.pdf. Accessed 17 Oct 2019)
7. American Speech-Language-Hearing Association: Telepractice. https://www.asha.org/PRPSpecificTopic.aspx?folderid=8589934956&section=Key_Issues. Accessed: 17 Oct 2019
8. American Physical Therapy Association: Telehealth. http://www.apta.org/telehealth/. Accessed: 17 Oct 2019
9. Cowan, K.E., McKean, A.J., Gentry, M.T., Hilty, D.M.: Barriers to use of telepsychiatry: clinicians as gatekeepers. Mayo Clin. Proc. **94**(12), 2510–2523 (2019)
10. Miller, G.: Physician and patient attitudes toward technology in medicine (2016). https://www.medscape.com/features/slideshow/public/technology-in-medicine. Accessed 29 June 2020
11. Kunst, M., Chaturvedi, N., Plantevin, L., Di Filippo, V., Meyer, D., Rebhan, C.: Rising physician dissatisfaction in Europe signals an urgent need for change. https://www.bain.com/insights/europe-front-line-of-healthcare-report-2018/. Accessed 18 June 2020
12. De Grood, C., Raissi, A., Kwon, Y., Santana, M.: Adoption of e-health technology by physicians: a scoping review. J. Multidiscip. Healthc. **9**, 335–344 (2016)

SwapMyMood: User-Centered Design and Development of a Mobile App to Support Executive Function

Tracey D. Wallace⬥ and John T. Morris(✉)⬥

Crawford Research Institute, Shepherd Center, Atlanta, GA 30309, USA
john.morris@shepherd.org

Abstract. This paper describes the research and development of the Swap-MyMood smartphone application designed to support use of evidence-based executive function strategies by people with traumatic brain injury. Executive dysfunction is a common sequela of traumatic brain injury (TBI) resulting in diminished cognitive-behavioral functioning. Problem-solving and emotion regulation are cognitive-behavioral functions that are often disrupted by changes in the executive control system. SwapMyMood is an electronic version of the Executive Plus/STEP program, a set of clinical techniques taught to people living with brain injury to help them 1) identify and implement solutions to problems encountered in daily life and 2) to utilize the emotion cycle to understand and regulate emotional responses to these problems. The Executive Plus/STEP program has until now relied on paper-based instruction and use. Input from target users – people with brain injury and clinical professionals who teach this program to their patients – has contributed to key refinements of features and functioning of the mobile app. Data gathered from target user participation in the user-centered design process are presented. Future directions for ongoing development of technologies to support executive function strategies are also discussed.

Keywords: eHealth · Brain injury · Executive function · Problem solving · Emotion regulation

1 Introduction

The paper describes the research and development of the SwapMyMood smartphone application designed to support use of evidence-based executive function strategies by people with traumatic brain injury (TBI). SwapMyMood is an electronic version of the Executive Plus/STEP program, a set of clinical techniques taught to people living with brain injury to help them 1) identify and implement solutions to problems encountered in daily life and 2) utilize the emotion cycle to understand and regulate their emotional responses to these problems. Data gathered from target users who participated in the design process are presented. Future directions for ongoing development of technologies to support executive function strategies are also discussed.

Executive dysfunction is a common sequela of traumatic brain injury (TBI) resulting in diminished cognitive-behavioral functioning. Problem-solving and emotion

K. Miesenberger et al. (Eds.): ICCHP 2020, LNCS 12377, pp. 259–265, 2020.
https://doi.org/10.1007/978-3-030-58805-2_31

regulation are cognitive-behavioral functions that are often disrupted by changes in the executive control system. Such changes can impact a person's independence community integration. Cognitive rehabilitation literature supports systematically training metacognitive strategies—particularly problem-solving strategies—to support executive functioning in people with TBI [1–4]. The literature supports use of a comprehensive, formal model of problem-solving [3–6].

The Executive Plus/STEP program is an evidence-based model incorporating instruction in metacognitive strategy and training in formal problem-solving to support problem-solving (using SWAPS strategy) and emotion regulation (using Emotion Cycle strategy). An RCT of the Executive Plus/STEP program concluded it is efficacious in improving self-reported post-TBI executive function and problem solving [7].

2 State of the Art

The Executive Plus/STEP program was adapted for use in Shepherd Center's SHARE Military Initiative, a comprehensive rehabilitation program focused on assessment and treatment of service members with TBI and Post-Traumatic Stress Disorder (PTSD). Data gathered using the National Outcome Measurement System (NOMS) created by the American Speech-Language-Hearing Association (ASHA) were used to evaluate program outcomes following implementation of this adapted approach within the SHARE program. Program outcomes data were analyzed for 95 clients with chronic symptoms of TBI who received this problem-solving intervention, revealing 86% improved by at least one level on the Adult NOMS Problem Solving Functional Communication Measure and 54% improved by two or more levels.

Despite successful adaptation and implementation of the Executive Plus/STEP program, many SHARE clients report difficulty recalling the multiple steps in the interventions, recalling which strategies they have used successfully and initiating strategy use under stress. When learning the strategies, clients routinely refer to a written workbook that describes the Executive Plus/STEP program interventions. But they often do not have the workbook with them for support when problems arise.

We developed the SwapMyMood mobile app for iOS to make the Executive Plus/STEP program more accessible and useful wherever the user may be. SwapMyMood is designed to assist people with TBI in using evidence-based methods to maximize problem-solving and emotion regulation. The goal was to make it portable while including functionality enabled by the electronic interface and cloud-based storage/interaction. Development of a smartphone app makes information contained in the workbook more accessible and portable by providing an easily navigable electronic version of these tools which can be carried in the user's pocket. The electronic version also has the potential to provide users with added support for completing each step in the intervention and recalling previous strategies used, which can be saved and retrieved quickly.

3   Research and Development of SwapMyMood

Development of SwapMyMood employed user-centered design principles by including target users throughout the design process [8, 9]. The initial design concept was led by a speech-language pathologist with expertise in TBI cognitive rehabilitation and a psychologist with expertise in TBI/PTSD.

Seven SMEs (3 speech pathologists, 3 Clinical Psychologists/Social Workers and 1 author or the Executive Plus/STEPS Manual) and 6 target users with TBI contributed to the development via interviews, sit-by demonstrations and take-home testing. Interviews and sit-by demonstrations lasted approximately 60 min. Take-home testing lasted 2 weeks.

Participants with TBI were recruited from the SHARE Military Initiative at Shepherd Center. Subject matter experts were recruited from the researchers' professional networks. The inclusion criteria of participants with TBI are listed below:

- Traumatic brain injury – Greater than 2 weeks post-onset.
- Identified by their speech-language pathologist and behavioral health provider as an appropriate candidate to use the SWAPS and Emotion Cycle interventions.
- 18 years of age, or older.
- Functional hearing & vision.
- Ability to follow 2 step directions (English speaking).
- Functional reading.

Inclusion criteria for the Subject Matter Experts (SME) were: 1) licensed clinician in the United States, and 2) experience using the SWAPS and Emotion Cycle interventions with people with TBI.

4   Results

The Executive Plus/STEP program is complex with a numerous actions that require users to input information related to problems they are facing and aspects of the emotion cycle the observe in their current state. Translating the substantial training manual into an app requires considerable effort to ensure intelligibility of the overall flow and perceivability of the information presented.

Feedback from interviews and sit-by demonstrations informed solution features, including:

- Guidance through the multiple steps of problem-solving and emotion regulation.
- Inclusion of video tutorials.
- User selected customization options.
- Links to strategy banks and useful tips based on the Executive Plus/STEP manual.
- Functionality to record, edit and save information input for future reference.
- Functionality to send strategy plans to a caregiver via email.

Seven SMEs and 4 target users with TBI participated in sit-by demonstrations. Most gave positive feedback:

- "It looks great."
- "Really well-designed."
- "That's really cool."
- "I like it. It's not as clunky as I thought it was going to be."

Target users with TBI identified specific features or qualities of SwapMyMood that were strongly appreciated and those that were cause for concern (Table 1). They liked the accessibility of the digital format compared to the paper-based manual, and they like other features like recall and prompting of the user with information previously entered and the phone-a-friend feature. User concerns focused on the complexity like the inability to view all the text on some screens and the number of dropdown menus and options within those menus. The original version of the app that served as the basis for testing also had a limited color palette, which was also not perceived as ideal. Enhancements made to the app based on feedback include:

- Design changed to permit optimal viewing when screen is in vertical position.
- Reduction of dropdown boxes.
- Ability to edit and email strategy plans.

Table 1. Summary of feedback from sit-by target users.

Most favored features	Concerns
Accessibility of digital mobile format	Can't see all text when phone is vertical
Strategy prompting & recall of entered information	Too many dropdown boxes
Phone a friend is "crucial"	Need more color schemes
Ability to review past strategy plans	Need to be able to edit entries
Using app during stress is "grounding"	

As part of our user-centered design process, we invited two target users with TBI to use the app in their daily lives for two weeks to allow the user to explore the solution more fully and under more varied conditions. Results show greater knowledge and use of the problem solving and emotion regulation techniques in the Executive Plus/STEP program by Target User 1 (Table 2).

Table 2. Summary of feedback from take-home target user 1.

	Before testing app	After testing app
How well do you know use of SWAPS	I know it a little	I know it well
How well do you know use of the emotion cycle?	I know it a little	I know it well
How often do you use your SWAPS and Emotion Regulation workbooks/ worksheets (asked before) or the app (asked after)?	Less than half the times when I use the strategies	Most of the times when I use the strategies

Target User 2 reported no change in the levels of knowledge and use over the testing period: high levels of knowledge of problem solving and emotion regulation techniques and moderate levels of use of these techniques (Table 3).

Table 3. Summary of feedback from take-home target user 2.

	Before testing app	After testing app
How well do you know use of SWAPS	I know it well	I know it well
How well do you know use of the emotion cycle?	I know it well	I know it well
How often do you use your SWAPS and Emotion Regulation workbooks/worksheets (asked before) or the app (asked after)?	Less than half the times when I use the strategies	Less than half the times when I use the strategies

5 Discussion: Scientific and Practical Contribution to the Field

User-centered design resulted in several iterations of the SwapMyMood app and continues to inform work on major version updates currently underway. Initial interviews, sit-by testing sessions and take-home testing supported the general concept of developing an app-based version of the Executive Plus/STEP intervention. Notably, the take home testing participant who expressed little confidence in his ability to use the strategies reported a marked increase in confidence after using the app for 2 weeks. He also reported using the app for support more frequently than he used the paper workbook prior to using the app.

Informed by a user-centered design approach, the SwapMyMood mobile app extends findings from other research on problem solving and executive functioning by people with brain injury. Rath, Hennessy and Diller (2003) found that social problem solving (SPS) is an important component of community integration following traumatic brain injury (TBI). These researchers stressed the importance of assessing a persons' confidence in their ability to cope with problems after brain injury; a focus on objective test scores alone may lead to under-detection of disabling problem-solving deficits. SwapMyMood provides a portable set of potentially useful tools and allows the user and clinician to track historical problem-solving performance in daily life.

Other researchers have developed and tested of an electronic version of an intervention to support emotion regulation or problem solving, but not both. Ehlhardt, et al. report on development and evaluation of a web-based program to support problem-solving skills after brain injury [10]. Other evidence-based electronic solutions include BEST Connections suite of mobile apps for people with cognitive limitations including those caused by brain injury. The suite includes 4 discrete but integrated solutions for planning and self-management, not for problem solving and emotion regulation. These solutions, however, point to the utility of electronic supports for people with brain injury and other conditions that cause executive function challenges.

6 Conclusion and Future Directions

Additional development of the app is currently underway. Version 2.0 will be released on Android and iOS in June 2020. It will include enhanced navigation, including the ability to pause/resume the problem-solving process in order to complete the emotion cycle to regulate emotions which may be interfering with effective problem solving. The new version also will improve display of summaries of each problem-solving instance and retrieval of previous problem-solving instances. The visual design of the interface – logo, colors, general layout of each screen – will be enhanced, as well.

Launch of SwapMyMood 2.0 will allow testing for clinical efficacy. The team will conduct a pragmatic clinical trial to compare outcomes in people with TBI who use SwapMyMood versus the paper workbook. Improvement in executive functioning, frequency of app use, types of problems encountered, strategies selected and satisfaction with outcomes of strategy use will be assessed. Study design will be a between-subjects test with random assignment to two groups of clients in Shepherd Center's SHARE military and veterans rehabilitation: 1) those receiving conventional training in the Executive Plus/STEP program and use of the workbook only; and 2) those receiving conventional training with the workbook and the SwapMyMood mobile app, with subsequent use of the SwapMyMood app only. Participants in both groups will utilize the Executive Plus/STEP program in their respective formats for 1 month. Participant use of each format will be recorded in weekly conversations with their speech therapist during treatment sessions. Additionally, use of the mobile app will be recorded in the app's Amazon Web Services (AWS) cloud-based reporting system.

The R&D team is already planning version 3.0 which will incorporate machine learning (ML) and artificial intelligence (AI) to support context awareness and predictive modeling to anticipate the user's need to perform either or both problem-solving and the emotion cycle. The team expects that these features and functions will enhance support for the user by delivering timely prompts, reminders and engagement, while minimizing risk of over-communicating with the user.

Acknowledgements. Development and testing of SwapMyMood was supported by the Rehabilitation Engineering Research Center for Community Living, Health and Function (LiveWell RERC) funded by a grant from the National Institute on Disability, Independent Living, and Rehabilitation Research (NIDILRR) in the United States Department of Health and Human Services (grant no. 90RE5028).

References

1. Gordon, W.A., Cantor, J., Ashman, T., Brown, M.: Treatment of post-TBI executive sysfunction: application of theory to clinical practice. J. Head Trauma Rehabil. **21**(2), 156–167 (2006)
2. Cicerone, K.D., Goldin, Y., Ganci, K., et al.: Evidence-based cognitive rehabilitation: systematic review of the literature from 2009 through 2014. Arch. Phys. Med. Rehabil. **100** (8), 1515–1533 (2019)

3. Haskins, E., Cicerone, K., Trexler, L.: Cognitive Rehabilitation Manual: Translating Evidence-Based Recommendations into Practice. Beta Edition, ACRM Publishing, Reston (2011)
4. Tate, R., Kennedy, M., Ponsford, J., Douglas, J., Velikonja, D., Bayley, M., Stergiou-Kita, M.: INCOG recommendations for management of cognition following traumatic brain injury, part III, executive functions and self-awareness. J. Head Trauma Rehabil. **29**(40), 338–352 (2014)
5. Rath, J.F., Simon, D., Langenbahn, D.M., Sherr, R.L., Diller, L.: Group treatment of problem-solving deficits in outpatients with traumatic brain injury: a randomized outcome study. Neuropsychol. Rehabil. **13**(4), 461 (2003)
6. Rath, J.F., Hradil, A.L., Litke, D.R., Diller, L.: Clinical applications of problem-solving research in neuropsychological rehabilitation: addressing the subjective experience of cognitive deficits in outpatients with acquired brain injury. Rehabil. Psychol. **56**(4), 320–328 (2011)
7. Cantor, J., Ashman, T., Dams-O'Connor, K., Dijkers, M.P., Gordon, W., et al.: Evaluation of the STEP intervention for executive dysfunction after traumatic brain injury: a randomized controlled trial with minimization. Arch. Phys. Med. Rehabil. **95**(1), 1–9 (2014)
8. Luna, D., Quispe, M., Gonzalez, Z., Alemrares, A., Risk, M., Garcia, A.M., Otero, C.: User-centered design to develop clinical applications. Literature review. Stud. Health Technol. Inform. **216**, 967 (2015)
9. International Organization for Standardization: ISO FDIS 9241–210, Ergonomics of human system interaction–Part 210: Human-centered design for interactive systems. ISO (2010)
10. Powell, L.E., et al.: The development and evaluation of a web-based programme to support problem-solving skills following brain injury. Disabil. Rehabil. Assist. Technol. **14**(1), 21–32 (2019)

Survey of User Needs: Mobile Apps for mHealth and People with Disabilities

Ben Lippincot[1] , Nicole Thompson[1] , John Morris[1(✉)] ,
Mike Jones[1] , and Frank DeRuyter[2]

[1] Crawford Research Institute, Shepherd Center, Atlanta, GA 30309, USA
john.morris@shepherd.org
[2] Duke University Medical Center, Durham, NC 27705, USA

Abstract. This paper presents data and analysis from survey research conducted by the Rehabilitation Engineering Research Center on Information and Communication Technology Access for Mobile Rehabilitation (mRehab RERC) on the use and unmet needs for mHealth mobile apps by people with disabilities in the United States. Quantitative and qualitative data are reported on user experiences with mHealth apps to map the behavior, interests and needs of people with specific types of disability (physical, cognitive, sensory, emotional/psychological, and speech). Summary results are presented for all respondents and each disability type. Slightly more than half of the participants in this sample (53.2%) reported using mHealth apps. Fitness and exercise apps were the mHealth apps most used by respondents with disabilities, followed by hospital/clinical portal apps. Symptom and disease management apps are the least commonly used, even though these would seem to be important for people with chronic conditions. Text-based responses regarding unmet needs for mHealth apps can be sorted into accessibility needs and functionality needs. In general, respondents with sensory limitations were more likely to identify accessibility needs. However, all disability groups identified both types of unmet needs. These results can help inform research and development efforts to provide mHealth apps that meet the needs of people with disabilities.

Keywords: mHealth · Mobile apps · User needs · Survey research

1 Introduction

This article presents data and analysis from survey research conducted by the Rehabilitation Engineering Research Center on Information and Communication Technology Access for Mobile Rehabilitation (mRehab RERC) on the use and unmet needs for mHealth mobile apps by people with disabilities in the United States. The paper focuses on several key questions related to the user experience with mobile health apps in order to map the behavior, interests and needs of people with specific types of disability (physical, cognitive, sensory, emotional/psychological, and speech). Survey response data for the following questions are presented and discussed:

K. Miesenberger et al. (Eds.): ICCHP 2020, LNCS 12377, pp. 266–273, 2020.
https://doi.org/10.1007/978-3-030-58805-2_32

- Do you use any mHealth apps?
- Which types of mHealth apps do you use to maintain your health? (exercise and fitness, diet and nutrition, lifestyle and stress, clinical portals, and disease/symptom management)
- Which specific mHealth apps do you use?
- What do you want in an mHealth app that you currently have not found to meet your needs? (open-ended question)

Summary results for all respondents are presented and for each disability. This analysis provides a detailed view of the use and unmet needs for mHealth mobile apps by people with disabilities in the United States and possibly by extension in other countries.

2 Background

Consumers and healthcare providers have considerable interest and high expectations for mHealth [1]. About half of patients recently surveyed in the United States predict that mHealth technologies will improve the convenience, cost and quality of healthcare in the next three years [2], and 96% of current mHealth app users believe the apps help improve their quality of life [3]. Six in 10 doctors and payers believe that their widespread adoption is inevitable, and 7 in 10 believe health apps will encourage patients to take more responsibility for their health [4].

The opportunities offered by mHealth technologies are substantial. The World Health Organization (WHO) views "digital health" solutions as a key tool to strengthen national health systems to support the goal of Universal Health Coverage (UHC). According to the WHO: "Digital technologies provide concrete opportunities to tackle health system challenges, and thereby offer the potential to enhance the coverage and quality of health practices and services" [5].

Despite the expected benefits of mHealth early evidence suggests that people with disabilities are not well represented in the growth of mobile healthcare, and particularly the proliferation of mobile health software applications (mHealth apps) for smartphones and tablets [6, 7]. This underrepresentation could widen health disparities between the general population and people with disabilities, and perhaps more fundamentally fail to take advantage of new and effective ways of engagement in personal health management.

3 Methodology

The mRehab RERC staff at Shepherd Center in Atlanta, Georgia USA has conducted user needs research with people with disabilities on assistive and accessible technology since 2001. We pioneered the "network model" of user-centered research with people with disabilities with the creation in that year of our Consumer Advisory Network (CAN), a national network of people with all types of disabilities and diverse demographic backgrounds [8–10]. This network model involves two levels of user-centered research: 1) national survey research involving the entire network, and 2) small-n narrowly focused research on specific questions related to assistive and accessible technology.

Since 2001 RERC research staff has conducted national survey research on smart phone use by people with disabilities, hearing aid compatibility (HAC) of mobile phones, use of mobile phones by elders, wearable technology, smart speakers and smart home technology, among other lines of inquiry. In 2017 our staff replicated this model to facilitate user-centered research with people with disabilities for Microsoft by establishing the established the Accessibility User Research Collective (AURC) [10].

More recently our team has developed and implemented a research agenda related to mHealth and related mobile apps and technologies. Building on this base of knowledge, the study team drafted a new survey in January 2020 focusing on the mHealth apps (general types and specific apps) used by people with disabilities and, as importantly, how people with disabilities find useful and usable mHealth apps. The study team solicited input on questionnaire design from our external advisors with disabilities and other professionals who work with people with disabilities and our mRehab RERC colleagues. The questionnaire consists of 45 questions organized in the following sections:

1. Demographics
2. Disability and use of assistive technology
3. Use of mobile devices and apps
4. Use of mHealth mobile apps
5. Discovering and using new mobile apps

Data were collected from April 14 to June 10, 2020. Participants were recruited primarily through the Consumer Advisory Network (CAN) developed and maintained since 2001. We also recruited via other disability organizations in the United States with which we have collaborated for many years and through the researchers' personal networks of people with disabilities. Data were collected in January and February 2019 using convenience sampling methods and online data collection on the Survey Monkey web-based platform. Although no protected health information (PHI) was collected in this survey, the Survey Monkey platform does meet the privacy and security requirements of the United States Health Insurance Portability and Accountability Act of 1996 (HIPAA), which establishes essential policies and practices for protecting patient health information from unnecessary and unauthorized access.

4   Results

Response data were analyzed using SPSS version 22. A total of 412 individuals with various types of disability, including physical, sensory, cognitive, emotional and speech limitations, responded to our requests for participation.

Mean age of respondents in our sample is 51.1 years with a standard deviation of 15.5 years, indicating that approximately two-thirds of the sample is between the ages of 35 and 67 (Table 1). Approximately 79% of respondents identified as white/Anglo, which is somewhat higher than the national average for the general population in the

United States. Just over half the sample is female, reflecting very closely the gender distribution for the general population. Slightly more than 2 in 5 respondents (41%) reported annual household income of $50,000 or higher, which is below the national median household income for the general population and seems appropriate for the population of people with disabilities due to more limited employment opportunities.

Table 1. Demographic background of respondents (n = 412).

Age – mean (years)	51.1
Age - standard deviation (years)	15.5
Race/ethnicity (% white/Anglo)	79.4
Gender (% female)	51.7
Education (% completed bachelor's degree or higher)	65.8
Annual household income (% $50,000 or higher)	41.0

Table 2 shows the functional limitations included in the survey questionnaire. Notably, many respondents reported having more than one functional limitation, which is due to the likelihood that people will have multiple comorbidities resulting from a single injury, disease or chronic condition. For instance, difficulty walking is correlated with difficulty using arms and/or hands.

Table 2. Functional difficulties of respondents.

Disability type	Number	Percent
Worry, nervousness, anxiety	50	12.1
Difficulty thinking	50	12.1
Difficulty speaking	19	4.6
Difficulty learning	34	8.3
Difficulty using arms	44	10.7
Difficulty using hands, fingers	62	15.0
Difficulty walking, standing	98	23.8
Fatigue or limited stamina	59	14.3
Low vision (even with glasses)	60	14.6
Blind (without usable vision)	112	27.2
Hard of hearing	84	20.4
Deaf (unable to hear)	50	12.1

Slightly more than half of the participants in this sample (53.2%) report using mHealth apps. Two categories of mHealth apps – fitness/exercise and hospital/clinical portal apps – are the most used by respondents, followed by lifestyle, diet/nutrition, and disease management apps (Table 3).

Table 3. Types of mHealth apps used by respondents (percentage of respondents).

Disability type	Fitness, exercise	Diet, nutrition	Lifestyle, stress, sleep	Hospital or clinic portal	Disease, symptom mgmt.
Worry, nervousness, anxiety	42.0	20.0	36.0	32.0	10.0
Difficulty thinking	40.0	24.0	30.0	36.0	12.0
Difficulty speaking	15.8	15.8	10.5	26.3	15.8
Difficulty learning	35.3	26.5	26.5	38.2	8.8
Difficulty using arms	20.5	15.9	15.9	34.1	11.4
Difficulty using hands, fingers	25.8	14.5	17.5	30.6	17.7
Difficulty walking, standing	26.5	13.3	15.3	28.6	16.3
Fatigue or limited stamina	35.6	28.0	23.7	33.9	22.0
Low vision (even with glasses)	41.7	23.3	20.0	30.0	46.7
Blind (without usable vision)	46.4	18.8	20.5	30.4	11.6
Hard of hearing	38.1	11.9	15.5	26.2	9.5
Deaf (unable to hear)	42.0	12.0	20.0	26.0	6.0

These results suggest that people with disabilities use many of the same types of apps used by the general population, likely reflecting the commercial availability of these apps. Fitness and exercise apps are numerous and are built into major smartphones running the iOS and Android operating systems. Also, in the United States many hospital systems offer and promote the use of clinical portal apps that allow for scheduling medical visits, accessing laboratory results, tracking vital signs, and communicating asynchronously with healthcare providers. Indeed, the most frequently used app was MyChart, the patient portal owned by and integrated into Epic, electronic medical record platform most widely used by hospitals and health systems in the United States. MyChart claims to have over 100 million users. Among fitness apps, Fitbit and Under Armour's MyFitnessPal were the most commonly used.

Notably, disease and symptom management apps are the least commonly used type of apps reported by respondents. One might expect that such apps would attract considerable interest among people with disabilities. These results might suggest that such apps do not enjoy the technical and marketing support of general fitness apps and patient portal apps.

Specific observations can be made about app use by people with specific disabilities. Individuals with blindness are most likely to use mHealth apps to track their fitness and exercise. Those who experience chronic fatigue and limited stamina use diet and nutrition apps most. Individuals who reported frequent worrying, nervousness and anxiety report use mHealth apps for lifestyle, stress, and sleep the most. Those with low vision, use disease/symptom management apps the most by a wide margin.

Table 4 summarizes responses to the open-ended question on the types of features, functions, and entire apps that respondents would like to have, but so far have not found in the app marketplaces. These responses can be sorted into accessibility needs (e.g., picture-based calorie counter, haptic feedback) and needs for specific functionality (e.g., sync health information from multiple healthcare providers, diabetes monitor that allows users to enter notes). In general, respondents with sensory limitations focused more on accessibility than did respondents with other disabilities. Still, respondents in each of the disability groups identified needs for both enhanced access and expanded functionality.

Table 4. Needs for mHealth apps identified by disability type.

Disability type	Needs for mHealth apps
Worry, nervousness, anxiety	• Guaranteed privacy • Goal and habit tracking • Universal app - all health/medical in one place
Difficulty thinking	• Picture-based calorie counter • Widgets on home screen to track health symptoms • Simple medication management system • Sync health information from multiple providers
Difficulty speaking	• Reputable review of apps by doctor or organization
Difficulty learning	• Ability to build personalized fitness regimen • Real-time suggestions based on health data/progress
Difficulty using arms	• Ability to measure heart rate and temperature • Ability monitor pain management, seizures, and O2 • Better movement monitoring for wheelchair users
Difficulty using hands, fingers	• App to schedule appointments • Apps to measure and track blood measure • Alerts when health measures out of normal range
Difficulty walking, standing	• Accuracy measuring physical activity/movement • App about spinal cord injury • Suggestions for wheelchair users
Fatigue or limited stamina	• Better nutrition app • Diabetes monitor that allows entering notes • Homeopathic, naturopathic, organic medicines info

(*continued*)

Table 4. (*continued*)

Disability·type	Needs for mHealth apps
Low vision (even with glasses)	• Accessible health records and exportable data • Gamification of exercises, like walking
Blind (without usable vision)	• Accessibility (labeled buttons and links) • Exportable personal health data • Less cluttered way to access step count • Exercise app that describes the exercises
Hard of hearing	• Haptic feedback controls • Real-time speech to text conversion
Deaf (unable to hear)	• Virtual clinic visits with captioning, ASL interpreter

5 Conclusion

Mobile health apps are an essential element in the mHealth technology ecosystem. Their variety and ubiquity endow them with considerable potential to improve health and expand healthcare access. Yet, most are designed and engineered by and for people without disabilities – people without substantial accessibility challenges and with neurotypical body functioning (normal blood pressure, heart rate, calorie consumption, gait, etc.). Concerted and continuous efforts to identify the experiences and needs for mobile health apps by people disabilities is critical to realizing the potential for expanded inclusion offered by mHealth/eHealth.

This survey of consumers with disabilities and mHealth mobile apps serves as the cornerstone for our ongoing effort to track consumer use patterns and preferences, and it supports our efforts to provide information on the usability of mHealth apps by people with specific disabilities directly to these same consumers. In order to respond to the rapid pace of change in consumer technology and track consumer perceptions, experiences and preferences over time, we plan to update, refine and conduct this key consumer survey regularly.

Survey results also support two key initiatives of the mRehab RERC: 1) provide an mHealth app accessibility clearinghouse with consumer reviews of specific mHealth apps; and 2) conduct an annual call for proposals from external developers working in the area of mHealth apps for people with disabilities. We will use the information gathered through the mHealth apps survey to identify promising apps worthy of in-depth testing and to help inform the types of mHealth apps we are most interested in funding for development each year.

Acknowledgements. The authors thank the hundreds of people with disabilities who partici-pated in this research project. This research is supported by the Rehabilitation Engineering Research Center on Information and Communications Technology Access for Mobile Rehabil-itation (mRehab RERC), which is funded by a 5-year grant from the National Institute on Disability, Independent Living and Rehabilitation Research (NIDILRR) in the U.S. Department of Health and Human Services (grant number 90REGE0011). The opinions contained herein are those of the mRehab RERC and do not necessarily reflect those of the U.S. Department of Health and Human Services or NIDILRR.

References

1. Zweig, M., Shen, J., Jug, L.: Healthcare Consumers in a Digital Transition. Rock Health. www.rockhealth.com/reports/healthcare-consumers-in-a-digital-transition. Accessed 22 May 2020
2. Price Waterhouse and Coopers: Emerging mHealth: Paths for Growth (2013). https://www.pwc.com/gx/en/healthcare/mhealth/assets/pwc-emerging-mhealth-full.pdf. Accessed 23 May 2020
3. Research Now. Are Mobile Health Apps Good for Our Health? (2015). https://www.researchnow.com/en-US/PressAndEvents/News/2015/March/research-now-study-are-mobile-medical-apps-good-for-our-health-infographic.aspx?language=en-US. Accessed 18 May 2020
4. Research Now. mHealth Apps Supporting a Healthier Future (2015). www.researchnow.com/blog/mhealth-apps-supporting-a-healthier-future-infographic. Accessed 14 May 2020
5. World Health Organization: WHO Guideline: Recommendations on Digital Interventions for Health System Strengthening. World Health Organization, Geneva (2019)
6. Jones, M., Morris, J., DeRuyter, F.: Mobile healthcare and people with disabilities: current state and future needs. Int. J. Environ. Res. Public Health **15**(3), 1–13 (2018)
7. DeRuyter, F., Jones, M., Morris, J.: Mobile health apps and needs of people with disabilities: a national survey. J. Technol. Persons Disabil. **6**, 229–245 (2019)
8. Jones, M., DeRuyter, F., Thompson, N., Norelli, J., Morris, J.: Survey of user needs for ICT – community living by people with disabilities. J. Technol. Persons Disabil. **6**, 148–160 (2018)
9. Morris, J., Mueller, J.: Blind and deaf consumer preferences for android and iOS smartphones. In: Langdon, P.M., Lazar, J., Heylighen, A., Dong, H. (eds.) Inclusive Designing: Joining Usability, Accessibility, and Inclusion. Springer, London (2014). https://doi.org/10.1007/978-3-319-05095-9_7
10. Morris, J., Thompson, N., Lippincott, B., Lawrence, M.: Accessibility user research collective: engaging consumers in ongoing technology evaluation. Assist. Technol. Outcomes Benefits **13**, 38–56 (2019)

Innovation and Implementation in the Area of Independent Mobility Through Digital Technologies

Implementation and Innovation in the Area of Independent Mobility Through Digital Technologies

Introduction to the Special Thematic Session

David Banes[1]([⊠]), Riccardo Magni[2], and Florian Brinkmann[3]

[1] Access and Inclusion Services, Milton Keynes, UK
david@davebanesaccess.org
[2] Centro Orientamento Ausili Tecnologici Associazione Onlus, Umbria, Italy
[3] Institute of Transportation Systems, German Aerospace Center (DLR),
Cologne, Germany

Abstract. Digital technologies are having a profound impact upon all phases of mobility for persons with a disability. In this paper, the different stages of travel are reflected upon their potential pain points for travelers with a diverse range of needs. Furthermore, solutions in which emerging digital technologies are offering solutions to historic barriers are derived. The paper thereby reflects upon the five contributions to the special thematic session "Implementation and Innovation in the area of independent mobility through digital technologies" of the 17th ICCHP.

Keywords: Travel · Transport · Assistive technology · Inclusion · Technology · Innovation · Emerging technology · Technology trends · Independence

1 Introduction

Independent mobility is often cited as a requirement of people with a disability in seeking to increase opportunities for full access to education, employment, and daily living [17]. The European Accessibility Act[1] takes the obligations deriving from the UN convention on persons with disabilities and aims to ensure equal opportunities for all to enjoy seamless, accessible, and independent travel [4]. The goal of European Project TRIPS (TRansport Innovation for disabled People needs Satisfaction) is to design, describe and demonstrate practical steps to empower people with disabilities to play a central role in the design of inclusive digital mobility solutions.

We are witnessing fast progress in the development of mobility solutions, Ride Pooling, E-Scooter Rental (Sharing), Moped Taxi/Scooter Taxi, Car Sharing, Bike Sharing (including electric bikes). Yet not all of them are designed and operated in a way that they are accessible to everyone and only few research projects address the

---

[1] https://eur-lex.europa.eu/legal-content/EN/TXT/?uri=COM%3A2015%3A0615%3AFIN.

© Springer Nature Switzerland AG 2020
K. Miesenberger et al. (Eds.): ICCHP 2020, LNCS 12377, pp. 277–285, 2020.
https://doi.org/10.1007/978-3-030-58805-2_33

challenge of accessibility in the context of new mobility systems [14]. Recent innovations in both assistive and accessible technologies, such as natural interfaces, wearable technologies and artificial intelligence suggest new ways in which navigation, orientation and wayfinding can be made accessible for people with a variety of needs including those with cognitive, sensory, physical impairments and the elderly.

For many people with disabilities, the barriers identified when travelling are often related to a lack of information to inform planning [11]. Digital assistive technologies impact across the entire journey through provision and ease of access to infrastructure, environment, points of interest, and the form of transportation itself. In seeking to understand the pain points within a journey, the model developed for accessible public transport in Australia provides a relevant framework [3]. These include:

- Pre-journey planning: decisions about using transportation that are made based on available information.
- Journey start and end: usually outside the transport system. For example, travelling from home to the stop, station or terminal along a footpath,
- Transport stop/station: locations that transport services operate to and from.
- Transport service: the conveyance that enables the journey, the 'on board experience', as well as the scheduling/routing of services
- Interchange: places where service or mode transfers take place.
- Return journey planning: reversing the journey for return or onward journey.
- Disruption to business-as-usual: this includes planned and unplanned disruption to transport services or along the journey start and end sections.
- Supporting infrastructure: this supports the journey and includes mid and end of trip infrastructure such as toilets, drinking fountains, wayfinding and seating

At each stage, we can explore where emerging technologies impact and promote ease of access. The five papers of the special thematic session address the different phases of the journey and propose solutions for making transport more accessible.

1.1   Pre-journey Planning

People with a disability may need to expend considerable time and effort at this stage to feel confident that they can efficiently and safely complete their journey. This contrasts with other customers who can often make more spontaneous public transport travel decisions.

The paper "AccessKB: Linked Open Data for Accessible Travel" addresses the topic of pre-journey planning by using open data for creating an accessible travelling decision support.

During this phase, users are seeking information to confirm the accessibility of all parts of the journey. Their decision making during this phase is influenced by experience and the experience of friends and family. Building confidence around the accessibility of the entire trip is key to enabling and encouraging more people to use a form of transport for their travel needs.

Emerging technologies can help to address some of the potential barriers at this early stage. For instance, natural interfaces offer more diverse and accessible ways for people with disabilities to interact with information [2]. Speech interfaces such as

Amazon's Alexa allow natural language to be used for enquiries, which are then spoken out supporting people with a visual or another form of impairment. An example might be "Alexa what time is the next bus to the airport" The system is location-aware and can understand the likelihood that you are searching for a route to the nearest airport. Such systems may then prompt with further information such as "do you want to know about later buses?".

AI can help us in planning journeys [5] by suggesting and recommending the best options for a journey. For instance, if we needed to get to the airport, we might enquire, what the best way to the airport, we might get asked whether we mean the fastest, most direct or cheapest journey and then recommend a solution based on refining the query. Over time the system can learn from our choices how we personally define "best" and retains that when responding to similar future enquiries.

The internet of things, when integrated with AI or machine learning, allows us to plan our journey based on the real-time experience of others with similar needs. For instance, the technology could form a planning support system which would inform the user that "people using a wheelchair near you, travelling to the airport by taxi take on average 22 min to reach the destination or 36 min by bus". Such systems could automatically then prompt users with questions such as "would you like us to book a taxi for you?"

Digital payment methods such as https://upipayments.co.in/digital-payment/ also allow travelers to pay or authorize payment at this stage, reducing the need to pay at kiosks or counters at stations, or to find cash or debit cards when boarding or departing a taxi or shared ride. Services such as Uber offer the ability to have payment pre-authorized and made automatically when the journey is complete.

VR as described by Neuburger Beck, and Egger, [10] can help to have a realistic simulation of the crucial phases of journey planning, to assist in choosing best options or preparing a user for the journey itself, anticipating views and operations (access, drive and use means of transportation).

The paper "How can I succeed in planning a trip with my disability? Identifying Gaps in the Travel Chain" reflects upon existing applications for trip planning and seamless navigation and identify gaps. The authors derive requirements for an automated generation of accessible indoor maps.

1.2   Journey Start and End, Including Entry and Exit from Transport Systems

To enter the transport system, people need to move from their current location to a transport point of access or to leave the system to enter a destination. People with a disability face challenges because of a lack of information about the environment they are entering. This is also a challenging part of the journey for providers and operators as they may have little or no control over conditions around the entrance and exit points and links to destinations.

The paper "Co-production of knowledge for designing inclusive digital mobility solutions – the methodological approach and process of the TRIPS project" addresses different phases of the journey by collecting requirements of users concerning different transport systems. The authors aim to identify barriers of using public transport means by using qualitative methods.

Digital technologies can enhance this phase of the journey in a variety of ways. The Internet of Things allows for real-time tracking of transport, [9] which can be communicated to a person with a disability to aid them in leaving their location to reach the access point for the carrier. These can include both outdoor navigations, based upon GPS systems and indoor systems utilizing beacons. Ideally, these systems are integrated and seamless. Wearable technology and machine learning offer the opportunity to record the maximum time taken by the user to reach that point [6] and warn the person well in advance that they need to be leaving to reach the access point on time. For people with a disability, this reduces the risk of missing crucial transportation which may incur costs and add to frustration.

Augmented Reality such as that used by Google Maps[2] can indicate specific access points for both the passenger and the provider of the service. Meeting points can be displayed in AR, and can be used to show locations of bus stops or platforms which are permanent access points. Both points of access and routes to temporary access points, including ride-sharing collection points for services such as UBER[3] or the direct route to temporary transport such as eScooters or other shared vehicles.

Such AR systems can also take account of the need for easy routing to an access point, avoiding both fixed and temporary barriers to the desired location and reducing the risks of missing a transport connection.

Wearable and location-based technologies can support ticketless access and keyless unlocking of rental vehicles when the user is in proximity [12]. The automation of such services can be of value to those with cognitive impairment who may find codes complex to repeat into a keypad, and the provider can be assured that the vehicle will be automatically locked such as when the user is more than 10 m from the vehicle.

1.3 Transport Access Point

This stage is concerned with the person's experience at the access point, from their arrival until they board the vehicle or conveyance. Transport access points may be as simple as a sign or stop marker or as complex as a multi-modal interchange where different services converge.

In the study undertaken by DIRD [3] People with disability highlighted issues at this point in the journey, including:

- lack of shade and shelter
- sufficient space for mobility devices
- visual and audio 'clutter' associated with advertising or general street/road signage
- issues around identifying and hailing their service

---

[2] https://support.google.com/maps/answer/144361?co=GENIE.Platform%3DiOS&hl=en#:~:text=Share%20a%20map%20or%20location&text=Or%2C%20find%20a%20place%20on,the%20place's%20name%20or%20address.&text=Share.,the%20link%20to%20the%20map.

[3] https://help.uber.com/riders/article/what-are-suggested-pickup-locations?nodeId=9edf05bf-ac3a-4cf8-b08e-76e9ca767f7f.

- late changes to departure points
- difficulty in boarding a vehicle.

In larger transport settings such as bus, air or rail terminals, movement between drop-off points and access points for the next stage can be challenging.

Location-based services will allow the virtual access point to be shared with the provider and the precise details to be agreed such as that offered by UBER and other ride sharing services This allows a point of access to be confirmed, that has the facilities required by the passenger for their comfort and convenience. Choosing a virtual access point can also be eased with the addition of further data around the location indicating potential places with shade and shelter or other facilities for personal care.

The both papers "Analysis of Indoor Maps Accounting the Needs of People with Impairments" and "Considering Time-critical Barriers in Indoor Routing for People with Disabilities" address the challenge of indoor navigation.

5G offers opportunities for information on services to be delivered in a range of formats (image maps, videos.) in real-time. The speed of 5G connections allows multiple data sources to be integrated, including the location of the vehicle, the likely journey time and any immediate changes that are needed.

Next IOTs directly connected to 5G support services will allow for many passengers, the ability to automate the booking and payment system using wearable or portable technologies, reducing the risk of errors in payment, or reservation. The move towards cashless and contactless facilities makes payment both safer and more accessible for disabled passengers.[4] [15].

1.4 Transport Service

This phase involves the user's interaction with the vehicle and potentially any driver or other user of the vehicle. People may need assistance to board and exit in the form of ramp deployment or other aid; onboard communication should help build the confidence of the passenger that such services are prepared for arrival. Requirements of the in-vehicle stage may be different depending on the mode of travel and the length of the journey. Current Guidance in countries such as the UK[5] places the onus upon the person with a disability to ensure that the station or destination is both accessible and informed of arrival times.

During this stage of the journey, 5G and location-based services allow users to receive and share real-time ongoing travel data. The ability to share real-time travel locations can be especially valuable to some of the most vulnerable in society who can be monitored for safe arrival and greeted, and any additional support required provided. The ability to share locations and arrival in technologies offered by a range of transport

---

[4] "Transit and Contactless Open Payments: An Emerging Approach for Fare Collection" - A Smart Card Alliance Transportation Council White Paper.

[5] https://orr.gov.uk/__data/assets/pdf_file/0018/41517/accessible-travel-policy-guidance-for-train-and-station-operators.pdf.

providers including ride sharing and bus companies, alongside those integrated into mobile handsets can facilitate this.

For those with communication impairments, AI supports access to real-time communication with the transport provider, including real-time transcriptions of speech, word prediction and text to speech for communication [13]. It could be a help for all passengers, also those with a cultural disadvantage, considering language barriers in international contexts. Text can be augmented by symbols to aid understanding for those with literacy impairments or other forms of communication need.

Increased personalization of services can be established based upon the actual records of transport use and travel preferences [16]. Hence if a passenger has always required a wheelchair accessible vehicle than that is automatically ordered. If the passenger has needed help boarding a vehicle, such as a chair stored, this is instantly communicated to the provider when the booking is made. Equally, the accessibility of onboard services, including washrooms or restaurants, could benefit from the application of modular automation/robotics helping passengers to reach and use services. Such services are especially valuable to people with a disability in planning longer journeys.

1.5   Interchange

People with disabilities may need to transfer to another transport system, mode or route at a point during their journey. To do this, they exit the service, navigate their way through an interchange to the next service, and then board. Changing services or modes occurs at an interchange. Transfers need to be efficient and easy to use to maintain confidence and reduce stress.

People with a disability are less likely to embark on public transport journeys that involve interchanges as it adds complexity and uncertainty to their trip [3].

To address this, a range of new technologies can contribute. AR and location-based services offer the opportunity for real-time navigation through an interchange, [8] with live updated directions based on the movements of others. As with other such services, the ability to track the progress of users, including those with specific needs helps the passenger to be confident that they have the time and the optimal route for to reach the next stage of their journey.

AI applied to the analysis of other user movement take informed in real-time the passenger with a disability whether the planned transfer time is realistic or if they should make alternate plans. Such systems can alert the provider of a service that a passenger with additional needs is en-route and to request a delay or other accommodation to facilitate their transfer. The paper Evaluation of Feasibility and Requirements of Audio Navigation System for Older Adults offers a solution to the issues of indoor navigation for people with a disability that are often encountered during this phase of a journey.

1.6   Return/Next Journey Planning

Once people have reached a destination, they may need to return to their origin, or will need to undertake an onward journey to a second destination. Users should be able to quickly find the start of their return journey by re-tracing their travel path to locate an access point and board services.

People with disability may arrange any further or return journey as part of their pre-journey planning. Travel plans may be fixed on returning on a specific service at a particular time. If their circumstances change, or if changes are made by service operators, it can be challenging to re-plan their return journey.

Research [7] would suggest that AI and location-based services have potential to support the recording of a journey and helping to plan a return or onward journey. One of the challenges experienced by those with disabilities at this stage is the uncertainty of departure times from the new location. The technologies can be used to maintain a live update on options for the next phase of the journey as the day progresses and this can be communicated on an ongoing basis with the use of high-speed 5G connectivity.

Similarly, AI and location-based services can offer real-time updates to plans taking account of data from other passengers planning to use similar routes and forms of transport. Sensors held with mobile and portable devices, and wearable technologies can track ease of movement and update planning options for the next stage of journeys.

For those with cognitive impairments, the capacity to have a journey replayed in reverse with VR and AR will add clear contextual information in unfamiliar contexts. Equally where an onward or return journey requires the person with a disability to make the journey using a different route or form of transport, then it is helpful for them to review a simulation of the journey before starting the next steps.

1.7 Disruption

Any journey may be subject to disruptions. These might include cancellations, closure of a service, weather-related interruptions, vehicle breakdown, vehicle and transport replacements, or evacuation of a vehicle or station due to an emergency.

Disruptions can be planned or unplanned. A planned outage is generally well managed with advance notice, and alternate arrangements can be put in place to minimise the effects of disruption on planning journey. Many of the lessons learned from emergency evacuation planning such as those suggested by Alexander et al. [1] can inform other responses to disruption, the mainstreaming of such information into everyday use may help prepare people with a disability to cope when a crisis does arise. Unplanned disruptions are more challenging, as information about the nature of the interruption, and alternate arrangements can be difficult to source and communicate.

DIRD [3] note that when disruption occurs, people should be made aware of the situation, how they should respond, and whether there are alternative arrangements in place for them to complete their journey. People with a disability say that disruptions are highly stressful, and the possibility of disruption is a significant barrier to their participation in public transport journeys. Emerging technologies can help anticipate potential problems and fund mitigations rapidly.

AI can interpret live data to predict and anticipate disruptions based on real-time data. Such real time data is employed in applications such as Waze[6] which tracks and

---

[6] https://www.waze.com/forum/viewtopic.php?f=6&t=205657.

analyses travel times from other app users to assist in planning and route changes. Unlike other users, those with disabilities need to understand options that are both available and accessible. The sharing of information on real-time disruption and arrival times can help ensure that destinations are aware of arrival times and can support those who are vulnerable.

Information gleaned from possible services linked through IoT can suggest the locations of alternate travel options through a mobile or portable device including the availability of rentable and usable vehicles in nearby neighborhoods.

1.8   Supporting Infrastructure for the Journey

People interact with a supporting infrastructure throughout their journey. This may include physical infrastructure such as bathroom facilities, drinking fountains, signage, seating, shelter, lighting, maps, and timetables. It also consists of the service provider infrastructure such as customer service, other operator staff and those involved in their journey. Both are critical to the experience of people with a disability while travelling. Interactions with service staff, drivers and other support people often define the success of a journey. In such settings, location-based services offer real-time information about surrounding and nearby facilities that are accessible and usable to a person with a specific need. Such data can also be used as part of planning a journey access point, destination, or interchange where users are aware that they may need such facilities.

Such information can be presented through AR on services such as Google Maps to offer instant redirection information to appropriate facilities on demand.

Access to information should allow users to personalize the data according to their needs: 5G technologies offer the capacity to draw together all the information needed on to a mobile phone or other device.

2   Conclusion

People with disabilities face potential pain points at every stage of the mobility process. Addressing these had traditionally been both frustrating and time consuming and may have acted as a deterrent to travel for many. The speed and ease of use of digital technologies address not only the specific pain points but also the underlying stress created by reducing the complexity planning and making a journey. As the ease of planning improves, there is likely to be added pressure on transport providers to accommodate increase numbers of people with disabilities seeking to travel and hence increase demand for accessible transport solutions.

Acknowledgement. The information outlined in this paper is based upon that undertaken for the TRIPS project which has received funding from the European Union's Horizon 2020 research and innovation programme under grant agreement No 875588 and reflects only the author's view and the European Commission is not responsible for any use that may be made of the information it contain.

References

1. Alexander, D., Gaillard, J.C., Wisner, B.: Disability and Disaster. The Routledge Handbook of Hazards and Disaster Risk Reduction, pp. 413–423. Routledge, London/New York (2012)
2. Balasuriya, S.S., Sitbon, L., Bayor, A.A., Hoogstrate, M., Brereton, M.: Use of voice activated interfaces by people with intellectual disability. In: Proceedings of the 30th Australian Conference on Computer-Human Interaction, pp. 102–112 (December 2018)
3. DIRD: The whole journey: a guide for thinking beyond compliance to create accessible public transport journeys Government of Australia (2017)
4. European Commission: European accessibility act (2020). https://ec.europa.eu/social/main. jsp?catId=1202&langId=en
5. Ghanim, M.S., Shaaban, K., Miqdad, M.: An Artificial Intelligence Approach to Estimate Travel Time along Public Transportation Bus Lines (2020)
6. Harms, T., Olaru, D., Pattison, C.: Active travel: using wearable technology to analyse daily travel behaviour. In: 41st Australasian Transport Research Forum (ATRF) 2019, ACT, Canberra (October 2019)
7. Huang, H., Gartner, G., Krisp, J.M., Raubal, M., Van de Weghe, N.: Location based services: ongoing evolution and research agenda. J. Locat. Based Serv. 12(2), 63–93 (2018)
8. Kasprzak, S., Komninos, A., Barrie, P.: Feature-based indoor navigation using augmented reality. In: 2013 9th International Conference on Intelligent Environments, pp. 100–107. IEEE (July 2013)
9. Kumbhar, M., Survase, M., Mastud, P., Salunke, A., Sirdeshpande, S.: Real time web based bus tracking system. Int. Res. J. Eng. Technol. (IRJET) 3(02), 632–635 (2016)
10. Neuburger, L., Beck, J., Egger, R.: The 'Phygital'tourist experience: the use of augmented and virtual reality in destination marketing. In: Tourism Planning and Destination Marketing, vol. 183 (2018)
11. Park, J., Chowdhury, S.: Investigating the barriers in a typical journey by public transport users with disabilities. J. Transp. Health 10, 361–368 (2018)
12. Reger, L.: 1.4 the road ahead for securely-connected cars. In: 2016 IEEE International Solid-State Circuits Conference (ISSCC), pp. 29–33. IEEE (2016)
13. Shaheen, S., Bell, C., Cohen, A., Yelchuru, B.: Travel Behavior: Shared Mobility and Transportation Equity, prepared for Office of Policy & Governmental Affairs, Federal Highway Administration, Report No. PL-18-007 (2017). https://www.fhwa.dot.gov/policy/otps/shared_use_mobility_equity_final.pdf
14. Smart Card Alliance: Transit and contactless open payments: an emerging approach for fare collection. White paper, Smart Card Alliance, Princeton (2011)
15. Wansley, A.T., Chen, R., Liu, S.Y.: U.S. Patent Application No. 13/956,182 (2014)
16. Warren, N., Ayton, D., Manderson, L.: Mobility issues for people with disabilities. In: Michalos, A.C. (ed.) Encyclopedia of Quality of Life and Well-Being Research. Springer, Dordrecht (2014). https://doi.org/10.1007/978-94-007-0753-5_1826
17. Wise, P.H.: Emerging technologies and their impact on disability. Future Child. 22(1), 169–191 (2012). https://doi.org/10.1353/foc.2012.0002

AccessibleMaps: Addressing Gaps in Maps for People with Visual and Mobility Impairments

Claudia Loitsch[1(✉)], Karin Müller[2], Christin Engel[1], Gerhard Weber[1],
and Rainer Stiefelhagen[2]

[1] Institute for Applied Computer Science, Human-Computer-Interaction,
Technische Universität Dresden, Dresden, Germany
{claudia.loitsch,christin.engel,gerhard.weber}@tu-dresden.de
[2] Study Centre for the Visually Impaired, Karlsruhe Institute of Technology,
Karlsruhe, Germany
{karin.e.mueller,rainer.steifelhagen}@kit.edu

Abstract. Persons with visual and mobility impairments often have problems when planning and implementing a trip to unknown buildings due to the inaccessibility of the built environment, the unavailability of reliable information, and missing mobility-supporting applications for indoor environments. One reason is the lack of barrier-free indoor maps enriched with accessibility information to support the diverse needs of people with disabilities. This paper provides a comprehensive review of user requirements, mobility-related applications and digital maps. We identify different gaps in supporting indoor mobility, *i.e.* lack of (i) dedicated requirement analyses for mobility in unknown buildings, (ii) procedures to improve the coverage of digital indoor maps, (iii) standards for barrier-free map representations and (iv) location-based indoor services that meet the needs of people with disabilities. Besides, we introduce the AccessibleMaps project, which addresses some of these gaps by automatically generating indoor maps enriched with accessibility features.

Keywords: Accessibility features · Indoor maps · People with Visual and Mobility Impairments

1 Introduction

Travelling and mobility are a matter of course in today's professional life. However, people with Visual and Mobility Impairments (VMI) often have problems with navigating to new locations, orientating in unfamiliar places or finding a specific point of interest. Good preparation is therefore essential in order to identify possible barriers in advance. It includes gathering information about the

---

C. Loitsch and K. Müller—Contributed equally to this research.

K. Miesenberger et al. (Eds.): ICCHP 2020, LNCS 12377, pp. 286–296, 2020.
https://doi.org/10.1007/978-3-030-58805-2_34

route, departure and arrival time, accommodation, exact address and meeting point at the destination.

In addition to this general information, accessibility aspects of the whole trip must be considered. Especially the information need regarding navigation and security is very high [1]. It is important for people with mobility and visual impairments to know both the facilitators that improve access and barriers that impede participation [30]. However, searching for this information is time-consuming and hardly possible without help, as the relevant information is only partially available or not available at all. Even with support, the search is often not successful.

Thus, the knowledge about the following two aspects play a major role in the successful planning and execution of a trip: (1) accessibility features of walkways, public transport, and buildings as well as possible barriers and whether this information is reliable and comprehensible enough to meet individual needs; (2) availability of apps that support planning & orientation, safety, and navigation.

While many projects, laws and guidelines focus on improving the accessibility of public transport as well as outdoor environments, indoor accessibility is not much discussed. Although there are many regulations in the architectural field regarding barrier-free buildings (e.g. ISO 21542:2011-12), there is less research on how this information can be made available to users. In this paper, we present our research project AccessibleMaps which aims to improve the accessibility of buildings by generating individualised, rich indoor maps for people with VMI. To this end, we first analyze existing approaches that aim to improve the mobility of people with VMI. On that basis, we identify gaps for indoor environments and propose a concept to support planning and orientating in unknown buildings.

2 Analysis of Existing Applications

Many applications aim to improve the mobility of people with VMI in different parts of the travel chain. Maps are important for both the planning phase and for orientation at a particular location. Navigation instructions, as well as real-time environmental information, are useful for finding an accessible route or avoiding obstacles and barriers locally. In the following sections, requirements for mobility supporting applications are collected and challenges of existing map-based applications are identified.

2.1 Requirements for Mobility Supporting Applications for People with VMI

Applications that support people with VMI in their orientation differ in terms of presentation, provided information and characteristics, input and output modalities, addressed target groups as well as supported use cases. Nonetheless, general requirements can be derived from the need for information about the accessibility of the whole trip. In Table 1, we shortly summarise some of the requirements with examples regarding information about navigation and safety (R1.1–R1.5), public transport (R2.1–R2.3), the user interface (R3.1–R3.3), maps and

Table 1. List of requirements and examples for information regarding navigation and safety (R1.1–R1.5); public transport (R2.1–R2.3); user interfaces (R3.1–R3.3); maps and databases (R4.1–R4.4); interaction with a system (R5.1–R5.2).

No	Requirement	Example
R1.1	Provide information about difficult situations for orientation	Equipment at crossings, open spaces finding entrances
R1.2	Make environmental features available	Curbs, stairs, fences, ground changes
R1.3	Provide precise GPS signal to allow precise positioning	One roadside can be accessible while the other is not
R1.4	Include information about obstacles	Construction sites, poles
R1.5	Provide information about safer paths	Detour with traffic lights
R2.1	Availability of accessible information about public transport	Timetables, stops
R2.2	Accessibility of the equipment of public transport	Non-level access between platforms of trains, busses, stops
R2.3	Availability of supporting services	Assistance when changing transportation
R3.1	Provide both a graphical and textual interface	For persons with VMI
R3.2	Integrate accessibility features	Layout, text design, touch
R3.3	Observe usability aspects	Intuitiveness, compactness, clarity
R4.1	Allow to add accessibility features	Accessible restrooms, tactile pavings, lowered curbs, ramps
R4.2	Use common available standards	*E.g.* for smartphone apps
R4.3	Provide flexible data structure	Information filters, extensibility
R4.4	Ensure mechanisms to facilitate updating of data	Publicly available data, crowd-sourcing mechanisms
R5.1	Ability to work with assistive technologies	Audio and tactile communication, screenreaders
R5.2	Allow hands-free navigation	Cane, guide dog, control of wheelchair already occupies hands

databases (R4.1–R4.4), as well as interaction with a system (R5.1–R5.2). These requirements were gathered from the analysis of various projects for navigation [7,8,16,18,33], from different studies [22,24,27,31,32,38], services [19] and legal guidelines [2,35].

2.2   Map Coverage of the Entire Travel Chain

Digital maps are the core of many accessible mobile applications designed to support people with VMI in planning and orientating as well as navigation throughout the entire travel chain. Maps for public transportation are increasingly available and an aid for travellers to support route finding tasks from a start to a destination [3]. Outdoor maps are ubiquitous and include street maps, geo-coding, searches, and routing functionality. The mapping is based on satellite images or high-resolution images taken, for example, by Google. In contrast, it is much harder to collect data for buildings. Floor plans created *e.g.* by architects are typically not freely available and mostly not suitable to bring this data into a structured map format [10]. Indoor environments, therefore, have the lowest map coverage, as the creation of databases with floor plans is currently proprietary and costly. Solving this problem through open, scalable and affordable indoor maps is essential to enable seamless support of navigation and orientation along the entire travel chain in the future.

2.3   Accessibility Information in Digital Maps

Commonly known geographical maps such as Google Maps, Apple Maps, or OpenStreetMap (OSM) provide general data on roads, railways, rivers, forests, houses but neglect information on their accessibility. Promising are Volunteered Geographic Information (VGI) approaches that collect location-based accessibility information [6] like Wheelmap[1] or Access Together[2]. A challenge of VGI approaches is to ensure high quality and accuracy of the annotations collected by the volunteers as well as scalability. When volunteers include people without disabilities who have not been previously trained, the information collected on accessibility may not meet the needs of people with disabilities [39]. Automated procedures can improve scalability, for instance by segmenting video footages of wheelchair usage to detect challenging spaces such as rough dropped curbs [26], by computer vision techniques and machine learning to acquire accessibility issues from image databases [37], or by simulation of accessibility space, analysing architectural floor plans [20]. However, fully automated solutions can lead to inaccurate or outdated information, for instance when images show barriers that do no longer exist [15]. However, the level of detail of information provided by VGI and automated approaches varies considerably as there is no standard that describes the information need of people with disabilities and their specific requirements for independent mobility. Another aspect, which has been only marginally addressed so far, is how to keep annotated information up-to-date. This is a key problem, as people with disabilities need very accurate and up-to-date information on the accessibility of the environment in order to be able to travel successfully without (or with little) assistance.

---

[1] SOZIALHELDEN e.V. - Wheelmap, https://wheelmap.org/, Retrieved April 3 2020.
[2] Access Together. http://www.accesstogether.org/, Retrieved April 3 2020.

2.4   Making Digital Maps Available

Apart from collecting and enriching maps with information on spatial accessibility, another important aspect is how maps are made accessible to people with disabilities. Since digital maps are usually displayed graphically and accessed by touch or mouse, they often cause barriers, especially for people with visual impairments and people with limited mobility in the upper body. A central problem is the lack of comparable standards for barrier-free maps, software or websites (*e.g.* WCAG [35]). However, some of these guidelines can be adopted to make maps accessible, *e.g.* to provide easier language and easily understandable symbols. For people with visual impairments, though, a wide range of methods already exists, including tactile maps, virtual acoustic maps, virtual tactile maps, accessible maps on touch devices, augmented paper-based tactile maps or tactile maps in Braille [25]. However, the most commonly used method, which constitutes tactile printing, is costly and time-consuming to produce and is primarily used for travel planning. During a trip, up-to-date information is usually required that may not be available on previously printed materials. Various researchers investigated the automatic generation of haptic maps for self-printing [4,13,14,17,29,36] or developed multi-modal applications to better address challenges such as Braille labelling and feature annotation [23] or to explore maps on a pin-matrix display [40]. Although the number of approaches to automatically create tactile maps is constantly growing [34], there is no holistic approach that can handle different representations and interaction modalities simultaneously. Furthermore, there is currently a lack of solutions that address different user groups, in particular, their specific needs and preferences for certain usage contexts. People with multiple disabilities, *e.g.* a visual and mobility impairment, have to collect information from different sources about the accessibility of their surroundings, especially in indoor environments. Thus, the diversity of end-users must be targeted by individual presentations, multi-modal interactions and personalised user interfaces and diverse accessibility information.

2.5   Map-Based Apps for Navigation & Environmental Information

In the past, a huge variety of mobility aids and applications relying on digital maps were developed to support the navigation and orientation of people with disabilities especially for **outdoor environments**. Many of them are specialised in routing to support outdoor navigation by *turn-by-turn instructions* (*e.g.* Seeing Eye GPS App[3], Lazzus[4] , Ariadne GPS[5], ViaOpta Nav[6], Routago Assist[7]). Some applications focusing on *landmark-based navigation and*

---

[3] Seeing Eye GPS App. http://www.senderogroup.com/products/seeingeyegps/index.html Retrieved March 30, 2020.

[4] Lazzus. http://lazzus.com/, Retrieved March 30, 2020.

[5] Ariadne GPS. https://www.ariadnegps.eu/, Retrieved April 4, 2020.

[6] ViaOpta Nav. https://apps.apple.com/de/app/viaopta-nav/id908435532, Retrieved April 4.

[7] Routago Assist. https://routago.de/en/assist_en/, Retrieved April 4, 2020).

orientation provide further semantic information about environments related to pathways (*e.g.* tactile paving, ramps, steps, slopes, type of doorway, obstacles) or floor transition (*e.g.* elevators, escalators, stairs) such as BlindSquare[8] or NavCog [28]. Unlike outdoor environments where GPS is available, comparable navigation systems for **indoor environments** like LowViz Guide Indoor Navigation[9] require the augmentation of the physical environment with Beacons [28], passive radio frequency identification (RFID) [5,11] or Near Field Communication tags (NFC) [12]. Those localisation approaches are suitable for test scenarios but not for large-scale deployment as the augmentation of the physical environment with RFID, NFC or Bluetooth *etc.* require still high implementation and maintenance effort and thus lack scalability. Sensor-based systems (*e.g.* the vOICe application, Navatar [9]) are less dependent on infrastructure and therefore less expensive but they depend on specific hardware and are less precise. In particular, the accuracy of the localisation must be far more accurate in the vicinity of buildings and inside buildings to ensure safe support for people with disabilities. Providing a robust and accurate positioning infrastructure that allows seamless localisation between outdoor and indoor areas is a crucial challenge and prerequisite for uniform support services during the travel chain.

3   The AccessibleMaps Project

The review of user requirements, mobility-related applications and digital maps presented in Sect. 2 showed that current approaches mainly focus on isolated mobility aspects to support orientation and navigation scenarios. The interior is the area that is least considered. In particular, there is a lack of (i) dedicated requirement analyses for mobility in unknown buildings, (ii) procedures to improve the coverage of digital indoor maps, (iii) standards for barrier-free map representations and (iv) location-based indoor services that meet the needs of people with disabilities. Bridging this gap is essential for the development of a system that covers the entire travel chain and can be used in practice for diverse user groups. As a basis, an automated method is needed to generate highly adaptable, rich indoor maps and to collect useful accessibility features about buildings.

In our AccessibleMaps project, we address the following three gaps to improve the development of location-based services in indoor spaces:

1. Poor coverage of indoor maps
2. Lack of accessibility information and timeliness of information
3. Insufficient accessibility of maps

Figure 1 shows the concept of our project. We pursue two objectives. One is to generate indoor maps enriched with accessibility features automatically and to

---

[8] BlindSquare. http://www.blindsquare.com/, Retrieved March 30, 2020.
[9] LowViz Guide Indoor Navigation. https://indoo.rs/solution/visually-impaired/, Retrieved April 4, 2020.

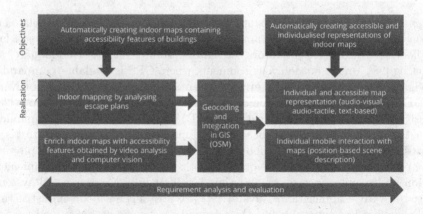

Fig. 1. Project plan for accessible maps which describe goals and envisaged realisation steps.

provide these algorithms for many and diverse stakeholders (gap (1) and (2)). The second objective is the automatic generation of accessible representations of indoor maps for different usage contexts and users (gap (3)). To achieve these objectives, we are currently working on the following activities:

1. **Automatic Indoor Mapping:** Analysis of escape plans and extraction of building features through image processing and machine learning. The use of simultaneous localisation and mapping (SLAM) methods to improve the accuracy of building layout and localise features (*e.g.* columns).
2. **Enrichment of indoor maps with accessibility features:** Identify and locate building features (*e.g.* barriers and accessibility features) by video footage and computer vision approaches.
3. **Integration into OSM:** Modeling of indoor maps enriched with accessibility features by extending the OSM scheme Simple Indoor Tagging (SIT). Since our maps are geo-referenced, they contribute to easier indoor localisation.
4. **Creation of interactive, personalised map representations:** Adaptation of the generated maps to specific user needs (*e.g.* audio-tactile maps, audio-visual maps, textual descriptions) and individual contexts, especially to improve mobile usage with barrier-free interaction techniques (*e.g.* voice and touch interaction).

In-house solutions for the creation of indoor maps are costly and time-consuming. It is, therefore, necessary to provide automated solutions for mapping buildings in order to significantly increase the availability of indoor maps for public buildings. To achieve this goal, we are developing algorithms for the automatic analysis of escape plans, which are available and mandatory for most public buildings and workplaces in Germany (including hotels, office buildings, schools and others). Escape plans contain basic safety information and pointers to places of interest and are constantly updated. The design follows certain legal design principles and symbols[10]. Based on the design guidelines and symbolism on escape plans, image processing algorithms can be used to recognise the basic features of a building (*e.g.* building structure, rooms, doors). The result of this step is additionally compared and enriched with specific map information determined by SLAM algorithms. This step is used to improve accuracy and to detect obstacles.

In a further step, we analyse videos of indoor environments, recorded by a wearable camera, using state-of-the art computer vision methods to deduce specific indoor accessibility features which are not detectable from escape plans (*e.g.* different kind of stairs, tactile pavings, braille labels). We will also extract individual object features that are needed to assess the accessibility of a building (*e.g.* door width, height of stairs, elevator size).

For integrating the generated indoor maps as well as the detected objects into OSM, we will develop specific localisation algorithms based on visual odometry that enable us to estimate position and orientation of the camera as well as the relative position to the objects. We will also investigate the application of SLAM methods to localise accessibility features more precisely. Furthermore, we will extend the data schema SIT for modelling accessibility features of buildings comprehensively. This is necessary as SIT supports only few accessibility tags such as *wheelchair accessibility yes/no* or *door width*[11].

To make the generated maps available for many and diverse users, we develop adaptable user interfaces that support the generation of personalised map representations. Therefore, we investigate which accessibility information and which level of detail is needed for different use cases, *e.g.* for planning a business trip at home versus orienting oneself within a building. The generated maps should support various interaction techniques for mobile use. Besides tactile maps, innovative interaction techniques such as speech, gestures or touch which can be used with mobile devices will be explored. The results comprise tailored representations of indoor maps that are valuable for users with various needs as they can judge whether a building is barrier-free for their specific needs based on the available accessibility features. To achieve this, we will create customisable user profiles that respond to specific needs and preferences, and on the basis of which certain types of information and map displays will be generated.

4   Conclusion

Many approaches aim to support barrier-free travel for people with disabilities. In our work, however, we have identified crucial gaps that need to be closed to support the entire travel chain. In particular, indoor maps are hardly available, which means that important information is missing to enable people with disabilities to successfully and independently find a location in a building with existing applications during a journey. We propose an automated generation process to

---

[10] The international regulation DIN 23601 or national such as "Technical rules for workplaces" (ASR; Germany).

[11] https://wiki.openstreetmap.org/wiki/Key:door, Retrieved April 10, 2020.

fill this gap, leading to richer indoor maps with tailored information on building accessibility. This will improve the availability of accessible, highly customisable and scalable indoor maps for different users. The results can have a significant impact on the development of a fully accessible travel chain, as seamless navigation and orientation support will be possible. By providing such maps, the involvement of people with VMI should also be improved in the professional sector so that independent travel becomes possible.

Acknowledgements. The project is funded by the German Federal Ministry of Labour and Social Affairs (BMAS) under the grant number 01KM151112.

References

1. Banovic, N., Franz, R.L., Truong, K.N., Mankoff, J., Dey, A.K.: Uncovering information needs for independent spatial learning for users who are visually impaired. In: Proceedings of the 15th International ACM SIGACCESS Conference on Computers and Accessibility, ASSETS 2013. Association for Computing Machinery, New York (2013)
2. Bundesministerium der Justiz und für Verbraucherschutz: Verordnung zur Schaffung barrierefreier Informationstechnik nach dem Behindertengleichstellungsgesetz (Barrierefreie-Informationstechnik-Verordnung - BITV 2.0), March 2020
3. Burch, M., Kurzhals, K., Weiskopf, D.: Visual task solution strategies in public transport maps. In: ET4S@ GIScience, pp. 32–36 (2014)
4. Červenka, P., Břinda, K., Hanousková, M., Hofman, P., Seifert, R.: Blind friendly maps. In: Miesenberger, K., Bühler, C., Penaz, P. (eds.) ICCHP 2016. LNCS, vol. 9759, pp. 131–138. Springer, Cham (2016). https://doi.org/10.1007/978-3-319-41267-2_18
5. Chumkamon, S., Tuvaphanthaphiphat, P., Keeratiwintakorn, P.: A blind navigation system using RFID for indoor environments. In: 5th International Conference on Electrical Engineering/Electronics, Computer, Telecommunications and Information Technology, ECTI-CON 2008, vol. 2, pp. 765–768 (2008)
6. Cruz, I., Campelo, C.E.C.: Improving accessibility through VGI and crowdsourcing. In: Crowdsourcing: Concepts, Methodologies, Tools, and Applications, chap. 20, pp. 374–392. Information Resources Management Association (2019)
7. Darvishy, A., Hutter, H.P., Seifert, A.: August 2016
8. DBSV: Anforderungen an satellitengestützte Navigationssysteme für blinde und sehbehinderte Menschen, March 2020
9. Fallah, N., Apostolopoulos, I., Bekris, K., Folmer, E.: The user as a sensor: navigating users with visual impairments in indoor spaces using tactile landmarks. In: Proceedings of the Conference on Human Factors in Computing Systems, pp. 425–432 (2012)
10. Froehlich, J.E., et al.: Grand challenges in accessible maps. Interactions **26**(2), 78–81 (2019)
11. Ganz, A., Schafer, J., Gandhi, S., Puleo, E., Wilson, C., Robertson, M.: PERCEPT indoor navigation system for the blind and visually impaired: architecture and experimentation. Int. J. Telemed. Appl. (2012)
12. Ganz, A., Schafer, J.M., Tao, Y., Wilson, C., Robertson, M.: PERCEPT-II: smartphone based indoor navigation system for the blind. In: 2014 36th Annual International Conference of the IEEE Engineering in Medicine and Biology Society,

EMBC 2014, pp. 3662–3665. Institute of Electrical and Electronics Engineers Inc., November 2014

13. Götzelmann, T., Pavkovic, A.: Towards automatically generated tactile detail maps by 3D printers for blind persons. In: Miesenberger, K., Fels, D., Archambault, D., Peñáz, P., Zagler, W. (eds.) ICCHP 2014. LNCS, vol. 8548, pp. 1–7. Springer, Cham (2014). https://doi.org/10.1007/978-3-319-08599-9_1

14. Hänßgen, D.: HaptOSM - creating tactile maps for the blind and visually impaired. In: Mensch und Computer 2015 - Workshop, pp. 405–410. Walter de Gruyter GmbH, August 2015

15. Hara, K., Froehlich, J.E.: Characterizing and visualizing physical world accessibility at scale using crowdsourcing, computer vision, and machine learning. ACM SIGACCESS Access. Comput. (113), 13–21 (2015)

16. HFC Human-Factors-Consult GmbH: OIWOB - Orientieren, Informieren, Warnen. Orientierungshilfe für Blinde, October 2019. http://www.oiwob.de/start

17. Jacob, R., Mooney, P., Corcoran, P., Winstanley, A.C.: Haptic-GIS: exploring the possibilities. SIGSPATIAL Spec. 2(3), 13 (2010)

18. Jaunich, P.: m4guide - mobile multi-modal mobility guide AP 820 Auswertung der Befragung zur Ausgangssituation und den Anforderungen der Nutzer. BLIC, Januar 2014. http://docplayer.org/7733335-M4guide-mobile-multi-modal-mobility-guide-ap-820-auswertung-der-befragung-zur-ausgangssituation-und-den-anforderungen-der-nutzer.html

19. Karimi, H.A., Zhang, L., Benner, J.G.: Personalized accessibility map (PAM): a novel assisted wayfinding approach for people with disabilities. Ann. GIS 20(2), 99–108 (2014)

20. Kostic, N., Scheider, S.: Automated generation of indoor accessibility information for mobility-impaired individuals. In: Lecture Notes in Geoinformation and Cartography, vol. 217, pp. 235–252. Kluwer Academic Publishers (2015)

21. Melfi, G., Müller, K., Schwarz, T., Jaworek, G., Stiefelhagen, R.: Understanding what you feel: a mobile audio-tactile system for graphics used at schools with students with visual impairment. In: Proceedings of the 2020 CHI Conference on Human Factors in Computing Systems, CHI 2020, pp. 1–12. Association for Computing Machinery, New York (2020). https://doi.org/10.1145/3313831.3376508

22. Meyers, A.R., Anderson, J.J., Miller, D.R., Shipp, K., Hoenig, H.: Barriers, facilitators, and access for wheelchair users: substantive and methodologic lessons from a pilot study of environmental effects. Soc. Sci. Med. 55(8), 1435–1446 (2002)

23. Miele, J.A., Landau, S., Gilden, D.: Talking TMAP: automated generation of audio-tactile maps using Smith-Kettlewell's TMAP software. Br. J. Vis. Impairment 24(2), 93–100 (2006)

24. Park, J., Chowdhury, S.: Investigating the barriers in a typical journey by public transport users with disabilities. J. Transp. Health 10, 361–368 (2018)

25. Research and Development Working Group (RDWG) of W3C: Accessible Maps, April 2020. https://www.w3.org/WAI/RD/wiki/Accessible_Maps

26. Rodger, S., Jackson, D., Vines, J., McLaughlin, J., Wright, P.: JourneyCam: exploring experiences of accessibility and mobility among powered wheelchair users through video and data. In: Proceedings of the 2019 CHI Conference on Human Factors in Computing Systems, CHI 2019. Association for Computing Machinery, New York (2019)

27. Saha, M., Fiannaca, A.J., Kneisel, M., Cutrell, E., Morris, M.R.: Closing the gap: designing for the last-few-meters wayfinding problem for people with visual impairments. In: The 21st International ACM SIGACCESS Conference on Computers

and Accessibility, ASSETS 2019, pp. 222–235. Association for Computing Machinery, New York (2019)

28. Sato, D., Oh, U., Naito, K., Takagi, H., Kitani, K., Asakawa, C.: NavCog3: an evaluation of a smartphone-based blind indoor navigation assistant with semantic features in a large-scale environment. In: Proceedings of the 19th International ACM SIGACCESS Conference on Computers and Accessibility, pp. 270–279. Association for Computing Machinery, Baltimore (2017)

29. Taylor, B., Dey, A., Siewiorek, D., Smailagic, A.: TactileMaps.net: a web interface for generating customized 3D-printable tactile maps. In: ASSETS 2015 - Proceedings of the 17th International ACM SIGACCESS Conference on Computers and Accessibility, pp. 427–428. Association for Computing Machinery Inc., New York, October 2015

30. Thapar, N., et al.: A pilot study of functional access to public buildings and facilities for persons with impairments. Disabil. Rehabil. **26**(5), 280–289 (2004)

31. Völkel, T., Kühn, R., Weber, G.: Mobility impaired pedestrians are not cars: requirements for the annotation of geographical data. In: Miesenberger, K., Klaus, J., Zagler, W., Karshmer, A. (eds.) ICCHP 2008. LNCS, vol. 5105, pp. 1085–1092. Springer, Heidelberg (2008). https://doi.org/10.1007/978-3-540-70540-6_163

32. Völkel, T., Weber, G.: RouteCheckr: personalized multicriteria routing for mobility impaired pedestrians. In: Proceedings of the 10th International ACM SIGACCESS Conference on Computers and Accessibility, Assets 2008, pp. 185–192. Association for Computing Machinery, New York (2008)

33. Vollrath, M., Leske, K., Friedrich, B., Axer, S.: Innerstädtische Mobilitätsunterstützung für Blinde und Sehbehinderte: InMoBS: Schlussbericht: Teilvorhaben Technische Universität Braunschweig. Technische Universität Braunschweig (2015)

34. Wabinski, J., Moscicka, A.: Automatic (tactile) map generation–a systematic literature review. ISPRS Int. J. Geo-Inf. **8**(7), 293 (2019)

35. WAI: web content accessibility guidelines, March 2020. http://www.w3.org/TR/WCAG/

36. Watanabe, T., Yamaguchi, T., Koda, S., Minatani, K.: Tactile map automated creation system using OpenStreetMap. In: Miesenberger, K., Fels, D., Archambault, D., Peňáz, P., Zagler, W. (eds.) ICCHP 2014. LNCS, vol. 8548, pp. 42–49. Springer, Cham (2014). https://doi.org/10.1007/978-3-319-08599-9_7

37. Weld, G., Jang, E., Li, A., Zeng, A., Heimerl, K., Froehlich, J.E.: Deep learning for automatically detecting sidewalk accessibility problems using streetscape imagery. In: The 21st International ACM SIGACCESS Conference on Computers and Accessibility, ASSETS 2019, pp. 196–209. Association for Computing Machinery, New York (2019)

38. Williams, M.A., Hurst, A., Kane, S.K.: "pray before you step out": describing personal and situational blind navigation behaviors. In: Proceedings of the 15th International ACM SIGACCESS Conference on Computers and Accessibility, ASSETS 2013. Association for Computing Machinery, New York (2013)

39. Zeng, L., Kühn, R., Weber, G.: Improvement in environmental accessibility via volunteered geographic information: a case study. Univ. Access Inf. Soc. **16**(4), 939–949 (2016). https://doi.org/10.1007/s10209-016-0505-9

40. Zeng, L., Weber, G.: Exploration of location-aware you-are-here maps on a pin-matrix display. IEEE Trans. Hum.-Mach. Syst. **46**(1), 88–100 (2016)

AccessKB: Linked Open Data
for Accessible Travel

Chaohai Ding[✉], E. A. Draffan, and Mike Wald

Web and Internet Science Group, School of Electronics and Computer Science,
University of Southampton, Southampton SO17 1BJ, UK
{c.ding,ead,mw}@ecs.soton.ac.uk

Abstract. Recent developments in Information Communication Technologies and digital map services have empowered aspects of digital inclusion, which can benefit people with disabilities with an increasingly wider range of information regarding accessible travel. However, accessibility data collection and management is one of the grand challenges in the area of accessible map information and accessible travel research. Most research projects in this area are still in the early stages of development, leading to difficulties in the provision of sufficient data about the barriers encountered by people with disabilities. This results in time-consuming searches for physical accessibility data. This paper presents an approach for accessibility data management and accessibility modelling, by introducing the AccessKB, a Linked Data-driven knowledge base designed for barrier-free or accessible travel.

Keywords: Linked data · Open accessibility data · Accessible travel · Accessibility data management

1 Introduction

According to the Family Resources Survey 2018/19 (FRS)[1], there were 14.1 million (21%) of the people reported with a disability in 2018/19, an increase from 11.3 million (19%) in 2008/09. This survey also showed that mobility impairments were the most prevalent mentioned in the report, accounting for 48% of the total number of those with disabilities. This is where an individual's mobility is affected due to a functional or structural issue that causes activity limitations or difficulties. Independent travelling for people with disabilities remains one of the top difficulties. This is not just because there has always been a large sector of the population who have mobility impairments. More recently this has been caused by the complexity of modern public transport, inaccessible transport hubs, facilities and services, and the absence of accessibility information about these facilities or services. Moreover, research has shown that it can be very time consuming and financially costly for those with mobility impairments to

---

[1] https://www.gov.uk/government/statistics/family-resources-survey-financial-year-201819.

© Springer Nature Switzerland AG 2020
K. Miesenberger et al. (Eds.): ICCHP 2020, LNCS 12377, pp. 297–304, 2020.
https://doi.org/10.1007/978-3-030-58805-2_35

find relevant accessibility information [6]. With the recent development of ICTs and digital map services, there were a group of researchers focus on this inter-disciplinary research related to accessible map and accessible travel. Froehlich et al. [3] concluded that there were five grand challenges in the research area of accessible map, including data collection, data management, modelling, accessi-ble maps and user foci. As one of the fundamental challenges, there were some research and recent applications such as 'wheelmap.org' applied corwdsourcing to improve the data quantity, but often failed to provide data quality[2]. There-fore, as a linked open data knowledge base for accessible travel, AccessKB aims to manage accessibility and model accessibility needs with the goal to contribute to the research of accessible map information development by providing barrier free travelling decision support for individuals.

2   Related Works

Although accessible travel has been listed as one of the top difficulties for people with mobility disabilities, there have been a limited number of research projects working on these fundamental challenges. ASK-IT project [1] is one of early projects that combined activity theory with content modelling to improve the travelling experience for people with mobility disabilities. Users were catego-rized into different groups: lower limb impairment, wheelchair users, upper limb impairment, upper body impairment, physiological impairment, psychological impairment, cognitive impairment, vision impairment, hearing impairment, and communication production/receiving impairment [8]. AEGIS [5] was another project, which used an ontology to model and integrate accessible information between users and devices. The modelling was based on their special needs and interactions, namely users with visual, hearing, motion, speech and cognitive impairments. OASIS [7] established an open ontology driven architecture to integrate and standardize accessible services to benefit to the quality of life of all aged people. Most importantly, this project proposed a hyper-ontology app-roach that could match determine correspondences between concepts with other ontologies from different domains. In summary, one of the challenges exposed by these projects has been data availability and it has always been difficult to find a publicly available, high quality and structured accessibility data sets. Addi-tionally, these projects were also faced with the challenge of data reusability and interoperability. There remain no standard guidelines for accessibility data, and no standard data models to represent the accessibility data. It also has been difficult to link accessibility requirements with the facilities by using accessi-bility modelling. Therefore, the use of Linked Data principles to accessibility data provided a fundamental improvement in data collection, management and accessibility modelling.

3   Methodology

In order to develop the knowledge base for accessible travel, it is important to understand the accessibility requirements of people with mobility disabilities.

The method applied in this research was based on the study conducted by Wiethoff et al. [8], which combined the Activity Theory and International Classification of Functioning, Disability and Health (ICF) code. Functional difficulties and activity limitations in travelling scenarios can be classified into different functional categories (presented in Table 1): 1. lower limb limitations, 2. user with upper limb limitations, 3. upper body limitations.

Table 1. Classification of mobility difficulties and limitations

Category	Sub-category	Limitation description
Lower limb limitations	Light walking limitations	Can walk 1/4 mile but not more distance and can climb 10 steps without rest
	Severe walking limitations	Very difficult or cannot walk 1/4 mile or very difficult or cannot climb 10 steps
	Wheelchair (manual)	Use manual wheelchair
	Wheelchair (power)	Use the powered wheelchair
Upper limb limitations	Upper limb limitations	Only one upper limb functionalities or both weak upper limbs functionalities, or no upper limb functionalities
Upper body limitations	Light upper body limitations	Weak upper body functionalities
	Severe upper body limitations	Very week or no upper body functionalities

3.1 Requirements Study

There was an online survey conducted to study the user requirements for accessible travelling data. People with mobility impairments having difficulties with public transport were asked to take part in the survey via an online website, social networking, a mailing list of interested groups and personal interviews. The questionnaire used the a 4-point Likert Scale for the candidate's answers to the proposed questions (i.e. 4 = Strongly Agree, 3 = Agree, 2 = Disagree, 1 = Strongly Disagree). Overview, there were 48 valid participant responses. 23% of the respondents were aged from between 18 to 35 years old and 77% of the respondents were aged from 36 to 64 years old. Based on the statistical analysis of the results, the most important accessible facilities in the transport hubs, such as train stations were: a lift to all (90.32%), an accessible entrance (87.10%), road slope to the place (83.87%), the road surface (83.33%) to the place, accessible car park around the building (83.33%), and accessible toilets (80.65%). For those questions on accessibility requirements for public transportation such as bus or train, the most important accessible faciliti were: ramps access (93.33%), accessible interchange (83.33%), accessible ticket machine (80.00%), accessible toilet (76.67%), and personal assistance (73.33%). As a conclusion, the analysis of this requirement study for accessible travel for those with a range of mobility impairments provided the evidence to aid the development of the ontologies and reasoning rules; thereby contributing to the development of the knowledge base.

3.2 Ontologies for Accessible Travel

An Ontology is the "formal, explicit specification of a shared conceptualization" [4]. Applying an ontology to model an accessibility requirement specification process has been applied in several projects, such as the AccessOnTo project, which integrated the standard checklist into the requirement specification [9], WTO-ICF Ontology and ASK-IT Ontology [8]. However, none of these ontologies fully met the requirements for accessible travel. Some ontologies were proposed and developed based on the aforementioned requirement's study, namely, a mobility difficulty ontology, place accessibility ontology and transport accessibility ontology. There were a list of core vocabularies and ontologies used in accessible travelling domain (presented in Table 2), such as FOAF (Friend Of a Friend) ontology, Geo Ontology, Simple Knowledge Organization System (SKOS) Schema, Places Ontology and spatialrelations ontology.

Table 2. Ontologies for accessible travel domain

Core Ontology	Namespace
FOAF	http://xmlns.com/foaf/0.1/\cdot
geo	http://www.w3.org/2003/01/geo/wgs84_pos#
SKOS	http://www.w3.org/2004/02/skos/core#
Schema	http://schema.org/
Places Ontology	http://purl.org/ontology/places#
spatialrelations	https://www.ordnancesurvey.co.uk/docs/ontologies/spatialrelations.owl
Proposed Ontology	Namespace
Mobility Difficulty Ontology	http://purl.org/net/ontology/modo#
Place Accessibility Ontology	http://purl.org/net/ontology/paco#
Transport Accessibility Ontology	http://purl.org/net/ontology/taco#

The Mobility Difficulty Ontology (MODO) aimed to be a lightweight ontology to model users' categorization of concepts based on their mobility limitations and their difficulties accessing public transport and places generally. This ontology applied Negative Property Assertion Pattern (NPAs) to distinguish the categories of mobility limitations. Although, built-in OWL2 (Web Ontology Language), negative object property assertions were not reasoning with the

Semantic Web Rule Language (SWRL) so one of proposed solutions was to apply the reasoning rule in the data querying phase, where the SPARQL1.1 was supporting the negation feature. For example, there were two negative object property assertions applied in *Category NNL* (No-Upper-Limb-Limitation, No-Upper-Body-Limitation, Light-Walking-Limitation) class to validate the ontology consistency, which could be represented as following SWRL rules: information of physical places and built environment.

```
Person(?p)^hasNoUpperLimbLimitation(?p,?ull)^
 ↪ UpperLimbLimitation(?ull)^hasNoUpperBodyLimitation(?p,?
 ↪ ubl)^UpperBodyLimitation(?ubl)^hasLowerLimbLimitation(?
 ↪ p,?lowerLimbLimitation)^LightWalkingLimitation(?
 ↪ lowerLimbLimitation) -> CategoryNNL(?p)
```

The Place Accessibility Ontology (PACO) was used to model the accessibility information of physical places and built environment. There was a list of existing ontologies used to model places, buildings and spatial things, such as Places ontology, ifcOwl ontology and LinkedGeoData ontology. However, ifcOWL was a formal description of the Building Information Modelling (BIM) data, which was extremely complex for usage in the accessible travelling domain. Places ontology was a lightweight ontology to describe geographical places and reused as intended, to describe places or buildings of interest. LinkedGeoData was the Linked Data of Open Street Map, which was used as a geographical reference. *Place* class in PACO ontology was equivalent to *schema:Place* in Schema vocabulary and *Building* class was the subclass of the class *geo:SpatialThing*. Classes *Facility* and *Service* could also be presented with the following syntax:

```
spatialrelations:contains (Building, BuildingPart)
rdfs:subClassOf (Entrance, BuildingPart)
rdfs:subClassOf(Floor, BuildingPart)
rdfs:subClassOf(Room, BuildingPart)
spatialrelations:contains (Building, BuildingPart)^rdfs:
    ↪ subClassOf (Entrance, BuildingPart)
-> spatialrelations:contains (Building, Entrance)
spatialrelations:contains (Building, BuildingPart)^rdfs:
    ↪ subClassOf(Floor, BuildingPart)
-> spatialrelations:contains (Building, Floor)
```

The Transport Accessibility Ontology (TACO) was the transport accessibility ontology built on top of The Linked General Transit Feed Specification (LinkedGTFS[2]) vocabularies, which was mapped from the GTFS towards the Resource Description Framework (RDF). Therefore, the TACO ontology reused Linked GTFS ontologies and imported the PACO ontology to describe the accessibility information of physical places in the public transport domain, such as the stations, stops, and terminals. Moreover, class like *Facility* and *Service* were designed to describe on board accessibility facilities and services such

---

[2] http://vocab.gtfs.org/terms#.

as AccessibleSeat, AccessibleTable and AccessibleToilet and PersonalAssistance. TACO also reused accessibility related vocabularies in the LinkedGTFS ontology, *WheelchairBoardingStatus* class, which represented the different status of wheelchair boarding.

4   Data Publishing and Reasoning

The previous section demonstrated the study of the accessibility requirements for people with mobility impairments. The ontologies for accessible travel were also introduced to address the urgent needs for quality accessibility data collection, management, and accessibility modeling in the research area of accessible travel. This section introduces the publication methods for the accessibility data as the AccessKB by applying the proposed ontologies. In order to publish the users' specifications as Linked Data, the syntax below has been provided as an example: user instance *Person_1* with following limitations: no upper limb limitation, no upper body limitation and has light walking limitation.

```
PREFIX rdf:<http://www.w3.org/1999/02/22-rdf-syntax-ns#>
PREFIX modo:<http://purl.org/net/ontology/modo#>
PREFIX owl:<http://www.w3.org/2002/07/owl#>
<modo:Person_1>
        rdf:type modo:Person .
        rdf:type owl:NamedIndividual .
        modo:hasNoUpperLimbLimitation modo:UpperLimbLimitation .
        modo:hasNoUpperBodyLimitation modo:UpperBodyLimitation .
        modo:hasLowerLimbLimitation mod:LowerLimbLimitation .
```

Having gathered the data about a person's limitations, as defined in the syntax above, a set of inference rules automatically defined the individual instance into the corresponding categories. The following syntax statement shows the customized OW2L-RL rule set written in the GraphDB, which represented the inference rules for class *CategoryNNL*.

```
Prefices {
    rdf: http://www.w3.org/1999/02/22-rdf-syntax-ns#
    modo: http://purl.org/net/ontology/modo#
} Rules {
    id:category_nnl
    x <rdf:type> <modo:Person>
    x <modo:hasNoUpperLimbLimitation> <modo:UpperLimbLimitation>
        <modo:hasNoUpperBodyLimitation> <modo:UpperBodyLimitation>
        <modo:hasLowerLimbLimitation> <mod:LowerLimbLimitation> }
```

As a result, the reasoning engine embedded in the GraphDB could apply the forwarding chaining strategy to infer the person into the class *CategoryNNL* automatically. Figure 1 demonstrates the result by embedding this rule set into the knowledge base. The triple with object (*modo:CategoryNNL*) was the implicit context inferred by the rule engine. The explicit context was the asserted statement and the implicit context was the inferred statement. Compared with applying a rule-based inference to publish the dataset, using SPARQL directly to insert the rule set into the triple store would keep reasoning rules up to date for inference.

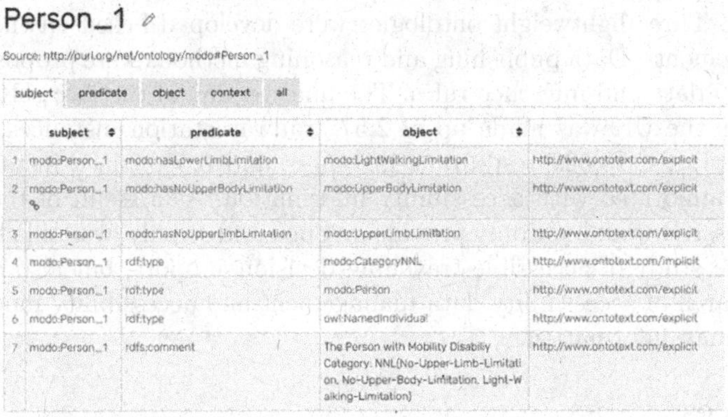

Person_1 ✎

Source: http://purl.org/net/ontology/modo#Person_1

subject	predicate	object	context	all

	subject ⬍	predicate ⬍	object ⬍	
1	modo:Person_1	modo:hasLowerLimbLimitation	modo:LightWalkingLimitation	http://www.ontotext.com/explicit
2	modo:Person_1	modo:hasNoUpperBodyLimitation	modo:UpperBodyLimitation	http://www.ontotext.com/explicit
3	modo:Person_1	modo:hasNoUpperLimbLimitation	modo:UpperLimbLimitation	http://www.ontotext.com/explicit
4	modo:Person_1	rdf:type	modo:CategoryNNL	http://www.ontotext.com/implicit
5	modo:Person_1	rdf:type	modo:Person	http://www.ontotext.com/explicit
6	modo:Person_1	rdf:type	owl:NamedIndividual	http://www.ontotext.com/explicit
7	modo:Person_1	rdfs:comment	The Person with Mobility Disability Category: NNL(No-Upper-Limb-Limitation, No-Upper-Body-Limitation, Light-Walking-Limitation)	http://www.ontotext.com/explicit

Fig. 1. Person instance inferred by OWL2-RL rule set

Place accessibility ontology provided vocabularies to represent the accessibility facilities and services within the built environment described in the following steps:

1. Publish the place area data within which the building is geographically located.
2. Publish the building data including name, geographic information, category, organization and contact etc.
3. Publish the accessible facilities and services connecting all floors, such as the lifts and stairs.
4. Publish rooms, accessible facilities and services on each floor.

Publishing accessibility data of the *Station* class was similar to the steps of publishing the place accessibility of built environment described above. Proposed steps were as follows:

1. Publish the instance of target built environment in the public transport class (i.e. stations, terminals or stops).
2. Publish instances of accessible facilities and services in all floors or platforms, such as lifts and stairs.
3. Publish instances of rooms, accessible facilities and services within each floor or platform.

5   Conclusion

This paper set as its goal the presentation of a research study applying semantic web technologies for accessibility data management and modelling to construct a knowledge base for automatic accessible travel decision support. It also aimed to address a grand challenge in the area of accessible map information. Classification of user groups based on mobility impairments affecting physical activity were introduced. Three lightweight ontologies were developed based on the study of user requirements. Data publishing and reasoning methods were proposed for the accessibility data and inference rules. The final version of the AccessKB dataset from across the UK was made up of 2,577 railway station instances, 362 tube station instances, 10,629 restaurant instances and 6,586 place instances published and annotated with accessibility information. As a result of the research work, AccessKB would not only provide an open and readily available knowledge base for the study of accessible travelling decision support, but also contribute to the research of accessibility data management and accessibility modelling for accessible map information.

References

1. Bekiaris, E., Panou, M., Mousadakou, A.: Elderly and disabled travelers needs in infomobility services. In: Stephanidis, C. (ed.) UAHCI 2007. LNCS, vol. 4554, pp. 853–860. Springer, Heidelberg (2007). https://doi.org/10.1007/978-3-540-73279-2_95

2. Ding, C., Wald, M., Wills, G.: A survey of open accessibility data. In: Proceedings of 13th International Web for All Conference - W4A 2014, pp. 73–80. ACM, Seoul (2014). https://doi.org/10.1145/2596695.2596708. http://eprints.soton.ac.uk/364209/

3. Froehlich, J.E., et al.: Grand challenges in accessible maps. Interactions 26(2), 78–81 (2019). https://doi.org/10.1145/3301657

4. Guarino, N., Oberle, D., Staab, S., Studer, R.: Handbook on Ontologies, pp. 1–17. https://doi.org/10.1007/978-3-540-92673-3

5. Korn, P., Bekiaris, E., Gemou, M.: Towards open access accessibility everywhere: the ÆGIS concept. In: Stephanidis, C. (ed.) UAHCI 2009. LNCS, vol. 5614, pp. 535–543. Springer, Heidelberg (2009). https://doi.org/10.1007/978-3-642-02707-9_60

6. Schmöcker, J.D., Quddus, M.A., Noland, R.B., Bell, M.G.: Mode choice of older and disabled people: a case study of shopping trips in London. J. Transp. Geogr. 16(4), 257–267 (2008). https://doi.org/10.1016/j.jtrangeo.2007.07.002

7. Vanderheiden, G., Treviranus, J.: Creating a global public inclusive infrastructure. In: Stephanidis, C. (ed.) UAHCI 2011. LNCS, vol. 6765, pp. 517–526. Springer, Heidelberg (2011). https://doi.org/10.1007/978-3-642-21672-5_57

8. Wiethoff, M., Sommer, S.M., Valjakka, S., Van Isacker, K., Kehagias, D., Bekiaris, E.: Specification of information needs for the development of a mobile communication platform to support mobility of people with functional limitations. In: Stephanidis, C. (ed.) UAHCI 2007. LNCS, vol. 4555, pp. 595–604. Springer, Heidelberg (2007). https://doi.org/10.1007/978-3-540-73281-5_63

9. Wooldridge, M., Jennings, N., Kinny, D.: The Gaia methodology for agent-oriented analysis and design. Auton. Agents Multi-Agent Syst. 3(3), 285–312 (2000). https://doi.org/10.1023/A:1010071910869

Analysis of Indoor Maps Accounting the Needs of People with Impairments

Julian Striegl[✉], Claudia Loitsch, Jan Schmalfuss-Schwarz,
and Gerhard Weber

Chair of Human Computer Interaction, Technical University Dresden,
Andreas-Pfitzmann-Bau, Nöthnitzer Str. 46, 01187 Dresden, Germany
{julian.striegl,claudia.loitsch,
jan.schmalfuss-schwarz,gerhard.weber}@tu-dresden.de

Abstract. Digital indoor maps are still in early stages of development but the demand for indoor location-based services is increasing continuously. Especially people with disabilities can benefit from accurate indoor maps with information in regards to the accessibility of indoor environments. Currently there are no widely accepted open standards for the expression of accessibility information in indoor maps. Furthermore, there is a lack of methods to assess if indoor maps comply with the requirements of people with disabilities in terms of orientation and indoor navigation. To address this problem, this paper presents a first analysis of the quantity and quality of indoor maps exemplary for selected cities in OpenStreetMap. The results show that the number of mapped indoor environments in OpenStreetMap is still sparse. On average only one building per city has a completely mapped indoor environment and the number of buildings with accessibility information is even smaller. This indicates that crowd-sourcing approaches should be supported with automated mapping processes and an ongoing analysis of indoor maps accounting the needs of people with disabilities should be conducted in order to ensure the quality of provided indoor geospatial information.

Keywords: Indoor maps · Indoor navigation · Accessibility ·
Barriers · OpenStreetMap · Visual impaired people · Mobility impaired people

1 Introduction

Geographic maps are running the way we travel in private or professional context; in particular to navigate, do outdoor adventures, plan holidays or business trips, orientate in unknown places as well as finding locations or points of interest (POIs). Compared to outdoor, indoor maps are still in the early stages of development but this sector will grow significantly due to an increased demand from location-based service providers [8]. With this development, the question of modelling the accessibility of buildings in geographical information systems

---

The original version of this chapter was revised: an error in the surname of the second author was corrected. The correction is available at
https://doi.org/10.1007/978-3-030-58805-2_59

K. Miesenberger et al. (Eds.): ICCHP 2020, LNCS 12377, pp. 305–314, 2020.
https://doi.org/10.1007/978-3-030-58805-2_36

should be raised at an early stage as well, as there are no widely accepted open standards that cover the diversity of user needs, heterogeneous indoor environments, as well as varying interests of stakeholders. There is also a lack of methods to assess if indoor maps comply with the requirements of people with disabilities in terms of orientation and indoor navigation, e.g. through conformance tests. To address this problem, this paper presents an analysis of indoor maps exemplary for OpenStreetMap (OSM). OSM is entirely crowd-sourced and provides free access and usage of maps and their underlying geographic data. We developed a web service that queries and analyses the OSM database according to quantitative criteria in order to evaluate the coverage of indoor maps for cities, federal states or countries. In addition, qualitative criteria are applied to assess the tagging of accessibility information about a building. The paper focuses on the results of the first analysis for selected cities and discusses the main problems with tagging environmental accessibility in indoor maps.

2   Understanding the User Needs

As stated by Froehlich et al. [6], modelling environmental accessibility is a complex open research question that requires the understanding of the user needs and abilities and a related analysis and assessment of accessibility and barriers. People with disabilities need granular information about the layout, orientation features (i.e. landmarks) as well as temporal relations (e.g. obstacles such as construction sites) to find their way independently. Mobility impaired people (wheelchair users and non-wheelchair users) primarily require structural information as they experience barriers such as narrow doors or passages, lack of or non-functioning elevators and escalators, lack of handrails, uneven walking surfaces and heavy doors [15]. Furthermore, mobility-impaired people rely on information such as slope of a path, stairs, ramps [17] floor covering [14], and opening of doors (auto or manual) [4]. Visually impaired people also require structural information such as handrails. Additionally, this user group specifically relies on wayfinding information and can experience barriers in complex and confusing buildings or buildings with bad lighting conditions [15]. Visually impaired people use auditory cues (e.g. echo from building fronts, the sound of stores and restaurants), olfactory information (e.g. smells from restaurants) as well as tactile information (e.g. cane tactile feedback, floor texture, change of ground composition) for orientation and way finding [1,17]. Accordingly, it is useful for visually impaired people to know, for instance, if the noise level in a building is high or low, where the bakery is located in the station, where pedestrian flows pass, where tactile pavings are. In addition, information about the availability and location of braille signs is helpful because many visually impaired people have troubles in locating them [1]. Landmarks for open spaces are crucial to help visually impaired people not to lose their position and relation to the environment [1].

3   State of the Art

Currently, there are no statistics and evaluations focusing on the quantity and quality of indoor maps in general and specifically in terms of accessibility. Commercial providers such as Google Maps or Apple Maps have closed APIs and limit the access to maps and data according to their own conditions. Google Maps itself states that indoor maps for over 10.000 locations are available worldwide[1]. However, due to the limited API access an analysis of the quality of those indoor maps - especially in the context of accessibility - cannot be conducted. Apple Maps introduced its indoor program rather recently in 2019 and thus has a far smaller amount of available indoor locations[2]. Furthermore, those platforms focus almost exclusively on the mapping of POIs and are lacking information about physical accessibility [6]. Moreover, data providers are hardly able to commercially capture indoor data for large areas in order to account for the high demand for indoor navigation solutions and indoor location-based services, because the level of detail required is too high to achieve with traditional mapping methods [12]. This makes the volunteered geographic information (VGI) approach of OSM for capturing and providing information about indoor environments highly promising [7]. When compared to professional manufacturers of geographic information, VGI can compete in accuracy and quality while at the same time providing the resulting spatial data freely [19].

For that reason, OSM is used by international and European projects such as the CAP4Access project for the collection of accessibility information [9,13]. In the accessibility domain, there are specific projects focusing on tagging buildings accessible for wheelchair users. The Wheelmap[3] project combines crowd-sourcing based data collection with map visualization in order to enable users to find wheelchair accessible places. Project Sidewalk[4] and the AccessMap[5] project take a similar approach in order to provide interactive visualizations of pedestrian accessibility. Other approaches such as the AXSMap[6] project or the crowd-sourcing project Access Together[7] focus not only on mobility-impaired people but also on the collection and providence of accessibility information in urban areas for users with visual or hearing impairments. While those projects are a first step towards accessible digital maps, there is still a high degree of variability in regards to mapped accessibility information and overall the amount of accessibility data is scarce [2]. Furthermore, existing projects tend to focus more on outdoor environments in urban areas instead of indoor [3]. To increase

---

[1] Google Maps - Indoor FAQ, https://maps.google.com/help/maps/indoormaps/faqs. html, Access date: 24.03.2020.

[2] Apple Maps Indoor Program, https://developer.apple.com/videos/play/wwdc2019/ 245/, Access date: 24.03.2020.

[3] Wheelmap.org, https://wheelmap.org/, Access date: 25.03.2020.

[4] Project Sidewalk, https://sidewalk-sea.cs.washington.edu/developer, Access date: 25.03.2020.

[5] AccessMap project, https://www.accessmap.io/, Access date: 25.03.2020.

[6] AXSMap, https://www.axsmap.com/, Access date: 26.03.2020.

[7] Access Together, http://www.accesstogether.org/, Access date: 26.03.2020.

scalability, a multitude of automated methods for indoor mapping and modelling (IMM) have emerged. IMM looks back on a long scientific tradition and has brought forth numerous approaches and technologies as reviewed by Zlatanova et al. [20]. SLAM methods, for example, have proven to be suitable for surveying buildings and localization [5]. Methods include the use of photographed escape plans for extracting spatial information of a building [16] or the appliance of statistical segmentation to interpret floor plans and extract specific information [10]. Kostic and Scheider investigated the automatic computation of spacial information to assess if indoor environments provide enough space for wheelchair users [11]. Automated methods for indoor mapping are promising to significantly increase the number of indoor maps. However, the current focus is on the recognition of elementary features such as rooms, corridors, and doors. The detection and integration of extensive accessibility features are not sufficiently considered by automated IMM approaches. A general problem of existing approaches is that tagged data is not continuously validated and evaluated to ensure sufficient quality of indoor maps enriched with accessibility information. To address this problem, we present an analysis of indoor maps subsequently.

4 Analysis of Indoor Maps in OSM

OSM is one of the most successful VGI projects [18]. It follows the peer production model and aims for the provision of free to use and editable map data, thus providing a promising solution for collecting and maintaining data for indoor environments [7]. In most cases, the mapping of buildings in OSM is mainly related to the outer shape of buildings and mapped information about the inner structure is still sparse [7]. Nevertheless, in coherence with an increasing need for indoor navigation solutions and indoor location based-services an accelerating increase of indoor specific tagging can be seen in OSM [7]. Furthermore, OSM strives to make maps and information on accessibility available to people with disabilities[8]. Users can provide information on the structure of pavements and specific tags can be used to capture whether certain objects (such as traffic lights) or facilities (such as cinemas) provide audio signals or voice interfaces. For mobility-impaired people the existence of steps, ramps, inclines and handrails can be mapped and public infrastructure can be marked as accessible by wheelchair. The following section describes the analysis conducted to evaluate the current state and extend of accessible indoor spatial information in OSM.

4.1 Materials and Methods

To analyse the quantity and quality of existing indoor maps in OSM the Overpass API[9] was used. The read-only API responds to requests with custom selected

---

parts of the OSM map data and is optimized for data consumers. The used requests where formed based on tags specific for the mapping of indoor areas with the *Simple Indoor Tagging* (SIT) schema of OSM. In the past, several possible tagging schemas for the expression of indoor environments in OSM have been proposed, with IndoorOSM[10] and SIT[11] being the most prominent solutions. Of those two solutions SIT was chosen by the OSM community for its simpler, clearer structure that does not rely on complex relational models. SIT extends the OSM platform by introducing several tags for the description of indoor environments. The propagated tags range from a coarse-grained to a fine-grained description of the indoor environment, as the VGI approach of OSM works best if contributors can chose the level of detail of added spatial information. The bare minimum of needed tags for a working indoor map in

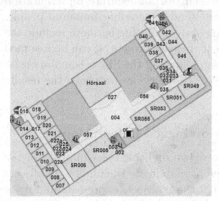
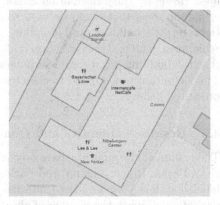

(a) Building with completely mapped in-door environment

(b) Building with mapped POI positions

Fig. 1. Comparison of two buildings with mapped indoor environments following the SIT schema. OpenLevelUp: https://openlevelup.net, access date: 11.06.2020

OSM are the *min_level* and *max_level* tag on the building polygon or the building relation and the *level* tag on POIs inside the building. To define specific indoor elements of a certain level, the *indoor* tag can be used. With the four basic indoor elements *room*, *area*, *wall* and *corridor* the floor plan of a building can be modeled. However, in most cases buildings get merely tagged with the *indoor:yes* key-value pair - which does not belong to the SIT schema - and more detailed information on the indoor environment is often missing. The *indoor:wall* key-value pair is for example only used in 5% of *indoor*-tag occurrences in order to

---

[10] IndoorOSM Tagging Schema, https://wiki.openstreetmap.org/wiki/Proposed_features/IndoorOSM, Access date: 24.03.2020.

[11] Simple Indoor Tagging, https://wiki.openstreetmap.org/wiki/Simple_Indoor_Tagging, Access date: 24.03.2020.

map the position of walls inside a building[12]. This indicates that most buildings lack detailed indoor information despite having the *indoor:yes* key-value pair. An example of this predicament can be seen in Fig. 1. Both of the displayed buildings are mapped correctly following the SIT schema. However, only the building in Fig. 1a has a completely mapped indoor environment. Figure 1b shows only some POIs and has no further information on the building structure. Hence, the completeness and quality of indoor geospatial information in OSM needs further investigation to determine if the platform could be used to provide accessibility information for indoor environments.

Definition of Completeness: As mentioned above, merely the *min_level* and *max_level* tag have to be defined in OSM in combination with *level* tags for POIs inside the building to provide a coarse-grained description of the inside of buildings. However, this information is not sufficient for an accurate representation of indoor areas that could be used to assist blind or mobility impaired people. Henceforth, a building (and its indoor elements) should furthermore include the *room*, *area*, *wall* and *corridor* tag. If all those tags are present, it can be assumed that the building has a complete indoor map following the SIT schema in OSM. This definition was applied to the Overpass API query and returned the results presented below.

4.2   Results – Quantity and Quality of Tagged Indoor Maps

The results of the quantitative analysis are shown in Table 1 as examples for the cities Berlin, Rome, Vienna, and Paris. The rows indicate the number of objects labeled with the *building*-key (indicating that those objects express a building or part of a building), the number of objects labeled to be in an indoor environment (marked with the *indoor = yes* tag) and the number of objects that comply with the aforementioned definition of completeness using SIT-Tags (i.e. including *min_level*, *max_level* and *indoor:room—area—wall—corridor*). The result set of objects comprise relations, ways and nodes as those are the basic OSM elements.

Table 1. Quantitative analysis of the current state of indoor maps in OSM using the SIT schema. (State: 2020-04-10)

City	Berlin	Rome	Vienna	Paris
Count of objects marked with *building = ** tag	470719	361771	232423	403927
Objects marked with *indoor = yes* tag	5350	666	10515	4262
Objects with SIT-Tags	3755	2102	1699	4104

Two main statements can be derived from the collected data. Firstly, for all European cities, there is a strong imbalance between the number of objects

---

[12] TagInfo, https://taginfo.openstreetmap.org/keys/indoor#overview, Access date: 02.04.2020.

marked as buildings and the number of objects marked to be in an indoor environment with the *indoor = yes* key-value pair. This indicates that the number of mapped indoor environments is sparse, regardless of the used indoor tagging schema. Secondly, even though SIT is the tagging schema currently chosen for indoor mapping by the OSM community, only a small percentage of objects have SIT associated tags. Overall, the quantity of indoor maps in OSM seems low.

Furthermore, the quality of mapped indoor spatial information in regards to accessibility is of utter importance when analysing how existing indoor maps in OSM suit the requirements of people with disabilities. Therefore, based on the data presented in Table 1, mapped buildings were further analysed in regards to their consistency in used indoor tags, their completeness of provided indoor geospatial information and mapped accessibility specific features such as elevators, ramps, provided braille information and tactile pavings. In contrast to other XML-based languages, OSM XML has no strict standardization. Users can define their key-value pairs and tag objects with them. This leads to several inconsistencies in OSM data sets. The *building*-key is for example only intended for outlines of buildings or single nodes associated to a building. Relations are not supposed to be tagged with the building key. However, for the city of Berlin 2501 relations and worldwide over 715000 relations are incorrectly tagged with the *building*-key. Furthermore, as described in Sect. 4.1, both the *min_level* and *max_level* are needed for buildings in order to meet the minimal requirements for SIT in OSM. However, the results show an incorrect usage of this specification for at least 502 objects as the *min_level*-tag is used 3184 times and the *max_level*-tag is used 2682 times worldwide[13].

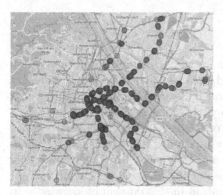 

(a) All SIT tags in Vienna   (b) All SIT tags which belong to SIT complete buildings in Vienna

Fig. 2. Comparison of all SIT tags and SIT complete buildings in Vienna. Overpass Turbo: http://overpass-turbo.eu/, access date: 06.05.2020

---

[13] Tag Info, https://taginfo.openstreetmap.org/, Access date: 09.04.2020.

On average, only 6.75 buildings per city fulfilled the minimal SIT requirements (see Table 2, first row) and on average only one building per city met the requirements of SIT completeness defined in Sect. 4.1 (see Table 2, second row). An example of the discrepancy between the number of buildings with SIT tags and the number of buildings that fulfill the definition of SIT completeness can be seen in Fig. 2. The quality of indoor information in regards to accessibility was even more sparse (see Table 2, row 3–5). In the complete data set only four buildings included mapped accessibility features for mobility-impaired people (e.g. ramps, elevators) and none of the analysed cities had buildings with mapped accessibility features for visually impaired people (e.g. braille, tactile paving) and a SIT conform completeness.

Table 2. Qualitative analysis of indoor maps of buildings in OSM in regards to the completeness of indoor mapping and indoor accessibility features for people with mobility impairments (PMI) and people with visual impairments (PVI). (State: 10.04.2020)

City	Berlin	Rome	Vienna	Paris
Buildings (SIT minimal)	6	9	7	5
Buildings (SIT complete)	1	0	3	0
Buildings with features for PMI	1	0	3	0
Buildings with features for PVI	0	0	0	0
Buildings with features for PMI & PVI	0	0	0	0

4.3   Discussion

People with disabilities have a high demand for accessibility information to develop orientation strategies in new and unknown environments and to get informed on permanent as well as temporal barriers. This information need is broadly investigated, in particular for mobility-impaired and visually impaired people as elaborated in Sect. 2. The results of the presented analysis clearly show, (1) the coverage of indoor maps is currently very low, (2) indoor tagging schemes are incorrectly and inconsistently applied, and (3) accessibility features are only available to a very limited extent. Reasons for these issues are manifold. First and foremost, there is a lack of standardization in this domain of knowledge in comparison to other accessibility domains, where diverse regulations and guidelines increased awareness and provided support for implementing accessibility in web and software environments, as well as user interfaces. A lack in standardization is also a hurdle when analyzing the state of accessible indoor maps in OSM. Due to the VGI structure of OSM and the loose standardization that can be extended by every user through new tags, the use of tags can vary from user to user - and therefore from object to object. Furthermore, different mapping solutions for buildings exist and even though the SIT schema is the currently chosen standard, the number of buildings mapped with the schema is still sparse and in many cases, the indoor areas of buildings are not mapped correctly or only partly. The number of mapped indoor accessibility features is even smaller and currently not appropriate to support people with disabilities with navigation and orientation in buildings. An improvement of the situation can be achieved by innovative evaluation tools that are capable of checking whether indoor maps comply with current tagging specifications (e.g. SIT) as well as proving feedback and corrections to contributors of the OSM community. The analysis presented in this paper is based on an analysis tool prototype which is currently under development and will be made available to the community in the future.

5   Conclusion

While several projects on the providence of accessibility information on outdoor areas exist - such as those presented in Sect. 3 - more projects taking similar approaches for indoor environments are needed. Due to the level of detail of geospatial information in indoor environments, the mapping process for those spaces should be automated as far as possible. Crowd-sourcing approaches should be supported through the providence of mapping and analysis tools for indoor environments, as both the addition of mapped indoor environments with accessibility features as well as a continuous analysis of the extent of available accessibility information in indoor spaces is needed to develop indoor navigation solutions and indoor location-based services for people with disabilities.

Acknowledgement. The project is funded by the Federal Ministry of Labour and Social Affairs (BMAS) under the grant number 01KM151112. Preliminary work for the implemented analysis tool has been done by Sebastian Rottmann.

References

1. Alkhanifer, A.A.: The role of situation awareness metrics in the assessment of indoor orientation assistive technologies that aid blind individuals in unfamiliar indoor environments. Dissertation, Rochester Institute of Technology (2015)
2. Bakillah, M., Mobasheri, A., Rousell, A., Hahmann, S., Jokar, J., Liang, S.H.: Toward a collective tagging Android application for gathering accessibility-related geospatial data in European cities. Parameters **10** (2014)
3. Benner, J.G.: Ontology of accessibility in the context of wayfinding for people with disabilities. ProQuest Dissertations and theses, p. 735 (2017)
4. Ding, D., et al.: Design considerations for a personalized wheelchair navigation system. In: Proceedings of the Annual International Conference of the IEEE Engineering in Medicine and Biology, pp. 4790–4793 (2007)
5. Durrant-Whyte, H., Bailey, T.: Simultaneous localisation and mapping (SLAM): part II the state of the art. Robot. Autom. Mag. 1–10 (2006)
6. Froehlich, J.E., et al.: Grand challenges in accessible maps. Interactions **26**(2), 78–81 (2019)

7. Goetz, M., Zipf, A.: Extending OpenStreetMap to indoor environments: bringing volunteered geographic information to the next level. In: Urban and Regional Data Management: UDMS Annual 2011, pp. 51–62 (2011)
8. Grand view research: digital map data - market analysis from 2016 to 2027. Technical report (2019)
9. Haklay, M.: How good is volunteered geographical information? A comparative study of OpenStreetMap and ordnance survey datasets. Environ. Plan. **37**(4), 682–703 (2010)
10. de las Heras, L.P., Ahmed, S., Liwicki, M., Valveny, E., Sánchez, G.: Statistical segmentation and structural recognition for floor plan interpretation: notation invariant structural element recognition. Int. J. Doc. Anal. Recogn. **17**(3), 221–237 (2014). https://doi.org/10.1007/s10032-013-0215-2
11. Kostic, N., Scheider, S.: Automated generation of indoor accessibility information for mobility-impaired individuals. In: Lecture Notes in Geoinformation and Cartography, vol. 217, pp. 235–252. Kluwer Academic Publishers (2015)
12. Laakso, M., Sarjakoski, T., Sarjakoski, L.T.: Improving accessibility information in pedestrian maps and databases. Cartographica **46**(2), 101–108 (2011)
13. Mobasheri, A., Zipf, A., Francis, L.: OpenStreetMap data quality enrichment through awareness raising and collective action tools-experiences from a European project. Geo-Spat. Inf. Sci. **21**(3), 234–246 (2018)
14. Park, J., Chowdhury, S.: Investigating the barriers in a typical journey by public transport users with disabilities. J. Transp. Health **10**, 361–368 (2018)
15. Thapar, N., et al.: A pilot study of functional access to public buildings and facilities for persons with impairments. Disabil. Rehabil. **26**(5), 280–289 (2004)
16. Tschorn, G., Kray, C., Broelemann, K.: Extracting indoor map data from public escape plans on mobile devices (2013)
17. Völkel, T., Kühn, R., Weber, G.: Mobility impaired pedestrians are not cars: requirements for the annotation of geographical data. In: Miesenberger, K., Klaus, J., Zagler, W., Karshmer, A. (eds.) ICCHP 2008. LNCS, vol. 5105, pp. 1085–1092. Springer, Heidelberg (2008). https://doi.org/10.1007/978-3-540-70540-6_163
18. Wang, Z., Niu, L.: A data model for using OpenStreetMap to integrate indoor and outdoor route planning. Sensors **18**(7), 2100 (2018)
19. Zielstra, D., Zipf, A.: A comparative study of proprietary geodata and volunteered geographic information for Germany, vol. 2010 (2010)
20. Zlatanova, S., Sithole, G., Nakagawa, M., Zhu, Q.: Problems in indoor mapping and modelling. In: International Archives of the Photogrammetry, Remote Sensing and Spatial Information Sciences - ISPRS Archives, vol. 40, pp. 63–68. International Society for Photogrammetry and Remote Sensing (2013)

Considering Time-Critical Barriers in Indoor Routing for People with Disabilities

Jan Schmalfuß-Schwarz[✉], Claudia Loitsch[✉], and Gerhard Weber

Fakultät Informatik, Technische Universität Dresden, Dresden, Germany
{jan.schmalfuss-schwarz,claudia.loitsch}@tu-dresden.de

Abstract. The usage of indoor map applications is growing and their importance is also increasing within the group of people with disabilities. Therefore, different approaches were already developed to support the users on their way. Though, these solutions don't prevent them from running into a dead end because of unknown insurmountable barriers. These barriers are often not included inside the data set of a building since they have no fixed locations and are temporary. For this reason, it is important to classify them on their characteristics and to develop a system that detects them and makes them available for routing applications. To address this, we present a classification of barriers founded on their time dependency within this paper and show an exemplary subdivision based on the three barrier types stairs, defect elevator, and wet floor. Furthermore, we draft a first proposal for the possibilities of developing an adaptive system for routing people with disabilities that captures time-critical barriers.

Keywords: Indoor routing · Indoor navigation · Indoor maps · Time-critical barriers · Visual impaired people · Mobility impaired people · Accessibility · People with disabilities · Inclusive mobility

1 Introduction

Mobility is a fundamental aspect of our daily life. Moreover, to overcome ways is a complex problem that does not only addresses outdoor areas, but also the orientation and navigation inside buildings. While research of outdoor mobility is well advanced, mobility inside buildings offers multi-layered problems which have yet to be explored. The market for different indoor map applications is growing at the same time [2]. To approach these problems Zlatanova et al. have analysed the status of indoor modelling and mapping and described a variety of current issues, for instance, dynamic barriers that occur due to crowds [12]. Froehlich et al. discuss five different challenges which contain data collection, data management and modelling with the main focus being the solving of "transient problems" such as a defect elevator [1]. Although temporal barriers have been recognized as one challenge respecting indoor modelling and mapping, only little research

© Springer Nature Switzerland AG 2020
K. Miesenberger et al. (Eds.): ICCHP 2020, LNCS 12377, pp. 315–322, 2020.
https://doi.org/10.1007/978-3-030-58805-2_37

has been conducted in this regard. Dynamic barriers are not yet specified in detail and their implications on existing and future routing applications are not discussed. This gap is addressed in this paper.

This paper presents a classification of barriers and their different types based on temporal characteristics. Besides, an adaptive system is discussed which should capture dynamic barriers before users with disabilities run into them.

2   State of the Art

Nowadays we have different geographic information systems (GIS). The most famous are Google Maps, Apple Maps and OpenStreetMap[1]. The first two providers have a closed API so that the access to develop applications is limited. The last one is an open-source project which is based on a crowd-sourcing approach. This arbitrary data access has the advantage that everyone can add and edit the information. Moreover, everyone can develop applications with the free data set for manifold user groups. Another strength, which can be seen as a weakness as well, is the simple expandability of the data format because everybody can define own tags for different objects of relations, nodes and ways. That is why we need a standard for the representation of buildings within OSM. For this specification the OSM Community offers an indoor data model called Simple Indoor Tagging (SIT)[2] which supports, for instance, half floors and repeating elements on different floor levels such as stairs or rooms about two or more floors. Additionally, different projects use the data set of OSM to support people with disabilities such as Wheelmap[3] which utilise particular tags to classify if a building is fully, partially or not accessible with wheelchairs.

Furthermore, we have to consider the various aid systems for people with disabilities as well as systems which collect data about the building's construction and barriers inside the building. The first type of these systems support users on their way and alert them if obstacles are in front of them. Therefore, they use RGB cameras and partially depth sensors to detect different kinds of obstacles [4,6,10,11]. In this regard, several papers discuss different approaches, but at the same time, these cannot protect people with disabilities from being unable to continue on their way due to an insurmountable barrier. Another problem is the question of how we collect floor plans of a building. Hence Tschorn et al. have developed a processing pipeline that transforms an escape plan into a building plan [9]. In contrast, De las Heras et al. use a picture of an architectural floor plan to recognize a simplified building plan [3]. The resulting building plans contain elements such as walls, rooms, stairs and describe the basic building construction. In the end, there are dynamic barriers which are characterised by a specific lifetime. For instance, crowd-sourcing systems are used to collect

---

[1] OpenStreetMap, https://openstreetmap.org/, Access Date: 2020-04-10.

[2] OpenStreetMap - Simple Indoor Tagging, https://wiki.openstreetmap.org/wiki/Simple_Indoor_Tagging, Access Date: 2020-04-10.

[3] Wheelmap.org, https://wheelmap.org/, Access date: 2020-04-10.

dynamic barriers in an outdoor environment because their mapping is difficult [7,8].

The actual research of indoor mobility focuses often on systems that support the user in real-time. The systems can detect barriers in the immediate environment of the user and alert them in case of detection. On the one hand, this is useful to save people with disabilities from hazards. On the other hand, reorientation and additional time are required to find the way insofar as the barrier is insurmountable. This additional effort has to be prevented to relieve the user from further stressful situations. Therefore, it is necessary to develop systems that recognize unknown barriers (without being tied to the user) and make the information about them available before the user reaches them. Hence, the routing application can pay attention to known insurmountable barriers and compute ways without them.

3   Classification of Barriers

The consequence of the current challenge described in Sect. 2 results in the urgency to define different types of barriers. In this context, we have to consider barriers with a dynamic character inside a building. Those barriers are also insurmountable for people with specific disabilities.

3.1   Time-Critical Barriers

The amount of static (non-time-critical) barriers contains mainly structural barriers inside a building, for example, stairs for wheelchair users (see Definition 2). In contrast to this type, we can classify dynamical barriers with a temporal dependence which have a fixed but most unknown starting and ending time (see Definition 1). So, we conclude that barriers can be classified based on their duration (see Theorem 1) and want to define them as time-critical barriers. If a building has a freely accessible indoor map, non-time-critical barriers are often mapped inside. However, time-critical barriers must always be kept up to date. Furthermore, these barriers can be predictable and unpredictable, such as large crowds on train stations, defect elevators and escalators or a wet floor due to contamination, while maintenance work or weekly cleaning are predictable. Besides, maintenance works are unique events, whereas weekly cleaning is a recurrent event in a fixed interval. A full schema is represented in Fig. 1a.

In the best case, time-critical predictable barriers belong to the set of known barriers which also include non-time-critical barriers. For example, a recurring cleaning of the hallway every Monday from 9 a.m. till 10 a.m. can be permanently added to the data set of the building.

Theorem 1. *Barriers can be classified based on their time frame.*

Definition 1 (time-critical barriers). *Time-critical barriers are such barriers that have a duration which means that they have a fixed known or unknown starting and ending time.*

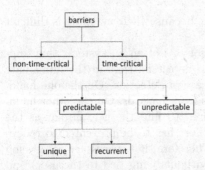

(a) Division of barriers based on their temporal dependence

(b) Division of barriers based on their surmountability

Fig. 1. The schemes show two classifications of barriers that are relevant for orientation and navigation.

Definition 2 (non-time-critical barriers). *Non-time-critical barriers are such barriers that have no fixed duration.*

3.2 Insurmountable Barriers

Additionally, barriers can be surmountable and insurmountable (see Theorem 2). The term surmountable barriers means that an impaired person has a higher effort to overcome them (see Definition 3). Insurmountability comprises all barriers which force a person with a disability to take a different way (see Definition 4). In addition to these two classifications, there is also the possibility that people with similar disabilities or the same person in different contexts can surmount the same barrier or not (as shown in Fig. 1b). For example, a large crowd of people can vary in difficulty for people with the same disabilities because they have a different experience for the given situation. Furthermore, a barrier can be surmountable with the help of an assistant but insurmountable without additional help.

Theorem 2. *Barriers can be classified in surmountable and insurmountable barriers when taking into account the specific needs of the user and of the context.*

Definition 3 (surmountable barriers). *Surmountable barriers are such barriers which require higher effort from the user in order to overcome them.*

Definition 4 (insurmountable barriers). *Insurmountable barriers are such barriers which the user cannot overcome.*

At the end of this section we want to give a little overview over three different barriers and their classification inside the shown schemes as shown in Table 1.

Table 1. Overview of three different barriers that were mentioned in [1,6] and their possible classification in the shown system.

barrier	Stairs	Defect elevator	Wet floor
User group	Mobility/ visual impaired	Mobility impaired	Mobility/visual impaired
Time-critical	No	Yes	Yes
Predictable	–	No	Yes (e.g. recurring cleaning)/no
Unique	–	–	No (e.g. recurring cleaning)/ –
Surmountable	Individual	no	individual

4   Adaptive System for Indoor Routing

Based on the aforementioned considerations, systems for indoor routing should combine a user tied routing solution which is based on an enriched indoor map that contains non-time-critical barriers and time-critical barriers. On the one hand, this can ensure that people with disabilities are safe on their way. On the other hand, it is important that they do not end up in dead ends caused by barriers.

Zlatanova et al. has shown, that indoor mapping and routing has many interlinked components [12]. In addition to this work, an overall system has to be adaptive to the special needs of different users which increases its complexity. Paramythis et al. discuss such an adaptive system that consider the needs of the user to model a user-specific "world" [5].

These findings and assumptions result in a first proposal for such a system which is shown in Fig. 2. The main components are subdivided into data collection, data modelling as well as routing applications, that mutually impact each other. Furthermore, legal aspects and user requirements represent two superordinate aspects which influence the main parts of the system.

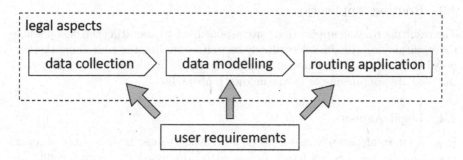

Fig. 2. The schema shows a proposal for an overall system design.

4.1   Data Collection

The data collection is a dynamic progressive process. This part should detect time-critical barriers on their own, collect information about them, and control, if they still exist or if they have changed.

With the condition that non-time-critical barriers like architectonic barriers are known, the subsystem has to address insurmountable unpredictable time-critical barriers. Besides, the data collection part should also be sensitive for insurmountable predictable time-critical barriers if they are unknown.

To achieve this, several strategies have to be examined. One kind of them can be based on autonomous robots or on fixed cameras which observe the building. Moreover, these systems can use the same technologies such as user tied detection systems. Alternatively, it is conceivable to develop a crowd-sourcing solution. For instance, an application where users can report barriers. Furthermore, the different approaches need to be evaluated concerning their accuracy and their possible uses in different contexts like various types of buildings.

4.2   Data Modelling

The data model is the main part of the system that has to deal with different kinds of barriers and information about them. At the same time, it has to communicate with different methods for the data collection as well as different kinds of routing applications. Depending of the context, it has to handle different volumes and types of input data and pre-processed them in the best possible way for routing applications, too. Therefore, one central aspect is a dynamic representation of time-critical barriers within the model and how we can save additional information about them. This also includes the end user, which means that the data model must incarnate a world that is tailored to his needs. Secondary, the information obtained in the data collection must be made freely available inside an indoor map and should be based on a unified vocabulary. In the best case, this can ensure that a multitude of routing applications is developed that are adapted to the different needs of the users.

4.3   Routing Application

The resulting routing applications are responsible for generating the best possible route, displaying the data accordingly as well as guiding the user along the best possible route based on landmarks or instructions. In addition, they must warn the user of spontaneous or as yet unknown obstacles.

4.4   Legal Aspects

In addition to aforementioned aspects, legal aspects must be taken into account. For example, on the one hand, it has to be discussed if personal rights are violated when barriers are detected using cameras and how user data may be processed. On the other hand, we have to analyse which kind of information can be published depending on the type of building.

4.5   User Requirements

Finally, the user requirements must be considered. The needs of the different user groups play a major role in the entire system. So it is necessary to discuss which information must be recorded for various time-critical barriers and how they can be represented inside the data model, as well as how specific information can be made available for the special needs of people with disabilities. In the end, the resulting routing applications also have to be adapted to different users.

5   Conclusion

Time-critical barriers represent a crucial aspect within the mobility of people with disabilities inside of buildings. Therefore, they have to be recognized and made available for routing applications so that the user is not guided into a dead end. These aspects are not considered properly by current research on mobility-aided orientation and navigation systems. This gap is addressed in this paper. A first step for this is - as presented in this paper - the specification of these barriers based on their temporal component in order to be able to identify them more easily. The next steps are now a comprehensive analysis of further barriers and the division of these into the classification schema in order to check its practicability. Furthermore, the collected time-critical barriers must be considered in their specific environment. Moreover, it is necessary to develop and evaluate optimised approaches for the resulting scenarios. Finally, the result provides an improved data set for a variety of routing applications inside buildings which have been developed for people with disabilities. Therefore, we have proposed a first draft of an adaptive system that supports a user-centred routing to protect them from injuries and to prevent users from running into a dead end because the time-critical barrier is insurmountable.

Acknowledgement. This work was partially funded by the Federal Ministry of Labour and Social Affairs (BMAS) under the grant number 01KM151112.

References

1. Froehlich, J.E., et al.: Grand challenges in accessible maps. Interactions **26**(2), 78–81 (2019)
2. Grand View Research: Digital Map Data - Market Analysis From 2016 to 2027. Technical report (2019)
3. de las Heras, L.-P., Ahmed, S., Liwicki, M., Valveny, E., Sánchez, G.: Statistical segmentation and structural recognition for floor plan interpretation. Int. J. Doc. Anal. Recogn. (IJDAR) **17**(3), 221–237 (2014). https://doi.org/10.1007/s10032-013-0215-2
4. Jafri, R., Khan, M.M.: User-centered design of a depth data based obstacle detection and avoidance system for the visually impaired. Hum. Centric Comput. Inf. Sci. **8**(1), 1–30 (2018). https://doi.org/10.1186/s13673-018-0134-9

5. Paramythis, A., Weibelzahl, S., Masthoff, J.: Layered evaluation of interactive adaptive systems: framework and formative methods. User Model. User Adapt. Inter. **20**(5), 383–453 (2010). https://doi.org/10.1007/2Fs11257-010-9082-4
6. Patil, K., Jawadwala, Q., Shu, F.C.: Design and construction of electronic aid for visually impaired people. IEEE Trans. Hum. Mach. Syst. **48**(2), 172–182 (2018)
7. Qin, H., Aburizaiza, A.O., Rice, R.M., Paez, F., Rice, M.T.: Obstacle characterization in a geocrowdsourced accessibility system. ISPRS Ann. Photogrammetry Remote Sens. Spat. Inf. Sci. **2**(3W5), 179–185 (2015)
8. Rice, M.T., et al.: Crowdsourcing techniques for augmenting traditional accessibility maps with transitory obstacle information. Cartography Geogr. Inf. Sci. **40**(3), 210–219 (2013)
9. Tschorn Supervisor, G., Kray Co-Supervisor, C., Broelemann, K.: Extracting indoor map data from public escape plans on mobile devices (2013)
10. Xiao, H., Li, Z., Yang, C., Yuan, W., Wang, L.: RGB-D sensor-based visualtarget detection and tracking for an intelligent wheelchair robot in indoorsenvironments. Int. J. Control Autom. Syst. **13**(3), 521–529 (2015)
11. Zeng, L., Simros, M., Weber, G.: Camera-based mobile electronic travel aids support for cognitive mapping of unknown spaces. In: Proceedings of the 19th International Conference on Human-Computer Interaction with Mobile Devices and Services, MobileHCI 2017, pp. 1–10. Association for Computing Machinery Inc, New York, USA (2017)
12. Zlatanova, S., Sithole, G., Nakagawa, M., Zhu, Q.: Problems in indoor mapping and modelling. In: International Archives of the Photogrammetry, Remote Sensing and Spatial Information Sciences - ISPRS Archives, vol. 40, pp. 63–68. International Society for Photogrammetry and Remote Sensing (2013)

3D Audio Navigation - Feasibility and Requirements for Older Adults

Elke Mattheiss[1], Georg Regal[2], Christian Vogelauer[3], and Hugo Furtado[1(✉)]

[1] Dreamwaves GmbH, Marxergasse 24/2, 1030 Vienna, Austria
hugo@dreamwaves.io
[2] AIT Austrian Institute of Technology, Center for Technology Experience,
Giefinggasse 2, 1210 Vienna, Austria
[3] Austrian Association in Support of the Blind and Visually Impaired,
Jägerstraße 36, 1200 Vienna, Austria
http://www.dreamwaves.io

Abstract. Independent mobility is crucial for maintaining the quality of life of older adults. However, independent navigation outdoors can become a challenge due to various physical changes and impairments in old age. In earlier work we have developed an acoustic augmented reality guidance system to guide blind and visually impaired people intuitively using virtual 3D audio sounds as way-points. In this work we investigate if the same acoustic augmented reality guidance can be used by older adults, as there are two important challenges: a) often older adults suffers from age related hearing impairments which might affect the ability of localizing sound in 3D and b) the specifics of the life circumstances and technology usage may differ substantially from the requirements of visually impaired people. In this paper we present our first approaches to tackle these two challenges. We have assessed the ability of older adults in localizing sound in 3D space and investigated which requirements need to be considered to create a guidance system that is useful and easy to use. Our results show that despite sometimes severe and asymmetrical hearing impairments, older adults are still able to localize sounds. We also found that in order to use such a guidance system older adults also need an additional visual user interface which supports conventional methods of navigating, e.g. overview of the route.

Keywords: Interaction design · Acoustic augmented reality · Navigation · Older adults

1 Introduction and Background

Independent mobility is crucial for maintaining the quality of life of older adults. However, navigational tasks can become a challenge due to various physical changes and impairments in old age.

© Springer Nature Switzerland AG 2020
K. Miesenberger et al. (Eds.): ICCHP 2020, LNCS 12377, pp. 323–331, 2020.
https://doi.org/10.1007/978-3-030-58805-2_38

Different approaches for navigation aids for older adults (cf. Werner et al. [14]) and for visually impaired people have been proposed and developed, ranging from research approaches (cf. Duarte et al. [4]) towards available commercial products, e.g. indoors[1], wayfindr[2]. Related work often focuses on technical implementation of the navigation support system (e.g. [7,15]). In terms of user interface, presented solutions in related work often rely on (synthesized) vocal messages (e.g [1]) or tactile interfaces (e.g. [10]). However, studies have shown that navigation with spatial sound is faster and associated with less cognitive stress than spatial speech such as the indications "left" and "right" cf. [8].

Building on the concept of spatial sound, during the last year, we developed a non-visual pedestrian navigational tool using binaural virtual audio to guide blind and visually impaired people in the street. To provide an unobtrusive tool we designed to use virtual acoustic way-points that are positioned in the real world and that can be heard using spatial audio. Thus the developed system can be seen as an acoustic augmented reality system. To guide a user along a route the way-points can be heard by the users and by following one point after the other the user is guided along the desired route.

As our experiences with blind and visually impaired people were positive we aim to extend that approach also to other user groups, especially older adults. Older adults have similar constraints as they also need tools that are easy and intuitive to use and adapted to their needs and workflows. Motivated by this similarity, we are conducting an exploratory project to evaluate whether our navigation app can be adapted for older adults (>65y). Our analysis considers challenges with spatial audio due to hearing impairments as well as specifics of the life circumstances and technology usage which affect product usability for this group.

On the one hand as stated by [6, p. 39] older adults want technologies that meet their individual needs, support them in their usual activities (social integration, security), and are easy to use. Thus we aim to get insights into the needs and considerations of older adults for navigational technology. On the other hand age related hearing impairment affects about 37% of the population between ages 60 and 70 and about 60% for people aged 70 or older [5].

The perception of spatial audio and the assessment of sound direction is learned early in childhood. But, it is not clearly understood to which extent age related hearing impairment affects sound localization. Existing studies are controversial. In [13] the authors show comparable sound localization performance in the horizontal plane for younger, middle aged and older adults, even with age-related high-frequency hearing loss. However, in [3] the authors found that for tones of certain frequencies, localization in the horizontal plane declines with advancing age, which is especially connected with limitations in the processing of temporal cues. Also [2] described that with decreasing hearing ability, spatial hearing can also be impaired. Again, these limitations are related to characteristics of the audio. Therefore, it is necessary to investigate the ability of older

---

[1] https://indoo.rs/.

[2] https://www.wayfindr.net.

adults to localize sounds for our specific navigation system where indeed we rely mainly on localization on the horizontal plane and can control the specific frequency content and duration of the localization tones.

Our work consists of two main contributions. Firstly, we could show that older adults (>65y) are able to identify the direction of sound sources, thus contributing to the state of the art of the currently controversial results in related work. Secondly, we investigated specific strategies and requirements of this target group when navigating in the street, and the resulting requirements for an acoustic augmented reality system.

2   Materials and Methods

2.1   3D Sound Localization

To assess whether age-related hearing impairments influence 3D sound localization we implemented standard localization experiments in the lab [12].

The test consists of presenting the participants with binaural virtual audio (BVA) stimuli through headphones. The participant then points in the direction of the sound and that indication is compared with the ground truth. For realistic BVA stimuli we acquired the head-related transfer functions (HRTFs) for each of the participants.

In the study we included 18 participants, all with age >65y. Participant information is shown in Table 3. 3 of the participants had moderate to severe visual impairment (barely no vision; left eye blind, right eye 25%; only can read very large fonts) and 3 were fully blind. All of the participants had age related hearing impairments i.e. had some loss of hearing although only clinically related with age and not with any other condition. Due to physical limitations, 3 of the participants could not have their HRTF measured. In this case, we used a generic HRTF from a database. Participants received 75 EUR remuneration.

2.2   Focusgroup

To gather insights regarding navigation strategies and route planning we conducted a focusgroup with 4 participants.

Participant information is shown in Table 1. We invited older adults with and without hearing impairments, age related vision impairments, but no severe visual or motor impairments. All participants also participated in the 3D Sound localization experiments described in Sect. 2.1. Participants received 30 EUR remuneration.

The focus group duration was 2 h. After a short introduction round of the overall goal of the project and the goal of the focusgroup, each participant and the facilitators introduced themselves. Afterwards different questions were discussed in the group. First planning routes to unknown places were discussed followed by navigation strategies when on the go and specific questions about navigation devices.

During the focus group 3 facilitators were present, one for moderation and two for taking notes and asking additional questions.

Table 1. Participants in the focusgroup

ID	Gender	Age	Visual impairment	Hearing impairment
1	Female	71–80	Not corrected	Mild
2	Female	71–80	Corrected	Mild
3	Female	61–70	Corrected	Mild
4	Male	71–80	Corrected	Mild

Table 2. Participants in the behavioural observation

ID	Gender	Age	Visual impairment	Hearing impairment
1	Male	61–70	Corrected	None
2	Female	61–70	Corrected	None
3	Female	71–80	None	Hearing aid
4	Female	61–70	Corrected	None

2.3 Behavioural Observation and Contextual Interview

To deepen the insights gained in the focusgroup with 4 participants, we conducted a observation of older adults on the go and contextual interviews.

Participant information is shown in Table 2. As in the focusgroup we invited older adults with and without hearing impairments, age related vision impairments, but no severe visual or motor impairments. None of the participants had participated in the previous focusgroup but all participants also participated in the 3D Sound localization experiments described in Sect. 2.1. Participants received 30 EUR remuneration.

During the observations, participants were accompanied while planning and navigating a (short) unknown route. Besides a video recording, the test facilitator recorded the procedure and problems in a protocol. After the navigation, semi-structured contextual interviews were conducted. In the interviews participants were questioned about their navigation habits, issues and problems, as well as the usage of assistive navigation devices.

3 Results

3.1 3D Sound Localization

Table 3 and Fig. 1 summarize the results for the localization experiments. The blue bars in the figure indicate the localization error in the horizontal plane in degrees for each of the participants. The yellow dashed line (long dashes) shows the average error in this cohort, the green solid line shows the localization error for the average of the population and the red dashed line (short dashes) the error if pointing at chance. The mean localization error among all participants was of 23.4° while the maximum was of 34.9° and the minimum of 16.5°. There was no significant difference between the errors of the sighted and visually impaired users (23.2° and 23.7° respectively).

Table 3. Summary of the localization experiments results.

ID	Nr. items	Age	Visual impairment	Lateral error
1	300	61–70	Corrected	16.54
2	300	71–80	Corrected	34.72
3	300	61–70	Corrected	17.37
4	200	61–70	Corrected	24.31
5	300	71–80	Corrected	22.26
6	200	71–80	Corrected	24.31
7	300	61–70	Corrected	19.64
8	300	61–70	Corrected	18.28
9	300	71–80	No	24.29
10	300	61–70	Corrected	21.59
11	300	71–80	No	20.48
12	300	61–70	No	34.91
13	200	61–70	Severe	26.62
14	300	61–70	Blind	19.69
15	300	61–70	Blind	26.9
16	300	61–70	Severe	24.63
17	300	61–70	Blind	24.73
18	300	71-80	Moderate	19.51

3.2 Focusgroup

The focusgroup revealed insights into planning and navigation strategies of older adults.

Most participants still like to walk (even long distances) if it is possible for them. Some participants mentioned that they prefer to walk or taking longer in a specific public transport route in order to avoid big crowds of people, touristic, noisy, busy and confusing places. Also sometimes walking is chosen as an intentional strategy to avoid certain transportation modes, e.g. one participant stated that she avoids using the subway if possible. Nevertheless using public transportation is important and should therefore also be implemented in an augmented acoustic navigation aid, even if the main use case is supporting navigation by foot.

Most participants mentioned that they like to pre-plan their trips, some with paper maps or desktop personal computer (PC) applications. Using this

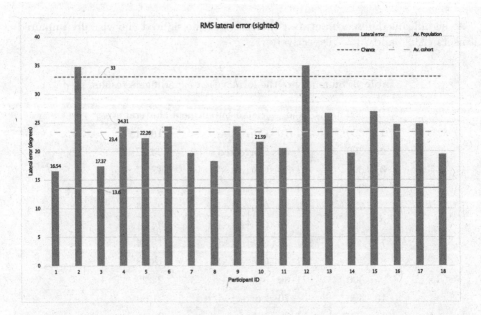

Fig. 1. Summary of the localization experiments results. The (blue) vertical bars indicate the localization error in the horizontal plane in degrees for each of the participants. The (solid - green) bottom-line shows the error for the average of the population, the (dashed - yellow) middle-line shows the average error in this cohort, and the (dotted - red) top-line the error if pointing at chance. (Color figure online)

pre-planning they try to memorize orientation points of interest, landmarks or cardinal points to get to the final destination. Most participants mentioned that they use a combination of online (mostly a map on the PC beforehand) and analogue, handwritten notes for navigation. Smart devices (e.g. phones) are mostly seen as a fallback in case they are uncertain or lost. Participants mentioned that an overview of the route is important, especially so they can make their own decisions and overrule the proposals by the system if needed. Also, users stated that they try to avoid navigation aids while on the go to keep mentally fit.

Some participants mentioned that they prefer to ask direction on the way, instead of checking themselves as they believe this is more time efficient. In general, time is an important aspect when planning and navigating. Participants stated that they need to have enough time (e.g. calculating with buffer time and thus starting early than needed) so they can take time for decisions and also don't need to hurry, which will lead to mistakes.

3.3   Behavioural Observation and Contextual Interview

The behavioural observations and contextual interviews revealed insight into planning and navigation strategies of older adults.

Regarding navigation strategy all 4 participants planned their routes in advance and (tried to) memorize the route so they can navigate without aid when on the go. All 4 participants stated that safety is important for them when planning or selecting routes. All 4 Participants stated that they use assistance (smartphones, asking others for help) only when uncertain, especially when they were not sure where to go. Although 3 out of 4 participants mentioned that they prefer turn by turn instructions, all 4 participants stated that they need an overview of the complete route. This is an important insight that needs to be addressed when designing an acoustic augmented reality system for navigation. We propose to use multi modal interaction by providing a visual routing overview on the phone, that can be accessed when necessary, but does not have to.

An important question is if a navigation system should provide constant feedback when walking in the right direction or to provide information only in case of error or decision points. All 4 participants stated that they want audio feedback when walking in the wrong direction, but only one person said she wants also feedback confirming she is walking in the right direction.

A crucial issue for the proposed augmented acoustic reality navigation system, is the fact that 3 out of 4 participants expressed a strong aversion to wearing headphones while navigating. But none of the participants has ever tried open headphones or bone conduction headphones.

4   Discussion

Regarding the localization experiments, the mean localization error among all the participants was of $23.4°$. The average error for the general population is of $13.6°$. This difference may have been influenced by the way how we implemented the localization experiments. The typical experiment needs a very long training period (400 sound points only for training) in order to avoid errors when pointing to the perceived sound location i.e. when the participant understands the location of the sound correctly but cannot point in the correct location. As this is very time consuming (several hours) and because our participants were $>65y$, we decided to shorten the training phase considerably (100 points). So, a larger final localization error is expected as the pointing error is included. Having this in mind, even with this added error, the tests show that the participants can localize sound as they are much better then pure chance.

The observations, interviews and focus-group discussion revealed that participants plan their routes in advance, memorized the route and used assistance only in case of uncertainty. Nevertheless they are willing to use technological assistance if needed. Due to the preferred usage only in cases of uncertainty it is important to present appropriate information for such uncertain situations.

Also it is important to provide an overview of the route, as this was mentioned as important in the focus-group and confirmed also in the contextual interviews. Thus we propose that the accompanying smartphone app should provide visual overview of the route.

Based on this information we suggest that an acoustic augmented reality navigation system should support navigation on the go, but behave very unobtrusively. We believe that the proposed approach of acoustic way points placed in the real world that the user needs to follow simply by hearing, is unobtrusive enough to be accepted.

One important aspect is to understand the best strategy to place the waypoints and provide the proper cues to convey distance. Early experiments showed us that the waypoints cannot be too close to each other but should not be too further away either. The ideal distance seems to be somewhere between 5 and 10 meters. Conveying distance is still an open topic as using HRTFs only is not enough. A common approach, which simulates sound propagation, is to add distance dependent low-pass filtering and reverberation to the waypoint sound source [9]. Varying the tempo and pitch are also important cues as high pitch and fast tempo are generally associated to proximity and urgency [11]. These possibilities need to be thoroughly investigated in future work.

Wearing headphones while navigating was seen quite negatively by the users, although no user reported experience with open headphones. Such open headphones would allow hearing acoustic augmentation as well as the real surrounding. As this needs to be experienced first hand, different hardware solutions need to be be further investigated in future research.

5   Conclusion

Independent navigation can become a challenge due to various physical changes and impairments in old age. We have developed an acoustic augmented reality guidance device to guide people intuitively using virtual 3D audio. Within this work we investigated if older adults are able to identify the direction of sound sources and strategies and requirements of older adults for using such a navigation aid.

We presented the results of an audio experiment, a focus group and behavioural observations. We could show that older adults (>65y) are able to identify the direction of sound sources and and we gathered insights into the strategies of this target group for navigating in the street as well as the requirements for an acoustic augmented reality guidance device.

Acknowledgments. We would like to thank all participants for their participation and their valuable feedback. We would also like to thank the OEAW for conducting the 3D sound localization experiments. This work was partially funded by the FFG under grant Nr. 873764 - Project "3D Audio Navigation" in the program "benefit - call 2018".

References

1. Ahmetovic, D., Gleason, C., Kitani, K.M., Takagi, H., Asakawa, C.: NavCog: turn-by-turn smartphone navigation assistant for people with visual impairments or blindness. In: Proceedings of the 13th Web for All Conference, pp. 1–2 (2016)

2. Akeroyd, M.A., Gatehouse, S., Blaschke, J.: The detection of differences in the cues to distance by elderly hearing-impaired listeners. J. Acoust. Soc. Am. **121**(2), 1077–1089 (2007)

3. Dobreva, M.S., O'Neill, W.E., Paige, G.D.: Influence of aging on human sound localization. J. Neurophysiol. **105**(5), 2471–2486 (2011). https://doi.org/10.1152/jn.00951.2010. pMID: 21368004

4. Duarte, K., Cecílio, J., Furtado, P.: Overview of assistive technologies for the blind: Navigation and shopping. In: 2014 13th International Conference on Control Automation Robotics and Vision (ICARCV), pp. 1929–1934. IEEE (2014)

5. Fritze, T., Teipel, S., Óvári, A., Kilimann, I., Witt, G., Doblhammer, G.: Hearing impairment affects dementia incidence. An analysis based on longitudinal health claims data in Germany. PLoS One **11**(7), 1–19 (2016). https://doi.org/10.1371/journal.pone.0156876

6. Georgieff, P.: Ambient assisted living: Marktpotenziale IT-unterstützter Pflege für ein selbstbestimmtes Altern. MFG-Stiftung Baden-Württemberg (2008)

7. Kamiński, Ł., Stepnowski, A., Demkowicz, J.: Wearable system supporting navigation of the blind. Int. J. Geol. **5**(2), 34–40 (2011)

8. Klatzky, R.L., Marston, J.R., Giudice, N.A., Golledge, R.G., Loomis, J.M.: Cognitive load of navigating without vision when guided by virtual sound versus spatial language. J. Exp. Psychol.: Appl. **12**(4), 223 (2006)

9. Liljedahl, M., Lindberg, S.: Sound parameters for expressing geographic distance in a mobile navigation application. In: Proceedings of the 6th Audio Mostly Conference: A Conference on Interaction with Sound. AM 2011, pp. 1–7. Association for Computing Machinery, New York (2011). https://doi.org/10.1145/2095667.2095668

10. Mann, S., et al.: Blind navigation with a wearable range camera and vibrotactile helmet. In: Proceedings of the 19th ACM International Conference on Multimedia, pp. 1325–1328 (2011)

11. May, K., Sobel, B., Wilson, J., Walker, B.: Auditory displays to facilitate object targeting in 3D space, pp. 155–162 (June 2019). https://doi.org/10.21785/icad2019.008

12. Middlebrooks, J.C.: Virtual localization improved by scaling nonindividualized external-ear transfer functions in frequency. J. Acoust. Soc. Am. **106**(3), 1493–1510 (1999). https://doi.org/10.1121/1.427147

13. Otte, R., Agterberg, M., van Wanrooij, M., Snik, A., Opstal, J.: Age-related hearing loss and ear morphology affect vertical but not horizontal sound-localization performance. J. Assoc. Res. Otolaryngol.: JARO **14**, 261–273 (2013). https://doi.org/10.1007/s10162-012-0367-7

14. Werner, C., Moustris, G.P., Tzafestas, C.S., Hauer, K.: User-oriented evaluation of a robotic rollator that provides navigation assistance in frail older adults with and without cognitive impairment. Gerontology **64**(3), 278–290 (2018)

15. Yang, G., Saniie, J.: Indoor navigation for visually impaired using AR markers. In: 2017 IEEE International Conference on Electro Information Technology (EIT), pp. 1–5. IEEE (2017)

How to Improve Interaction with a Text Input System

Text Input with Foot Gestures Using the Myo Armband

Krzysztof Dobosz[(⊠)] [iD] and Mirosław Trzcionkowski

Department of Algorithmics and Software, Silesian University of Technology,
Akademicka 16, Gliwice, Poland
krzysztof.dobosz@polsl.pl, mirotrz839@student.polsl.pl

Abstract. This article describes the study in the area of alternative text entry. The aim of the project was to use the Myo band to detect foot gestures using EMG or acceleration signals for the special needs of people with physical disabilities. The Myo controller in the form of a band attached to the leg below the calf is responsible for detecting signals of a change in muscle tension. It can also be applied directly to the foot and measure the change in acceleration caused by the movement of the foot. Myo sends data to the application that uses it to control the virtual keyboard. The research confirmed that foot gestures allowed the user to enter text. The results obtained are comparable to other methods of linear alphabet scanning.

Keywords: Text input · Text entry · Myo armband · Gesture controller · Foot gestures · Motor disability · Virtual keyboard

1 Introduction

Some research on HCI is focused on interfaces for people with motor disabilities. In the future gesture control which can be used in our day lives. Hence, smart homes can also be controlled by Myo armband, because it can also be used to control various other electronic home devices or robots [19]. However, people with paresis of hands or without hands will not be able to take full advantage of gesture control options, or it will be very difficult for them [11].

People who are already born with the inability to use the upper limbs, throughout their life acquire skills that allow the efficient use of feet at eating, drinking, cooking, dressing and even applying makeup. Some of them are able to perform tasks that require great craftsmanship, which even the most able-bodied people would not be able to do. The feet allow you to grip objects and very accurately manipulate them. However, it should be noted that all such activities require practice, and people performing them are disabled for many years - from childhood or even from birth.

This work was co-financed by SUT grant for maintaining and developing research potential.

The problem is providing the opportunity to perform basic tasks for people that have not yet learned how to use legs at an advanced level or need the help temporarily. One such action is entering text that can be sent via messengers, social media and the Internet in general.

2 Background

The area of foot gestures already was studied. Foot movements can be detected in a water vessel [8], however it is useless in everyday use. Foot gestures can be also detected by built-in accelerometer on the smartphone located in a pocket [21] when the user is mobile. Another approach uses force sensors incorporated in the sole and an accelerometer attached to the shoe has already been used to interact with entities of a 3D virtual environment displayed on a mobile device [14]. The position of the foot can also be recorded by a camera [16]. The overall concept of foot control has already been patented [7,15].

So far many researchers have proved that gesture controllers can be great support for paresis of the hands. The Myo armband is a gesture controller that was produced to be worn on the forearm. It uses a set of electromyographic (EMG) sensors, a gyroscope, accelerometer and magnetometer to recognize gestures. The concept of using the EMG sensors is not new. The muscle communicator can use EMG activity to move a cursor, and then to perform selected action, especially text entry. It has already been confirmed that the use of EMG techniques can be a support in HCI solutions, and in particular in the field of text input [22].

EMG-based system can classify four-finger gestures as including pinching or holding a travel mug [20]. Another solution is a framework using multi-channel EMG sensors in order to classify 72 Chinese sign language. Next one classified 20 stationary letter gestures from the Brazilian Sign Language (LIBRAS) alphabet [1]. However, acceleration signals play there a much more significant role in this method than EMG [23]. 27 gestures were defined and then recognized using Bayes classifier with 90% accuracy in the study, where high-density EMG sensor array with 192 electrodes was utilized for detection and recognition subtle finger gestures [3]. Some studies verified systems for pattern-recognition-based strategies of myoelectric control [5]. Another researchers proposed an algorithm to estimate the overall arm motion using the Myo armband attached to the upper arm [2]. A forearm-based EMG system that can recognize fine-grained thumb gestures, including left swipes, right swipes, taps, long presses and user-defined complex motions with high accuracy [10].

A gesture controller worn on a leg was already used to detect the set of foot movements for a soccer game on a mobile phone [13]. Finally, foot gestures can be used for typing. People with motor disorders can enter text in different ways [18]. When one of the user's feet has attached an accelerometer-equipped mobile device, then simple gestures can be detected and interpreted as Morse code signals [17].

Looking through related works, it was noticed that there are no methods to control the keyboard by foot gestures. The aim of the project was to use the Myo armband to detect foot gestures using EMG or acceleration signals for the special needs of people with physical disabilities.

3 Method

3.1 The Concept

Myo is a gesture control armband consisting of a band of eight EMG muscle sensors and an inertial measurement unit (IMU), which is an electronic device that measures and reports a body's specific force, angular rate, and sometimes the orientation of the body, using a combination of accelerometer, gyroscope, and magnetometer. When worn on a user's forearm, Myo detects the user's hand gestures and arm motion. Such gestures as fist, wave in, wave out, fingers spread, and double tap are recognized with high accuracy over 97% [4,6]. The communication with external data receiver is wireless, so the user will not have to worry about tangling or breaking the wires.

The entire armband design is extensible and, according to the specifications, its circumference at maximum tension can reach 34 cm (13.4 in.). This allows the user to place it on the calf at a height sufficient to measure muscle tension (Fig. 1(a)). However, this can cause some problems when it comes to taking measurements. In the case of people with a large circumference of the lower leg, the sensors will be at a greater distance from each other than in the case of people with a smaller body structure, so part of the impulses appearing in the area between EMG sensors may not be captured.

Changing the foot position can be recognized not only by testing muscle tension, but also by monitoring the acceleration signals of the IMU. For this purpose, however, the band must be worn on foot (Fig. 1(b)).

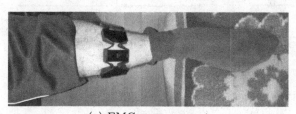 

(a) EMG measurement (b) Measurement by IMU

Fig. 1. Myo controller workplace

The data provided by the IMU can be used to support the process of recognizing foot gestures or even to prepare a completely separate, alternative method that does not use EMG data. Bluetooth technology is used to transfer data to the research tool made in a form of application running on a PC computer.

3.2 Gesture Detection

Four characteristic gestures were selected for the study, which should allow the user to control the virtual keyboard application (Fig. 2).

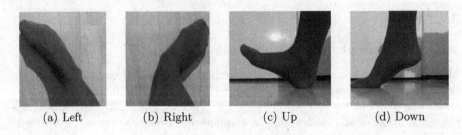

| (a) Left | (b) Right | (c) Up | (d) Down |

Fig. 2. Foot gestures

First defined gesture was *left*. It was done by rotation the foot to the left in a horizontal plane, without changing the position of the heel and knee. Similarly, the *right* gesture is performed. The next two proposed gestures are *up* and *down*. *Up* meant a gesture consisting in raising fingers up without tearing the heel from the ground. Whereas *down* means raising the heel up while keeping toes on the ground, as if "standing on toes".

First of proposed approaches was based on EMG signals collected from eight muscle sensors (Fig. 3). These data were used to clear interpretation of the assumed simple gestures.

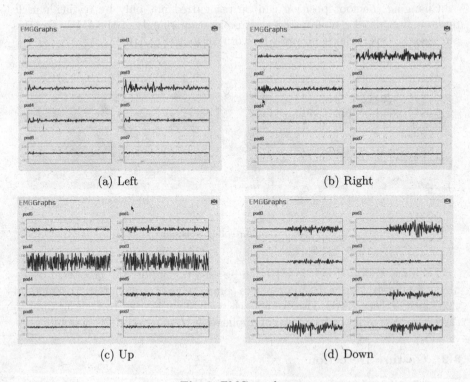

Fig. 3. EMG results

The *pull toes up* gesture was also considered (Fig. 4), consisting of raising the foot without lifting the toes and heel from the ground. However, that was rejected at the initial stage of work due to the convergence of measurements with the gesture *up*.

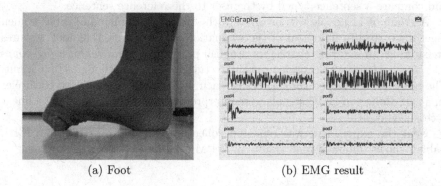

| (a) Foot | (b) EMG result |

Fig. 4. Foot with pull toes up

The second of the described approaches of foot gesture detection is fully based on data provided from the band's IMU module. First, the initial state of the IMU module is saved from the description placed on the foot. Then, when moving the foot, the acceleration value is read from the IMU. Obtained measurements in the form of quaternion coefficients are converted into rotation angles. Obtained values, after exceeding a certain threshold, allow to detect assumed simple gestures. After initial testing, it was decided to set the 0.2 rad threshold value.

3.3   Text Input Method

For the purposes of assessing the prepared methods of gesture recognition, a research tool was developed to collect data from the Myo armband. This tool not only interpreted the gestures performed with the foot gestures on a regular basis, but also translated it into actions related to navigation on the virtual linear keyboard. The set of gestures was responsible for:

- *left* - moving the virtual indicator to the preceding letter (i.e. change the selected letter from "B" to "A") or removing one character from the already entered text,
- *right* - move the virtual indicator to the next letter (i.e. change the selected letter from "A" to "B") or enter a space,
- *up* - confirmation of the selected character and entering it into the text field,
- *down* - modifier of actions performed by *left* and *right* so that the indicated character will be deleted or a space is entered accordingly.

4   Evaluation and Discuss

Proposed methods of text input were implemented as research tool in a form of standalone application fo personal computer. The application allows the user to receive and collect data form Myo armband, measure a time of the experiment and compare a sentence typed by the user to the reference sentence.

A group of 11 people was involved in the study: eight men and three women (age range 20–49). The goal of the evaluation was to verify that foot gestures are suitable for entering characters. English pangram *the quick brown fox jumps over the lazy dog* was chosen to evaluate the proposed methods of text input. The pangram was typed three times by each participant wearing Myo controller on a calf. Collected EMG signals were interpreted as gestures controlling a linear access keyboard.

Next the experiment was repeated collecting acceleration data from IMU. Table 1 shows obtained final results in WPM (*Words Per Minute*) units.

Table 1. Obtained WPM values

	Person	1	2	3	4	5	6	7	8	9	10	11	AVR
EMG	Mean	1.16	1.22	1.23	1.49	1.41	1.31	1.33	1.24	1.12	1.07	0.97	**1.23**
	MSE	0.21	0.16	0.12	0.04	0.18	0.12	0.16	0.13	0.07	0.21	0.11	0.14
IMU	Mean	1.23	1.27	1.46	1.79	1.71	1.75	1.49	1.56	1.23	1.38	1.16	**1.46**
	MSE	0.03	0.16	0.02	0.12	0.17	0.08	0.07	0.23	0.03	0.19	0.07	0.10

The approach using EMG signals was more problematic than a method based on acceleration signals. Initial attempts did not result in the text being entered correctly. Putting the band too low or too high on the calf makes gesture detection more difficult. Moreover, the return movement of the foot to the neutral position required muscle tone, and this led to random actions. For example, it happened that after a long hold of the foot in the "right" gesture, when the foot returned to the neutral position, for a moment the "left" gesture was recognized, which practically prevented the selection of the right letter. In order to reduce the scale of the problem, a history of recognized gestures has been added to the research tool so that several consecutive measurements clearly indicate which gesture is being performed. This enabled the error-free use of the virtual keyboard, but unfortunately reduced the typing fluency because gestures were recognized late. Hence, the final results obtained in the approach with EMG signals are worse than in the approach with acceleration signals.

5   Conclusions

Despite many works on recognizing gestures from mobile sensors, none focused on foot gestures for the needs of text entry. This study confirmed that foot gestures allowed people to enter a text. This result is very important especially for people with paresis of hands. Two different (but combinable) approaches were verified: EMG data gathered from muscle sensors and acceleration signals taken from the inertial measurement unit. The obtained results (EMG - 1.23 WPM, IMU - 1.46 WPM) are comparable to other methods consisting of linear alphabet scanning. Related works of the single-switch scanning, presented obtained results as 1.48 WPM [9] and in the range 1.28–1.51 WPM [12].

The use of EMG sensors gave slightly worse results. The reason lies in the anatomical differences in the calves of the study participants. Slight differences in the position of the band also affect the detection of gestures. Putting the band too low or too high on the calf makes it more difficult to apply a gesture that would be correctly detected.

To improve both proposed approaches, the tool application should be calibrated before every test. Text input by foot gestures can also be improved by using a virtual keyboard with complexity better than linear that allows the user to reach the expected characters in fewer moves. These issues will be the subject of future work.

References

1. Abreu, J.G., Teixeira, J.M., Figueiredo, L.S., Teichrieb, V.: Evaluating sign language recognition using the Myo armband. In: 2016 XVIII Symposium on Virtual and Augmented Reality (SVR), pp. 64–70. IEEE (2016)
2. Akhmadeev, K., Rampone, E., Yu, T., Aoustin, Y., Le Carpentier, E.: A testing system for a real-time gesture classification using surface EMG. IFAC-PapersOnLine 50(1), 11498–11503 (2017)
3. Amma, C., Krings, T., Böer, J., Schultz, T.: Advancing muscle-computer interfaces with high-density electromyography. In: Proceedings of the 33rd Annual ACM Conference on Human Factors in Computing Systems, pp. 929–938 (2015)
4. Boyali, A., Hashimoto, N., Matsumoto, O.: Hand posture and gesture recognition using Myo armband and spectral collaborative representation based classification. In: 2015 IEEE 4th Global Conference on Consumer Electronics (GCCE), pp. 200–201. IEEE (2015)
5. Chen, X., Wang, Z.J.: Pattern recognition of number gestures based on a wireless surface EMG system. Biomed. Signal Process. Control 8(2), 184–192 (2013)
6. Cognolato, M., et al.: Hand gesture classification in transradial amputees using the Myo armband classifier* this work was partially supported by the swiss national science foundation Sinergia Project# 410160837 MeganePro. In: 2018 7th IEEE International Conference on Biomedical Robotics and Biomechatronics (Biorob), pp. 156–161. IEEE (2018)
7. Everett, J.B., Turnquist, L.L., Stevens, T.M., Coutts, D.D., Groenland, M.: Foot gesture-based control device, US Patent App. 15/521,023, 23 Nov 2017
8. Gunawardena, K.L., Hirakawa, M.: GestureTank: a gesture detection water vessel for foot movements. ICTER 8(2), 1 (2016)
9. Hoppestad, B.S.: Current perspective regarding adults with intellectual and developmental disabilities accessing computer technology. Disabil. Rehabil.: Assist. Technol. 8(3), 190–194 (2013)

10. Huang, D., Zhang, X., Saponas, T.S., Fogarty, J., Gollakota, S.: Leveraging dual-observable input for fine-grained thumb interaction using forearm EMG. In: Proceedings of the 28th Annual ACM Symposium on User Interface Software and Technology, pp. 523–528 (2015)

11. Jacko, J.A.: Human-computer interaction: interaction techniques and environments. In: Jacko, J.A. (ed.) Proceedings of 14th International Conference, HCI International 2011, Orlando,FL, USA, 9–14 July 2011, vol. 6762. Springer, Heidelberg (2011). https://doi.org/10.1007/978-3-642-21605-3

12. Koester, H.H., Simpson, R.C.: Method for enhancing text entry rate with single-switch scanning. J. Rehabil. Res. Dev. **51**(6), 995 (2014)

13. Lavoie, T., Menelas, B.A.J.: Design of a set of foot movements for a soccer game on a mobile phone. Comput. Games J. **5**(3–4), 131–148 (2016)

14. Menelas, B.A.J., Otis, M.J.: Use of foot for direct interactions with entities of a virtual environment displayed on a mobile device. In: 2013 IEEE International Conference on Systems, Man, and Cybernetics, pp. 3745–3750. IEEE (2013)

15. Nurse, M.A., Meschter, J.C., Pisciotta, J.C., Schrock, A.M., Rauchholz, W.F.: Foot gestures for computer input and interface control, US Patent 9,002,680, 7 Apr. 2015

16. Paelke, V., Reimann, C., Stichling, D.: Foot-based mobile interaction with games. In: Proceedings of the 2004 ACM SIGCHI International Conference on Advances in Computer Entertainment Technology, pp. 321–324. ACM (2004)

17. Pedrosa, D., Pimentel, M.D.G.C.: Text entry using a foot for severely motor-impaired individuals. In: Proceedings of the 29th Annual ACM Symposium on Applied Computing, pp. 957–963. ACM (2014)

18. Polacek, O., Sporka, A.J., Slavik, P.: Text input for motor-impaired people. Univ. Access Inf. Soc. **16**(1), 51–72 (2015). https://doi.org/10.1007/s10209-015-0433-0

19. Rawat, S., Vats, S., Kumar, P.: Evaluating and exploring the Myo armband. In: 2016 International Conference System Modeling and Advancement in Research Trends (SMART), pp. 115–120. IEEE (2016)

20. Saponas, T.S., Tan, D.S., Morris, D., Balakrishnan, R., Turner, J., Landay, J.A.: Enabling always-available input with muscle-computer interfaces. In: Proceedings of the 22nd Annual ACM Symposium on User Interface Software and Technology, pp. 167–176 (2009)

21. Scott, J., Dearman, D., Yatani, K., Truong, K.N.: Sensing foot gestures from the pocket. In: Proceedings of the 23nd Annual ACM Symposium on User Interface Software and Technology, pp. 199–208. ACM (2010)

22. Yang, Q., Zou, Y., Zhao, M., Lin, J., Wu, K.: ArmIn: explore the feasibility of designing a text-entry application using EMG signals. In: Proceedings of the 15th EAI International Conference on Mobile and Ubiquitous Systems: Computing, Networking and Services, pp. 117–126. ACM (2018)

23. Zhang, X., Chen, X., Li, Y., Lantz, V., Wang, K., Yang, J.: A framework for hand gesture recognition based on accelerometer and EMG sensors. IEEE Trans. Syst. Man Cybern.-Part A: Syst. Hum. **41**(6), 1064–1076 (2011)

Application of Gesture Interface to Transcription for People with Motor Dysfunction

Ikushi Yoda[1]([⊠]), Tsuyoshi Nakayama[2], Kazuyuki Itoh[2],
Daisuke Nishida[3], and Katsuhiro Mizuno[3]

[1] Advanced Industrial Science and Technology (AIST),
Tsukuba 305-8560, Japan
i-yoda@aist.go.jp
[2] Research Institute, National Rehabilitation Center for Persons with Disabilities,
Tokorozawa 359-8555, Japan
[3] National Center of Neurology and Psychiatry, Kodaira 187-8551, Japan

Abstract. We previously developed a gesture interface for people with motor dysfunction using an RGB-D camera. We collected 226 gesture data from 58 individuals with motor dysfunction and classified the data. We then developed multiple recognition modules based on the data. The interface has nine modules for recognizing various types of gestures. For this study, we had a person with a disability use this interface in combination with an input device he had been using trackball for a transcription task. We set two gesture-input switches from the movement of two sites on his body that were easy for him to move. The user performed character input in the on-screen keyboard by using the trackball and separately operated the sound player using our gesture interface. He continued this activity using this combination daily use for half a year. He was able to reduce the input time by half. We are now supplying AAGI for Japanese people with motor dysfunction freely. We will supply AAGI for foreign users through our home page in next year.

Keywords: Gesture interface · Assistance for people with motor dysfunction · Augmentative and alternative communication · Gesture recognition

1 Introduction

1.1 Background

Individuals with severe motor dysfunction or other physically disabilities have difficulty operating an input device such as a mouse, keyboard, or remote controller when trying to use computers or home appliances. "Augmentative and alternative communication [1]" is available to help these individuals use information and communications technology devices, and devices using scanning input software are in wide use [2–5].

Various types of physical switches are available and in use for entering data into software applications, but such devices must fit the needs of the particular user and must be adjustable to correspond to the long-term physical changes in the user. In

© Springer Nature Switzerland AG 2020
K. Miesenberger et al. (Eds.): ICCHP 2020, LNCS 12377, pp. 343–347, 2020.
https://doi.org/10.1007/978-3-030-58805-2_40

addition, some people with disabilities cannot control the intensity of their movements due to involuntary movement that could damage the physical device.

1.2   AAGI

To address these issues, we previously developed a non-contact and non-constraining gesture interface called the Alternative and Augmentative Gesture Interface (AAGI) using an RGB-D camera [6–10].

In these previous studies, we collected gesture data from people with disabilities and classified the data. A total of 226 gestures were collected from 58 individuals with motor dysfunction and the voluntary movements were classified on the basis of body part. We then developed nine recognition modules based on the data. These nine modules are (1) finger, (2) head, (3) strong wink, (4) mouth/tongue, (5) shoulders, (6) knees, (7) foot tapping, (8) front objects, and (9) slight movement.

Figure 1 shows the configuration of the AAGI. The user's gesture is captured with the RGB-D camera, which is connected to a PC. The AAGI recognizes the captured gesture, and the user is able use that gesture as a software switch in a PC or environment-control application. The AAGI semi-automatically adjusts the gesture to fit the individual user, keeping down the cost of continual usage compared to conventional physical switches. The AAGI was designed so that multiple modules can function in parallel. For this reason, multiple gestures can be recognized simultaneously if they are within the same angle of camera view.

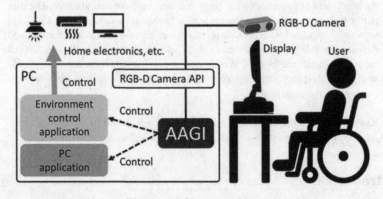

Fig. 1. AAGI components.

2   Transcription Task

During our previous studies a person with disability have worked for transcription of the municipal assembly minutes. The person had muscular dystrophy, so he could only use a trackball as an input device. He could control the trackball precisely, but he had weak muscle function, particularly for long-distance moving of a pointer.

Table 1 summarizes the environmental setup, and Fig. 2 an image of the monitor. He continued changing between the on-screen keyboard and sound player for transcription by using the trackball only, so he had to constantly switch between these two applications because it is troublesome to change between two applications without using a physical keyboard.

Table 1. Environment for transcription in the user.

OS	Windows10
Input device	Trackball
Character input	Microsoft OSK (on screen keyboard)
Word processor	Google Docs
Sound player	Voitex, Asuka 21 Ltd.

3   Combination of Gesture and Currently Used Device

3.1   Combination with Current Device

The AAGI was originally developed for people with severe motor dysfunction who are not able to use currently input devices. For this study, we had applied the AAGI to the above-mentioned user in combination with a trackball that he had been using. Specifically, he performed input characters input in the on-screen keyboard by using the trackball as he had been doing. He separately operated the sound player by using the AAGI too. In other words, there was no need for him to change between the two applications using just the trackball.

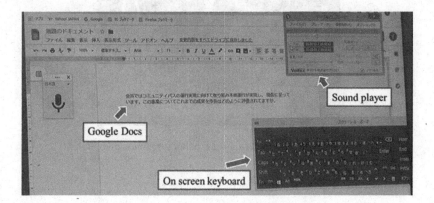

Fig. 2. Monitor image.

3.2   Application of Gesture Interface

The user first used the AAGI. As mentioned above, the AAGI has nine recognition modules and each user has to choose the module that best meets his/her needs. The user could not move the lower part of his body but could perform small tasks with his upper body. He had to use both hands to operate the trackball (Fig. 3). Therefore, using the slight-movement module, we decided to use the slight movement of the head and left thumb to add two software switches. The top of Fig. 3 illustrates the entire environment. The user performed transcription on the laptop by using the trackball. The bottom of Fig. 3 shows an image of the recognition monitor of the AAGI. The AAGI recognized the movements inside the two blue rectangles (head and left thumb). From the movements at these two sites, the AAGI recognized them as input from the two switches input. Regarding the correspondence between the laptop operations and the gestures, we set head movement to start/stop the sound player and left-thumb movement to rewind based on the needs of the user.

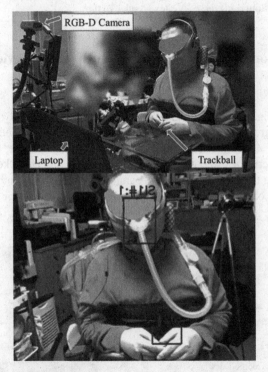

Fig. 3. Top: Entire environment, bottom: monitor of AAGI.

3.3   Application of Gesture Interface

After the application of the gesture, the user used a combination of the trackball and AAGI for transcription in the normal work. At the time of the use start, the interface made semiautomatic adjustments and learned from the last initial setting, and the user started the transcription task. He continued this activity using this combination for half a year.

We also carried out a basic evaluation on character-input speed. It took the user 1 min 12 s to input one sentence consisting of 34 Japanese characters without the AGGI and 36 s with it, i.e. half the input time.

4   Conclusion and Future Work

We had a person with a disability use our AAGI in combination with an input device (trackball) he had been using for a transcription task. We developed two software input switches from movements at two sites on his body that he easily moved and assigned them to operating two applications. The participant was able to do reduce his input time by half mainly by completely separating the two software operations using the AAGI and trackball. Furthermore, he was able to perform this type of transcription task for half a year.

Three more individuals are now starting to use the AAGI for the same purpose. Of course, the sites for switch input and types of input devices they use differ. However, the basic structure is the same. Increasing the types of applications and automating daily gesture adjustment is necessary and will be addressed in future work.

We have started to supply AAGI for Japanese people with motor dysfunction freely from last year. The users are related two hospitals mainly. All information is described in our home page [10]. We will supply AAGI for foreign users through our home page in next year.

Acknowledgments. This study was supported by the TATEISHI SCIENCE AND TECH-NOLOGY FOUNDATION 2020 S and AMED 20dk0310095h0102 in Japan.

References

1. Pino, A., et al.: Augmentative and alternative communication systems for the motor disabled. In: Disability Informatics and Web Accessibility for Motor Limitation, 1st edn, pp. 105–152. IGI Global (2013). Chapter 4
2. Microsoft Window OSK (On-Screen Keyboard). https://support.microsoft.com/en-us/help/10762/windows-use-on-screen-keyboard. Accessed 15 June 2020
3. Technotool, Ltd., OperateNavi TT. https://opnv.ttools.co.jp/. Accessed 15 June 2020
4. Hearty Radder Supporter. http://heartyladder.net/. Accessed 15 June 2020
5. Hitachi KE Systems, Ltd., Den-no-shin. https://www.hke.jp/products/dennosin/denindex.htm. Accessed 15 June 2020
6. Yoda, I., et al.: Augmentative and Alternative Gesture Interface (AAGI): multi modular gesture interface for people with severe motor dysfunction. Tecnol. Diability **31**(Supplement 1), S140–S141 (2019)
7. Yoda, I., Itoh, K., Nakayama, T.: Modular gesture interface for people with severe motor dysfunction: foot recognition. In: Proceedings of AAATE 2017 (Harnessing the Power of Technology to Improve Lives), pp. 725–732. IOS Press (2017)
8. Yoda, I., Ito, K., Nakayama, T.: Long-term evaluation of a modular gesture interface at home for persons with severe motor dysfunction. In: Antona, M., Stephanidis, C. (eds.) UAHCI 2016. LNCS, vol. 9738, pp. 102–114. Springer, Cham (2016). https://doi.org/10.1007/978-3-319-40244-4_11
9. Yoda, I., Itoh, K., Nakayama, T.: Collection and classification of gestures from people with severe motor dysfunction for developing modular gesture interface. In: Antona, M., Stephanidis, C. (eds.) UAHCI 2015. LNCS, vol. 9176, pp. 58–68. Springer, Cham (2015). https://doi.org/10.1007/978-3-319-20681-3_6
10. Augmentative and Alternative Gesture Interface (AAGI). http://gesture-interface.jp/en/. Accessed 15 June 2020

Tecla Sound: Combining Single Switch and Speech Access

Hemanshu Bhargav[1](✉), Ijaz Ahmed[2](✉), Margot Whitfield[1](✉),
Raaga Shankar[1](✉), Mauricio Meza[2](✉), and Deborah I. Fels[1](✉)

[1] Ryerson University, 350 Victoria St., Toronto, Canada
{hbhargav, margot.whitfield,
raaga.shankar, dfels}@ryerson.ca
[2] Komodo OpenLab, Toronto, Canada
ijaz.ahmad@ryerson.ca, mauricio@kmo.do

Abstract. Using single switch scanning with a mobile Smartphone can often be frustrating and slow to use. Phone functions, such as answering a call, either have specific timeout imitations that are set by service providers or may not be accessible using non-standard access methods. Single switch scanning can take longer than these timeout settings allow, resulting in missed calls or becoming stuck in endless automated call option menu loops. The Tecla single switch-scanning system has been augmented with a simple speaker dependent, limited vocabulary, offline speech recognizer to offer users one solution to this dilemma. Users decide on and record applicative words for specific phone functions, such as "answer," that can then be used instead of selecting that item from a scanning array. Given that speech production is often faster than selection from a scanning array, the user will be able to avoid the timeout limitation of their smartphone.

Keywords: Single switch use · Switch access · Accessibility speech recognition · Mobile devices

1 Introduction

Single switch interfaces are used by individuals who can only produce a single intentional and consistent physical action to activate a control [1]. Individuals with quadriplegia and other motor impairments, Cerebral Palsy, Multiple Sclerosis, and other diagnoses, require alternative access to computers and mobile devices [2]. Speech impairments may also be present in individuals with these diagnoses [2, 3]. The single switch interface involves one switch that is coupled with a method of presenting possible options, one at a time, often as a scanning array. The user presses the switch to indicate a selection once the desired option appears. The types of applications that are commonly used with single switches and scanning arrays are: environmental and wheelchair controls; general computer hardware and software; and specialized or dedicated alternative access systems such as speech generation devices. However, dedicated or specialized access systems can be expensive and have limited functionality. Instead, being able to access mainstream applications allows users to learn and

© Springer Nature Switzerland AG 2020
K. Miesenberger et al. (Eds.): ICCHP 2020, LNCS 12377, pp. 348–354, 2020.
https://doi.org/10.1007/978-3-030-58805-2_41

gain experience with those applications rather than adopting a specialized application which can be more expensive, inflexible or less readily available.

Mainstream desktop (e.g., macOS) and mobile operating systems (e.g., iOS and Android) now incorporate switch access accessibility features [4], which enable access to individuals who are unable to use standard interfaces like touch screens, keyboard or pointer devices.

While mobile devices are now, more than ever, natively accessible to single switch/scanning devices. However, using a single switch remains a very slow process. Todman [3] reports that typical word entry rates for single switch users are 2–5 words per minute, even with word prediction (compared to typical touch-typing keyboard rates of 20–45 words per minute). Assistive voice recognition with word prediction can reduce the number of required keystrokes by as much as 69% [5, 6].

If additional methods can be found to augment single switch technologies, which do not involve more physical movement, then the time it takes to access functionality, options or enter selections may increase. One relatively new and recently more robust technology is automatic speech recognition (ASR). As Rudzciz [7] states, "Since dysarthric speech is often 10 to 17 times slower than normal, ASR is seen as a viable alternative to improve communicatively in computer-assisted interaction" [pp. 248].

However, built-in ASR systems (voice assistants) on smartphones are designed for clear and unambiguous speech production and require an Internet connection. They also rely on remote data sets to perform recognition and do not allow users to personalize the voice models (such as what is used with speaker dependent systems), which can improve recognition [8]. A single switch user may be disconnected from the Internet or have mobile data deactivated, which then disables their smartphone's onboard speech recognition system. However, speaker dependent systems, such as Dragon Naturally Speaking, can be expensive and are often not intended to be integrated with single switch interfaces. Thus, any ASR system that complements single switch use must be accurate, inexpensive and robust without Internet connectivity.

In this paper, a Bluetooth enabled, limited vocabulary ASR application for use with the Tecla single switch interface is described. A use-case example is also presented to describe how the system could be used by single-switch users.

2 System Description

2.1 Switch Scanning and Mobile Devices

In mobile devices, switch accessibility features provide access to native, standard functionality. When a single switch scanning user receives a phone call, the scanning frame scans through all elements of call answering functions, one at a time. This is a time sensitive task and depending on the scanning settings of the user, the call may be missed before the answer button is scanned by the system. While some voice assistants in mobile devices may allow the user to answer a phone call, there is no option to hang up by voice, as the microphone is in use by the phone app during a call. This could lead to users to become "stuck" in corporate menus or voicemail systems, if they do not have alternative access to their device such as switch access.

2.2 Speech Interface Augmenting Tecla's Single Switch Functions

As a result of difficulties with the time restrictions for answering and hanging up functions experienced by Tecla users, we wanted to augment the single-switch system with a limited functionality speech interface. However, an important criterion was to implement a limited-phrase offline speech recognizer, so that Tecla users do not require Internet access in order to use it. In addition, this system could be used in parallel to phone use. Limited word/phrase encoding that can be user-specified, called a "hot-word," is possible as there are only a few time-dependent phone functions such as "answer" or "hang-up the phone".

There were a number of possible options for offline natural language processers (NLPs) including Picovoice [9] PocketSphinx [10], Snowboy [11], Kaldi [12] and Mozilla's DeepSpeech [13]. We selected the Snowboy system as it uses a neural network, which classified true/false for "wake-word" detection, allows developer modifications, and was optimized for limited hotword detection. Wake-word detection was necessary for mode-switching, so that hotwords were not confused with speech utterances that could occur in another application such as a phone conversation. Other offline NLPs required enterprise licensing (Picovoice), had disproportionately high false positives [14, pp.67] and poor "word-error rate" scores [10], did not provide wake-word support (Kaldi and Mozilla DeepSpeech), or were not intended for consumer deployment (Kaldi).

As shown in Fig. 1, the Tecla speech interface begins with an "initial setup" which prompts the user to configure a set of predefined phrases. The user begins by specifying their language choice, age, speech pattern, and microphone settings, as these are required by Snowboy in order to optimize the speech detection algorithm for particular technical voice parameters. The user is then presented with 15 default phrases such as answer, which can be used, edited or replaced (see Fig. 2).

To qualify as a hotword, restrictions are placed on user input such that commands are a minimum of ten characters in length, so that voice commands are sufficiently distinct in sound. To train the system, the user is prompted to record three samples voicing the phrase using whichever words/sounds that they can repeat. Once successful training occurs, a Snowboy "personal model" is generated for each voice command, specific to each user (see Fig. 1). This process is repeated until the user has trained the system for all of the desired hotwords.

To reduce the effects of variability in dysarthric speech, users are encouraged to record voice samples for their commands at various times of the day, each time assigning a command which is similar in enunciation to previous commands, which serve the same function. As the Snowboy system only permits three samples for training, this process will ensure that the "personal model" is not corrupted from environment noise and so that variations of the command that a user with dysarthric speech may speak are included in the model.

Audio samples must be recorded at frequency of 16 kHz to ensure the Snowboy recognizer accepts them for training [11]. Although most USB microphones can record at this frequency, mass-market, open source microphones, which comply with the Tecla Shield 3.0's small space, are fewer. As such, the Seeed Sound Dac for speech recognition is the default microphone for the system and functions independently from the phone microphone. Gain and sensitivity for the microphone are user adjustable and can be adjusted to accommodate different levels of speech production quality—including dysarthric speech.

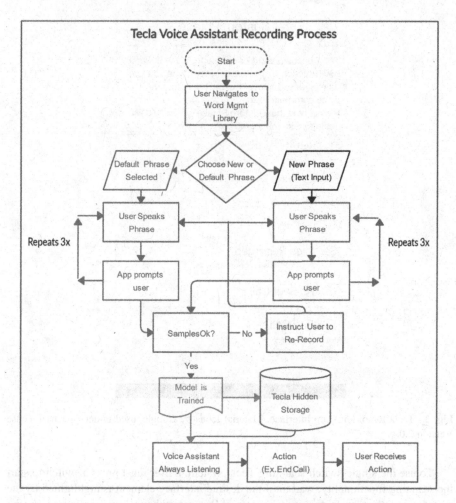

Fig. 1. Data flow during recording.

3 Use Case/Example Scenario

Instead of using the Tecla single switch/scanning solution for all phone actions, using voice commands would allow a user to replace some physical hardware/relay switch functionality with voice commands. The following scenario of the receipt and answering of a phone call on a user's smartphone is outlined and compared between the "single-switch only" version of Tecla and the speech augmented version.

Fig. 2. Tecla Recording App Interface. Material Icons by Google, used under Apache License Version 2.0.

To use the single-switch scanning Tecla system, a user must press a switch to start the scanning functionality, wait until the desired interface element is highlighted by the system, and then press the switch again. Most smartphones are configured by the cellular service provider to ring for a specific number of times (e.g., for the Rogers service provider, the number of rings is nine) [15]. Once that time is exceeded, the phone reverts to voicemail. The time to activate the "answer call" item on the scanning menu is longer than allowed by the service provider. It is thus difficult to answer the phone within the designated number of rings, and calls are often missed. To perform the same tasks with the speech recognition system, the user would voice the command used for the "answer" function. This takes only the time to voice that single command.

While the number of commands that have been selected for use with the Snowboy offline recognizer is 15, it is sufficient to accommodate a number of phone-specific functions that are difficult to complete with single-switch scanning. In addition to answering or ending a call, a command could be set to perform a gesture such as turning a page, or scrolling, or used as a modifier to use a switch with a secondary function. For example, the new Xbox adaptive controller uses switches as inputs to play games and allow users to create different layouts. Similarly, a voice command on the Tecla system could be used to allow users to switch between layouts – a switch between racing and adventure games is one possible scenario.

3.1   Limitations

The current speech recognizer is an open source tool for personal use, which is subjected to market interest and support from the community of developers. If the development community no longer wishes to support the tool, then there will be a potential risk to future development, troubleshooting or support. A different speech recognizer must be considered if this occurs.

4   Future Work

The next steps in this research is to carry out user studies with current Tecla single-switch-scanning users to determine the acceptability, usability and usefulness of the Tecla scanning/speech system for managing telephone functions in a smartphone. Time to access the various phone functions will be a key variable. The target user group must include users with varying levels of speech production ability, articulacy, severe dysarthria and environments with varying noise levels.

Acknowledgements. Funding is generously provided by the Accessible Technology Program of Innovation, Science and Economic Development Canada.

References

1. Koester, H.H., Simpson, R.C.: Method for enhancing text entry rate with single-switch scanning. J. Rehabil. Res. Dev. **51**(6), 995–1012 (2014)
2. Koester, H.H., Arthanat, S.: Text entry rate of access interfaces used by people with physical disabilities: a systematic review. Assistive Technol. **30**, 151–163 (2018). https://doi.org/10.1080/10400435.2017.1291544
3. Todman, J.: Rate and quality of conversations using a text-storage AAC system: single-case training study. Augmentative Altern. Commun. **16**, 164–179 (2000). https://doi.org/10.1080/07434610012331279024
4. Apple Inc.: Use Switch Control to navigate your iPhone, iPad, or iPod touch. https://support.apple.com/en-ca/HT201370
5. Swiffin, A., Arnott, J., Pickering, J.A., Newell, A.: Adaptive and predictive techniques in a communication prosthesis. Augmentative Altern. Commun. **3**, 181–191 (1987). https://doi.org/10.1080/07434618712331274499
6. Matiasek, J., Baroni, M., Trost, H.: FASTY—a multi-lingual approach to text prediction. In: Miesenberger, K., Klaus, J., Zagler, W. (eds.) ICCHP 2002. LNCS, vol. 2398, pp. 243–250. Springer, Heidelberg (2002). https://doi.org/10.1007/3-540-45491-8_51

7. Rudzicz, F.: Production knowledge in the recognition of dysarthric speech (2011). http://search.proquest.com/docview/920144730/abstract/B15CC1C7A3F437CPQ/1

8. Nuance Communications: Dragon Speech Recognition - Get More Done by Voice. https://www.nuance.com/dragon.html

9. Embedded Wake Word & Voice Commands - Picovoice. https://picovoice.ai/products/porcupine/

10. Huggins-Daines, D., Kumar, M., Chan, A., Black, A.W., Ravishankar, M., Rudnicky, A.I.: Pocketsphinx: a free, real-time continuous speech recognition system for hand-held devices. In: 2006 IEEE International Conference on Acoustics Speech and Signal Processing Proceedings, vol. 1 (2006). https://doi.org/10.1109/ICASSP.2006.1659988

11. Kitt, A.I., Chen, G.: Snowboy, a Customizable Hotword Detection Engine—Snowboy 1.0.0 documentation. http://docs.kitt.ai/snowboy/

12. Povey, D., et al.: The Kaldi speech recognition toolkit

13. Mozilla: Welcome to DeepSpeech's documentation!—DeepSpeech 0.7.3 documentation. https://deepspeech.readthedocs.io/en/v0.7.3/?badge=latest

14. Rosenberg, D., Boehm, B., Stephens, M., Suscheck, C., Dhalipathi, S.R., Wang, B.: Parallel Agile – Faster Delivery, Fewer Defects, Lower Cost. Springer, Cham (2020). https://doi.org/10.1007/978-3-030-30701-1

15. Rogers Communications: Set up additional features for your Home Phone voicemail - Rogers. https://www.rogers.com/customer/support/article/set-up-additional-features

Increasing the Efficiency of Text Input in the 8pen Method

Krzysztof Dobosz$^{(\boxtimes)}$ ⓘ and Mateusz Pindel

Department of Algorithmics and Software, Silesian University of Technology,
Akademicka 16, Gliwice, Poland
krzysztof.dobosz@polsl.pl, matepin927@student.polsl.pl

Abstract. The purpose of this work is to improve the 8pen method
to increase text input speed. Authors proposed calculation of Layout
Factor based on gesture energy cost calculated as number of Curve Drawn
Per Character (CDPC) and the cost of transition between two letters
neighboring in a text. Then the letters were arranged in four different
layouts: alphabetically, using the frequency of unigrams, bigrams and
trigrams in English. The best result was estimated for letter order based
on bigrams. However, after user evaluation the best results were achieved
for trigrams (almost 20 WPM). That underlines the importance of easy
transition between letters while entering the text.

Keywords: 8pen · Text entry · Text input · Virtual keyboard

1 Introduction

Text entry is a common functionality of many ICT devices. Although it is easy for
most people to enter text, sometimes it is a big challenge for people with physical
disabilities. It is very important to offer alternative methods of typing text to
support the integration of people with disabilities in society. There are many
different physical impairments that cause many obstacles in using smartphones
intended for most people. Therefore, to provide access to computer technology,
many techniques and methods of interaction are used [7], among others those
that facilitate the text input. However, studies in the field of text input is not
focused exclusively on the development of new methods and approaches, but
also on improving the existing ones.

This article discusses improving the 8pen method to increase its efficiency.

2 Background

The progress of mobile technologies has resulted in many new methods of text
input using touch screens. There are several interesting approaches in the area of

This work was co-financed by SUT grant for maintaining and developing research
potential.

free-hand writing. First should be mention two projects based on straight lines for a single letter composing. First one is the *EdgeWrite* [14], utilized a special template with a square hole and a stylus; a user needed to write the symbols with the stylus along the edges and diagonals of the hole. The second one under the name *GrooveWrite* [1] - instead of a square, used a seven-segment layout. One of the oldest methods (1993) of smooth typing was gesture-based system the *Unistrockes* [4]. Its symbols bare little resemblance to Roman letters. Each letter is associated to a short gesture. The most frequent letters are represented with straight lines. Next one, the *Graffity-stroke* [2] is a text entry system that uses strokes resembles its assigned Roman letters. This was intended to facilitate learning. Another system - *MoonTouch* [5] is a technique based on an enhanced version of the Moon alphabet. It consists of a set of simple symbols made as similar as possible to the Roman alphabet. It should also be mentioned the method of continuous writing Braille code [3], which also leads to various shapes representing single letters. Many methods that use hand movement can be used for touchless writing. There are a lot of studies devoted to the problem of hand gesture recognition described in a literature surveys [6,9,11].

A separate field in the area of text input are studies about thee use of smooth gestures to navigate a specific keyboard layout. Since the spread of mobile devices with touch screens, gestures in the form of swipes on their surface have become widely used. Hence, many solutions for fully swipe keyboards [13], or as support for keys [12] have already been patented. One of the little-known, but very interesting solutions, is the 8pen method, hardly at all described in the literature although its implementations for Android OS are known. So far the 8pen method has been compared to one and two-hand QWERTY-based virtual keyboard, and swipe text input. The study presented its advantage of the 8pen method in a contactless onscreen keyboard interface where these based techniques have been adopted [10].

The purpose of this work is to improve the 8pen method so that it can compete with other virtual keyboards that use swipes on the touchscreen.

3   The 8pen Method

3.1   Concept

The 8pen solution has been introduced for mobile platforms. This text entry technique based on a special virtual keyboard layout. The area that is used for writing is a circle divided into four parts, the letters are located on the edges of the quarters. At the start the user has to touch the central region of the keyboard. Next the user selects one of the four sectors (up, down, right, left) by moving the finger across its area. This limits the number of letters available only to those visible in the selected sector. Next, an expected letter is selected by moving the finger in one of two directions: clockwise (letters: W, P, K, M) or counterclockwise (letters: Q, O, J, N). The direction corresponds to the set of letters where will be selected for an expected letter. The number of sectors crossed in the turn indicates the successive letter on the boundary. Going through the first border (Fig. 1), the first letter 'Q' is selected from the set, continuing movement until the second border intersects, causes the selection of the second letter 'O' and so until the desired letter is obtained. After reaching the expected letter, the user makes a move inside the circle so that the finger is again in the central region of the keyboard.

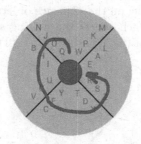

Fig. 1. Selection of "J" on the 8pen layout.

The 8pen method itself is very versatile and can provide acceptable results in terms of speed and precision of text input. However, like all other methods, it uses a certain arrangement of characters that can be random or precisely chosen.

3.2   Gesture Energy Cost

The pointer route (finger on the touch screen) to reach the selected letter, it can be short or long, depending on its location. Considering the trajectory of motion needed to select a sign, a CDPC (*Curve Drawn Per Character*) measure was proposed, i.e. the number of curves drawn for a given letter. This measure will assess the complexity of the moves, which the user will need to enter the text. On the Fig. 2. The CDPC value for entering the letter "Q" equals 3 (on the left), while entering the letter "O" requires 4 moves (on the right side).

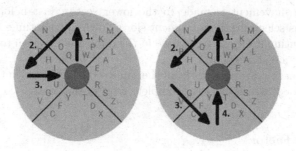

Fig. 2. Calculation of CDPC

3.3 Transition Cost

A characteristic feature of the 8pen method is the use of movements reminiscent of drawing the digit '8' or circles, because they are natural movements and can be performed in one sequence without breaks. Unfortunately, the letter setting and the variety of vocabulary do not allow the user to perform only natural movements. In some cases, the gesture should be stopped and started in the opposite direction. Depending on the sequence of letters entered, the movement may be slower or faster, which affects the writing speed. In this situation, we can introduce the concept of the Transition Cost (TC) needed to start drawing the next letter (Fig. 3).

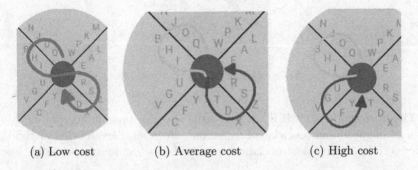

(a) Low cost   (b) Average cost   (c) High cost

Fig. 3. Examples of typing character sequences with different energy costs

The following cost values have been assumed in this work (Fig. 4):

1 - for gestures performed in a circle or through the center in a straight line - these are the most natural movements that do not require stopping; in this case, at the end, there is a move to the right or upper sector and a left turn;
2 - when after the gesture the upper sector is selected again, but this time the turn has been made to the right, which causes a slight break in the natural movement of the circle;
3 - when the movement is made to the lower sector, just before the end of the previous selection, the movement slows down or sometimes even stops so that the continuation can take place in the opposite direction to the assumed natural circular movement;
4 - when the next gesture starts from the same sector from which the movement has just ended, which causes a complete stop in the center.

3.4 Layout Factor

The usual approach to testing usability and efficiency of a virtual keyboard relies on practical tests with human users. Unfortunately, such tests are time-consuming. Therefore, the quality of a given layout (arrangement of letters) can

Fig. 4. Gesture energy costs.

be assessed by calculating the appropriate Layout Factor (1) depended on the CDPC and TC values.

$$LF = \frac{CDPC}{NoC} + \frac{TC}{NoT} \qquad (1)$$

where:

    CDPC - Curve Drawn Per Character;
    NoC - Number of Characters;
    TC - Transition Cost;
    NoT - Number of Transitions.

    The calculation of the LF should be made for a representative text of a given national language.

3.5 Arrangement of Letters

The order of letters in the layout was defined in the following steps (Fig. 5):

1. Selection of the sector,
2. Selection of the circle of letters,
3. Selection of the place in the sector on a proper circle

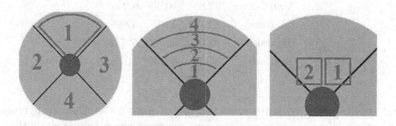

Fig. 5. Steps in the process of inserting letters

    Then the letters were arranged in four different sequences: alphabetically, using the frequency of unigrams, bigrams, and trigrams in English (Fig. 6).

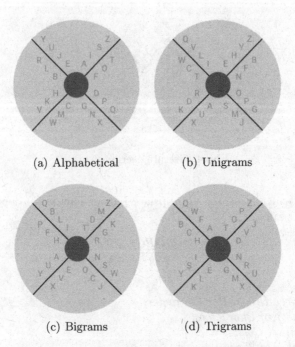

(a) Alphabetical   (b) Unigrams

(c) Bigrams   (d) Trigrams

Fig. 6. Letter arrangement in the layout

3.6 Evaluation

There were used twenty sentences in English taken from [8] to calculate the *LF* indicator for different layouts. Table 1 shows average values of sentence parameters calculated for different letter arrangement in the 8pen layout.

Table 1. Calculated layout parameters

Order	CPDC	TC	LF
Alphabetical	92.85	40.95	6.255
Unigrams	**81.30**	43.15	5.886
Bigrams	82.05	40.50	**5.745**
Trigrams	84.30	**38.50**	5.755

The results obtained show that the use of n-grams in the arrangement of letters has an effect on reducing the energy spent when typing with the 8pen method. The average sum of gesture energy cost in a sentence (CDPC) has the lowest value for the arrangement of characters according to the frequency of occurrence of individual letters (unigrams) in English. The average cost of transition between letters is the lowest for a layout based on trigrams. However, the best LF factor was obtained for a layout using bigram order.

Next, a group of eight volunteers involved in the study evaluated the four proposed layouts. The 8pen method with four different letter arrangement was implemented in the form of mobile application. Each participant had five attempts to enter a chosen test sentence making gestures on the smartphone touchscreen. The illustration (Fig. 7) presents the progress in learning a new arrangements of letters. Learning to write using the 8pen method is not difficult due to the smoothness of the gestures performed. However, the difficulty of the evaluation resulted from the different placement of the letters during the experiments. In general, all results improved as experience grew. The best result was achieved for trigrams, when typing speed has reached the value almost 19 WPM. This means that the cost of transitions between letters is more important than the gesture energy cost when a single letter is entered.

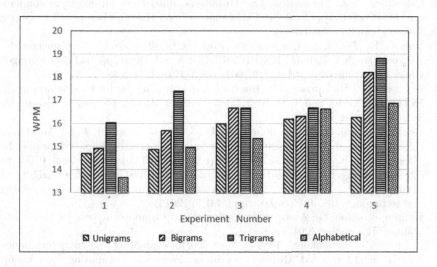

Fig. 7. Results obtained in five trials

4   Conclusions

The paper describes the original method of calculating the layout factor for 8pen method. This parameter based on gesture energy cost calculated as number of Curve Drawn Per Character (CDPC) and the cost of transition between two letters neighboring in a text. The best result was obtained by a layout based on bigrams and trigrams - the result were very similar. The layout using unigrams got worse, while the worst was the alphabetical order. During the user tests, the theoretical assumptions were confirmed, the best results were obtained by layouts using bigrams, and trigrams, although the trigram order gave the best result. This means the fluent transition between entered letters is more important than its complexity represented by single gesture energy cost. This observation is particularly relevant for all alternative text input methods for people with motor deficits.

In this studies, it was also found that estimates also play a very important role. In a research where many different systems would be tested, a properly defined factor allows to reject practical tests for cases with low performance in calculations.

References

1. Al Faraj, K., Mojahid, M., Vigouroux, N.: GrooveWrite: a multi-purpose stylus-based text entry method. In: Miesenberger, K., Klaus, J., Zagler, W., Karshmer, A. (eds.) ICCHP 2008. LNCS, vol. 5105, pp. 1196–1203. Springer, Heidelberg (2008). https://doi.org/10.1007/978-3-540-70540-6_180
2. Castellucci, S.J., MacKenzie, I.S.: Graffiti vs. unistrokes: an empirical comparison. In: Proceedings of the SIGCHI Conference on Human Factors in Computing Systems, pp. 305–308 (2008)
3. Dobosz, K., Depta, T.: Continuous writing the braille code. In: Miesenberger, K., Kouroupetroglou, G. (eds.) ICCHP 2018. LNCS, vol. 10897, pp. 343–350. Springer, Cham (2018). https://doi.org/10.1007/978-3-319-94274-2_48
4. Goldberg, D., Richardson, C.: Touch-typing with a stylus. In: Proceedings of the INTERACT 1993 and CHI 1993 Conference on Human Factors in Computing Systems, pp. 80–87 (1993)
5. Heni, S., Abdallah, W., Archambault, D., Uzan, G., Bouhlel, M.S.: An empirical evaluation of MoonTouch: a soft keyboard for visually impaired people. In: Miesenberger, K., Bühler, C., Penaz, P. (eds.) ICCHP 2016. LNCS, vol. 9759, pp. 472–478. Springer, Cham (2016). https://doi.org/10.1007/978-3-319-41267-2_66
6. Ibraheem, N.A., Khan, R.Z.: Survey on various gesture recognition technologies and techniques. Int. J. Comput. Appl. **50**(7) (2012)
7. Kouroupetroglou, G.: Assistive Technologies and Computer Access for Motor Disabilities. IGI Global (2013)
8. MacKenzie, I.S., Soukoreff, R.W.: Phrase sets for evaluating text entry techniques. In: CHI 2003 Extended Abstracts on Human Factors in Computing Systems, pp. 754–755 (2003)
9. Mitra, S., Acharya, T.: Gesture recognition: a survey. IEEE Trans. Syst. Man Cybern. Part C: Appl. Rev. **37**(3), 311–324 (2007)
10. Nowosielski, A.: Evaluation of touchless typing techniques with hand movement. In: Burduk, R., Jackowski, K., Kurzyński, M., Woźniak, M., Żołnierek, A. (eds.) Proceedings of the 9th International Conference on Computer Recognition Systems CORES 2015. AISC, vol. 403, pp. 441–449. Springer, Cham (2016). https://doi.org/10.1007/978-3-319-26227-7_41
11. Sarkar, A.R., Sanyal, G., Majumder, S.: Hand gesture recognition systems: a survey. Int. J. Comput. Appl. **71**(15) (2013)
12. Tran, P.K.: Touch-screen keyboard with combination keys and directional swipes, US Patent App. 12/713,175, 1 Sept 2011
13. Westerman, W.C., Lamiraux, H., Dreisbach, M.E.: Swipe gestures for touch screen keyboards, US Patent 8,059,101, 15 Nov 2011
14. Wobbrock, J.O., Myers, B.A., Kembel, J.A.: EdgeWrite: a stylus-based text entry method designed for high accuracy and stability of motion. In: Proceedings of the 16th Annual ACM Symposium on User Interface Software and Technology, pp. 61–70. ACM (2003)

SlideKey: Impact of In-depth Previews for a Predictive Text Entry Method

Mathieu Raynal[1]([✉]) and Benoit Martin[2]

[1] ELIPSE Team, IRIT, University of Toulouse, Toulouse, France
`mathieu.raynal@irit.fr`
[2] LCOMS, University of Lorraine, Metz, France
`benoit.martin@univ-lorraine.fr`

Abstract. Last decade has seen the democratization of small sensitive devices. But text entry solutions remain faithful to the AZERTY or QWERTY layout or to the 12-key mobile phone keypad. We propose SlideKey which is based on FOCL. It uses a linear keyboard whose layout changes according to probabilities. Key selection is operated with the four directional keys. SlideKey integrates a preview of the two-next layouts to ease user to planify his next interactions. Preliminary tests show a not significant gain in performance when the preview is used.

Keywords: Slidekey · Soft-keyboard · Character prediction · Preview

1 Introduction

With the use of Smartphones, soft keyboards are heavily used. But, before this massive use on Smartphone, soft keyboards already existed on traditional computers. Used with a suitable pointing device, soft keyboards allow people with motor disabilities to replace the physical keyboard. Thus, the soft keyboard makes it possible to enter messages or text on the computer, and consequently, to perform the same tasks as with a physical keyboard.

However, text input using these devices is often very slow. Indeed, these systems being used by means of a cursor or a pointer, it is necessary to move this cursor from one key to another to be able to enter the different characters. Typing text on a physical keyboard can be done with 10 fingers. Therefore, if fingers are well distributed above the keyboard, it is not necessary to move the same finger from one key to another, but to use two separate fingers to enter two successive characters. That's why text input in physical keyboard is much faster.

To compensate for this decrease in input speed, soft keyboards are often coupled with word prediction systems. The most commonly used solutions are to offer the user the most likely words in the form of a list displayed near the soft keyboard [2]. However, these systems are only effective if the desired word is present in the list. In any case, it is often necessary to enter several characters before you can access the word in the list [3].

© Springer Nature Switzerland AG 2020
K. Miesenberger et al. (Eds.): ICCHP 2020, LNCS 12377, pp. 363–370, 2020.
https://doi.org/10.1007/978-3-030-58805-2_43

To improve the input speed, one method is to use a character prediction system. This solution consists of predicting the next character. This makes it easier to point the keys containing the most probable characters either by enlarging these keys [1,6], by adding additional keys [7], or by increasing the speed of the pointer according to its position [8]. But, this type of solution is mostly used for single-switch scanning using a virtual keyboard [4]. This type of keyboard uses a cursor that switches from one key to another automatically after a delay: for example FOCL [5] or Sybil [10]. When the cursor is on the correct character, the user validates the selection by means of a contactor. After each character entered, the cursor is replaced at the beginning of the keyboard. Therefore, in a single-switch scanning keyboard, without character prediction, if a character is away from the cursor, the user will have to wait for the cursor to move to all keys preceding the desired key. With a character prediction system, the characters are rearranged on the keyboard after each user input, and the most likely characters are positioned closest to the cursor. This limits the number of movements to be performed.

However, the integration of dictionary raises many questions including the cognitive overload induced by the visual inspection of the proposal, the different way to display the proposals to ease navigation, etc. The advantage of such a system resides on a gain higher than the cost that is induced or on a higher user satisfaction. In a broader dialogue context, [11] has shown the benefits of preview. This is important to reduce the cognitive overload caused by the prediction system. Thus, we propose SlideKey a single-switch scanning keyboard that combines a predictive system to a system of preview.

2   SlideKey

SlideKey relies on FOCL the keyboard proposed by Scott MacKenzie [5]. Keys are presented on a line in order of their probability of occurrence, taking into account the last or the last two one characters. The selection is done using three keys, two to move from left to right the cursor represented by a blue rectangle, the third for validation.

SlideKey uses the principle of FOCL while distributing characters on a ring. Figure 1 shows its basic layout. The prefix that represents the last six characters entered is displayed in order to prevent the user from unnecessary looks to the input area. $\forall i \leq 0, L_i$ denotes the last entered letters. L_0 is the last one, L_{-1} the previous one and so, on.

As FOCL, letters are presented using one line but they are distributed on a ring. The set S of n letters actually used contains alphabetical characters and the space character. The ring is partially visible: only eleven letters are displayed to take into account the constraints of the small interactive devices. $\forall j \; with \; j \in [1, n], L_{1,j}$ denotes one possible letter of the keyboard. The current letter is presented at the middle in the red selection frame ($L_{1,1}$ in Fig. 1). Unlike FOCL, it is fixed: the characters move (the ring rotates). The prefix and the current letter uses a similar background color to facilitate the reading of the word being typed. The choice is done with the left and right directions. The down direction validates the current character and the top direction deletes the last entered one.

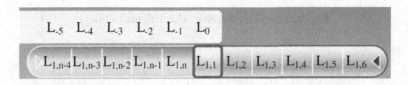

Fig. 1. Basic layout of SlideKey (Color figure online)

We note:

- $P(l, s)$ the probability of character $l \in S$ to follow the suite of characters $s = (s_i)_{i \in N}$ with $s_i \in S - \{space\}$.
- $Last_k$ the last k entered characters. If one or more space characters occur in the last four characters, we consider only the last characters from the last space character.

When validating, the current character is added to the prefix and next possible characters are displayed from left to right from the selection frame. If $Last_4$ is empty (at the beginning or after a space character), characters are displayed in alphabetical order, the character 'A' first and space character at the end. On the contrary, the more probable character is presented in the selection frame and next ones are displayed in order of probability. We have:

$$\sum_{j=1}^{n} P(L_{1,j}, Last_4) = 1 \tag{1}$$

and

$$\forall j \in [1, n-1], P(L_{1,j}, Last_4) \leq P(L_{1,j+1}, Last_4) \tag{2}$$

As the ring is closed, we find $L_{1,n}$ the least common character at the left of the selection frame. In normal use, navigation should mainly use down and right. The left navigation and the display at the left of the selection frame should be only useful at the beginning of a word when characters are displayed in alphabetical order and in case of exceeding the desired character.

When deleting a character, it is removed from the prefix and the letter most likely to succeed to the corrected prefix is displayed as the new current one.

Figure 2 shows a screenshot of running SlideKey. The user as yet entered the prefix "BONJO" and the system proposes the next characters. The most probable, 'U', is displayed in the selection frame. Others, 'N', 'I', 'E', 'T', 'L', ... 'M', 'W', 'X', 'Z', 'space', are displayed from left to right in order of probability.

SlideKey is based on the availability of a in-depth preview through two additional lines as shown in Fig. 3.

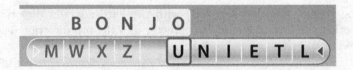

Fig. 2. Running SlideKey (Color figure online)

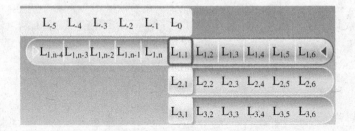

Fig. 3. Basic layout of SlideKey with preview

The second line shows the arrangement in case of validation of the current character $L_{1,1}$. We have:

$$\sum_{j=1}^{n} P(L_{2,j}, Last_3 L_{1,1}) = 1 \qquad (3)$$

and

$$\forall j \in [1, n-1], P(L_{2,j}, Last_3 L_{1,1}) \leq P(L_{2,j+1}, Last_3 L_{1,1}) \qquad (4)$$

The third line shows the arrangement in case of validation of the most probable character $L_{2,1}$. We have:

$$\sum_{j=1}^{n} P(L_{3,j}, Last_2 L_{1,1} L_{2,1}) = 1 \qquad (5)$$

and

$$\forall j \in [1, n-1], P(L_{3,j}, Last_2 L_{1,1} L_{2,1}) \leq P(L_{3,j+1}, Last_2 L_{1,1} L_{2,1}) \qquad (6)$$

With this preview, W the set of suites of characters that are viewable with the in-depth preview is:

$$W = \bigcup_{j \in [1,n]} \{prefix L_{1,1} L_{2,1} L_{3,j}\} \bigcup \bigcup_{j \in [2,n]} \{prefix L_{1,1} L_{2,j}\} \bigcup \bigcup_{j \in [3,n]} \{prefix L_{1,j}\}$$

$$(7)$$

The prefix and the most probable character of each line uses the same background color to ease reading of $prefix L_{1,1} L_{2,1} L_{3,1}$, the most probable suite of characters.

Figure 4 shows a screenshot of running SlideKey with the in-depth preview. When the current character is validated the second and third line move up and the third line is replaced by the new prediction. Only one line is new for the user. But if the current character is not the intended one, the second and the third lines are useless: when the current character changes, the first line shifts left or right and the second and the third lines change totally (Fig. 4).

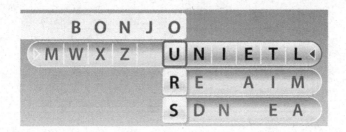

Fig. 4. Running SlideKey with the in-depth preview (Color figure online)

Generally, with the dynamic layout the cognitive load is important. The preview should allow anticipating the interaction to be performed to achieve the desired characters but it can involve a visual and cognitive overload too. It is difficult to quantify the influence of these parameters on the performance and the user satisfaction without conducting an experiment in real situation.

3   Experimentation

Participants - Height participants, two female and six male, participated in the experiment. They ranged in age from 22 to 40. There were seven right-handed and all are computer specialists.

Apparatus - The experiment was conducted on a Dell laptop running on windows. A joystick was attached to the system and was the only device used by participants. We chose for this first experimentation to restrict us to a soft keyboard which contained only the 26 characters of the Latin alphabet and the space character. Moving on the keyboard was made using the directional arrows of a joystick. Experimental software including the keyboard and the prediction system was done in Java. Data collection was performed with the platform E-Assist [9]. All data were saved in an XML file.

Design - Each subject had to perform two exercises of copy with SlideKey: one with the preview and one without preview. For each exercise, the subjects had to copy out 22 words which were the same for the two exercises. Words were chosen as the most usually used in the maternal language of the users and as to represent a maximum of different co-occurrences. Before each exercise, subjects have a training session where they had to type 12 words with the system proposed. We used a counterbalanced, within-subjects design.

Procedure - The word to be copied was presented on a line, and the word being typed by the user appeared on the line below (Fig. 5). The text entry errors were not displayed on the screen. Instead there was a visual and audio feedback signaling the error and the strip did not move until the subject entered the right character. At the end of each word, the participant had to enter the space character.

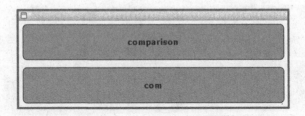

Fig. 5. Experimental device

4   Results and Discussion

Table 1 shows the mean time that participants have to type a word (MTword), and more precisely the mean time to enter a character when this one is the most likely (MTchar). On average, participants entered a word in 7756 ms without the preview, whereas they needed only 7534 ms with the preview. Thus they gain on average 3% of time with the preview relatively to SlideKey without preview. However, these results remain to be confirmed because the statistical test performed (ANOVA) showed no significant differences between the two systems ($F = 0.59418$ with $p = 0.44133$).

Table 1. Mean time (in ms) to input a word (MTword) and a character when it is the most likely (MT_{char}).

Heading level	MT_{word}	MT_{char}
With preview	7.534	585
Without preview	7.756	691

However, a closer analysis shows significant differences between the two methods tested. The first significant difference is the input of a character which is the best result of the prediction system. Indeed, after the validation of a character, the most likely character appears in the selection frame (red outline on Fig. 6). With preview, before entering the current character, we can see which character has the best chance of succeeding him in the yellow area just below the selection frame. In this case, after entering the current character, the next character is entered just by another tap on the down arrow of the joystick. We see a significant difference ($F = 42.164$, $p < 0.0001$) between the time required to input this character with SlideKey with preview and without preview (cf. Table 1). On average, participants entered this character in 691 ms without the preview, whereas they needed only 585 ms with the preview (that is to say that text input time decrease on average 15.

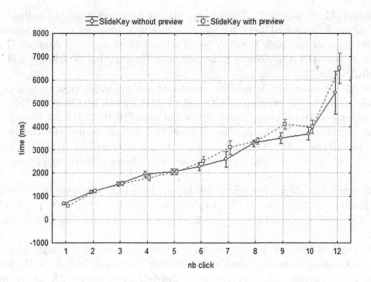

Fig. 6. Mean time to enter a character according to its position on the line

Finally, we see in Fig. 6 that, depending on the character position on the line, the system with preview is useful or not. The limit of the efficiency of preview is the 5th character. This shows that the system of preview is useful when the user can view the position of the next character. However, if the next character to enter is not previewed (because too far down the prediction list), the preview becomes more disruptive to the user.

5   Conclusion

We presented SlideKey, a soft keyboard offering a preview of the two next character layouts to help the user with the following interactions. Preliminary tests show that preview offers a significant gain when the most likely character indicated by the prediction is the character to enter. However, on all typed characters, even if a gain is observed, it is too small to be significant.

These results confirm our proposal for these preliminary tests. The prediction module was reset for each word. Thus, the module n-gram was "underutilized" in early word for lack of character. Hopefully better prediction results with phrases and thus a significant gain. In addition, results show that the preview is useful if the next character to enter is previewed. Then, we plan to increase the number of characters at the right of the current one by reducing the space at its left. These works will be tested later.

References

1. Aulagner, G., François, R., Martin, B., Michel, D., Raynal, M.: Floodkey: increasing software keyboard keys by reducing needless ones without occultation. In: Proceedings of the 10th WSEAS International Conference on Applied Computer Science, pp. 412–417. World Scientific and Engineering Academy and Society (WSEAS) (2010)
2. Badr, G., Raynal, M.: WordTree: results of a word prediction system presented thanks to a tree. In: Stephanidis, C. (ed.) UAHCI 2009. LNCS, vol. 5616, pp. 463–471. Springer, Heidelberg (2009). https://doi.org/10.1007/978-3-642-02713-0_49
3. Badr, G., Raynal, M.: Evaluation of WordTree system with motor disabled users. In: Miesenberger, K., Klaus, J., Zagler, W., Karshmer, A. (eds.) ICCHP 2010. LNCS, vol. 6180, pp. 104–111. Springer, Heidelberg (2010). https://doi.org/10.1007/978-3-642-14100-3_17
4. MacKenzie, I.S.: Modeling text input for single-switch scanning. In: Miesenberger, K., Karshmer, A., Penaz, P., Zagler, W. (eds.) ICCHP 2012. LNCS, vol. 7383, pp. 423–430. Springer, Heidelberg (2012). https://doi.org/10.1007/978-3-642-31534-3_63
5. MacKenzie, S.: Mobile text entry using three keys. In: Proceedings of the second Nordic Conference on Human-Computer Interaction, pp. 27–34. ACM (2002)
6. Merlin, B., Raynal, M.: Evaluation of SpreadKey system with motor impaired users. In: Miesenberger, K., Klaus, J., Zagler, W., Karshmer, A. (eds.) ICCHP 2010. LNCS, vol. 6180, pp. 112–119. Springer, Heidelberg (2010). https://doi.org/10.1007/978-3-642-14100-3_18
7. Raynal, M.: KeyGlasses: semi-transparent keys on soft keyboard. In: Proceedings of the 16th International ACM SIGACCESS Conference on Computers & Accessibility, pp. 347–349 (2014)
8. Raynal, M., MacKenzie, I.S., Merlin, B.: Semantic keyboard: fast movements between keys of a soft keyboard. In: Miesenberger, K., Fels, D., Archambault, D., Peñáz, P., Zagler, W. (eds.) ICCHP 2014. LNCS, vol. 8548, pp. 195–202. Springer, Cham (2014). https://doi.org/10.1007/978-3-319-08599-9_30
9. Raynal, M., Maubert, S., Vigouroux, N., Vella, F., Magnien, L.: E-assiste: a platform allowing evaluation of text input systems. In: 3rd International Conference on Universal Access in Human-Computer Interaction (UAHCI 2005), Las Vegas, USA (2005). https://hal.archives-ouvertes.fr/hal-01761479
10. Schadle, I.: Sibyl: AAC system using NLP techniques. In: Miesenberger, K., Klaus, J., Zagler, W.L., Burger, D. (eds.) ICCHP 2004. LNCS, vol. 3118, pp. 1009–1015. Springer, Heidelberg (2004). https://doi.org/10.1007/978-3-540-27817-7_149
11. Sellen, A.J., Kurtenbach, G.P., Buxton, W.A.: The prevention of mode errors through sensory feedback. Hum.-Comput. Interact. **7**(2), 141–164 (1992)

Literacy Toy for Enhancement Phonological Awareness: A Longitudinal Study

Carlos Ramos-Galarza[1,2](✉) ⓘ, Hugo Arias-Flores[2] ⓘ,
Omar Cóndor-Herrera[2] ⓘ, and Janio Jadán-Guerrero[2] ⓘ

[1] Facultad de Psicología, Pontificia Universidad Católica del Ecuador,
Av. 12 de Octubre y Roca, Quito, Ecuador
caramos@puce.edu.ec

[2] Centro de Investigación en Mecatrónica y Sistemas Interactivos MIST/Carrera
de Ingeniería en Ciencias de la Computación/Maestría en Educación mención
Innovación y Liderazgo Educativo/Carrera de Psicología/Carrera de
Administración, Universidad Tecnológica Indoamérica,
Av. Machala y Sabanilla, Quito, Ecuador
{hugoarias, omarcondor, janiojadan}@uti.edu.ec

Abstract. In this report it is presented the results of a longitudinal pre-experimental study, it was realized a technological intervention to stimulate the phonological awareness through a tangible reading toy based on the RFID technology, consisting of a teddy bear and 30 letters in 3D from the Spanish alphabet. This study started with a sample of 200 children, from them, there were selected 17 children aged between 6 and 7 years (M_{age} = 6.47, SD = .51) with a phonological disorder from an educative institution. The procedure consisted of obtaining pre-test and post-test values with the Evaluation of Phonological Awareness (PECFO). Sampling inclusion criteria considered children presenting problems of phonemes' recognition and its relationship with graphemes. During 30 weeks it was realized an intervention with the technological toy and at the end of the sessions, it was applied the post-test. Results of phonological awareness showed statically significant differences among the pre (M = 12.88, SD = 3.53) and post-test (M = 17.17, SD = 2.96) this contributes to the empirical evidence of the intervened group improvement in this cognitive function $t_{(16)}$ = −3.67, p = .002. From this research it is projected proposing technological innovations contributing in the treatment of children's cognitive difficulties.

Keywords: Phonological awareness · Literacy toy · Inclusive toys · RFID · PECFO

1 Introduction

Cognitive development is a central issue in the context of technological innovations for children's disorders treatment. Because of it, in this article, it is reported a longitudinal pre-experimental study, where it was realized an interactive device for children to improve their phonological development. Following, the benefits of technology usage in the treatment of cognitive difficulties are described, as well as the proposal of a

K. Miesenberger et al. (Eds.): ICCHP 2020, LNCS 12377, pp. 371–377, 2020.
https://doi.org/10.1007/978-3-030-58805-2_44

reading tangible toy, as technological innovation, for the treatment of phonological awareness' difficulties. Afterward, it is explained the longitudinal pre-experimental study carried out.

1.1   Benefits of Technological Usage for Cognitive Issues

The use of ICT inserted in the educative field allows generating new forms of production, representation, diffusion and knowledge accessibility [1], which represents a constant innovation for education.

The use of a variety of devices and technological resources, adding modern students' innate abilities for using them, makes possible offering educative interactive innovations, different to those accustomed [2], which allows students to enjoy the learning process, generating on them an inner motivation, these emotions influence not just in motivation but improving significantly learning experience and academic achievements [3].

1.2   Technological Devices Used in Phonological Awareness and Cognitive Difficulties

Plenty studies are approaching technological usage to work on cognitive difficulties and phonological awareness, an example of it is the Project called Petit Ubinding, that has been designed by the University of Barcelona [4], which measured the impact of an educative method to stimulate reading in children belonging to the first grade of primary school, including on-line learning sessions. Another study conducted in a sample of deaf students about reading, orthography, and phonological abilities found that technological usage allows the improvement of these abilities [5]. On the other hand, the usage of computer-assisted pronunciation training (CAPT) is used in learning a second language for a variety range of age and technological use supports children identifying phonemes and bad-word pronouncing, suggesting to users the option to improve these errors [6]. There are other alphabetization programs based on the web offered possibilities, which have reported positive evidence improving phonological abilities that were worked on, such as phoneme-grapheme correspondence, segmentation of phonemes and word fluency [7].

Another field in this same research line is the usage of toys and inclusive games for children with disabilities rehabilitation, and in the same manner, these could be used in children presenting learning disorders such as dyslexia, dysgraphia, and dyslalia, reflecting excellent results in the learning process [8, 9]. The previous investigation about the usage of web extension assisting reading and writing problems reported significant results of treating these issues, as well as increasing motivation and child's working frequency [10].

Implementing the usage of technological tools is substantive in children's initial reading process, as it is evidenced in the longitudinal study of early reading development through technological media. Intervened children with this type of stimulation improve the automatic integration of letters and sounds and a variety of measures that assess early reading and language abilities [20].

1.3   The Necessity to Create a Friendly Device for Children with Cognitive Difficulties

Children must be prepared to acquire abilities and knowledge in the actual world and the application of technology in the learning environment will allow them to use their thinking abilities to reach social and emotional development [11, 12]. Learning environments enriched with technology in its variety [13, 14] will improve attention levels, motivation, knowledge and students' abilities in a positive way, especially in children with language disorders and special education [15, 16].

1.4   Technological Proposal to Work with Phonologic Awareness

The proposal of a tangible reading toy is based on one of the already mentioned literature, in which it was developed a literacy kit called Kiteracy (Kit for Literacy) to generate interaction of children with Down's Syndrome in the learning process. The study realized was based on a qualitative technique, using recorded sessions in video with twelve children with Down's Syndrome belonging to an institute from Spain. This technological proposal is presented in three interactive ways: cardboard cards, a tablet and a technological radiofrequency (RFID) toy and tangible objects.

The task was conducted by special education teachers and 12 children presenting Down's Syndrome. There were design three experimental sessions with every child consisting of pair-work (professor-child). From these sessions, it was possible identifying that tangible interaction offers an enjoyable moment for children. Surveys and interviews' data collected from the information given by professors revealed that tangible objects offered higher adaptability to create reading pedagogic strategies [21].

Taking into consideration this experience and with positive results in the interaction, a new research question appeared, "It is possible to use the kit to stimulate phonological awareness in children with non-special conditions", to do it, it was necessary to make a kit's adaptation to Ecuadorian context, creating a kit called Kiteracy-PiFo (Fig. 1) based on the Picto-Phonic (PiFo) alphabetization methodology, which is composed by a teddy bear with an RFID lector incorporated and 30 labels representing alphabet's letters. There were manufactured 25 kits to conduct the pre-experimental longitudinal study, to assess the effectiveness of interventions in children aged between 6 and 7 years [22].

Fig. 1. Tangible reading toy Kiteracy-Pifo.

The teddy bear contained cards RFID with the technical specification LANMU Smart ID Card Reader EM4099 USB – Proximity Sensor of 125 kHz. Also, there were used 30 cardboards made of plastic RFID with letters in pieces made of foaming material. The software allows the association between the card´s coding and phonemes sound, the visualization of the grapheme and the interactive video of trace and vocalization.

2 Method

2.1 Research Design

There was applied a pre-experimental longitudinal study since it was worked with a group of students presenting alterations in the phonological awareness.

2.2 Participants

The sample started with 200 students, from them, 17 children aged between 6 and 7 years with phonological alterations were selected (Mage = 6.47, SD = .51). According to gender, 6 (35.3%) were females and 11 (64.7%) were males. These children belonged to the educative private system of Quito- Ecuador.

2.3 Instruments

For obtaining pre and post-test values, it was used the phonological awareness evaluation test (PECFO) [17], this test allows evaluating phonological awareness development in children.

2.4 Procedure

The pre-experimental longitudinal study was conducted in an educative institution. It started with the pre-test phonological awareness test. Afterward, it was realized a technological intervention with the device to improve phonological awareness for 30 weeks. Finally, in the post-test, the impact of this technological intervention was analyzed.

It is important to highlight that this research was approved by the Ethical Committee of Investigation with human beings of the University Indoamerica of Ecuador. Participant's representatives were asked to sign the informed consent of voluntary participation and children were asked to give their assent by signing in a form as well, of accepting being part of the study. Throughout this research ethical standards of investigation with human beings were followed, protecting participants' physical and psychological integrity at all times.

2.5 Statistical Analysis

Once the statistical hypotheses were proven, it was conducted a comparison of means with a T-test procedure for related samples between the pre and post-test realized. Also, there were applied statistical central tendency and dispersion measures to characterize the data.

3   Results

In the beginning, descriptive values found were analyzed in the different measures. Table 1 shows these values.

Table 1. Descriptive results of the variables valued. Note: Mn (minimum), Mx (maximum), M (mean) and SD (Standard Deviation).

Measure	Mn	Mx	M	SD
Pre-test	4.00	18.00	12.88	3.53
Post-test	11.00	23.00	17.17	2.96

The second analysis realized was the comparison of means between the pre and post-test of the phonological awareness variable. Table 2 shows the results found.

Table 2. Comparison realized between the pre and post-test of the linguistical variable valued.

	M	SD	Mn	Mx	T	Df	Sig.	D
Pre-test vs. Post-test	−4.29	4.82	−6.77	−1.82	−3.67	16	.002	.68

Figure 2 presents phonological awareness means' differences of pre and post-test.

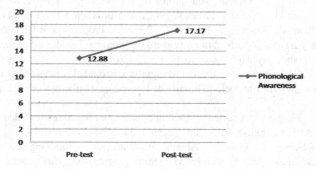

Fig. 2. Pre and post-test means differences.

4   Conclusions

This work reports an investigation that analyzed the impact of the technological development of Kiteracy-Pifo to intervene in the phonological awareness difficulties in children aged between 6 and 7 years.

Results found affirmed that its application has positive results since there were found statistically significant improvements in the phonological awareness between the pre and post-test. Results found in this investigation are concordant with the results found in previous research such as the one conducted by Thompson et al. [18] and Gilakjani and Rahimy [19], who have reported that technological use improves the oral phoneme-grapheme decoding precision as well as reading rating, contributing to significant improvement in pronunciation learning; this allows to affirm that children with learning difficulties will be benefited with reading, pronunciation, phonological awareness and writing abilities learning through technological use.

The future investigation that is proposed is related to the creation, production, and implementation of new technological inclusive devices contributing to the treatment of children with cognitive difficulties, as well as the implementation of these devices in usual educative contexts to stimulate cognitive processes.

Acknowledgments. The authors thank Universidad Tecnológica Indoamérica for funding this study through the project "Aplicación piloto del Kit Kiteracy para fortalecer el aprendizaje de lectura en niños y niñas de educación inicial" coordinated by Soledad Males and Ana Carolina Márquez.

References

1. de Pérez, A.M., Tellera, M.: Las TIC en la educación: nuevos ambientes de aprendizaje para la interacción educativa. Revista de Teoría y Didáctica de las Ciencias Sociales **18**, 83–112 (2012)
2. Borba, M., Askar, P., Engelbrecht, J., Gadanidis, G., Llinares, S., Sanchéz, M.: Aprendizaje mixto, e-learning y aprendizaje móvil en la educación matemática. ZDM Math. Educ. **48**, 589–610 (2016)
3. Anaya, A., Anaya, C.: "Motivar para aprobar o para aprender" estrategias de motivación del aprendizaje para los estudiantes. Tecnología Ciencia Educación **25**(1), 5–14z (2010)
4. López, J., Pina, V., Ballesta, S., Bordoy, S., Pérez, L.: Proyecto petit Ubinding: método de adquisición y mejora de la lectura en primero de primaria. Estudio de eficacia, Revista de Logopedia, Foniatría y Audiología **40**(1), 12–22 (2020)
5. Gonzáles, V., Domínguez, A.: Lectura, ortografía y habilidades fonológicas de estudiantes sordos con y sin implante coclear. Revista de Logopedia, Foniatría y Audiología **39**(2), 75–85 (2019)
6. Agarwal, C., Pinaki, C.: A review of tools and techniques for computer aided pronunciation training (CAPT) in english. Educ. Inf. Technol. **24**, 3731–3743 (2019)
7. Mak, B., Cheung, A., Guo, X., Abrami, P., Wade, A.: Examining the impact of the ABRACADABRA (ABRA) web-based literacy program on primary school students in Hong Kong. Educ. Inf. Technol. **22**, 2671–2691 (2017)
8. dos Santos Nunes, E.P., da Conceição Júnior, V.A., Giraldelli Santos, L.V., Pereira, M.F.L., de Faria Borges, L.C.L.: Inclusive toys for rehabilitation of children with disability: a systematic review. In: Antona, M., Stephanidis, C. (eds.) UAHCI 2017. LNCS, vol. 10277, pp. 503–514. Springer, Cham (2017). https://doi.org/10.1007/978-3-319-58706-6_41
9. El Kah, A., Lakhouaja, A.: Developing effective educative games for arabic children primarily dyslexics. Educ. Inf. Technol. **23**, 2911–2930 (2018)
10. Pařilová, T.: DysHelper – the dyslexia assistive approach user study. In: Miesenberger, K., Kouroupetroglou, G. (eds.) ICCHP 2018. LNCS, vol. 10896, pp. 478–485. Springer, Cham (2018). https://doi.org/10.1007/978-3-319-94277-3_74
11. Ejikeme, A.N., Okpala, H.N.: Promoting children's learning through technology literacy: challenges to school librarians in the 21st century. Educ. Inf. Technol. **22**(3), 1163–1177 (2017). https://doi.org/10.1007/s10639-016-9481-13
12. Adam, T., Tatnall, A.: The value of using ICT in the education of school students with learning difficulties. Educ. Inf. Technol. **22**, 2711–2726 (2017). https://doi.org/10.1007/s10639-017-9605-2

13. Alghabban, W.G., Salama, R.M., Altalhi, A.H.: Mobile cloud computing: an effective multimodal interface tool for students with dyslexia. Comput. Hum. Behav. **75**, 160–166 (2017)
14. Halloluwa, T., Vyas, D., Usoof, H., et al.: Gamification for development: a case of collaborative learning in Sri Lankan primary schools. Pers. Ubiquit. Comput. **22**, 391–407 (2018). https://doi.org/10.1007/s00779-017-1073-6
15. Cakir, R., Korkmaz, O.: The effectiveness of augmented reality environments on individuals with special education needs. Educ. Inf. Technol. **24**, 1631–1659 (2019). https://doi.org/10.1007/s10639-018-9848-6
16. Khlaisang, J., Songkram, N.: Designing a virtual learning environment system for teaching 21st century skills to higher education students in ASEAN. Tech. Know. Learn. **24**, 41–63 (2019). https://doi.org/10.1007/s10758-017-9310-7
17. Varela, V., De Barbieri, Z.: Prueba de evaluación de conciencia fonológica - PECFO (Phonological Awareness Assessment Test). Editorial BIOPSIQUE (2012)
18. Thompson, R., et al.: Effective instruction for persisting dyslexia in upper grades: adding hope stories and computer coding to explicit literacy instruction. Educ. Inf. Technol. **23**, 1043–1068 (2018)
19. Gilakjani, A., Rahimy, R.: Factors influencing iranian teachers' use of computer assisted pronunciation teaching (CAPT). Educ. Inf. Technol. **24**, 1715–1740 (2019)
20. Clayton, F., West, G., Sears, C., Hulme, C., Lervåg, A.: A longitudinal study of early reading development: letter-sound knowledge, phoneme awareness and RAN, but not letter-sound integration, predict variations in reading development. Sci. Stud. Read. **24**(2), 91–107 (2020). https://doi.org/10.1080/10888438.2019.1622546
21. Jadan-Guerrero, J., Jaen, J., Carpio, M.A., Guerrero, L.A.: Kiteracy: a kit of tangible objects to strengthen literacy skills in children with down syndrome. In: Proceedings of the 14th International Conference on Interaction Design and Children (IDC 2015), pp. 315–318. Association for Computing Machinery, New York (2015). https://doi.org/10.1145/2771839.2771905
22. Jadán-Guerrero, J., Ramos-Galarza, C., de los Angeles Carpio-Brenes, M., Calle-Jimenez, T., Salvador-Ullauri, L., Nunes, I.L.: Phonological awareness intervention and basic literacy skill development with Kiteracy-PiFo. In: Nunes, I.L. (ed.) AHFE 2020. AISC, vol. 1207, pp. 319–325. Springer, Cham (2020). https://doi.org/10.1007/978-3-030-51369-6_43

Human Movement Analysis
for the Design and Evaluation
of Interactive Systems and Assistive
Devices

Human Movement Analysis for the Design and Evaluation of Interactive Systems and Assistive Devices: Introduction to the Special Thematic Session

Lilian Genaro Motti Ader[1]([✉]) [iD] and Mathieu Raynal[2] [iD]

[1] CeADAR, SPHPSS, University College Dublin, Dublin, Ireland
`lilian.mottiader@ucd.ie`
[2] IRIT, ELIPSE Team, University of Toulouse, Toulouse, France
`mathieu.raynal@irit.fr`

Abstract. Human movement analysis is the assessment of users' body or segments of the body, their movements and position in space, and can be used to identify patterns or variations for an individual or group of people. This short paper present ten studies selected to the Special Thematic Section on human movement analysis and their contribution to the design and evaluation of interactive systems or assistive devices, aiming at fostering digital inclusion, autonomy and quality of life for people with disabilities.

Keywords: Motion-based interaction · Sensors · Gesture recognition · Assistive technologies

1 Introduction to the Special Thematic Session

The evaluation of prototypes and systems often takes completion time and accuracy as success criteria. This usually involves how the user uses their pointing device or text entry system, and therefore the movements they make to be able to use them. The advances in technologies, in particular motion sensors and wireless communications, allow the access to information to be extended beyond the graphic interfaces, creating opportunities interaction in the physical space, embracing new possibilities for detecting body movements as input for interaction [2,3]. Furthermore, the evaluation of users' movements is helpful to understand the difficulties they during interaction with technologies [5,7,8].

Human movement analysis, or the assessment of users' body or segments of the body, their movements and position in space, is used to identify patterns or variations for an individual or group of people [1,4]. For people with disabilities, this represent new opportunities to be explored, designing interaction techniques

K. Miesenberger et al. (Eds.): ICCHP 2020, LNCS 12377, pp. 381–383, 2020.
https://doi.org/10.1007/978-3-030-58805-2_45

and assistive devices to address individual needs. However, when the accessibility factors are not carefully considered, instead of promoting digital inclusion, technologies can create barriers and new situation of disability.

The papers selected for this Special Thematic Session on human movement analysis present how design and evaluation of interactive systems and assistive devices take into account the different users' skills, across many applications, to support activities related to daily living, mobility, communication and socialization. Authors of the selected papers address the needs of people in situation of disability related to physical impairment affecting lower or upper limbs (e.g., quadriplegic persons, wheelchair users), movement disorders (e.g., Cerebral Palsy), fine motor control (e.g., rheumatoid arthritis), or yet people with chronic degenerative diseases (e.g., dementia).

The process of acquisition and analysis of data related to the human movement has many challenges [6], and can be referred in terms of

- design evaluation (i.e. ergonomics, feedback),
- machine processing (i.e. sensors, gesture recognition)
- and human factors (i.e. users skills, morphology, fatigue).

The selected studies present the design evaluation for interfaces enabling the adaptation of mainstream technologies (e.g., touchscreen on smartphones), with the possibility of adding assisted devices (e.g., tongue track pad, head motion sensors) or bespoke aids (e.g., joystick handles). Examples of the tasks include: playing digital musical instruments from head rotation, sending an email using a tongue track pad or using a spoon with the aid of a vision-based feeding robotic arm. The design of the graphical interfaces has been carefully considered, measuring the effects of targets positions, sizes and distances to correctly map users' movements to the cursors and targets in different plans.

The technologies used for assessing users' movements or morphology vary according to the designed space of interaction and users skills, and included body-worn devices, such as Oral User Interface Controller, Received Signal Strength Indicator (RSSI) based smart wearable bracelet, or external sensors. Inertial Measurement Units – IMUs were used to record movements from users (e.g., head motion) or from assistive devices (e.g., crutches). Following the purposes of each study, participants skills were evaluated with additional devices, including mouse, touchscreen, eye trackers, microphones, cameras, pressure sensors or RGB Depth sensors (e.g., Microsoft Kinect). To a better fit with the users' anatomy, three-dimmensional (3D) scan and printing techniques were used to recreate users' hands anatomy. When considering mobility, the volume and physical constraints of assistive devices should be taken into account for comfort and safety, for example, to estimate wheelchair stability from a 3D mapping of the environment.

For all the selected studies, the assessment of users' skills is a very important stage in the design process, in order to identify existing limitations or restrictions in their motor control. The design of graphical interfaces of bespoke adaptations will then be optimized to facilitate access, ergonomics and comfort of use. With the current advances in sensing technologies, added to the possibilities of applying machine learning techniques, the processing of individuals' movement, not only to improve gesture recognition, but also to enable the distinction between voluntary or involuntary movements.

Human movement analysis has a great potential to improve design and evaluation of interactive systems and assistive devices. The papers presented in this Special Thematic Section show how human movement analysis can contribute to the assessment of the users' skills, in different context of use of technologies, in order to support people with special needs and improve their autonomy and quality of life.

Acknowledgements. L. G. M. A. receives funding from the EU H2020 under the Marie Skłodowska-Curie Career-FIT fellowship (Co-fund grant No. 713654).

References

1. Ader, L.G.M., McManus, K., Greene, B.R., Caulfield, B.: How many steps to represent individual gait? In: Proceedings of the 12th ACM SIGCHI Symposium on Engineering Interactive Computing Systems, pp. 1–4 (2020). https://doi.org/10.1145/3393672.3398638
2. Bergé, L.P., Dubois, E., Raynal, M.: Design and evaluation of an "around the smartphone" technique for 3D manipulations on distant display. In: Proceedings of the 3rd ACM Symposium on Spatial User Interaction, pp. 69–78 (2015). https://doi.org/10.1145/2788940.2788941
3. Bossavit, B., Marzo, A., Ardaiz, O., Pina, A.: Hierarchical menu selection with a body-centered remote interface. Interact. Comput. **26**(5), 389–402 (2014). https://doi.org/10.1093/iwc/iwt043
4. Bossavit, B., Pina, A.: Designing educational tools, based on body interaction, for children with special needs who present different motor skills. In: 2014 International Conference on Interactive Technologies and Games, pp. 63–70. IEEE (2014). https://doi.org/10.1109/iTAG.2014.16
5. Irwin, C.B., Yen, T.Y., Meyer, R.H., Vanderheiden, G.C., Kelso, D.P., Sesto, M.E.: Use of force plate instrumentation to assess kinetic variables during touch screen use. Univ. Access Inf. Soc. **10**(4), 453–460 (2011). https://doi.org/10.1007/s10209-011-0218-z
6. Motti Ader, L.G., et al.: HCI challenges in human movement analysis. In: Lamas, D., Loizides, F., Nacke, L., Petrie, H., Winckler, M., Zaphiris, P. (eds.) INTERACT 2019. LNCS, vol. 11749, pp. 725–730. Springer, Cham (2019). https://doi.org/10.1007/978-3-030-29390-1_70
7. Motti Ader, L.G., Vigouroux, N., Gorce, P.: Movement analysis for improving older adults' performances in HCI: preliminary analysis of movements of the users' wrists during tactile interaction. In: Zhou, J., Salvendy, G. (eds.) ITAP 2017. LNCS, vol. 10298, pp. 17–26. Springer, Cham (2017). https://doi.org/10.1007/978-3-319-58536-9_2
8. Young, J.G., Trudeau, M., Odell, D., Marinelli, K., Dennerlein, J.T.: Touch-screen tablet user configurations and case-supported tilt affect head and neck flexion angles. Work **41**(1), 81–91 (2012). https://doi.org/10.3233/WOR-2012-1337

Alzheimer's Garden: Understanding Social Behaviors of Patients with Dementia to Improve Their Quality of Life

Gloria Bellini[1] ⓘ, Marco Cipriano[1] ⓘ, Nicola De Angeli[1] ⓘ,
Jacopo Pio Gargano[1](✉) ⓘ, Matteo Gianella[1] ⓘ, Gianluca Goi[1],
Gabriele Rossi[1], Andrea Masciadri[2] ⓘ, and Sara Comai[2] ⓘ

[1] Alta Scuola Politecnica (Politecnico di Milano and Politecnico di Torino),
Milano, Italy
{gloria.bellini,marco.cipriano,nicola.deangeli,jacopopio.gargano,
matteo.gianella,gianluca.goi,gabriele.rossi}@asp-poli.it
[2] Dipartimento di Elettronica, Informazione e Bioingegneria, Politecnico di Milano,
Via Ponzio 34/5, 20133 Milano, Italy
{andrea.masciadri,sara.comai}@polimi.it
http://www.asp-poli.it

Abstract. This paper aims at understanding the social behavior of people with dementia through the use of technology, specifically by analyzing localization data of patients of an Alzheimer's assisted care home in Italy. The analysis will allow to promote social relations by enhancing the facility's spaces and activities, with the ultimate objective of improving residents' quality of life. To assess social wellness and evaluate the effectiveness of the village areas and activities, this work introduces measures of sociability for both residents and places. Our data analysis is based on classical statistical methods and innovative machine learning techniques. First, we analyze the correlation between relational indicators and factors such as the outdoor temperature and the patients' movements inside the facility. Then, we use statistical and accessibility analyses to determine the spaces residents appreciate the most and those in need of enhancements. We observe that patients' sociability is strongly related to the considered factors. From our analysis, outdoor areas result less frequented and need spatial redesign to promote accessibility and attendance among patients. The data awareness obtained from our analysis will also be of great help to caregivers, doctors, and psychologists to enhance assisted care home social activities, adjust patient-specific treatments, and deepen the comprehension of the disease.

Keywords: Ambient Assisted Living · Data-driven design · Social behavior · Social wellness assessment

K. Miesenberger et al. (Eds.): ICCHP 2020, LNCS 12377, pp. 384–393, 2020.
https://doi.org/10.1007/978-3-030-58805-2_46

1   Introduction

In 1990, only 6% of the world population was aged 65 years or over, 10% in 2019 and by 2050 the number is projected to rise to 15%, potentially surpassing that of adolescents, according to the United Nations forecast [1]. As a consequence, requests for assistance, which are already on the rise and having an impact on health-care systems worldwide, will further intensify. One of the leading causes of dependency and disability in the elderly is dementia, a chronic degenerative disease that affects memory, visuospatial abilities, domain and functional cognition, attention, and problem solving capabilities. The number of affected people is quite high: 5–8% of people aged 60 and over suffer from dementia, rising to 50% when considering people over 85 [2].

Alzheimer's disease (AD) is the most frequent form of dementia consisting in a severe progressive neurological pathology in which the main cognitive functions of an individual are compromised. This disease significantly affects the quality of life and, so far, medical sciences have not been able to find an effective treatment to halt or reverse its progression. However, recent studies have found that engaging in social relationships and activities could delay the cognitive decline of AD patients [3].

Alzheimer's Garden is a joint project of Politecnico di Milano and Politecnico di Torino that aims to understand the social behavior of AD patients living in a healthcare facility and to promote sociability among them to improve their quality of life and slow down the progression of the disease. The subject of our case study is *Il Paese Ritrovato* (see Sect. 3), an Ambient Assisted Living (AAL) facility in Italy featuring an advanced technological infrastructure. Specifically, this project assesses both the degree of relations among residents and the popularity of the facility spaces as an indicator of accessibility by measuring the attendance of the patients throughout an observation period, identifying the most preferred locations and the ones in need of enhancements.

2   State of the Art

Activities play a crucial role in enabling people with AD to live a life as satisfying as possible, allowing them to pursue their own hobbies and interests, creating immediate pleasure, restoring dignity and enabling friendships [4]. It has been shown that high social engagement reduces the rate of cognitive decline by 91% [5]. On the contrary, both actual social isolation, including having a small social network and participating in few activities with others, and perceived social isolation, that is, feeling lonely, are robustly associated with AD progression and cognitive decline [6].

Spatial solutions, especially those focused on accessibility, play an important role in promoting socialization between patients. Van Hecke et al. [7] state that when AD patients are not allowed to leave a dementia special care unit, it is important to provide sufficient freedom of movement and social interaction within the unit, including access to private outdoor space. This freedom of movement is crucial for patients walking through the unit without a specific destination. This statement is reinforced by the research of Ferdous et al. [8] proving architectural configuration affects the type of conversations likely to occur in certain locations within assisted care homes and, consequently, social relations.

The research team Lab.I.R.Int of the Design Department of Politecnico di Milano with Lapo Lani and Ivo Cilesi describes the concept of *therapeutic habitat* to define good design for Alzheimer's patients [9]. It recognizes the value of intangible environmental features that act as activators of opportunities for social relationships, conversations and daily rituals, improving the wellbeing of patients. Several outdoor environments do not adequately address accessibility issues concerning people with AD, as they often are disorientating, difficult to interpret and navigate, and threatening or distressing for them [10].

3   Case Study: Il Paese Ritrovato

Il Paese Ritrovato [11] is the first Alzheimer's assisted care home in the form of a village ever built in Italy. Officially opened in 2018 by La Meridiana [12] in the city of Monza, the village is developed as a traditional, small Italian town with streets, squares and gardens. The facility is composed of 8 units, each hosting 8 single rooms with private services and common areas, accounting for a total of 64 residents. At its core there are common facilities such as a church, a café, shops and a theatre to recreate the safe and stimulating environment typical of a small village. Several brain-stimulating activities are organized in multisensory rooms and labs, including pet therapy, music therapy, aromatherapy, and entertainment clubs. Building exteriors are painted each with a different color, taking inspiration from those of the close neighborhoods of Monza to evoke a feeling of resemblance in residents as if they were walking in familiar streets. Caregivers assume different roles beside their own (e.g., gardener, hairdresser, barista) to make the whole environment even more realistic.

The typical resident of *Il Paese Ritrovato* is a person with a fair level of self-reliance and independence, able to move around the village autonomously. All residents were diagnosed with mild to moderate AD, in the worst cases resulting in spontaneous confabulation, temporal and spatial context confusion, and personality and behavioral changes leading to occasional delirium [13]. Residents usually establish strong bonds with caregivers, who play a fundamental role in their daily routines, including eating together and conducting social activities.

4   Methodology and Results

A monitoring system, previously implemented by Masciadri et al. [14], collects residents' localization data through a Received Signal Strength Indicator (RSSI) based smart wearable bracelet every 10 seconds and stores the history of visited areas inside the village for every resident into a database at the end of each day [14]. Residents are informed about the localization system, and gave the rights to La Meridiana Due who is responsible for the data collection and treat-ment process. The necessary data for this study was preprocessed to guarantee the anonymity of the residents before being provided to the research team.

Taking into account the data at our disposal and following our main objec-tives, we develop our analysis on two main aspects: residents' social interactions and their behavior towards the village areas.

4.1 Assessing Patients Sociability: The Relational Index

Assessing residents' wellbeing, specifically their social behavior, only through their localization data is a hard task. We resort to the Relational Index $RI_{i,j}^d$ [14]: an indicator that aims to estimate the degree of relation between persons i and j on day d taking into account the amount of time they spend together in the same place. We extend it by introducing the Individual Relational Index for person i on day d:

$$RI_i^d = \frac{\sum_{j \in A^d \setminus \{i\}} {RI_{i,j}^d}^2}{|A^d| - 1}, \tag{1}$$

where A^d is the set of active users on day d. This index estimates quite accurately the sociability of person i on day d, and can be further extended to the entire community, for instance, by averaging over its members. Observing the value of the Relational Index and its trend over time, it is possible to discriminate between more and less sociable patients outlining a social profile for each of them. Furthermore, social isolation can be easily identified by observing decays in the patient's Individual Relational Index curve and changes in the visited places over time. Figure 1 shows an example plot of the Individual Relational Index. The change in late September could be investigated further by doctors and caregivers. Figure 2 shows an example of user profiling based on the Relational Index for a quite sociable resident. Figure 2a shows the average percentage of time spent in the village areas during a period of time of fifteen days, while Fig. 2b specifies it over the different times of the day.

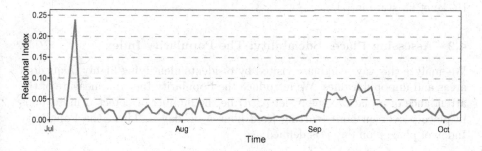

Fig. 1. An example of patient's Individual Relational Index plot

In our analysis, we perform a *multiple linear regression* in which the Rela-tional Index is the response variable. Applying *ordinary least squares* we estimate the correlation between the Relational Index and the following variables: season, temperature, weather, patient's bedroom floor (ground or first), predisposition to walk on a specific day, and patient's average hourly walked distance. Furthermore, we build a *contingency matrix* and perform a χ^2 *independence test* to study the correlation of the Relational Index with the aforementioned variables considered individually.

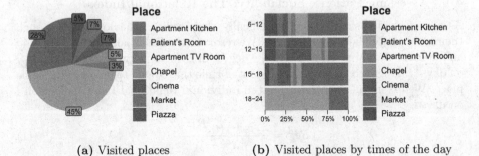

(a) Visited places   (b) Visited places by times of the day

Fig. 2. An example of patient's Localization Profile

These two models were chosen because of their high reliability, their statistical relevance, and consistency. The low *p-values* obtained from the linear regression and the dependencies in the contingency table highlight the strong correlation between the considered variables and the patients' sociability. The only irrelevant variable is the weather. This is both due to its multicollinearity with other variables such as temperature and season, but also to the fact that most facilities are indoors, making this factor less influential on the behavior of residents. Our analysis confirms that accommodating residents with dementia on the top floor should only occur when strictly necessary (e.g., to prevent patients exiting from dementia special care units), adopting thoughtfully designed solutions, as Van Hecke et al. state in [7].

4.2 Assessing Places Sociability: The Popularity Index

We analyze the way places are visited by residents identifying highly frequented areas and unpopular ones. We introduce the Popularity Index: a measure of the attendance of a place. Namely, let $n_p^d(h)$ be the number of detected individuals in place p over an hour starting from hour h on day d. Then, the Popularity Index of place p on day d is defined as:

$$PI_p^d = \frac{1}{|A^d||D|} \sum_{h \in D} n_p^d(h), \tag{2}$$

where A^d is the set of active users on day d, and D is the set of hours in which users are generally awake. We apply typical methodologies proper of Functional

Data Analysis [15] in order to detect common features and patterns among the places of the facility. We first embed data in a suitable space through a smoothing procedure. Then, we perform *functional k-means clustering* [16] detecting non-trivial and peculiar trends exhibiting some sort of time dependence (see Fig. 3), thus obtaining four clusters of places.

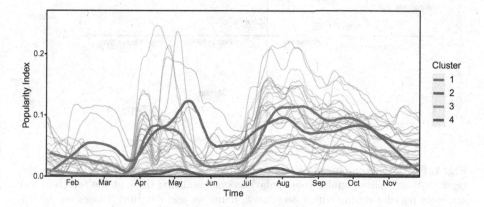

Fig. 3. Popularity Index plot and identified clusters of places

The thicker curves in the foreground, representing the identified clusters, are the main Popularity Index trends distinguished inside *Il Paese Ritrovato*: we observe which places are more frequented (clusters 1 and 2) and which are less popular (clusters 3 and 4). Places belonging to the different clusters are depicted in Fig. 4. Note that cluster 2 is generally more popular than cluster 1 during the first half of the year, while we may observe an opposite behavior in the second half; cluster 3 shows an increasing popularity in the second half of the observance period; cluster 4 is stable and represents those areas that are barely visited by the residents.

This procedure groups together places exhibiting a similar trend during the observation period. As a consequence, the metric introduced for clustering is blind towards constant shifts. More specifically, clusters 1 and 2 show higher curves, but only represent an average trend. Hence, places belonging to these clusters may be not so popular.

To enrich the aforementioned results, we perform a *functional principal component analysis* (FPCA) [17] detecting those features clustering may leave unseen. Through the first two principal components, obtained as perturbations with respect to the average curve, we are able to explain more than 80% of the total variance. The considered principal components are summarized through FPCA scores, preserving the respective component interpretation and resulting in a clearer graphical representation. The score of the first principal component captures the variance in the popularity of a place with respect to the average value for the whole observation period. Considering the two halves of the observation period, the score of the second principal component rewards a place for its popularity in the first half and penalizes it for its popularity in the second half.

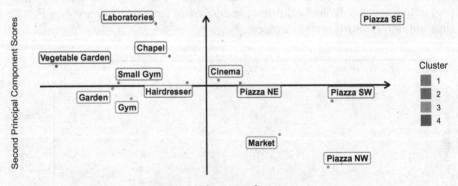

Fig. 4. Functional components scores scatter plot for public social places. Places on the right (left) are quite popular (unpopular) among residents; those at the top (bottom) are more popular during winter and spring (summer and autumn). Places on the left definitely need enhancements.

This analysis truly extends the results obtained through clustering, since we can observe strong coherence in the outcomes, constituting highly reliable and valid hypotheses for future interventions. Combining the results of the presented analyses, we can clearly identify neglected places in need of enhancements. For instance, the outdoor areas, namely the vegetable garden and the garden, are rarely frequented.

4.3 Accessibility and Neglected Spaces

Il Paese Ritrovato is a modern ensemble of buildings and does not present accessibility issues attributable to architectural barriers. The main spaces for community life in the village are located on the ground floor and are arranged in the center of the square to be easily identifiable and available to the residents. The two main outdoor locations of the village, the garden and the vegetable garden, are also easily accessible. However, these spaces cover peripheral areas of the village, being situated on the edges of the structure. This causes the residents to rarely spend time outside, as they usually do not pass by these open spaces unless it is their intention.

It would be desirable to make these areas more attractive, as gardens provide excellent sensory stimuli to the residents. Olfactory and auditory stimuli are extremely important for their mental health, since the associations between senses and memories are hardly affected by AD progression [18]. We therefore aim to work on intangible features of the external environment such as sounds, smells, lights, and climate to create therapeutic micro-habitats that provide tactile and sound stimuli, therefore improving residents wellbeing.

5   Conclusions and Future Work

In this work, we analyzed localization data to gather insights on the behavior of the residents of *Il Paese Ritrovato* to design solutions for the improvement of their social life and wellbeing. We extended the notion of Relational Index [14] to single individuals and investigated its statistical correlation with other variables by means of a *linear regression* and a χ^2 *independence test*, observing and explaining why it is influenced by all of them except for the weather. We also examined the popularity of different areas of the facility by leveraging *functional k-means clustering* and *functional principal component analysis*, identifying well-functioning social areas and those in need of enhancements, such as the outdoor places.

The insight obtained from the analysis performed on the Relational Index could be game-changing for caregivers and psychologists, contributing to the overall assessment of patients wellbeing. Monitoring the Relational Index trend identifying decays - indicating the patient is starting to isolate themselves - could also offer a precious hint to doctors on the disease progression, leading to the development of better personalized treatments. Moreover, comprehending the way both domain specific and domain agnostic variables influence socialization could be used to build advanced predictive tools for the estimation of the Relational Index over time. This measure can be also used to study the relationship between two specific patients, spotting recurring behavioral patterns and identifying best friendships.

Furthermore, we intend to combine the statistical and accessibility analyses of the social places of *Il Paese Ritrovato* to plan, propose and finally introduce new social activities, as well as spatial modifications to the village facilities, such as sensory maps. Once the activity revision and space redesign are carried out, we plan to evaluate them through further detailed analyses. For instance, as a graphical tool, we intend to design the social network of the village where the connection between two residents depends on their Relational Index. This will serve to observe the formation of social clusters and analyze their change over time.

Finally, we plan to implement a dynamic social activities scheduler aimed to promote active aging through the daily proposal of new engaging activities, including physical ones to exploit their positive effects [19], tailored to the preferences of residents, as described by Costa et al. [20], in a user-centered perspective.

References

1. World Population Ageing 2019. Technical report, Department of Economic and Social Affairs, United Nations (2019)
2. Dementia, World Health Organization. https://www.who.int/news-room/fact-sheets/detail/dementia. Accessed 15 Apr 2020
3. Ya-Hsin Hsiao, C.H.C., Gean, P.W.: Impact of social relationships on Alzheimer's memory impairment: mechanistic studies. J. Biomed. Sci. **25**(3) (2018). https://doi.org/10.1186/s12929-018-0404-x

4. Mace, N.L.: Principles of activities for persons with dementia. Phys. Occup. Ther. Geriatr. **5**(3), 13–28 (1987). https://doi.org/10.1080/J148v05n03_03
5. Barnes, L.L., Mendes de Leon, C.F., Wilson, R.S., Bienias, J.L., Evans, D.A.: Social resources and cognitive decline in a population of older African Americans and whites. Neurology **63**(12), 2322–2326 (2004). https://doi.org/10.1212/01.WNL.0000147473.04043.B3
6. Wilson, R.S., et al.: Loneliness and risk of Alzheimer disease. Arch. Gen. Psychiatry **64**(2), 234–240 (2007). https://doi.org/10.1001/archpsyc.64.2.234
7. Liesl Van Hecke, I.V.S., Heylighen, A.: How enclosure and spatial organization affect residents' use and experience of a dementia special care unit: a case study. Health Environ. Res. Des. J. **12**, 1–15 (2018)
8. Ferdous, F., Moore, K.D.: Field observations into the environmental soul: spatial configuration and social life for people experiencing dementia. Am. J. Alzheimer's Dis. Other Dement.® **30**(2), 209–218 (2015)
9. Biamonti, A.: Design & Alzheimer: Dalle esperienze degli Habitat Terapeutici al modello GRACE. Serie di architettura e design, Franco Angeli Edizioni (2018)
10. Blackman, T., et al.: The accessibility of public spaces for people with dementia: a new priority for the 'open city'. Disabil. Soc. **18**(3), 357–371 (2003)
11. Il Paese Ritrovato. https://ilpaeseritrovato.it. Accessed 15 Apr 2020
12. Cooperativa La Meridiana. https://cooplameridiana.it. Accessed 15 Apr 2020
13. Alzheimer's Association: Stages of Alzheimer's. https://www.alz.org/alzheimers-dementia/stages. Accessed 15 Apr 2020
14. Masciadri, A., Comai, S., Salice, F.: Wellness assessment of Alzheimer's patients in an instrumented health-care facility. Sensors **19**(17), 36–58 (2019). https://doi.org/10.3390/s19173658
15. Ramsay, J., Silverman, B.: Functional Data Analysis. Springer, New York (2005). https://doi.org/10.1007/b98888
16. Sangalli, L.M., Secchi, P., Vantini, S., Vitelli, V.: K-mean alignment for curve clustering. Comput. Stat. Data Anal. **54**(5), 1219–1233 (2010). https://doi.org/10.1016/j.csda.2009.12.008
17. Pearson, K.: On lines and planes of closest fit to systems of points in space. Phil. Mag. **2**(11), 559–572 (1901). https://doi.org/10.1080/14786440109462720
18. Valla, P.: Alzheimer: architetture e giardini come strumento terapeutico. Guerini e Associati (2002). https://books.google.it/books?id=i5RQAAAAMAAJ
19. Vernooij-Dassen, M., Vasse, E., Zuidema, S., Cohen-Mansfield, J., Moyle, W.: Psychosocial interventions for dementia patients in long-term care. Int. Psychogeriatr. **22**, 1121–1128 (2010)
20. Costa, A., Rincon, J.A., Carrascosa, C., Novais, P., Julian, V.: Activities suggestion based on emotions in AAL environments. Artif. Intell. Med. **86**(3), 9–19 (2018). https://doi.org/10.1016/j.artmed.2018.01.002

Predicting Wheelchair Stability While Crossing a Curb Using RGB-Depth Vision

Aryan Naveen, Haitao Luo, Zhimin Chen, and Bing Li[(✉)]

Department of Automotive Engineering, Clemson University,
4 Research Dr., Greenville, SC 29607, USA
bli4@clemson.edu

Abstract. Handicapped individuals often rely heavily on various assistive technologies including wheelchairs and the purpose of these technologies is to enable greater levels of independence for the user. In the development of autonomous wheelchairs, it is imperative that the wheelchair maintains appropriate stability for the user in an outdoor urban environment. This paper proposes an RGB-Depth based perception algorithm for 3D mapping of the environment in addition to dynamic modeling of the wheelchair for stability analysis and prediction. We utilize RTAB Mapping in combination with Poisson Reconstruction that produced triangular mesh from which an accurate prediction of the stability of the wheelchair can be made based on the normals and the critical angle calculated from the dynamic model of the wheelchair.

Keywords: Wheelchair stability · Dynamics model · Computer vision · SLAM · Mesh generation · 3D reconstruction

1 Introduction

Individuals with cognitive, motor or sensory impairment, whether it is due to disability or disease, often rely heavily on wheelchairs. As of 2015, there were 2.7 million wheelchair users in the United States [3]. Autonomous wheelchairs have the ability to enable a higher level of independence for handicapped individuals, however the margin for error is small. Maintaining wheelchair stability goes a long way in preventing injuries to the user. This requirement-while traversing a dynamic outdoor urban environment- is extremely important and there are a wide array of terrains that an autonomous wheelchair must handle and ensure stability for the user.

In addition to avoiding obstacles, the terrain in many scenarios can pose hazards as they can cause orientations of a wheelchair that results in rollover. Essentially, in order to effectively accomplish this task of ensuring stability for the wheelchair the system must have a high level understanding of the surrounding terrain. Of course this presents numerous challenges that must be accounted

© Springer Nature Switzerland AG 2020
K. Miesenberger et al. (Eds.): ICCHP 2020, LNCS 12377, pp. 394–401, 2020.
https://doi.org/10.1007/978-3-030-58805-2_47

for in order to develop a robust solution for stability prediction of an autonomous wheelchair. The first main challenge is understanding and mapping the environment accurately despite high levels of data noise. Multiple research works have focused on building different 3D maps of a given environment with different information for the wheelchair. Murakara et. al analyzed the integration of vision and laser range finders to construct a 2 dimensional indoor safety map for a wheelchair [5]. Furthermore, Zhao et. al implemented a graph based SLAM approach for building a grid point cloud semantic map for indoor navigation of an autonomous wheelchair [7].

Another challenge is understanding the environment-wheelchair interaction. The parameters of the terrain needed for an unstable configuration (coefficient of friction and gradient) must be determined in terms of wheelchair parameters. In addition, modeling has been performed to account for various types of suspensions, chassises, and drive systems [4,6]. In our case we treat the wheelchair as a rigid body and do not need to account for these factors as wheelchairs use simple differential drive without any suspension thereby simplifying the model. Furthermore, specific to wheelchairs, Candiotti et. al perform stability analysis with their novel electric power wheelchair, MEBot, based on analyzing the movement of the center of mass of the wheelchair [2].

This paper proposes an RGB-Depth based perception algorithm for 3D mapping of the environment in addition to dynamic modeling of the wheelchair for stability analysis and prediction. We employ RTAB mapping- based on graph SLAM- to construct a three dimensional pointcloud of the terrain and then convert the pointcloud to triangular mesh using Poisson Reconstruction. We then use the normals from the triangular mesh along with the dynamic model of the wheelchair to predict the stability of the wheelchair.

2   Curb Mapping

2.1   3D Mapping and Pointcloud Generation

To solve the problem of building a 3D map of the "safety zone" we employed RTAB which uses graph based SLAM algorithm to construct a pointcloud as shown in Fig. 1. In graph based SLAM, the idea is to arrange the collected data in the form of a graph consisting of nodes and links. A node in the graph contains the pose of the sensor, x_i, and the raw data, D, at a specific time step t, while a link contains the measurement constraints w_t and v_t. The Maximum Likelihood Principle (MLE) is used to then optimize the graph. We implemented this algorithm through a ROS package with an IntelRealsense D435i stereo camera.

2.2   3D Mesh Generation

The goal of mesh generation is to ensure that the mesh conform to the geometric characteristics of the generated pointcloud. We decided to employ Poisson Surface Reconstruction [1], proposed by Kazhdan et. al, because it highly resilient to data noise which will surely be encountered in a generated 3D map from an outdoor environment.

The problem of computing the indicator function boils down to finding the scalar function X, indicator function, whose gradient best approximates a vector field V defined by the sample S. Given a solid M, whose boundaries is Γ_M, and a smoothing filter $F(q)$, where $F_p(q) = F(q - p)$, a vector field $\vec{V}(q)$ can be derived based on the input pointcloud S.

$$\vec{V}(q) = \sum_{s \in S} |\zeta_s| F_{s.p}(q) s.N \qquad (1)$$

Then the indicator function, X, can by applying the divergence operator to V because X laplacian is equal to the divergence of V.

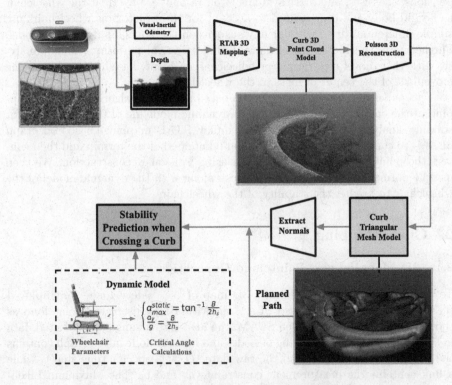

Fig. 1. 3D mapping and stability prediction pipeline

3   Dynamic Model of the Wheelchair Rollover Stability

The modeling process is based on the following assumptions: (1) the whole wheelchair is equivalent to rigid body, (2) the wheelchair is symmetrical with the middle plane of the wheels on both sides, and the center of mass lies on the middle plane, (3) the four-wheeled wheelchair model is equivalent to a two-wheeled model, where the two wheels in contact with the ground are equivalent to a longitudinal middle position, and the center of mass is located on this plane.

Figure 2 is a diagram of the wheelchair's static roll dynamics model. The following relationships between the forces at points A and C are given: $F_i + F_o = mg\cos(\alpha)$ and $F_{si} + F_{so} = mg\sin(\alpha)$. Using these relations, the net force on the inner tire, F_1, and on the outer tire, F_2, can be derived in relation to the wheelchair parameters, h_s and B, by simplying applying the lever rule.

$$\begin{cases} F_1 = (1 - \dfrac{B + (h_s \tan(\alpha) + \frac{B}{2})}{B})mg \\ F_2 = \dfrac{B - (h_s \tan(\alpha) + \frac{B}{2})}{B}mg \end{cases} \qquad (2)$$

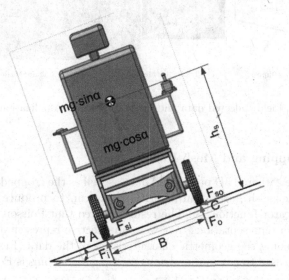

Fig. 2. Static model of wheelchair static rollover

Using the derived net forces for each tire, the conditions required for rollover in both a static and dynamic state can be calculated. In both situations when the wheelchair is at the critical rollover angle, the net force of the outer tire is 0. This condition is used to evaluate the maximum roll angle, a_{max}^{static}, and wheelchair dynamic rollover threshold, $\frac{a_y}{g}$.

$$\begin{cases} a_{max}^{static} = \tan^{-1}\dfrac{B}{2h_s} \\ \dfrac{a_y}{g} = \dfrac{B}{2h_s} \end{cases} \qquad (3)$$

The above relations are used to evaluate the wheelchair's anti rollover capability.

4   Experiment

For the data collection using the IntelRealsense D435i, we implemented the
SLAM based 3D mapping approach outlined above to construct maps of various
curb terrains. The maps generally consisted of 2 m of road or flat elevation
followed by some obstacle, approximately 1 m wide, and then another terrain
such as grass or a ramp for another 2 m to provide sufficient area for simulation
purposes. The maps were constructed on an intel core i7, running ROS kinetic on
Ubuntu 16.04. Visualization of the produced meshes from the proposed pipeline
compared to the RGB image of the obstacle can be seen in Fig. 3.

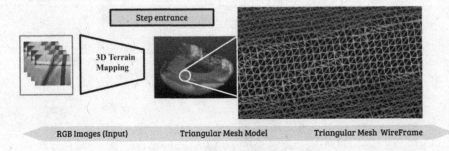

Fig. 3. Field collected data and mesh generation visualization results

4.1   3D Mapping and Mesh Result

From both the gathered 3D pointcloud data as well as the cropped 3D pointcloud
data the same mesh generation algorithm was run to produce the isosurface
from the indicator function, X. The results proved that Poisson reconstruction
produced mesh representations that were an effective representation for the 3D
map while keeping the geometric characteristics of the data (Fig. 1). The mesh
quality metric used to assess the various meshing algorithms is Edge Root Mean
Square (ERMS) as $ERMS_\mu = \frac{1}{N}\sum_{t\in\Lambda_t}\sqrt{\frac{t_{L1}^2+t_{L2}^2+t_{L3}^2}{3}}$ where Λ_T is the set of
all triangles that make up the different meshes, and t_{L1}, t_{L2}, t_{L3}, are the legs of
triangle $t \in \Lambda_t$. N is also the number of triangles in a given mesh.

Table 1 shows that the most optimal configuration for the mesh generation is Poisson Reconstruction after a subsample of $K = 0.7$, because Poisson
Reconstruction's time complexity is polynomial. Furthermore, the extremely low
ERMS for Poisson compared to the other methods demonstrates that the normal
vectors calculated from the triangular mesh will be more accurate which enables
better stability prediction.

4.2   Dynamic Simulation on Field Collected Data

Establish the dynamic model of the wheelchair in ADAMS as seen in Fig. 4.
Among the parameters of the wheelchair, the three-dimensional size of the

Table 1. Performance of mesh generation algorithms

Edge Root Mean Square			
K	0.5	0.7	0.9	0.97
Poisson Reconstruction — $O(m^3 log(m))$			
μ	0.00665	**0.00478**	0.00413	0.00429
Alpha Shapes — $O(m^2)$			
μ	0.01596	0.01398	0.01268	0.01232
Delaunay Triangulation — $O(mlog(m))$			
μ	0.02621	0.02498	0.024193	0.02394

wheelchair (length $\times$ width $\times$ height) is 1000×710 mm $\times 1320$ mm, the wheelbase B is 650 mm, the wheelbase L is 575 mm, and the wheelchair's distance to the mass centroid from the ground h_s is 451 mm. Taking into account the user's weight in the dynamic model of the wheelchair, the mass of the system now includes both the wheelchair's mass(65 kg) and the mass of the user (100 kg), producing a total mass (m) of 165 kg. The four tire specifications of the wheelchair are 205/55 R16, this tire model uses magic formulas and is suitable for wheelchair roll stability analysis. Import field collected terrain data as ".rdf" file into ADAMS to generate 3D road simulation model as seen in Fig. 4.

(a) Lateral sliding   (b) Roll over

Fig. 4. Wheelchairs simulation in ADAMS on field collected data

The variations in both the acceleration as well as the posture angle as shown in Fig. 5 demonstrate the anti-tipping characteristic of the wheelchair in the simulated environment. Both charts have similar trends in the sense that while driving over the initial flat road the values were relatively steady compared to the fluctuations caused by traversing the curb as well as the rugged terrain behind the curb.

Figure 4 also shows two kinds of unstable status of wheelchair when simulated in ADAMS, Fig. 4 (a) is the lateral sliding statue and Fig. 4 (b) is the rollover status. From Table 2, the critical rollover angle increases with increasing terrain coefficient of friction. When the terrain friction coefficient is less than 0.6, the unstable state of the wheelchair is represented by lateral sliding, otherwise it is

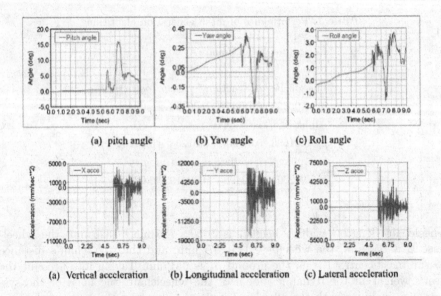

(a) pitch angle   (b) Yaw angle   (c) Roll angle

(a) Vertical acceleration   (b) Longitudinal acceleration   (c) Lateral acceleration

Fig. 5. Stability analysis results from ADAMs simulation

rollover. In addition, the terrain rollover angle of 25° is the dividing line between roll and sliding, and the friction coefficient of the corresponding terrain is 0.6. When the coefficient of terrain friction is greater than 0.6, the roll angle of the wheelchair fluctuates around 25° with little change.

Table 2. Wheelchair critical rollover stability w.r.t. terrain friction coefficients

No	Coefficient of friction of terrain	Critical rollover angle (°)	Unstable state
1	0.2	8.2	Sliding
2	0.4	18.2	Sliding
3	0.6	22.8	Sliding
4	0.8	25.2	Rollover
5	1.0	25.8	Rollover
6	1.2	26.2	Rollover
7	1.4	26.5	Rollover

5 Conclusion

In this paper we have proposed a robust pipeline for 3D mapping of terrain for autonomous wheelchairs. In addition, we also developed a dynamic model for a wheelchair to be used for stability analysis and prediction. We utilize RTAB Mapping in combination with Poisson Reconstruction to produce triangular mesh (Fig. 3) from which normals can be extracted to enable stability predictions. An area of improvement in our work is the time complexity of the mesh generation algorithm. Although, poisson reconstruction was selected due to it's distinct characteristic of being resistant to data noise, it presents a poor time complexity that in this paper was dealt with by simply subsampling the 3D pointcloud. Also another interesting area to investigate is the influence of other terramechanical properties of terrain on stability of wheelchairs. In the future, the big picture plan for this work is to be integrated into a comprehensive autonomous wheelchair to help enable greater independence/mobility for a population that is handicapped.

References

1. Bolitho, M., Kazhdan, M., Burns, R., Hoppe, H.: Parallel poisson surface reconstruction. In: Bebis, G., Boyle, R., Parvin, B., Koracin, D., Kuno, Y., Wang, J., Wang, J.-X., Wang, J., Pajarola, R., Lindstrom, P., Hinkenjann, A., Encarnação, M.L., Silva, C., Coming, D. (eds.) ISVC 2009. LNCS, vol. 5875, pp. 678–689. Springer, Heidelberg (2009). https://doi.org/10.1007/978-3-642-10331-5_63
2. Candiotti, J., et al.: Kinematics and stability analysis of a novel power wheelchair when traversing architectural barriers. Top. Spinal Cord Inj. Rehabil. 23(2), 110–119 (2017). https://doi.org/10.1310/sci2302-110
3. Koontz, A.M., et al.: Wheeled mobility. BioMed research international (2015). https://doi.org/10.1155/2015/138176
4. Levesley, M., Kember, S., Barton, D., Brooks, P., Querin, O.: Dynamic simulation of vehicle suspension systems for durability analysis. In: Materials Science Forum - MATER SCI FORUM, vol. 440–441, pp. 103–110 (01 2003). https://doi.org/10.4028/www.scientific.net/MSF.440-441.103
5. Murarka, A., Modayil, J., Kuipers, B.: Building local safety maps for a wheelchair robot using vision and lasers. In: The 3rd Canadian Conference on Computer and Robot Vision (CRV06) (2006). https://doi.org/10.1109/crv.2006.20
6. Schofield, B., Hagglund, T., Rantzer, A.: Vehicle dynamics control and controller allocation for rollover prevention. In: 2006 IEEE International Conference on Control Applications (2006). https://doi.org/10.1109/cca.2006.285884
7. Zhao, C., Hu, H., Gu, D.: Building a grid-point cloud-semantic map based on graph for the navigation of intelligent wheelchair. In: 2015 21st International Conference on Automation and Computing (ICAC) (2015). https://doi.org/10.1109/iconac.2015.7313995

Gait Patterns Monitoring Using Instrumented Forearm Crutches

Marien Narváez[✉][iD] and Joan Aranda[iD]

Department of Automatic Control (ESAII), Polytechnic University of Catalonia,
Barcelona, Spain
marien.cristina.narvaez@upc.edu

Abstract. Crutches are one of the most common assistive devices used in rehabilitation for lower limbs. Improper use of them results in extended recovery periods and even cause damage and pain to the limb. Many existing studies demonstrated that correctly using crutches requires an understanding of the disability or injury of the patient, gait patterns as well as user and crutch interaction during rehabilitation. In this work, a prototype was developed to monitor in real-time the exerted axial force and the tilt angles involved in each gait cycle at a prescribed gait pattern. The prototype is composed for an instrumented forearm crutch with a wireless measurement system. Four gait patterns were tested experimentally in three healthy users. Promising results were obtained that induces the possibility to identify automatically the performed pattern and even typical errors while using forearm crutches. The proposed system opens up a valid alternative to individualize therapy by monitoring the user gait using crutches in the rehabilitation process.

Keywords: Assistive tecnologies · Forearm crutches · Crutch gait · Gait monitoring · Instrumented crutch

1 Introduction

Forearm crutches or elbow crutches are assistive devices designed to help individuals walk with reduced Weight-Bearing (WB) on the affected lower extremity. These devices also have the function to improve balance, to assist the propulsion, to reduce the compressive force on one or both lower limbs and can help relieve pain in the affected limb [6,7].

Sensorized devices can provide objective and quantitative data to adapt the therapy to the patient, to monitor the daily activities, and to assess the recovery status of the user. It is significantly recognized that the improper use of crutches may lengthen the rehabilitation period or even cause further damage [6,9,11]. In general, this problem can be tackled by using instrumented crutches to monitor the involved parameters during the gait. For instance, the axial force allows knowing the support needs of the patient and also, the crutch motion represents relevant information for the therapist to define the gait performance.

The original version of this chapter was revised: the chapter was changed to non-open access. The correction to this chapter is available at https://doi.org/10.1007/978-3-030-58805-2_58

K. Miesenberger et al. (Eds.): ICCHP 2020, LNCS 12377, pp. 402–410, 2020.
https://doi.org/10.1007/978-3-030-58805-2_48

Consequently, the monitoring of these variables can instruct the user into the correct use of the crutches during recovery, and avoid other injuries or even a painful experience due to the wrong use of the device.

Walking with any assistive device modifies the gait pattern. Hence, different structures for walking with crutches are pre-established according to specific patient requirements. The literature review shows different prototypes and systems [2,4,5,8,9] with the purpose of analyzing involved variables in walking with crutches. However, these research projects do not present enough information about monitoring the different gait patterns. In order to monitor the behavior of the applied force and the tilt angles into a gait pattern, a system with low cost-sensors was developed and installed on a forearm crutch [9]. The present paper shows the results of monitoring parameters of four gait patterns and the choosed descriptors for the gaits. Moreover, it presents the discussion of the obtained data and possible future works.

2   Gait Training Using Crutches

There are diverse ways to walk with crutches that depend on a specific injury or disability [1,12,13]. Gait patterns rely on the user's ability to move the feet reciprocally, tolerate full load on each leg, lift the body off the floor by extending the elbows and pressing on the hands, and maintain balance [6]. The structure of gait patterns is defined according to different parameters, including the delay between the crutch and foot placement, the number of points in contact with the ground, and the laterality [1]. In this context, the points indicate the number of floor contacts on a perpendicular line to the direction of walking in one gait cycle, as shown in Fig. 1. Determining which gait is more beneficial depends on

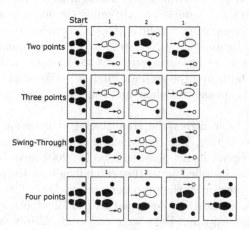

Fig. 1. Sequence of gait patterns using forearm crutches. Shaded areas represent WB, numbers show the time frame in the sequence of the gait, when ground contacts land synchronously. Arrows indicate the advance of the foot or the crutch. Modified of [1,3]

the lower-limb strength of the user and the impaired side. For example, Four-point gait is the slowest and the most stable pattern and two-point gait, that is similar to regular gait pattern, is the second slowest gait pattern [12]. During Swing-Through gait, the user lands and pivots over a crutch, repeated and acute stresses of crutch hand/arm support go through the user's wrist, elbow, and shoulder joints [11], noticeably the energy cost of this pattern is the highest.

Conforming to the literature, a study of crutch gait requires the incorporation of variables to measure the human performance (physical or psychological responses), and dynamic aspects of crutch locomotion during walking. In line with the dynamic parameters, walking with crutches implies the study of the applied forces to the upper limbs, which carry the body during the gait cycle, as well as kinematic measurements. Gait crutch walking includes an understanding of gait variables additionally: angles, displacement, cycle times, phase ratio, step length, cadence velocity and acceleration, as cited in [1,7].

The exerted force, crutch angles and the relationship between the phases within the walking cycle are essential parameters, in order to examine the crutch walk behaviour under prescribed gait patterns. Measurements of time, such a contact time can indicate a gait pattern change. Joint angles show the trajectory of the crutch during walking and phase ratio, or swing/stance ratio compares the relative percentage of each stance or swing portion during one step.

3 Methods

3.1 Instrumented Crutch Description

The prototype consists of one crutch and a wireless measurement system. The axial force applied for the user is sensorized, employing strain gauges. The sensors were integrated and connected in bridge configuration inside the handle of the crutch. The signals pass through a conditioning circuit, consisting of a low pass filter and an instrumentation amplifier (INA 126). Also, the orientation of the crutch is measured by using the BNO080 Inertial Measurement Unit (IMU). Tilt angles (pitch and roll) estimations were sent to the microcontroller. The angles are relative to the body and the ground. Pitch (θ) is the angle between a crutch, and the vertical axis in sagittal plane and roll (ϕ) is the angle with the ground in the frontal plane.

The microcontroller drives the conditioning, conversion and the wireless transmission of the signals. The components, as mentioned earlier, were assembled on a printed circuit board powered by a 5v, 2600 mAh battery. The entire circuit is inside a box installed under the crutch handle on the outer side. Figure 2 depicts the block diagram of the proposed system. [1].   The central processing unit consists of a standard PC equipped with a Bluetooth receiver to process and record data in real-time. Data were collected, with a sampling frequency of 75 Hz. The magnitude of the force and the tilt angles were calibrated and measured, based on z-$axis$ and x-$axis$ as seen in Fig. 2 a. By multiple tests and electronic and programming adjustments, the data show good repeatability and linearity in the force measurement.

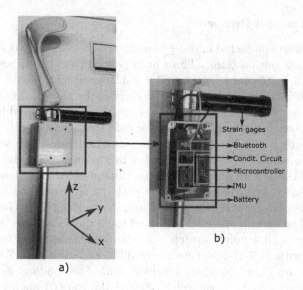

Fig. 2. Instrumented crutch with components. a) Installed circuit on the crutch and reference axes. b) Circuit board with the main components

3.2   Data Processing

After each experiment, the obtained data from IMUs were filtered with a ten-point moving average filter to attenuate the dynamic accelerations. The signal force was smoothed using a Gaussian filter to reduce the effect of noise. As discussed in previous literature, the movement of the crutch can be divided into the Swing and Stance phases [1,11,13]. This segmentation was performed for each gait cycle in order to know the appropriate descriptors for each defined pattern. Segmentation was performed by analyzing the pitch angle signal (after observation and several qualitative and quantitative analyzes of the signal). It was considered that from the lowest position of the angle to the maximum point reached by the crutch, the movement is in the swing phase. When the angle lowers to its lowest position, the stance phase ends. This entire movement corresponds to a walking cycle.

According to the aim of this work, attention was focussed in vertical forces, pitch and roll angle, and swing and stance phases. Data was summarized finding mean, median and standard deviation for the data of interest. Finally, the descriptors of each pattern were estimated according to force and temporal parameters: time and force intervals for swing and stance phases, maximum force during a cycle and ratios of force and time between the phases. All the data was validated using an RGBD camera that allowed to support the validity and relevance of the data.

3.3   Experimental Protocol

Experiments were conducted in order to monitor and to indetify the behaviour of four crutch walk gait patterns . Three healthy volunteers (mean age ± standard deviation, 27.3 ± 2.5 years; height, 160.4 ± 4.2 cm; weight, 55.3 ± 7.02 kg) participated of this study. Due to the homogeneity of the participants in the experiment, we did not consider it necessary to normalize the measured force. None of the users had any orthopedic condition, or pain that could modify their natural walking patterns, besides none of them ever used crutches. They were instructed and trained to handle the forearm crutches in a proper mode and walk in each gait pattern. Users were asked to use the instrumented crutch with the right arm and to watch four videos where the patterns are explained by phyosioterapists. Besides, the experiments were planned according to a Guide [10] and the (Fig. 1). The participans were requested to do the tests three times for three minutes. From 2 to 4 points crutch gait, the users were asked to perform the experiments with Full-Weight-Bearing (FWB), and with Non-Weight-Bearing (NWB)for Swing-Through, which means a single foot landing. Force data was collected concurrently with the pitch (θ) and the roll (ϕ) angles into the gait cycle. The software contains an algorithm to self-calibrating both sensors after each trial.

4   Results

As pictured in Fig. 3, there are notable differences between each gait pattern tested. In 2-Points for one gait cycle, the maximum force applied for the user happens when the crutch starts to go down until it hits the ground (stance phase). That is when (θ) reaches the minimum value, correspondingly with frame 1 in the sequence in 1. Subsequently, when the left crutch leaves the ground and land on the opposite side, then (θ) is at its maximum (swing phase). The gait cycle repeats throughout the gait. Larger peak forces and bigger motions at angles in the Swing-Through gait compared with 2-Points, 3-Points and 4-Points. The 4-Points pattern is the slowest in its execution since it involves the movement of lower and upper extremities. The appreciable variations in ϕ angle are due to the movements that the user makes to position the crutch and also the dynamic accelerations.

The results in Table 1 show the summarized data of the ratios of time and force for Swing/Stance phases, in conjunction with the mean and standard deviation of the maximum force during a gait cycle. Smaller values (close to zero) in Swing-Stance time ratio means that more time is spent in the swing phase, while values close or greater than one means that the most extended phase is the stance. Otherwise, smaller values (close to zero) in Swing-Stance force ratio, means that greater force is applied in the stance phase. Therefore, the force values in the swing phase are not relevant. Values close to one or greater than one implies that the force was applied significantly in the swing phase. In general, the time ratios for 2 and 3 points showed significant differences concerning the 4 points and Swing-Through gait. For 4 points and Swing-Through, the time

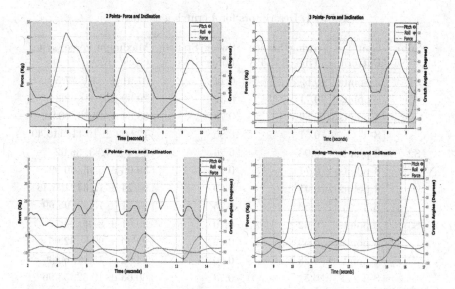

Fig. 3. Crutch angles and force measurements for four gait patterns. The blue line represents the axial force applied over the crutch in the gait cycle. The red line indicates the inclination (pitch angle) and the dotted green line indicates the roll angle. The shaded intervals represent the swing phase. (Color figure online)

during stance phase is higher than time for 2 and 3 points gait. Moreover, the values of the ratio force for 2 and 3 points gait are lower than 4 points and Swing-Through. For 4 points and Swing-Through patterns, the force is applied during the two phases, although it continues the largest in the stance phase. The maximum forces reached inside a cycle were 122.02 Kg ± 16.1 for Swing-Trough gait and 94.24 Kg for 4 points. The smaller values were obtained during 2 and 3 points patterns (29.01 Kg ± 8.03 and 29,89± 9.41).

5   Discussion

This study provides the results of monitoring four gait patterns with crutches and their relationship with the chosen descriptors. We hypothetically considered that the measured data could be segmented in the swing and stance phases and thus find descriptors that would automatically identify each gait pattern. However, the segmentation was carried out using the pitch angle and not the force, as proposed [4,5]. With this approach, we obtained satisfactory results within each phase, and that allowed us to make the distinction we wanted to explore. In this work, the obtained force and angles values remained similar in proportion to the results of the studies mentioned above, and the difference is mostly statistical. Interesting details came out when we considered the individual data of each pattern Table 1. It is clear that for Swing-Trough is required more force from the upper extremity to perform the movement and maintain the

Table 1. Descriptors for 4 crutch gait patterns.

Subj	Gait Pattern	Swing/Stance Time Ratio	Swing/Stance Force Ratio	Maximum Force Gait Cycle (Kg)
S1	2 points	0.69	0.14	37.91 ± 5.61; 37.56
	3 points	0.71	0.32	29.89 ± 9.41; 32.34
	4 points	0.59	0.73	68.84 ± 13.68; 60.94
	S-T	0.51	0.85	122.02 ± 16.11; 119.49
S2	2 points	0.96	0.26	34.4 ± 7.83; 36.62
	3 points	0.77	0.36	39.06 ± 5.13; 40.99
	4 points	0.41	0.69	94.24 ± 19.34; 105.48
	S-T	0.59	0.75	97.71 ± 16.89; 95.69
S3	2 points	0.62	0.10	29.01 ± 8.03; 29.77
	3 points	0.69	0.32	29.09 ± 9.58; 32.05
	4 points	0.38	0.60	54.02 ± 15.42; 60.30
	S-T	0.51	0.73	60.63 ± 19.52; 53.96

Notes: The descriptors are indexed as mean ±; median for each gait pattern for 3 subjects. S-T corresponds to Swing-Through gait.

balance. The crutches propel the body forward while the legs are swung to past them. For all the subjects Maximum forces were obtained in this pattern. The graph for 4-Points pattern and the collected data suggest that the segmentation should include more gait phases due to the four movements to complete a cycle, as can be seen in Fig. 3 the beginning of each action in the sequence cannot be precisely identified from the graph. Even though the participants (healthy people) in the experiment were instructed on how walking with the crutches in each gait pattern, it is necessary to carry out experiments with patients with injuries, to a better understanding of the association among the parameters and the tested patterns.

6   Conclusions and Future Works

One of the primary motivation of this work is the individualization of rehabilitation therapies for gait recovery, through the monitoring of the parameters involved in the gait with crutches. Instrumented crutches for gait monitoring are a convenient tool to know the recovery status of the patient in rehabilitation. This work presented the development of a system to measure the force and the position of the crutch with acceptable accuracy within an indoor environment, and also the results of monitoring four gait patterns. According to data in the table and the graph, it is possible to observe the pre-established sequence for the users and to identify the executed pattern. In this way, therapists could use this data to determine the patient's performance taking into account the prescribed WB and the pattern. The gait patterns need to match with physical capabilities and specific characteristics of the user. Further research on this topic will investigate the relation between the WB and each one of the gait patterns and the forces through the affected limbs. Besides, the gait patterns could be classified using the descriptors mentioned above while the user walks with the crutches, ergo online. Future works could investigate too the correlation between gait patterns and injuries or particular conditions. Disabilities affect gait parameters differently. Being the applied force to the crutch is a critical parameter, it is necessary for future experiments to provide a system with biofeedback for the user. So the user will have better learning and understanding of gait patterns during training.

References

1. Rasouli, F., Reed, K.B.: Walking assistance using crutches: a state of the art review. J. Biomech. **98**, 109489 (2020)
2. Acosta L, M., Frigola Bourlon, M.: iMuleta : Muletas sensorizadas para la detección del paso. Trabajo de Fin de Máster. Universitat Politécnica de Catalunya (2019)
3. Musculoskeletal Disorders. https://nursekey.com/musculoskeletal-disorders/. Accessed 24 Mar 2020
4. Merrett, G.V., Ettabib, M.A., Peters, C., Hallett, G., White, N.M.: Augmenting forearm crutches with wireless sensors for lower limb rehabilitation. Meas. Sci. Technol. **21**(12), 124008 (2010)
5. Sesar, I., Zubizarreta, A., Cabanes, I., Portillo, E., Torres-Unda, J., Rodriguez-Larrad, A.: Instrumented crutch tip for monitoring force and crutch pitch angle. Sensors **19**(13), 2944 (2019)
6. Edelstein, J.: 36 - canes, crutches, and walkers. In: Atlas of Orthoses and Assistive Devices, 5th Edn. Elsevier Inc. (2019)
7. Li, S., Armstrong, C.W., Cipriani, D.: Three-point gait crutch walking: variability in ground reaction force during weight bearing. Arch. Phys. Med. Rehabil. **82**(1), 86–92 (2001)
8. Chen, Y. F., Napoli, D., Agrawal, S. K., Zanotto, D.: Smart crutches: towards instrumented crutches for rehabilitation and exoskeletons-assisted walking. In: Proceedings of the IEEE RAS and EMBS International Conference on Biomedical Robotics and Biomechatronics (2018)
9. Sardini, E., Serpelloni, M., Lancini, M.: Wireless instrumented crutches for force and movement measurements for gait monitoring. IEEE Trans. Instrum. Meas. **64**(12), 3369–3379 (2015)
10. Oxford University Hospitals NHS Trust. Using Elbow Crutches Instruction for patients (2015)
11. Capecci, D., Kim, S.H., Reed, K.B., Handzic, I.: Crutch tip for swing-through crutch walking control based on a kinetic shape. In: IEEE International Conference on Rehabilitation Robotics (ICORR), pp. 612–617 (2015)

12. Lee, J., et al.: Analysis of plantar foot pressure during the non- crutch, two-point, and four-point crutch gait. Gait and Posture **23**(3), 489–493 (2011)
13. Youdas, J.W., Kotajarvi, B.J., Padgett, D.J., Kaufman, K.R.: Partial weight-bearing gait using conventional assistive devices. Arch. Phys. Med. Rehabil. **86**(3), 394–398 (2005)

Personalized Arm Gesture Recognition Using the HMM-Based Signature Verification Engine

Jacek Szedel[✉] [iD]

Department of Algorithmics and Software, Silesian University of Technology,
Akademicka 16, 44-100 Gliwice, Poland
Jacek.Szedel@polsl.pl

Abstract. Gesture-based interfaces can significantly improve access to computer technologies for people with disabilities. However, the gestures of the disabled can be very unstable, which means that standard gesture recognition solutions may occur not applicable in this case. In this study, a personalized arm gesture recognition system is presented. It uses automatic handwritten signature verification (ASV) techniques which deal with the instability of human motion processes by default. The proposed gesture-based HCI framework involves the Microsoft Kinect sensor, the data acquisition module, and the formerly tested HMM offline signature verification engine. The evaluation process included intentional, non-intentional and randomly distorted gestures converted into images. The confusion matrices and receiver-operation characteristic (ROC) analysis were used to evaluate the accuracy of the system. The performed tests showed that the applied ASV software could effectively recognize unstable gestures, even when the evaluation set included both random and distorted gesture patterns.

Keywords: Gesture recognition · Motor disabilities ·
Human-Computer Interaction · Kinect · Hidden Markov Model ·
Offline signature verification

1 Introduction

Human gesture recognition is an important research direction in the area of human-computer interaction (HCI). The last two decades have been a period of particular progress in this field, which resulted in applications ranging from highly reliable control systems to those designed for entertainment purposes [10]. The growing availability of sensing devices and SDKs also provides an opportunity to improve access to computer technologies for impaired people. Gesture interfaces have already been reported to be a valuable tool to help in visual, speech and hearing, mobility, and general disabilities. Since many disabled people need an individual approach, and their gestures can be very unstable, the developed recognition tools should use personalized characteristics and cope with

© Springer Nature Switzerland AG 2020
K. Miesenberger et al. (Eds.): ICCHP 2020, LNCS 12377, pp. 411–420, 2020.
https://doi.org/10.1007/978-3-030-58805-2_49

their intra-personal variability at the same time. Additionally, to encode larger command sets, they should handle more complex patterns and structures. These properties are very common to the domain of handwriting recognition, and in particular, to the area of automatic signature verification (ASV). This issue has been a subject of intensive research for almost four decades. As the very satisfying results have been reported in many papers (and confirmed in competitions), researchers extend their scope of interest to other fields, including both medical and health applications [2,5,8]. Furthermore, ASV systems, or their selected components, may be utilized outside of their primary application area, with no direct relations to signatures. In other words, it is possible to use (or adapt) those systems to perform the classification of patterns other than handwriting. This approach may be associated with a variety of input devices, like external or wearable motion sensors. This association creates the possibility of developing new ASV based health and medical applications, as well as the applications supporting assistive technologies and the HCI solutions dedicated to people with disabilities.

The following work addresses the last of the aspects mentioned above. The goal is to create a gesture recognition interface which uses the already implemented and tested signature verification engine as a classifier. The engine is based on the Hidden Markov Model (HMM), and it is the result of research conducted by the author for several years. The solution is still being developed and improved in its primary application range. Independently, the gesture recognition topic is now a subject of interest as a useful way of exploiting the already developed solutions. The system described in this paper uses Microsoft Kinect for the input. However, its architecture is open to other sources. It is destined to be an HCI tool for people with partial motor disabilities, as they are less able to perform stable gestures required by other solutions.

2   Related Work

2.1   Gesture Recognition for General Purposes

After years of sustained progress, gesture recognition is both extensive and manifold. Developed methods analyze positions and movements of different body parts, like face, arms, hands, fingers, or the whole body. Also, there are many input devices and acquisition methods, gesture types, interpretation levels, and application domains. This variety of categories generates a large number of possible configurations. Since it is impossible to pertain to all of them in the frame of this work, the remaining part contains references to the recent state-of-the-art papers directly related to arm posture and movement recognition, which is also an intensively researched topic. Zhang et al. [12] used elastic strain sensors and information fusion methods for arm and hand gesture recognition. The data acquisition device designed and applied in that study consists of a wearable glove and bands armed in several string sensors measuring the movements of shoulder joints, elbow joints, wrist joints, and metacarpophalangeal joints. Reported experiments concerned four aspects of human gesture analysis: arm/hand motion recognition, general gesture recognition, static hand gesture recognition, static and dynamic gesture recognition. A study by Zeng et al. [11] describes tracking arm movements using the radio frequency (RF) sensing and micro-Doppler (MD) signatures. Two machine learning techniques - dynamic time wrapping (DTW) and long short-term memory (LSTM) were applied in association with the neural network (NN) classifier. The gesture set included: pushing arms, pulling them back, crossing and opening arms, crossing arms, rolling arms, giving a stop sign, pushing and opening arms. The best accuracy was achieved for the DTW based NN classifier. Arm gesture recognition research also concerns less demanding and more pervasive acquisition devices like gaming sensors or smartwatches. For example, Paraskevopoulos et al. [4] applied several widely used classifiers for real-time arm gesture recognition based on 3D skeletal data captured by the Microsoft Kinect sensor. The input data were described by features extracting angles and displacements of skeleton joints. The authors introduced a testing protocol based on a dataset, including 820 gestures composed of four "swipes" of both hands (swipe up/down in/out). Shen [9] presented a method of arm posture inference using the inertial measurement unit (IMU) of a smartwatch. The author derived the relationship between wrist orientation and possible wrist/elbow locations based on observations from human kinematic. The inference procedure uses the hidden Markov model and the Viterbi algorithm.

2.2   Gesture Recognition and Disabilities

Gesture recognition and its applications are particularly important for the sake of supporting people with disabilities. There are many fields and ways that can turn out helpful in this context. One of the topics being researched for many years is recognition of the sign language: mainly with the view of removing barriers between the abled and the speech and hearing disabled. Raghuveera et al. [7] presented the Indian sign language recognition system using Microsoft Kinect depth data. In this approach, hands are segmented using the k-Mean clustering. The authors used the local binary pattern (LBP), the histogram of gradients (HOG) and speed-up robust features (SURF). The accuracies achieved by the system for all features were approximately equal. The sign language is a sophisticated communication method, and it can be cumbersome in some situations. Thus, there is a need for using less complex gesture sets. Priatama et al. [6] reported a system recognizing five gestures of a raised hand. The system uses the discrete wavelet transform (DWT) for feature extraction and the convolutional neural network (CNN) for classification. There are also hardware solutions with embedded software reported in recent papers. In [1], Ail et al. introduced a useful tool for the speech impaired, namely the hand gesture-based vocalizer. The developed system consists of a glove with flexible sensors attached to each finger, and a controller including voice synthesizer and the LCD. Gestures of the user's hand are associated with the corresponding commands that the device displays and vocalizes. Another crucial research area of applying gesture recognition for the benefits of impaired people is assistive technology. One of the researchers' goals is to exploit (or design) more comfortable sensors that produce meaningful signals even when the impairment restricts body movements. Esposito et al. [3] presented a new piezoresistive sensors array armband for hand movement recognition. The device is a band armed with three force-sensitive resistors (FSR). It is worn on the forearm. Raw voltage signals are pre-processed, segmented, and then the feature extraction is performed. The evaluation procedure considered eight hand gestures. Different machine learning techniques were applied, among others, the SVM with linear function basis. This classifier was finally implemented in a real-time PC controller.

3   The Proposed Approach

3.1   System Architecture

The implemented research environment consists of the standard Microsoft Kinect sensor and its software, the data acquisition (DA) module, and the automatic signature verification (ASV) engine; Fig. 1(a) depicts the overall system workflow and its architecture. The DA module is responsible for acquiring data, converting them into the desired format, and transferring them to other system components. It is designed to support different input data sources. For this particular configuration, only the Kinect skeletal data are under consideration; they are converted into the static form, namely into binary images.

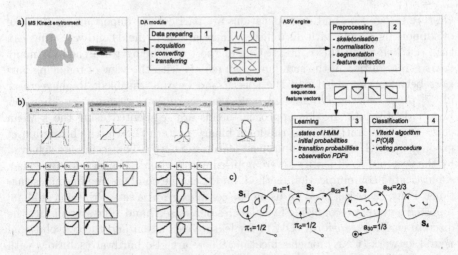

Fig. 1. The illustration of the proposed system: (a) - the architecture and the basic system workflow, (b) - examples of processed gestures and their corresponding models, (c) - the visualization of a sample model.

The second component of the presented environment is the HMM-based ASV engine. As mentioned earlier, the key idea is to exploit its abilities to cope with unstable and personalized patterns like handwritten signatures in terms of in-air gestures, in particular those performed by disabled people. The ASV engine is responsible for the machine learning part of the presented framework. This part consists of two processes: model learning and gesture classification. In the first scenario, the learning set of gestures is processed, then the parameters of HMMs are computed for each class of gestures. In the second scenario, the data of the gesture to be recognized are transferred to the engine. Then, the gesture is scored for all the models by calculating the probability $P(O|\lambda)$, so that the gesture in question, represented by the observation sequence O, can be generated by the model λ_k representing the k-th gesture class. The Viterbi algorithm is used for that purpose.

3.2   The ASV Engine

As mentioned above, the ASV engine pursues two scenarios: model learning and gesture classification. Both are preceded by the preprocessing stage, in the frame of which the images are skeletonized, normalized, and segmented. Finally, the feature extraction is performed. The first step aims at making the gesture lines one pixel wide. This feature is required for subsequent segmentation step using the line tracing algorithm. The iterative thinning algorithm is used for skeletonization. In the second step, the image normalization is performed. It involves only the translation of the image centroid into the image area center: it is assumed that the size and rotation are the important features of a gesture. The next step of the preprocessing stage is image segmentation. In this step, the lines of the skeleton are analyzed by a procedure through which endpoints, intersections, and crossings are found. The line tracing is performed from each of these points. The result of the tracing is the set of image segments. The segments are sorted in the order that they appear on the image. This produces the sequence of segments - Fig. 1(a). The last step of the preprocessing stage is feature extraction. Here, a set of ten geometrical features is extracted for all segments treating them as separate images.

The learning stage is performed for a set of labelled samples. For each gesture class, a few learning images have to be supported. They are sequentially processed, and their segments are classified using a clustering algorithm. When a new segment is being classified, its Euclidean distance to other clusters is checked. Each cluster has its hypersphere-shaped border. The segment is assigned to the closest cluster if its corresponding feature space point lies inside its border. Oppositely, a new cluster is created, and the segment in consideration is assigned to it. Each of the clusters formed this way is considered to be a state of the HMM. The order in which segments are assigned to the model states, and the number of segments assigned to each state determine values of the transition and initial probability matrices a_{ij} and π_i. The examples of segmented gestures and their models are shown in Fig. 1(b), a sample model is visualized on Fig. 1(c). Further, the observation distributions have to be computed. In the presented modelling strategy, the HMM observations are vectors of features extracted from subsequent segments of the signature. Thus, the observations are both continuous and multidimensional. To associate the model states with the observations, the procedure of estimating observation probability density functions was proposed. In this procedure, the initial, discrete distributions are calculated, concerning feature values observed in a particular state. Then, initial distributions are iteratively re-estimated by an appropriate smoothing algorithm. The iterative smoothing leads in effect to continuous density functions comparable to Gaussian mixtures.

In the classification stage, a sequence of segments from the gesture to be recognized is processed by the Viterbi algorithm. The most likely transition paths are reproduced for all gesture classes enrolled in the system. The probabilities of generating the sequence in question are computed along these paths. The class with the maximum probability is preliminarily selected as the one to be recognized. The additional reference set of learning samples is then used to evaluate the acceptance threshold. The voting procedure performed on the reference set determines whether or not the preliminarily selected class is finally recognized.

4   Evaluation and Results

The evaluation procedure considered the following main scenario: a set of gestures was recorded and learned by the system. Then, the gestures were presented to the participants. Finally, after preceding exercises, participants were asked to playback the gestures that had been shown to them. Two datasets of gestures were collected - A and B. The dataset A was recorded in the early stage of the project and used to verify currently developed functionality. It contains a total of 156 samples of six classes recorded by three persons. The subset of 96 of them was recorded intentionally (they are referred to as regular gestures), the remaining 60 are casual gestures. The dataset B was captured for final testing. It includes 600 regular and 100 casual gesture samples. They were recorded by three persons, the samples of whom were stored as separate databases (we refer to them as partitions). The example gestures that represent all classes from both datasets are shown in Figs. 2(a) and 2(b).

The evaluation included three experiments having different objectives. The first experiment was performed to determine the optimal number of learning samples per a single gesture class ($\#T$), the second to evaluate the general accuracy of the proposed framework, and the third to check how the system behaves when the original gestures are distorted by noise. A single experiment consisted of several series of tests. In each test, samples were selected randomly from learning and testing sets. In all experiments, the testing set contained 5 regular and 5 casual gestures, and it did not involve the samples used for learning. The set that was used to elaborate thresholds contained 3 images. In experiments two and three, regular as well as casual gesture scenarios were considered. In the first scenario, the testing set contained only intentionally recorded gestures; in the second, also casual gestures were included. When casual gestures were not considered, the general error rate (ER) was evaluated using only the maximum $P(O|\lambda)$ criterion (the threshold was only monitored). In the opposite case, system performance was assessed using the receiver operating

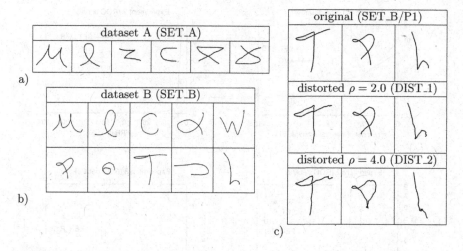

Fig. 2. The gesture samples used for testing: (a), (b) - examples from datasets A and B, (c) - examples of selected original gestures and their distorted versions (experiment 3).

characteristics (ROC) curves and the equal, or the average error rates (ERR, AER). Both the maximum $P(O|\lambda)$ and the threshold criterion were used.

As mentioned earlier, the objective of the first experiment was to establish the optimal number of learning samples per a single class of gestures ($\#T$). The experiment consisted of 5 series of tests (10 tests per series). A different value of $\#T$ was considered in each series, namely 6, 7, 8, 9, and 10. The experiment was performed separately for the dataset A and for one of the partitions of the dataset B (only one partition was used to simplify the procedure; the second experiment showed that the system achieves similar accuracy for all partitions, so it had no major influence on $\#T$). The results of experiment 1 are depicted in Fig. 3(a). The minimum error rates were achieved for $\#T = 9$ for both datasets (A and B/P1). The error rate for $\#T = 9$ ER $= 2.24\%$.

The second experiment was performed to evaluate the general accuracy of the proposed framework for both regular and casual gesture scenarios. It included 4 series of 10 tests. The first series of tests concerned the dataset A, and the remaining series applied to the individual partitions of the dataset B. The results of experiment 2 are summarized in Table 1. For the regular gesture scenario, the system achieved the accuracy of ER $= 2.84\%$. The accuracy for the casual gesture scenario was evaluated using the ROC analysis. The system computed the false rejection rates (FRR) and the false acceptance rates (FAR). In the context of the following work, the term "false acceptance" meant the recognition of a casual gesture, and the term "false rejection" referred to the situation when a regular gesture was not recognized. Figure 3(b) shows the ROC curve obtained in experiment 2, Fig. 3(c) presents the details of the analysis. The equal error rates (ERR) are marked with grey vertical lines; EER_REF is a line on which FRR equals FAR. The resulting EER for both datasets (A and B) is 4.71%.

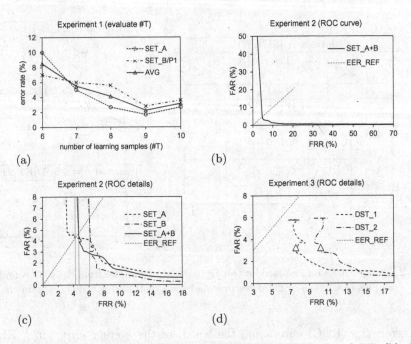

Fig. 3. The visualization of results: (a) - experiment 1: evaluation of $\#T$, (b), (c) - experiment 2: general system evaluation; the ROC curve and its details, (d) - experiment 3: system evaluation with distorted gestures; the ROC curve details.

The objective of the third experiment was to check the behavior of the system in the situation when it had to cope with unstable movements. To perform this part of the evaluation procedure, gestures were recorded not only as images but also as the sequences of 2D coordinates. A procedure that adds noise to these sequences and converts them into images - required by the ASV engine - was implemented. In this stage of the research, a simple Gaussian gesture floating formula was applied: for each point of the gesture (x_i, y_i), $x_i^* = x_i + \delta x_i$, $y_i^* = y_i + \delta y_i$, where $\delta x_1 = 0, \delta y_1 = 0, \delta x_{i+1} = \delta x_i + \mathcal{N}(0, \rho), \delta y_{i+1} = \delta y_i + \mathcal{N}(0, \rho), (x_i^*, y_i^*)$ are the distorted coordinates. The examples of the original gesture images and the relevant noised samples are presented in Fig. 2(c). The results were evaluated in the same fashion as in experiment 2. The partition P1 of the dataset B was used for tests. Two distortion levels were considered: DIST_1 ($\rho = 2.0$) and DIST_2 ($\rho = 4.0$). The error rate for the regular gesture scenario is 6.20%. The equal error rate was not applicable, because the FAR and FRR values in the function of the threshold coefficient did not cross, which demonstrated with the ROC curve not developed for the whole threshold coefficient range - Fig. 3(d). Instead, the minim average error rate AER_{min} was evaluated as the $min((FAR+FPR)/2)$ (triangle markers on ROC lines). The obtained AER_{min} = 5.87%, and the relevant FRR = 8.83%, FAR = 2.90%. The summary results are presented in the second part of Table 1.

Table 1. The summary results of experiment 2 and experiment 3.

Experiment 2		
	No casual gestures	With casual gestures
Dataset/partition	ER (%)	EER (%)
SET_A	1.67	4.27
SET_B	3.07	6.10
SET_A+B	2.84	4.71
Experiment 3		
Noise parameters	ER (%)	AER_{min} (FRR, FAR) (%)
DIST_1 $(\mu = 0.0, \rho = 2.0)$	5.80	5.22 (7,51, 2,94)
DIST_2 $(\mu = 0.0, \rho = 4.0)$	6.60	6.51 (10.16, 2.86)
AVG	6.20	5.87 (8.83, 2.90)

5   Conclusion and Future Work

The following work verified the ability to apply the automated signature verification technology for recognition of in-air arm gestures. It was shown that the ASV engine could recognize gesture patterns, also when the testing set included casual gestures that were not involved in the learning stage. Moreover, the proposed system was tested with gestures distorted by random noise, and the achieved accuracies remained satisfying. These features are highly desirable for computer-human interfaces designed with the view of increasing the accessibility of computer technologies for impaired people. Another important feature of the presented system is the fact that it does not require fixed gesture sets. This enables system personalization at the level of user-defined gestures relevant to his or her motor abilities. The system can also be personalized at the level of adjusting its parameters. This concerns both the parameters of the DA module and the ASV engine. The DA module parameters related to the gesture capturing process occurred particularly important. Thus, the users had to be involved in its development and customization process, which increased the final usability of the gesture capturing interface.

There are certainly some open challenges and problems to be resolved in the future. One of them is further adaptation of the ASV engine parameters and procedures to the specificity of the gesture recognition task. Several modifications have been made so far. The most crucial were the changes made in the characteristics of image segments to be less sensitive to line instability and to be more focused on the overall segment shape. The issue that has to be addressed in the future is also the modification of the HMM scaling procedure. At present, the results of the calculations are scaled to preserve the floating-point precision, because signature models have many states and require a large number of multiplications of small factors. The scaling procedure is vital in the case of signatures but not in the case of gestures which generate significantly smaller models, and thus it can have a negative influence on results. It is believed that appropriate adaptation of the scaling procedure should result in better performance and better receiver operator characteristics. The objective of future activities is also: to test the system for a broader group of participants, to perform real-time testing, to integrate the developed framework with the operating system in the layer of controlling applications, and to implement interfaces for other sensors capable of acquiring gesture-like activities (like eye-tracking and touch devices).

The software environment created in this work is an essential part of the ongoing research on the interface destined to control the operating system by people with partial motor disabilities. The research is co-financed by SUT grant for maintaining and developing research potential.

References

1. Ail, S., Chauhan, B., Dabhi, H., Darji, V., Bandi, Y.: Hand gesture-based vocalizer for the speech impaired. In: Vasudevan, H., Gajic, Z., Deshmukh, A.A. (eds.) Proceedings of International Conference on Wireless Communication. LNDECT, vol. 36, pp. 585–592. Springer, Singapore (2020). https://doi.org/10.1007/978-981-15-1002-1_59
2. Diaz, M., Ferrer, M., Impedovo, D., Malik, M., Pirlo, G., Plamondon, R.: A perspective analysis of handwritten signature technology. ACM Comput. Surv. **51**(5), 117 (2018)
3. Esposito, D., et al.: A piezoresistive array armband with reduced number of sensors for hand gesture recognition. Front. Neurorobotics **13**, 114 (2020)
4. Paraskevopoulos, G., Spyrou, E., Sgouropoulos, D., Giannakopoulos, T., Mylonas, P.: Real-time arm gesture recognition using 3D skeleton joint data. Algorithms **12**(5), 108 (2019)
5. Pirlo, G., Diaz, M., Ferrer, M.A., Impedovo, D., Occhionero, F., Zurlo, U.: Early diagnosis of neurodegenerative diseases by handwritten signature analysis. In: Murino, V., Puppo, E., Sona, D., Cristani, M., Sansone, C. (eds.) ICIAP 2015. LNCS, vol. 9281, pp. 290–297. Springer, Cham (2015). https://doi.org/10.1007/978-3-319-23222-5_36
6. Priatama, M.B., Novamizanti, L., Aulia, S., Candrasari, E.B.: Hand gesture recognition using discrete wavelet transform and convolutional neural network. Bull. Electr. Eng. Inform. **9**(3), 996–1004 (2020)
7. Raghuveera, T., Deepthi, R., Mangalashri, R., Akshaya, R.: A depth-based Indian sign language recognition using microsoft kinect. Sādhanā **45**(1), 34 (2020). https://doi.org/10.1007/s12046-019-1250-6
8. Renier, M., et al.: A correlational study between signature, writing abilities and decision-making capacity among people with initial cognitive impairment. Aging Clin. Exp. Res. **28**(3), 505–511 (2016). https://doi.org/10.1007/s40520-016-0549-y
9. Shen, S.: Arm posture tracking using a smartwatch. In: Proceedings of on MobiSys 2016 PhD Forum (Ph.D. Forum 2016), pp. 9–10. ACM, New York (2016)
10. Yasen, M., Jusoh, S.: A systematic review on hand gesture recognition techniques, challenges and applications. PeerJ Comput. Sci. **5**, e218 (2019)
11. Zeng, Z., Amin, M.G., Shan, T.: Arm motion classification using time-series analysis of the spectrogram frequency envelopes. Remote Sens. **12**(3), 454 (2020)
12. Zhang, Y., et al.: Static and dynamic human arm/hand gesture capturing and recognition via multiinformation fusion of flexible strain sensors. IEEE Sens. J. **20**(12), 6450–6459 (2020)

Digital Design of Aids for Activities
of Daily Living

Tom Saey, Kris Cuppens[(✉)], Tessa Delien, Mario Broeckx,
and Veerle Creylman

Thomas More University of Applied Sciences, Mobilab & Care, Geel, Belgium
{tom.saey,kris.cuppens}@thomasmore.be

Abstract. People with physical disabilities and people with moderate, severe to profound intellectual disabilities often need aids for activities of daily living (AADLs). Currently almost all of them are provided with prefabricated aids which often do not fit well or insufficiently. A bespoke aid would be an added-value here. In this paper, approaches to design such bespoke AADLs with different technical complexities are elaborated. As an example the implementation and workflow of two cases are covered: a bespoke joystick handle for an electric wheelchair and a plate-raiser. For both cases, an overview of the practical implementation is given, including the technical considerations. Also an implementation is provided using a 3D scan of the end-user or object on which the AADL is fitted, and one that is usable without 3D scan. The choice of implementation strategy is based on the needs of the end-user, and the preferences of the health care professional who designs the aid. By providing different options for health care professionals to design (and produce) bespoke AADLs, this study aims to lower the threshold to provide end-users with bespoke AADLs that are better tailored to their needs, more specifically when the bespoke AADLs would benefit them better than the prefabricated ones. Hereby, this study aims to contribute to the quality of life and participation of the end-users.

Keywords: Digital design · Bespoke aids · Disability · ADL · 3D printing

1 Introduction and State of the Art

People with physical disabilities, for example as a result of stroke or rheumatoid arthritis, and people with moderate, severe to profound intellectual disabilities often need aids for activities of daily living (AADLs) to help them perform activities in daily living (ADL). Currently almost all of them are provided with prefabricated aids. From conversations with multiple allied health professionals (such as occupational therapists and physiotherapists, further referred to as professionals) it appears that these aids often do not fit well or insufficiently. A bespoke aid would be an added-value here.

Additive manufacturing is a technique for fabricating geometries from three-dimensional (3D) model data. According to Ngo et al. (2018) one of the trending applications are biomedical applications due to the customization and patient-specific necessities, small production quantities and easy public access [1]. Although some

K. Miesenberger et al. (Eds.): ICCHP 2020, LNCS 12377, pp. 421–428, 2020.
https://doi.org/10.1007/978-3-030-58805-2_50

AADLs produced by professionals are a good example of such patient-specific necessities with small production quantities, the use of additive manufacturing in applications to help people with disabilities to perform ADL is mainly focused on the production of orthotics and prosthetics [2–4]. However, there are some recent studies that investigate the impact of applying digital techniques in occupational therapy [5–8].

To enable professionals to produce bespoke AADLs by the means of additive manufacturing, we have set up a project to generate a general workflow to give them guidelines to work with digital techniques (3D scanning, 3D modelling, 3D printing). To set-up this general workflow, 35 different cases are elaborated in 9 different care centers and patient organizations, such as a center for the visually impaired, a center for children with profound intellectual and multiple disabilities, the organization for people with ALS, the organization for people with rheumatic disorders and the organization of sports for people with disabilities. A multidisciplinary group, consisting of engineers, professionals and the end-users of the bespoke AADLs elaborates every case. The different steps of this process shall be discussed later in this paper.

The developed workflow include protocols for 3D measurement, 3D design, 3D printing and product finishing. They describe 1) methods for 3D scanning, taking into account end-user specific characteristics and the desired functionality of the needed AADLs, 2) different software tools ranging from low-end/simple design software to more extensive but complex design software that can be used for the 'freeform' design of bespoke AADLs, 3) integration of anatomical shapes into the digital design of bespoke AADLs to ensure optimal fit and function, 4) the choice of 3D printing technique and material which depends on the complexity and end-user specific clinical and technical requirements of each bespoke AADL, 5) different types of finishing (e.g. coatings) for bespoke AADLs that come into contact with skin, food or water.

The chosen cases have different complexities, as some are parametric designs that only require a few input parameters (such as the length or height), while others are fitted to the exact shape of a body part or object, and require a 3D scan.

In this paper, the implementation and workflow from 3D scanning to 3D design of two different cases are covered:

- A bespoke joystick handle for an electric wheelchair
- A plate-raiser

2 Methods and Implementation

2.1 Study Setup

The two cases that are covered in this paper are part of a larger study (Assist3D: 3D printing of bespoke aids) that was approved by the Ethics Committee of the Jessa Hospital, in Hasselt, Belgium (registration number: B243201941203). Within this larger study 35 different AADLs are developed using 3D scanning, digital design and 3D printing.

The aim of this pilot study is not to compare the digitally designed and 3D-printed AADLs with conventionally manufactured AADLs. The aim is to determine whether the use of 3D scanning, digital design and 3D printing for the production of AADLs is feasible and where, according to end-users and/or professionals, adjustments are needed. Therefore different 3D scanning methods, digital design software and 3D printing techniques are compared to each other.

In addition to the comparative study between different digital tools and printing techniques, the end-user's satisfaction with the use of digitally designed and 3D-printed AADLs is examined. The values are used to identify the points for improvement of the AADLs, to improve them in a next iteration and optimize the workflow.

Selection of End-Users. In the larger study, a maximum of 35 end-users will be recruited across the 9 care centers and patient organizations. The end-users (or the parents/guardian) are contacted by an employee of the center/organization, the study is explained to them and they are asked whether they want to participate in the study or not. Inclusion criteria:

- The end-user has a disability ((sensory) motor, cognitive, visual or auditory)
- The end-user needs a personalized or non-personalized AADL
- The end-user is at least 4 years old

Study Design. End-users that meet the inclusion and exclusion criteria are recruited. Once an end-user is recruited, the same steps of the design process are followed.

1. A multidisciplinary group consisting of at least a professional (if possible from the care organization) and a researcher of the study, possibly supplemented by a person with a more technical background in 3D printing, have a discussion together with the end-user. During this assessment interview, the end-user's needs and the possibilities and requirements for an AADLs are identified. The end-user thinks along during this process and, together with the group, offers possible solutions to his or her question;
2. The designer (researcher or professional), with the support of the multidisciplinary group, goes through the steps of measurement (if necessary), digital design, production and finishing.
3. The digital design is presented to the end-user. Before starting production, he/she can formulate proposals for improvement.
4. The bespoke AADL is produced using 3D printing;
5. The device is delivered to the end-user and the use is explained;
6. After a minimum of 3 weeks, the D-QUEST questionnaire is administered to the end-user (or, if necessary, by the parents, guardian, family) under the supervision of the professional.

2.2 Bespoke Joystick Handle for an Electric Wheelchair

Most manufacturers offer a limited set of different joystick designs to help the most common group of end-users. However, some people have limited fine motor skills and/or hand grasp function, and therefore can't use this limited set of different joystick handles. For people with limited fine motor skills but enough palmar grasp function, enlarging the joystick handle can be a solution. For other people with a lack of hand grasp function and fine motor skills a personalized design that perfectly fits the end-user's anatomy can be the solution. Hence, the desired complexity of a bespoke joystick can range from a simple design (e.g. a cylinder or a sphere with a bigger radius compared to the conventional joystick), all the way to a truly personalized joystick design based on a 3D scan of the anatomy of the end-user's hand.

(Radial) Palmar Grasp Joystick Handle. A center for children and adults with profound intellectual and multiple disabilities asked for a bespoke joystick handle. Due to an intellectual disability, the adolescent end-user has an intact palmar grasp function, but very limited fine motor skills and therefore can't use one of the existing joystick designs. A few simple tests with toys were performed to find out which palmar grasp and grasp position was possible for this end-user. These tests clarified that the end-user prefers a horizontal radial palmar grasp and has no specific preference for one hand or the other. Therefore, the joystick design needs to be useable with both hands.

Since a simple design is sufficient in this case, a free and low-end 3D design software tool, Tinkercad (Autodesk ®), is used. After a short initial introduction of the software, a professional designed a model existing of (Fig. 1 - left): two solid cylinders that are combined as a handle and one hollow cylinder that is used to cut out a hole at the bottom of the handle to connect the handle to the joystick of the wheelchair. The upper cylinder is rounded to avoid injury by sharp edges. The length, width and height of this handle can be adapted to the measures of the hand of each end-user. The hole at the bottom is centered for stability and has the exact measures of the pin of the joystick of the wheelchair to optimize the fit of the handle (Fig. 1 - middle). The 3D design was exported as an stl file and imported into Meshmixer (Autodesk ®). Within Meshmixer the final model was remeshed and smoothed as the model from Tinkercad results in a rather coarse mesh.

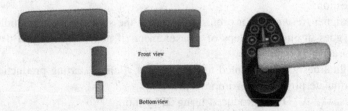

Fig. 1. Left: three cylinders to create the joystick handle: two solid cylinders that are combined as handle and one cylinder to cut the hole to connect the handle to the joystick of the wheelchair; middle: different views of the (radial) palmar grasp joystick, right: the printed palmar grasp joystick attached to the actual joystick.

Personalized Joystick Handle Based on a 3D Scan of the Hand. The center for children and adults with profound intellectual and multiple disabilities also asked for a bespoke joystick handle for an adolescent with intellectual disability and partially developed hands, and therefore lacks fine motor skills and hand grasp function. Due to the lack of hand grasp function, a personalized joystick handle based on a 3D scan of the partially developed hand is proposed.

It was difficult to make a direct 3D scan of the hand, due to spasticity of the hand muscles and the fact that it was very difficult to keep the end-user's hand in a fixed position during the time needed to make a good 3D scan. Therefore, an intermediate step with a silicone cast was used to capture the 3D shape of the hand and wrist.

A two-component malleable silicone (Vosschemie Benelux) approved for skin contact was applied to the end-user's hand. A professional positioned the hand and kept it in the required position until the silicone had cured (after approximately 5 min). Subsequently this silicone cast was 3D scanned with the Artec Leo 3D scanner (Artec LEO, Artec 3D Luxembourg) in order to obtain a digital representation of the end-user's palmar surface (Fig. 2A). The raw 3D scan files were processed with the Artec Studio software (Artec 3D, Luxembourg) using global registration and outlier removal algorithms (Fig. 2B). The processed 3D scan was exported as stl file. In a next step this stl file was imported into Meshmixer.

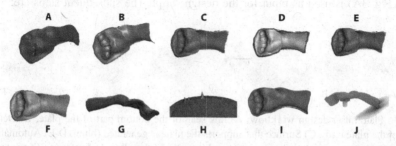

Fig. 2. Design workflow. A) Silicone cast scan, B) processed scan in Artec 3D software, C) region selection in Meshmixer that will be used in the design of the bespoke joystick, D) boundary smoothing, E) selection inversion to trim off all parts of the mesh outside this selection, F) remaining part after mesh trimming, G) resulting model after applying 3.5 mm offset, H) offset mesh with spikes due to small overlapping triangles near the mesh edge, I) Smoothed offset mesh, J) personalized joystick handle with connector.

The part of the 3D scan that was used in the further design of the bespoke joystick was selected (Fig. 2C) and the boundary of the selected area was smoothed (Fig. 2D). Next, the selection was inverted in order to select all parts of the mesh that can be trimmed off (Fig. 2E). The remaining mesh was offset with a 3.5 mm distance which provided a good balance between the volume (hence price) and required mechanical properties such as stiffness.

For the offset to give a good result, one should make sure the mesh does not contain any defects or small overlapping triangles near the mesh edge (Fig. 2H). Once the result of the offset is good, the sharp edges of the offset mesh are smoothed (Fig. 2I). As a final step a connector similar to the connector used in Fig. 1 is added to the design by means of a boolean union operation (Fig. 2J). This connector can either be designed in a low-end CAD software like Tinkercad or a high-end software like Fusion 360 (Autodesk®).

2.3   Plate-Raiser

For people with limited upper-limb fine and gross motor skills it is often difficult to eat without spilling food. A way to reduce this problem is to shorten the distance between their plate and mouth by means of a plate-raiser. If the end-user is using common circular plates, such a plate-raiser can be designed based on simple measurements of the plate diameter. However, often they use a special kind of high sided plate (Manoy high sided plate) that allows them to eat one handed more easily. It is more difficult to design a plate-raiser for this this type of plate purely based on measurements. For this reason, a CAD engineer developed a parametric Rhino Grasshopper (Rhinoceros®, McNeel) script that allows the design of a plate-raiser for irregular plates based on a 3D scan of the bottom side of the plate. We also developed a script that did not make use of a 3D scan but of a 2D scan or image of the (contour of) the plate. In the next paragraphs, only the version based on the 3D scan is elaborated.

The plate was 3D scanned with an Artec EVA scanner (Artec 3D) while placed on a table with the bottom side facing upwards. The scan includes part of the table. This 3D scan (Fig. 3A) is used as input for the design script. The subsequent steps are:

A   B   C   D   E   F

Fig. 3. Plate raiser design workflow: A) raw scan of the bottom part of the plate, B) Detected edge of the plate (red), C) Surface that supports the plate is generated (blue), D-E) Automatically generated plate-raiser based on user input and the scan of the plate, F) Image of 3D printed and coated plate-raiser, containing the plate. (Color figure online)

- The 3D scan is automatically aligned with the world coordinate system:
    - A local coordinate system (LCS) is defined: the xy plane of the LCS is defined by a plane fitted through the naked edge vertices of the mesh (hence, through the scanned table). The orientation of the positive z axis is defined as the direction towards the largest volume of the mesh. The origin of the LCS is defined as the center of the plate.
    - The transformation needed to align the LCS with the world coordinate system is calculated. The same transformation is applied to the mesh.
- To detect the edge of the plate (Fig. 3B), the xy plane is translated a small distance (0.5 mm) along the positive z axis. The intersection curve between this plane and the mesh is the edge of the plate.
- The surface that will support the plate is generated (Fig. 3C). In order to make sure that this support surface will fit the plate perfectly, the region of the plate's mesh that needs to be supported is converted to a surface. Once the support surface is generated, the rest of the plate-raiser is automatically generated based on the desired parameters (plate-raiser height, thickness, …) defined by the end-user (Fig. 3D–E). Although it is initially complex to write, no programming skills are needed to use

the script. An allied health care professional can use this script by taking a scan of the plate for which the plate raiser will be designed.

3 Discussion

In this paper, approaches to develop bespoke AADLs with different technical complexities are elaborated. As an example the implementation and workflow of two different cases are covered: a bespoke joystick handle for an electric wheelchair and a plate-raiser. For every case, the workflow consists of different choices that have to be made. The first choice is the level of personalization: is there a need for an exact fit and is a 3D scan of either the end-user or another object necessary? This is not only case specific but also end-user specific. In the examples discussed previously, different levels of personalization are given. For the bespoke joystick, for some end-users with an intact palmar grasp function, there is no need for a scan of the hand, while for the end-user without hand grasp function this is beneficial.

When making a 3D scan, two elements need to be considered: which scanner is used and how to post-process the scan data? The choice of scanner (e.g. a low-end scanner such as the Structure Sensor (Occipital) mounted on a tablet or a high-end scanner such as the Leo Scanner, (Artec 3D)) depends on the required and allowed accuracy, resolution, scanning area, portability of the scanner, preparation time, scanning time and ease of operation [9]. While a low-end scanner needs less preparation time and is easy to operate, a high-end scanner will result in a more accurate scan with a higher resolution. In post-processing, a clean-up of the scan is needed. As discussed in the workflow of the personalized joystick handle, this involves selecting the required scan area and smoothing the scan.

A next step in the workflow is the 3D design. Here, a choice has to be made in complexity of the software tools. This depends on the complexity of the bespoke AADL, the need of parametrization and the preference of the designer. If the complexity of the design is relatively low, simple CAD-software tools such as the freely online available Tinkercad can be used. Such software allows the user to design simple geometric shapes with little experience and hence is ideal for a broad group of professionals. If the design involves a scan, the slightly more complex Meshmixer software allows for the combination of an stl file of a scan with simple geometry. If a more complex geometry is necessary, more complex software tools such as Rhino in combination with Grasshopper or Fusion 360 are needed. Here, the possibility arises to make easy-adjustable parametric designs. Hence, although the professional might not be designing himself, after making the parametric design available, this can be used to make different AADLs based on different scans/parameters. This once more lowers the threshold for non-technical designers to make bespoke AADLs that are more adapted to the end-users. Different user-friendly online platforms exist to make the design available for a broad range of users.

A last step in the digital workflow of a bespoke AADL is the choice of which additive manufacturing technique is used with which material and which finishing (such as coatings) is applied after production. Although a complete discussion is outside the scope of this paper, it is worth mentioning that the examples discussed above are printed in polyamide 12 with the HP Multi Jet Fusion technique.

After 3D-printing the bespoke AADLs and delivering them to the end-users, the D-QUEST questionnaire is used to evaluate their satisfaction, to adjust the designs and optimize the workflows.

4 Conclusion

This paper discussed a workflow to design AADLs with different levels of complexity. Different strategies are available, which all depend on the needs of the end-user and the preference of the professionals. A digital process to design bespoke joystick handles for an electric wheelchair and a plate-raiser is discussed. As there is still an unfulfilled need in the health care sector for a better and more broad access to bespoke AADLs, this study can have a positive impact on the clinical field. It lowers the threshold to digitally design and 3D print bespoke AADLs by professionals, hence giving end-users access to aids better fitted to their needs.

References

1. Ngo, T.D., Kashani, A., Imbalzano, G., Nguyen, K.T., Hui, D.: Additive manufacturing (3D printing): a review of materials, methods, applications and challenges. Compos. Part B: Eng. **143**, 172–196 (2018)
2. Barrios-Muriel, J., Romero-Sánchez, F., Alonso-Sánchez, F.J., Rodríguez Salgado, D.: Advances in orthotic and prosthetic manufacturing: a technology review. Materials **13**(2), 295 (2020)
3. Creylman, V., Muraru, L., Pallari, J., Vertommen, H., Peeraer, L.: Gait assessment during the initial fitting of customized selective laser sintering ankle foot orthoses in subjects with drop foot. Prosthet. Orthot. Int. **37**(2), 132–138 (2013)
4. Paterson, A.M., Bibb, R., Campbell, R.I., Bingham, G.: Comparing additive manufacturing technologies for customised wrist splints. Rapid Prototyp. J. **21**(3), 230–243 (2015)
5. Brown, C., Hurst, A.. VizTouch: automatically generated tactile visualizations of coordinate spaces. In: Proceedings of the Sixth International Conference on Tangible, Embedded and Embodied Interaction, pp. 131–138 (2012)
6. Buehler, E., et al.: Sharing is caring: assistive technology designs on thingiverse. In: Proceedings of the 33rd Annual ACM Conference on Human Factors in Computing Systems, pp. 525–534 (2015)
7. Lunsford, C., Grindle, G., Salatin, B., Dicianno, B.E.: Innovations with 3-dimensional printing in physical medicine and rehabilitation: a review of the literature. PM&R **8**(12), 1201–1212 (2016)
8. Medola, F.O., Fortulan, C.A., Purquerio, B.D.M., Elui, V.M.C.: A new design for an old concept of wheelchair pushrim. Disabil. Rehabil: Assist. Technol. **7**(3), 234–241 (2012)
9. Rosicky, J., Grygar, A., Chapcak, P., Bouma, T., Rosicky, J. Application of 3D scanning in prosthetic & orthotic clinical practice. In: Proceedings of the 7th International Conference on 3D Body Scanning Technologies, pp. 88–97 (2016)

A Multimodal Communication Aid for Persons with Cerebral Palsy Using Head Movement and Speech Recognition

Tomoka Ikeda[1], Masakazu Hirokawa[2]([⊠]) [iD], and Kenji Suzuki[2]([⊠]) [iD]

[1] Intelligent and Mechanical Interaction Systems, University of Tsukuba,
Tsukuba, Japan
ikeda@ai.iit.tsukuba.ac.jp
[2] Faculty of Engineering, Information and Systems, University of Tsukuba,
Tsukuba, Japan
hirokawa_m@ieee.org, kenji@ieee.org

Abstract. In this study, we proposed a multimodal communication aid for persons with cerebral palsy. This system supports their interpersonal communication based on utterance recognition and head movement detection. To compensate for the inaccuracy of utterances owing to oral motor impairment in persons with cerebral palsy, vowel string-based word prediction and decision behavior detection via head movement measurement were implemented. The proposed system was tested by a participant with cerebral palsy and the obtained results were compared with those for conventional communication aid tools such as transparent communication boards. Our results confirmed that the time required for communication using our proposed method was shorter than that required using the conventional communication tools.

Keywords: Cerebral palsy · Communication aid · Speech recognition · Gesture recognition.

1 Introduction

Cerebral palsy (CP) is a group of permanent movement disorders that appear in early childhood. Communication through speech is difficult for persons with CP owing to poor oral motor control; however, they might be able to participate in spoken conversation with the help of speech assistive tools.

Currently, persons with CP can communicate with others via several different approaches. First, they could express their intentions via some means based on which their conversation partner could determine the target word one character at a time; this method is the most popular communication assistance approach used by persons with CP. Second, persons with CP could use touch panels or other similar devices to communicate with others. Because the symptoms of CP are diverse, in the first approach, the communication partners should understand the specific symptoms of the person with CP they are assisting in

© Springer Nature Switzerland AG 2020
K. Miesenberger et al. (Eds.): ICCHP 2020, LNCS 12377, pp. 429–436, 2020.
https://doi.org/10.1007/978-3-030-58805-2_51

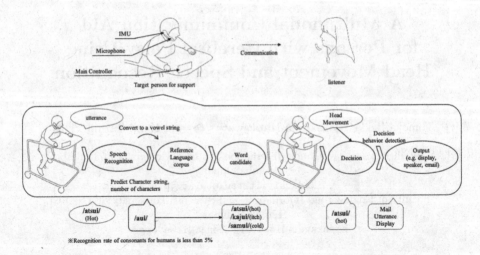

Fig. 1. Proposed multimodal communication assistance approach for persons with CP

communication, especially their involuntary movements. In addition, considering the second approach, it might be difficult for persons with CP to communicate through small buttons on a touch screen or device owing to their involuntary movements, which are more likely to occur when they try to move their body. Furthermore, these involuntary movements also make it difficult to capture their movements using a camera for vision-based communication assistance systems [5,7,8].

To overcome the above mentioned issues faced by persons with CP while communicating using these existing approaches, in this study, we propose a multimodal communication assistance system that enables persons with CP to verbally communicate with others at a comfortable speed using utterances and head movements.

In this paper, first, we present information on the communication approach used by a person with CP and the manner in which their communication partner recognizes their intended characters, and subsequently, their intended words. Then, we describe the proposed communication assistance system along with its practical applications; it should be noted that this system was designed to support conversations in Japanese. Finally, we discuss possible improvements to the proposed system and user feedback on it.

2   Method

In our study, we observed a typical conversation between a person with CP and a healthy communication partner, which was then used as the basis of the interaction structure used to design our proposed system. In particular, the communication partner attempts to understand the communication intention or intended

Table 1. Features of the language corpus used in this study

	Number of characters in a word						Total
	2	3	4	5	6	7	
Number of unique vowel strings	6	26	21	7	1	1	62
Maximum number of words with a common vowel string	3	5	2	1	1	1	5
All	19	50	23	7	1	1	101

Algorithm 1. Estimating a decision based on head movements [1]

Require: t: Current time, $v_S(t), v_L$: Variance of the pitch angles at each time, p_t: Pitch angle, T_S, T_L: Two different time windows, α: Empirically determined threshold
  while $True$ **do**
    $v_S(t) = V\,[p_t]_{t-T_S}^{t}$
    if $v_S(t)/v_L(t) > \alpha$ **then**
      decision behavior is performed
    else
      continue
    end if
  end while

---

word of the person with CP by listening to their utterance. However, if the communication partner does not understand their utterance, the communication partner then shows characters on a board and observes the feedback received from the person with CP in the form of head movements, such as nodding.

Based on these observations, we designed a multimodal communication system to identify utterances and detect head movements of persons with CP to enable communication between them and others; our proposed approach is depicted in Fig. 1. In the Japanese language, all characters can be represented using combinations of a consonant and a vowel. However, because uttering consonants requires delicate lip movements, it is difficult for persons with CP to clearly pronounce characters with consonant sounds [6]. Therefore, we focused on the vowel sounds in the characters, and used them in the form of a "vowel string" to recognize the utterance of a person with CP thereby reducing the number of candidate words the person with CP might be trying to convey. In our proposed approach, if no word corresponding to the uttered vowel string was found in the language corpus, the vowel string was modified based on the entries in the language corpus; in particular, the language corpus consists of words frequently used by a person with CP. Then, to enable the selection of a word from the list of candidate words based on the identified or estimated vowel string, head movement was considered as a means to express "confirmation" by the person with CP. These candidate words are displayed on the primary controller of our proposed system one after another after a certain interval of time; thus, when the word that a user want to convey is displayed, the user can move their head to make a selection [4]. This head movement is an easy one for persons with CP, which is also often used by their communication partners to determine the intention of the former, especially those who have difficulty in conscious movements owing to simultaneously occurring involuntary movements.

For the speech classification described above, we created a language corpus with 101 words based on an interview with a parent. A support vector machine was trained with 12-dimensional Mel-frequency cepstral coefficients to classify vowel strings.

Table 1 shows the features of the language corpus used for utterance correction and word prediction in our proposed system. From the information presented in the table, it can be observed that the maximum number of suggested words displayed on the controller of the proposed system is five.

To estimate the decision behavior of a person with CP based on their head movements, we implemented the algorithm shown in Algorithm 1 [6]. In particular, $v_s(t)$ and $v_l(t)$ denote the variances of the pitch angle at time t using two different time windows T_S and T_L, respectively. When the ratio between the two variance values exceeds the empirically determined threshold α, the head movement is considered as a decision behavior and the word displayed at that time could be conveyed to others through email, voice, or on a terminal display. In this study, T_S and T_L were set as 0.5 s and 15 s, respectively.

3   Experiments

To validate our proposed system, three experiments were conducted wherein a 20-year-old, male subject with athetosis-type CP used our proposed system. Informed consent was obtained from the participant before the experiments.

3.1   Speech Recognition

First, we conducted an experiment to verify the speech recognition accuracy of our proposed system. While collecting utterance data from the participant, it was observed that more than 90% of the participant's utterances were unvoiced because of motor speech disorders even though the participant intended to utter sound. However, we recorded 14 sets of "a", "i", "ɯ", "e", and "o" sounds. The obtained utterance data were segmented using a sliding window of 50 ms with an overlap of 40 ms. Then, vowel identification was performed for each segment to calculate the correct recognition rate.

The recognition rate for voiced sounds was 86.1%, while that for unvoiced sounds was 61.0%. When the final result was determined via a majority vote, the correct answer was given for voiced sounds. In contrast, in the case of unvoiced sounds, the utterances for "a" and "o" were frequently confused, which resulted in a reduction in the recognition rate.

No Reaction   Reaction

Fig. 2. Experiment outline

Table 2. Classification results

Precision	Recall	F-score
0.625	0.857	0.72

3.2   Decision Behavior

Next, we examined the recognition performance of our proposed system for head movements. We asked the participant to perform a simple reaction task to visual stimuli. The framework of this experiment is shown in Fig. 2. We prepared three blank sheets and one sheet with a circle drawn on it; these sheets were randomly shown to the participant one at a time. The participant was instructed to perform a head movement when the sheet with the circle was presented. We measured the average reaction time of the participant to the visual stimulus (i.e., the presentation of the sheet with the circle) to determine the participant's decision behavior and compared it with that obtained using our proposed system.

The precision, recall, and F-score for the obtained experimental results are listed in Table 2. In particular, the average time taken by the participant to respond to the visual stimuli was 0.4 s.

3.3   Usability Testing

Finally, we conducted a pilot study to evaluate the time required for communication and interviews by users using our proposed method compared with using conventional communication aids such as transparent communication boards and switches.

Table 3. Time required for each process

	Time (s)
Speech	5
Speech recognition word prediction	20.2
Word selection	2.5

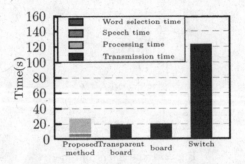

Fig. 3. Comparison with conventional methods

To investigate the limitations of the proposed method in terms of processing time, we separately measured the utterance time, processing time for utterance recognition and word prediction, and time for word selection, because it is difficult to determine the number of characters via speech recognition. These timing results are listed in Table 3. From the obtained results, it can be observed that the processing time for speech recognition and word prediction was 20.2 s, which was 72.9% of the total time. However, as shown in Fig. 3, the proposed method could convey the word intended by the user in a similar time compared with the use of conventional communication boards.

Furthermore, to improve the usability of our proposed system in the future, we collected opinions from the participant and their communication partner; some of those opinions are as follows: the communication partner wanted to be informed of the vocabulary of the person with CP as well as the difficulty of using the proposed device. In addition, the participant wanted functionality to be included to output a series of word strings as well as that for a reply function in the system.

4   Discussion and Conclusion

Based on our experiments, the positive recognition rate for utterances using our proposed system was about 60%; however, for word prediction using a personalized corpus, word candidates with 3 to 5 characters could be reduced to about 10%. These results indicate that it is realistic to use utterance recognition as a communication aid approach for persons with CP because it enhances word prediction by reducing the number of candidate words, thereby reducing the error in word recognition.

Furthermore, it was also found that breathing sounds could be misidentified as utterances. Therefore, it is necessary to distinguish breathing sounds from unvoiced utterances.

During the investigation of decision behavior recognition based on head movements, motions other than the target behavior caused by involuntary movements. However, as indicated by the results in Table 2, the proposed method could successfully detect the target decision behavior with a high recall value.

Using the proposed method, the utterance time and the time required for word selection were shorter than those obtained using other conventional communication assistance methods; moreover, the processing time could be further reduced by increasing the computational power of the processor used for the proposed system and improving the underlying algorithm. In addition, our proposed approach could be easily extended to assist persons with CP in composing sentences.

Only Japanese were considered in this study. However, the proposed method can be applied for the case of multiple languages if we create the language corpus from individuals. We consider that it is efficient to narrow down the word candidates with voice and gesture recognition.

In conclusion, we proposed a multimodal communication assistance system to assist persons with CP to communicate with others in realtime. The speech recognition results obtained using our proposed system indicated that our method could support communication for persons with CP as well as dysarthria. Compared with conventional communication assistance methods, communication using our proposed method required a shorter time. Though there is room for improvement, to the best of our knowledge, our proposed communication assistance system for persons with CP is faster than any similar, currently available method.

Moreover, our method has other potential communication applications; for example, our system could be linked with chat applications on smartphones. Furthermore, the built-in spellcheck function on smartphones could allow communication between persons with CP and others who otherwise would have difficulties understanding them as well as improve the vocalizations of persons with CP. Moreover, the addition of a reply function for communication partners could increase the communication opportunities for persons with CP and support their learning.

References

1. Bharti, P., Panwar, A., Gopalakrishna, G., Chellappan, S.: Watch-dog: detecting self-harming activities from wrist worn accelerometers. IEEE J. Biomed. Health Inform. **22**(3), 686–696 (2017)
2. Guerrier, Y., Kolski, C., Poirier, F.: Proposition of a communication system used in mobility by users with physical disabilities, focus on cerebral palsy with athetoid problems. In: 2013 International Conference on Advanced Logistics and Transport, pp. 269–274 (2013)
3. Hochstein, D.D., McDaniel, M.A., Nettleton, S.: Recognition of vocabulary in children and adolescents with cerebral palsy: a comparison of two speech coding schemes. Augment. Altern. Commun. **20**(2), 45–62 (2004). https://doi.org/10.1080/07434610410001699708
4. Farwell, L.A., Donchin, E.: Talking off the top of your head: toward a mental prosthesis utilizing event-related brain potentials. Electroencephalogr. Clin. Neurophysiol. **70**(6), 510–523 (1988)

5. Shor, J., et al.: Personalizing ASR for dysarthric and accented speech with limited data. In: Proceedings of Interspeech 2019, pp. 784–788 (2019). https://doi.org/10.21437/Interspeech.2019-1427
6. Ohnishi, S., Kojima, C., Yokchi, K.: Articulation analysis of athetoid children. Jpn. Soc. Logop. Phoniatr. **33**, 221–226 (1992)
7. Niwa, T., Torii, I., Ishii, N.: Development of communication tool for physically handicapped with involuntary movements by line-of-sight detection. In: 2016 4th International Conference on Applied Computing and Information Technology, pp. 253–238 (2016). https://doi.org/10.1109/ACIT-CSII-BCD.2016.056
8. Takiguti, T., Ariki, Y.: Multimodal assistive technologies for people with articulation disorders. In: ICT Innovation Forum, pp. 784–788 (2013)
9. Guerrier, Y., Naveteur, J., Kolski, C., Poirier, F.: Communication system for persons with cerebral palsy. In: Miesenberger, K., Fels, D., Archambault, D., Peňáz, P., Zagler, W. (eds.) ICCHP 2014. LNCS, vol. 8547, pp. 419–426. Springer, Cham (2014). https://doi.org/10.1007/978-3-319-08596-8_64

Experimental Evaluation of Three Interaction Channels for Accessible Digital Musical Instruments

Nicola Davanzo$^{(\boxtimes)}$ ⓘ and Federico Avanzini ⓘ

Laboratory of Music Informatics, Department of Computer Science,
University of Milan, Via Celoria 18, 20133 Milan, Italy
{nicola.davanzo,federico.avanzini}@unimi.it

Abstract. Accessible Digital Musical instruments (ADMIs) dedicated to people with motor disabilities represent a relevant niche in accessibility research. The designer is often required to exploit unconventional physical interaction channels, different from hands and fingers. Although comprehensive evaluation methods for Digital Musical Instruments in general are found in literature, little has been done both in ADMIs evaluation and the analysis of suitable interaction channels from a Human-Computer Interaction perspective. In this work the performance of breath, gaze pointing and head movements is analyzed, in terms of movement speed and stability, through a simple experiment. These interaction channels could be exploited in the design of ADMIs dedicated to quadriplegic musicians. The proposed experiment has similarities with past Fitts Law evaluation tests. Results are discussed proposing possible mappings between channels and musical performance parameters. These results could also be useful to inform the design of different interface types.

Keywords: Accessible interfaces · Accessible Digital Musical Instruments · Performance metrics · Fitts' Law

1 Introduction

Among the technologies dedicated to people with physical, cognitive, and sensory impairments, ADMIs (Accessible Digital Musical Instruments) are gradually gaining attention, while the research on this topic has expanded considerably in recent years [4]. Musical activities provide benefits in terms of health, learning and concentration skills, while being an important cultural and social inclusion factor [2,11,21]. Frid's work [4] shows that a considerable percentage of existing ADMIs are dedicated to users with physical impairments. Such instruments, particularly those dedicated to quadriplegic performers, require to exploit interaction channels other than fingers, which are common to many traditional acoustic musical instruments: gaze pointing, head and face movement, breath, tongue, EEG, etc. Within the literature of Digital Musical Instruments (DMIs) in general, one challenge is the definition of proper evaluation metrics [14,17,20].

K. Miesenberger et al. (Eds.): ICCHP 2020, LNCS 12377, pp. 437–445, 2020.
https://doi.org/10.1007/978-3-030-58805-2_52

The problem is even more complex for ADMIs. In particular, little work was done to evaluate interaction channels suitable for quadriplegic users.

A widely used model in HCI research is Fitts Law, which predicts human performance in target acquisition tasks, in terms of *throughput*. Its most recent formulation [12] is as follows:

$$T = a + b \log_2 \left(\frac{D}{W} + 1 \right) \tag{1}$$

where T is the movement execution time, D and W are the target distance and width, respectively, while a and b are empirical constants. The logarithmic term is usually referred to as *ID* (Index of Difficulty). The ISO 9421-9 experimental procedure [12,20], often used to verify Fitts' Law, prescribes an experimental methodology employing 1D and 2D target selection tasks. In light of our specific objectives, the experiment reported next is not fully compliant with the standard. Specifically: (a) some of the analyzed channels offer only one degree of freedom; (b) an additional one would be necessary to make a selection (e.g. mouse click), which is not possible with the investigated channels; (c) we are also interested in movement *stability*; (d) the target width has been kept fixed to standardize stability measurements. The introduction of stability measurement denotes an important difference with Fitts' Law related experiments: an high stability, which is not obvious given the nature of the channels and sensors, is potentially very useful in musical interfaces interaction, e.g. for keeping a stable pitch or volume selection.

Gaze, breath, and head interactions have been analyzed in previous works. Gaze pointing is a consolidated interaction channel [18], and several gaze based ADMIs exist [3,19]. Hornof [5] and Baath [1] evaluate gaze in rhythmic tasks. Breath is widely used in traditional instruments, as well as in accessible interfaces [9,13]. Head movement is also employed for instance in wheelchair control [13] and is used in ADMIs control [6,8]. Its kinematics has been widely studied [16].

The main contribution for this work is the evaluation of three alternative channels (gaze pointing, breath, head movements), in terms of two characteristics useful for musical interaction: movement *speed* and *stability*. The evaluation occurred through a simple experiment, described in Sect. 2. Results are exposed in Sect. 3. In light of these, possible usages of the aforementioned in musical interfaces and ADMIs are discussed in Sect. 4. It should be however highlighted that these results could be useful also to inform the design of different types of interfaces other than musical ones.

2   Experiment

2.1   Procedure

The experimental GUI is shown in Fig. 1. Interaction takes place on the *interaction bar* (dark gray). A marker (in red) indicates the center of the *target zone*

Fig. 1. A screenshot of the interface used to run the experiment. (Color figure online)

(light gray). The *cursor* (in white) can only be moved horizontally within the limits of this bar, using one interaction condition.

Seven conditions were considered (see Sect. 2.2 for details): hand (considered solely as a benchmark for the remaining ones), gaze (raw or smoothed), breath, head (yaw, pitch, roll). For each condition, five target distances were tested: *D200, D300, D500, D700* and *D900* (numbers indicate distance, as a proportion of D1000). Subjects were required to (1) move the cursor to the target as quickly as possible; (2) once reached, keep it in the center of the target as stably as possible. A within-subject procedure was used. Each subject performed 15 trials for each condition. The first 5 trials were used as training and discarded in subsequent analysis, while the remaining 10 presented the 5 distances twice. Conditions and distances were randomized across subjects.

Each trial was initiated by the subject through a key press, after which a target appeared on the far left. The subject had to position the cursor inside the target for two seconds. The test then entered two main phases. **Selection phase:** an acoustic warning signalled the appearance of a new target to the right at a given distance, and the subject had 5 seconds to make a target selection (after this time, the trial was declared as failed); a selection was valid only if the cursor remained within the target for at least 1 second (not counted in the reported selection time). **Stability phase:** after selection, the subject had to keep the cursor as centered and stable as possible on the target, for 2 s, after which a new acoustic signal notified the end of the trial.

A one minute break was provided between conditions, to switch the setup. The total session time was around 30 min. At the end of the session, a questionnaire was presented with 6 questions, with answers provided on a 7-value Likert scale (higher is better), to investigate personal perception of testers on each interaction channel. Questions were as follows:

(a) **Fatigue.** Did you feel fatigue, tiredness, or pain during the execution? (High = not fatiguing)
(b) **Usability.** Did you find the interaction easy and comfortable or frustrating? (High = easy)
(c) **Precision.** Did you find the interaction accurate and precise? (High = very precise)
(d) **Involuntary movements.** During the test, did you perceive involuntary movements which affected the position of the cursor? (High = no)
(e) **Speed.** Did you find the selection method quick and fast? (High = very fast)

(f) **General opinion.** Give a general rating of these channels as interaction methods. (High = excellent)

2.2   HW/SW Setup

The experiment was run on an Apple MacBook Pro (2017) with Windows 10 (started via Bootcamp) and a dual-core Intel Core i5 CPU at 2.3 GhZ, 8 GB RAM LPDDR3 at 2133 MHz, Intel Iris Graphics 640 GPU with 1536 MB VRAM. Sensors and screen were connected via a Thunderbolt/USB+VGA port adapter. A 21-inch VGA monitor at 1920 × 1080 px resolution was used. The physical length of the interaction bar on the screen was 24.7 cm (out of a 47.7 cm screen width). The software (test automation, data recording, GUI) was developed in C#.[1]

Interaction occurring through a physical channel is inextricably linked to the type, setup and quality of the used sensor. Thus, the experiment actually evaluates channel-sensor pairs.

Hands (Mouse). We used a high-end gaming mouse, namely a *Corsair M65 Pro* equipped with a 12,000 DPI resolution optical sensor. Sensitivity was set to 1500 DPI.

Gaze point (Eye Tracker). Only horizontal movements were evaluated. We used a *Eye Tribe* device, with a sampling rate of 60 Hz and an accuracy of 0.5-1.0° on the visual field [15]. Two setups were used, raw and smooth. In the latter, a natively available smoothing filter was activated.

Breath (Breath sensor). An *ad-hoc* sensor was built using a *NXP MPX5010DP* low-pressure sensor with a range of $0-10$ KPa, a sensitivity of 1 mV/mm and a response time of 1 ms. It was interfaced to the computer through an *Arduino Uno* microcontroller. A rubber tube with an interchangeable mouthpiece was connected to the sensor inlet. At zero pressure, the cursor is positioned to the left end of the interaction bar, while the right end is reached with a pressure of 5 kPa, which is a comfortable value for all subjects [10]. The sampling rate was $\sim$200 Hz.

Head (Head Tracker). An *ad-hoc* head tracker was built using the *MPU-6050 (GY-521)* 6DoF accelerometer and gyroscope integrated sensor, interfaced to the computer through an *Arduino Nano* microcontroller. For each head rotation axis, the range required to move the cursor from the left to the right ends was 40° ([−20°, +20°]), and the natural rest position corresponded to the cursor placed at the center. The sampling rate was $\sim$100 Hz.

3   Results

A sample of 16 subjects, aged between 22 and 47, participated in the experiment. None had previous experiences with the investigated interaction channels except

---

[1] Source code available under a GNU-GPLv3 license at https://github.com/Neeqstock/HanDMIs-TestSuite.

for the mouse, and in one case the breath (some experience in saxophone playing). The initially planned number of subjects (25–30), could not be attained due to the onset of the COVID-19 epidemic in Italy (Feb. 2020).

All subjects were able-bodied: although this is a limitation, this is a preliminary test providing a benchmark for subsequent experimentation. Moreover, it must be noted that a quadriplegic user may have the same level of control as an able-bodied user for the analyzed interaction channels.

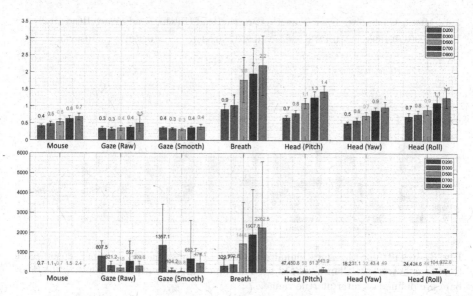

Fig. 2. Results for *selection time* (upper plot) and *selection stability* (lower plot). Error bars represent the standard deviation. Bar colors refer to the various distances (see legend). (Color figure online)

Figure 2 shows the results, where the following trials were removed as outliers: (1) trials failed due to expired time; (2) trials with wrong movements due to a reported misunderstanding of the task; (3) trials ranking outside the 10th and 90th percentile interval. Failure for expired time occurred only for Gaze (Raw) (1 for D900) and Breath (1 for D300, 2 for D500, 9 for D700, 10 for D900).

Selection times (upper plot in Fig. 2) were averaged across trials for distances and conditions. Two terms influencing these values can be noticed: a reaction time (formalized by the a parameter in the Fitts Law model) and an additive term related to the distance traveled (whose slope is defined by the b parameter). A least square linear regression was run to estimate a and b, and a subsequent ANOVA revealed an non-significant difference ($p = 0.487$) between the a parameters, suggesting comparable reaction times for all channels. In order to obtain a more accurate estimate for the b parameter, the model was then adjusted by imposing the same value for a in all channels, and linear regression on the adjusted model provided the results reported in Table 1. A subsequent ANOVA resulted in statistically significant difference for the b values ($p \ll 0.001$). Post-hoc pairwise tests with Bonferroni-Holm correction revealed non-significant differences only in the following pairs: [Mouse - Gaze (Raw)] ($p = 0.23$), [Gaze (Raw) - Gaze (Smooth)] ($p = 0.21$), [Head (Roll) - Head (Pitch)] ($p = 0.21$). All remaining pairs showed significant differences with $p < 0.05$.

Table 1. Estimates of b parameters for each interaction channel.

	Mouse	Gaze (raw)	Gaze (Smooth)	Breath	Head (Pitch)	Head (Yaw)	Head (Roll)
b	0.2304	0.1896	0.1273	0.8637	0.5315	0.3537	0.4690

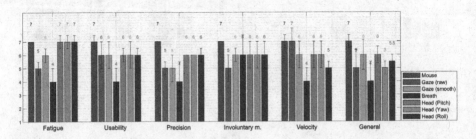

Fig. 3. Results for the questionnaire divided by question and channel-sensor pairs (higher is better). Median has been used as a measure of central tendency, while error bars are defined as interquartile range.

The stability value for each trial was computed as the variance of the cursor position within the stability phase. After outliers removal (same as above), the variances were averaged within single distances and conditions (lower plot in Fig. 2. All head related channels exhibit high stability, comparable to the mouse. The gaze point stability is negatively affected by both the sensor output and the natural instability of fixations [18]. Interestingly, the Gaze (Smooth) condition does not improve compared to Gaze (Raw). Breath is visibly more unstable especially for large distances, with large deviations. Subjects reportedly found it difficult to keep a stable pressure in the case of large distances, given that the required pressure was greater.

The questionnaires provided additional indications: results are provided in Fig. 3. With regard to *Fatigue*, Head was found not to be comparable to Mouse, while some fatigue for Gaze was indicated (in particular in the raw condition) and Breath. *Usability* of the various channels was lower than Mouse but generally comparable, except for Breath, which scored very low values. Mouse *Precision* was found to be superior, followed by Head, Gaze and Breath, consistently with results on stability. Mouse interaction was perceived free of *Involuntary movements*, while some were noted for all the other channels, notably Gaze (raw): this can be explained by the erratic movements of the cursor. *Velocity* of Gaze was perceived as comparable to Mouse, consistently with the test results, while the worst judged were Head (roll) and Breath. Excluding Mouse, *General* ratings showed a preference for Gaze (smooth) and Head (Yaw), while Breath ranked lowest.

4   Discussion and Conclusions

The channels considered in this work are independent from each other, being based on different physical degrees of freedom, and may therefore be used together for musical interactions.

Gaze interactions resulted to be very fast, and only weakly dependent on the target distance (especially in the Smooth formulation). This supports the choice of this channel for note selections (e.g., EyeHarp [19], or Netytar [3]). Although, given the nature of gaze and related sensors, stability is not particularly high, several solutions can be devised to deal with this issue [5].

On the other hand, the relatively low upper limit for the number of saccades per second [5] may lead to a reconsideration of head related channels for note selections. The three head channels have comparable performance. Yaw performs better, possibly due to (1) familiarity with this movement; (2) larger rotational range; (3) congruence between rotation direction and cursor movement, resulting in a more natural mapping. Little exploration has been carried out in this regard, even if some DMIs exploit Pitch and Yaw (e.g., Magic Flute [6] and Jamboxx [8]). Roll may instead be mapped to pitch bend, vibrato or other musical parameters.

Breath had comparatively lower scores in tests and questionnaires. The variability also appears to be very high, especially for large distances. Despite its widespread application in assistive technologies, it performed poorly in precise target selection tasks. However it can reconsidered for musical interaction given the following observations. First, breath is naturally linked to the regulation of sound intensity (e.g. while singing or playing aerophones). Furthermore, the emission of breath is associated to the sensation of energy being injected by the performer into the instrument. This doesn't happen for the other analyzed channels, as the cursor remains still in any position in absence of movement. Hunt [7] highlights how this sensation can result in a natural mapping with sound intensity. Other configurations should be explored even for the channel-sensor pairs analyzed in this work: for example, the position of the cursor could be mapped to the derivative of the head movement speed. Finally, it should be important to perform experiments with quadriplegic users. This could be achieved by proposing the same experimental setting or, given the heterogeneity of this last category, through proper case studies on differentiated users.

Acknowledgements. We would like to offer our special thanks to Daniele Zago (from University of Padova, Italy) for advising us on statistical analysis, and to Mattia Galante (from University of Milan, Italy) for the great help given by assisting the testers.

References

1. Bååth, R., Strandberg, T., Balkenius, C.: Eye tapping: how to beat out an accurate rhythm using eye movements. In: Proceedings of 11th International Conference on New Interfaces for Musical Expression (NIME 2011), NIME 2011, Oslo (May 2011)
2. Cross, I.: The nature of music and its evolution. In: Hallam, S., Cross, I., Taut, M. (eds.) The Oxford Handbook of Music Psychology, pp. 3–13. Oxford University Press, Oxford (2009)
3. Davanzo, N., Dondi, P., Mosconi, M., Porta, M.: Playing music with the eyes through an isomorphic interface. In: Proceedings of the Workshop on Communication by Gaze Interaction - COGAIN 2018, pp. 1–5. ACM Press, Warsaw (2018)
4. Frid, E.: Accessible digital musical instruments—a review of musical interfaces in inclusive music practice. Multimodal Technol. Interact. **3**(3), 57 (2019)
5. Hornof, A.J.: The prospects for eye-controlled musical performance. In: Proceedings 14th International Conference on New Interfaces for Musical Expression (NIME 2014), NIME 2014, Goldsmiths, University of London (July 2014)
6. Housemate: Magic Flute (nd). http://housemate.ie/magic-flute/. Accessed 8 June 2019
7. Hunt, A., Wanderley, M.M., Paradis, M.: The importance of parameter mapping in electronic instrument design. J. New Music Res. **32**(4), 429–440 (2003)
8. Jamboxx: Jamboxx (nd). https://www.jamboxx.com/. Accessed 8 June 2019
9. Jones, M., Grogg, K., Anschutz, J., Fierman, R.: A sip-and-puff wireless remote control for the Apple iPod. Assist. Technol. **20**(2), 107–110 (2008)
10. Lausted, C.G., Johnson, A.T., Scott, W.H., Johnson, M.M., Coyne, K.M., Coursey, D.C.: Maximum static inspiratory and expiratory pressures with different lung volumes. BioMed. Eng. OnLine **5**, 29 (2006)
11. Lubet, A.: Music, Disability, and Society. Temple University Press, Philadelphia (2011)
12. McKenzie, S.: Fitts' law. In: Norman, K.L. Kirakowski, J. (eds.) Handbook of Human-Computer Interaction, vol. 1, pp. 349–370. Hoboken (2018)
13. Mougharbel, I., El-Hajj, R., Ghamlouch, H., Monacelli, E.: Comparative study on different adaptation approaches concerning a sip and puff controller for a powered wheelchair. In: Proceedings of the 2013 Science and Information Conference, pp. 597–603. London (October 2013)
14. O'Modhrain, S.: A framework for the evaluation of digital musical instruments. Comput. Music J. **35**(1), 28–42 (2011)
15. Ooms, K., Dupont, L., Lapon, L., Popelka, S.: Accuracy and precision of fixation locations recorded with the low-cost eye tribe tracker in different experimental setups. J. Eye Mov. Res. **8**(1) (2015)
16. Sarig-Bahat, H.: Evidence for exercise therapy in mechanical neck disorders. Man. Ther. **8**(1), 10–20 (2003)
17. Shima, K., Tsuji, T., Kandori, A., Yokoe, M., Sakoda, S.: Measurement and evaluation of finger tapping movements using log-linearized Gaussian mixture networks. Sensors **9**(3), 2187–2201 (2009)
18. Sibert, L.E., Jacob, R.J.K.: Evaluation of eye gaze interaction. In: Proceedings of SIGCHI Conference on Human Factors in Computing Systems, CHI 2000, pp. 281–288. Association for Computing Machinery, The Hague (April 2000)
19. Vamvakousis, Z., Ramirez, R.: The EyeHarp: a gaze-controlled digital musical instrument. Front. Psychol. **7**, article 906 (2016)

20. Wang, F., Ren, X.: Empirical evaluation for finger input properties in multi-touch interaction. In: Proceedings of 27th International Conference on Human Factors in Computing Systems (CHI 2009), pp. 1063–1072. ACM Press, Boston (2009)
21. Williams, K.E., Berthelsen, D., Nicholson, J.M., Walker, S., Abad, V.: The effectiveness of a short-term group music therapy intervention for parents who have a child with a disability. J. Music Ther. **49**(1), 23–44 (2012)

iFeedingBot: A Vision-Based Feeding Robotic Arm Prototype Based on Open Source Solution

Settapong Phalaprom and Prajaks Jitngernmadan[(✉)]

Burapha University, Chon Buri 20131, Thailand
prajaks@buu.ac.th

Abstract. Giving the people with physical disabilities or elderly the possibility of eating unaided is to bring them back a piece of quality of living. In this work, we demonstrated how a vision-based feeding robotic arm prototype can be implemented using hardware and software open source solution. Two important aspects have been identified, 1) this concept is a low-cost solution that is affordable for people with physical disabilities or elderly in low-income countries, and 2) the solution embraces image processing and artificial intelligence technology for the user's facial landmark detection, which can be used to control the feeding procedure. The result shows that our vision-based feeding robotic arm prototype functions as expected. This concept can be utilized in healthcare section for relieving caregivers' load on feeding tasks.

Keywords: Robotic arm · Vision-based · Open source

1 Introduction

For some people with motoric disabilities or elderly, the unaided eating is one of the common but difficult tasks to master. This simple routine is much harder to be achieved if the person has other disabilities in combination. They may need the support of a caregiver and such a session lasts maybe at least 60 min; time that can be used for more necessary things. From the described situation, it would be good to help disable people or elderly to control the eating procedure unaided. In addition, this solution can relieve the load of the caregivers, too.

This work is aimed to design and develop a vision-based feeding robotic arm prototype based on open source software and low-cost hardware. This feeding robotic arm is equipped with an artificial intelligence (AI) and image processing concept with user-centered design. The potential users will act naturally during eating such as open their mouth and then the feeding robotic arm starts to function. The hardware design will be based on off-the-shelf electronic parts and devices. This will keep the cost of the prototype as low as possible. However, to have enough calculation power for AI and image processing operations, a high performance experimental board such as Raspberry Pi 4 is still needed. We believe that this kind of low-cost, open source prototype will be a solution for people with physical disabilities or elderlies who need help from caregivers when they are at the table. Especially, for those who live in low-income countries and they may not have possibility accessing to expensive commercial solutions.

© Springer Nature Switzerland AG 2020
K. Miesenberger et al. (Eds.): ICCHP 2020, LNCS 12377, pp. 446–452, 2020.
https://doi.org/10.1007/978-3-030-58805-2_53

2   State of the Art

Robotic arms have been using in assistive field for more than 2 decades [1] now, and win more attention lately due to the demographic change in many countries. Beside the design and development for helping people with disabilities, some of the robotic arms are used for helping the elderly. In the assistive field, the approach of the robotic arm development differs into 2 categories, the one-task robotic arm and the general or multi-purpose one, as follows:

2.1   One-Task Robotic Arm

This kind of robotic arms is designed and developed for doing just one task, in this case "feeding" robotic arm. Followings are some of the Feeding Robotic Arms, which have been researched and implemented. The first worth mentioned feeding robotic arm may be the Handy1 system [1], which was developed in 1987 by Mike Topping. It was used to assist a boy with cerebral palsy to eat without caregiver's help. In 2003, Soyama, Ishii, and Fukase had published a work entitled "The Development of Meal-Assistance Robot 'My Spoon'" [2], which is a table-top feeding robotic arm equipped with different kinds of sensors and actuators. It operates in 3 modes, namely the manual, semi-automatic, and automatic one. My Spoon is currently running in commercial version. Another commercial automatic feeding robotic arm is the so-called Obi [3], which is developed by Robert Grace in 2016. Like My Spoon, Obi can be placed on the top of a table and helps the user eating unaided. It is designed to be a robotic dining companion for people with disabilities. Another one is the work from Candeias, Rhodes, Marques, Costeira, and Veloso entitled "Vision Augmented Robot Feeding" [4], which was published in 2019 and it uses image processing technology and visual feedback for robotic arm operation.

2.2   Multi-purpose Robotic Arm

This kind of robotic arms is mostly designed to be attached to a wheelchair for convenient use. The robotic arms can be used for general purposes, such as grasping a bottle of water, open a cabinet door, grasping a spoon for eating, etc. They use different kinds of assistive technologies in order to function semi-automatically or manually with a user controlling joystick. The work of Driessen, Kate, Liefhebber, Versluis, and van Woerden entitled "Collaborative Control of the Manus Manipulator" [5] published in 2005 describes an assistive device called MANUS, which can be mounted to a wheelchair. The system is a 6 degree of freedom (DOF) rehabilitation robot with sensor-based and user control combined in a collaborative controller. It uses a gripper for multi-purpose operations. Another assistive robotic arm is the so-called JACO [6], which is running by Kinova, a company based in Canada. This robotic arm is equipped with a sophisticated gripper, which can be controlled using a joystick. An end-user can use this robotic arm for e.g. grasp a bottle of water and pour water into a glass, grasp an object, open a door, etc.

Though these robotic arms are useful and helpful for people with disabilities, they have one common important weak point, namely their high cost. This is a very important aspect, especially when the end-users are in low-income countries and may not have an access to this kind of technology. Another issue is the control of the system. Some have to be controlled using a joystick, which cannot be operated without another functioning motoric organ. To tackle these problems, iFeedingBot has been designed to be low-cost and intelligent enough to detect user's mouth movement. Thus, it can operate semi-automatically.

3   The Methodology

Our approach for designing and implementing the vision-based feeding robotic arm prototype based on open source solution is divided into 2 parts, the hardware and the software solution.

3.1   Hardware Overview

The hardware configuration is based on Raspberry Pi 4 Model B [7] that is used as a processing unit of the system. Figure 1 (a) illustrates the hardware overview of the system. A 6-Degree of Freedom (DOF) robotic arm with 5 servo motors is attached and controlled using a PCA9685 servo driver board [8]. This driver board communicates over I2C bus system and needs only 2 pins to control 16 servo motors over PWM signal. With this concept, we can control angle of a servo motor freely (between 0°–180°). For image processing and artificial intelligence purpose, a Pi camera with 8MP resolution is attached to the system. The system responses are delivered to an end-user via 3 devices, namely the Red and Green LEDs for system readiness indication, a loud speaker for voice feedback, and a 16 × 2 LCD display for text message response. In addition, a spoon is modified and attached to a servo motor at the end of the robotic arm for food taking. Figure 1 (b) depicts the wiring and connection of the electrical components of the purposed system.

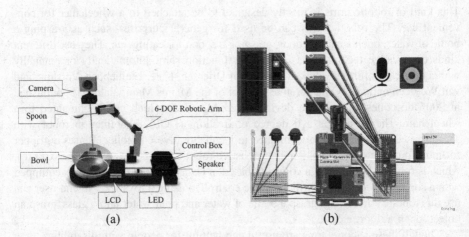

Fig. 1. (a) Hardware design overview, (b) Servo motor control circuit

As mentioned above, the hardware design of this system keeps the cost as low as possible. The whole material cost is not over 250 USD (it depends on where the components are purchased). Table 1 shows some of the specification details of the purposed system.

Table 1. Hardware specification

List	Specification
Size	60 × 25 × 35 cm
Working radius	30 cm
Weight	3.5 kg
Control unit	Raspberry Pi 4, CPU 1.5 GHz/RAM 2 GB
Degree of freedom	6
Camera resolution	2592 × 1944 pixels
Materials	Wooden base, Aluminum (Arm/Box), Plastics
Total material cost	≈ 250 USD

3.2 Software Solution

Based on Facial Landmark Detection using open source OpenCV [9] and dlib library [10], which is a combination of Image Processing and Artificial intelligence, the software architecture has been designed as shown in Fig. 2. The Raspbian serves as an operating system for system resource management. The OpenCV is used for face localization within the given image. The face bounding box ((x, y)-coordinates of the face in that image) can be then obtained. The dlib library is shipped with the so-called Face Landmark Detector, which is implemented using "One Millisecond Face Alignment with an Ensemble of Regression Trees" concept published by Kazemi and Sullivan [11]. The key facial structures in the face region, such as mouth, right eye, left eye, etc., can be detected. This face landmark detector can be used to detect facial landmarks (location of 68 (x, y)-coordinates on a face) in real-time with high quality predictions (see Fig. 2 (b)). Our feeding robotic arm uses mouth detection and localization to determine whether the end-user open his/her mouth or not (see Fig. 2 (c)).

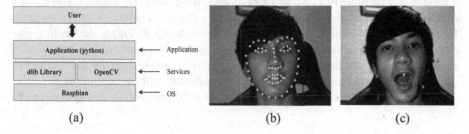

(a)   (b)   (c)

Fig. 2. (a) Software layer, (b) Key facial structures in the face region, (c) Mouth movement

The shows how the iFeedingBot system works. The camera takes the pictures of the end-user and send them to the face detection process, which will find out where the face bounding box locates. If the system detects a face, it will call the mouth detection process. If not, it will acquire more pictures from the camera. In the next step, the system tries to detect the mouth. If it detects one, it will consider, whether the mouth is opening or not. If yes, it will start the feeding procedure by sending the PWM signal to control the servo motors and bring them into the pre-defined position. If not, it will acquire the new pictures from the camera, and the whole procedure starts from the beginning (Fig. 3).

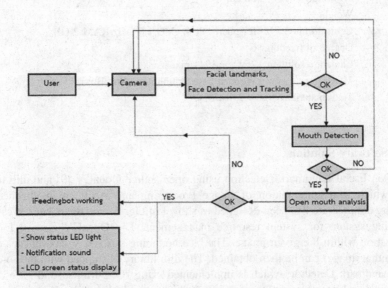

Fig. 3. System flowchart of image processing and operation steps

4   The Results

Figure 4 (a) shows the result of the implementation of the designed vision-based feeding robotic arm prototype. From the hardware point of view, the system consists of a control box (Raspberry Pi 4), an LCD display, a 6-DOF robotic arm, a bowl, and a camera. The open source software is used for face and facial landmark detection. In the feeding-ready mode, the end-users can open their mouth to trigger the feeding procedure. After the food has been taken from the spoon, the system will go into standby mode for a while, and then it will go into feeding-ready mode again for the next mouth opening. In this manner, the end-users can eat naturally without controlling any other input devices, such as switch or joystick. Figure 4 (b) depicts how this system can be setup.

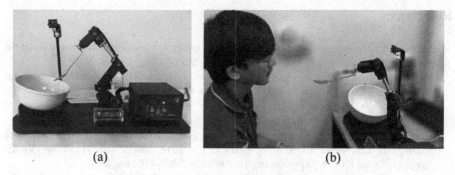

Fig. 4. (a) Actual system, (b) iFeedingBot in action

The commercial feeding robotic arms offered in the market are still very expensive, especially for those people with disabilities in low-income countries. We hope this vision-based feeding robotic arm prototype based on open source solution can be one of the contributions demonstrating possibility of approaching low-cost feeding robotic arms. The recent technology in the field of image processing and artificial intelligence can be implemented with pre-defined models and data sets. This enhances the design and implementation of such feeding robotic arms.

5   Conclusion and Future Work

With the material cost under 250 USD we demonstrated that such a vision-based feeding robotic arm can be designed and implemented. The system embraces the image processing and artificial intelligence technology through open source software for detecting the user's facial landmark structures and movement. This give us the possibility to detect the user's mouth moves. We take advantage of this feather and creating a sophisticated system that works with the user's natural behaviors of mouth movement. From the cost point of view, this vision-based feeding robotic arm is low-income country friendly and potentially affordable.

In the future, we will enhance the system in both software and hardware aspects. In the hardware aspect, the system will be equipped with more sophisticated electronic components such as stepping motors or ultrasonic sensors. The stepping motors should allow the robotic arm move with smooth and gentle motion. The ultrasonic sensors can let the system measure the distance between the spoon and the user's mouth. In the software aspect, the algorithm for locating the user's mouth position should be developed and implemented. This will let us move the spoon to the right position automatically. In addition, the Speech Recognition technique should be used in case of more natural operability. Furthermore, the User Research should be done with the target group for more usability, user acceptance, and better user experience.

Acknowledgment. This work is done at Digital Media and Interaction Research Laboratory (DMI), Faculty of Informatics, Burapha University. We are deeply grateful for the grant and supports from Faculty of Informatics.

References

1. Topping, M.: An overview of the development of handy 1, a rehabilitation robot to assist the severely disabled. J. Intell. Robot. Syst. **34**, 253–263 (2002)
2. Soyama, R., Ishii, S., Fukase, A.: The development of meal-assistance robot 'My Spoon'. In: Proceedings of the 8th International Conference on Rehabilitation Robotics, 2003, pp. 88–91 (2003)
3. Grace, R.: Obi feeds more than the imagination. Plast. Eng. **72**, 18–22 (2016)
4. Candeias, A., Rhodes, T., Marques, M., Costeira, J.P., Veloso, M.: Vision augmented robot feeding. In: Leal-Taixé, L., Roth, S. (eds.) ECCV 2018. LNCS, vol. 11134, pp. 50–65. Springer, Cham (2019). https://doi.org/10.1007/978-3-030-11024-6_4
5. Driessen, B., Liefhebber, F., Kate, T.T., van Woerden, K.: Collaborative control of the MANUS manipulator. In: 2005 IEEE 9th International Conference on Rehabilitation Robotics, Chicago, IL, 28 June–1 July 2005, pp. 247–251. IEEE, Piscataway (2005)
6. Kinova: Jaco—Robotic arm—Kinova. KINOVA JACO Assistive robotic arm. https://www.kinovarobotics.com/en/products/assistive-technologies/kinova-jaco-assistive-robotic-arm. Accessed 14 Apr 2020
7. Raspberry Pi Foundation: Raspberry Pi 4 Model B specifications – Raspberry Pi. https://www.raspberrypi.org/products/raspberry-pi-4-model-b/specifications/. Accessed 15 Apr 2020
8. Sunfounder: PCA9685 16 Channel 12 Bit PWM Servo Driver – Wiki. http://wiki.sunfounder.cc/index.php?title=PCA9685_16_Channel_12_Bit_PWM_Servo_Driver. Accessed 15 Apr 2020
9. OpenCV: OpenCV. https://opencv.org/. Accessed 15 Apr 2020
10. King, D.: dlib C++ Library. http://dlib.net/. Accessed 15 Apr 2020
11. Kazemi, V., Sullivan, J.: One millisecond face alignment with an ensemble of regression trees. In: 2014 IEEE Conference on Computer Vision and Pattern Recognition (CVPR), Columbus, OH, USA, pp. 1867–1874. IEEE (2014)

Development of Smart-Phone Interfaces for Tongue Controlled Assistive Devices

Silvia Maddalena Rossi[✉], Nicholas Marjanovic,
and Hananeh Esmailbeigi

University of Illinois at Chicago, Chicago, IL 60607, USA
{srossi3, nmarja2, hesmai2}@uic.edu

Abstract. Enabling individuals with upper limb disabilities to interact independently with smartphones is challenging. Our team has developed discreet
Bluetooth-enabled intraoral wearable devices that utilize the tongue in order to
allow for independent interaction with smartphones. This paper presents on
custom applications that are paired with the developed button-based intraoral
device and the trackpad-based intraoral device. Initially, user study surveys were
conducted in order to identify the most common needs of the target population.
The prominent needs identified were the ability to independently type and place
phone calls. These identified features were implemented in the developed
applications. The applications also featured six tongue-training environments.
Each tongue-training environment is designed to enhance an aspect of the
tongue's strength and precision for optimized interaction with the intraoral
wearable devices. To assess the implementation of the developed applications,
an expert user participated in the iterative design process. Also, in order to
assess the target population's feedback in regard to the developed applications, a
follow-up survey was distributed. Our aim is to be able to utilize the intraoral
wearable devices and applications to bridge the technological divide which
affects individuals with paralyzing disabilities to the upper limbs.

Keywords: Assistive technology · Smartphone interfaces · Intraoral wearable
device

1 Introduction

According to the World Health Organization's report on disability, more than 13.3% of
the world's population is affected by mental or physical disabilities [1]. In the USA,
1.7% of the population lives with paralysis. 27% of these cases are consequences of
spinal cord injuries [2]. When these injuries affect the upper limbs, the individual loses
their ability to independently interact with everyday technologies, such as smartphones
and computers. The currently available assistive devices that aim to address this loss
are either voice recognition devices or devices that utilize the head and neck movement. The voice recognition assistive devices hinder the user's privacy by requiring
them to speak out loud. The head and neck-based assistive devices require bulky
equipment that attracts unwanted attention. Both of these shortcomings result in a low
adoption rate of these categories of assistive devices [3]. To address these issues, a new

© Springer Nature Switzerland AG 2020
K. Miesenberger et al. (Eds.): ICCHP 2020, LNCS 12377, pp. 453–460, 2020.
https://doi.org/10.1007/978-3-030-58805-2_54

category of assistive devices that concentrates on the unique connection of the tongue to the brain has been developed. The Hypoglossal nerve and the Vagus nerve bypass the spinal cord and allow for the direct communication between the tongue and the brain; hence, enabling the tongue to maintain its functionality after spinal cord injury. Intraoral assistive devices utilize this feature and allow the user to control various external devices using their tongue. Some of the better known intraoral assistive devices are the Tongue Drive System (TDS) [4], the intraoral Tongue Drive System (ITDS) [5], the Intraoral Tongue Computer Interface (ITCI) [6] and the TongueToSpeech (TTS) [7]. All of these devices - except for TTS - either require additional units outside the oral cavity or modifications to the oral cavity. The applications developed for these intraoral assistive devices often do not enable accessing the evolving core functionalities of smartphones.

In this paper, we present our work on two novel intraoral wearable assistive device and their custom applications, that allow the user to interact with the core functionalities of smartphones. The two versions of the discreet Bluetooth-enabled intraoral wearable devices are the button-based intraoral device (Oral User Interface Controller) and the trackpad-based intraoral device (Tongue Trackpad User Interface Controller). The applications are developed, according to a user-centered design process, with the objective of simplifying communication for basic interaction with smartphones.

2   Materials and Methods

2.1   Hardware

Our team has developed a novel platform of discreet Bluetooth-enabled intraoral wearable assistive devices that are controlled with the tongue. The two most recent versions of the developed devices are the Oral User Interface Controller (O-UIC) [8] and the Tongue Trackpad User Interface Controller (TT-UIC) [9, 10] (Fig. 1).

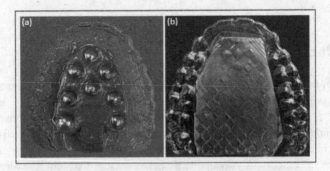

Fig. 1. (a) The O-UIC device; (b) The TT-UIC device.

The O-UIC device interacts with the applications using eight discrete capacitive contact pads. It achieves the typing goal by providing a "T9 (Text on 9 keys) Format" interaction. Characters are assigned to each touch-sensitive capacitive contact pad of the device and the user can circulate between them in order to type the character of interest. The TT-UIC device interacts with the applications through continuous control of a cursor. Both of the intraoral devices are stand-alone and do not require any external units or modifications to the oral cavity. The tongue's intentional interactions with the wearables are detected through the capacitive sensors embedded in the devices. These interactions are then coded into cursor control and commands and transmitted to the smartphones via Bluetooth Low Energy (BLE) communication.

2.2   Software Application

The development framework for the applications is React Native (Facebook, 2015). This framework allows for efficient cross-platform development and optimization, as well as providing libraries for BLE communication.

Communication of the Custom Applications. Due to the core difference in the communication flow among the two intraoral devices, an application is developed for each one. The O-UIC device communicates with the smartphone through a string of characters sent at 2.5 Hz frequency. The string identifies the selected capacitive contact pad and is decoded by the custom application's BleManager (a React Native component). The TT-UIC device, on the other hand, utilizes the Human Interface Device (HID) protocols. It sends packets of information directly to the smartphone's Operative System (OS), allowing for it to be recognized as a mouse. This feature enables the TT-UIC device to control any Bluetooth-enabled interface without requiring a custom application.

Design Principles of the Custom Applications. The O-UIC device custom application is required for the user to be able to interact with the smartphone; basically, without the application, the device is not recognizable by the smartphone. The application's design principle is to provide visual feedback of the pad's location and content to the user in order to enable the typing task (Fig. 2.a). On the other hand, when using the TT-UIC device, the user has the option to directly interact with the smartphone's native interfaces. However, the default smartphone's on-screen components are optimized for fingertip interactions, hence making it difficult for the tongue to have precise control over the small keyboard keys, icons, and buttons. Therefore, the design principle followed for the custom application is to simplify the tongue's interaction with the smartphone and to increase its precision of cursor control (Fig. 2.b).

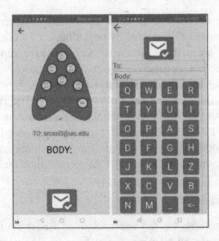

Fig. 2. (a) Email screen of the O-UIC application (b) and the TT-UIC application.

The TT-UIC custom keyboard layout was designed to optimize the tongue's interaction with the application. The dimensions of the custom keys were calculated by the analysis of the Difficulty Index (DI) present in Fitts Law for pointing interactions [11]. The DI is defined as the ratio of the distance between the targets (A) to the target's width (W). In our case, the maximum distance for both the custom application and the default on-screen components is constant and equal to the screen's width. Therefore, DI is calculated as 1/Width. The DI for the default keyboard of the smartphone (used for the development of the application) is 0.028. The DI for the custom keyboard is 0.016, which theoretically should make it 43% easier for the tongue to interact with the custom keyboard.

2.3 User-Centered Design Process

Survey. To identify the most common needs of the target population, a survey was distributed amongst the intended population. The survey was in accordance with the University of Illinois at Chicago (UIC) Institutional Review Board (IRB) protocol number 2017-0550. Eighteen potential users participated in the survey, of which 50% expressed interest in adopting intraoral assistive devices. The prominent functionalities identified were easy access to placing SOS calls and independent interactions with keyboards. The analysis of the survey data also highlighted the need for the interface to accommodate visually impaired users. Hence, the built-in functionalities of React Native `accessibilityLabel` and `accessibilityHint` were utilized to allow for each component to be compatible with voice-over readers. The applications were developed to accommodate for the needs identified through the survey.

Evaluation and Iteration. The Keystroke Level Model (KLM) was utilized to theoretically calculate the time required to perform various tasks using the developed custom applications. The KLM analysis estimates the theoretical time needed by a proficient user to perform a task by breaking it down into building blocks and adding up the theoretical time for execution of each block. The tasks studied were placing a SOS call, placing a ten-digit phone call, and sending an eleven-character email. An iterative design process was utilized in order to test the effective functioning of the tasks and to identify the areas of improvement. In this process an expert user was asked to perform the same tasks using both intraoral assistive devices. The results of the theoretical KLM analysis are presented in Table 1.

Table 1. KLM theoretical times of execution for each task using the two devices and interfaces.

	SOS call	Phone call	Email
O-UIC device [s]	2.65	22.85	30.2
TT-UIC device [s]	2.65	29.15	34.45

O-UIC Device User Testing. In addition to the expert user performing each task once and testing its correct functioning, the functioning of the O-UIC device was evaluated in regard to its efficiency as a T9 typing device. Nine users were asked to use the O-UIC device to type a pangram, hence the device was tested as a typing device and the Characters per Minute rate (CPM) was recorded [8].

TT-UIC Device User Testing. The tasks studied to evaluate the functionally of the application were the above mentioned three tasks and an additional task of sending an 11-character text message. The expert user was instructed to perform each of the tasks four times, one after the other using the custom application. The same four tasks were also executed four times, using the TT-UIC device while interfacing with the smart-phone's native environment. This aimed to compare the usability of the custom application and the native environment.

Feedback Survey. After the applications were developed and implemented, a follow-up survey was distributed to the target population. The survey included a description of the applications and assessed the user's feedback in regard to the implemented functionalities.

2.4 Tongue Training Environments

Studies have demonstrated that training the tongue, like any other muscle in the body, increases the tongue's eight muscles' strength and precision [12]. Therefore, the applications also featured six tongue-training environments. Each tongue-training environment is designed to enhance an aspect of the tongue's strength and precision for optimized interaction with the intraoral wearable devices. These environments are designed based on six hypotheses, that aim to be tested in future studies. The same expert users who performed the evaluation of the application also evaluated the functioning of the six environments, by testing them three consecutive times. The results of conducting each taring can be accessed by the user in the form of graphs, which could be used to track potential improvements over time.

3 Results

During the functional evaluation of both devices and their applications, it was observed that the user could accidentally trigger the SOS call. Therefore, a control mechanism was implemented in which three consecutive clicks are required in the O-UIC application to activate this feature. Also, a pop-up button needs to be selected in order to confirm intention in the TT-UIC application.

The average Characters per Minute (CPM) of the nine users' trials is 16.72 CPM for the inexperienced users. For an experienced user it is 32.67 CPM [8]. This, together with the confirmed compatibility of the device with the custom interface, proves it to be a viable solution

The results of the four trials with the TT-UIC device using the application and the native smartphone environment are presented in Table 2.

Table 2. Average time and errors (and standard deviation) required to perform each task by the expert user while interacting with the TT-UIC application or the native smartphone environment.

	SOS call	Phone call	Email	Text message
Average application time [s]	2.53 ± 0.35	50.25 ± 1.48	68.75 ± 2.86	71 ± 4.74
Average application errors	0	0.75 ± 0.43	0	1 ± 1
Average native environment time [s]	21.9 ± 2.57	65.18 ± 13	76.75 ± 5.8	109.5 ± 20.2
Average native environment errors	0	1.25 ± 0.8	2.25 ± 0.43	2 ± 0.7

The comparison between the native environment and the custom application results shows the effectiveness of the simplification. For the theoretical calculation of the simplification, a 43% was expected. The lowering of the DI allows for an average improvement in the time needed of 39.6%, accompanied by a lowering of the error rate by 63.3%.

Feedback Survey Results. A follow-up survey was distributed amongst the targeted population. Five potential users participated in the survey. Though this represents a limited sample, the overall response proved interest in the applications and devices by the intended population. The responses are summarized in Table 3, in which we can see the average answer to the feedback questions asked. Each question required the selection of an agreement level, from "strongly disagree" (1) to "strongly agree" (5).

Table 3. Summary of the answers given to the questions in the feedback survey. The answers were given on an agreement scale with 1 being "strongly disagree" and 5 being "strongly agree". The table shows the average value and standard deviation of the responses. 5 users answered the survey.

Survey questions	O-UIC device	TT-UIC device
I think that I would be able to use this system independently after it is placed inside the oral cavity	4.6 ± 0.49	4.4 ± 0.8
I think this system would positively impact my daily activities	3.6 ± 0.8	2.6 ± 1.02
I think this system would assist me in my interaction with my smartphone and computer	3.4 ± 1.02	3.2 ± 1.32
Overall interest in the wearable device and the associated application	2.8 ± 0.98	3.2 ± 1.32

4 Discussion

Two custom intraoral assistive devices were developed by our team. The applications that are paired with the developed button-based intraoral device and the trackpad-based intraoral device were evaluated in this paper. Through the conducted survey it was concluded that the developed applications would provide a viable solution for individuals interested in discreet independent interactions with smartphones. The theoretical time presented in Table 1, demonstrates the minimum time needed for a proficient user to execute a task at the peak of their learning curve. From the average time and errors presented in Table 2, it is evident that the custom application simplifies interaction with the smartphone and increases the precision of the interaction. The time needed to perform the tasks is higher than the theoretical time calculated via KLM, but it is expected that a proficient user would reach that speed of interaction. The follow-up survey confirmed the potential interest of the target population in the proposed intraoral devices and their associated applications. The expert user assessed the functionalities of the six developed training environments and all were proved compatible and executable with the TT-UIC device.

5 Conclusion

In this work, we presented on intraoral wearable devices and their associated applications. These assistive devices could be adopted by paralyzed individuals who strive to regain privacy and independence in their interaction with smartphones. We proposed two devices, the button-based intraoral device and the trackpad-based intraoral device, each catering to a subcategory of users' preferences. We acknowledge the limited user study of the current paper. Future steps will include extensive user testing, including the target population. Also, testing of the tongue-training environments would be conducted.

References

1. World Health Organization. Summary World Report On Disability. World Health, pp. 1–24 (2011)
2. Armour, B.S., Courtney-Long, E.A., Fox, M.H., Fredine, H., Cahill, A.: Prevalence and causes of paralysis - United States, 2013. Am. J. Public Health **106**(10), 1855–1857 (2016)
3. Parette, P., Scherer, M.: Assistive technology use and stigma. Educ. Train. Dev. Disabil. **39**, 217–226 (2004)
4. Kim, J., et al.: The tongue enables computer and wheelchair control for people with spinal cord injury. Sci. Transl. Med. **5**(213), 213ra166 (2013). https://doi.org/10.1126/scitranslmed.3006296
5. Kong, F., Sahadat, M.N., Ghovanloo, M., Durgin, G.D.: A stand-alone intraoral tongue-controlled computer interface for people with tetraplegia. IEEE Trans. Biomed. Circuits Syst. **13**(5), 848–857 (2019)
6. Andreasen Struijk, L.N.S., Bentsen, B., Gaihede, M., Lontis, E.: Error-free text typing performance of an inductive intra-oral tongue computer interface for severely disabled individuals. IEEE Trans. Neural Syst. Rehabil. Eng. **25**(11), 2094–2104 (2017)
7. Marjanovic, N., Piccinini, G., Kerr, K., Esmailbeigi, H.: TongueToSpeech (TTS): wearable wireless assistive device for augmented speech. In: Proceedings of the Annual International Conference of the IEEE Engineering in Medicine and Biology Society (EMBC), pp. 3561–3563 (2017)
8. Tomback, M.: The Oral User Interface Controller (O-UIC): An Assistive Communication Device (2019)
9. Soresini, G.: Distribution analysis of the tongue's free-exploration pattern using an oral wearable device (2020)
10. Bondavalli, D.: Tongue trackpad: an augmentative and assistive device aimed at enhancing digital life (2020)
11. MacKenzie, T.: Fitt's law. Hum.-Comput. Interact. **7**, 91–139 (1992)
12. Svensson, P., Romaniello, A., Arendt-Nieisen, L., Sessle, B.J.: Plasticity in corticomotor control of the human tongue musculature induced by tongue-task training. Exp. Brain Res. **152**(1), 42–51 (2003)

Application of Multi Materials Additive Manufacturing Technique in the Design and Manufacturing of Hand Orthoses

Sai Advaith Venumbaka[1](✉) (ID), Mario Covarubias[1] (ID),
Giacomo Cesaro[2], Alfredo Ronca[2], Cristina De Capitani[2],
Luigi Ambrosio[2], and Andrea Sorrentino[2] (ID)

[1] Department of Mechanical Engineering, Politecnico di Milano, Via Previati,
23900 Lecco, Italy
saiadvaith.venumbaka@mail.polimi.it
[2] Institute for Polymers, Composites and Biomaterials (CNR), Via Previati 1/C,
23900 Lecco, Italy

Abstract. The objective of this study is to demonstrate the possibility of obtaining a completely customized orthosis through the use of multi-material 3-D printing technique. Additive manufacturing with multi-material enables to print objects with two different materials at the same time. Two immiscible materials Polylactic Acid (PLA), Thermoplastic Polyurethane (TPU) are chosen to give the orthosis a good trade-off between flexibility and rigidity. Results show that with this innovative technology it is possible not only create complex functional geometries but also to overcome some of the issues associated with traditional immobilization techniques (plaster of Paris splints). Tensile and impact tests are performed on 3D printed specimens to analyze their toughness, rigidity and flexibility. Three different prototypes are developed varying the composition and the organization of the materials used. Results show that the proposed approach is capable of addressing all the issues associated with conventional plaster casts.

Keywords: Orthosis · 3D printing · Polylactic Acid (PLA) · Thermoplastic Polyurethane (TPU) · Multi-material printing · Tensile test · Impact test

1 Introduction

Millions of fractures that occur every year around the world are immobilized in a similar way for centuries. Typically, plaster of Paris is used to immobilize and hold the injured limbs in place until healing is confirmed. This orthopaedic technique makes use of cotton bandage combined with calcined gypsum, which hardens after it has been made wet. Due to the weight of the resulting cast, the patient was largely confined to bed during the period of fracture healing. The additional issue associated with the use of the Plaster of Paris casts are: deep vein thrombosis, soft tissue swelling, pressure sores; venous congestion, lack of breathability, comfort, waterproofing and aesthetics [1].

© Springer Nature Switzerland AG 2020
K. Miesenberger et al. (Eds.): ICCHP 2020, LNCS 12377, pp. 461–468, 2020.
https://doi.org/10.1007/978-3-030-58805-2_55

3D-printed orthosis, which has recently been reported in media, are lightweight, well-ventilated, waterproof, and aesthetically pleasing [4, 5]. Despite the numerous vantages offered by these techniques, several issues already exist. The lack of materials and the poor mechanical properties of the printed objects play a critical role determining the acceptance rate the patients. Abrasion caused by the skin rubbing against a rough surface of some 3D printed orthosis is another important limitation of these techniques.

This paper proposes the use of a multi-material 3D printing technology to manufacture innovative orthoses. A soft (TPU) and rigid material (PLA) are printed simultaneously to allow for different properties.

2 State of the Art

The typical function of any orthoses is to enhance the patient's ability to function and improve quality of life by supporting the alignment of the bone position, immobilization and stabilization. 3D printing has already proven record of manufacturing custom based orthoses according to patient specifications. The customization however requires a dedicated design phase that addresses all the major specifications such as the fit, aesthetics etc. To assist the design phase, Shih et al. proposed a cloud-based design system called Cyber Design and Additive Manufacturing (CDAM) [6]. The CDAM system aims at shortening the delivery and improving the fit and comfort of custom orthoses. The system is composed of four main features such as the digital scanning; a cloud-based design software that enables clinicians to access scanned point cloud data on the geometry of patients limb; a cloud-based manufacturing software that generates tool paths and process parameters for additive manufacturing; the evaluation using Inertia Measurement Unit (IMU) for measurement of the limb motion for gait analysis.

Companies such as ActivArmor, Xkelet Easy Life SL, Summit ID, Andiamo, Evill Design, MediPrint are currently producing orthoses using 3D printing in the market according to the patient specifications. The noteworthy point is that providing a parametric design allows the patient to choose from a wide range of options that fits their body and style. This leads to the fact that aesthetics is very important at the design stage which makes patients proud of wearing the orthoses.

On the other hand, printing time is a major issue to be addressed. Being a layer by layer process 3D printing takes forever. Due to the increasing research done throughout many years in the field of 3D printing, nowadays there are many printers available in the market that prints very fast reducing the print time drastically. For instance, Superfast printers like Carbon M1 manufactured by company Carbon 3D which uses a state of art Digital Light Synthesis technology known as CLIP (Continuous Liquid Interface Process) [7] is able to print 25 times faster than a traditional 3D printer.

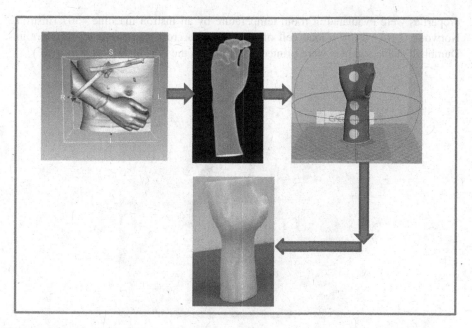

Fig. 1. Process showing the development of Orthosis, Step 1: Segmentation of DICOM data, Step 2: STL Image of hand, Step 3: 3D cast is modelled for the arm which is then printed, Step 4: Final 3D Printed Orthosis

3 Materials and Methodology

The two materials used in this work are polylactic acid (PLA) and thermoplastic polyurethane (TPU). In particular, the following commercial materials were chosen PLA light blue from FILOALFA® (extrusion temperature 205 °C); medical-grade TPU 95A black from Lubrizol Advanced Materials Inc. (extrusion temperature 225 ° C). The PLA filament is rigid and brittle whereas the TPU is a semi-flexible material with excellent mechanical resistance to abrasion, impact, laceration and chemistry to oils and greases.

Fused deposition modelling (FDM) is the technology used to fabricate the orthoses with a multi material approach. A dual-extrusion CREATBOT F430 machine (nozzle diameter 0.4 mm) and the Cura 3.1.0 software were used. Generally, a 3D scanner is used to scan the hand part to directly extract the STL format of the model or in most cases the CT scan is taken and then it is converted from Dicom to STL format using an open-source medical imaging software called Slicer 3D. In this research the CT scan is used to extract the STL file. The process flow showing the development of orthoses is shown in Fig. 1. To enable the dual extrusion the design is made in two parts and then merged together during slicing in Cura 3.1.0. Figure 2 shows the image with two designs to be merged. To evaluate how 3D printing parameters affect mechanical properties, different specimens are printed with an infill percentage of 100%. Tensile properties were evaluated at room temperature by an Instron machine 4507 (Instron, Norwood, USA) using a load cell of 100kN and a crosshead speed of 10 mm/min. Dumbbell shape samples were printed according to the ASTM D1708 standard.

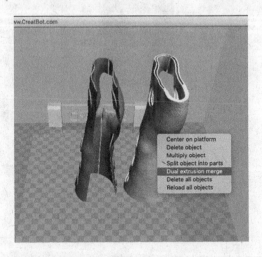

Fig. 2. Image showing two designs to be merged

Charpy impact tests were performed to correlate the energy absorption of the different materials with fibers orientation and layer thickness. Samples (13.0 mm wide (w) 2.5 mm thick (t) and 60 mm long) with a notch depth-to-width ratio of 0.3 were fractured at room temperature by using impact energy of 3.6 J and an impact speed of 1 m/s. An instrumented apparatus (CEAST Mod. 6545) equipped with a Charpy pendulum hammer (mass: 3.65 kg) was used.

4   R&D Work

Mechanical tests on 3D printed PLA, TPU tensile and Charpy specimens are carried out to validate the performance of the cast structure and identify the potential risk of the structural collapse due to concentrated stresses. Experimental results for tensile tests are reported in Table 1 for both materials used. As expected, PLA show the higher tensile strength, whereas TPU has lower elastic modulus and higher elongation at break. Results for the impact tests are reported in Table 2. Moreover, TPU material showed higher impact strength. In summary, TPU showed typical elastomeric behavior with low stiffness and good flexibility. In contrary, PLA has very high rigidity with very less flexibility.

The cast is modeled as funnel-shaped geometry using Meshmixer which allows the manipulation of the STL files and creates smooth edges. The cast structure includes two different materials, ventilation structure and opening gap for hygienic purposes and wearing comfort.

Table 1. Tensile test results for PLA and TPU samples

Description	PLA	TPU
Percentage of strain at peak (%)	3.06	161.3
Load at peak (KN)	2.578	0.5441
Stress at peak (MPa)	49.58	10.46
% strain at break	3.454	188.6
Load at break (KN)	2.512	0.5218
Stress at break (MPa)	48.31	10.03
Youngs modulus (MPa)	2244	47.14

Table 2. Impact test results for PLA and TPU samples

	PLA	TPU
Force (N)	303.66	304.78
Time (ms)	0.510	14.110
Velocity (m/s)	0.97	−0.03
Energy (Joules)	0.06	1.79

The cast can be adjusted to accommodate swelling from injured limbs during treatment. To allow for the multi-material printing the design is developed in two parts and later they are merged together using slicer software Cura 3.1.0. Figure 2 shows the two designs on the Cura platform that are to be merged and printed with two different materials.

The cast is fabricated with a layer height of 0.3 mm. The thickness of the cast selected is 5 mm to improve the stiffness of the device. Finally, to close the orthoses after the person wears it for better fit and immobilization a Velcro strip can be used to close the orthoses.

5 Discussion

Three different prototypes are developed:

1. PLA-TPU-PLA (66% PLA AND 33%TPU): The outer layers in this configuration are printed using PLA and the inner layers are printed using TPU. Hand orthosis manufactured with this configuration show high resistance to bending due to high flexural modulus and high stiffness of PLA. However, PLA is very hard and its contact with the skin causes irritation. This is a problem because it affects the comfort of the person wearing it.

2. TPU-PLA-TPU (66% TPU AND 33% PLA): Hand orthosis manufactured with this configuration shows a significant bending deformation compared to the configuration above. Since the outer layers in this configuration are made up of TPU (which has low flexural modulus and stiffness compared to PLA), the bending is good and still the PLA layers inside will resist some of the bending leading to lower plastic

deformation of the orthosis. Beyond this from the practical point of view, the TPU material is very soft, so the contact with the skin is good which reduces the chances of skin irritation improving the comfort of the person wearing it. From the above-mentioned reasons it can be concluded that this configuration will fulfill the needs of the patient.

3. Only TPU (100% TPU): The orthosis manufactured with this configuration show high flexibility (due to low flexural modulus and stiffness of TPU) since all of it is printed with TPU. From a manufacturing point of view the prototype made only with TPU is easier to manufacture (also single material printing is easier compared to multi-material printing), but there are chances that the orthosis may deform plastically if it is removed and worn a number of times leading to change in its fit which affects the healing process. Due to the above-mentioned reasons it can be concluded that TPU-PLA-TPU exhibits good trade-off between flexibility and rigidity thus allowing for the patient comfort (Fig. 3).

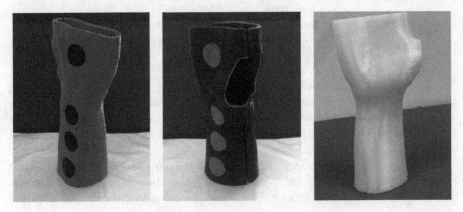

Fig. 3. From left to right Prototype 1, Prototype 2, Prototype 3

6   Scientific and Practical Impact to the Orthotics Field

Multi-materials 3D printing allows obtaining 3D-printed orthosis with 1/10 of weight in comparison with traditional alternatives. Medical technicians with a few years of experience can design cast within 20 min using the proposed technique. The image-based design minimizes the distortion during the healing process because of the best fit geometry. The soft structure reducing the risk of cutaneous complications and potentially improves treatment efficacy and increases patients' satisfaction. Moreover, the thermoplastic materials used are fully recyclable and thus reusable at the device end of life. It causes less to zero harm to the environment.

Also, the cost associated with the 3D printing of hand orthosis is less compared to the traditional casts in the long run. Although start-up costs can be high, the cost of individual unit production is relatively low. Considering all of the factors mentioned above it can be concluded that Additive Manufacturing is all set to take over the traditional methods of orthosis and prosthesis.

7 Conclusions

Although Plaster of Paris is still used as splinting material extensively, it still suffers from many drawbacks as a heavyweight, low breathability, inability to get wet or be cleaned. The application of multi-material 3D printing to produce orthosis promises higher levels of compliance amongst patients who are required to wear a wrist orthosis and can address the problems associated related to plaster casts. Figure 4 shows the person wearing prototype 2 as it is proven feasible in terms of mechanical properties and comfort to patients due to contact with TPU.

Fig. 4. Image of Person wearing prototype 2

A short interview conducted with the person who wore prototype 2 has revealed that the cast is very light in weight, the contact with the skin is good (due to soft nature of TPU) and there is no difficulty wearing the orthoses as she was able to perform her tasks without any problem.

The creation of a waterproof, washable, lightweight, static, or removable padded cast is the goal to improve the quality of life and compliance of patients with immobilization regimens. These cast qualities can have a tremendous impact on the wearer's experience, especially in children, the elderly, athletes, and those whose skin needs to be observed regularly.

However, there are some limitations that are worth discussing. Limitations like high capital cost to buy a laser 3D scanner and the time taken to manufacture the orthoses. A typical 3D printer to manufacture end products may cost anywhere between 10000 to 120000 euros and a laser 3D scanner can range between 5000 to 6000 euros. However, the material cost is lower and once the capital cost is recovered the cost to produce one piece is lower than the plaster casts. Another major issue that is pulling back 3D printing from being prototyping to real-time manufacturing technique is the print time. With the recent advancements in the field of 3D printing there are companies like Carbon3D who are manufacturing super-fast 3D printers which can print 25 times faster than the traditional 3D printer. If these kinds of 3D printers are made economic 3D printed orthoses have the potential to greatly impact quality of life in patients with orthopedic injuries requiring immobilization.

References

1. Fitch, M.T., Nicks, B.A., Pariyadath, M., McGinnis, H.D., Manthey, D.E.: Basic splinting techniques. New Engl. J. Med. **359**, e32 (2008). https://doi.org/10.1056/NEJMvcm0801942
2. Lin, H., Shi, L., Wang, D.: A rapid and intelligent designing technique for patient-specific and 3D-printed orthopedic cast. 3D Printing Med. **2**(1), 1–10 (2016). https://doi.org/10.1186/s41205-016-0007-7
3. Lunsfort, C., Grindle, G., Salatin, B., Dicianno, B.E.: Innovations with 3-dimensional printing in physical medicine and rehabilitation: a review of the literature. PM&R J. **8**(12), 1201–1212 (2016). https://doi.org/10.1016/j.pmrj.2016.07.003
4. Chen, Y.-J., Lin, H., Zhang, X., Huang, W., Shi, L., Wang, D.: Application of 3D–printed and patient-specific cast for the treatment of distal radius fractures: initial experience. 3D Printing Med. **3**(1), 1–9 (2017). https://doi.org/10.1186/s41205-017-0019-y
5. Chen, R.K., Jin, Y., Wensman, J., Shih, A.: Additive manufacturing of custom orthoses and prostheses–a review. J. Addit. Manufact. **12**(A), 77–89 (2016). https://doi.org/10.1016/j.addma.2016.04.002
6. Shih, A., Park, D., Yang, Y., Chisena, R., Wu, D.: Cloud-based design and additive manufacturing of custom orthoses. Procedia CIRP **63**, 156–160 (2017)
7. Carbon. Carbon - The World's Leading Digital Manufacturing Platform (2020). https://www.carbon3d.com/

Service and Care Provision in Assistive Environments

Designing Nostalgic Tangible User Interface Application for Elderly People

Way Kiat Bong[✉] , Florian Mäußer, Margot van Eck,
Diogo De Araujo, Jorg Tibosch, Tobias Glaum, and Weiqin Chen

OsloMet – Oslo Metropolitan University,
Postboks 4, St. Olavs Plass, 0130 Oslo, Norway
wayki@oslomet.no

Abstract. Our elderly population faces challenges in accepting and using new digital technology, and tangible user interface (TUI) can contribute as a more intuitive user interface in addressing these challenges. Studies have shown that nostalgic memories trigger positive emotions, which can provide better experiences for elderly people in learning and using new technology. However, the use of nostalgia in TUI for elderly people has been little and therefore the understanding on how nostalgia can contribute in TUI promoting technology acceptance among elderly people is limited. In order to address this knowledge gap, in this study we have created a nostalgic TUI application for elderly people through three iterations of design, development and evaluation. The results show that by adopting the element of nostalgia into the TUI application, elderly people could learn to use new technology in a more intuitive way. They could relate the new technology to their old positive memories. However, they had expectations that the TUI application would work exactly like the old fashioned way. Through the research process, we gathered and reflected on the lessons learned, which can serve as guidelines for using the concept of nostalgia in designing TUI application for elderly people's technology acceptance.

Keywords: Tangible user interface · Nostalgia · Elderly people

1 Introduction

Recent studies have been focusing on improving elderly's acceptance and use of information and communication technology (ICT). The use of ICT among elderly people can have positive impacts on their daily life, but many elderly people are not benefiting from it as they felt "intimidated" and "anxious" with the new technology [1]. Thus, while designing ICT for elderly people, it is crucial to ensure that ICT appears inviting, user-friendly and easy to use. Tangible user interface (TUI) allows the users to interact with the digital information using everyday physical objects [2], which can result in more intuitive and effortless use of ICT. It has therefore been identified as having the potential in addressing elderly people's challenges in accepting and using new technology [3–5].

In order to achieve a design of TUI that is inviting, user-friendly and easy to use, the concept of nostalgia can be used. According to Sedikides and Wildschut [6],

K. Miesenberger et al. (Eds.): ICCHP 2020, LNCS 12377, pp. 471–479, 2020.
https://doi.org/10.1007/978-3-030-58805-2_56

nostalgia is a self-relevant, most of the time positive than negative emotions that link one to his or her past. Therefore, it can help people in finding meaning in their lives by primarily increasing social connectedness, i.e. a sense of belongingness and acceptance, and secondarily by augmenting self-continuity (a sense of connection between one's past and one's present). Studies have shown that nostalgic memories can trigger positive memories [6, 7]. These positive emotions can contribute in providing better user experiences for elderly people in terms of learning and using new technology.

However, the use of nostalgia in TUI for elderly people has been little. Nilsson, Johansson [7] developed a nostalgic TUI prototype, named "Nostalgia". It consisted a textile runner and an old fashioned radio placed on a table. By pressing on the runner, a choice would be made for listening to the news or music. Although the study indicated that using nostalgia could promote technology acceptance among elderly participants, Nilsson, Johansson [7] stated that their work focused more on the process of a participatory design instead of the understanding why Nostalgia gained good acceptance among them. In another similar works, Seo, Sungkajun [8] demonstrated the potential of their interactive plants among the elderly people living in an assisted living facility. However, the ways how the nostalgic TUI application could promote better technology acceptance was not clearly illustrated.

In this study we aim to investigate how nostalgia can contribute in designing TUI application for better technology acceptance among elderly people by designing and developing a nostalgic TUI application for them. While improving elderly's technology acceptance, we hoped that they could have more social interaction through the use of TUI application. In this paper, through our research process, we gathered and reflected upon the lessons learned in using the concept of nostalgia in designing TUI for elderly people.

2   Prototypes

The TUI application's main functionality is to enable elderly people to develop new potential friendship by making calls to other users who had the same interest. It was developed through three iterations of design, development and evaluation. We involved two elderly participants (P1 and P2) to evaluate the prototype in each iteration. Both of them were above 70 years old and had been using ICT actively. They were recruited since they were interested and had experience working in helping other elderly people in using ICT. P2 even involved in giving talks and seminars to inspire elderly people to use ICT. By having them to evaluate the prototype, we hoped that their feedback could contribute to a better designed TUI application for elderly ICT users.

During the evaluation, the prototype was first presented to them. They were then interviewed to provide their feedback about the prototype. Questions related to the design of the prototype, for instance its size and weight, the way they would use the prototype and so forth were asked. Using the gathered feedback, we improved the design and further developed the prototype in the next iteration.

2.1 Iterations of Design, Development and Evaluation

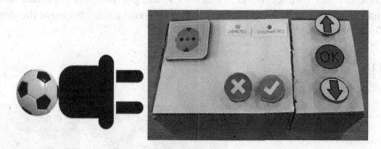

Fig. 1. Plug and play paper prototype with interest plug (to the left) and console box (to the right)

In the first iteration, the group produced a low fidelity paper prototype that consisted of a box with plugs (Fig. 1). The idea was inspired by the old fashioned plug and play gaming console. A symbol object representing an interest was attached to a plug. For instance, a football representing sports is attached to a plug in Fig. 1. The user was expected to connect the 'interest plug' onto a socket on the console box to find other users with the same interest. The console box together with several interest plugs (sports, news, music, literature, travel, etc.) were presented to P1. During the evaluation, P1 had problem understanding the prototype. He commented that the plug and play gaming console was not familiar to him, since he was not interested in such games. After explaining to him, the evaluation continued. Despite the difficulty in understanding the design, he provided his opinion regarding the functionality, size, weight and overall design of the TUI prototype.

Using the gathered feedback, the group decided to make another paper prototype in the second iteration so that they could compare the two designs. To make the nostalgic TUI application appeared more familiar to a larger group of users, the group decided to adopt the design of an old fashioned telephone. During the evaluation, we presented P2 the paper prototype of plug and play console (Fig. 1), and the paper prototype of old fashioned telephone (Fig. 2).

Fig. 2. Old fashioned telephone paper prototype

She was asked about her opinion about both prototypes. She preferred the telephone over the plug and play box. The telephone was found to be more familiar to her and therefore easier to understand. Same as P1, she provided her feedback about the functionality, size, weight and so forth, so that we could further improve the design of the TUI telephone in the next iteration.

2.2   TUI Telephone

Fig. 3. TUI telephone (to the left) and its 12-key keypad (to the right)

In the third iteration, a high fidelity prototype of the TUI telephone was created. As illustrated in Fig. 3, it consisted of an old fashioned TUI telephone (size 20 cm × 20 cm × 20 cm) connecting to a tablet. In the tablet there was a calling app installed. An Arduino board was embedded in the TUI telephone to inform the actions performed on the TUI telephone to the calling app in the tablet via Bluetooth.

There were 12 buttons on the TUI telephone, which was the same as the standard 12-key telephone keypad (10 digits, star sign and hash sign). The size was 3 cm × 3 cm for the square-shape buttons and 3 cm-diameter for the round buttons. Based on the feedback from the evaluation in the second iteration, for the design of 12-key TUI telephone keypad, we included eight interests (news, music, sports, movies, theatre, literature, family and travel), one button for emergency, two buttons indicating 'Previous' and 'Next' to navigate while selecting contacts on the tablet, and one 'OK' button to select a contact. There were a red light and a green light on the top right corner of the TUI telephone. When the users were making calls, the green light would turn on. The red light would flash when the call ended.

To use the TUI telephone, the users needed to pick up the handset and then press on a particular interest button. The action would trigger a list of online users who had the same interest displayed on the calling app in the tablet. They could then choose to make a call to one of the online users. In order to simulate nostalgic user experience, the users were also expected to use the handset while talking on the phone. The calls were limited to audio only without video, as we attempted to keep the functionality as simple as possible for the elderly users.

3 Final Evaluation

3.1 Participants and Tasks

Testing tasks were added into the evaluation in the third iteration. P1 who has involved in testing previous prototypes participated in the final evaluation. In addition, we set up a booth at a senior center and recruited five walk-in visitors (four females and one male) aged above 65 years old to participate in the final evaluation. All of them were ICT literate users and they performed the testing tasks individually at a time at the cafeteria at the senior center. All testers were asked to use the TUI telephone to make a call to someone based on their interests. They were observed while performing the testing tasks.

3.2 Results

Both P1 and all five participants from the senior center liked and understood the design of the TUI telephone easily, as they could immediately relate the design of the TUI telephone to their old fashioned telephone. However, there were a few aspects that raised concerns among the participants.

First, they commented that the size of TUI telephone was too big. Most of them were concerned that the telephone might be too heavy to carry around for the other elderly people. On the other hand, it might then be suitable for elderly people who had special needs, for instance those who had visual impairment or problem with muscle control. For elderly people with visual impairment, the font size in the calling app had to be big, or they should be able to voice over correctly. The buttons on the keypad could be incorporated with braille as well. P1 suggested to provide options for the users to choose their own color and size for the telephone. Black color appeared to be slightly sad to him. Other usability issues included the color contrast on the buttons was not sufficient and the placement of the buttons and the labels was too close, which caused the shadow of the button to fall on the labels (refer Fig. 3 to the right).

In terms of the way of using the TUI telephone, some participants did not understand completely that the TUI telephone was used to interact with the calling app installed in the tablet. They thought the TUI telephone was a stand-alone device. In addition, they were confused as they were expecting that a telephone number would be needed to make a call. They wondered how they could dial the number when it only showed interests on the keypad. After explaining to them that the numbers were not required and they should use interest buttons to find other users, they understood the idea. We expected the participants to press an interest button first, then pick up the handset and choose an online contact to make a call. However, while conducting the testing tasks, the participants showed the other way around. After clarifying with them, we understood that they were used to picking up the phone first, only then they would press the number buttons to make a call.

All participants were willing to test and try out the TUI telephone because they were interested in new technology and used ICT very often. Since they were already experienced ICT users, they were unsure if the TUI telephone would be suitable for elderly ICT users like them. On the other hand, they agreed that it could reach out to their peers who were more skeptical towards new technology. The use of TUI telephone was commented more suitable to be use in a group setting than individual, home setting. They suggested that a group of elderly senior center visitor could use it together and call to elderly users at other senior centers. Lastly, they suggested more functionalities could be provided than just simply calling someone based on interests. For elderly people, they often needed to call to organizations providing services such as hospital, senior center, bank and so forth.

4 Discussion

This study supports the findings from previous studies in designing nostalgic TUI application for elderly people [5, 7–9], i.e. the nostalgic TUI telephone in this study managed to gain positive user experience among elderly people. It appeared intuitive, user-friendly and inviting for them. Through the entire research process, we gathered and reflected upon our lessons learned which can serve as guidelines for using the concept of nostalgia in designing TUI application for elderly people's technology acceptance.

First, nostalgia applies not only to the object, but also to the behavior. Our observation indicates that elderly people expected the TUI application to be used in the old fashioned way. For instance, they would pick up the handset first before pressing on any interest button. They also anticipated to dial telephone numbers and therefore had challenges understanding the concept of getting contact with users who had the same interest by pressing interest button. This finding is consistent of Li, Hu [10] who found out that the elderly users encountered difficulties when performing tasks which were different from their recalled memories, i.e. opening an incoming message using touch gesture. While designing a nostalgic TUI, or any nostalgic ICT application, this is an important factor to consider in terms of the elderly users' interaction with the application.

Second, a more commonly shared nostalgia can reach more diverse elderly user group. Examples of commonly shared nostalgic object include jukebox designed for people with dementia [11] and slots-machine for elderly people [10]. The authors from these studies claimed that the chosen nostalgic object could enhance familiarity for the target users by employing metaphor and thus providing intuitive interaction. In our study, the feedback from the elderly participants indicate that the design of an old fashioned telephone, which is a more commonly shared nostalgia was preferred over a plug and play gaming console.

Third, Nostalgia is for the present and the future. While triggering elderly people's positive emotions and old memories, it is important to remember that the design with nostalgia element shall aim for their present and future use, rather than leading them to be reluctant in accepting the new technology. Similar to Nilsson, Johansson [7] 's study, our findings indicate that nostalgic TUI application managed to trigger the elderly people's curiosity towards the new technology and we hope that such design could inspire them to be more open about their present and future ICT use.

Fourth, there will be gaps between the new technology and nostalgia, and it is important to reduce these gaps. It is difficult to have the new technology work exactly the same as the old fashioned way. The gap occurred when the elderly users' expectation was different from how the TUI telephone actually worked. One example was the TUI telephone would not require the elderly users to dial the numbers to make a call. Similarly in Li, Hu [10] 's study, the gap occurred when the incoming messages were in digital form and the users were not expecting to respond to them using touch gesture. It is important to take into consideration of these potential gaps when using the concept of Nostalgia in designing TUI application for elderly people. Such gaps can be addressed by providing facilitation and guided instructions. Li, Hu [10] suggested that paper instruction was necessary in order to provide text-based guidance to the elderly users.

We acknowledge that the design of TUI telephone was not completely TUI. By having the tablet as a display, the entire application was actually a combination of TUI and GUI (graphical user interface). However, the focus of the study was on designing and developing the TUI object, and we managed to identify the ways nostalgia can contribute in designing TUI application for better technology acceptance among elderly people. In addition, the use of mobile technology where the users are interacting with GUI has been heavily studied with the goal to address the special needs of elderly users in using these mobile technologies [12]. The future elderly ICT users might feel less "intimidated" and "anxious" with new technology. Combining TUI and GUI in a design of ICT application can be the trend for the future gerontechnology. The presented work might therefore serve as an inspiration for future studies that aim to achieve that.

Two major limitations in this study should be noted. First, limited number of elderly participants were involved in the process of design and evaluation of the prototypes. Second, they were not representatives of the target user group. The participants were experienced ICT users and had higher level ICT skills than target users of the prototype. The design of the prototype is at its preliminary stage and future development should address these limitations by involving more target users in the process.

5   Conclusion and Future Work

In summary, the paper demonstrates the process of design, development and evaluation of a nostalgic TUI application for the technology acceptance among elderly people. A list of lessons learned have been gathered and presented, which could provide better understanding in using the concept of nostalgia in designing TUI application for elderly people's technology acceptance. One of the implications of this study includes informing the researchers, designers and developers about the potential of adopting nostalgia in designing TUI or even general ICT tools for elderly users. Nostalgia triggers positive emotions and experiences of elderly people, and the nostalgic TUI application could therefore have a less "intimidating" and more inviting appearance for this user group. Such application could be potentially useful for people with dementia.

In the future, we hope to improve the design of the TUI telephone in two versions. First version is a TUI telephone with tablet while the other one is a purely TUI without the use of tablet. Both versions shall be further developed into fully functional prototypes. A comparative case study where both prototypes can be used and tested at senior centers by the elderly users will inform us more about the impacts of the nostalgic TUI telephone on elderly's technology acceptance and social interaction, along with their preferences in terms of the design of nostalgic TUI application. Elderly users with diverse abilities, preferences, ICT skills and so forth will be included in the case study.

References

1. Vroman, K.G., Arthanat, S., Lysack, C.: "Who over 65 is online?" Older adults' dispositions toward information communication technology. Comput. Hum. Behav. **43**, 156–166 (2015)
2. Ishii, H., Ullmer, B.: Tangible bits: towards seamless interfaces between people, bits and atoms. In: Proceedings of the ACM SIGCHI Conference on Human Factors in Computing Systems. ACM, Georgia (1997)
3. Bong, W.K., Bergland, A., Chen, W.: Technology acceptance and quality of life among older people using a TUI application. Int. J. Environ. Res. Public Health **16**(23), 4706 (2019)
4. Spreicer, W.: Tangible interfaces as a chance for higher technology acceptance by the elderly. In: Proceedings of the 12th International Conference on Computer Systems and Technologies, pp. 311–316. ACM, Vienna (2011)
5. Dubuc, L., Edge, D.: TUIs to ease: tangible user interfaces in assistive technology. In: Proceedings of the 3rd Cambridge Workshop on Universal Access and Assistive Technology (CWUAAT 2006). Citeseer, Cambridge (2006)
6. Sedikides, C., Wildschut, T.: Finding meaning in nostalgia. Rev. Gen. Psychol. **22**(1), 48–61 (2018)
7. Nilsson, M., Johansson, S., Håkansson, M.: Nostalgia: an evocative tangible interface for elderly users. In: CHI 2003 Extended Abstracts on Human Factors in Computing Systems, pp. 964–965. ACM, Florida (2003)
8. Seo, J.H., et al.: Grass: interactive tangible art to evoke older adults' nostalgia. In: Actas Segundo Congreso Internacional Arte Ciencia Ciudad ACC2015, pp. 284–289. Editorial Universitat Politècnica de València, València (2015)
9. Morganti, L., et al.: Building collective memories on the web: the Nostalgia Bits project. Int. J. Web Based Commun. **9**(1), 83–104 (2013)

10. Li, C., et al.: Story-me: design of a system to support intergenerational storytelling and preservation for older adults. In: Companion Publication of the 2019 on Designing Interactive Systems Conference 2019 Companion, pp 245–250. ACM, San Diego (2019)
11. Huber, S., et al.: Tangible objects for reminiscing in dementia care. In: Proceedings of the Thirteenth International Conference on Tangible, Embedded, and Embodied Interaction, pp. 15–24. ACM, Arizona (2019)
12. Iancu, I., Iancu, B.: Designing mobile technology for elderly. A theoretical overview. Technol. Forecast. Soc. Change **155**, 119977 (2020)

Assessment of Economic Value of Assistive Technologies Through Quality-Adjusted Work-Life Years (QAWLY)

Siny Joseph[1] and Vinod Namboodiri[2]([⊠])

[1] Kansas State University, Manhattan, KS 66506, USA
siny@k-state.edu
[2] Wichita State University, Wichita, KS 67260, USA
vinod.namboodiri@wichita.edu

Abstract. Assistive technologies (ATs) are commonly used to improve the quality of life of persons with disabilities. While their utility to a person is usually clear, their cost-effectiveness or economic value is often unclear. There are no tools for specifically assessing the cost-effectiveness of an AT. Such cost effectiveness analysis is often important in workplace contexts where an employer or other agencies are responsible for providing accommodations. In this paper a tool called Quality-Adjusted Work-Life Years (QAWLY) is introduced to measure how cost-effectiveness of AT can be assessed including considerations of extended work-life and improved quality/productivity at work. Case studies are presented that showcase how QAWLY can be used to provide economic data points to be used for decision making involving AT.

Keywords: Assistive technology · Economic value · Work

1 Introduction

Technological advances in health and social care have led to a plethora of assistive technologies (AT) that enable people with impairments or disabilities to ameliorate their impact to varying extents. There is an increasing awareness that there are many barriers, physical or otherwise, that impede opportunities for work, education, and participation by people with disabilities. Technology has tremendous potential for removing accessibility barriers. For example, mapping and localization systems deployed in public spaces support orientation and wayfinding, or to identify safe paths to traverse for wheelchair users [1–3].

Often ATs are developed with the claim of having the potential to improve the quality of life for people with disabilities [4, 5]. However, an important criteria for AT to be adopted is the consideration of its cost-effectiveness. This paper sets out to determine how one goes about answering such questions. We are interested in determining the economic value of adopting a potential AT for a person with a disability.

Potential tools/metrics for such assessment can be based on prior related work. Quality-Adjusted Life Years (QALY) is a well-known measure that attempts to show the extent to which a particular treatment or system extends life and improves the quality of life at the same time [6–8]. It is a tool aimed at incorporating all the essential

© Springer Nature Switzerland AG 2020
K. Miesenberger et al. (Eds.): ICCHP 2020, LNCS 12377, pp. 480–488, 2020.
https://doi.org/10.1007/978-3-030-58805-2_57

dimensions of health, ability, and length of life. It combines the effects of health interventions on morbidity (quality of life) and mortality (quantity of life) into a single index. QALY has been largely used by insurance providers to weigh the benefits of a drug or medical treatment for patients [8–10]. It has, however, come under a lot of criticism for its use for assessing disability and related quality of life [10].

Another potential tool for assessing cost effectiveness of AT is the disability-adjusted life year (DALY), which is a measure of overall disease burden, expressed as the number of years lost due to ill-health, disability or early death [11]. It was developed in the 1990s as a way of comparing the overall health and life expectancy in different countries. DALYs are calculated by combining measures of life expectancy as well as the adjusted quality of life during a burdensome disease or disability for a population. DALYs are related to the quality-adjusted life year (QALY) measure; however QALYs only measure the benefit with and without medical intervention and therefore do not measure the total burden. Also, QALYs tend to be an individual measure, and not a societal measure. Both DALYs and QALYs are forms of HALYs or health-adjusted life years. HALYs, including DALYs and QALYs, are especially useful in guiding the allocation of health resources as they provide a common numerator, allowing for the expression of utility in terms of dollar/DALY, or dollar/QALY [12].

To measure how the technology extends work-life and improves the quality of work at the same time for people with disabilities, we introduce in this paper an adaptation to QALY called QAWLY where QAWLY considers work-life instead of length of life.[1] This measure then follows the same process as QALY in determining the impact of technological adoptions on work morbidity and work mortality for people with disabilities. Specifically, this paper determines the value and impact of ATs for people with disabilities for workplaces and shows through case studies how QAWLY could be applied for common AT categories.

2 Introduction to QALY Computation

To calculate QALY, it is necessary to determine by how much not being in health impacts a person's quality of life. QALY's do this by assigning a number between 0 and 1, called a health utility, to the various conditions a person's health could be in. A 0 would represent the lowest possible quality of life, while a 1 would represent the highest possible quality of life. Health utilities are typically derived from surveys, which attempt to determine how much survey participants would prefer to be in one health state as compared to another. Health states do not correspond directly to specific disabilities- they instead represent the degree of impairment a person has in specific, limited categories of functioning (such as mobility, ability to perform tasks, etc.). However, most disabilities share some or all characteristics of a health state.

The steps to compute QALY starts with determining how having a disability impacts a person. This can be accomplished with the help of a survey. There are a number of

---

[1] QAWLY is an adaptation of QALY instead of DALY despite the similarities in the focus on disability because DALY measures the overall burden of the disease on the population as a whole, while QALY allows for determining the impact of AT on individuals.

survey instruments adopted for measuring the health utility, namely EQ-5D-3L developed by the EuroQol Group, the 8-item Health Utilities Index Mark 3 scale (HUI3), and the 6-item SF-6D scale developed from SF-36 [13]. The most common questionnaire is EQ-5D-3L, where three levels of severity are assigned to five dimensions of quality of life, namely, mobility, self-care, usual activities, pain/discomfort, and anxiety/depression. Similarly, HUI3 considers eight attributes of 5 to 6 levels. Other questionnaires to evaluate at-work disability and productivity loss are the Work Limitations Questionnaire (WLQ-25) [14] and Workplace Activity Limitation Scale (WALS).

After determining the health utility, the decimal is multiplied by the number of years (quantity of life) that the intervention is expected to cover. The quantity can be the number of years by which the system extends work-life, i.e., the number of years a person expects to use the system over their lifetime in being able to work effectively.

More formally, a person who is expected to benefit from a health intervention through an increase in health utility of u_1 to u_2 and a lifespan change from t_1 to t_2 is said to have gained $(u_2 t_2 - u_1 t_1)$ QALYs. This concept is illustrated in Fig. 1.

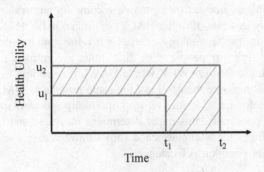

Fig. 1. QALY illustration

If the cost of an intervention is c, a cost effectiveness ratio (CER) is computed as

$$\text{CER} = \frac{c}{(u_2 t_2 - u_1 t_1)} \tag{1}$$

An intervention with a lower CER is considered to be a more cost effective intervention. This implies lower costs and/or higher utility is desirable. CERs have also been used with thresholds with interventions approved only when below a set threshold. In the past, the National Institute of Health and Clinical Excellence (NICE) in the UK has used pound 20,000–30,000 as a CER threshold.

Another related metric used with QALY is that of incremental cost effective ratio (ICER), it is useful if comparing two interventions. It is the incremental costs per number of QALYs gained and can be expressed as:

$$\text{ICER} = \frac{c_2 - c_1}{u_2 t_2 - u_1 t_1} \tag{2}$$

where c_2 and c_1 are the respective costs of the two interventions.

3 Adaptation of QALY to QAWLY

This section takes the existing theory on QALY and modifies to QAWLY. This adaptation helps determine the impact of AT in extending work-life and improving the quality of work. A major modification needed is to introduce the concept of work-life (the number of years a person wishes to stay in the workforce) as opposed to lifespan. Intuitively, a long-term investment on AT may not be cost effective if a person's work-life is expected to be much shorter than the useful-life of the AT. With this adaptation, we modify the lifespan based expression for time t used previously to the expression, $t(i) = \min(t, worklife(i))$, where $worklife(i)$ is the number of years left for a person i to be able to work till a widely accepted retirement age, as measured for a person with no disabilities from the population. If R is denoted this retirement age, then $worklife(i) = \max(R - age(i), 0)$ where $age(i)$ is the age of a person.

Consider an existing AT, say A, with a utility score u_A and another improved AT under consideration called B with a utility score u_B. Assume that A has a useful life of $t_A(i)$ for a person i going forward and B will have a useful life of $t_B(i)$. The QALYs gained by switching to B is then $u_B t_B(i) - u_A t_A(i)$. Consider that the total cost to acquire AT A and B are c_A and c_B. The incremental cost effectiveness ratio (ICER) then is the ratio $(c_B - c_A)/(u_B t_B(i) - u_A t_A(i))$. ATs with smaller values of ICER are considered more cost-effective than those with larger values. If an AT is being considered over a status quo with no AT, $c_A = 0$. The values of u_A and $t_A(i)$ could be the current utility for person i without an AT and $t_A(i) = t_B(i)$ because we are interested in comparing over the same time-frame as AT B. This gives a cost effectiveness ratio (CER) of any AT to be $c/(\Delta u t(i))$ where c is the cost of the AT, Δu is the change in utility (or impact) by the adoption of this AT and $t(i)$ is the useful-life of the AT (capped by work-life) over which it is assumed to provide a constant utility to the user. This assumption has been common in prior work too such as [6]. If utility is likely to change, then this can be construed as the average utility over this period.

Next we show a few examples of how QAWLY can be used in practice. The first step involves benchmarking with existing AT followed by incorporation of work-life.

Rollator: The rollator (also called a walker) is a commonly used mobility aid. It costs in the range $50–400 depending on construction quality and features. Its lifetime typically ranges from 3–5 years. In the study [6], the EQ-5D-3L instrument[2] showed a change in utility of about 0.05. Utilizing values from these ranges, the CER value with rollators can be computed (shown in Table 1) as 1000.

Hearing Aids: A hearing aid is also a common AT used to improve hearing capabilities. Cost of a pair of hearing aids (for both ears) typically ranges from $2000 to as much as $8000 depending on features, quality, and additional services provided with them. Lifespan of these aids is typically 3–7 years. In the study [6], a change of utility of 0.186 was determined using the HUI3 instrument (HUI3 is considered better than

---

[2] The best-case scenario would be to use modified WLQ-25 or WALS survey instrument generated values of health utility in the context of AT adoption. However, published utility estimates with AT adoption are only available using EQ-5D-3L instrument.

Table 1. CER benchmarking using known parameters from [6]

AT	Cost ($) C	Change in utility Δu	AT useful-life (years) t	CER
Rollator	200	0.05	4	1000
Hearing aid	2500	0.186	5	2688

EQ-5D-3L for capturing sensory impairments). Using values from these ranges, a CER of 2688 can be computed as shown in Table 1.

These two case studies with utility weights computed previously provide for an effective benchmark to compare with other AT products.

Now assume that the two ATs of Rollator and Hearing Aids were being used by persons for work scenarios and are supported by their employers as accommodations. Table 2 shows the CER computations for workers with three different ages: 60, 63, 67 in a country with a typical retirement age of 66.

Table 2. CER computations for varying work-life

AT	Cost ($) c	Change in utility Δu	AT useful-life (years) t	Work-life	CER
Rollator (age 60)	200	0.05	4	4	1000
Rollator (age 63)	200	0.05	4	3	1334
Rollator (age 67)	200	0.05	4	0	∞
Hearing aid (age 60)	2500	0.186	5	5	2688
Hearing aid (age 63)	2500	0.186	5	3	4480
Hearing aid (age 67)	2500	0.186	5	0	∞

These results show that when ATs are supported with a work-life shorter than the useful-life or lifespan of the device, the CERs increase to signify that the investment may not be as sound as compared to a younger person, unless the AT can be reused by someone else. These case studies also show the impact of maintenance of the AT can have on CERs; each year of life added to an AT is significant, especially for those ATs that have a small useful-life to begin with.

4 General Principles of Applying QAWLY

To simply exposition in general terms, we introduce the notion of cost per work-life year c_{wy} for any AT. This is simply, $c/worklife(i)$. For any AT to be cost-effective, the necessary condition for c_{wy} can be expressed as:

$$c_{wy} \leq \gamma_{CER} \Delta u \tag{3}$$

where γ_{CER} is the maximum CER that is deemed acceptable for that class of AT. For example, using c_{wy} results from Tables 1 and 2, for Rollators, or perhaps any mobility device, γ_{CER} could be in the range of 1000–1500 whereas AT for hearing challenges or in general sensory impairments could have a γ_{CER} in the range 2500–5000.

Intuitively, the condition above provides a price ceiling for an ATs adoption given cost-effectiveness of prior AT from which γ_{CER} is derived. A larger benefit in utility to the end-user allows for greater annual costs that may be acceptable to the end-user or those who support them (such as insurance and employers) that can be used for investment in research and development to develop the AT.

An alternate consideration in the design of AT is to look at how much benefits it must provide, for it to be under serious consideration. This can be answered by the condition for Δu expressed as: $\Delta u \geq c_{wy}/\gamma_{CER}$, with $0 \leq c_{wy} \leq \gamma_{CER}$.

Case studies with different ATs (computations shown in Table 3) are described next to show how the above theory of QAWLY can be used. To keep the exposition simple, it is assumed in all cases that work-life of the potential user is greater than the useful-life of the AT. When this is not true, the below calculations should adjust the number of years the AT will be used in computing annual costs.

Screen Reader: The JAWS screen reader costs $90/year. If a γ_{CER} of $2500 is used (CER for sensory impairment from Table 1), the potential increase in utility comes out to 0.036. This indicates that the JAWS screen reader is cost effective as long it provides capabilities that result in at least a utility weight increase of about 4%.

Smartphone App: Apps can range from free to up to $100 a year. For a free smartphone app we pick the SeeingAI app that allows blind individuals to recognize objects using a camera. With a γ_{CER} of $2500 (or any value for that matter), such an app is always cost-effective. The Seeing Eye GPS, an app that provides wayfinding information specific to blind individuals, costs $72 a year. Using the same γ_{CER}, this app can be considered cost-effective with a utility increase of 0.029 or about 3%.

Ergonomic Chair: The Herman Miller Mirra costs $1000 and comes with a 12-year warranty, for an annual cost of $83.33. Assuming it is for a user who will work longer than 12 years, using a γ_{CER} or 1000 from Table 1 for a mobility impairment AT, the minimum utility increase needed is 0.0834. An ergonomic chair therefore is considered effective as long it results in a utility increase of about 8%.

Wheelchair Ramps: Average wheelchair ramps for homes and small businesses (mostly individual use) cost around $2000 with a 10-year warranty, although there is a wide range in terms of where they are used and construction materials, length and height. With an average annual cost of $200 with a γ_{CER} of 1000, the minimum utility increase needed is 0.20 or 20%.

Wheelchair Ramps (Shared Use): Sturdy ramps built on a permanent basis for use by many individuals cost around $7500. These can last 20 or more years without much maintenance. If 5 employees at a workplace use a ramp, the annual cost is $75. With a

γ_{CER} of 1000, the minimum utility increase needed per person is 0.075. The same ramp with only one user would have needed a utility increase of 0.375. Thus, ATs with more number of users can be cost effective even if upfront costs are greater due to improved quality or scale needed.

Wayfinding Infrastructure (Shared Use): Recent apps for indoor navigation and wayfinding such as NavCog [1], GuideBeacon [2, 3] complementing outdoor GPS-based apps require infrastructure modifications such as the embedding of wireless devices called beacons typically at a density of about 10 per 1000 sq. ft. A five-story office building with 5000 sq. ft every floor will require 250 beacons. Addition beacons at entrances, stairways, and emergency exit locations may require another 50 beacons. Each beacon can cost around $25 and should last around 10 years with $5 in battery replacements over this life, requiring a cost of $9000 just for the beacon hardware. Assuming another $11,000 in cost for R & D and app development totaling $20,000 in costs resulting in an annual cost of $2000/year. Assuming 50 users use such a system (for example an employer of blind individuals at a manufacturing site), with a γ_{CER} of 2500, a minimum utility increase of 0.016 per person. If only one user uses this system, a utility increase of at least 0.8 would be needed. Such AT with large infrastructure costs need amortization of costs over a large number of users to be cost effective. If such a large user base exists, the minimum utility increase needed is quite minimal.

Table 3. Computing utility increases for AT adoption

AT	Annual cost ($) c_{wy}	Assumed minimum CER threshold γ_{CER}	Minimum utility increase (Δu) necessary for adoption
Screen reader	90	2500	0.036
App – seeing AI	0	2500	0
App – seeing eye GPS	72	2500	0.029
Ergonomic chair	83.34	1000	0.0834
Ramp (individual use)	200	1000	0.20
Ramp (shared use)	75	1000	0.075
Wayfinding (shared use)	40	2500	0.016

5 Limitations and Future Work

This work's primary contribution has been in connecting health utility and the concept of work-life as it applies to AT to assess cost effectiveness. Most health utility capturing instruments include various aspects of life, not just the work component. Thus, a better characterization of cost-effectiveness of AT for work should use instruments specific to work. The WALS (specifically for those with Rheumatoid Arthritis) and the WLQ-25 are potential options that need to be considered in future with the QAWLY model developed in this work to provide a more accurate picture. Because those instruments were not developed to be used in assessing ATs, they may need to be modified. This work has also been limited by being able to use only two ATs (and their associated utility values) for benchmarking CERs, with only one for mobility impairments and one for sensory impairments. Benchmark CER scores would have more confidence if more ATs could be added to Table 1. Computation of minimum utility benefits needed for a specific AT are more accurate for individual use ATs as there is less uncertainty about the number of potential users. For shared use AT such as ramps and navigation infrastructure, judging the number of potential users adds uncertainty and the best approach would be to work with a range of maximum and minimum likely users using past data. Given these limitations, QAWLY as introduced in this paper, is still a work in progress and much future work needs to be done in terms of designing instruments to assess utility weights for work, and deploying these instruments widely to gather statistics from individuals with a wide range of disabilities.

Acknowledgment. This work is supported by NSF (#1951864).

References

1. Ahmetovic, D., Gleason, C., Ruan, C., Kitani, K., Takagi, H., Asakawa, C.: NavCog: a navigational cognitive assistant for the blind. In: Proceedings of the 18th International Conference on Human-Computer Interaction with Mobile Devices and Services, MobileHCI 2016, pp. 90–99, New York (2016)
2. Cheraghi, S.A., Namboodiri, V., Walker, L.: GuideBeacon: beacon-based indoor wayfinding for the blind, visually impaired, and disoriented. In: IEEE Pervasive Communications (PerCom) (2016)
3. Cheraghi, S.A., Sharma, A., Namboodiri, V., Arsal, G.: SafeExit4All: an inclusive indoor emergency evacuation system for people with disabilities. In: W4A 2019: Proceedings of the 16th Web For All May 2019, Article No. 29, pp. 1–10 (2019)
4. Cook, M., Polgar, J.M., Essentials of Assistive Technologies, 1st edn. (2014)
5. Cook, M., Polgar, J.M., Encarnação, P.: Assistive Technologies: Principles and Practice. 5th edn. (2019)
6. Persson, J., Husberg, M.: Can we rely in QALYs for assistive technologies? Technol. Disabil. **24**, 93–100 (2012)
7. Weinstein, M.C., Torrance, G., McGuire, A.: QALYs: the basics. Value Health **12**(Suppl 1), S5–S9 (2009)
8. Quality-adjusted life years and the devaluation of life with disability, National Council on Disability. https://ncd.gov/sites/default/files/NCD_Quality_Adjusted_Life_Report_508.pdf. Accessed 6 Nov 2019
9. Solow, B., Pezalla, E.J.: Commentary: ISPOR's initiative on US value assessment frameworks: the use of cost-effectiveness research in decision making US insurers. Value Health **21**, 166–167 (2018)
10. Roland, D.: Obscure model puts a price on good health- and drives down drug costs. Wall Street J. (2019). https://www.wsj.com/articles/obscure-model-puts-a-price-on-good-healthand-drives-down-drug-costs-11572885123

11. WHO—Metrics: Disability-Adjusted Life Year (DALY)". WHO. Accessed 02 Jan 2020
12. Gold, M.R., Stevenson, D., Fryback, D.G.: HALYS and QALYS and DALYS, oh my: similarities and differences in summary measures of population health. Ann. Rev. Pub. Health **23**, 115–134 (2002)
13. Furlong, W.J., Feeny, D.H., Torrance, G.W.: Health Utilities Index Measurement System, Self-Complete Questionnaire Manual, Health Utilities Inc., Dundas (2002). http://www.healthutilities.com/
14. Lerner, D., Amick 3rd, B.C., Rogers, W.H., Malspeis, S., Bungay, K., Cynn, D.: The work limitations questionnaire. Med. Care **39**(1), 72–85 (2001)

Correction to: Gait Patterns Monitoring Using Instrumented Forearm Crutches

Marien Narváez[ID] and Joan Aranda[ID]

Correction to:
Chapter "Gait Patterns Monitoring Using Instrumented
Forearm Crutches" in: K. Miesenberger et al. (Eds.):
Computers Helping People with Special Needs, **LNCS 12377,**
https://doi.org/10.1007/978-3-030-58805-2_48

The original version of this chapter was revised. The chapter was published open access, but this has been reversed and the copyright is now © Springer Nature Switzerland AG.

The updated version of this chapter can be found at
https://doi.org/10.1007/978-3-030-58805-2_48

© Springer Nature Switzerland AG 2020
K. Miesenberger et al. (Eds.): ICCHP 2020, LNCS 12377, p. C1, 2020.
https://doi.org/10.1007/978-3-030-58805-2_58

Correction to: Analysis of Indoor Maps Accounting the Needs of People with Impairments

Julian Striegl, Claudia Loitsch, Jan Schmalfuss-Schwarz, and Gerhard Weber

Correction to:
Chapter "Analysis of Indoor Maps Accounting the Needs of People with Impairments" in: K. Miesenberger et al. (Eds.): *Computers Helping People with Special Needs*, **LNCS 12377, https://doi.org/10.1007/978-3-030-58805-2_36**

In an older version of this paper, there was error in the author name, "Claudia Lotisch" was incorrect. This has been corrected to "Claudia Loitsch".

The updated original version of this chapter can be found at
https://doi.org/10.1007/978-3-030-58805-2_36

Author Index

Printed in the United States
by Baker & Taylor Publisher Services

Printed in the United States
by Baker & Taylor Publisher Services